GEOGRAPHY 95/96

Tenth Edition

Editor

Gerald R. Pitzl
Macalester College

Gerald R. Pitzl, professor of geography at Macalester College, received his bachelor's degree in secondary social science education from the University of Minnesota in 1964 and his M.A. (1971) and Ph.D. (1974) in geography from the same institution. He teaches a wide array of geography courses and is the author of a number of articles on geography, developing world countries, and computers in social science education.

Annual Editions

A Library of Information from the Public Press

Cover illustration by Mike Eagle

The Dushkin Publishing Group, Inc.
Sluice Dock, Guilford, Connecticut 06437

This map has been developed to give you a graphic picture of where the countries of the world are located, the relationship they have with their region and neighbors, and their positions relative to the superpowers and power blocs. We have focused on certain areas to more clearly illustrate these crowded regions.

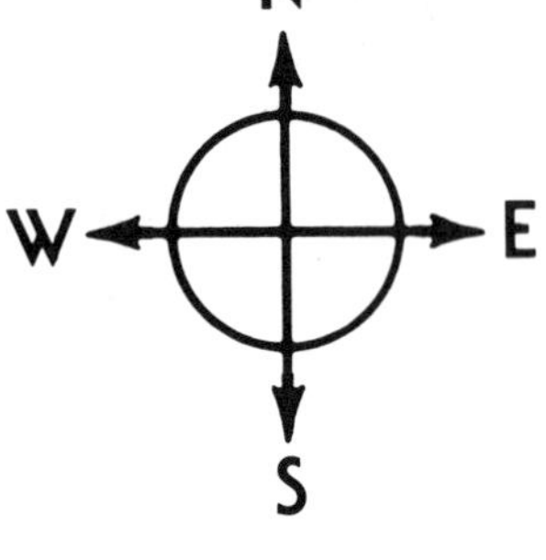

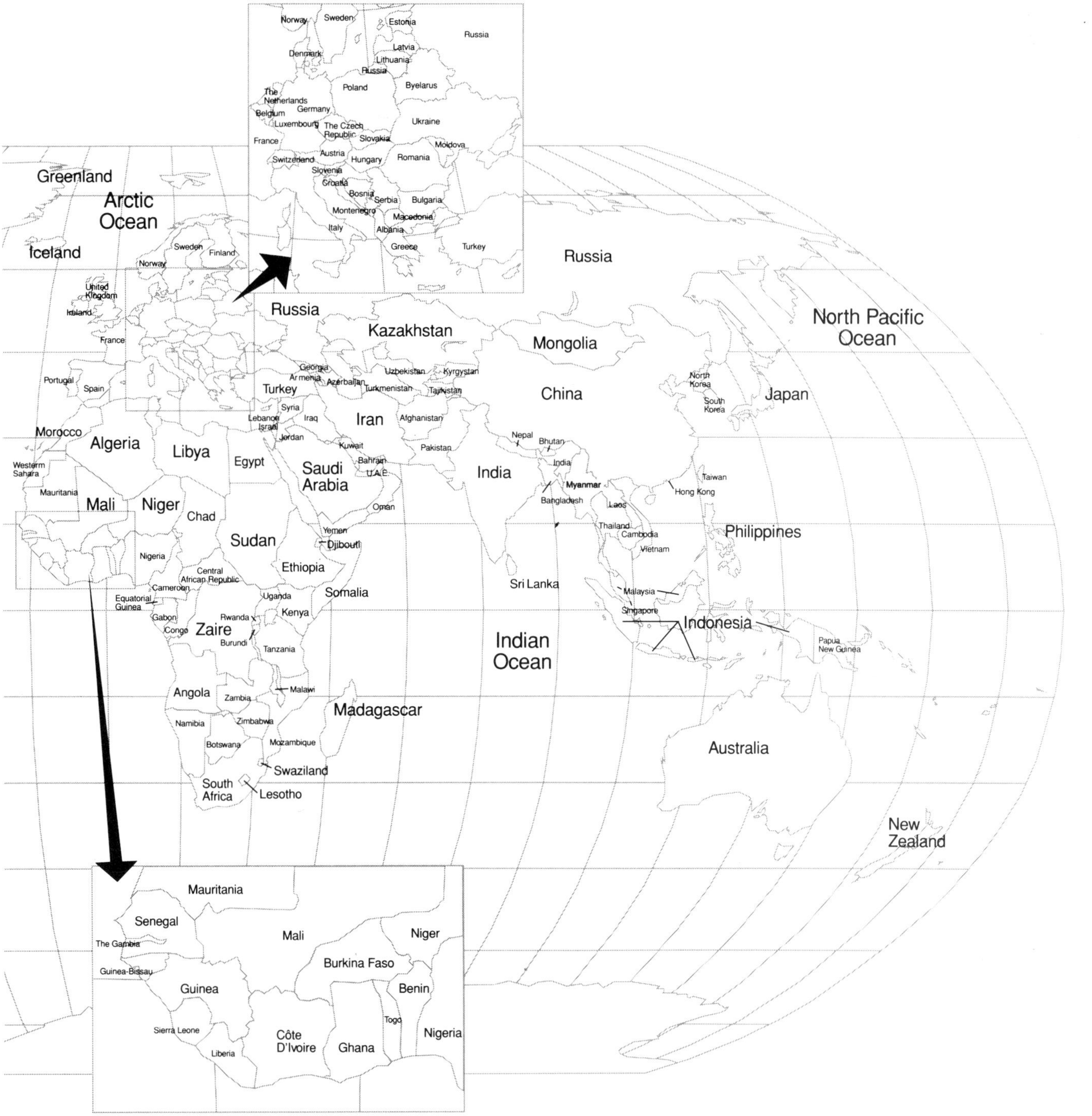
Norway
Sweden
Estonia
Russia
Denmark
Latvia
Lithuania
Russia
Poland
Byelarus
The Netherlands
Germany
Belgium
Luxembourg
The Czech Republic
Ukraine
France
Slovakia
Moldova
Austria
Switzerland
Hungary
Romania
Slovenia
Croatia
Bosnia
Serbia
Bulgaria
Montenegro
Macedonia
Italy
Albania
Greece
Turkey
Greenland
Arctic Ocean
Iceland
Sweden
Finland
Norway
United Kingdom
Ireland
France
Portugal
Spain
Russia
Kazakhstan
Mongolia
North Pacific Ocean
Russia
Georgia
Armenia
Azerbaijan
Uzbekistan
Kyrgyzstan
Turkey
Turkmenistan
Tajikistan
China
North Korea
South Korea
Japan
Syria
Lebanon
Israel
Iraq
Iran
Afghanistan
Morocco
Algeria
Libya
Egypt
Jordan
Kuwait
Nepal
Bhutan
Western Sahara
Saudi Arabia
Bahrain
U.A.E.
Pakistan
India
India
Taiwan
Mauritania
Mali
Niger
Chad
Oman
Myanmar
Bangladesh
Hong Kong
Laos
Sudan
Yemen
Djibouti
Thailand
Cambodia
Philippines
Nigeria
Ethiopia
Vietnam
Central African Republic
Cameroon
Sri Lanka
Equatorial Guinea
Uganda
Somalia
Malaysia
Kenya
Singapore
Indonesia
Gabon
Rwanda
Congo
Zaire
Burundi
Tanzania
Indian Ocean
Papua New Guinea
Angola
Malawi
Zambia
Madagascar
Namibia
Zimbabwe
Botswana
Mozambique
Australia
Swaziland
South Africa
Lesotho
New Zealand
Mauritania
Senegal
Mali
Niger
The Gambia
Burkina Faso
Guinea-Bissau
Guinea
Benin
Togo
Sierra Leone
Côte D'Ivoire
Ghana
Nigeria
Liberia

The Annual Editions Series

Annual Editions is a series of over 65 volumes designed to provide the reader with convenient, low-cost access to a wide range of current, carefully selected articles from some of the most important magazines, newspapers, and journals published today. Annual Editions are updated on an annual basis through a continuous monitoring of over 300 periodical sources. All Annual Editions have a number of features designed to make them particularly useful, including topic guides, annotated tables of contents, unit overviews, and indexes. For the teacher using Annual Editions in the classroom, an Instructor's Resource Guide with test questions is available for each volume.

Printed on Recycled Paper

VOLUMES AVAILABLE

Africa
Aging
American Foreign Policy
American Government
American History, Pre-Civil War
American History, Post-Civil War
Anthropology
Archaeology
Biology
Biopsychology
Business Ethics
Canadian Politics
Child Growth and Development
China
Comparative Politics
Computers in Education
Computers in Business
Computers in Society
Criminal Justice
Developing World
Drugs, Society, and Behavior
Dying, Death, and Bereavement
Early Childhood Education
Economics
Educating Exceptional Children
Education
Educational Psychology
Environment
Geography
Global Issues
Health
Human Development
Human Resources
Human Sexuality
India and South Asia
International Business
Japan and the Pacific Rim
Latin America
Life Management
Macroeconomics
Management
Marketing
Marriage and Family
Mass Media
Microeconomics
Middle East and the Islamic World
Money and Banking
Multicultural Education
Nutrition
Personal Growth and Behavior
Physical Anthropology
Psychology
Public Administration
Race and Ethnic Relations
Russia, the Eurasian Republics, and Central/Eastern Europe
Social Problems
Sociology
State and Local Government
Urban Society
Violence and Terrorism
Western Civilization, Pre-Reformation
Western Civilization, Post-Reformation
Western Europe
World History, Pre-Modern
World History, Modern
World Politics

Cataloging in Publication Data
Main entry under title: Annual editions: Geography. 1995/96.
1. Geography—Periodicals. 2. Anthropo-geography—Periodicals. 3. Natural resources—Periodicals. I. Pitzl, Gerald R., *comp.* II. Title: Geography.
910′.5 ISBN 1-56134-356-0 87-641715

Tenth Edition

Printed in the United States of America

Editors/ Advisory Board

Members of the Advisory Board are instrumental in the final selection of articles for each edition of Annual Editions. Their review of articles for content, level, currentness, and appropriateness provides critical direction to the editor and staff. We think you'll find their careful consideration well reflected in this volume.

To the Reader

In publishing ANNUAL EDITIONS we recognize the enormous role played by the magazines, newspapers, and journals of the *public press* in providing current, first-rate educational information in a broad spectrum of interest areas. Within the articles, the best scientists, practitioners, researchers, and commentators draw issues into new perspective as accepted theories and viewpoints are called into account by new events, recent discoveries change old facts, and fresh debate breaks out over important controversies.

Many of the articles resulting from this enormous editorial effort are appropriate for students, researchers, and professionals seeking accurate, current material to help bridge the gap between principles and theories and the real world. These articles, however, become more useful for study when those of lasting value are carefully *collected, organized, indexed,* and *reproduced* in a *low-cost format*, which provides easy and permanent access when the material is needed. That is the role played by *Annual Editions*.

Under the direction of each volume's *Editor*, who is an expert in the subject area, and with the guidance of an *Advisory Board*, we seek each year to provide in each *ANNUAL EDITION* a current, well-balanced, carefully selected collection of the best of the public press for your study and enjoyment. We think you'll find this volume useful, and we hope you'll take a moment to let us know what you think.

The articles in this tenth edition of *Annual Editions: Geography* represent the wide range of topics associated with the discipline of geography. The major themes of spatial relationships, regional development, the population explosion, and socioeconomic inequalities exemplify the diversity of research areas within geography.

The book is organized into five sections, each of which contains articles relating to themes within the discipline. Articles address the conceptual nature of geography and the global and regional problems in the world today. The latter theme reflects the geographer's concern with finding solutions to these serious global and regional problems. Regional problems, such as food shortages in the Sahel and the greenhouse effect, not only concern geographers but interest researchers from other disciplines as well.

The association of geography with other disciplines is important because expertise from a number of different fields will be necessary in finding solutions to some difficult problems. Geography should be involved in the search for solutions because the discipline has always been integrative. That is, geography uses evidence from many sources to answer the basic questions, "Where is it?" "Why is it there?" and "What is its relevance?" The articles emphasize the interconnectedness not only of places and regions in the world, but of thrusts to solutions to problems as well. No single discipline will have all of the answers to the problems facing the world today; the complexity of the issues is simply too great.

The articles in the first section of the book discuss particular aspects of geography as a discipline and provide examples of the topics presented in the remaining four sections. The middle three sections represent major themes in geography. The last section addresses important problems faced by geographers and others.

Articles in *Annual Editions: Geography 95/96* will be useful to both teachers and students in their study of geography. The anthology is designed to provide detail and case study material to supplement the standard textbook treatment of geography. The goals of this anthology are to introduce students to the richness and diversity of topics relating to places and regions on Earth's surface, to pay heed to the serious problems facing humankind, and to stimulate the search for more information on topics of interest.

I would like to express my gratitude to Barbara Wells-Howe for her help in preparing this material for publication. Her typing, organization of materials, and many helpful suggestions are greatly appreciated. Without her diligence and professional efforts, this undertaking could not have been completed. Special thanks are also extended to Ian Nielsen for his continued encouragement during the preparation of this new edition, and to Addie Raucci for her enthusiasm and helpfulness. A word of thanks must go, as well, to all those who recommended articles for inclusion in this volume and who commented on the overall organization of the volume. Peter O. Muller, Robert S. Bednarz, Vern Harnapp, and Owa Saarinen were especially helpful in that regard. Please continue to share your opinions by filling out the article rating form on the last page of this book.

Gerald R. Pitzl

Gerald R. Pitzl
Editor

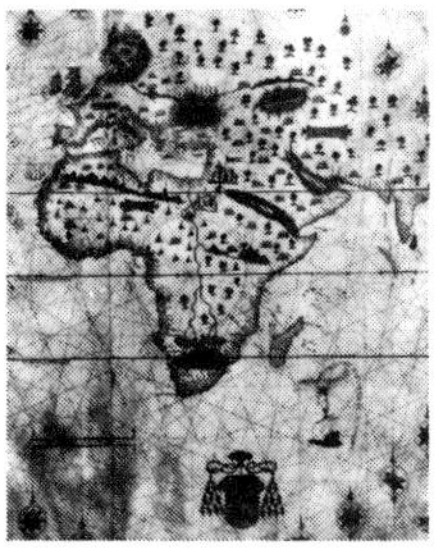

Unit 1

Geography in a Changing World

Eight articles discuss the discipline of geography and the extremely varied and wide-ranging themes that define geography today.

The concepts in bold italics are developed in the article. For further expansion please refer to the Topic Guide and the Index.

Unit 2

Land-Human Relationships

Six articles examine the relationship between humans and the land on which we live. Topics include the devastation of the oceans, the destruction of the rain forests, desertification, pollution, and the effects of human society on the global environment.

The concepts in bold italics are developed in the article. For further expansion please refer to the Topic Guide and the Index.

Unit 3

The Region

Eight selections review the importance of the region as a concept in geography and as an organizing framework for research. A number of world regional trends, as well as the patterns of area relationships, are examined.

The concepts in bold italics are developed in the article. For further expansion please refer to the Topic Guide and the Index.

The concepts in bold italics are developed in the article. For further expansion please refer to the Topic Guide and the Index.

Unit 4

Spatial Interaction and Mapping

Eight articles discuss the key theme in geographical analysis: place-to-place spatial interaction. Human diffusion, transportation systems, urban growth, and cartography are some of the themes examined.

The concepts in bold italics are developed in the article. For further expansion please refer to the Topic Guide and the Index.

Unit 5

Population, Resources, and Socioeconomic Development

Seven articles examine the effects of population growth on natural resources and the resulting socioeconomic level of development.

The concepts in bold italics are developed in the article. For further expansion please refer to the Topic Guide and the Index.

The concepts in bold italics are developed in the article. For further expansion please refer to the Topic Guide and the Index.

Topic Guide

This topic guide suggests how the selections in this book relate to topics of traditional concern to students and professionals involved with the study of geography. It is useful for locating articles that relate to each other for reading and research. The guide is arranged alphabetically according to topic. Articles may, of course, treat topics that do not appear in the topic guide. In turn, entries in the topic guide do not necessarily constitute a comprehensive listing of all the contents of each selection.

TOPIC AREA	TREATED IN:
Accessibility	25. Channel Tunnel
Agriculture	21. Low Water in the American High Plains 33. Can the Growing Human Population Feed Itself?
Arid Lands	12. Threat of Encroaching Deserts
Cartography	*See* Mapmaking
Climatic Change	8. Is Our Climate Unstable?
Coastlines	10. It Comes Down to the Coasts
Communication	23. Transportation and Urban Growth
Computer Mapping	29. Sense of Where You Are 30. New Cartographers
Conservation	7. Averting a Disaster 12. Threat of Encroaching Deserts
Core-Periphery	16. Africa's Geomosaic under Stress
Deforestation	11. Deforestation Debate
Demographic Transition	32. Vicious Circles
Desertification	12. Threat of Encroaching Deserts 19. Aral Sea Basin
Developing World	31. Population Policy Options 32. Vicious Circles
Development	32. Vicious Circles
Development Gap	36. Why Africa Stays Poor
Drought	21. Low Water in the American High Plains
Economic Development	10. It Comes Down to the Coasts 20. Does It Matter Where You Are? 32. Vicious Circles
Economic Geography	13. Environmental Problems of the Danube Delta
El Niño	4. What's Wrong with the Weather?
Environment	13. Environmental Problems of the Danube Delta 14. Action Plan to Clean Up the Baltic 37. Refugees: The Rising Flood
Erosion	5. Beaches on the Brink 12. Threat of Encroaching Deserts
Geographic Information Systems (GIS)	*See* Computer Mapping
Geography	2. American Geographies 20. Does It Matter Where You Are?
Geopolitical	3. Coming Anarchy 17. Middle East Geopolitical Transformation 22. Return of the Soviet Empire
Global	7. Averting a Disaster 15. Rise of the Region State 20. Does It Matter Where You Are?
Global Positioning System (GPS)	30. New Cartographers
Global Warming	4. What's Wrong with the Weather? 5. Beaches on the Brink
Greenhouse Effect	4. What's Wrong with the Weather?
Groundwater	18. Prairie Potholes 21. Low Water in the American High Plains
History of Geography	1. Four Traditions of Geography
Immigration	26. New White Flight
Industrialization	8. Is Our Climate Unstable?
Land Degradation	36. Why Africa Stays Poor
Landscape	2. American Geographies
Location	20. Does It Matter Where You Are?
Mapmaking	28. Alternative Route to Mapping History 29. Sense of Where You Are 30. New Cartographers

TOPIC AREA	TREATED IN:
Metropolitan	27. Asians in the Suburbs
Migration	24. Hispanic Migration and Population Redistribution 26. New White Flight 27. Asians in the Suburbs 35. We're All Minorities Now
Multicultural	35. We're All Minorities Now
Nation-State	3. Coming Anarchy 15. Rise of the Region State
Ozone Layer	*See* Greenhouse Effect
Place	2. American Geographies
Pollution	9. Troubled Waters 10. It Comes Down to the Coasts 14. Action Plan to Clean Up the Baltic
Population Growth	3. Coming Anarchy 7. Averting a Disaster 10. It Comes Down to the Coasts 24. Hispanic Migration and Population Redistribution 31. Population Policy Options 33. Can the Growing Human Population Feed Itself? 34. Landscape of Hunger 36. Why Africa Stays Poor
Prairie	18. Prairie Potholes
Rain Forests	11. Deforestation Debate
Refugees	37. Refugees: The Rising Flood
Region	3. Coming Anarchy 16. Africa's Geomosaic under Stress 17. Middle East Geopolitical Transformation 20. Does It Matter Where You Are? 24. Hispanic Migration and Population Redistribution 36. Why Africa Stays Poor
Region State	15. Rise of the Region State
Satellite	12. Threat of Encroaching Deserts
Shatterbelt	17. Middle East Geopolitical Transformation
Soil	7. Averting a Disaster
Spatial Patterns	28. Alternative Route to Mapping History 35. We're All Minorities Now
Suburbs	6. New Downtowns 27. Asians in the Suburbs
Sustainable Development	21. Low Water in the American High Plains
Third World	*See* Developing World
Transportation Systems	23. Transportation and Urban Growth 25. Channel Tunnel
Tribalism	3. Coming Anarchy
Underdeveloped Countries	*See* Developing World
Urban	6. New Downtowns 23. Transportation and Urban Growth
Water Conservation	9. Troubled Waters 19. Aral Sea Basin
Wetlands	13. Environmental Problems of the Danube Delta 18. Prairie Potholes

Geography in a Changing World

What is geography? This question has been asked innumerable times. It is a question that has not elicited a universally accepted answer, even from those who are considered to be members of the geography profession. The reason lies in the very nature of geography as it has evolved through time.

Geography is an extremely wide-ranging discipline, one that examines appropriate sets of events or circumstances occurring at specific places. Its goal is to answer certain basic questions.

The first question, "Where is it?" establishes the location of the subject under investigation. The concept of location is very important in geography, and its meaning extends beyond the common notion of a specific address or the determination of the latitude and longitude of a place. Geographers are more concerned with the relative location of a place and how that place interacts with other places both far and near. Spatial interaction and the determination of the connections between and among places are important themes in geography.

Once a place is "located," in the geographer's sense of the word, the next question is, "Why is it here?" For example, why are people concentrated in high numbers on the North China Plain, in the Ganges River Valley in India, and along the eastern seaboard in the United States? Conversely, why are there so few people in the Amazon Basin and the Central Siberian Lowlands? Generally, the geographer wants to find out why particular distribution patterns occur and why these patterns change over time.

The element of time is another extremely important ingredient in the geographical mix. The discipline is most concerned with the activities of human beings, and human beings bring about change. As changes occur, new adjustments and modifications are made in the distribution patterns previously established. Patterns change, for instance, as new technology brings about new forms of communication and transportation, and as once-desirable locations decline in favor of new ones. For example, people migrate from once-productive regions such as the Sahel when a disaster such as drought visits the land. Geography, then, is greatly concerned with discovering the underlying processes that can explain the transformation of distribution patterns and interaction forms over time. Geography itself is dynamic as it adjusts as a discipline to handle new situations in a changing world.

Geography is truly an integrating discipline. The geographer will assemble evidence from many sources in order to explain a particular pattern or ongoing process of change. Some of this evidence may even be in the form of concepts or theories borrowed from other disciplines. The first three articles of this unit provide insight into both the conceptual nature of geography and the development of the discipline over time.

Throughout its history, four main themes have been the focus of research work in geography. These themes or traditions, according to William Pattison in "The Four Traditions of Geography," link geography with earth science, establish it as a field that studies land-human relationships, engage it in area studies, and give it a spatial focus. Although Pattison's article first appeared over 30 years ago, it is still referred to and cited frequently today. Much of the geographical research and analysis engaged in today would fall within one or more of Pattison's traditional areas, but new areas are also opening for geographers. In a particularly thought-provoking essay, the eminent author Barry Lopez discusses local geographies and the importance of a sense of place. In Robert Kaplan's article, "The Coming Anarchy," a startling scenario is presented about the destruction of the social fabric of our planet.

Research into apparently abnormal weather shifts in recent years is addressed in the article "What's Wrong with the Weather?" An example of erratic weather and a much higher evidence of storminess is found in "Beaches on the Brink."

The article "The New Downtowns" provides an analysis of significant changes under way in the structure of

Unit 1

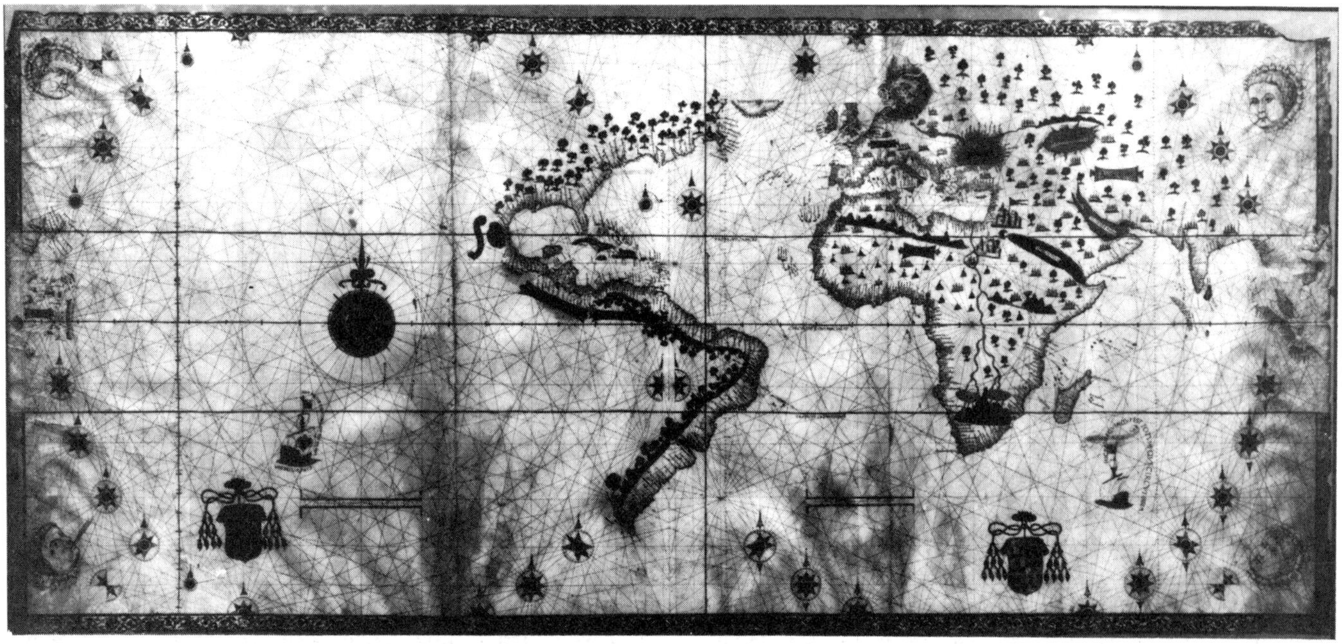

American cities due to the advent of shopping malls. In the article "Averting a Disaster," discussion centers on the serious problem of global soil loss. Finally, Melinda Bell looks at climatic change and the factors that bring it about in "Is Our Climate Unstable?"

Looking Ahead: Challenge Questions

Why is geography called an integrating discipline?

How is geography related to earth science? Can you give some examples of land-human relationships? What are area studies? Why is the spatial concept so important in geography? What is your definition of geography?

Why do history and geography rely on one another?

How have humans affected the weather? The environment in general?

How is individual behavior related to the understanding of environment?

Is change a good thing? Why is it important to anticipate change?

Do you understand what interconnectedness means in terms of places? Can you give examples of how you as an individual interact with people in other places? How are you "connected" to the rest of the world?

What do you think the world will be like in the year 2010? Are you pessimistic or optimistic about the future? Is there anything you can do about the future?

The Four Traditions of Geography

William D. Pattison

Late Summer, 1990

To Readers of the *Journal of Geography:*

I am honored to be introducing, for a return to the pages of the *Journal* after more than 25 years, "The Four Traditions of Geography," an article which circulated widely, in this country and others, long after its initial appearance—in reprint, in xerographic copy, and in translation. A second round of life at a level of general interest even approaching that of the first may be too much to expect, but I want you to know in any event that I presented the paper in the beginning as my gift to the geographic community, not as a personal property, and that I re-offer it now in the same spirit.

In my judgment, the article continues to deserve serious attention—perhaps especially so, let me add, among persons aware of the specific problem it was intended to resolve. The background for the paper was my experience as first director of the High School Geography Project (1961–63)—not all of that experience but only the part that found me listening, during numerous conference sessions and associated interviews, to academic geographers as they responded to the project's invitation to locate "basic ideas" representative of them all. I came away with the conclusion that I had been witnessing not a search for consensus but rather a blind struggle for supremacy among honest persons of contrary intellectual commitment. In their dialogue, two or more different terms had been used, often unknowingly, with a single reference, and no less disturbingly, a single term had been used, again often unknowingly, with two or more different references. The article was my attempt to stabilize the discourse. I was proposing a basic nomenclature (with explicitly associated ideas) that would, I trusted, permit the development of mutual comprehension **and** confront all parties concerned with the pluralism inherent in geographic thought.

This intention alone could not have justified my turning to the NCGE as a forum, of course. The fact is that from the onset of my discomfiting realization I had looked forward to larger consequences of a kind consistent with NCGE goals. As finally formulated, my wish was that the article would serve "to greatly expedite the task of maintaining an alliance between professional geography and pedagogical geography and at the same time to promote communication with laymen" (see my fourth paragraph). I must tell you that I have doubts, in 1990, about the acceptability of my word choice, in saying "professional," "pedagogical," and "layman" in this context, but the message otherwise is as expressive of my hope now as it was then.

I can report to you that twice since its appearance in the *Journal,* my interpretation has received more or less official acceptance—both times, as it happens, at the expense of the earth science tradition. The first occasion was Edward Taaffe's delivery of his presidential address at the 1973 meeting of the Association of American Geographers (see *Annals AAG,* March 1974, pp. 1–16). Taaffe's working-through of aspects of an interrelations among the spatial, area studies, and man-land traditions is by far the most thoughtful and thorough of any of which I am aware. Rather than fault him for omission of the fourth tradition, I compliment him on the grace with which he set it aside in conformity to a meta-epistemology of the American university which decrees the integrity of the social sciences as a consortium in their own right. He was sacrificing such holistic claims as geography might be able to muster for a freedom to argue the case for geography as a social science.

The second occasion was the publication in 1984 of *Guidelines for Geographic Education: Elementary and Secondary Schools,* authored by a committee jointly representing the AAG and the NCGE. Thanks to a recently published letter (see *Journal of Geography,* March-April 1990, pp. 85–86), we know that, of five themes commended to teachers in this source,

> The committee lifted the human environmental interaction theme directly from Pattison. The themes of place and location are based on Pattison's spatial or geometric geography, and the theme of region comes from Pattison's area studies or regional geography.

From *Journal of Geography,* Vol. 89, No. 5, September/October 1990, pp. 202-206. Reproduced with permission of the National Council for Geographic Education.

Having thus drawn on my spatial area studies and man-land traditions for four of the five themes, the committee could have found the remaining theme, movement, there too—in the spatial tradition (see my sixth paragraph). However that may be, they did not avail themselves of the earth science tradition, their reasons being readily surmised. Peculiar to the elementary and secondary schools is a curriculum category framed as much by theory of citizenship as by theory of knowledge: the social studies. With admiration, I see already in the committee members' adoption of the theme idea a strategy for assimilation of their program to the established repertoire of social studies practice. I see in their exclusion of the earth science tradition an intelligent respect for social studies' purpose.

Here's to the future of education in geography: may it prosper as never before.

W. D. P., 1990

Reprinted from the *Journal of Geography*, 1964, pp. 211-216.

In 1905, one year after professional geography in this country achieved full social identity through the founding of the Association of American Geographers, William Morris Davis responded to a familiar suspicion that geography is simply an undisciplined "omnium-gatherum" by describing an approach that as he saw it imparts a "geographical quality" to some knowledge and accounts for the absence of the quality elsewhere.[1] Davis spoke as president of the AAG. He set an example that was followed by more than one president of that organization. An enduring official concern led the AAG to publish, in 1939 and in 1959, monographs exclusively devoted to a critical review of definitions and their implications.[2]

Every one of the well-known definitions of geography advanced since the founding of the AAG has had its measure of success. Tending to displace one another by turns, each definition has said something true of geography.[3] But from the vantage point of 1964, one can see that each one has also failed. All of them adopted in one way or another a monistic view, a singleness of preference, certain to omit if not to alienate numerous professionals who were in good conscience continuing to participate creatively in the broad geographic enterprise.

The thesis of the present paper is that the work of American geographers, although not conforming to the restrictions implied by any one of these definitions, has exhibited a broad consistency, and that this essential unity has been attributable to a small number of distinct but affiliated traditions, operant as binders in the minds of members of the profession. These traditions are all of great age and have passed into American geography as parts of a general legacy of Western thought. They are shared today by geographers of other nations.

There are four traditions whose identification provides an alternative to the competing monistic definitions that have been the geographer's lot. The resulting pluralistic basis for judgment promises, by full accommodation of what geographers do and by plain-spoken representation thereof, to greatly expedite the task of maintaining an alliance between professional geography and pedagogical geography and at the same time to promote communication with laymen. The following discussion treats the traditions in this order: (1) a spatial tradition, (2) an area studies tradition, (3) a man-land tradition and (4) an earth science tradition.

Spatial Tradition

Entrenched in Western thought is a belief in the importance of spatial analysis, of the act of separating from the happenings of experience such aspects as distance, form, direction and position. It was not until the 17th century that philosophers concentrated attention on these aspects by asking whether or not they were properties of things-in-themselves. Later, when the 18th century writings of Immanuel Kant had become generally circulated, the notion of space as a category including all of these aspects came into widespread use. However, it is evident that particular spatial questions were the subject of highly organized answering attempts long before the time of any of these cogitations. To confirm this point, one need only be reminded of the compilation of elaborate records concerning the location of things in ancient Greece. These were records of sailing distances, of coastlines and of landmarks that grew until they formed the raw material for the great *Geographia* of Claudius Ptolemy in the 2nd century A.D.

A review of American professional geography from the time of its formal organization shows that the spatial tradition of thought had made a deep penetration from the very beginning. For Davis, for Henry Gannett and for most if not all of the 44 other men of the original AAG, the determination and display of spatial aspects of reality through mapping were of undoubted importance, whether contemporary definitions of geography happened to acknowledge this fact or not. One can go further and, by probing beneath the art of mapping, recognize in the behavior of geographers of that time an active interest in the true essentials of the spatial tradition—*geometry* and *movement*. One can trace a basic favoring of movement as a subject of study from the turn-of-the-century work of Emory R. Johnson, writing as professor of transportation at the University of Pennsylvania, through the highly influential theoretical and substantive work of Edward L. Ullman during the past 20 years and thence to an article by a younger geographer on railroad freight traffic in the U.S. and Canada in the *Annals* of the AAG for September 1963.[4]

One can trace a deep attachment to geometry, or positioning-and-layout, from articles on boundaries and population densities in early 20th century volumes of the *Bulletin of the American Geographical Society*, through a controversial pronouncement by Joseph Schaefer in 1953 that granted geographical legitimacy only to studies of spatial patterns[5] and so onward to a recent *Annals* report on electronic scanning of cropland patterns in Pennsylvania.[6]

One might inquire, is discussion of the spatial tradition, after the manner of the remarks just made, likely to bring people within geography closer to an understanding of one another and people outside geography closer to an understanding of geographers? There seem to be at least two reasons for being hopeful. First, an appreciation of this tradition allows one to see a bond of fellowship uniting the elementary school teacher, who attempts the most rudimentary instruction in directions and mapping, with the contemporary research geographer, who dedicates himself to an exploration of central-place theory. One cannot only open the eyes of many teachers to the potentialities of their own instruction, through proper exposition of the spatial tradition, but one can also "hang a bell" on research quantifiers in geography, who are often thought to have wandered so far in their intellectual adventures as to have become lost from the rest. Looking outside geography, one may anticipate benefits from the readiness of countless persons to associate the name "geography" with maps. Latent within this readiness is a willingness to recognize as geography, too, what maps are about—and that is the geometry of and the movement of what is mapped.

Area Studies Tradition

The area studies tradition, like the spatial tradition, is quite strikingly represented in classical antiquity by a practitioner to whose surviving work we can point. He is Strabo, celebrated for his *Geography* which is a massive production addressed to the statesmen of Augustan Rome and intended to sum up and regularize knowledge not of the location of places and associated cartographic facts, as in the somewhat later case of Ptolemy, but of the nature of places, their character and their differentiation. Strabo exhibits interesting attributes of the area-studies tradition that can hardly be overemphasized. They are a pronounced tendency toward subscription primarily to literary standards, an almost omnivorous appetite for information and a self-conscious companionship with history.

It is an extreme good fortune to have in the ranks of modern American geography the scholar Richard Hartshorne, who has pondered the meaning of the area-studies tradition with a legal acuteness that few persons would challenge. In his *Nature of Geography*, his 1939 monograph already cited,[7] he scrutinizes exhaustively the implications of the "interesting attributes" identified in connection with Strabo, even though his concern is with quite other and much later authors, largely German. The major literary problem of unities or wholes he considers from every angle. The Gargantuan appetite for miscellaneous information he accepts and rationalizes. The companionship between area studies and history he clarifies by appraising the so-called idiographic content of both and by affirming the tie of both to what he and Sauer have called "naively given reality."

The area-studies tradition (otherwise known as the chorographic tradition) tended to be excluded from early American professional geography. Today it is beset by certain champions of the spatial tradition who would have one believe that somehow the area-studies way of organizing knowledge is only a subdepartment of spatialism. Still, area-studies as a method of presentation lives and prospers in its own right. One can turn today for reassurance on this score to practically any issue of the *Geographical Review*, just as earlier readers could turn at the opening of the century to that magazine's forerunner.

What is gained by singling out this tradition? It helps toward restoring the faith of many teachers who, being accustomed to administering learning in the area-studies style, have begun to wonder if by doing so they really were keeping in touch with professional geography. (Their doubts are owed all too much to the obscuring effect of technical words attributable to the very professionals who have been intent, ironically, upon protecting that tradition.) Among persons outside the classroom the geographer stands to gain greatly in intelligibility. The title "area-studies" itself carries an understood message in the United States today wherever there is contact with the usages of the academic community. The purpose of characterizing a place, be it neighborhood or nation-state, is readily grasped. Furthermore, recognition of the right of a geographer to be unspecialized may be expected to be forthcoming from people generally, if application for such recognition is made on the merits of this tradition, explicitly.

Man-Land Tradition

That geographers are much given to exploring man-land questions is especially evident to anyone who examines geographic output, not only in this country but also abroad. 0. H. K. Spate, taking an international view, has felt justified by his observations in nominating as the most significant ancient precursor of today's geography neither Ptolemy nor Strabo nor writers typified in their outlook by the geographies of either of these two men, but rather Hippocrates, Greek physician of the 5th century B.C. who left to posterity an extended essay, *On Airs, Waters and Places*.[8] In this work, made up of reflections on human health and conditions of external nature, the questions asked are such as to confine thought almost altogether to presumed influence passing from the latter to the former, questions largely about the effects of winds, drinking water and seasonal changes upon man. Understandable though this uni-directional concern may have been for Hippocrates as medical commentator, and defensible as may be the attraction that this same approach held for students of the condition of man for many, many centuries thereafter, one can only regret that this narrowed version of the man-land tradition, combining all too easily with social Darwinism of the late 19th century, practically overpowered American professional geography in the first generation of its history.[9] The premises of this version governed scores of studies by American geographers in interpreting the rise and fall of nations, the strategy of battles and the construction of public improvements. Eventually this special bias, known as environmentalism, came to be confused with the whole of the man-land tradition in the minds of many people. One can see now, looking back to the years after the ascendancy of environmentalism, that although the spatial tradition was asserting itself with varying degrees of forwardness, and that although the area-studies tradition was also making itself felt, perhaps the most interesting chapters in the story of American professional geography were being written by academicians who were reacting against environmentalism while deliberately remaining within the broad man-land tradition. The rise of culture historians during the last 30 years has meant the dropping of a curtain of culture between land and man, through which it is asserted all influence must pass. Furthermore work of both culture historians and other geographers has exhibited a reversal of the direction of the effects in Hippocrates, man appearing as an independent agent, and the land as a sufferer from action. This trend as presented in published research has reached a high point in the collection of papers titled *Man's Role in Changing the Face of the Earth*. Finally, books and articles can be called to mind that have addressed themselves to the most difficult task of all, a balanced tracing out of interaction between man and environment. Some chapters in the book mentioned above undertake just this. In fact the separateness of this approach is discerned only with difficulty in many places; however, its significance as a general research design that rises above environmentalism, while refusing to abandon the man-land tradition, cannot be mistaken.

The NCGE seems to have associated itself with the man-land tradition, from the time of founding to the present day, more than with any other tradition, although all four of the traditions are amply represented in its official magazine, *The Journal of Geography* and in the proceedings of its annual meetings. This apparent preference on the part of the NCGE members *for defining geography in terms of the man-land tradition* is strong evidence of the appeal that man-land ideas, separately stated, have for persons whose main job is teaching. It should be noted, too, that this inclination reflects a proven acceptance by the general public of learning that centers on resource use and conservation.

Earth Science Tradition

The earth science tradition, embracing study of the earth, the waters of the earth, the atmosphere surrounding the earth and the association between earth and sun, confronts one with a paradox. On the one hand one is assured by professional geographers that their participation in this tradition has declined precipitously in the course of the past few decades, while on the other one knows that college departments of geography across the nation rely substantially, for justification of their role in general education, upon curricular content springing directly from this tradition. From all the reasons that combine to account for this state of affairs, one may, by selecting only two, go far toward achieving an understanding of this tradition. First, there is the fact that American college geography, growing out of departments of geology in many crucial instances, was at one time greatly overweighted in favor of earth science, thus rendering the field unusually liable to a sense of loss as better balance came into being. (This one-time disproportion found reciprocate support for many years in the narrowed, environmentalistic interpretation of the man-land tradition.) Second, here alone in earth science does one encounter subject matter in the normal sense of the term as one reviews geographic traditions. The spatial tradition abstracts certain aspects of reality; area studies is distinguished by a point of view; the manland tradition dwells upon relationships; but earth science is identifiable through concrete objects. Historians, sociologists and other academicians tend not only to accept but also to ask for help from this part of geography. They readily appreciate earth science as something physically associated with their subjects of study, yet generally beyond their competence to treat. From this appreciation comes strength for geography-as-earth-science in the curriculum.

Only by granting full stature to the earth science tradition can one make sense out of the oft-repeated addage, "Geography is the mother of sciences." This is the tradition that emerged in ancient Greece, most clearly in the work of Aristotle, as a wide-ranging study of natural processes in and near the surface of the earth. This is the tradition that was rejuvenated by Varenius in the 17th century as "Geographia Generalis." This is the tradition that has been subjected to subdivision as the development of science has approached the present day, yielding mineralogy, paleontology, glaciology, meterology and other specialized fields of learning.

Readers who are acquainted with American junior high schools may want to make a challenge at this point, being aware that a current revival of earth sciences is being sponsored in those schools by the field of geology. Belatedly, geography has joined in support of this revival.[10] It may be said that in this connection and in others, American professional geography may have faltered in its adherence to the earth science tradition but not given it up.

In describing geography, there would appear to be some advantages attached to isolating this final tradition. Separation improves the geographer's chances of successfully explaining to educators why geography has extreme difficulty in accommodating itself to social studies programs. Again, separate attention allows one to make understanding contact with members of the American public for whom surrounding nature is known as the geographic environment. And finally, specific reference to the geographer's earth science tradition brings into the open the basis of what is, almost without a doubt, morally the most significant concept in the entire geographic heritage, that of the earth as a unity, the single common habitat of man.

An Overview

The four traditions though distinct in logic are joined in action. One can say of geography that it pursues concurrently all four of them. Taking the traditions in varying combinations, the geographer can explain the conventional divisions of the field. Human or cultural geography turns out to consist of the first three traditions applied to human societies; physical geography, it becomes evident, is the fourth tradition prosecuted under constraints from the first and second traditions. Going further, one can uncover the meanings of "systematic geography," "regional geography," "urban geography," "industrial geography," etc.

It is to be hoped that through a widened willingness to conceive of and discuss the field in terms of these traditions, geography will be better able to secure the inner unity and outer intelligibility to which reference was made at the opening of this paper, and that thereby the effectiveness of geography's contribution to American education and to the general American welfare will be appreciably increased.

---

1. William Morris Davis, "An Inductive Study of the Content of Geography," *Bulletin of the American Geographical Society,* Vol. 38, No. 1 (1906), 71.

2. Richard Hartshorne, *The Nature of Geography,* Association of American Geographers (1939), and idem., *Perspective on the Nature of Geography,* Association of American Geographers (1959).

3. The essentials of several of these definitions appear in Barry N. Floyd, "Putting Geography in Its Place," *The Journal of Geography,* Vol. 62, No. 3 (March, 1963). 117–120.

4. William H. Wallace, "Freight Traffic Functions of Anglo-American Railroads," *Annals of the Association of American Geographers,* Vol. 53, No. 3 (September, 1963), 312–331.

5. Fred K. Schaefer, "Exceptionalism in Geography: A Methodological Examination," *Annals of the Association of American Geographers,* Vol. 43, No. 3 (September, 1953), 226–249.

6. James P. Latham, "Methodology for an Instrumental Geographic Analysis," *Annals of the Association of American Geographers,* Vol. 53, No. 2 (June, 1963). 194–209.

7. Hartshorne's 1959 monograph, *Perspective on the Nature of Geography,* was also cited earlier. In this later work, he responds to dissents from geographers whose preferred primary commitment lies outside the area studies tradition.

8. O. H. K. Spate, "Quantity and Quality in Geography," *Annals of the Association of American Geographers,* Vol. 50, No. 4 (December, 1960), 379.

9. Evidence of this dominance may be found in Davis's 1905 declaration: "Any statement is of geographical quality if it contains . . . some relation between an element of inorganic control and one of organic response" (Davis, *loc. cit.*).

10. Geography is represented on both the Steering Committee and Advisory Board of the Earth Science Curriculum Project, potentially the most influential organization acting on behalf of earth science in the schools.

The American Geographies: Losing Our Sense of Place

Americans are fast becoming strangers in a strange land, where one roiling river, one scarred patch of desert, is as good as another. America the beautiful exists—a select few still know it intimately—but many of us are settling for a homogenized national geography.

Barry Lopez

Barry Lopez has written The Rediscovery of North America *(Vintage), and his most recent book is* Field Notes *(Knopf).*

It has become commonplace to observe that Americans know little of the geography of their country, that they are innocent of it as a landscape of rivers, mountains, and towns. They do not know, supposedly, the location of the Delaware Water Gap, the Olympic Mountains, or the Piedmont Plateau; and, the indictment continues, they have little conception of the way the individual components of this landscape are imperiled, from a human perspective, by modern farming practices or industrial pollution.

I do not know how true this is, but it is easy to believe that it is truer than most of us would wish. A recent Gallup Organization and National Geographic Society survey found Americans woefully ignorant of world geography. Three out of four couldn't locate the Persian Gulf. The implication was that we knew no more about our own homeland, and that this ignorance undermined the integrity of our political processes and the efficiency of our business enterprises.

As Americans, we profess a sincere and fierce love for the American landscape, for our rolling prairies, freeflowing rivers, and "purple mountains' majesty"; but it is hard to imagine, actually, where this particular landscape is. It is not just that a nostalgic landscape has passed away—Mark Twain's Mississippi is now dammed from Minnesota to Missouri and the prairies have all been sold and fenced. It is that it has always been a romantic's landscape. In the attenuated form in which it is presented on television today, in magazine articles and in calendar photographs, the essential wildness of the American landscape is reduced to attractive scenery. We look out on a familiar, memorized landscape that portends adventure and promises enrichment. There are no distracting people in it and few artifacts of human life. The animals are all beautiful, diligent, one might even say well-behaved. Nature's unruliness, the power of rivers and skies to intimidate, and any evidence of disastrous human land management practices are all but invisible. It is, in short, a magnificent garden, a colonial vision of paradise imposed on a real place that is, at best, only selectively known.

> *To truly understand geography requires not only time but a kind of local expertise, an intimacy with place few of us ever develop.*

The real American landscape is a face of almost incomprehensible depth and complexity. If one were to sit for a few days, for example, among the ponderosa pine forests and black lava fields of the Cascade Mountains in western Oregon, inhaling the pines' sweet balm on an evening breeze from some point on the barren rock, and then were to step off to the Olympic Peninsula in Washington, to those rain forests with sphagnum moss floors soft as fleece underfoot and Douglas firs too big around for five people to hug, and then head south to walk the ephemeral creeks and sun-blistered playas of the Mojave Desert in southern California, one would be reeling under the sensations. The contrast is not only one of plants and soils, a different array say, of brilliantly colored beetles. The shock to the senses comes from a different shape to the silence, a difference in the very quality of light, in the weight of the air. And this relatively short journey down the West Coast would still leave the traveler with all that lay to the east to explore—the anomalous sand hills of Nebraska, the heat and frog voices of Okefenokee Swamp, the fetch of Chesapeake Bay, the hardwood copses and black bears of the Ozark Mountains.

No one of these places, of course, can be entirely fathomed, biologically or aesthetically. They are mysteries upon which we impose names. Enchantments. We tick the names off glibly but lovingly. We mean no disrespect. Our genuine desire, though we might be skeptical about the time it would take and uncertain of its practical value to us, is to actually know these places. As deeply ingrained in the American psyche as the desire to conquer and control the land is the desire to sojourn in it, to sail up and down Pamlico Sound, to paddle a canoe through Minnesota's boundary waters, to

From *Teacher Magazine*, February 1990, pp. 38-44. Reprinted by permission of Sterling Lord Literistic, Inc. Originally appeared in *Orion*, Autumn 1989, pp. 52-61.

walk on the desert of the Great Salt Lake, to camp in the stony hardwood valleys of Vermont.

To do this well, to really come to an understanding of a specific American geography, requires not only time but a kind of local expertise, an intimacy with place few of us ever develop. There is no way around the former requirement: If you want to know you must take the time. It is not in books. A specific geographical understanding, however, can be sought out and borrowed. It resides with men and women more or less sworn to a place, who abide there, who have a feel for the soil and history, for the turn of leaves and night sounds. Often they are glad to take the outlander in tow.

These local geniuses of American landscape, in my experience, are people in whom geography thrives. They are the antithesis of geographical ignorance. Rarely known outside their own communities, they often seem, at the first encounter, unremarkable and anonymous. They may not be able to recall the name of a particular wildflower—or they may have given it a name known only to them. They might have forgotten the precise circumstances of a local historical event. Or they can't say for certain when the last of the Canada geese passed through in the fall, or can't differentiate between two kinds of trout in the same creek. Like all of us, they have fallen prey to the fallacies of memory and are burdened with ignorance; but they are nearly flawless in the respect they bear these places they love. Their knowledge is intimate rather than encyclopedic, human but not necessarily scholarly. It rings with the concrete details of experience.

America, I believe, teems with such people. The paradox here, between a faulty grasp of geographical knowledge for which Americans are indicted and the intimate, apparently contradictory familiarity of a group of largely anonymous people, is not solely a matter of confused scale. (The local landscape is easier to know than a national geography.) And it is not simply ironic. The paradox is dark. To be succinct: The politics and advertising that seek a national audience must project a national geography; to be broadly useful that geography must, inevitably, be generalized and it is often romantic. It is therefore frequently misleading and imprecise. The same holds true with the entertainment industry, but here the problem might be clearer. The same films, magazines, and television features that honor an imaginary American landscape also tout the worth of the anonymous men and women who interpret it. Their affinity for the land is lauded, their local allegiance admired. But the rigor of their local geographies, taken as a whole, contradicts a patriotic, national vision of unspoiled, untroubled land. These men and women are ultimately forgotten, along with the details of the landscapes they speak for, in the face of more pressing national matters. It is the chilling nature of modern society to find an ignorance of geography, local or national, as excusable as an ignorance of hand tools; and to find the commitment of people to their home places only momentarily entertaining. And finally naive.

If one were to pass time among Basawara people in the Kalahari Desert, or with Kreen-Akrora in the Amazon Basin, or with Pitjantjatjara Aborigines in Australia, the most salient impression they might leave is of an absolutely stunning knowledge of their local geography—geology, hydrology, biology, and weather. In short, the extensive particulars of their intercourse with it.

In 40,000 years of human history, it has only been in the last few hundred years or so that a people could afford to ignore their local geographies as completely as we do and still survive. Technological innovations from refrigerated trucks to artificial fertilizers, from sophisticated cost accounting to mass air transportation, have utterly changed concepts of season, distance, soil productivity, and the real cost of drawing sustenance from the land. It is now possible for a resident of Boston to bite into a fresh strawberry in the dead of winter; for someone in San Francisco to travel to Atlanta in a few hours with no worry of how formidable might be crossings of the Great Basin Desert or the Mississippi River; for an absentee farmer to gain a tax advantage from a farm that leaches poisons into its water table and on which crops are left to rot. The Pitjantjatjara might shake their heads in bewilderment and bemusement, not because they are primitive or ignorant people, not because they have no sense of irony or are incapable of marveling, but because they have not (many would say not yet) realized a world in which such manipulation of the land—surmounting the imperatives of distance it imposes, for example, or turning the large-scale destruction of forests and arable land in wealth—is desirable or plausible.

In the years I have traveled through America, in cars and on horseback, on foot and by raft, I have repeatedly been brought to a sudden state of awe by some gracile or savage movement of animal, some odd wrapping of tree's foliage by the wind, an unimpeded run of dew-laden prairie stretching to a horizon flat as a coin where a pin-dot sun pales the dawn sky pink. I know these things are beyond intellection, that they are the vivid edges of a world that includes but also transcends the human world. In memory, when I dwell on these things, I know that in a truly national literature there should be odes to the Triassic reds of the Colorado Plateau, to the sharp and ghostly light of the Florida Keys, to the aeolian soils of southern Minnesota, and the Palouse in Washington, though the modern mind abjures the literary potential of such subjects. (If the sand and flood water farmers of Arizona and New Mexico were to take the black loams of Louisiana in their hands they would be flabbergasted, and that is the beginning of literature.) I know there should be eloquent evocations of the cobbled beaches of Maine, the plutonic walls of the Sierra Nevada, the orange canyons of the Kaibab Plateau. I have no doubt, in fact, that there are. They are as numerous and diverse as the eyes and fingers that ponder the country—it is that only a handful of them are known. The great majority are to be found in drawers and boxes, in the letters and private journals of millions of workaday people who have regarded their encounters with the land as an engagement bordering on the spiritual, as being fundamentally linked to their state of health.

One cannot acknowledge the extent and the history of this kind of testimony without being forced to the realization that something strange, if not dangerous, is afoot. Year by year, the number of people with firsthand experience in the land dwindles. Rural populations continue to shift to the cities. The family farm is in a state of demise, and government and industry continue to apply pressure on the native peoples of North America to sever their ties with the land. In the wake of this loss of personal and local knowledge from which a real geography is derived, the knowledge on which a country must ultimately stand, has [be]come something hard to define but I think sinister and unsettling—the packaging and marketing of land as a form of entertainment. An incipient industry, capitalizing on the nostalgia Americans feel for the imagined virgin landscapes of their fathers, and on a desire for adventure, now offers people a convenient though sometimes incomplete or even spurious geography as an inducement to purchase a unique experience. But the line between authentic experience and a superficial exposure to the elements of experience is blurred. And the real landscape, in all its complexity, is distorted even further in the public imagination. No longer innately mysterious and dignified, a ground from which experience grows, it becomes a curiously generic backdrop on which experience is imposed.

In theme parks the profound, subtle, and protracted experience of running a river is reduced to a loud, quick, safe equivalence, a pleasant distraction. People only able to venture into the countryside on annual vacations are, increasingly, schooled in the belief that wild land will, and should, provide thrills and exceptional scenery on a timely basis. If it does not, something is wrong, either with the land itself or possibly with the company outfitting the trip.

People in America, then, face a convoluted situation. The land itself, vast and differentiated, defies the notion of a national geography. If applied at all it must be applied lightly and it must grow out of the concrete detail of local geographies. Yet Americans are daily presented with, and have become accustomed to talking about, a homogenized national geography. one that seems to operate independently of the land, a collection of objects rather than a continuous bolt of fabric. It appears in advertisements, as a background in movies, and in patriotic calendars. The suggestion is that there can be national geography because the constituent parts are interchangeable and can be treated as commodities. In day-to-day affairs, in other words, one place serves as well as another to convey one's point. On reflection, this is an appalling condescension and a terrible imprecision, the very antithesis of knowledge. The idea that either the Green River in Utah or the Salmon River in Idaho will do, or that the valleys of Kentucky and West Virginia are virtually interchangeable, is not just misleading. For people still dependent on the soil for their sustenance, or for people whose memories tie them to those places, it betrays a numbing casualness, a utilitarian, expedient, and commercial frame of mind. It heralds a society in which it is no longer necessary for human beings to know where they live, except as those places are described and fixed by numbers. The truly difficult and lifelong task of discovering where one lives is finally disdained.

If a society forgets or no longer cares where it lives, then anyone with the political power and the will to do so can manipulate the landscape to conform to certain social ideals or nostalgic visions. People may hardly notice that anything has happened, or assume that whatever happens—a mountain stripped of timber and eroding into its creeks—is for the common good. The more superficial a society's knowledge of the real dimensions of the land it occupies becomes, the more vulnerable the land is to exploitation, to manipulation for short-term gain. The land, virtually powerless before political and commercial entities, finds itself finally with no defenders. It finds itself bereft of intimates with indispensable, concrete knowledge. (Oddly, or perhaps not oddly, while American society continues to value local knowledge as a quaint part of its heritage, it continues to cut such people off from any real political power. This is as true for small farmers and illiterate cowboys as it is for American Indians, native Hawaiians, and Eskimos.)

The intense pressure of imagery in America, and the manipulation of images necessary to a society with specific goals, means the land will inevitably be treated like a commodity; and voices that tend to contradict the proffered image will, one way or another, be silenced or discredited by those in power. This is not new to America; the promulgation in America of a false or imposed geography has been the case from the beginning. All local geographies, as they were defined by hundreds of separate, independent native traditions, were denied in the beginning in favor of an imported and unifying vision of America's natural history. The country, the landscape itself, was eventually defined according to dictates of Progress like Manifest Destiny, and laws like the Homestead Act which reflected a poor understanding of the physical lay of the land.

When I was growing up in southern California, I formed the rudiments of a local geography—eucalyptus trees, February rains, Santa Ana winds. I lost much of it when my family moved to New York City, a move typical of the modern, peripatetic style of American life, responding to the exigencies of divorce and employment. As a boy I felt a hunger to know the American landscape that was extreme; when I was finally able to travel on my own, I did so. Eventually I visited most of the United States, living for brief periods of time in Arizona, Indiana, Alabama, Georgia, Wyoming, New Jersey, and Montana before settling 20 years ago in western Oregon.

The astonishing level of my ignorance confronted me everywhere I went. I knew early on that the country could not be held together in a few phrases, that its geography was magnificent and incomprehensible, that a man or woman could devote a lifetime to its elucidation and still feel in the end that he had but sailed many thousands of miles over the surface of the ocean. So I came into the habit of traversing landscapes I wanted to know with local tutors and reading what had previously been written about, and in, those places. I came to value exceedingly novels and essays and works of nonfiction that connected human enterprise to real and specific places, and I grew to be mildly distrustful of work that occurred in no particular place, work so cerebral and detached as to be refutable only in an argument of ideas.

These sojourns in various corners of the country infused me, somewhat to my surprise on thinking about it, with a great sense of hope. Whatever despair I had come to feel at a waning sense of the real land and the emergence of false geographies—elements of the land being manipulated, for example, to create erroneous but useful patterns in advertising—was dispelled by the depth of a single person's local knowledge, by the serenity that seemed to come with that intelligence. Any harm that might be done by people who cared nothing for the land, to whom it was not innately worthy but only something ultimately for sale, I thought, would one day have to meet this kind of integrity, people with the same dignity and transcendence as the land they occupied. So when I traveled, when I rolled my sleeping bag out on the shores of the Beaufort Sea, or in the high pastures of the Absaroka Range in Wyoming, or at the bottom of the Grand Canyon, I absorbed those particular testaments to life, the indigenous color and songbird song, the smell of sun-bleached rock, damp earth, and wild honey, with some crude appreciation of the singular magnificence of each of those places. And the reassurance I felt expanded in the knowledge that there were, and would likely always be, people speaking out whenever they felt the dignity of the Earth imperiled in those places.

The promulgation of false geographies, which threaten the fundamental notion of what it means to live somewhere, is a current with a stable and perhaps growing countercurrent. People living in New York City are familiar with the stone basements, the cratonic geology, of that island and have a feeling for birds migrating through in the fall, their sequence and number. They do not find the city alien but human, its attenuated natural history merely different from that of rural Georgia or Kansas. I find the countermeasure, too, among Eskimos who cannot read but who might engage you for days on the subtleties of sea-ice topography. And among men and women who, though they have followed in the footsteps of their parents, have come to the conclusion that they cannot farm or fish or log in the way their ancestors did; the finite boundaries to this sort of wealth have appeared in their lifetime. Or among young men and women who have taken several decades of book-learned agronomy, zoology, silviculture and horticulture, ecology, ethnobotany, and fluvial geomorphology and turned it into a new kind of local knowledge, who have taken up residence in a place and sought, both because of and in spite of their education, to develop a deep intimacy with it. Or they have gone to work, idealistically, for the National Park Service or the fish and wildlife services or for a private institution like the Nature Conservancy. They are people to whom the land is more than politics and economics. These are people for whom the land is alive. It feeds them, directly, and that is how and why they learn its geography.

In the end, then, if one begins among the blue crabs of Chesapeake Bay and wanders for several years, down through the Smoky Mountains and back to the bluegrass hills, along the drainages of the Ohio and into the hill country of Missouri, where in summer a chorus of cicadas might drown out human conversation, then up the Missouri itself, reading on the way the entries of Meriwether Lewis and William Clark and musing on the demise of the plains grizzly and the sturgeon, crosses west into the drainage of the Platte and spends the evenings with Gene Weltfish's *The Lost Universe,* her book about the Pawnee who once thrived there, then drops south to the Palo Duro Canyon and the irrigated farms of the Llano Estacado in Texas, turns west across the Sangre de Cristo, southernmost of the Rocky Mountain ranges, and moves north and west up onto the slickrock mesas of Utah, those browns and oranges, the ocherous hues reverberating in the deep canyons, then goes north, swinging west to the insular ranges that sit like battleships in the pelagic space of Nevada, camps at the steaming edge of the sulfur springs in the Black Rock desert, where alkaline pans are glazed with a ferocious light, a heat to melt iron, then crosses the northern Sierra Nevada, waist-deep in summer snow in the passes, to descend to the valley of the Sacramento, and rises through groves of the elephantine redwoods in the Coast Range, to arrive at Cape Mendocino, before Balboa's Pacific, cormorants and gulls, gray whales headed north for Unimak Pass in the Aleutians, the winds crashing down on you, facing the ocean over the blue ocean that gives the scene its true vastness, making this crossing, having been so often astonished at the line and the color of the land, the ingenious lives of its plants and animals, the varieties of its darknesses, the intensity of the stars overhead, you would be ashamed to discover, then, in yourself, any capacity to focus on ravages in the land that left you unsettled. You would have seen so much, breathtaking, startling, and outsize, that you might not be able for a long time to break the spell, the sense, especially finishing your journey in the West, that the land had not been as rearranged or quite as compromised as you had first imagined.

After you had slept some nights on the beach, however, with that finite line of the ocean before you and the land stretching out behind you, the wind first battering then cradling you, you would be compelled by memory, obligated by your own involvement, to speak of what left you troubled. To find the rivers dammed and shrunken, the soil washed away, the land fenced, a tracery of pipes and wires and roads laid down everywhere and animals, cutting the eye off repeatedly and confining it—you had expected this. It troubles you no more than your despair over the ruthlessness, the insensitivity, the impetuousness of modern life. What underlies this obvious change, however, is a less noticeable pattern of disruption: acidic lakes, the skies empty of birds, fouled beaches, the poisonous slags of industry, the sun burning like a molten coin in ruined air.

It is a tenet of certain ideologies that man is responsible for all that is ugly, that everything nature creates is beautiful. Nature's darkness goes partly unreported, of course, and human brilliance is often perversely ignored. What is true is that man has a power, literally beyond his comprehension, to destroy. The lethality of some of what he manufactures, the incompetence with which he stores it or seeks to dispose of it, the cavalier way in which he employs in his daily living substances that threaten his health, the leniency of the courts in these matters (as though products as well as people enjoyed the protection of the Fifth Amendment), and the treatment of open land, rivers, and the atmosphere as if, in some medieval way. they could still be regarded as disposal sinks of infinite capacity, would make you wonder, standing face to in the wind at Cape Mendocino, if we weren't bent on an errant of madness.

The geographies of North America, the myriad small landscapes that make up the national fabric, are threatened—by ignorance of what makes them unique, by utilitarian attitudes, by failure to include them in the moral universe, and by brutal disregard. A testament of minor voices can clear away an ignorance of any place, can inform us of its special qualities; but no voice, by merely telling a story, can cause the poisonous wastes that saturate some parts of the land to decompose, to evaporate. This responsibility falls ultimately to the national community, a vague and fragile entity to be sure, but one that, in America, can be ferocious in exerting its will.

Geography, the formal way in which we grapple with this areal mystery, is finally knowledge that calls up something in the land we recognize and respond to. It gives us a sense of place and a sense of community. Both are indispensable to a state of well-being, an individual's and a country's.

One afternoon on the Siuslaw River in the Coast Range of Oregon, in January, I hooked a steelhead, a sea-run trout, that told me, through the muscles of my hands and arms and shoulders, something of the nature of the thing I was calling "the Siuslaw River." Years ago I had stood under a pecan tree in Upson County, Georgia, idly eating the nuts, when slowly it occurred to me that these nuts would taste different from pecans growing somewhere up in South Carolina. I didn't need a sharp sense of taste to know this, only to pay attention at a level no one had ever told me was necessary. One November dawn, long before the sun rose, I began a vigil at the Dumont Dunes in the Mojave Desert in California, which I kept until a few minutes after the sun broke the horizon. During that time I named to myself the colors by which the sky changed and by which the sand itself flowed like a rising tide through grays and silvers and blues into yellows, pinks, washed duns, and fallow beiges.

It is through the power of observation, the gifts of eye and ear, of tongue and nose and finger, that a place first rises up in our mind; afterward, it is memory that carries the place, that allows it to grow in depth and complexity. For as long as our records go back, we have held these two things dear, landscape and memory. Each infuses us with a different kind of life. The one feeds us, figuratively and literally. The other protects us from lies and tyranny. To keep landscapes intact and the memory of them, our history in them, alive, seems as imperative a task in modern time as finding the extent to which individual expression can be accommodated, before it threatens to destroy the fabric of society.

If I were now to visit another country, I would ask my local companion, before I saw any museum or library, any factory or fabled town, to walk me in the country of his or her youth, to tell me the names of things and how, traditionally, they have been fitted together in a community. I would ask for the stories, the voice of memory over the land. I would ask about the history of storms there, the age of the trees, the winter color of the hills. Only then would I ask to see the museum. I would want first the sense of a real place, to know that I was not inhabiting an idea. I would want to know the lay of the land first, the real geography, and take some measure of the love of it in my companion before stood before the painting or read works of scholarship. I would want to have something real and remembered against which I might hope to measure their truth.

THE COMING ANARCHY

How scarcity, crime, overpopulation, tribalism, and disease are rapidly destroying the social fabric of our planet

Robert D. Kaplan

Robert D. Kaplan is a contributing editor of The Atlantic. *His article in this issue will be expanded into a book he is writing for Random House, with support from the U.S. Institute of Peace and the Foreign Policy Research Institute.*

THE Minister's eyes were like egg yolks, an aftereffect of some of the many illnesses, malaria especially, endemic in his country. There was also an irrefutable sadness in his eyes. He spoke in a slow and creaking voice, the voice of hope about to expire. Flame trees, coconut palms, and a ballpoint-blue Atlantic composed the background. None of it seemed beautiful, though. "In forty-five years I have never seen things so bad. We did not manage ourselves well after the British departed. But what we have now is something worse—the revenge of the poor, of the social failures, of the people least able to bring up children in a modern society." Then he referred to the recent coup in the West African country Sierra Leone. "The boys who took power in Sierra Leone come from houses like this." The Minister jabbed his finger at a corrugated metal shack teeming with children. "In three months these boys confiscated all the official Mercedes, Volvos, and BMWs and willfully wrecked them on the road." The Minister mentioned one of the coup's leaders, Solomon Anthony Joseph Musa, who shot the people who had paid for his schooling, "in order to erase the humiliation and mitigate the power his middle-class sponsors held over him."

Tyranny is nothing new in Sierra Leone or in the rest of West Africa. But it is now part and parcel of an increasing lawlessness that is far more significant than any coup, rebel incursion, or episodic experiment in democracy. Crime was what my friend—a top-ranking African official whose life would be threatened were I to identify him more precisely—really wanted to talk about. Crime is what makes West Africa a natural point of departure for my report on what the political character of our planet is likely to be in the twenty-first century.

The cities of West Africa at night are some of the unsafest places in the world. Streets are unlit; the police often lack gasoline for their vehicles; armed burglars, carjackers, and muggers proliferate. "The government in Sierra Leone has no writ after dark," says a foreign resident, shrugging. When I was in the capital, Freetown, last September, eight men armed with AK-47s broke into the house of an American man. They tied him up and stole everything of value. Forget Miami: direct flights between the United States and the Mur-

From *The Atlantic Monthly,* February 1994, pp. 44-46, 48-49, 52, 54, 58-60, 62-63, 66, 68-70, 72-76.

tala Muhammed Airport, in neighboring Nigeria's largest city, Lagos, have been suspended by order of the U.S. Secretary of Transportation because of ineffective security at the terminal and its environs. A State Department report cited the airport for "extortion by law-enforcement and immigration officials." This is one of the few times that the U.S. government has embargoed a foreign airport for reasons that are linked purely to crime. In Abidjan, effectively the capital of the Côte d'Ivoire, or Ivory Coast, restaurants have stick- and gun-wielding guards who walk you the fifteen feet or so between your car and the entrance, giving you an eerie taste of what American cities might be like in the future. An Italian ambassador was killed by gunfire when robbers invaded an Abidjan restaurant. The family of the Nigerian ambassador was tied up and robbed at gunpoint in the ambassador's residence. After university students in the Ivory Coast caught bandits who had been plaguing their dorms, they executed them by hanging tires around their necks and setting the tires on fire. In one instance Ivorian policemen stood by and watched the "necklacings," afraid to intervene. Each time I went to the Abidjan bus terminal, groups of young men with restless, scanning eyes surrounded my taxi, putting their hands all over the windows, demanding "tips" for carrying my luggage even though I had only a rucksack. In cities in six West African countries I saw similar young men everywhere—hordes of them. They were like loose molecules in a very unstable social fluid, a fluid that was clearly on the verge of igniting.

"You see," my friend the Minister told me, "in the villages of Africa it is perfectly natural to feed at any table and lodge in any hut. But in the cities this communal existence no longer holds. You must pay for lodging and be invited for food. When young men find out that their relations cannot put them up, they become lost. They join other migrants and slip gradually into the criminal process."

"In the poor quarters of Arab North Africa," he continued, "there is much less crime, because Islam provides a social anchor: of education and indoctrination. Here in West Africa we have a lot of superficial Islam and superficial Christianity. Western religion is undermined by animist beliefs not suitable to a moral society, because they are based on irrational spirit power. Here spirits are used to wreak vengeance by one person against another, or one group against another." Many of the atrocities in the Liberian civil war have been tied to belief in *juju* spirits, and the BBC has reported, in its magazine *Focus on Africa,* that in the civil fighting in adjacent Sierra Leone, rebels were said to have "a young woman with them who would go to the front naked, always walking backwards and looking in a mirror to see where she was going. This made her invisible, so that she could cross to the army's positions and there bury charms . . . to improve the rebels' chances of success."

SIERRA LEONE IS A MICROCOSM OF WHAT IS OCCURRING IN WEST AFRICA AND MUCH OF THE UNDER-DEVELOPED WORLD: THE WITHERING AWAY OF CENTRAL GOVERNMENTS, THE RISE OF TRIBAL AND REGIONAL DOMAINS, THE UNCHECKED SPREAD OF DISEASE, AND THE GROWING PERVASIVENESS OF WAR.

Finally my friend the Minister mentioned polygamy. Designed for a pastoral way of life, polygamy continues to thrive in sub-Saharan Africa even though it is increasingly uncommon in Arab North Africa. Most youths I met on the road in West Africa told me that they were from "extended" families, with a mother in one place and a father in another. Translated to an urban environment, loose family structures are largely responsible for the world's highest birth rates and the explosion of the HIV virus on the continent. Like the communalism and animism, they provide a weak shield against the corrosive social effects of life in cities. In those cities African culture is being redefined while desertification and deforestation—also tied to overpopulation—drive more and more African peasants out of the countryside.

A PREMONITION OF THE FUTURE

West Africa is becoming *the* symbol of worldwide demographic, environmental, and societal stress, in which criminal anarchy emerges as the real "strategic" danger. Disease, overpopulation, unprovoked crime, scarcity of resources, refugee migrations, the increasing erosion of nation-states and international borders, and the empowerment of private armies, security firms, and international drug cartels are now most tellingly demonstrated through a West African prism. West Africa provides an appropriate introduction to the issues, often extremely unpleasant to discuss, that will soon confront our civilization. To remap the political earth the way it will be a few decades hence—as I intend to do in this article—I find I must begin with West Africa.

There is no other place on the planet where political maps are so deceptive—where, in fact, they tell such lies—as in West Africa. Start with Sierra Leone. According to the map, it is a nation-state of defined borders, with a government in control of its territory. In truth the Sierra Leonian government, run by a twenty-seven-year-old army captain, Valentine Strasser, controls Freetown by day and by day also controls part of the rural interior. In the government's territory the national army is an unruly rabble threatening drivers and passengers at most checkpoints. In the other part of the country units of two separate armies from the war in Liberia have taken up residence, as has an army of Sierra Leonian rebels. The government force fighting the rebels is full of renegade commanders who have aligned themselves with disaffected village chiefs. A premodern formlessness governs the battlefield, evoking the wars in medieval Europe prior to the 1648 Peace of Westphalia, which ushered in the era of organized nation-states.

As a consequence, roughly 400,000 Sierra Leonians are internally displaced, 280,000 more have fled to neighboring Guinea, and another 100,000 have fled to Liberia, even as 400,000 Liberians have fled to Sierra Leone. The third largest city in Sierra Leone, Gondama, is a displaced-persons camp. With an additional 600,000 Liberians in Guinea and 250,000 in the Ivory Coast, the borders dividing these four countries have become largely meaningless. Even in quiet zones none of the governments except the Ivory Coast's maintains the schools, bridges, roads, and police forces in a manner necessary for functional sovereignty. The Koranko ethnic group in northeastern Sierra Leone does all its trading in Guinea. Sierra Leonian diamonds are more likely to be sold in Liberia than in Freetown. In the eastern provinces of Sierra Leone you can buy Liberian beer but not the local brand.

In Sierra Leone, as in Guinea, as in the Ivory Coast, as in Ghana, most of the primary rain forest and the secondary bush is being destroyed at an alarming rate. I saw convoys of trucks bearing majestic hardwood trunks to coastal ports. When Sierra Leone achieved its independence, in 1961, as much as 60 percent of the country was primary rain forest. Now six percent is. In the Ivory Coast the proportion has fallen from 38 percent to eight percent. The deforestation has led to soil erosion, which has led to more flooding and more mosquitoes. Virtually everyone in the West African interior has some form of malaria.

Sierra Leone is a microcosm of what is occurring, albeit in a more tempered and gradual manner, throughout West Africa and much of the underdeveloped world: the withering away of central governments, the rise of tribal and regional domains, the unchecked spread of disease, and the growing pervasiveness of war. West Africa is reverting to the Africa of the Victorian atlas. It consists now of a series of coastal trading posts, such as Freetown and Conakry, and an interior that, owing to violence, volatility, and disease, is again becoming, as Graham Greene once observed, "blank" and "unexplored." However, whereas Greene's vision implies a certain romance, as in the somnolent and charmingly seedy Freetown of his celebrated novel *The Heart of the Matter*, it is Thomas Malthus, the philosopher of demographic doomsday, who is now the prophet of West Africa's future. And West Africa's future, eventually, will also be that of most of the rest of the world.

Consider "Chicago." I refer not to Chicago, Illinois, but to a slum district of Abidjan, which the young toughs in the area have named after the American city. ("Washington" is another poor section of Abidjan.) Although Sierra Leone is widely regarded as beyond salvage, the Ivory Coast has been considered an African success story, and Abidjan has been called "the Paris of West Africa." Success, however, was built on two artificial factors: the high price of cocoa, of which the Ivory Coast is the world's leading producer, and the talents of a French expatriate community, whose members have helped run the government and the private sector. The expanding cocoa economy made the Ivory Coast a magnet for migrant workers from all over West Africa: between a third and a half of the country's population is now non-Ivorian, and the figure could be as high as 75 percent in Abidjan. During the 1980s cocoa prices fell and the French began to leave. The skyscrapers of the Paris of West Africa are a façade. Perhaps 15 percent of Abidjan's population of three million people live in shantytowns like Chicago and Washington, and the vast majority live in places that are not much better. Not all of these places appear on any of the readily available maps. This is another indication of how political maps are the products of tired conventional wisdom and, in the Ivory Coast's case, of an elite that will ultimately be forced to relinquish power.

Chicago, like more and more of Abidjan, is a slum in the bush: a checkerwork of corrugated zinc roofs and walls made of cardboard and black plastic wrap. It is located in a gully teeming with coconut palms and oil palms, and is ravaged by flooding. Few residents have easy access to electricity, a sewage system, or a clean water supply. The crumbly red laterite earth crawls with foot-long lizards both inside and outside the shacks. Children defecate in a stream filled with garbage and pigs, droning with malarial mosquitoes. In this stream women do the washing. Young unemployed men spend their time drinking beer, palm wine, and gin while gambling on pinball games constructed out of rotting wood and rusty nails. These are the same youths who rob houses in more prosperous Ivorian neighborhoods at night. One man I met, Damba Tesele, came to Chicago from Burkina Faso in 1963. A cook by profession, he has four wives and thirty-two children, not one of whom has made it to high school. He has seen his shanty community destroyed by municipal authorities seven times since coming to the area. Each time he and his neighbors rebuild. Chicago is the latest incarnation.

Fifty-five percent of the Ivory Coast's population is urban, and the proportion is expected to reach 62 percent by 2000. The yearly net population growth is 3.6 percent. This means that the Ivory Coast's 13.5 million people will become 39 million by 2025, when much of the population will consist of urbanized peasants like those of Chicago. But don't count on the Ivory Coast's still existing then. Chicago, which is more indicative of Africa's and the Third World's demographic present—and even more of the future—than any idyllic junglescape of women balancing earthen jugs on their heads, illustrates why the Ivory Coast, once a model of Third World success, is becoming a case study in Third World catastrophe.

President Félix Houphouët-Boigny, who died last December at the age of about ninety, left behind a weak cluster of political parties and a leaden bureaucracy that discourages foreign investment. Because the military is small and the non-Ivorian population large, there is neither an obvious force to maintain order nor a sense of nationhood that would lessen the need for such enforcement. The economy has been shrinking since the mid-1980s. Though the French are working assiduously to preserve stability, the Ivory Coast faces a possibility worse than a coup: an anarchic implosion of criminal violence—an urbanized version of what has already happened in Somalia. Or it may become an African Yugoslavia, but one without mini-states to replace the whole.

Because the demographic reality of West Africa is a countryside draining into dense slums by the coast, ultimately the region's rulers will come to reflect the values of these shanty-towns. There are signs of this already in Sierra Leone—and in Togo, where the dictator Etienne Eyadema, in power since 1967, was nearly toppled in 1991, not by democrats but by thousands of youths whom the London-based magazine *West Africa* described as "Soweto-like stone-throwing adolescents." Their behavior may herald a regime more brutal than Eyadema's repressive one.

The fragility of these West African "countries" impressed itself on me when I took a series of bush taxis along the Gulf of Guinea, from the Togolese capital of Lomé, across Ghana, to Abidjan. The 400-mile journey required two full days of driving, because of stops at two border crossings and an additional eleven customs stations, at each of which my fellow passengers had their bags searched. I had to change money twice and repeatedly fill in currency-declaration forms. I had to bribe a Togolese immigration official with the equivalent of eighteen dollars before he would agree to put an exit stamp on my passport. Nevertheless, smuggling across these borders is rampant. *The London Observer* has reported that in 1992 the equivalent of $856 million left West Africa for Europe in the form of "hot cash" assumed to be laundered drug money. International cartels have discovered the utility of weak, financially strapped West African regimes.

The more fictitious the actual sovereignty, the more severe border authorities seem to be in trying to prove otherwise. Getting visas for these states can be as hard as crossing their borders. The Washington embassies of Sierra Leone and Guinea—the two poorest nations on earth, according to a 1993 United Nations report on "human development"—asked for letters from my bank (in lieu of prepaid round-trip tickets) and also personal references, in order to prove that I had sufficient means to sustain myself during my visits. I was reminded of my visa and currency hassles while traveling to the communist states of Eastern Europe, particularly East Germany and Czechoslovakia, before those states collapsed.

Ali A. Mazrui, the director of the Institute of Global Cultural Studies at the State University of New York at Binghamton, predicts that West Africa—indeed, the whole continent—is on the verge of large-scale border upheaval. Mazrui writes,

> In the 21st century France will be withdrawing from West Africa as she gets increasingly involved in the affairs [of Europe]. France's West African sphere of influence will be filled by Nigeria—a more natural hegemonic power. . . . It will be under those circumstances that Nigeria's own boundaries are likely to expand to incorporate the Republic of Niger (the Hausa link), the Republic of Benin (the Yoruba link) and conceivably Cameroon.

THE future could be more tumultuous, and bloodier, than Mazrui dares to say. France *will* withdraw from former colonies like Benin, Togo, Niger, and the Ivory Coast, where it has been propping up local currencies. It will do so not only because its attention will be diverted to new challenges in Europe and Russia but also because younger French officials lack the older generation's emotional ties to the ex-colonies. However, even as Nigeria attempts to expand, it, too, is likely to split into several pieces. The State Department's Bureau of Intelligence and Research recently made the following points in an analysis of Nigeria:

> Prospects for a transition to civilian rule and democratization are slim. . . . The repressive apparatus of the state security service . . . will be difficult for any future civilian government to control. . . . The country is becoming increasingly ungovernable. . . . Ethnic and regional splits are deepening, a situation made worse by an increase in the number of states from 19 to 30 and a doubling in the number of local governing authorities; religious cleavages are more serious; Muslim fundamentalism and evangelical Christian militancy are on the rise; and northern Muslim anxiety over southern [Christian] control of the economy is intense . . . the will to keep Nigeria together is now very weak.

Given that oil-rich Nigeria is a bellwether for the region—its population of roughly 90 million equals the populations of all the other West African states combined—it is apparent that Africa faces cataclysms that could make the Ethiopian and Somalian famines pale in comparison. This is especially so because Nigeria's population, including that of its largest city, Lagos, whose crime, pollution, and overcrowding make it the cliché par excellence of Third World urban dysfunction, is set to double during the next twenty-five years, while the country continues to deplete its natural resources.

Part of West Africa's quandary is that although its population belts are horizontal, with habitation densities increasing as one travels south away from the Sahara and toward the tropical abundance of the Atlantic littoral, the borders erected by European colonialists are vertical, and therefore at cross-purposes with demography and topography. Satellite photos depict the same reality I experienced in the bush taxi: the Lomé-Abidjan coastal corridor—indeed, the entire stretch of coast from Abidjan eastward to Lagos—is one burgeoning megalopolis that by any rational economic and geographical standard should constitute a single sovereignty, rather than the five (the Ivory Coast, Ghana, Togo, Benin, and Nigeria) into which it is currently divided.

As many internal African borders begin to crumble, a more impenetrable boundary is being erected that threatens to isolate the continent as a whole: the wall of disease. Merely to visit West Africa in some degree of safety, I spent about $500 for a hepatitis B vaccination series and other disease prophylaxis. Africa may today be more dangerous in this regard than it was in 1862, before antibiotics, when the explorer Sir Richard Francis Burton described the health situation on the continent as "deadly, a Golgotha, a Jehannum." Of the approximately 12 million people worldwide whose blood is HIV-positive, 8 million are in Africa. In the capital of the Ivory Coast, whose modern road system only helps to spread the disease, 10 percent of the population is HIV-positive. And war and refugee movements help the virus break through to more-remote areas of Africa. Alan Greenberg, M.D., a representative of the Centers for Disease Control in Abidjan, explains that in Africa the HIV virus and tuberculosis are now "fast-forwarding each other." Of the approximately 4,000 newly diagnosed tuberculosis patients in Abidjan, 45 percent were also found to be HIV-positive. As African birth rates soar and slums proliferate, some experts worry that viral mutations and hybridizations might, just conceivably, result in a form of the AIDS virus that is easier to catch than the present strain.

It is malaria that is most responsible for the disease wall that threatens to separate Africa and other parts of the Third World from more-developed regions of the planet in the twenty-first century. Carried by mosquitoes, malaria, unlike AIDS, is easy to catch. Most people in sub-Saharan Africa have recurring bouts of the disease throughout their entire lives, and it is mutating into increasingly deadly forms. "The

IT IS MALARIA THAT IS MOST RESPONSIBLE FOR THE DISEASE WALL THAT THREATENS TO SEPARATE AFRICA AND OTHER PARTS OF THE THIRD WORLD FROM MORE-DEVELOPED REGIONS OF THE PLANET IN THE TWENTY-FIRST CENTURY. IT IS MUTATING INTO INCREASINGLY DEADLY FORMS.

great gift of Malaria is utter apathy," wrote Sir Richard Burton, accurately portraying the situation in much of the Third World today. Visitors to malaria-afflicted parts of the planet are protected by a new drug, mefloquine, a side effect of which is vivid, even violent, dreams. But a strain of cerebral malaria resistant to mefloquine is now on the offensive. Consequently, defending oneself against malaria in Africa is becoming more and more like defending oneself against violent crime. You engage in "behavior modification": not going out at dusk, wearing mosquito repellent all the time.

And the cities keep growing. I got a general sense of the future while driving from the airport to downtown Conakry, the capital of Guinea. The forty-five-minute journey in heavy traffic was through one never-ending shanty-town: a nightmarish Dickensian spectacle to which Dickens himself would never have given credence. The corrugated metal shacks and scabrous walls were coated with black slime. Stores were built out of rusted shipping containers, junked cars, and jumbles of wire mesh. The streets were one long puddle of floating garbage. Mosquitoes and flies were everywhere. Children, many of whom had protruding bellies, seemed as numerous as ants. When the tide went out, dead rats and the skeletons of cars were exposed on the mucky beach. In twenty-eight years Guinea's population will double if growth goes on at current rates. Hardwood logging continues at a madcap speed, and people flee the Guinean countryside for Conakry. It seemed to me that here, as elsewhere in Africa and the Third World, man is challenging nature far beyond its limits, and nature is now beginning to take its revenge.

AFRICA may be as relevant to the future character of world politics as the Balkans were a hundred years ago, prior to the two Balkan wars and the First World War. Then the threat was the collapse of empires and the birth of nations based solely on tribe. Now the threat is more elemental: *nature unchecked.* Africa's immediate future could be very bad. The coming upheaval, in which foreign embassies are shut down, states collapse, and contact with the outside world takes place through dangerous, disease-ridden coastal trading posts, will loom large in the century we are entering. (Nine of twenty-one U.S. foreign-aid missions to be closed over the next three years are in Africa—a prologue to a consolidation of U.S. embassies themselves.) Precisely because much of Africa is set to go over the edge at a time when the Cold War has ended, when environmental and demographic stress in other parts of the globe is becoming critical, and when the post–First World War system of nation-states—not just in the Balkans but perhaps also in the Middle East—is about to be toppled, Africa suggests what war, borders, and ethnic politics will be like a few decades hence.

To understand the events of the next fifty years, then, one must understand environmental scarcity, cultural and racial clash, geographic destiny, and the transformation of war. The order in which I have named these is not accidental. Each concept except the first relies partly on the one or ones before it, meaning that the last two—new approaches to mapmaking and to warfare—are the most important. They are also the least understood. I will now look at each idea, drawing upon the work of specialists and also my own travel experiences in various parts of the globe besides Africa, in order to fill in the blanks of a new political atlas.

THE ENVIRONMENT AS A HOSTILE POWER

FOR a while the media will continue to ascribe riots and other violent upheavals abroad mainly to ethnic and religious conflict. But as these conflicts multiply, it will become apparent that something else is afoot, making more and more places like Nigeria, India, and Brazil ungovernable.

Mention "the environment" or "diminishing natural resources" in foreign-policy circles and you meet a brick wall of skepticism or boredom. To conservatives especially, the very terms seem flaky. Public-policy foundations have contributed to the lack of interest, by funding narrowly focused environmental studies replete with technical jargon which foreign-affairs experts just let pile up on their desks.

It is time to understand "the environment" for what it is: *the* national-security issue of the early twenty-first century. The political and strategic impact of surging populations, spreading disease, deforestation and soil erosion, water depletion, air pollution, and, possibly, rising sea levels in critical, overcrowded regions like the Nile Delta and Bangladesh—developments that will prompt mass migrations and, in turn, incite group conflicts—will be the core foreign-policy challenge from which most others will ultimately emanate, arousing the public and uniting assorted interests left over from the Cold War. In the twenty-first century water will be in dangerously short supply in such diverse locales as Saudi Arabia, Central Asia, and the southwestern United States. A war could erupt between Egypt and Ethiopia over Nile River water. Even in Europe tensions have arisen between Hungary and Slovakia over the damming of the Danube, a classic case of how environmental disputes fuse with ethnic and historical ones. The political scientist and erstwhile Clinton adviser Michael Mandelbaum has said, "We have a foreign policy today in the shape of a doughnut—lots of peripheral interests but nothing at the center." The environment, I will argue, is part of a terrifying array of problems that will define a new threat to our security, filling the hole in Mandelbaum's doughnut and allowing a post–Cold War foreign policy to emerge inexorably by need rather than by design.

OUR Cold War foreign policy truly began with George F. Kennan's famous article, signed "X," published in *Foreign Affairs* in July of 1947, in which Kennan argued for a "firm and vigilant containment" of a Soviet Union that was imperially, rather than ideologically, motivated. It may be that our post–Cold War foreign policy will one day be seen to have had its beginnings in an even bolder and more detailed piece of written analysis: one that appeared in the journal *International Security*. The article, published in the fall of 1991 by Thomas Fraser Homer-Dixon, who is the head of the Peace and Conflict Studies Program at the University of Toronto, was titled "On the Threshold: Environmental Changes as Causes of Acute Conflict." Homer-Dixon has, more successfully than other analysts, integrated two hitherto separate fields—military-conflict studies and the study of the physical environment.

In Homer-Dixon's view, future wars and civil violence will often arise from scarcities of resources such as water, cropland, forests, and fish. Just as there will be environmentally driven wars and refugee flows, there will be environmentally induced praetorian regimes—or, as he puts it, "hard regimes." Countries with the highest probability of acquiring hard regimes, according to Homer-Dixon, are those that are threatened by a declining resource base yet also have "a history of state [read 'military'] strength." Candidates include Indonesia, Brazil, and, of course, Nigeria. Though each of these nations has exhibited democratizing tendencies of late, Homer-Dixon argues that such tendencies are likely to be superficial "epiphenomena" having nothing to do with long-term processes that include soaring populations and shrinking raw materials. Democracy is problematic; scarcity is more certain.

Indeed, the Saddam Husseins of the future will have more, not fewer, opportunities. In addition to engendering tribal strife, scarcer resources will place a great strain on many peoples who never had much of a democratic or institutional tradition to begin with. Over the next fifty years the earth's population will soar from 5.5 billion to more than nine billion. Though optimists have hopes for new resource technologies and free-market development in the global village, they fail to note that, as the National Academy of Sciences has pointed out, 95 percent of the population increase will be in the poorest regions of the world, where governments now—just look at Africa—show little ability to function, let alone to implement even marginal improvements. Homer-Dixon writes, ominously, "Neo-Malthusians may underestimate human adaptability in *today's* environmental-social system, but as time passes their analysis may become ever more compelling."

While a minority of the human population will be, as Francis Fukuyama would put it, sufficiently sheltered so as to enter a "post-historical" realm, living in cities and suburbs in which the environment has been mastered and ethnic animosities have been quelled by bourgeois prosperity, an increasingly large number of people will be stuck in history, living in shantytowns where attempts to rise above poverty, cultural dysfunction, and ethnic strife will be doomed by a lack of water to drink, soil to till, and space to survive in. In the developing world environmental stress will present people with a choice that is increasingly among totalitarianism (as in Iraq), fascist-tending mini-states (as in Serb-held Bosnia), and road-warrior cultures (as in Somalia). Homer-Dixon concludes that "as environmental degradation proceeds, the size of the potential social disruption will increase."

Tad Homer-Dixon is an unlikely Jeremiah. Today a boyish thirty-seven, he grew up amid the sylvan majesty of Vancouver Island, attending private day schools. His speech is calm, perfectly even, and crisply enunciated. There is nothing in his background or manner that would indicate a bent toward pessimism. A Canadian Anglican who spends his summers canoeing on the lakes of northern Ontario, and who talks about the benign mountains, black bears, and Douglas firs of his youth, he is the opposite of the intellectually severe neoconservative, the kind at home with conflict scenarios. Nor is he an environmentalist who opposes development. "My father was a logger who thought about ecologically safe forestry before others," he says. "He logged, planted, logged, and planted. He got out of the business just as the issue was being polarized by environmentalists. They hate changed ecosystems. But human beings, just by carrying seeds around, change the natural world." As an only child whose playground was a virtually untouched wilderness and seacoast, Homer-Dixon has a familiarity with the natural world that permits him to see a reality that most policy analysts—children of suburbia and city streets—are blind to.

"We need to bring nature back in," he argues. "We have to stop separating politics from the physical world—the climate, public health, and the environment." Quoting Daniel Deudney, another pioneering expert on the security aspects of the environment, Homer-Dixon says that "for too long we've been prisoners of 'social-social' theory, which assumes there are only social causes for social and political changes, rather than natural causes, too. This social-social mentality emerged with the Industrial Revolution, which separated us from nature. But nature is coming back with a vengeance, tied to population growth. It will have incredible security implications.

"Think of a stretch limo in the potholed streets of New York City, where homeless beggars live. Inside the limo are the air-conditioned post-industrial regions of North America, Europe, the emerging Pacific Rim, and a few other isolated places, with their trade summitry and computer-information highways. Outside is the rest of mankind, going in a completely different direction."

WE are entering a bifurcated world. Part of the globe is inhabited by Hegel's and Fukuyama's Last Man, healthy, well fed, and pampered by technology. The other, larger, part is inhabited by Hobbes's First Man, condemned to a life that is "poor, nasty, brutish, and short." Although both parts will be threatened by environmental stress, the Last Man will be able to master it; the First Man will not.

The Last Man will adjust to the loss of underground water tables in the western United States. He will build dikes to save Cape Hatteras and the Chesapeake beaches from rising sea levels, even as the Maldive Islands, off the coast of India, sink into oblivion, and the shorelines of Egypt, Bangladesh, and Southeast Asia recede, driving tens of millions of people inland where there is no room for them, and thus sharpening ethnic divisions.

Homer-Dixon points to a world map of soil degradation in his Toronto office. "The darker the map color, the worse the degradation," he explains. The West African coast, the Middle East, the Indian subcontinent, China, and Central America have the darkest shades, signifying all manner of degradation, related to winds, chemicals, and water problems. "The worst degradation is generally where the population is highest. The population is generally highest where the soil is the best. So we're degrading earth's best soil."

China, in Homer-Dixon's view, is the quintessential example of environmental degradation. Its current economic "success" masks deeper problems. "China's fourteen percent growth rate does not mean it's going to be a world power. It means that coastal China, where the economic growth is taking place, is joining the rest of the Pacific Rim. The disparity with inland China is intensifying." Referring to the environmental research of his colleague, the Czech-born ecologist Vaclav Smil, Homer-Dixon explains how the per capita availability of arable land in interior China has rapidly declined at the same time that the quality of that land has been destroyed by deforestation, loss of topsoil, and salinization. He mentions the loss and contamination of water supplies, the exhaustion of wells, the plugging of irrigation systems and reservoirs with eroded silt, and a population of 1.54 billion by the year 2025: it is a misconception that China has gotten its population under control. Large-scale population movements are under way, from inland China to coastal China and from villages to cities, leading to a crime surge like the one in Africa and to growing regional disparities and conflicts in a land with a strong tradition of warlordism and a weak tradition of central government—again as in Africa. "We will probably see the center challenged and fractured, and China will not remain the same on the map," Homer-Dixon says.

Environmental scarcity will inflame existing hatreds and affect power relationships, at which we now look.

SKINHEAD COSSACKS, JUJU WARRIORS

IN the summer, 1993, issue of *Foreign Affairs*, Samuel P. Huntington, of Harvard's Olin Institute for Strategic Studies, published a thought-provoking article called "The Clash of Civilizations?" The world, he argues, has been moving during the course of this century from nation-state conflict to ideological conflict to, finally, cultural conflict. I would add that as refugee flows increase and as peasants continue migrating to cities around the world—turning them into sprawling villages—national borders will mean less, even as more power will fall into the hands of less educated, less sophisticated groups. In the eyes of these uneducated but newly empowered millions, the real borders are the most tangible and intractable ones: those of culture and tribe. Huntington writes, "First, differences among civilizations are not only real; they are basic," involving, among other things, history, language, and religion. "Second . . . interactions between peoples of different civilizations are increasing; these increasing interactions intensify civilization consciousness." Economic modernization is not necessarily a panacea, since it fuels individual and group ambitions while weakening traditional loyalties to the state. It is worth noting, for example, that it is precisely the wealthiest and fastest-developing city in India, Bombay, that has seen the worst intercommunal violence between Hindus and Muslims. Consider that Indian cities, like African and Chinese ones, are ecological time bombs—Delhi and Calcutta, and also Beijing, suffer the worst air quality of any cities in the world—and it is apparent how surging populations, environmental degradation, and ethnic conflict are deeply related.

Huntington points to interlocking conflicts among Hindu, Muslim, Slavic Orthodox, Western, Japanese, Confucian, Latin American, and possibly African civilizations: for instance, Hindus clashing with Muslims in India, Turkic Muslims clashing with Slavic Orthodox Russians in Central Asian cities, the West clashing with Asia. (Even in the United States, African-Americans find themselves besieged by an influx of competing Latinos.) Whatever the laws, refugees find a way to crash official borders, bringing their passions with them, meaning that Europe and the United States will be weakened by cultural disputes.

Because Huntington's brush is broad, his specifics are vulnerable to attack. In a rebuttal of Huntington's argument the Johns Hopkins professor Fouad Ajami, a Lebanese-born Shi'ite who certainly knows the world beyond suburbia, writes in the September-October, 1993, issue of *Foreign Affairs*,

> The world of Islam divides and subdivides. The battle lines in the Caucasus . . . are not coextensive with civilizational fault lines. The lines follow the interests of

states. Where Huntington sees a civilizational duel between Armenia and Azerbaijan, the Iranian state has cast religious zeal . . . to the wind . . . in that battle the Iranians have tilted toward Christian Armenia.

True, Huntington's hypothesized war between Islam and Orthodox Christianity is not borne out by the alliance network in the Caucasus. But that is only because he has misidentified *which* cultural war is occurring there. A recent visit to Azerbaijan made clear to me that Azeri Turks, the world's most secular Shi'ite Muslims, see their cultural identity in terms not of religion but of their Turkic race. The Armenians, likewise, fight the Azeris not because the latter are Muslims but because they are Turks, related to the same Turks who massacred Armenians in 1915. Turkic culture (secular and based on languages employing a Latin script) is battling Iranian culture (religiously militant as defined by Tehran, and wedded to an Arabic script) across the whole swath of Central Asia and the Caucasus. The Armenians are, therefore, natural allies of their fellow Indo-Europeans the Iranians.

Huntington is correct that the Caucasus is a flashpoint of cultural and racial war. But, as Ajami observes, Huntington's plate tectonics are too simple. Two months of recent travel throughout Turkey revealed to me that although the Turks are developing a deep distrust, bordering on hatred, of fellow-Muslim Iran, they are also, especially in the shantytowns that are coming to dominate Turkish public opinion, revising their group identity, increasingly seeing themselves as Muslims being deserted by a West that does little to help besieged Muslims in Bosnia and that attacks Turkish Muslims in the streets of Germany.

In other words, the Balkans, a powder keg for nation-state war at the beginning of the twentieth century, could be a powder keg for cultural war at the turn of the twenty-first: between Orthodox Christianity (represented by the Serbs and a classic Byzantine configuration of Greeks, Russians, and Romanians) and the House of Islam. Yet in the Caucasus that House of Islam is falling into a clash between Turkic and Iranian civilizations. Ajami asserts that this very subdivision, not to mention all the divisions within the Arab world, indicates that the West, including the United States, is not threatened by Huntington's scenario. As the Gulf War demonstrated, the West has proved capable of playing one part of the House of Islam against another.

True. However, whether he is aware of it or not, Ajami is describing a world even more dangerous than the one Huntington envisions, especially when one takes into account Homer-Dixon's research on environmental scarcity. Outside the stretch limo would be a rundown, crowded planet of skinhead Cossacks and *juju* warriors, influenced by the worst refuse of Western pop culture and ancient tribal hatreds, and battling over scraps of overused earth in guerrilla conflicts that ripple across continents and intersect in no discernible pattern—meaning there's no easy-to-define threat. Kennan's world of one adversary seems as distant as the world of Herodotus.

Most people believe that the political earth since 1989 has undergone immense change. But it is minor compared with what is yet to come. The breaking apart and remaking of the atlas is only now beginning. The crack-up of the Soviet empire and the coming end of Arab-Israeli military confrontation are merely prologues to the really big changes that lie ahead. Michael Vlahos, a long-range thinker for the U.S. Navy, warns, "We are not in charge of the environment and the world is not following us. It is going in many directions. Do not assume that democratic capitalism is the last word in human social evolution."

Before addressing the questions of maps and of warfare, I want to take a closer look at the interaction of religion, culture, demographic shifts, and the distribution of natural resources in a specific area of the world: the Middle East.

THE PAST IS DEAD

BUILT on steep, muddy hills, the shantytowns of Ankara, the Turkish capital, exude visual drama. Altindag, or "Golden Mountain," is a pyramid of dreams, fashioned from cinder blocks and corrugated iron, rising as though each shack were built on top of another, all reaching awkwardly and painfully toward heaven—the heaven of wealthier Turks who live elsewhere in the city. Nowhere else on the planet have I found such a poignant architectural symbol of man's striving, with gaps in house walls plugged with rusted cans, and leeks and onions growing on verandas assembled from planks of rotting wood. For reasons that I will explain, the Turkish shacktown is a psychological universe away from the African one.

To see the twenty-first century truly, one's eyes must learn a different set of aesthetics. One must reject the overly stylized images of travel magazines, with their inviting photographs of exotic villages and glamorous downtowns. There are far too many millions whose dreams are more vulgar, more real—whose raw energies and desires will overwhelm the visions of the elites, remaking the future into something frighteningly new. But in Turkey I learned that shantytowns are not all bad.

Slum quarters in Abidjan terrify and repel the outsider. In Turkey it is the opposite. The closer I got to Golden Mountain the better it looked, and the safer I felt. I had $1,500 worth of Turkish lira in one pocket and $1,000 in traveler's checks in the other, yet I felt no fear. Golden Mountain was a real neighborhood. The inside of one house told the story: The architectural bedlam of cinder block and sheet metal and cardboard walls was deceiving. Inside was a *home*—order, that is, bespeaking dignity. I saw a working refrigerator, a television, a wall cabinet with a few books and lots of family pictures, a few plants by a window, and a stove. Though the streets become rivers of mud when it rains, the floors inside this house were spotless.

Other houses were like this too. Schoolchildren ran along with briefcases strapped to their backs, trucks delivered cooking gas, a few men sat inside a café sipping tea. One man sipped beer. Alcohol is easy to obtain in Turkey, a secular state where 99 percent of the population is Muslim. Yet there is little problem of alcoholism. Crime against persons is infinitesimal. Poverty and illiteracy are watered-down versions of what obtains in Algeria and Egypt (to say nothing of West Africa), making it that much harder for religious extremists to gain a foothold.

My point in bringing up a rather wholesome, crime-free slum is this: its existence demonstrates how formidable is the fabric of which Turkish Muslim culture is made. A culture this strong has the potential to dominate the Middle East once again. Slums are litmus tests for innate cultural strengths and weaknesses. Those peoples whose cultures can harbor extensive slum life without decomposing will be, relatively speaking, the future's winners. Those whose cultures cannot will be the future's victims. Slums—in the sociological sense—do not exist in Turkish cities. The mortar between people and family groups is stronger here than in Africa. Resurgent Islam and Turkic cultural identity have produced a civilization with natural muscle tone. Turks, history's perennial nomads, take disruption in stride.

The future of the Middle East is quietly being written inside the heads of Golden Mountain's inhabitants. Think of an Ottoman military encampment on the eve of the destruction of Greek Constantinople in 1453. That is Golden Mountain. "We brought the village here. But in the village we worked harder—in the field, all day. So we couldn't fast during [the holy month of] Ramadan. Here we fast. Here we are more religious." Aishe Tanrikulu, along with half a dozen other women, was stuffing rice into vine leaves from a crude plastic bowl. She asked me to join her under the shade of a piece of sheet metal. Each of these women had her hair covered by a kerchief. In the city they were encountering television for the first time. "We are traditional, religious people. The programs offend us," Aishe said. Another woman complained about the schools. Though her children had educational options unavailable in the village, they had to compete with wealthier, secular Turks. "The kids from rich families with connections—they get all the places." More opportunities, more tensions, in other words.

My guidebook to Golden Mountain was an untypical one: *Tales From the Garbage Hills*, a brutally realistic novel by a Turkish writer, Latife Tekin, about life in the shantytowns, which in Turkey are called *gecekondus* ("built in a night"). "He listened to the earth and wept unceasingly for water, for work and for the cure of the illnesses spread by the garbage and the factory waste," Tekin writes. In the most revealing passage of *Tales From the Garbage Hills* the squatters are told "about a certain 'Ottoman Empire' . . . that where they now lived there had once been an empire of this name." This history "confounded" the squatters. It was the first they had heard of it. Though one of them knew "that his grandfather and his dog died fighting the Greeks," nationalism and an encompassing sense of Turkish history are the province of the Turkish middle and upper classes, and of foreigners like me who feel required to have a notion of "Turkey."

But what did the Golden Mountain squatters know about the armies of Turkish migrants that had come before their own—namely, Seljuks and Ottomans? For these recently urbanized peasants, and their counterparts in Africa, the Arab world, India, and so many other places, the world is new, to adapt V. S. Naipaul's phrase. As Naipaul wrote of urban refugees in *India: A Wounded Civilization*, "They saw themselves at the beginning of things: unaccommodated men making a claim on their land for the first time, and out of chaos evolving their own philosophy of community and self-help. For them the past was dead; they had left it behind in the villages."

Everywhere in the developing world at the turn of the twenty-first century these new men and women, rushing into the cities, are remaking civilizations and redefining their identities in terms of religion and tribal ethnicity which do not coincide with the borders of existing states.

IN Turkey several things are happening at once. In 1980, 44 percent of Turks lived in cities; in 1990 it was 61 percent. By the year 2000 the figure is expected to be 67 percent. Villages are emptying out as concentric rings of *gecekondu* developments grow around Turkish cities. This is the real political and demographic revolution in Turkey and elsewhere, and foreign correspondents usually don't write about it.

Whereas rural poverty is age-old and almost a "normal" part of the social fabric, urban poverty is socially destabilizing. As Iran has shown, Islamic extremism is the psychological defense mechanism of many urbanized peasants threatened with the loss of traditions in pseudo-modern cities where their values are under attack, where basic services like water and electricity are unavailable, and where they are assaulted by a physically unhealthy environment. The American ethnologist and orientalist Carleton Stevens Coon wrote in 1951 that Islam "has made possible the optimum survival and happiness of millions of human beings in an increasingly impoverished environment over a fourteen-hundred-year period." Beyond its stark, clearly articulated message, Islam's very militancy makes it attractive to the downtrodden. It is the one religion that is prepared to *fight*. A political era driven by environmental stress, increased cultural sensitivity, unregulated urbanization, and refugee migrations is an era divinely created for the spread and intensification of Islam, already the world's fastest-growing religion. (Though Islam is spreading in West Africa, it is being hobbled by syncretization with animism: this makes new converts less apt to become anti-Western extremists, but it also makes for a weakened version of the faith, which is less effective as an antidote to crime.)

In Turkey, however, Islam is painfully and awkwardly forging a consensus with modernization, a trend that is less apparent in the Arab and Persian worlds (and virtually invisible in Africa). In Iran the oil boom—because it put development and urbanization on a fast track, making the culture shock more intense—fueled the 1978 Islamic Revolution. But Turkey, unlike Iran and the Arab world, has little oil. Therefore its development and urbanization have been more gradual. Islamists have been integrated into the parliamentary system for decades. The tensions I noticed in Golden Mountain are natural, creative ones: the kind immigrants face the world over. While the world has focused on religious perversity in Algeria, a nation rich in natural gas, and in Egypt, parts of whose capital city, Cairo, evince worse crowding than I have seen even in Calcutta, Turkey has been living through the Muslim equivalent of the Protestant Reformation.

Resource distribution is strengthening Turks in another way vis-à-vis Arabs and Persians. Turks may have little oil, but their Anatolian heartland has lots of water—the most important fluid of the twenty-first century. Turkey's Southeast Anatolia Project, involving twenty-two major dams and irrigation systems, is impounding the waters of the Tigris and Euphrates rivers. Much of the water that Arabs and perhaps Israelis will need to drink in the future is controlled by Turks. The project's centerpiece is the mile-wide, sixteen-story Atatürk Dam, upon which are emblazoned the words of modern Turkey's founder: "*Ne Mutlu Turkum Diyene*" ("Lucky is the one who is a Turk").

Unlike Egypt's Aswan High Dam, on the Nile, and Syria's Revolution Dam, on the Euphrates, both of which were built largely by Russians, the Atatürk Dam is a predominantly Turkish affair, with Turkish engineers and companies in charge. On a recent visit my eyes took in the immaculate offices and their gardens, the high-voltage electric grids and phone switching stations, the dizzying sweep of giant humming transformers, the poured-concrete spillways, and the prim unfolding suburbia, complete with schools, for dam employees. The emerging power of the Turks was palpable.

Erduhan Bayindir, the site manager at the dam, told me that "while oil can be shipped abroad to enrich only elites, water has to be spread more evenly within the society. . . . It is true, we can stop the flow of water into Syria and Iraq for up to eight months without the same water overflowing our dams, in order to regulate their political behavior."

Power is certainly moving north in the Middle East, from the oil fields of Dhahran, on the Persian Gulf, to the water plain of Harran, in southern Anatolia—near the site of the Atatürk Dam. But will the nation-state of Turkey, as presently constituted, be the inheritor of this wealth?

I very much doubt it.

THE LIES OF MAPMAKERS

WHEREAS West Africa represents the least stable part of political reality outside Homer-Dixon's stretch limo, Turkey, an organic outgrowth of two Turkish empires that ruled Anatolia for 850 years, has been among the most stable. Turkey's borders were established not by colonial powers but in a war of independence, in the early 1920s. Kemal Atatürk provided Turkey with a secular nation-building myth that most Arab and African states, burdened by artificially drawn borders, lack. That lack will leave many Arab states defenseless against a wave of Islam that will eat away at their legitimacy and frontiers in coming years. Yet even as regards Turkey, maps deceive.

It is not only African shantytowns that don't appear on urban maps. Many shantytowns in Turkey and elsewhere are also missing—as are the considerable territories controlled by guerrilla armies and urban mafias. Traveling with Eritrean guerrillas in what, according to the map, was northern Ethiopia, traveling in "northern Iraq" with Kurdish guerrillas, and staying in a hotel in the Caucasus controlled by a local mafia—to say nothing of my experiences in West Africa—led me to develop a healthy skepticism toward maps, which, I began to realize, create a conceptual barrier that prevents us from comprehending the political crack-up just beginning to occur worldwide.

Consider the map of the world, with its 190 or so countries, each signified by a bold and uniform color: this map, with which all of us have grown up, is generally an invention of modernism, specifically of European colonialism. Modernism, in the sense of which I speak, began with the rise of nation-states in Europe and was confirmed by the death of feudalism at the end of the Thirty Years' War—an event that was interposed between the Renaissance and the Enlightenment, which together gave birth to modern science. People were suddenly flush with an enthusiasm to categorize, to define. The map, based on scientific techniques of measurement, offered a way to classify new national organisms, making a jigsaw puzzle of neat pieces without transition zones between them. "Frontier" is itself a modern concept that didn't exist in the feudal mind. And as European nations carved out far-flung domains at the same time that print technology was making the reproduction of maps cheaper, cartography came into its own as a way of creating facts by ordering the way we look at the world.

In his book *Imagined Communities: Reflections on the Origin and Spread of Nationalism*, Benedict Anderson, of Cornell University, demonstrates that the map enabled colonialists to think about their holdings in terms of a "totalizing classificatory grid. . . . It was bounded, determinate, and therefore—in principle—countable." To the colonialist, country maps were the equivalent of an accountant's ledger books. Maps, Anderson explains, "shaped the grammar" that would make possible such questionable concepts as Iraq, Indonesia, Sierra Leone, and Nigeria. The state, recall, is a purely Western notion, one that until the twentieth century applied to countries covering only three percent of the earth's land area. Nor is the evidence compelling that the state, as a governing ideal, can be successfully transported to areas outside the industrialized world. Even the United States of America, in the words of one of our best living poets, Gary Snyder, consists of "arbitrary and inaccurate impositions on what is really here."

Yet this inflexible, artificial reality staggers on, not only in the United Nations but in various geographic and travel publications (themselves by-products of an age of elite touring which colonialism made possible) that still report on and photograph the world according to "country." Newspapers, this magazine, and this writer are not innocent of the tendency.

According to the map, the great hydropower complex emblemized by the Atatürk Dam is situated in Turkey. Forget the map. This southeastern region of Turkey is populated almost completely by Kurds. About half of the world's 20 million Kurds live in "Turkey." The Kurds are predominant in an ellipse of territory that overlaps not only with Turkey but also with Iraq, Iran, Syria, and the former Soviet Union. The Western-enforced Kurdish enclave in northern Iraq, a consequence of the 1991 Gulf War, has already exposed the fictitious nature of that supposed nation-state.

On a recent visit to the Turkish-Iranian border, it occurred to me what a risky idea the nation-state is. Here I was on the legal fault line between two clashing civilizations, Turkic and Iranian. Yet the reality was more subtle: as in West Africa, the border was porous and smuggling abounded, but here the people doing the smuggling, on both sides of the border, were Kurds. In such a moonscape, over which people have migrated and settled in patterns that obliterate borders, the end of the Cold War will bring on a cruel process of natural selection among existing states. No longer will these states be so firmly propped up by the West or the Soviet Union. Because the Kurds overlap with nearly everybody in the Middle East, on account of their being cheated out of a state in the post-First World War peace treaties, they are emerging, in effect, as *the* natural selector—the ultimate reality check. They have destabilized Iraq and may continue to disrupt states that do not offer them adequate breathing space, while strengthening states that do.

Because the Turks, owing to their water resources, their growing economy, and the social cohesion evinced by the most crime-free slums I have encountered, are on the verge of big-power status, and because the 10 million Kurds within Turkey threaten that status, the outcome of the Turkish-Kurdish dispute will be more critical to the future of the Middle East than the eventual outcome of the recent Israeli-Palestinian agreement.

AMERICA'S fascination with the Israeli-Palestinian issue, coupled with its lack of interest in the Turkish-Kurdish one, is a function of its own domestic and ethnic obsessions, not of the cartographic reality that is about to transform the Middle East. The diplomatic process involving Israelis and Palestinians will, I believe, have little effect on the early- and mid-twenty-first-century map of the region. Israel, with a 6.6 percent economic growth rate based increasingly on high-tech exports, is about to enter Homer-Dixon's stretch limo, fortified by a well-defined political community that is an organic outgrowth of history and ethnicity. Like prosperous and peaceful Japan on the one hand, and war-torn and poverty-wracked Armenia on the other, Israel is a classic national-ethnic organism. Much of the Arab world, however, will undergo alteration, as Islam spreads across artificial frontiers, fueled by mass migrations into the cities and a soaring birth rate of more than 3.2 percent. Seventy percent of the Arab population has been born since 1970—youths with little historical memory of anticolonial independence struggles, postcolonial attempts at nation-building, or any of the Arab-Israeli wars. The most distant recollection of these youths will be the West's humiliation of colonially invented Iraq in 1991. Today seventeen out of twenty-two Arab states have a declining gross national product; in the next twenty years, at current growth rates, the population of many Arab countries will double. These states, like most African ones, will be ungovernable through conventional secular ideologies. The Middle East analyst Christine M. Helms explains,

> Declaring Arab nationalism "bankrupt," the political "disinherited" are not rationalizing the failure of Arabism . . . or reformulating it. Alternative solutions are not contemplated. They have simply opted for the political paradigm at the other end of the political spectrum with which they are familiar—Islam.

Like the borders of West Africa, the colonial borders of Syria, Iraq, Jordan, Algeria, and other Arab states are often contrary to cultural and political reality. As state control mechanisms wither in the face of environmental and demographic stress, "hard" Islamic city-states or shantytown-states are likely to emerge. The fiction that the impoverished city of Algiers, on the Mediterranean, controls Tamanrasset, deep in the Algerian Sahara, cannot obtain forever. Whatever the outcome of the peace process, Israel is destined to be a Jewish ethnic fortress amid a vast and volatile realm of Islam. In that realm, the violent youth culture of the Gaza shantytowns may be indicative of the coming era.

The destiny of Turks and Kurds is far less certain, but far more relevant to the kind of map that will explain our future world. The Kurds suggest a geographic reality that cannot be shown in two-dimensional space. The issue in Turkey is not simply a matter of giving autonomy or even independence to Kurds in the southeast. This isn't the Balkans or the Caucasus, where regions are merely subdividing into smaller units, Abkhazia breaking off from Georgia, and so on. Federalism is not the answer. Kurds are found everywhere in Turkey, including the shanty districts of Istanbul and Ankara. Turkey's problem is that its Anatolian land mass is the home of two cultures and languages, Turkish and Kurdish. Identity in Turkey, as in India, Africa, and elsewhere, is more complex and subtle than conventional cartography can display.

A NEW KIND OF WAR

To appreciate fully the political and cartographic implications of postmodernism—an epoch of themeless juxtapositions, in which the classificatory grid of nation-states is going to be replaced by a jagged-glass pattern of city-states, shanty-states, nebulous and anarchic regionalisms—it is necessary to consider, finally, the whole question of war.

"Oh, what a relief to fight, to fight enemies who defend themselves, enemies who are awake!" André Malraux wrote in *Man's Fate*. I cannot think of a more suitable battle cry for many combatants in the early decades of the twenty-first century. The intense savagery of the fighting in such diverse cultural settings as Liberia, Bosnia, the Caucasus, and Sri Lanka—to say nothing of what obtains in American inner cities—indicates something very troubling that those of us inside the stretch limo, concerned with issues like middle-class entitlements and the future of interactive cable television, lack the stomach to contemplate. It is this: a large number of people on this planet, to whom the comfort and stability of a middle-class life is utterly unknown, find war and a barracks existence a step up rather than a step down.

"Just as it makes no sense to ask 'why people eat' or 'what they sleep for,'" writes Martin van Creveld, a military historian at the Hebrew University in Jerusalem, in *The Transformation of War*, "so fighting in many ways is not a means but an end. Throughout history, for every person who has expressed his horror of war there is another who found in it the most marvelous of all the experiences that are vouchsafed to man, even to the point that he later spent a lifetime boring his descendants by recounting his exploits." When I asked Pentagon officials about the nature of war in the twenty-first century, the answer I frequently got was "Read Van Creveld." The top brass are enamored of this historian not because his writings justify their existence but, rather, the opposite: Van Creveld warns them that huge state military machines like the Pentagon's are dinosaurs about to go extinct, and that something far more terrible awaits us.

The degree to which Van Creveld's *Transformation of War* complements Homer-Dixon's work on the environment, Huntington's thoughts on cultural clash, my own realizations in traveling by foot, bus, and bush taxi in more than sixty countries, and America's sobering comeuppances in intractable-culture zones like Haiti and Somalia is startling. The book begins by demolishing the notion that men don't like to fight. "By compelling the senses to focus themselves on the here and now," Van Creveld writes, war "can cause a man to take his leave of them." As anybody who has had experience with Chetniks in Serbia, "technicals" in Somalia, Tontons Macoutes in Haiti, or soldiers in Sierra Leone can tell you, in places where the Western Enlightenment has not penetrated and where there has always been mass poverty, people find liberation in violence. In Afghanistan and elsewhere, I vicariously experienced this phenomenon: worrying about mines and ambushes frees you from worrying about mundane details of daily existence. If my own experience is too subjective, there is a wealth of data showing the sheer frequency of war, especially in the developing world since the Second World War. Physical aggression is a part of being human. Only when people attain a certain economic, educational, and cultural standard is this trait tranquilized. In light of the fact that 95 percent of the earth's population growth will be in the poorest areas of the globe, the question is not whether there will be war (there will be a lot of it) but what kind of war. And who will fight whom?

Debunking the great military strategist Carl von Clausewitz, Van Creveld, who may be the most original thinker on war since that early-nineteenth-century Prussian, writes, "Clausewitz's ideas . . . were wholly rooted in the fact that, ever since 1648, war had been waged overwhelmingly by states." But, as Van Creveld explains, the period of nation-states and, therefore, of state conflict is now ending, and with it the clear "threefold division into government, army, and people" which state-directed wars enforce. Thus, to see the future, the first step is to look back to the past immediately prior to the birth of modernism—the wars in medieval Europe which began during the Reformation and reached their culmination in the Thirty Years' War.

Van Creveld writes,

> In all these struggles political, social, economic, and religious motives were hopelessly entangled. Since this was an age when armies consisted of mercenaries, all were also attended by swarms of military entrepreneurs. . . . Many of them paid little but lip service to the organizations for whom they had contracted to fight. Instead, they robbed the countryside on their own behalf. . . .
>
> Given such conditions, any fine distinctions . . . between armies on the one hand and peoples on the other were bound to break down. Engulfed by war, civilians suffered terrible atrocities.

Back then, in other words, there was no "politics" as we have come to understand the term, just as there is less and less "politics" today in Liberia, Sierra Leone, Somalia, Sri Lanka, the Balkans, and the Caucasus, among other places.

Because, as Van Creveld notes, the radius of trust within tribal societies is narrowed to one's immediate family and guerrilla comrades, truces arranged with one Bosnian commander, say, may be broken immediately by another Bosnian commander. The plethora of short-lived ceasefires in the Balkans and the Caucasus constitute proof that we are no longer in a world where the old rules of state warfare apply. More evidence is provided by the destruction of medieval monuments in the Croatian port of Dubrovnik: when cultures, rather than states, fight, then cultural and religious monuments are weapons of war, making them fair game.

Also, war-making entities will no longer be restricted to a specific territory. Loose and shadowy organisms such as Islamic terrorist organizations suggest why borders will mean increasingly little and sedimentary layers of tribalistic identity and control will mean more. "From the vantage point of the present, there appears every prospect that religious . . . fanaticisms will play a larger role in the motivation of armed conflict" in the West than at any time "for the last 300 years," Van Creveld writes. This is why analysts like Michael Vlahos are closely monitoring religious cults. Vlahos says, "An ideology that challenges us may not take familiar form, like the old Nazis or Commies. It may not even engage us initially in ways that fit old threat markings." Van Creveld concludes, "Armed conflict will be waged by men on earth, not robots in space. It will have more in common with the struggles of primitive tribes than with large-scale conventional war." While another military historian, John Keegan, in his new book *A History of Warfare*, draws a more benign portrait of primitive man, it is important to point out that what Van Creveld really means is *re-primitivized* man: warrior societies operating at a time of unprecedented resource scarcity and planetary overcrowding.

Van Creveld's pre-Westphalian vision of worldwide low-intensity conflict is not a superficial "back to the future" scenario. First of all, technology will be used toward primitive ends. In Liberia the guerrilla leader Prince Johnson didn't just cut off the ears of President Samuel Doe before Doe was tortured to death in 1990—Johnson made a video of it, which has circulated throughout West Africa. In December of 1992, when plotters of a failed coup against the Strasser regime in Sierra Leone had their ears cut off at Freetown's Hamilton Beach prior to being killed, it was seen by many to be a copycat execution. Considering, as I've explained earlier, that the Strasser regime is not really a government and that Sierra Leone is not really a nation-state, listen closely to Van Creveld: "Once the legal monopoly of armed force, long claimed by the state, is wrested out of its hands, existing distinctions between war and crime will break down much as is already the case today in . . . Lebanon, Sri Lanka, El Salvador, Peru, or Colombia."

If crime and war become indistinguishable, then "national defense" may in the future be viewed as a local concept. As crime continues to grow in our cities and the ability of state governments and criminal-justice systems to protect their citizens diminishes, urban crime may, according to Van Creveld, "develop into low-intensity conflict by coalescing along racial, religious, social, and political lines." As small-scale violence multiplies at home and abroad, state armies will continue to shrink, being gradually replaced by a booming private security business, as in West Africa, and by urban mafias, especially in the former communist world, who may be better equipped than municipal police forces to grant physical protection to local inhabitants.

Future wars will be those of communal survival, aggravated or, in many cases, caused by environmental scarcity. These wars will be subnational, meaning that it will be hard for states and local governments to protect their own citizens physically. This is how many states will ultimately die. As state power fades—and with it the state's ability to help weaker groups within society, not to mention other states—peoples and cultures around the world will be thrown back upon their own strengths and weaknesses, with fewer equalizing mechanisms to protect them. Whereas the distant future will probably see the emergence of a racially hybrid, globalized man, the coming decades will see us more aware of our differences than of our similarities. To the average person, political values will mean less, personal security more. The belief that we are all equal is liable to be replaced by the overriding obsession of the ancient Greek travelers: Why the differences between peoples?

THE LAST MAP

IN *Geography and the Human Spirit,* Anne Buttimer, a professor at University College, Dublin, recalls the work of an early-nineteenth-century German geographer, Carl Ritter, whose work implied "a divine plan for humanity" based on regionalism and a constant, living flow of forms. The map of the future, to the extent that a map is even possible, will represent a perverse twisting of Ritter's vision. Imagine cartography in three dimensions, as if in a hologram. In this hologram would be the overlapping sediments of group and other identities atop the merely two-dimensional color markings of city-states and the remaining nations, themselves confused in places by shadowy tentacles, hovering overhead, indicating the power of drug cartels, mafias, and private security agencies. Instead of borders, there would be moving "centers" of power, as in the Middle Ages. Many of these layers would be in motion. Replacing fixed and abrupt lines on a flat space would be a shifting pattern of buffer entities, like the Kurdish and Azeri buffer entities between Turkey and Iran, the Turkic Uighur buffer entity between Central Asia and Inner China (itself distinct from coastal China), and the Latino buffer entity replacing a precise U.S.-Mexican border. To this protean cartographic hologram one must add other factors, such as migrations of populations, explosions of birth rates, vectors of disease. Henceforward the map of the world will never be static. This future map—in a sense, the "Last Map"—will be an ever-mutating representation of chaos.

The Indian subcontinent offers examples of what is happening. For different reasons, both India and Pakistan are increasingly dysfunctional. The argument over democracy in these places is less and less relevant to the larger issue of governability. In India's case the question arises, Is one unwieldy bureaucracy in New Delhi the best available mechanism for promoting the lives of 866 million people of diverse languages, religions, and ethnic groups? In 1950, when the Indian population was much less than half as large and nation-building idealism was still strong, the argument for democracy was more impressive than it is now. Given that in 2025 India's population could be close to 1.5 billion, that much of its economy rests on a shrinking natural-resource base, including dramatically declining water levels, and that communal violence and urbanization are spiraling upward, it is difficult to imagine that the Indian state will survive the next century. India's oft-trumpeted Green Revolution has been achieved by overworking its croplands and depleting its watershed. Norman Myers, a British development consultant, worries that Indians have "been feeding themselves today by borrowing against their children's food sources."

Pakistan's problem is more basic still: like much of Africa, the country makes no geographic or demographic sense. It was founded as a homeland for the Muslims of the subcontinent, yet there are more subcontinental Muslims outside Pakistan than within it. Like Yugoslavia, Pakistan is a patchwork of ethnic groups, increasingly in violent conflict with one another. While the Western media gushes over the fact that the country has a woman Prime Minister, Benazir Bhutto, Karachi is becoming a subcontinental version of Lagos. In eight visits to Pakistan, I have never gotten a sense of a cohesive national identity. With as much as 65 percent of its land dependent on intensive irrigation, with wide-scale deforestation, and with a yearly population growth of 2.7 percent (which ensures that the amount of cultivated land per rural inhabitant will plummet), Pakistan is becoming a more and more desperate place. As irrigation in the Indus River basin intensifies to serve two growing populations, Muslim-Hindu strife over falling water tables may be unavoidable.

"India and Pakistan will probably fall apart," Homer-Dixon predicts. "Their secular governments have less and less legitimacy as well as less management ability over people and resources." Rather than one bold line dividing the subcontinent into two parts, the future will likely see a lot of thinner lines and smaller parts, with the ethnic entities of Pakhtunistan and Punjab gradually replacing Pakistan in the space between the Central Asian plateau and the heart of the subcontinent.

None of this even takes into account climatic change, which, if it occurs in the next century, will further erode the capacity of existing states to cope. India, for instance, receives 70 percent of its precipitation from the monsoon cycle, which planetary warming could disrupt.

Not only will the three-dimensional aspects of the Last Map be in constant motion, but its two-dimensional base may change too. The National Academy of Sciences reports that

> as many as one billion people, or 20 per cent of the world's population, live on lands likely to be inundated or dramatically changed by rising waters. . . . Low-lying countries in the developing world such as Egypt and Bangladesh, where rivers are large and the deltas extensive and densely populated, will be hardest hit. . . . Where the rivers are dammed, as in the case of the Nile, the effects . . . will be especially severe.

Egypt could be where climatic upheaval—to say nothing of the more immediate threat of increasing population—will incite religious upheaval in truly biblical fashion. Natural catastrophes, such as the October, 1992, Cairo earthquake, in which the government failed to deliver relief aid and slum residents were in many instances helped by their local mosques, can only strengthen the position of Islamic factions. In a statement about greenhouse warming which could refer to any of a variety of natural catastrophes, the environmental expert Jessica Tuchman Matthews warns that many of us underestimate the extent to which political systems, in affluent societies as well as in places like Egypt, "depend on the underpinning of natural systems." She adds, "The fact that one can move with ease from Vermont to Miami has nothing to say about the consequences of Vermont acquiring Miami's climate."

Indeed, it is not clear that the United States will survive the next century in exactly its present form. Because America is a multi-ethnic society, the nation-state has always been more fragile here than it is in more homogeneous societies like Germany and Japan. James Kurth, in an article published in *The National Interest* in 1992, explains that whereas nation-state societies tend to be built around a mass-conscription army and a standardized public school system, "multicultural regimes" feature a high-tech, all-volunteer army (and, I would add, private schools that teach competing values), operating in a culture in which the international media and entertainment industry has more influence than the "national political class." In other words, a nation-state is a place where everyone has been educated along similar lines, where people take their cue from national leaders, and where everyone (every male, at least) has gone through the crucible of military service, making patriotism a simpler issue. Writing about his immigrant family in turn-of-the-century Chicago, Saul Bellow states, "The country took us over. It *was* a country then, not a collection of 'cultures.'"

During the Second World War and the decade following it, the United States reached its apogee as a classic nation-state.

During the 1960s, as is now clear, America began a slow but unmistakable process of transformation. The signs hardly need belaboring: racial polarity, educational dysfunction, social fragmentation of many and various kinds. William Irwin Thompson, in *Passages About Earth: An Exploration of the New Planetary Culture*, writes, "The educational system that had worked on the Jews or the Irish could no longer work on the blacks; and when Jewish teachers in New York tried to take black children away from their parents exactly in the way they had been taken from theirs, they were shocked to encounter a violent affirmation of negritude."

Issues like West Africa could yet emerge as a new kind of foreign-policy issue, further eroding America's domestic peace. The spectacle of several West African nations collapsing at once could reinforce the worst racial stereotypes here at home. That is another reason why Africa matters. We must not kid ourselves: the sensitivity factor is higher than ever. The Washington, D.C., public school system is already experimenting with an Afrocentric curriculum. Summits between African leaders and prominent African-Americans are becoming frequent, as are Pollyanna-ish prognostications about multiparty elections in Africa that do not factor in crime, surging birth rates, and resource depletion. The Congressional Black Caucus was among those urging U.S. involvement in Somalia and in Haiti. At the *Los Angeles Times* minority staffers have protested against, among other things, what they allege to be the racist tone of the newspaper's Africa coverage, allegations that the editor of the "World Report" section, Dan Fisher, denies, saying essentially that Africa should be viewed through the same rigorous analytical lens as other parts of the world.

Africa may be marginal in terms of conventional late-twentieth-century conceptions of strategy, but in an age of cultural and racial clash, when national defense is increasingly local, Africa's distress will exert a destabilizing influence on the United States.

This and many other factors will make the United States less of a nation than it is today, even as it gains territory following the peaceful dissolution of Canada. Quebec, based on the bedrock of Roman Catholicism and Francophone ethnicity, could yet turn out to be North America's most cohesive and crime-free nation-state. (It may be a smaller Quebec, though, since aboriginal peoples may lop off northern parts of the province.) "Patriotism" will become increasingly regional as people in Alberta and Montana discover that they have far more in common with each other than they do with Ottawa or Washington, and Spanish-speakers in the Southwest discover a greater commonality with Mexico City. (*The Nine Nations of North America*, by Joel Garreau, a book about the continent's regionalization, is more relevant now than when it was published, in 1981.) As Washington's influence wanes, and with it the traditional symbols of American patriotism, North Americans will take psychological refuge in their insulated communities and cultures.

RETURNING from West Africa last fall was an illuminating ordeal. After leaving Abidjan, my Air Afrique flight landed in Dakar, Senegal, where all passengers had to disembark in order to go through another security check, this one demanded by U.S. authorities before they would permit the flight to set out for New York. Once we were in New York, despite the midnight hour, immigration officials at Kennedy Airport held up disembarkation by conducting quick interrogations of the aircraft's passengers—this was in addition to all the normal immigration and customs procedures. It was apparent that drug smuggling, disease, and other factors had contributed to the toughest security procedures I have ever encountered when returning from overseas.

Then, for the first time in over a month, I spotted businesspeople with attaché cases and laptop computers. When I had left New York for Abidjan, all the businesspeople were boarding planes for Seoul and Tokyo, which departed from gates near Air Afrique's. The only non-Africans off to West Africa had been relief workers in T-shirts and khakis. Although the borders within West Africa are increasingly unreal, those separating West Africa from the outside world are in various ways becoming more impenetrable.

But Afrocentrists are right in one respect: we ignore this dying region at our own risk. When the Berlin Wall was falling, in November of 1989, I happened to be in Kosovo, covering a riot between Serbs and Albanians. The future was in Kosovo, I told myself that night, not in Berlin. The same day that Yitzhak Rabin and Yasser Arafat clasped hands on the White House lawn, my Air Afrique plane was approaching Bamako, Mali, revealing corrugated-zinc shacks at the edge of an expanding desert. The real news wasn't at the White House, I realized. It was right below.

What's Wrong with the

PHILIP ELMER-DEWITT

JUST WHEN SUMMER SHOULD HAVE been coming in, it snowed last week in Colorado, punctuating several days of unseasonable 32°C (90°F) weather with enough snowfall to close three mountain highways. Paris was hit with a torrential rainstorm—the worst in a decade—that crippled the city, poisoned the Seine with sewer effluent, and clogged the river with 300 tons of dead fish. In one hour in early May, a squall dumped a record 110 mm (4⅓ in.) of rain on Hong Kong, turning steep city streets into rushing rivers and killing five. In the Middle East this January, the wettest, coldest winter in recent memory was capped by a storm that blanketed Amman, Damascus and Jerusalem with much more snow than anyone there had seen for 40 years.

If it continues as it has begun, 1992 could turn out to be almost as bizarre as 1991, a year in which North America's spring arrived in winter, its summer in spring and its winter in autumn. The period from December 1991 to March 1992 has already gone into the National Weather Service's record books as the warmest winter in at least 97 years. It hardly rained at all in rainy Seattle in May. Texas in January was swamped with twice as much precipitation as normal, and Southern California, where it never rains, was socked with floodwaters so powerful they carried cars out to sea. Africa is having its worst drought in 50 years, and eastern Australia, which is supposed to have summer when the northern hemisphere has winter, had to do without this year. Instead of balmy days and bright sunshine, Melbourne racked up a record 12 consecutive days of rain and the coldest January in 137 years, which is as far back as anyone Down Under kept track.

What is going on? Experts say fluctuations from normal readings are, well, normal and that weird weather is the rule, not the exception. But the highs and lows and wets and drys over the past two years have been so extreme that anxious questions are arising. Could these outbursts of wacky weather be related to those fires from the gulf war? That hole in the ozone layer? The global warming trend that environmentalists have been predicting for so many years?

The questions are more than idle speculation. This week at the Earth Summit in Rio de Janeiro, world leaders will be adding their signatures to a treaty to prevent climate change, a document that was significantly weakened during presummit negotiations, in part because of U.S. contentions that the threat of global warming has been overblown. But the Bush Administration's skepticism must contend with the direct experience of millions of citizens who are worried that when the weather gets as odd as it has been of late, something must be wrong.

Scientists, however, are more cautious than the umbrella-carrying public. Even climatologists who believe that global warming may eventually trigger extreme weather variations like the ones we are experiencing say it is too early to prove a direct connection. The outbreak of freakish weather could also have been partly caused by one or more of several large-scale atmospheric events now under way. The main suspects, in descending order of likelihood:

EL NIÑO. To meteorologists, the weather phenomenon named after the Christ child is not a theory but a recognizable and recurrent climatological event. Every few years around Christmastime, a huge pool of warm seawater in the western Pacific begins to expand eastward toward Ecuador, nudging the jet streams off course and dis-

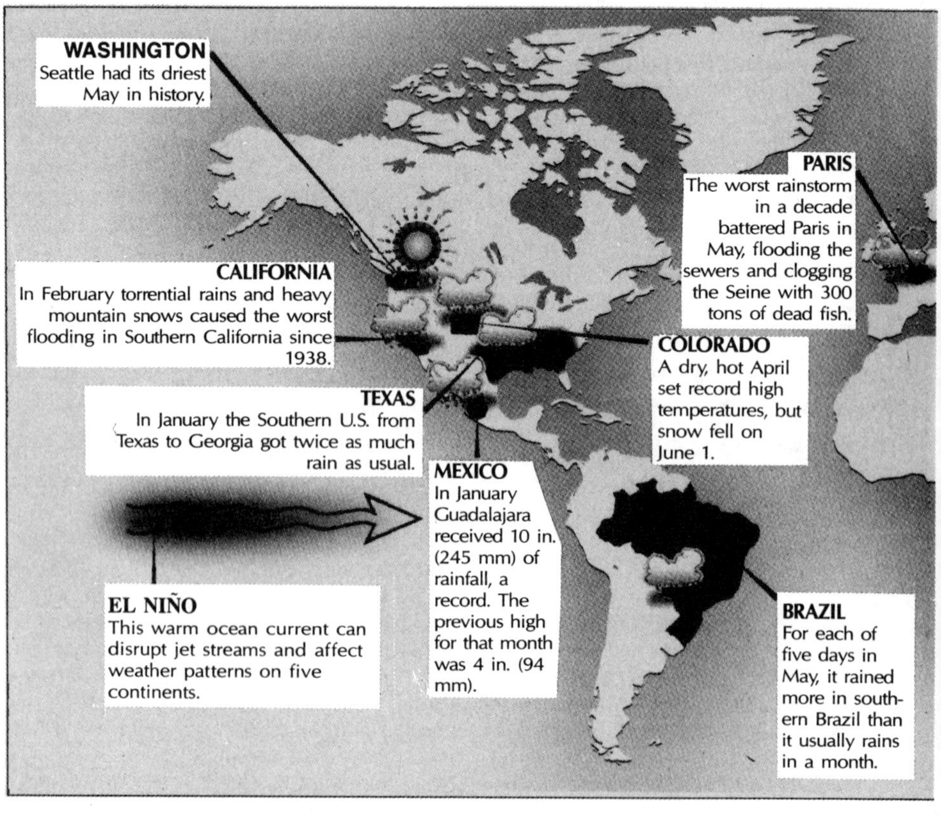

Weather?

There's nothing unusual about unusual weather. But global warming, a volcano and a stray ocean current may be making things even freakier.

rupting weather patterns across half the earth's surface. The El Niño that began last year and is now breaking up has been linked to record flooding in Latin America, the unseasonably warm winter in North America and the droughts in Africa.

PINATUBO. The full effects of the eruption of Mount Pinatubo in the Philippines last June—probably the largest volcanic explosion of the 20th century—are starting to be felt this year. The volcano heaved 20 million tons of gas and ash into the stratosphere, where they formed a global haze that will scatter sunlight and could lower temperatures—by half a degree Fahrenheit—for the next three or four years. Smoke from the gulf-war fires, by contrast, never reached the stratosphere and had no measurable effect on the world's weather.

GREENHOUSE GASES. It is known that the level of CO_2, methane and other heat-trapping gases in the atmosphere has increased 50% since the start of the Industrial Revolution. Measurements also indicate that the world's average temperature has increased 1°F over the past 100 years. The rest is conjecture. Computer models suggest that as the buildup of greenhouse gases continues, average temperatures could jump 3°F to 9°F over the next 60 years. Some scientists speculate that even a small rise in average temperatures could lead to greater extremes in weather patterns from time to time and place to place.

The problem with sorting out these influences is that they interact in complex ways and may, to some extent, cancel each other out. Pinatubo's cooling effects could counteract the warming caused by greenhouse gases, at least over the short term. At the same time, El Niño's warming influence seems to have suppressed the early cooling effects of Pinatubo's global haze.

Predicting the weather is, in the best of circumstances, a game of chance. Even with the most powerful supercomputers, forecasters will never be able to see ahead more than a couple of weeks with any accuracy. Climatologist Stephen Schneider of the National Center for Atmospheric Research compares the typical weather forecast to guessing what bumpers a pinball will hit after it has left the flipper. "What's happening now," he says, "is we're tilting the machine in several directions at once."

Of course, there have always been volcanic eruptions, and the tales of El Niño date back at least to the Spanish conquistadors. Old-timers can point to freak weather occurrences that put the Los Angeles floods to shame, like the 1928 storm that bombarded southwestern Nebraska with hailstones the size of grapefruit. Or the blizzard of 1888 that buried the Eastern Seaboard in snowdrifts the size of four-story buildings. "There is a record set somewhere every day," says Steve Zebiak, an atmospheric scientist at Columbia University's Lamont-Doherty Geological Observatory.

What is new is that for the first time some of the influences that shape our weather are man-made. Experts say it could be 20 or 30 years before they know for certain what effect the buildup of greenhouse gases, the destruction of ancient forests or the depletion of the ozone layer have had. Policymakers looking for excuses not to halt those trends will always be able to point to scientific uncertainty. As Schneider puts it, "We're insulting the system at a faster rate than we can understand." The risk is that by the time we understand what is happening to the weather, it may be too late to do anything about it. ***—Reported by David Bjerklie/ New York, with other bureaus***

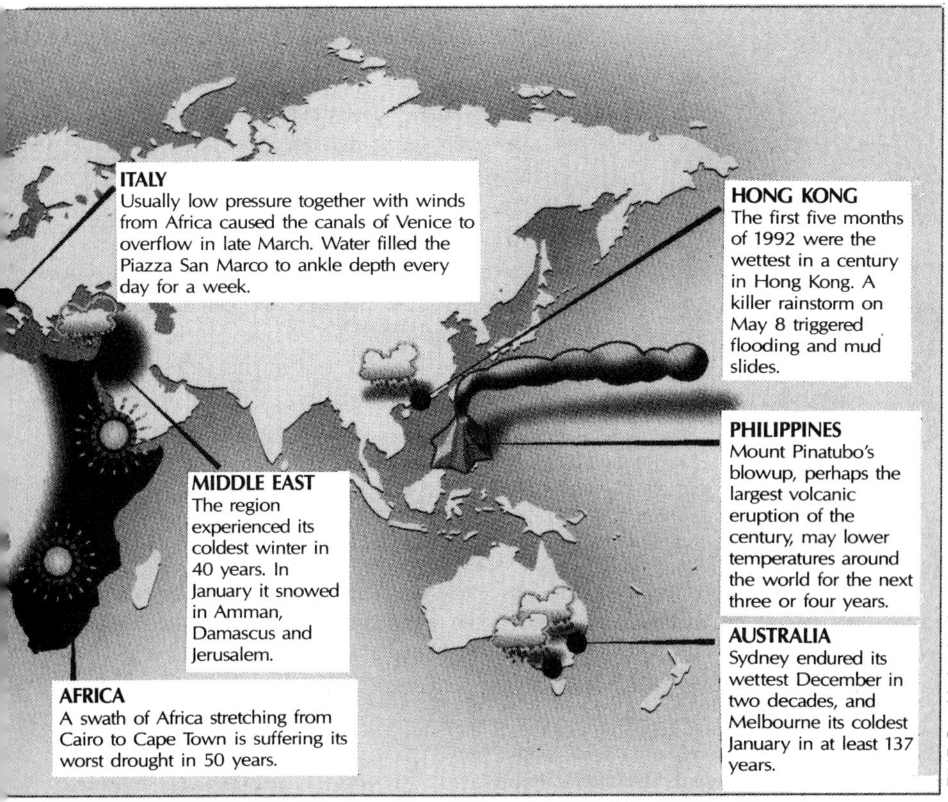

TIME Graphic by Joe Lertola

BEACHES ON THE BRINK

Retreat of the shoreline is nature's response to a rising sea level. Recent storms have renewed the debate over attempts to hold it in place.

Ruth Flanagan

Ruth Flanagan is an associate editor at Earth magazine. While reporting this story, she visited North Carolina and the storm-ravaged coasts of New Jersey and Long Island.

The most striking sight along the island of Westhampton Beach has traditionally been architectural: the contemporary summer homes of well-heeled New Yorkers lined up along the dunes. But after a severe storm blasted the town last December, it was nature, not culture, that commanded attention. The storm sliced through the slender barrier island, carving an inlet hundreds of yards wide that severed the community's only road. The sea swallowed much of the beach, stranding houses in the surf. More than 80 collapsed on their spindly pilings. After each one fell, it took a mere 20 minutes for the waves to chew up the clapboard and spit it all out as flotsam.

The same northeaster claimed millions of cubic yards of sand—and millions of dollars in property—along 200 miles of the coast from the Hamptons in New York to Long Beach Island in southern New Jersey. It also threw into relief fundamental questions about the future of coastal development, particularly on the barrier islands that fringe most of the U.S. Atlantic and Gulf coasts. Since the 1800s, most of these sandy strips have been narrowing. Though gentle swells in spring and summer restore sand, overall the islands have been slimming down year after year.

Many people fear the islands are in deep trouble. The very term "coastal erosion" has become a rallying cry, inspiring herculean attempts to immobilize retreating shorelines. People have tried trapping sand, pumping sand, even building walls that transform chunks of barrier islands into giant sandboxes. Most of these measures do protect property. But in the long run, none stop shoreline erosion. And some do much more harm than good.

"What we're doing as a nation is trying to maintain the status quo and keep everything in place," says Norbert Psuty, associate director of the Institute of Marine and Coastal Sciences at Rutgers University. "It's a losing battle."

It's also a confusing battle. Is the goal to save beaches or the property sidled up to the shore? On some barrier islands, such as Miami Beach and Atlantic City, storm damage and shoreline retreat could threaten billions of dollars' worth of beach-front development. In areas like these, many people feel we have no choice but to hold the ocean at bay—even though stabilizing shores with seawalls and other structures destroys natural beach systems. In many regions, however, people are moving toward "softer" solutions, such as replenishing beaches with sand from offshore. A few planners and residents are even starting to discuss what may be politically painful but ultimately necessary option: strategic retreat from the sea.

Human beings have undoubtedly accelerated erosion on many barrier islands. But according to Orrin Pilkey, a coastal geologist at Duke University, the main reason most islands are narrowing worldwide appears to be nature itself: rising sea level. About 20,000 years ago, during the Ice Age, much of the Atlantic Ocean's water was locked up in massive continental ice sheets. As a result, sea level along the U.S. East Coast was about 450 feet lower than it is now. As the climate warmed, the ice sheets began to melt and sea level rose rapidly. About 4,000 years ago, the rise slowed, but in the 1800s it picked up again. Since then the sea has crept up at an average rate of one foot per century. The amount of land being swallowed up differs from place to place, depending on other conditions such as the slope of the land. Even a small sea level rise generally has a marked effect on barrier islands because their slope is gentle.

Yet the sea's advance doesn't threaten the integrity of island systems, Pilkey says. In fact, he believes that by slimming down, the islands are actually securing their long-term survival.

Geologic evidence shows that barrier islands naturally tighten their belts when the sea rises. Then, after tens, hundreds or thousands of years, they become slender

From *Earth* magazine, November 1993, pp. 24-33.

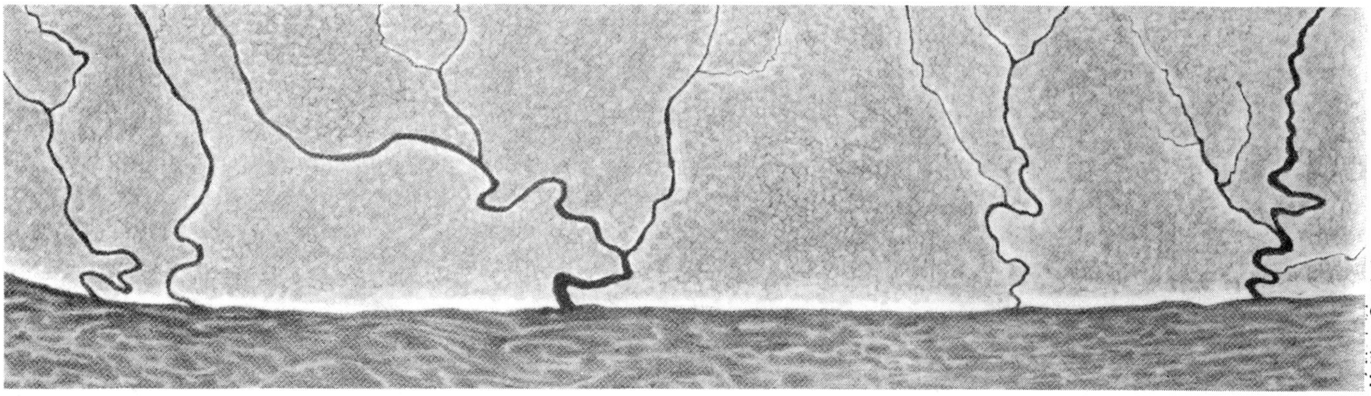

EVOLUTION OF A SHORELINE: ***Phase 1, 20,000 years ago.*** *Ice Age glaciers are advancing, causing sea level to drop. No barrier islands line the shore, which lies far seaward of today's coast. Rivers flowing through the low-lying coastal plain empty directly into the ocean; there are no estuaries.*

enough for even trifling storms to transfer sand clear across their widths. At that critical point the narrowing stops. Storms then remove sand from the front side of the islands and add it to the back. By this process, the islands migrate inland in pace with the rising sea. If the sea rises slowly enough, moving islands don't usually smash into mainland coasts. Instead, the shorelines behind the islands retreat at the same time. The two landmasses move back in step, like partners in a tango.

The encroaching ocean doesn't really damage the recreational beach either, Pilkey says. The swath of sand we plunk our towels on doesn't actually erode in response to sea level rise. It simply moves back, remaining the same width while the island as a whole narrows down. Erosion becomes a problem only when we put up immobile structures. As Pilkey puts it, "Coastal erosion is not a problem for beaches. It's only a problem for buildings."

It's not surprising that barrier island management is a major concern in the United States. Although these strips of sand fringe nearly every flat-lying coastal plain in the world, North America is blessed with the longest barrier island chain of all. These islands extend in a perforated line running parallel to the mainland some 2,700 miles from Long Island all the way to the Yucatan Peninsula. Some are highly developed and bear little resemblance to their natural state. Others remain wild. A few, like Cumberland Island in Georgia, are plump. A few other, like Assateague off the Maryland coast, are wisp-thin and low-lying and are migrating swiftly toward the mainland.

But varied as they are, all barrier islands share a few common features. They form only on gently sloping coastal plains. They require both sufficient sand and strong enough waves to move the sand about. And though sea level rise is now eroding many of them, they all required rising seas to form in the first place.

To demonstrate how barrier islands evolve, Orrin Pilkey takes his students to Shackleford Banks on North Carolina, an uninhabited island a half-mile wide and 7.5 miles long in Cape Lookout National Seashore. Today, much of the island is covered with a roller coaster of high dunes. The interior is forested with cedars and gnarled live oaks. Salt marsh thrives behind the island in a sheltered lagoon. Shackleford's front side is a long stretch of tawny beach behind which clumps of sea oats cling to hummocks of sand. The island looks sturdy and permanent.

But 20,000 years ago, when ice sheets to the north were still growing, there was no barrier island there or anywhere along the Atlantic Coast. Shackleford was part of a vast, forested plain, including what is now the submerged continental shelf. The plain was flatter than Kansas and extended seaward 40 miles.

Several thousand years later, the ice sheets began melting and the sea began to encroach. River valleys on the plain drowned and widened into estuaries. Only the high areas between the valleys were left jutting above water into the sea, forming protruding headlands. Then, as soon as the headlands emerged, waves began eroding them away. The waves generally approached the shore at an angle, forming longshore currents that carried huge loads of suspended sand picked up from the eroding headlands. When the waves lost energy, they deposited their sand in linear spits across the mouths of the estuaries.

At the same time, dunes were forming on the spits. Fair weather waves pushed sand onto the beach from the inner continental shelf. Winds carried some of this sand to the interior of the island, and plants like Shackleford's sea oats held much of it in place. Storms and hurricanes transported huge volumes of sand to the island's interior through gaps between the dunes. This supply allowed secondary ranks of dunes to form.

Finally, the spits broke free from the mainland and became true islands. Sometimes storms broke the spits into separate islands by carving inlets through them. In other cases, the spits gained their independence by more gradual means: Rising sea level flooded the lowlands behind the dunes, transforming the ridges of sand into

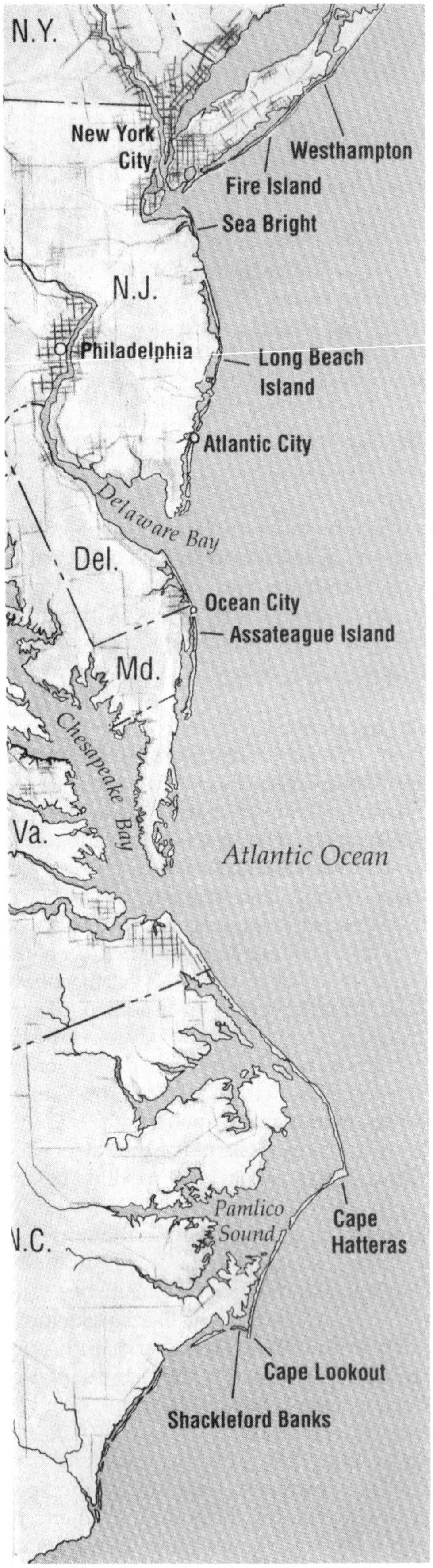

EARTH: Lee Vande Visse

Stephen G. Maka

THE NATURAL BEACH

Vegetation helps stabilize the talcum-fine sand just inland of the beach on Cumberland Island in Georgia (above). Farther inland on this wide barrier island near the Florida border are thick forests of moss-draped live oak.

Jack Dermid

North Carolina's Cape Lookout lighthouse (above) stands on a classic barrier island. The ocean beach is to the right. Sheltered behind dunes are grasses, shrubs and trees. The lagoon lies to the left. Salt marshes are common in calm lagoon waters, such as those behind Bear Island, N.C. (below).

Jack Dermid

islands and the former lowlands into quiet salt marsh lagoons.

Once they were cast out on their own, the barrier islands could take care of themselves. They no longer needed the eroding headlands to provide them with sand. Instead, waves brought in a steady supply from the shoreface, the submerged part of the beach. The islands sustained themselves for thousands of years in this state of dynamic balance, constantly changing in response to the action of waves and wind.

This doesn't mean that the going has always been easy for the barrier islands. For some periods between 18,000 and 6,000 years ago, sea level rose at the rate of five feet per century—about five times faster than it's rising today, Pilkey says. Some of these rapid rises must have caused many islands to disappear completely. During other periods, barrier islands migrated quickly enough to keep up with the rise. Many of these migrating islands have even preserved records of their travels. On Shackleford, for instance, bits of pearlescent oyster shell rest in the sand on the ocean side of the island. The oysters didn't live along the unprotected oceanfront. They grew on the other side of the island, in the shelter of a quite lagoon. Since then, the island has migrated back, plowing over its former lagoon.

People have been building permanent structures on barrier islands for only a tiny sliver of time, starting with a few scattered settlements in the 1700s. But by a quirk of fate, the development of the islands overlaps with a turning point in their history. After remaining stable for thousands of years, sea level began to rise during the 1800s, according to Pilkey. Thus, permanent settlement came at a time when most islands had already begun slimming and preparing to move.

Intensive development on barrier islands is an even more recent phenomenon. Construction boomed after World War II, spurred on by post-war prosperity, and has continued at a dizzying rate ever since. The most recent surge of development occurred in the past 25 years—a period in which thousands of hotels, condominiums and beach homes have sprung up. Significantly, this boom also coincides with a stint of unprecedented calm weather along the Atlantic coast. Many scientists consider this an unlucky break: The relative rarity of severe storms and hurricanes may have led people to overestimate the safety of barrier islands.

"In the last three decades or so, we've had very very few storms on the East Coast, and it's encouraged people to develop without fear," Rutgers' Norbert Psuty says. Perhaps then it's no coincidence that the number of homes located in coastal and riverine "high hazard areas" rose 40 percent from 1966 to 1989.

Pilkey fears that a general lack of experience with storms and hurricanes has also encouraged risky construction practices that transform relatively safe islands into dangerous ones. He is seriously concerned, for example, about the removal and "notching" of dunes, the

Michael Baytoff

A boardwalk and high-rise gambling halls line the shore in Atlantic city, N.J. (above). The beach here depends on periodic replenishment efforts, in which massive amounts of sand are added to compensate for erosion. In Seaside Park, N.J. (below), houses are densely packed nearly up to the surf line.

Robert Perron

THE DEVELOPED BEACH

On Long Beach Island in New Jersey, summer homes lie behind a barrier of dunes. These homes are less protected from the sea than they may seem. As sea level rises, Long Beach Island may eventually migrate inland right out from under them.

Michael Baytoff

Matthew Groshek

*EVOLUTION OF A SHORELINE: **Phase 2, 17,000 years ago.** Glaciers are melting and sea level is rising. The mouths of rivers drown and widen into estuaries. High areas between the estuaries are left as headlands. Sand eroding from the headlands is deposited in spits that grow steadily longer across the mouths of the estuaries—barrier islands in the making.*

building of houses on areas of beach that once were inlets, and the construction of roads that cut direct, perpendicular paths to the beach—standard practice on many barrier islands.

"In a big storm, a surge can cut through those roads like a knife through hot butter," Pilkey says. The roads not only usher in stormwaters, but often cut off residents' only access to escape routes.

Intensive shoreline development has already put many towns on a collision course with the everchanging islands. But when clashes occur, the islands generally suffer as much damage as their human inhabitants. Once communities place immobile structures near the shore, coastal erosion inevitably becomes a problem, and people often feel compelled to stabilize the beaches to protect themselves and their property. Sadly, rigid stabilization generally degrades and sometimes destroys the beaches that attracted development in the first place.

No stabilizing structures illustrate this process quite as dramatically as seawalls. Massive and unyielding, they run along beaches as a barricade against the waves. (Smaller parallel-lying obstructions, such as revetments and bulkheads, are also part of the seawall family.) People have often erected seawalls as a defensive measure following devastating storms or hurricanes. In 1900, for instance, the worst hurricane disaster in U.S. history struck Galveston, Texas, killing 6,000 people. In response, the survivors built the largest protective seawall ever placed on a barrier island.

Today, seawalls armor much of the developed shoreline. Many have done their job admirably, protecting homes and other buildings that otherwise would probably have tumbled into the sea. But seawalls extract a high toll for their services. Obviously, they block easy access to the beach and blot out the view. More importantly, though, they narrow and, according to Pilkey, even eliminate beaches.

Many geologists and engineers consider the seawall at the historic town of Sea Bright, N.J., a kind of object lesson: an example of the final, sorry consequences of hemming in a moving shore. In the late 1800s, Sea Bright was one of several island resort communities along a barrier spit in northern New Jersey that boasted a broad, sandy beach. A railroad running through the town to nearby Sandy Hook helped transport thousands of people each year to the prized bathing grounds in the area. In the early 1900s, a seawall was constructed to protect the railroad. Today, the gray, fortresslike wall in Sea Bright dominates the shoreline, looming 15 to 18 feet high and stretching more than six miles.

Unfortunately, the wall is protecting the town at the beach's expense. As the spit has slimmed down, the beach has narrowed dramatically in front of the wall. This process, called "passive erosion," occurs whenever a static structure is placed on a retreating shore. Psuty and Pilkey believe the wall has also caused "active erosion." Its presence caused the sea floor in front of it to steepen. The steep grade increased the storm-wave energy striking the shoreline, accelerating erosion and making it impossible for incoming waves to deposit sand from the continental shelf. Today, northern Sea Bright has no beach. Just big waves and a very big wall.

In places like Sea Bright where erosion is severe, communities often erect other structures specifically designed to build up the beaches. Groins and jetties are wall-like sand traps that run perpendicular to the shore, interrupting the transport of sand across the coast by longshore currents. Groins are used to widen a particular beach. Jetties (basically long groins) protect harbors and inlets. These devices line thousands of developed barrier shores.

Both groins and jetties can be very effective at building up beaches. Yet their drawbacks are obvious. Wherever they plump up one stretch of beach, they starve others down the coast. They work, essentially, by "robbing Peter to pay Paul." This often leads to a domino effect: Once one groin is in place, another is needed at the beach next door.

Matthew Groshek

EVOLUTION OF A SHORELINE: ***Phase 3, 14,000 years ago.*** *High water from storms occasionally washes over the spits, breaking their connections with the mainland and carving inlets across the strands. The result: a line of barrier islands guarding the mainland, with quiet salt-marsh lagoons in between. Currents deliver replenishing sand to the forested, dune-lined islands, which are now in dynamic balance.*

Jack Dermid

Sand bags (above) offer meager protection from the waves, which have taken a bite out of the beach at South Nags Head, N.C.

Courtesy: Moss Archives Sea Bright, N.J.

THE DAMAGED BEACH

The ocean crashes against a seawall in northern Sea Bright, N.J. (above). In this very spot in 1931 (below), bathers set up their umbrellas on a sandy strip called Highland Beach. The seawall, built in the early 1900s to protect the railroad, hastened the beach's demise by cutting off its supply of replenishing sand.

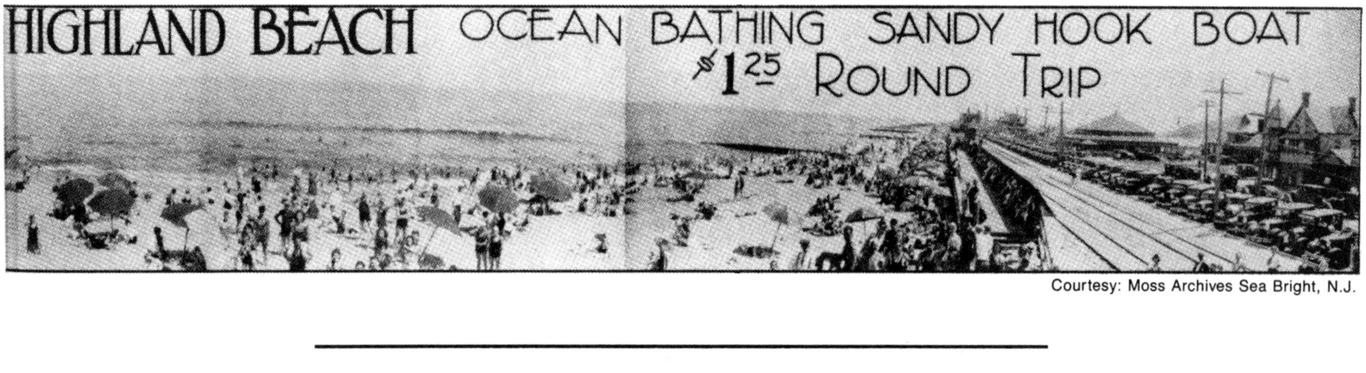

Courtesy: Moss Archives Sea Bright, N.J.

Matthew Groshek

EVOLUTION OF A SHORELINE: ***Phase 4, today . . . and the future.*** *With few exceptions, barrier islands are slimming down as sea level rise resumes after a hiatus of several thousand years. Waves and wind push sand from the ocean side of the narrow islands to the lagoon side, taking from the front and adding to the back. In this way, some islands are migrating shoreward. They could eventually crash into the mainland—especially where seawalls and other protective constructions prevent the mainland coast from retreating.*

The shifting sands of Assateague Island in Maryland and Virginia demonstrate the tremendous impact jetties can have. In 1933, the Army Corps of Engineers built jetties on either side of an inlet separating the Maryland beach resort of Ocean City from Assateague. The corps' purpose was to keep the inlet open for navigation, but the jetties had an unintended impact. They trapped sand to the north, providing Ocean City with the bonus of a wider recreational beach. But they prevented sand from reaching the northern part of Assateague on the other side of the inlet. As a result, this part of the island has slimmed considerably and moved back toward the mainland. Today, the northern part of the island is migrating rapidly toward a boat channel. This situation is sure to create an interesting management dilemma in the near future.

In the last few decades, however, barrier island communities have been building fewer and fewer structures to stabilize shores. Instead, most have embraced "beach replenishment" or "nourishment" to repair coastal erosion. Replenishment involves adding sand to beaches, both to provide recreational opportunities and to buffer property from storms. Sometimes the sand is dredged from silted harbors; in other cases, it's pumped from offshore bars or other parts of the coastal system. According to a report in the *Journal of Coastal Management*, more than 400 miles of U.S. shoreline were replenished as of 1987.

But even replenishment has its down side. Sand of the right size and texture may be hard to obtain. Dredging sand may also disrupt marine organisms and other parts of the coastal system, Pilkey says. And replenished beaches are often expensive and frustratingly short-lived. "It's all sacrificial sand," explains Diane Abell, a landscape architect at Fire Island National Seashore in New York. "We know a storm will come eventually and wash it all away."

Past replenishment projects have shown widely varying results. According to a report by Pilkey and his colleague Tonya Clayton, Ocean City, N.J., replenished a stretch of beach at a cost of $5.2 million in 1982. Two and a half months and 18 northeasters later, the beach had disappeared. On the other hand, the sand pumped onto 10.5 miles of Miami Beach between 1976 and 1981 (at a cost of $54 million) is still in place. The project even won a preservation award from the American Shore and Beach Preservation Association, Pilkey and Clayton report. It also received the Golden Fleece Award from Senator William Proxmire for wasting the taxpayers' money.

There is one other solution to coastal erosion. We could stop intervening and let the ocean advance. We could stop rebuilding storm-damaged buildings, for instance, and instead move them back as needed in step with the shore. We could let sand go where waves and wind transport it.

Though it's very controversial, the idea of retreat is creeping into the corners of coastal policy. A number of states, such as South Carolina, North Carolina and Maine, have adopted strong regulations prohibiting hard stabilization. At the federal level, the Army Corps of Engineers is now required to weigh the costs and benefits of retreat along with other solutions. Years ago, Pilkey says, many people would have scoffed at such an approach.

In the mid-1980s, Nags Head, N.C., adopted strict standards requiring that new beach homes be constructed on deep lots so that the houses have room to move back. "We consciously adopted the principal of retreat as part of our land-use planning," says Donald Bryan, the town's former mayor.

Of course, retreat is not practical on densely populated islands like Miami Beach or Atlantic City, where vast sums of money are tied up in shoreline development and where there is little, if any, room for buildings and utilities to move back. But even in smaller communities, retreat is sure to be painful. It could shrink the tax base, creating economic and political fallout. Requiring people to move from their homes would be emotionally wrenching as well.

LESSONS FOR THE FUTURE

A ruined home lies in the surf off Fire Island, N.Y., after last December's storm (right). Efforts to control the sea often have unanticipated results. A good example is a jetty protecting an inlet bordering Ocean City, Md., (below). It blocked the flow of sand to Assateague Island (foreground), which has thinned and migrated toward the mainland.

Diane Abell

Judy Johnson

But the rising costs of fighting the sea will undoubtedly force more communities to consider retreat in the near future. For instance, Psuty predicts that the exorbitant cost of replenishing the beach and maintaining the seawall at Sea Bright will ultimately compel people to abandon the area.

Nationally, reimbursing coastal dwellers for damage they incur from storms and hurricanes has helped put pressure on the National Flood Insurance Program. But obviously it is not only coastal disasters that soak up these funds. In July, the severe flooding in the Midwest completely drained the program's coffers. Additional money could come from federal taxpayers in a coastal emergency. This is hardly comforting though, since a single year of bad storms can cost up to $4 billion.

The expense of maintaining barrier islands for development thus raises issues of fairness, such as who pays and who benefits. After bad storms strike, taxpayers may be asked to foot the bill not only for insurance payments but also for beach repairs. Following last December's northeaster, city officials and property owners in Westhampton and nearby Fire Island clamored for aid in closing newly opened inlets, arguing that the channels posed a risk to the islands' ecosystems. The property owners claim that ocean water moving through the inlets threatens shellfish in the bays. But the inlets don't damage the system in general, or the islands in particular—only the people who depend on them to stay the same year after year.

A few things, at least, are certain: Our problems on barrier islands are not going to go away, especially if global warming accelerates the sea's rise. Some scientists believe the warming may also increase the frequency of coastal storms, making barrier islands and spits more vulnerable in the future.

But even without global warming, the sea will continue to encroach. The islands will continue to move. And, in the long run, we may have no choice but to get out of the way.

After a century of evolution, shopping malls are now urban centers, with post offices, hotels, counseling centers, and even amusement parks—all in a weather-protected, safe, clean place. Now signs of real life are starting to appear

The New Downtowns

Witold Rybczynski

Witold Rybczynski is a professor of architecture at McGill University, in Montreal. Rybczynski's books include Home: A Short History of an Idea *(1986),* Waiting for the Weekend *(1991), and* Looking Around: A Journey Through Architecture *(1992).*

Every two or three weeks I go to the mall. I drive, of course, and leave my car in the large lot. I don't dislike parking lots except at night, when they feel spooky, although not as spooky as underground parking garages: thanks to the movies, an underground garage always makes me think of echoing footsteps, screaming tires, gunshots. I read the bumper stickers and look at what people display on the rear-window shelf. There are rarely any interesting-looking cars: the mall I go to is patronized by small-town folk and farmers who tend to drive pickup trucks and Japanese compacts.

Inside the mall the atmosphere is enlivened by families eating lunch in the food court, excited teenagers swarming at the video arcade, young parents trailing children on the way to the movie theater. I suppose that my academic colleagues would find this unsophisticated version of urbanity depressing (although you can get a reasonable espresso here), and would probably refer darkly to "hyperconsumerism" and "artificial reality." But I am more encouraged than depressed. People are walking, they are rubbing shoulders, they are in a shared space.

Among urban sophisticates references to malls are invariably accompanied by a smirk or a sigh, but for most Americans shopping malls are an accepted part of everyday life, just like freeway commuting, fast food, garage sales, and backyard barbecues. Like these institutions, malls are resolutely middlebrow. Although there are plenty of upscale malls that cater to the rich, the classic mall is not an effete oasis of luxury—nor is it the utilitarian strip of the poor neighborhood. It's the so-called regional mall, generally defined as having more than 400,000 square feet of retail space and at least one department store—the equivalent of a fair-sized downtown shopping area. According to the National Research Bureau, at the end of last year the country contained 38,966 operating shopping centers, of which 1,835 were large regional malls.

Exemplary Models

Critics of shopping malls talk about the "malling of America" as if it were a sudden phenomenon, but it has taken almost a hundred years for the mall to become a feature of both the urban and the suburban landscape. Harvey Rabinowitz, who teaches in the school of architecture and urban planning of the University of Wisconsin, in Milwaukee, cites the shopping mall in explaining how changes often occur in building. According to Rabinowitz, in free-market societies new ideas about how to organize the urban environment are frequently introduced not by city planners or architects but by individual businessmen in the private sector. If these ideas are popular with the public, they become what he calls exemplary models, and go on to be widely imitated. In the past such urban models have included the English housing terrace, popularized in the eighteenth century by the Bath architect-developer John Wood the Elder, and quickly copied by speculative builders across Georgian Britain. Other examples: the department store, originated by Parisian entrepreneurs in the 1860s and popularized throughout Europe and America after millions of foreigners visited Paris for the great exhibitions of the late 1800s; and the high-rise business district. This last model began to appear in the 1880s in Chicago, the product of technological invention (steel-frame construction, the elevator), land speculation, and the desire for architectural splendor. So powerful was the image of the downtown skyline that it was quickly reproduced across the continent and finally around the world.

Exemplary models originate in response to economic and social forces in the marketplace, but their success is

From *The Atlantic Monthly,* May 1993, pp. 98-102, 104-106.

also due to refinement and modification during their later evolution. The history of the shopping mall is replete with experimentation and a host of small inventions. The shopping cart, for example, introduced in the 1930s, greatly facilitated the operation of supermarkets, which were a prominent feature of early shopping centers. The food court is the convivial focus of many contemporary malls; its successful introduction in the early 1970s by The Rouse Company and The Pyramid Companies was a milestone of shopping-center design.

The shopping center emerged in the early 1900s in the suburbs that encircled American cities. Suburbs of the time tended to be chiefly residential and to depend on the traditional downtown for shopping. The first suburban commercial centers had three identifiable features: they consisted of a number of stores built and leased by a single developer, they were usually situated at an important intersection, and they provided plenty of free, off-street parking. Roland Park Shopping Center, which opened at the turn of the century, about five miles north of downtown Baltimore, is listed by the *Guinness Book of World Records* as the first shopping center; it had only six establishments. It was followed by Market Square in Lake Forest, near Chicago (1916), and Country Club Plaza, which opened in 1925 in Kansas City, and became well known thanks to its proselytizing owner, Jesse Clyde Nichols. These "shopping villages" consciously recalled small-town shopping districts, both in their architecture, which was carefully traditional, and in their layout, which integrated them into the surrounding neighborhood—the stores faced the street and the parking lots were usually in the rear.

Some Depression-era shopping villages, such as Highland Park, in suburban Dallas (1931), and the Farmers Market chain, in California, did include stores oriented to a private pedestrian walkway, which presaged the inward-looking shopping centers of the future. Highland Park combined a variety of commercial tenants, not only retail stores but also a pharmacy, a bank, a beauty salon, a barbershop, a theater, and offices. Farmers Markets were the 1930s equivalents of today's discount warehouses, and to keep prices low they were built on cheap land at the edges of cities; since most people drove to go shopping, the peripheral location was not an inconvenience. This did not escape the attention of developers, who understood that with almost universal car ownership the pool of potential customers for any single shopping center—those who lived within a five-minute drive, say, rather than within a five-minute walk—had grown very large.

The spread of shopping centers was slowed by the Depression and the Second World War. According to Kenneth T. Jackson, a Columbia University professor and the author of *Crabgrass Frontier*, a history of American suburbanization, in 1946 there were still only eight shopping centers in the entire United States. What was needed was an exemplary model, and it arrived in the form of the regional shopping center. It is generally agreed that the first such shopping center was Northgate, which opened on the outskirts of Seattle in 1950. The architect, John Graham Jr., devised a long open-air pedestrian way that was a sort of carless street, lined with a department store and a number of smaller stores. The idea was that the department store, which is called an anchor, would attract people, who would then walk—and shop—along the way. In addition to stores, Northgate included several freestanding structures: a gas station, a drive-in bank, and a movie theater. Like all future suburban shopping centers, it was built next to a highway. The inward-oriented buildings were surrounded by a 4,000-car parking lot that took up about three quarters of the fifty-acre site.

The convenience of "one-stop shopping" appealed to many people, and during the 1950s the construction of shopping centers, in tandem with the expansion of suburbs, began in earnest; the total went from about a hundred centers nationwide in 1950 to about 3,700 a decade later. Not only were there more centers but also they were bigger. One of the largest was Northland, in Detroit, which opened in 1954 and provided more than a million square feet of rentable space and parking for 7,400 cars. The 250-acre area around the center was planned to accommodate a host of nonretail buildings, including offices, research laboratories, apartments, a hospital, and a hotel. This made Northland probably the first example of what the *Washington Post* reporter Joel Garreau would later call an "edge city," in his book of the same title.

A New Way to Shop

THE RAPID PROLIFERATION OF SHOPPING CENters was not just a function of suburban growth. It also signified a change in the shopping habits of Americans. These new shopping places were competing directly with the traditional downtown shopping district, and in most cases they were winning. According to Bernard Frieden and Lynne Sagalyn, professors of urban studies and the authors of *Downtown, Inc.: How America Rebuilds Cities* (1989), from 1948 to 1954, in the midst of a nationwide economic boom, the downtown share of retailing fell by a fourth in thirteen of the largest metropolitan areas, and the profit margins of downtown department stores sank lower than they had been even in the Depression.

In 1960 Buckminster Fuller proposed the construction of a huge dome that would cover a fifty-block area in midtown Manhattan. Fuller pointed out that such a dome would prevent snow and rain from falling on the protected area, and would control the quality of the air. Most people dismissed the outlandish idea—like many of Fuller's inventions, it was part in earnest, part publicity stunt. Perhaps they shouldn't have. Indeed, Fuller's vision of urban life taking place in an artificially controlled environment had been realized several years before.

In 1956 a shopping center that would become the exemplary model for the next three decades opened in Edina, a suburb of Minneapolis. Southdale (the early centers all seem to have been named after compass points) was not particularly large, just over half a million square feet of retail space, and it followed the usual pattern of buildings surrounded by parking lots. But it included a striking innovation: the public walking areas were not outdoors but indoors, air-conditioned in the summer and heated in the winter. The architect, Victor Gruen, a transplanted Viennese and a prolific designer of shopping centers (he had been the architect of Northland), cited the glass-roofed nineteenth-century gallerias of Milan and Naples as his inspiration, even if the bland, modernistic interior of Southdale did not much resemble its Italian antecedents. Indoor shopping streets are attractive anywhere the climate is marked by hot, humid summers or harsh winters or both, and enclosed shopping malls began to appear in the cold Midwest and Northeast, in the South and Southwest, in hot southern California, and in the wet Northwest—that is, everywhere.

From 1960 to 1970 more than 8,000 new shopping centers opened in the United States—twice as many as in the previous decade. The great majority of the regional centers followed the example of Southdale and provided enclosed walking areas. To optimize this extra investment, the new centers were built on two or even three levels (this idea, too, had been introduced at Southdale), which meant that walking distances were reduced and shopping centers could house even more stores. In 1970 the Galleria in suburban Houston, which did recall its Italian namesakes, opened with more than 1.5 million square feet of retail and commercial space; the following year Woodfield, outside Chicago, provided two million square feet of shopping under one roof. During the 1980s malls got even larger: the Del Amo Fashion Center, in Torrance, California, enclosed three million square feet, and the mother of all malls—the Ghermezian brothers' West Edmonton Mall, in Alberta—covers 5.2 million square feet. In all, from 1970 to 1990 about 25,000 new shopping centers were built in the United States: every seven hours during that period a new shopping mall opened its doors to the public.

And the mall was not only a suburban phenomenon. It became a key ingredient of the urban revitalization that was taking place throughout the seventies and eighties. Charleston; Stamford, Connecticut; White Plains, New York; Salt Lake City; Minneapolis; Philadelphia; and Chicago were all sites of large downtown malls. In Boston, Baltimore, and New York, The Rouse Company, a major shopping-center developer, built so-called festival marketplaces, which were really shopping malls in waterfront settings; they were often shoehorned into rehabilitated dockside buildings.

The Galleria, in Houston, whose centerpiece was a year-round ice-skating rink, added yet another ingredient to the exemplary model. The developer, Gerald Hines, incorporated a variety of nonretail uses not in separate buildings, as had been done before, but within the mall. The lobbies of the hotel and office buildings, for example, could be entered directly from the enclosed space. This was not as dramatic as roofing over public spaces, but its effect on the environment was just as great. Both developers and the public began to think of malls not merely as shopping conveniences but as urban places in which someone could enjoy spending several hours. Although retail functions continued to dominate, mall developers added recreation facilities like health and athletic clubs and were also able to attract banks, brokerage houses, and medical centers. It has become increasingly common for malls to fulfill civic functions, with public libraries (Saint John, New Brunswick, and Tucson, Arizona), the USO (Hampton, Virginia), a city-hall branch office (Everett, Washington), and federal and state agencies. The Sports Museum of New England, in East Cambridge, Massachusetts, is housed in a mall, and so is a children's museum in Ogden, Utah. The Board of Education of Ottawa has been operating a storefront classroom in a shopping mall since November of 1987, and a local high school recently opened a counseling center in the West Edmonton Mall. Just as noncommercial spaces are showing up in shopping malls, malls are popping up in unexpected places: York University, in suburban Toronto, recently added a shopping mall to its campus, and Pittsburgh's new airport includes a mall with more than a hundred stores, three food courts, and, appropriately enough, a chiropractor.

Private Property or Public Forum?

THE APPEARANCE of noncommercial tenants in shopping malls has made them even more like traditional downtowns, but it has also raised the issue of public access. Are malls private property, as many mall owners have always maintained, or have they become, as the American Civil Liberties Union has argued, public places that should be obliged to observe the principles of free speech—to allow unlimited access to community groups, including petitioners and political demonstrators? Understandably, mall owners have not been keen on the idea of having abortion groups arguing their cases in the food court, or of hosting a violent altercation between the Ku Klux Klan and its opponents (this actually happened, in a Connecticut mall in the mid-1980s). Such altercations are just the sort of thing that mall shoppers want to get away from. In a 1990 Gallup poll 73 percent of respondents said that shopping centers shouldn't have to allow political gatherings. It is disingenuous, however, for developers to argue that they are merely merchants. They have become city builders, and as such should be prepared to take the bad—or at least the awkward—with the good.

In 1968 the U.S. Supreme Court ruled that shopping malls could not interfere with individuals' exercise of their First Amendment rights. But in a 1972 ruling (*Lloyd Corp. v. Tanner et al.*) the court reversed itself and held that the First Amendment did not require shopping centers to allow the distribution of war-related leaflets. So matters stood until 1980, when a unanimous ruling on a public-access case concerning a mall in California held that the state constitution granted greater free-speech rights than the U.S. Constitution, which effectively made public access a state issue. So far other states have tended to support the notion that malls are private property; ten state supreme courts have ruled against public access. Only five states have supported it, and then only in fairly limited forms—to groups soliciting signatures for a state initiative, for example, or to candidates seeking signatures to qualify for a place on the ballot.

But the example of California malls may in the long run be influential. If large regional malls want to be a part of the community and attract a broad cross-section of the population, it is in their interest to allow access to local nonprofit groups. Although not legally required to do so, a small number of mall owners are beginning to do exactly that. The Rouse Company provides a booth for community activities in its mall in Columbia, Maryland, and encourages its mall managers elsewhere to make similar accommodations; so does The Edward J. DeBartolo Corporation, of Youngstown, Ohio, the nation's largest shopping-center developer and manager.

Another reason that mall owners may eventually support the idea of public access is that since the California ruling the state's access requirements have proved to be neither troublesome nor expensive, despite the fears of some developers. In 1991 the giant Hahn Company, which owns and operates thirty malls in California, signed an agreement with the ACLU which permits leafleting and canvassing in designated locations in most of its malls. Robert L. Sorensen, the vice-president of Hahn, told *Shopping Centers Today*, an industry monthly, "We haven't seen expenses rise because of it, and I don't think it's costing us shoppers."

A Place to Play

WORK AND PLAY, SHOPPING AND RECREATION, community promotion and public protest—the mall now houses more and more of the activities of the traditional downtown, including that newest of urban industries, tourism. With its skating rink and glass-roofed promenade, Houston's Galleria quickly became a tourist attraction. The builders of the West Edmonton Mall provided not only a skating rink but also an amusement park, an aviary, a dolphin pool, an artificial lagoon with a submarine ride, a floating replica of the *Santa Maria*, and the world's largest indoor water park, complete with an artificial beach and rolling surf—all calculated to draw vacationers in addition to shoppers.

"We expect that a third of our visitors will be tourists coming from more than a hundred and fifty miles away," says Michael Dorsey, a spokesman for the Mall of America, the recently opened 4.2-million-square-foot mall in Bloomington, Minnesota, outside Minneapolis. The Mall of America expects to attract an average of about 100,000 people a day when it is fully operational; during the first three months after its opening, last August, nearly a million people a week visited the mall. Indeed, according to the owners, the Mall of America is expected to draw more visitors than Walt Disney World or the Grand Canyon.

The Mall of America is an extremely large shopping mall—four department stores, about 360 specialty stores to date, more than forty restaurants and food outlets—but the three-level retail area is not particularly remarkable, only bigger than most. What is unusual is the fact that the stores are grouped around a huge (seven-acre) glass-roofed courtyard containing an amusement park with twenty-three rides, two theaters, and dozens of smaller attractions. Although the courtyard is usually described as a theme park (it's called Camp Snoopy), anyone looking for the technological theatricality and sophisticated gimmickry of a Walt Disney World will be disappointed. The attendants are dressed like camp counselors (at first I mistook them for fundraising Boy Scouts), but otherwise there is little attempt at simulation; the rides are tame and the atmosphere is unpretentious, almost homely. At night the sparkling lights, hurdy-gurdy music of the merry-go-round, excited children, and screams of the riders on the roller coaster that races overhead recall the gaiety of a carnival midway at a county fair.

The layout of the Mall of America is reminiscent of what was probably the world's first building to combine shopping and recreation—the eighteenth-century incarnation of the Palais Royal, in Paris. The developer of that project was the Duc de Chartres, whose family home in Paris, beside the Louvre, had an extremely large garden. The duke, chronically short of funds, engaged the architect Victor Louis to design a pleasure garden *à l'anglaise* that also included commercial spaces and apartments for rent. The Palais Royal opened in 1784 to immediate accolades, and it dominated Parisian social life for fifty years. Like many developers since, the duke did not reap the profits of his brilliant idea. Financially ruined by the heavy investment, he was forced to sell off most of the project.

The Palais Royal (which still exists, although today it is a quiet place) consisted of a five-story arcaded building on three sides of a large landscaped courtyard about 100 yards by 300 yards; the fourth side, which was never completed, was closed by wooden stalls. At the ground level were glass-fronted shops along the two-story arcade, but there were also a variety of other establishments: cafés, eating places, social clubs, gambling rooms, music rooms, auction rooms, a puppet show, a silhouette show, a waxworks, several small hotels, a Turkish bath, and a theater (which later became the home of the Comédie Française). The upper floors contained apartments and rooms, many rented by the high-priced prostitutes for which the Palais became famous. The central courtyard was not merely a pleasure garden; it also contained a circular roofed amphitheater—the Cirque Royal—for public performances, concerts, and balls.

Most of the establishments of the Palais were luxurious and

could be afforded only by the rich—or by army officers on a spree—but the arcades and the garden were open to all except the poorest classes (who were invited in on only three special days of the year), and they were places where aristocrat and bourgeois mixed. The Palais Royal merged shopping with entertainment and pleasure with leisure. "Should an American savage come to the Palais Royal," the Russian novelist Nikolai Karamzin wrote, "in half an hour he would be most beautifully attired and would have a richly furnished house, a carriage, many servants, twenty courses on the table, and, if he wished, a blooming Laïs who each moment would die for love of him."

Clearly, the Mall of America has a ways to go. In its own middle-American way, though, it too aspires to be a "place for fun in your life," as its theme song puts it. This ambition is evident in the nightclub area, which shares the fourth level of the mall with a fourteen-screen cineplex that includes a 4,000-seat theater. Although the stores in the mall close at 10:00 P.M., the nightclubs, which include a sports bar, a comedy club, and a country-and-western supper club, stay open until 1:00 A.M. Combine neon, nighttime, loud music, alcohol, and cruising singles, and the resulting atmosphere (it reminded me of a sort of midwestern Times Square—there was a whiff, but only a whiff, of sin) is not what one usually associates with shopping malls.

Re-creating Downtowns

NOT EVERYONE AGREES THAT MALLS COULD become a new version of the old Main Street. Kenneth Jackson observes in *Crabgrass Frontier* that because they are so self-contained and so uniform, shopping malls in fact represent almost the opposite of downtown areas: "They cater exclusively to middle-class tastes and contain no unsavory bars or pornography shops, no threatening-looking characters, no litter, no rain, and no excessive heat or cold."

In fact large malls do cater to a variety of tastes—they have to. The Mall of America has the usual array of fast-food outlets arranged around two food courts, several "family" restaurants (with occasional live entertainment), an assortment of inexpensive steakhouses, several mainstream Italian eateries, an upscale restaurant serving California cuisine, and a Wolfgang Puck pizza and pasta emporium, the first one outside California. Admittedly, that is less than could be found in a comparable area of Manhattan, but it does represent greater diversity than one would encounter in most small cities.

The idea that malls cater to only one taste in shopping is likewise unsupported by the evidence: the Mall of America contains Bloomingdale's and The Gap, Brooks Brothers and Sam Goody, Godiva Chocolatier and Radio Shack, Brookstone and video arcades. The number of stores may be greater than at other malls, but their variety is typical. There are even, arguably, pornography shops, in the form of video stores, and plenty of threatening-looking (to me, at least) teenagers—but no panhandlers, which is of course why people like to go to malls. It is true that malls are clean, but the notion that urbanity is somehow represented by litter is surely more a sad comment on the miserable state of most American downtowns (Parisian streets are virtually litter-free) than it is a serious criticism.

Because people in malls are protected from rain and from extremes of heat and cold, does that really disqualify malls as urban? The first completely enclosed shopping spaces, or *passages,* emerged in the center of Paris in the early 1800s (many still exist and are well worth a visit). These glass-roofed arcades were widely imitated across the Continent and in England. Nineteenth-century London and Paris also had shopping bazaars, and Milan its famous gallerias; these were large, often multilevel shopping arcades with independent stalls, covered by impressive roofs constructed of cast iron and glass. One of the few surviving examples of a shopping-bazaar building is the splendid GUM department store in Moscow, completed in 1893. Beside the high-blown, extravagant interiors of the Victorian shopping bazaars and department stores, which celebrated shopping and consumerism on a scale unrivaled before or since, the architecture of most contemporary shopping malls appears downright modest.

Still, Jackson does have a point. Downtown areas are made up of open as well as enclosed public spaces—Central Park as well as the concourse of Grand Central Station—and most developers, in their rush to enclose malls completely, may have missed an important opportunity to provide a greater diversity of experience. At least one major mall offers an alternative exemplary model: Horton Plaza, opened by The Hahn Company in downtown San Diego in 1985. The architect, Jon Jerde, turned the tables on the now-traditional enclosed mall and put all the public areas outdoors. Horton Plaza is unorthodox in other ways: it is the most colorful shopping center built since 1925, when Jesse Clyde Nichols included a tower imitating Seville's Giralda in his Spanish-Moorish–style Country Club Plaza, in Kansas City. Jerde also designed the Mall of America, but whereas that is architecturally unadventurous, Horton Plaza is a *tour de force* that includes bits and pieces of almost every stylistic period in history—Egyptian, Renaissance, Moorish, Art Deco, Victorian, Mediterranean. The result resembles a Cecil B. De Mille backlot. It is, needless to say, a popular success.

Horton Plaza is in southern California, but the example of festival marketplaces like Boston's Faneuil Hall Marketplace and Baltimore's Harborplace demonstrates that the use of outdoor spaces is a good idea: it makes shopping malls more stimulating, more pleasurable, and more traditionally urban. Maurice Sunderland, the Calgary-based architect who designed the West Edmonton Mall and prepared the preliminary plans for the Mall of America, is currently working on several large malls that will combine indoor and outdoor areas. I recently asked him whether he thought that malls could eventually become mini-cities. "They haven't reached that stage yet," he answered, "but they could."

One thing that is required to make malls more truly urban is the introduction of some form of permanent housing, which would provide a resident population in addition to shoppers. Housing for the elderly would seem particularly appropriate, not only because of the proximity to shops and indoor promenades but also because malls in many cities are well served by mass transportation.

In the past, developers resisted the use of malls for noncommercial purposes, including housing. Today this has changed. Increasingly, large urban malls are being built with the co-sponsorship of city governments. In half of the thirty-nine downtown shopping-mall projects studied by Bernard Frieden and Lynne Sagalyn, the public share was between 20 and 50 percent of total development cost. In the case of Horton Plaza, the city of San Diego contributed $33 million. As cities become active partners in mall development, social considerations come into play. Cities have already negotiated with mall developers for additional public spaces, mass-transit facilities, and civic spaces such as theaters. Housing should be next.

Power Centers

THE CHIEF OBSTACLE TO THE FURTHER SOCIALizing of the shopping mall may be a new, competitive form of shopping center—what developers call the power center. Power centers are usually moderate in size (about 200,000–400,000 square feet); instead of an assortment of small stores anchored by a department store, they include only two or three deep-discount, or "category-killer," stores—enormous self-service specialty stores with large inventories and low prices. But bargains are not the only attraction. These streamlined centers reflect the desire of many consumers to devote less time to shopping. According to Keith Foxe, of the International Council of Shopping Centers, the average visitor to a power center spends only forty-five to fifty minutes there, as compared with an average of three hours in a regional mall (or more than four hours in the Mall of America). The same desire accounts for the popularity of huge general-merchandise warehouses, which resemble department stores with shopping carts and which are designed to shorten, not prolong, shopping time. Not surprisingly, power centers and discount warehouses, unlike malls, don't have extensive public spaces for strolling. Indeed, in many of them the only public domain is the parking lot. Although some power centers do include nonretail businesses, such as day-care centers and coffee shops, they do not seem likely to develop the same semi-public character as the regional mall, or at least not soon.

The power center is a poor substitute for the shopping mall, which is poised to become a real urban place. The mall is beginning to integrate a variety of commercial and noncommercial functions, to deal with the thorny issue of public access, and to find an architectural balance between enclosed and open public space. In many cases part-public ownership is also changing its character. And it remains, for most Americans, the chief place to meet fellow citizens in a noncombative environment—not behind the wheel of a car but on foot, malling about.

Soil loss is accelerating and land that is needed to feed the world's growing population is being degraded. Disaster lies ahead unless the loss of soil is halted

AVERTING A DISASTER

Over the next 20 years, up to 345 million acres (140 million hectares) of fertile land—an area nearly equal in size to Alaska—is expected to lose much of its agricultural value, says the Food and Agriculture Organisation (FAO) of the United Nations. Urgent action is needed to halt the loss, or food problems in developing countries will worsen

Some 745 million acres (305 million hectares) of arable land, an area nearly equal in size to Western Europe, has already been damaged by man-made soil degradation, meaning it has lost much of its agricultural productivity, says a group of 250 soil scientists consulted by the Netherlands-based International Soil Reference and Information Centre.

Another 2.25 billion acres (910 million hectares) of once-rich land—an area larger than Australia—has become moderately degraded, which means that it has suffered a decline in productivity. If no restoration is undertaken on such land, it may be strongly degraded in the near future.

"Analysis of man-made land degradation," says FAO director-general Edouard Saouma, "raises a fundamental question—are we going to have enough good land to feed the extra 2.6 billion people who will be on this planet by the year 2025?"

Only 11 percent of the world's land area has no limits on its use for agriculture. Some 28 percent of land area is too dry; 23 percent has chemical imbalances; 10 percent is too wet; 6 percent is permanently frozen; and the soil is too shallow on the remaining 22 percent.

Soil is, in effect, a non-renewable resource. Once destroyed, it is practically gone forever. Under most conditions, soil is formed at a rate of 1 inch every 250-1,200 years. In all, it usually takes 3000-12,000 years to make agricultural productive land.

FAO says the planet is currently losing up to 17.5 million acres—an area nearly as large as Ireland—of cultivated land a year due to soil degradation. If the process is not halted, it would negate all agricultural gains from the opening of new lands to farming and pasture over the next 20 years.

"Land degradation is now proceeding so rapidly that few African countries can hope to achieve sustainable agriculture in the near future, while serious food consequences could eventually be felt as well in Latin America and Asia," says Saouma.

Land degradation can at least partially be blamed for the famines in Ethiopia in the 1970s and 80s, along with low rainfall, population growth and civil war.

Degradation

In the past 45 years, about 11 percent of the world's vegetated surface has suffered either moderate or strong degradation. By region, the best estimates suggest that in Africa 4 percent of the land has been strongly degraded, in Asia 4 percent, South America 1.4 percent, North America 1.3 percent and Europe 2.3 percent.

Are we going to have enough good land to feed the extra 2.6 billion people who will be on this planet by the year 2025?

The countries with the biggest land degradation problems in Asia are China, India, Thailand, Vietnam; in Africa they are Burkina Faso, Burundi, Ethiopia, Madagascar, Lesotho, Rwanda, Morocco; in Latin America, they are Brazil, Costa Rica, El Salvador, and Panama.

Soil erosion is a natural phenomenon, but man has increased the rate of degradation of the natural process by at least 2.5 times, faster than the Earth can recover in many regions. The three main causes of land degradation are overgrazing, destructive agricultural practices and deforestation.

* Overgrazing is the most prevalent cause of soil damage, responsible for 35 percent of all erosion, the most important type of degradation, while continual trampling by herds compacts the soil and reduces its capacity to retain moisture.
* Destructive agricultural practices and mismanagement of land account for 27 percent of degraded areas, much of which has occurred in North America. These include such practices as repeated conventional tillage with heavy equipment, and mismanagement such as steep land being cultivated down the slope. The US Government has spent about $18 billion since the 1930s to reduce the effects of soil erosion and currently spends about $1 billion a year for the effort, but still loses some 6 billion tons of top soil yearly.
* Deforestation is one main causes of the Earth's degraded land, mostly in Asia and South America. The latest FAO study shows that 380 million acres (154 million hectares) of tropical forest were lost between 1981 and 1990. More than 70 percent of the deforestation took place in the rain forests of Latin America, Asia and the Pacific. The remaining occurred in Africa's forests and savannah woodlands.

From *International Agricultural Development*, November/December 1993, pp. 7-10. Reprinted by permission.

Once land has been deforested, it takes 15 years of idleness for the land to recover its nutrient value.

Insidious

Land degradation is an insidious process—rarely is land in full production one year and out of production the next. Instead, crop yields begin to fall as degradation proceeds. Eventually, arable land becomes scrub, and finally, scrub becomes barren land.

Even the better soils of many parts of the Third World are getting less productive, says the FAO, marking a decline in fertility in the very areas where there is an urgent need for sharp production increases.

The main reason for this process is the continuous "mining" of plant nutrients without adequate replenishment. FAO commissioned one recent study that discloses the depletion rate of nutrients on arable land in sub-Saharan African countries now averages 44 pounds (20 kilos) of nitrogen a year, 22 pounds of phosphorus (10 kilos) and 44 pounds of potassium (20 kilos) per hectare.

The use of plant nutrients provides the quickest and surest way of boosting crop production, but fertilizers are in many cases too costly for small farmers and can cause serious pollution if not applied properly.

In addition, land is being taken out of production because of the increased presence of man-made chemicals and pollution in the environment, such as industrial or urban waste accumulation, or excessive use of pesticides, oil spills etc. Industrial accidents have also played a part, such as the Soviet nuclear accident at Chernobyl, which affected major but scattered areas of northern Europe.

It is usually the best crop land that is disappearing most rapidly, warns the FAO, especially because of urban expansion, road building, mining, industry and recreation.

There are four ways in which land, once stripped of its protection by overgrazing, poor agricultural practices or deforestation, is degraded:

* Build-up of salts: this can happen when poorly drained land is irrigated in hot climates. The sun evaporates the surface water, leaving behind the salts. At the same time, inadequate drainage causes the water table to rise, bringing salt water into contact with plant roots, which kills them. Worldwide, about 100 million acres (40 million hectares) out of a total of 500 million irrigated acres (200 million irrigated hectares) are either waterlogged, affected by salt, or both. The process limits the use of irrigation.
* Physical and biological damage: soil may be physically damaged when it is repeatedly worked by heavy equipment in wet weather, or when it is compacted around water holes in pasture land. It is difficult to return compacted soil to full productivity. Damage occurs when soils are deprived of their essential fertilizers and organic matter. Crop rotation and good farming practices can prevent the problem.
* Wind erosion—large areas of the world are affected by wind erosion, one of the key causes of land degradation and eventual desertification. Wind erosion occurs when soil is left bare of vegetation to block the wind. It is particularly severe in arid and semi-arid areas following over-stocking and over-grazing, with 22.4 percent of Africa north of the equator and 35.5 percent of the Near East affected by it. Under the worst conditions, 60 tons of soil can be blown off one acre (150 tons per hectare) of land in an hour.
* Water erosion—this is the most common form of erosion, causing massive damage in nearly all developing countries. It is especially found where steep land is being unwisely farmed and where gently sloping land is left exposed to the effects of heavy rain for any length of time.

About 25 billion tons of soil are washed away each year

Worldwide, about 25 billion tons of soil are being washed away each year, going first into the world's rivers and finally into the oceans.

China's Huang River, the most sediment-laden river in the world, annually carries away 1.6 billion tons of soil into the East China Sea. During a short storm in Tanzania a few years ago, scientists found that a field they were studying lost 2 inches (5cm) of topsoil over its whole surface in just a few hours.

In the United States, the annual loss of top soil from crop land still averages nearly 12 tons per hectare, with some 50 million tons of plant nutrients lost nationwide every year—nutrients which must be replaced by expensive fertilizers. The United States has lost about one-third of its top soil since farming began.

The FAO analysis shows that most nations in Africa and South America are still using only a relatively small proportion of arable land available to them. Most nations in Asia, however, are approaching the limits of their arable land, while some nations in the Near East such as Jordan, Yemen and Egypt have passed beyond that point and have been forced to cultivate land unsuitable for agriculture.

Africa

Africa has some of the world's more serious land and food problems, as well as much of its greatest potential. Much of the continent's land base is environmentally fragile and easily damaged. Large areas of cropland, woodland and forest have already been seriously degraded. Sustainable production in Africa, whether crops, livestock or fuelwood, depends on systems of land use that maintain soil fertility and reduce erosion and other kinds of degradation.

An FAO study stresses that if Africa can overcome its problems, it could produce enough food, fuel and fibre to support a population very much larger than 660 million people now living there. About 2.1 billion acres (840 million hectares), or 30 percent of Africa's land area, is potentially cultivable. In 1990 less than one-fourth of this area was actually being cultivated.

But land resources are unevenly distributed with countries such as Zambia and Zaire having large reserves while countries like Rwanda, Ethiopia and Lesotho have little, if any, new land to bring into production.

Over the centuries, African farmers and pastoralists have developed effective systems of land use compatible with their environments, such as nomadic grazing in the semi-arid areas, and shifting cultivation in the humid tropics—which served to conserve fertility as it allowed a long fallow period during which soil fertility would build up to its previous level, and nomadic grazing in the semi-arid areas.

Problems arose in many African nations when their populations started to increase, and the pressure on land resources became more severe. There is no longer enough land available to allow long fallow periods; more and larger herds are competing for forage over the same range and, placing all other traditional systems of land use under increasing strain.

Farmers have responded by trying to cultivate new land, although most of the best land was already in use. As a result, expansion is taking place mostly in marginal areas—steep land, land in regions of uncertain rainfall and land with poorer eroding soils. This is radically changing the African landscape—large areas of forest have been destroyed and much traditional pasture has been put under the plow. Given their limited resources, African farmers cannot put sufficient nutrients into this type of marginal soil to replace what is being taken off the land—through water or wind erosion or by the crops themselves. This is now bringing severe degradation to many regions for the first time.

As much as 34 percent of African land, which is not already desert, is now under threat of desertification. In addition, deforestation is proceeding 45 times faster than reforestation in tropical Africa. In the early 1980s, an estimated 9.2 million acres (3.7 million hectares) of forest lands were lost each year. The estimate for the early 1990s is 10.3 million acres (4.1 million hectares) per year.

The destruction of forests is mainly the result of people clearing land for agriculture. Both slash-and-burn agriculture, when land is not allowed to lie fallow as long as traditional practices dictate, and permanent clearing for modern farms, are taking a toll, as well as the search for fuelwood and growing frequency and severity of forest and bush fires.

"Conservation is not a high priority for hungry people", says Saouma, "farmers have to make sure that they and their families survive today. The 21st century is too far off for them."

Water conditions over much of Africa are changing. With less vegetative cover to protect against the impact of raindrops that cause surface scaling, less rain infiltrates the soil. Runoff increases, stream flows fluctuate more and more and flooding becomes more frequent and extensive. These conditions lead to erosion and as a result, sediment loads in rivers are increasing, dams are filling with silt, hydro-electric schemes are being damaged, navigable waterways are being blocked and water is deteriorating. Both crop yields and the inland fish catch fall.

FAO studies indicate that more than 35 percent of land north of the equator is affected by either erosion or salinity. An FAO study shows that sediment levels are increasing at approximately 5 percent per year in Nigeria, Tanzania and Zimbabwe, 4.3 percent in the Sudan and 3.2 percent in Tunisia.

"Such conditions lead directly to human suffering and misery," Saouma points out, "unless the present trend is reversed, many African nations may soon face the famines suffered by Somalia, Sudan and Ethiopia, all at least partly due to land degradation.

As an example of what can happen in one country, an FAO study of Zimbabwe suggests that erosion carries away an annual average of 1.6 million tons of nitrogen, 15.6 million tons of organic matter and 240,000 tons of phosphorus. Nitrogen and phosphorus losses are from the arable land were about three times the level of total fertilizer applied in the country in the 1984-85 season.

If fertilizers were applied to compensate for these losses, the cost would have been $1.5 billion per year in 1985 and even more today. The implication of these figures is a massive "hidden" cost on the economy of Zimbabwe—and almost certainly a similar cost on nearly every other African country.

Rehabilitation

To assist nations struggling with land degradation, FAO has launched an International Scheme for the

The effects of erosion. Pictured in Tunisia ***Cr:WFP/FAO/F Botts***

Conservation and Rehabilitation of African Lands.

This African programme can provide a framework for solutions that can be utilized in other continents as well. The alternative, at least for Africa, and maybe elsewhere, could be famine.

The importance of this issue was highlighted in the 1986 FAO study "African Agriculture: the next 25 years". One of the major recommendations of that study was that a conservation strategy should be developed for the continent, and this led to the new international scheme. Its purpose is to provide a means by which African countries can develop their own programmes to fight land degradation.

The scheme—which came into action in 1991—is designed to enable countries to tailor these programs to meet their own individual needs; it also provides a mechanism through which countries are able to systematically appraise their land resources and needs and then develop the necessary policies, strategies and programs in collaboration with potential donor organizations, funding, institutions, technical assistance agencies and non-governmental organizations (NGOs).

Networks to exchange knowledge and experience are being encouraged under the scheme, which also provides for activities, such as specialized training and research, to be handled at a sub-regional or regional level. To date the following countries have applied to join in the scheme: Benin, The Central African Republic, Ghana, Madagascar, Mali, Malawi, Morocco and Togo.

An approach has been developed called Integrated Plant Nutrition Systems (IPNS). Its objectives are the complementary use of renewable organic sources of plant nutrients along with mineral fertilizers. FAO says that IPNS is environmentally sound, socially acceptable and economically viable.

In Bangladesh and Pakistan, for instance, animal wastes prevail as sources of organic matter, while in Indonesia, biological nitrogen fixation comes first, followed by recycling of legume crop residues, rice straw and animal wastes.

FAO says, therefore, that it is possible to rehabilitate the land, first by a series of physical measures, then by a balanced and adequate nutrient supply in the area where it has been depleted the most.

"You can see how the land can be rehabilitated in the United States, for example," says Mr.Robert Brinkman, Chief of FAO's Soil Resources, Management and Conservation Service. "In the Appalachian Belt along the U.S. East Coast in the early part of the nation's history, the region suffered from all the same problems of land degradation that is now occurring in the developing world. In photos taken 50 years ago, you will find bare, denuded hillsides, with major gullies scarring the land. Now the upper hills are forested again, and well-selected lower places are devoted to arable and grazing land. There is now a balanced use of the land, with good protection for the hills. The U.S. is an example of what can work."

The FAO also points out that Europe was once on the verge of serious soil degradation, but was saved by the widespread use of fertilizers. However, the pendulum is now swinging the other direction.

"The system in Europe went into a new kind of disequilibrium with the use of too much nitrogen on grazing land," Mr Brinkman says. "In some areas with intensive grazing, Europeans began putting on 600 kilos of nitrogen per hectare of land (535 pounds per acre) per year, mainly from mineral fertilizer application, which in some cases is seriously endangering the land—but Europe is at least free of the spectre of nutrient depletion."

The science of soil conservation has existed for little more than 50 years, during which most attempts to control land degradation have been directed mainly at preventing or reducing soil loss. Soil erosion was seen as a physical process, to be controlled mainly by physical measures. It was not recognized as a consequence of the more fundamental problems of incorrect land management and lack of vegetative covers.

Farmers, pastoralists and those who relied on woodlands and forests for their livelihoods were often regarded as part of the problem, rather than as the potential solution. The FAO has learned that future programs to tackle land degradation must find out why land is being misused and how to motivate land users to correct it. Benefits must be immediately obvious.

Deforestation—one of the main causes of degraded land. Pictured in Brazil *Cr: Marcus Santilli/Earthscan*

"What the world needs are well-planned, long-term national and regional land conservation and rehabilitation programs, with strong political support and adequate funding," says Edouard Saouma, "land use planning and land zoning could provide long-term solutions, but conservation programs that arrest land degradation are urgently needed."

This article is based on material supplied by FAO.

Is our climate UNSTABLE?

A new record of past climates suggests that the Northern Hemisphere has repeatedly snapped from balmy to frigid conditions in a matter of years. Could the greenhouse effect cause our currently stable climate to snap again?

Melinda Bell

Melinda Bell is a freelance science writer and high school biology teacher living in Logan, Utah.

Surely we humans know how fickle climate can be. In our own lifetimes, we've seen floods and droughts, cold spells and heat waves. And centuries ago, people of the Northern Hemisphere experienced far more enduring climate shifts that literally shaped the course of history. It's probably no coincidence, for example, that the Vikings settled in Greenland in the 10th century, during a long period of unusually warm weather. Nor is it by chance that their colonies disappeared from Greenland six centuries later. By that time, the Little Ice Age had gripped the North Atlantic for several hundred years, clogging the sea with ice and severing the settlers' access to the outside world.

But it now appears these climatic shifts were decidedly puny compared with Earth's earlier history. In fact, new research suggests that for the last 10,000 years, the climate in the North Atlantic region has been remarkably benign compared with the dramatic instability that marked the preceding 200,000 to 250,000 years. The new findings show that for those earlier millenia, Greenland experienced climate swings more violent than any known in historic times, plummeting to ice age levels — or soaring out of them — in a matter of decades or years. Many scientists involved in the research speculate that extremely rapid but perhaps less severe climate swings may have also characterized the climate of much of the Northern Hemisphere.

The new research raises unsettling questions about how our climate works. For instance, if rapid shifts are the norm, why has the climate system remained stable for the past 8,000 to 10,000 years? Could our own industrial activities tip it back into convulsive shudders? Or perhaps more disturbingly, is radical climate change inevitable no matter what we do?

Scientists began puzzling over these problems last summer, after separate teams of European and American researchers analyzed two cylinders of ice, each about two miles long, pulled section by section from the Greenland ice sheet. Such ice cores trap chemicals, gases and bits of dust that were present in the snow that fell over Greenland for thousands of years and then became compressed into ice. By studying these components in the ice, scientists have obtained a detailed archive of many aspects of climate, including air temperatures, snowfall, and concentrations of greenhouse gases in the atmosphere. They have even discerned the annual snow layers in the younger ice. This enabled them to count back the years like the rings of a tree.

"The cores are essentially videotapes of the past 200,000 years," says Paul Mayewski, chief scientist for the American Greenland Ice Sheet Project 2 (GISP2). "Records like this never existed before."

The European study, called the Greenland Ice-Core Project (GRIP), and GISP2, which drilled 17.5 miles away, are not the first coring projects ever attempted in Greenland. But earlier cores were pulled from the flanks of the ice cap, where melting and flowing of the ice can distort the climate record. The GRIP and GISP2 cores were the first to have been drilled in the optimum location, on the lofty, nearly level summit of the cap, where ice flow and melting are minimal. The result is the most reliable and richly detailed climate record of the Northern Hemisphere ever recovered.

Last spring, findings from the GISP2 core proved that Greenland's climate during the last ice age fluctuated very rapidly. Then last summer came new findings from GRIP that astonished the scientific community. This work provides the first close look at an interglacial period other than our own, in this case, the Eemian interglacial (or Sangamon as it is called in North America), which lasted from about 115,000 to 135,000 years ago. Scientists had presumed that interglacials — warm, ice-free interludes between ice ages — were dependably stable, as ours has been for all of its 8,000 to 10,000 years. But the GRIP core showed that the Eemian climate had swung at least as wildly as the climate of ice age periods.

Why has the climate system remained stable for the past 8,000 to 10,000 years? Could our own industrial activities tip it back into convulsive shudders? Or perhaps more disturbingly, is radical climate change inevitable no matter what we do?

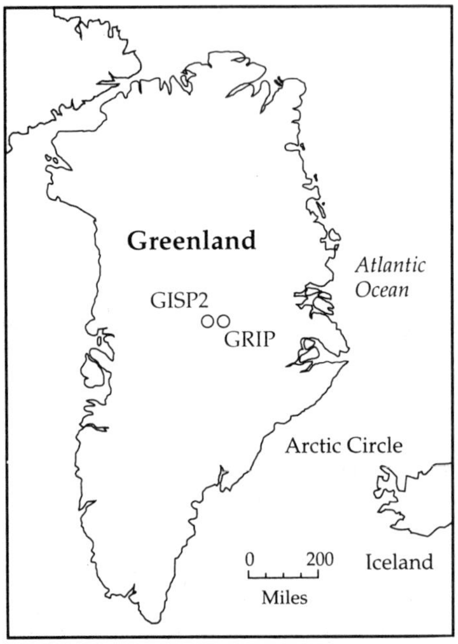

EARTH: Lee Vande Visse

So far, many of the researchers' clues to the Eemian climate come from measurements of the ratios of two slightly different types of oxygen, isotopes ^{16}O and ^{18}O, preserved in the ice. These ratios indicate air temperatures and show how temperatures over Greenland fluctuated season by season and year by year. When the air was warm, water vapor containing the heavier isotope, ^{18}O, condensed more readily than vapor containing ^{16}O. Thus, snow that fell during warmer periods contains proportionately more ^{18}O than snow deposited during cold spells. The researchers obtained further evidence for rapid climate shifts from other sources, such as dust and calcium ions in the ice layers. During cold periods, winds were strong, causing calcium-rich dust from loess deposits to blow across the ice sheet. Thus, differing amounts of dust in the layers indicate changing climatic conditions.

The results of these studies were dramatic indeed. Fossil records have already shown that the Eemian was generally a balmy time — so balmy, in fact, that hippos basked along the banks of the Thames River in the area that is now London. But the GRIP record shows that these warm conditions often gave way to prolonged cold. On two occasions, temperatures dove from 6.3 degrees Fahrenheit warmer than the present to 9 degrees F colder (levels equalling the mildest periods of the last ice age) in less than a few centuries and remained that way for thousands of years. More often, however, they plunged and rose even more abruptly, vacillating between preferred states. In one catastrophic cold snap, temperatures plummeted by 25 degrees F in a mere decade, only to rise again 70 years later.

The GRIP core also stretched back to an even earlier interglacial period, the Holstein, 100,000 years before the Eemian. Because the ice was greatly compressed at this depth, researchers have less detailed and reliable information on the Holstein. However, the oxygen isotope record shows that it too was wracked by significant temperature swings. The Holstein shifts were not as volatile as the Eemian shifts, but they were far more abrupt and severe than any known in recent times.

These findings shatter old notions of the Eemian and the Holstein as gentle, placid periods. But they are perhaps more important for what they may tell us about the present and future. Until now, scientists could reasonably assume that interglacials were stable by nature. This notion grew out of our experience of the Holocene gained from tree rings, pollen samples and other records, which show that its climate has always been relatively uniform. Though we had no finely detailed archive of past interglacials, available records suggested that they too were steady and mild.

But if the GRIP team are interpreting their data correctly, all bets are off. Scientists must now consider the possibility that the present stable climate is peculiar — and potentially fragile.

"Since we hadn't observed rapid and frequent change, we

hadn't really thought about whether our climate system is abnormal," explains Jim White, a geochemist at the University of Colorado's Institute of Arctic and Alpine Research. "Could our climate change very rapidly without any influence of ours? That question was never asked because it didn't seem like an obvious question to ask."

Now it is an obvious question to ask, White says. It's also a very difficult question to answer, given scientists' knowledge of past climate change. To understand why this is so, we need to take a step back, to the beginnings of ice core research.

When paleoclimatologists drilled their first deep ice core in western Greenland more than 40 years ago, they had no idea that Earth's climate had such an unruly past. They did know, however, that over the past two million years, the planet had experienced numerous ice ages. These ice ages waxed and waned roughly every 100,000 years, interrupted by relatively brief warm spells like today's interglacial. Though climate researchers are still debating what causes ice ages, many believe they are driven by slow changes in Earth's orbit around the sun and the angle of its axis.

But the picture of Earth's climate history has become much more complex over the years. Climate records pulled from ice cores and deep sea sediments revealed that the ice ages themselves were marked by climatic jiggles — intricate cycles within the larger cycles of glacial advance and retreat.

In the early 1970s, researchers turned up one of the first ill-fitting pieces of the climate puzzle in an ice core drilled near the margin of the Greenland ice sheet. The record revealed bizarre climatic oscillations: cycles of severe temperature swings accomplished in 500 to 2,000 years. Such shifts were much too swift to be caused by steady orbital changes. Many scientists initially dismissed the oscillations as aberrations in the ice core, perhaps representing periods of surface melting.

The Climatic Seesaw

The Holocene, the warm interglacial we've enjoyed for the last 8,000 to 10,000 years, was preceded by 250,000 years of much more abrupt and violent climatic swings. These graphs show how temperatures have risen and fallen during these two periods. The white portions of the larger graph indicate periods that were colder than the present. The gray portions of the graph indicate periods that were warmer than the present. During the Eemian interglacial, generally warm conditions gave way suddenly to cool on several occasions.

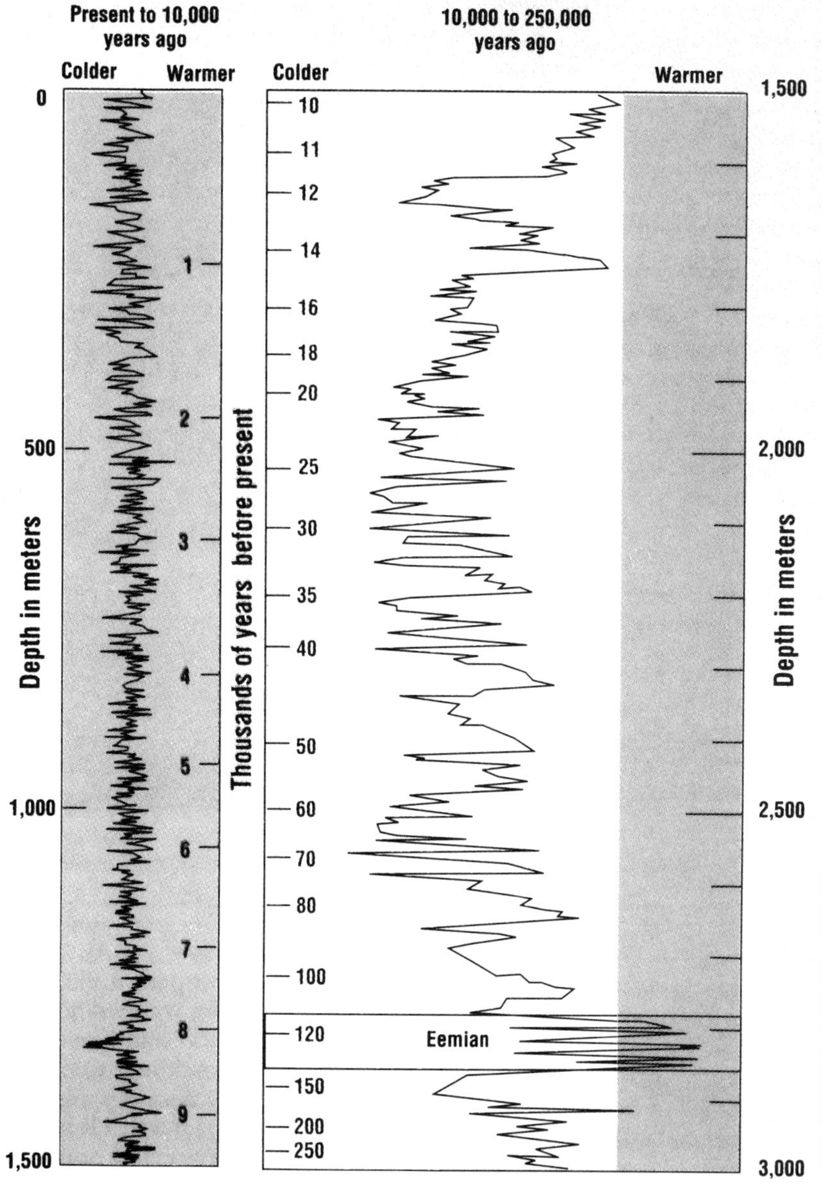

EARTH: Lee Vande Visse. Source: *Nature*

Eventually, however, the evidence arguing for abrupt shifts became too compelling to ignore. In 1992, the GISP2 researchers confirmed what other cores had hinted: that Greenland's climate did indeed fluctuate repeatedly during the last ice age, between 11,000 and 35,000 years ago. Surprisingly, the finely detailed core also revealed even more abrupt "flickers" within these fluctuations. Studies published last spring by GISP2 researchers showed that Greenland's climate see-sawed from glacial to interglacial conditions in just three years as the last ice age hiccupped to a close. For instance, Ken Taylor of the Desert Research Institute in

Lisa Barlow

A weather balloon rises near the drilling dome and science hut at the GISP2 site.

Reno, Nev., and his colleagues found that dust layers, associated with windy, glacial conditions, ended in just a few years at the close of the last ice age. And Richard Alley of Pennsylvania State University found that snow accumulations doubled during this same brief period of time as the atmosphere warmed and was able to hold more moisture.

"At first we thought rapid climate change meant a century. Then we found out that it meant a decade. Now we find out that it can mean years," White says.

Paleoclimatologists can explain at least some of these ice age shifts. Most of these theories center on the circulation of the North Atlantic Ocean, where a conveyor belt of ocean currents strongly influences climate. This conveyor pulls warm waters up from lower latitudes into the North Atlantic, bringing mild temperatures to otherwise inhospitable climes. Without it, roses wouldn't grow in Norway, for example. In winter, in fact, the amount of heat brought up to the region by this conveyor of warm water rivals the amount of heat the region derives from sunlight.

The conveyor is driven by the sinking of the currents in the far North Atlantic. As the currents sink to great depths, more warm surface waters from lower latitudes flow north to replace them. Along the way, these surface waters pass through warm latitudes, where evaporation increases their salinity and density. When they reach the cold North Atlantic, they sink, pulling in new warm waters and perpetuating the cycle.

Many scientists believe that a shutting off and on of the conveyor belt might explain some of the climatic wobbles during ice ages, an idea first proposed by Wallace Broecker of the Lamont Doherty Earth Observatory of Columbia University. Broecker theorized that warm spells during ice ages were intitiated when salinity rose in the North Atlantic, switching on the conveyor. The warm water that began to flow northward then set the stage for the conveyor to switch off. The warm water may have melted nearby ice, sending pulses of glacial meltwater into the North Atlantic. These pulses diluted the surface waters, decreasing their salinity and density until they no longer sank. The conveyor ground to a halt, and temperatures quickly dropped. When salinity rose, the conveyor started up again, causing temperatures to rise.

But there were probably other processes at work that scientists haven't yet fully pieced together. For instance, the ice age glaciers themselves may have affected climate as well, working in intricate syncopation with the ocean conveyor. During very cold periods, when the conveyor was turned off, enormous ice sheets steered cold winds around them, casting a chill over surrounding regions. But occasionally ice sheets appear to have collapsed, jerking the system into a warm phase.

Douglas MacAyeal, a glaciologist at the University of Chicago, thinks ice sheets may have collapsed after growing too large for their own good. Warmed by the insulation of their top layers and the heat from Earth's interior, their bottom layers began to melt and grow slushy. Eventually they disintegrated, sending out fleets of icebergs and plumes of meltwater across the Atlantic. After the ice sheets collapsed, the winds calmed and the ocean eventually warmed, allowing evaporation to enrich the surface waters with salt. The salty surface waters began to sink again, and the conveyor belt was reactivated, warming the North Atlantic once more.

Interestingly, these widely accepted explanations for the ice age shifts share a common theme: They depend on the presence of massive ice sheets to help trip the climate switches. For those concerned about our own climate's instability, this fact once offered a measure of comfort. It suggested that abrupt shifts were unlikely — and perhaps even impossible — during warm interglacials, when large ice sheets were absent. As science writer Richard Kerr explained in a May 1993 article in the journal *Science*, "The more climate researchers learn about the workings of climate in the last ice age,

Lisa Barlow

GISP2 researcher Bill Kimball cuts a segment of the core to prepare it for analysis.

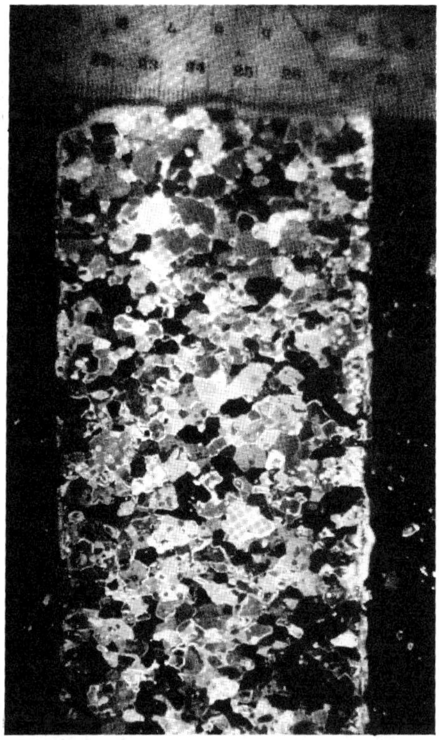

Bruce Vaughn

A thin section of the GISP2 ice core seen through polarized filters shows individual crystals [which would appear] in various colors and air bubbles in black. Polarized light interacting with the crystals produces the colors and provides information on grain size and crystal orientation. Scientists use this information to estimate the age of older ice layers.

the less they think the same switch is likely to flip in today's world."

With the new findings from GRIP, however, the ground rules have changed. We can no longer reassure ourselves that rapid shifts were strictly an ice-age phenomenon. Today's world may be vulnerable to rapid shifts after all.

Now scientists are also faced with the difficult task of explaining the Eemian and Holstein shifts. Many researchers suspect that the causes lie, at least in part, in a shutting on and off of the oceanic conveyor. But since scientists never had cause to explain interglacial climate shakes before, they have no well-formed answers as yet. Indeed, the GRIP data are forcing scientists to reconsider some basic questions about how climate works.

"It's like we had blinders on. Now we have to think about ways to accommodate changes of comparable or even greater severity in a world without much ice," says Scott Lehman, of the Woods Hole Oceanographic Institution in Massachusetts. "This is a new way of looking at the problem."

Or, as David Peel of the British Antarctic Survey of Cambridge University put it, "At the moment we're at a loss."

Is our climate likely to lapse into instability in the near future? Of course, no one knows. Until climate researchers learn what caused the Eemian swings, they can't determine the risk of similar swings' occurring today. It's possible, for instance, that the factors that caused instability in the past no longer exist. In other words, we

At first we thought rapid climate change meant a century. Then we found out that it meant a decade. Now we find out that it can mean years.

may just be lucky enough to live in a stubbornly stable time.

But the Eemian swings do give cause for concern. They may even offer an ominous warning of the

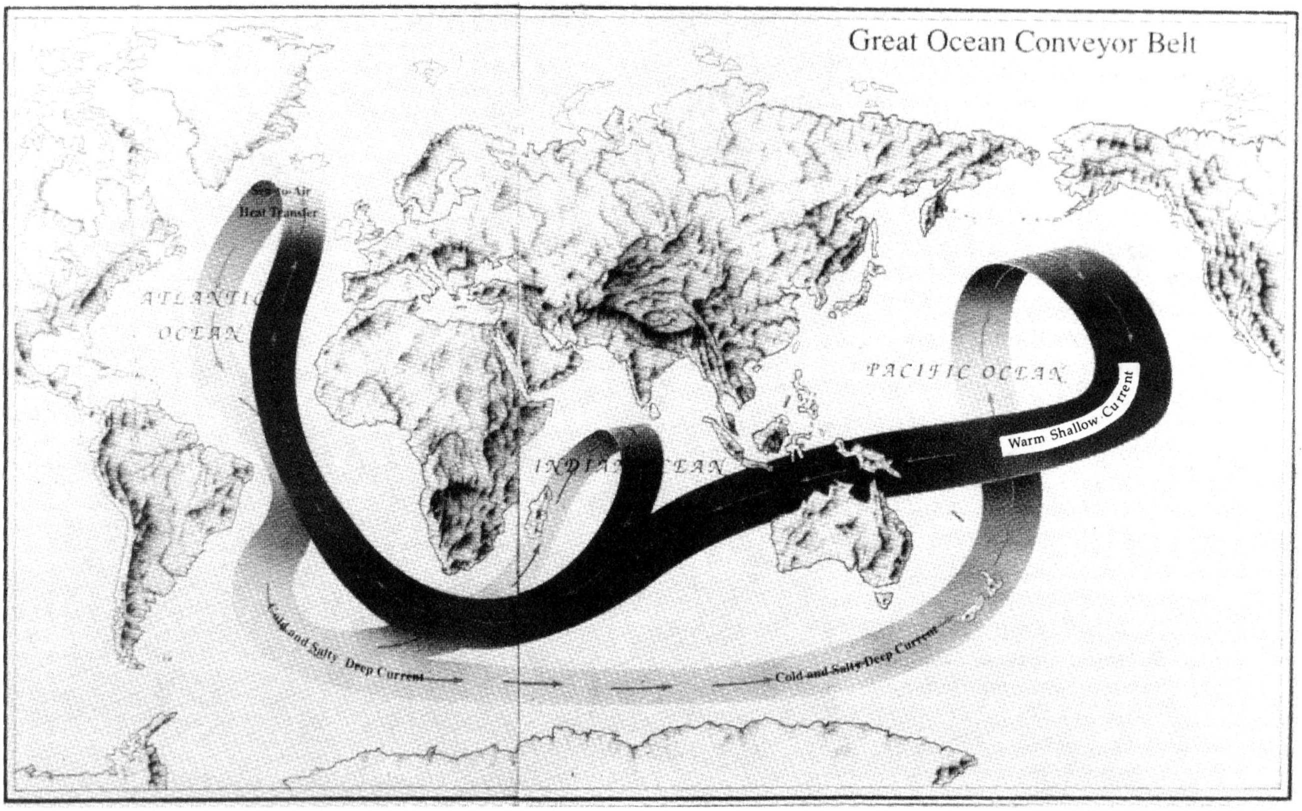

Joe LeMonnier/*Natural History*

Many scientists believe that a conveyor belt of ocean currents caused rapid climate shifts during the last ice age. In periods like the present, the conveyor draws warm waters from lower latitudes into the North Atlantic region. As the currents pass through the warm latitudes, evaporation increases their salinity and density. When they reach the far North Atlantic, they release their heat, sink to great depths and travel south. Meanwhile, new surface waters flow north to replace them. During the last ice age, the conveyor may have been switched off most of the time, allowing frigid cold to grip the North Atlantic. On occasion, however, it may have switched on, bringing a brief warm spell.

consequences of our industrial activities. Temperatures during the Eemian were generally about 3.6 degrees F warmer than they are today. This is toward the upper range of warming predicted for the next century by many computer climate models if emissions of greenhouse gases continue at the present rate. Thus, scientists fear that our continued greenhouse emissions could perhaps trigger convulsive, Eemian-like change again. Perhaps, ironically, we could send the warming world careening temporarily into cold, similar to the Eemian's frigid snaps.

However, the GRIP data also reduce climatologists' confidence in the specific predictions of warming by the computer models. Most models assume that increases in greenhouse gases have gradual effects on the climate system. The GRIP findings, by contrast, suggest that the system may respond to such changes unpredictably — suddenly jerking into a new state when it reaches a critical threshold.

All this raises disturbing possibilities. Many climatologists fear that we are ill-prepared to cope with even gradual climate shifts that are presumably associated with the greenhouse effect, such as overall warming and changes in precipitation patterns. So how would we cope with much more abrupt changes? White raised this question in a recent commentary on the GRIP findings in *Nature*: "Adaptation — the peaceful shifting of food-growing areas, coastal populations and so on — seemed possible, if difficult, when abrupt change meant a few degrees in a century. It now seems a much more formidable task, requiring global cooperation with swift recognition and response."

Clearly, the potential for such disruptions argues strongly for reducing our emissions of greenhouse gases. But it's also possible that we couldn't prevent rapid climate swings even if we tried. After all, the Eemian and Holstein shifts in Greenland occurred without any human prodding. Athough there's little question that our industrial activities can change the climate system, some of the system's switches may be completely beyond our control.

"These rapid changes occurred without human intervention, and that's challenging when you think about it. Even if we cleaned up our act, even if we lived in as perfect harmony with the natural ecosystems as we could, the system is still capable of changing," White says.

Before the GRIP and GISP2 researchers can draw any firm conclusions from the data, however, they have much more work to do. They are still analyzing the cores,

GISP2 scientists enjoy an after-dinner game of volleyball on the Greenland ice cap.

searching for additional "chemical fingerprints" to shed light on the nature, timing and scope of Greenland's climate shifts. Their ongoing studies of greenhouse gases trapped in tiny air bubbles, for example, may help identify the causes of the Eemian swings and may also offer new insights into the likely consequences of our own greenhouse emissions.

"These rapid changes occurred without human intervention, and that's challenging when you think about it. Even if we cleaned up our act, even if we lived in as perfect harmony with the natural ecosystems as we could, the system is still capable of changing."

Studies of greenhouse gases and other factors should also help them determine how widespread severe climate shifts were. Because greenhouse gases disperse widely and rapidly throughout the atmosphere, their concentrations can reveal changes on a global scale. The isotope record, by contrast, shows only that rapid temperature swings of very large magnitude occurred in Greenland.

The researchers strongly suspect that if changes in ocean circulation and other large-scale processes were involved, then lower latitudes in the Northern Hemisphere, such as Europe and North America, probably experienced significant climate swings as well. But as Willi Dansgaard, a GRIP member from the Niels Bohr Institute at the University of Copenhagen, points out, the shifts in lower latitudes were probably less pronounced than those seen in Greenland. Until the teams study further clues, however, they can't be sure.

Finally, the GRIP and GISP2 teams need to compare their results with one another to check for errors and reinforce their conclusions. This is especially important in the lower layers of the core, where the ice is more compressed and difficult to read. And collaborative studies with other climate records, such as an ice core drilled by a Russian team in Vostok, Antarctica, and deep-sea sediment samples are also critical. The climate record from the Vostok core and most deep-sea sediment samples are much less detailed than the GRIP and GISP2 cores, but they stretch back further in time. Thus, they will help fill in the big picture of climate change.

If these studies confirm the GRIP researchers' conclusions, the implications are undeniably significant. As Peel explains, "It's still early yet, and we don't want to put over an alarmist viewpoint. But we have found something very unusual that we can't explain with our present understanding of climate.

"We simply cannot take the stability of the last 8,000 years for granted."

Land-Human Relationships

Unit 2

The home of humankind is Earth's surface and the thin layer of atmosphere enveloping it. Here the human populace has struggled over time to change the physical setting and to create the telltale signs of occupation. Humankind has greatly modified Earth's surface to suit its purposes. At the same time, humankind has been influenced greatly by the very environment that it has worked to change.

This basic relationship of humans and land is important in geography. As you will recall, in unit 1 William Pattison identifies this relationship as one of the four traditions of geography. Geographers observe, study, and analyze the ways in which human occupants of Earth have interacted with the physical environment.

This unit presents a number of articles that illustrate the theme of land-human relationships. In some cases, the association of humans and the physical world has been mutually beneficial; in others, environmental degradation has been the result.

At the present time, the potential for major modifications of Earth's surface and the atmosphere is greater than at any other time in history. It is crucially important that the consequences of these modifications for the environment be clearly understood before such efforts are undertaken.

The first article in this unit delves deeply into the continued decline in fresh water quality in a number of major rivers in the United States. Next, Peter Weber draws attention to problems along populated oceanic coastlines because of pollution and environmental degradation in "It Comes Down to the Coasts."

Can the rain forests of Earth be saved? What is the climatic impact of their wholesale destruction? Richard Monastersky's article, "The Deforestation Debate," discusses a new NASA program to improve the assessments of global deforestation.

In the following article, William Stevens reports on recent studies indicating that desertification may not be as serious a problem as originally believed. The next two articles draw attention to large-scale water pollution in the European region with reports on attempts that are being made to reverse these damaging trends.

The articles presented in this unit provide a small sample of the many ways in which humans interact with the environment. The outcomes of these interactions may be positive or negative; they may enhance the position of humankind and protect the environment, or they may do just the opposite. Human beings are the guardians of the physical world; they have it in their power to protect, to neglect, or to destroy.

Looking Ahead: Challenge Questions

What are the long-range implications of atmospheric pollution? Can you explain the greenhouse effect?

How can the problem of regional transfer of pollutants be solved?

The manufacture of goods needed by humans produces pollutants that degrade the environment. How can this dilemma be solved?

What would be the climatic effect of the loss of the tropical rain forests?

Where in the world are there serious problems of desertification and drought? Why are these areas increasing in size?

What will be the major forms of energy in the next century?

How are you as an individual related to the land?

Can humankind do anything to ensure the protection of the environment?

TROUBLED WATERS

Two decades after passage of the Clean Water Act, American waterways no longer catch fire with chemical pollution, but they do carry invisible toxic waste that threatens fish and people. Congress tackles the issue this fall, but the answers may be as intricate as rivers themselves.

"Eventually all things merge into one, and a river runs through it."

—*Norman Maclean*

ANNETTE MCGIVNEY

ANNETTE MCGIVNEY *is associate editor of* Backpacker Magazine. *She lives on the Delaware River and sees pollution first-hand.*

For Norman Maclean, Montana's Big Blackfoot River was a pristine and spiritual place where any faithful fly fisherman could enjoy a near-religious experience, partaking in the best that nature had to offer. The trout-filled waters of the Blackfoot shaped Maclean's life and inspired him to write a book, *A River Runs Through It*, filled with romantic descriptions of the Blackfoot, which inspired Robert Redford to buy the screenplay rights and produce a movie about the beautiful river of Maclean's youth. Flyfishing, brotherhood, growing up in Montana—the Hollywood production had all the wholesome goodness of homemade bread, except for one thing. By the time Redford was ready to start filming two years ago, some 16 years after the book was published, the Big Blackfoot lacked the aesthetics necessary to serve as the setting for the movie.

Like many rivers in Montana, and in the rest of the U.S., the mighty Blackfoot has been broken by the resource-guzzling activities of humans and is no longer the proud water that Maclean described. The Montana locals weren't surprised that Redford and his crew had to simulate the Blackfoot, which hasn't supported a healthy fish population for at least 10 years. Its banks are scarred by clearcuts, and foul-looking mine waste slurps against road crossings. "The Blackfoot has been over-mined, over-cut, over-fished, over-recreated, and overlooked," says Becky Garland, president of the Big Blackfoot Chapter of Trout Unlimited, which is helping to revive the river.

Taken out of context, Maclean's words are prophetic—all of our land use practices and wastes have indeed merged into one, and our rivers run through it. Since Cleveland's Cuyahoga River caught fire in 1969, federal and state governments have worked hard to get the junk out of polluted waters. It's rare now to see a river topped with chemical foam, flowing bright red from industrial discharges, or reeking from raw sewage. But in many instances, these waters are not much healthier than they were two decades ago.

The Blackfoot is part of 2,279 miles of rivers and streams in Montana listed in the Environmental Protection Agency's (EPA) 1990 National Water Quality Inventory as having "elevated toxins." Nationwide, more than 28,000 river miles contained a hazardous level of toxins in 1990, and some 26 million fish were killed by pollution. "The public perception is that the rivers are cleaned up, that they're better than ever, because the goo is gone," says Kevin Coyle, president of American Rivers. "But if water quality is improving, then why are all the fish dying? Eventually, our rivers will look incredibly clean and they will be deadly." What worries him most is the invisible pollution that spills undetected from industry, and flows with rain water from every paved street and farmed field into rivers and streams. "Back in the 70s, people thought of water quality

> "The public thinks that the rivers are cleaned up because the goo is gone. If water quality is improving, why are all the fish dying?"

From *E Magazine*, September/October 1993, pp. 30-37.

in terms of gooey stuff washing up on the docks," he says. "Today, non-point source pollution is the major problem for rivers, and it's not usually something people can see. Poison runoff can even be aesthetic because the water looks so clear."

When the Clean Water Act (officially called the Federal Water Pollution Control Act) was passed in 1972, the mandate was broad: "to restore and maintain the chemical, physical and biological integrity of the nation's waters." But the immediate task was to stop municipalities and industries from dumping untreated or poorly treated wastes into public waters. And urban rivers like the Delaware, Potomac and Hudson, which once stunk from blocks away, are now popular spots for fishing, canoeing and picnicking. Much of the progress has come from improved wastewater treatment. The federal government has spent $56 billion on new treatment plants since the early 70s.

But controlling point-source discharges is about as far as the nation has gotten in meeting the goals of the Clean Water Act. Under the deadlines set out in 1972, by 1983 all of the nation's waters were to be fishable and swimmable. And by 1985, the discharge of any pollutant into U.S. waters was to have been eliminated. According to EPA's 1990 Water Quality Inventory, 37 percent of rivers and streams assessed did not meet fishing and swimming standards. The figure could be higher, since only 36 percent of the nation's 1.8 million river miles were monitored. And industrial releases of toxic substances into American waters still average 360 million pounds a year.

"Rivers are the catch basins for all our land use practices—farmers spraying their fields, homeowners spraying their lawns, logging, grazing, everything," Coyle says. "And our land use practices are causing aquatic species to go extinct at a rapid rate. The invertebrates are shouting out most loudly, telling us some rivers are dying."

A recent study by The Nature Conservancy found that 65 to 70 percent of bottom-of-the-food-chain aquatic species like crayfish and freshwater mussels are classified as rare to extinct, while only 11 to 14 percent of North American terrestrial species (birds, mammals and reptiles) are considered rare to extinct. Since freshwater mussels are filter-feeders and have little tolerance for water-borne pollutants, they have been seen as the proverbial canaries in the coal mine. "The unprecedented decline of mussels is nothing less than a red flag, a distress signal from our rivers, streams and creeks," says Nature Conservancy president John Sawhill. "We cannot ignore this warning and the degradation of water quality that it implies."

The Clean Water Act is up for reauthorization this year, and the need for the federal government to come to the rescue of rivers is just as urgent as it was in 1969. A preliminary bill was introduced in the Senate last June by Max Baucus (D-MT), head of the Committee on Environment and Public Works, and John Chafee (R-RI), the committee's ranking minority leader. Following summer hearings, the final bill is expected to be submitted to the Senate for approval early this fall.

"The House isn't as far along as the Senate with a reauthorization bill, but getting Clean Water Act legislation through this session is a top priority for Congress," says Robyn Roberts of the Clean Water Network, a coalition of 450 environmental and community organizations that want a "strengthened" Clean Water Act. Supported by national players like the Sierra Club, American Rivers and the National Wildlife Federation, as well as local grassroots groups, the Network wants a reauthorized Clean Water Act that will "eliminate the use of the nation's waters—and other parts of the environment—as dumping grounds for society's wastes." The Network also wants Congress to federalize water quality programs and make them less permissive, to focus on non-point source pollution, preserve wetlands, expand regulations of toxic discharges, and prevent clean waters from getting polluted. Many of these components already appear in the broad language and numerous amendments to the Clean Water Act, but federal and state agencies are failing to carry them out. "The law seems fine to me as it is written," says Nina Bell, executive director of Northwest Environmental Advocates (NEA) in Portland, Oregon. "It's just the implementation that stinks."

> "The industrialization of agriculture over the last two decades has had a tremendous effect on rivers. Farmers spray crops with all kinds of chemicals, and weeds with herbicides instead of tilling the land. And people wonder why the cancer rate is going up in Iowa."

Keeping Tabs

Over the past decade, local groups like NEA have led the fight against river degradation by spending a great deal of time policing the polluters to stay in compliance with water quality standards. The Willamette River no longer has rafts of sewage floating atop its waters or slime lining its banks. Municipal wastewater treatment plants have been built, industries must obtain discharge permits, and some 200 miles of greenway have been acquired for a large riverfront park system. In 1989, the U.S. Army Corps of Engineers described the Willamette as "one of the cleanest streams of comparable size in the nation," and the EPA often refers to it as an example of a river restoration success story.

The Willamette, however, is far from restored and requires constant management. Water levels are regulated by a series of 13 dams, most of the fish are hatchery stock, and waste discharges are diluted with impounded water. A 148-mile strip of the Upper Willamette has unsafe levels of dioxin, a carcinogenic byproduct of pulp mills and sewage treatment plants that use chlorine. Other toxins violate water quality standards in scattered sections of the river, including DDT, PCBs, chlordane, arsenic and heavy metals. On the Lower Willamette, Portland uses 43 antiquated storm drains called combined sewer outfalls (CSOs) which dump raw sewage into the river when it rains. "I wouldn't take my child swimming in the Willamette," Bell says. "There's too much sewage. You can see toilet paper floating by after a rain."

Even more frustrating than the pollution is the lack of information about it. "The fundamental problem is we don't have enough monitoring. The states aren't required by EPA to collect certain water quality data, so, like with the Willamette, information is very sketchy," Bell says. The Oregon Department of Environmental Quality has admitted as much: "The river's current water quality is not completely known. Much of the existing information on the river describes conventional water quality measurements, such as levels of dissolved oxygen. Insufficient information exists on other topics, such as the impact of toxins on the overall health of the river."

The Clean Water Act requires states to designate uses for rivers—usually fishing and/or swimming—and then report to the

EPA on whether or not those uses are met. The EPA offers guidelines, but the decision on which rivers to monitor and what testing methods to use is up to the states. Their information gets compiled by the EPA every two years for the National Water Quality Inventory, which typically only reports on about one third of the nation's river miles. And since every state has its own testing methods, the EPA can't combine all of the information into a national overview. "In times of limited resources, you have to monitor where there are suspected problems," says Elizabeth Jester Fellows, branch chief for monitoring in EPA's Office of Wetlands, Oceans and Watersheds. "Since only about one third of rivers are monitored in a two-year period, we are recommending that the states rotate their testing each period so more rivers are covered."

The EPA also encourages states to shift their focus from testing for the obvious—specific chemicals from point-source discharges—toward monitoring for non-point source pollution. But in 1991, the federal government gave less than $70 million to states for ambient water monitoring—assessing the quality of the aquatic environment rather than studying the effect of specific discharges. Federal monies for new wastewater treatment plants in 1991 totaled $6 billion. "Increased funding for monitoring is often viewed by Congress as a resource sink," says Fellows, "because it's hard to prove the money has been used effectively."

Richard Sparks, an aquatic ecologist with the State of Illinois, says, however, that river water quality won't improve unless the feds step up to the plate. "There needs to be more leadership from the federal government. States set up programs in response to federal requirements and grant opportunities. Most states are too strapped financially just to start up new water quality programs on their own," he says. "Our monitoring is supposed to provide a kind of 'state of the aquatic environment' report for the EPA, but I consider many of the measures the states use to gauge this as irrelevant." The EPA does recommend that states incorporate the use of biological criteria in their reporting and will require it by 1995. These methods, which involve counting the number of different aquatic species and the abundance of each, cost more than the chemical approach and require a staff of biologists—which most states don't have.

"The use of bio-criteria will result in the re-direction of money we currently spend on wastewater treatment plants to pay for the restoration of aquatic ecosystems," says James Karr, director of the Institute for Environmental Studies at the University of Washington. "Historically, states have concentrated on waters they suspected had toxic concentrations. Now, with bio-criteria, we're going to find problems in rivers the states thought were okay."

Pointless Pollution

When there is a blanket of dead fish covering a river just downstream from an industrial treatment plant, it's not hard for state and local authorities to find the source of the pollution and slap the guilty party with a fine. Non-point source pollution, however, is much more evasive—everyone is to blame, and no one is to blame. But there's no arguing with the fact that the agricultural industry is the primary culprit in polluting our nation's rivers. The EPA reports that 50 to 70 percent of impaired or threatened surface waters are affected by non-point source pollution from agricultural activities. According to the Conservation Foundation, nearly five tons of soil erode off of one acre of farmland each year in the U.S., carrying sediment (the number one pollutant), fertilizers, herbicides and insecticides into rivers and streams.

> "I wouldn't take my child swimming in the Willamette. You can see toilet paper floating by after a rain."

"The industrialization of agriculture over the last two decades has had a tremendous effect on rivers," says Kevin Coyle. "The U.S. decided it would maximize farm production and be the bread basket for the world. Farmers started spraying their crops with all kinds of chemicals, and spraying weeds with herbicides instead of tilling the land. There are more chemicals being used by farmers today than ever before. The EPA approves these substances, but they don't really monitor their potentially hazardous effects. And people wonder why the cancer rate is going up in Iowa?"

The 1990 Farm Bill encourages farmers to voluntarily participate in programs that minimize the use of chemicals and control agricultural runoff, but the financial incentives for these programs are not nearly as enticing as other U.S. Department of Agriculture (USDA) programs that encourage exploitation of the land. For example, more than two-thirds of U.S. cropland is enrolled in a program where farmers receive price supports based on the average crop yield over a five-year period. This discourages the farmer from rotating crops or letting the land lay dormant, which would reduce runoff into rivers as well as the need for pesticides.

An obvious step would be to place stricter land use regulations on the agricultural industry. But the notion of making farmers comply with federal requirements is politically taboo, and downright un-American in much of the country. "Voluntary action through education is more effective than regulation in addressing our environmental issues," says James Moseley, USDA assistant secretary for agriculture for natural resources and environment. "Prohibiting the use of certain chemicals and policing and fining polluters is not the best way to deal with water quality concerns, particularly in a diversified industry such as agriculture. Regulations undermine agriculture's flexibility in determining production options."

The other major cause of non-point source pollution is urban run-off. Poisonous substances wash down city streets and storm drains from everything and everyone—from residential landscaping to road construction to motor oil. But finding ways to control the conglomeration of wastes that merge into urban runoff is a new and evolving science. "There is a lot of emphasis being placed on figuring out how to deal with non-point source pollution," says Curtis Dalpra of the Interstate Commission on the Potomac River Basin. "A lot of methods for abating non-point in urban areas are not turning out to be as effective as people first thought they would be."

Accidentally Toxic

For all of the talk about non-point source pollution, toxic spills are still a serious threat to both water quality and public health. In 1990, 31 states reported concentrations of toxic contaminants in fish tissue that exceeded public health standards. Deadly substances like DDT, chlordane, PCBs and dioxin live for decades in a river's aquatic food chain. "Toxic spills and the legacy of toxic substances along riverbanks are a real problem," says Richard Sparks. "Industries have to meet requirements in order to get discharge permits, but accidents happen—and unless there's a fish kill, small spills often go undetected."

In fact, much to the surprise of unsuspecting river recreationists, accidents happen quite often. A U.S. Public Interest Research Group (U.S. PIRG) study has found that 21 percent of the nation's 7,185 major industrial and public waste treatment facilities are in serious or chronic violation of their discharge permits, and another 19 percent of the facilities report at least occasional violations. What's more, the study says, many of these facilities violate their permits on purpose because the cost of paying minimal fines to the EPA is less than that of investing in the equipment needed to comply with water quality standards. An occasional toxic spill may seem like a negligible crime, but the long-term cost to public health can be high. Sparks says that it takes many of these toxic substances decades to degrade, and as time passes the toxin "bio-magnifies" as it moves up the food chain. "A fish can tolerate a certain amount of mercury," he says, "but a human that eats several of those fish could get too big a dose." EPA studies show that dioxin bioaccumulates at very high rates, and that even immeasurably small quantities cause a range of health problems in humans from immunological disorders to cancer.

Since states want to promote clean looking rivers for recreational users, it's not uncommon to find waterways where the fish are known to contain toxins but there are no signs warning people of the danger. On a stretch of Virginia's scenic Shenandoah River there's an advisory against eating fish tainted with mercury from an industrial spill 17 years ago, but there are no signs. "People tore the signs down a long time ago and we haven't put them back up," says a Virginia Department of Health official.

"Citizens have a right to know when significant threats to their health or environment are present in their communities," says U.S. PIRG staff attorney Carolyn Hartman. "We want the Clean Water Act to require public postings on waterways that don't meet standards, or have a fishing or shellfish ban." U.S. PIRG and the Clean Water Network also support legislation to require dischargers to post a sign on the entrance of their facility that details what is going into the river and who people can contact for more information.

Congress added a section to the Clean Water Act in 1987 to accelerate efforts to control and eventually eliminate toxic point-source discharges into rivers. It requires states to identify and put on three EPA lists all sources of "priority" pollutants, and then stringently regulate those sites. A 1991 report by the U.S. General Accounting Office found, however, that the process of who gets listed is often politicized at the state and local levels. "Nationwide, EPA deleted a total of 309 facilities from the lists," says the report, primarily because "the fear of the negative image associated with being listed as a toxic pollutant discharger prompted certain industries to pressure states to make their water quality standards less stringent. In Alabama, this action resulted in nine out of 10 paper mills being deleted from the discharger list because they were no longer in violation of the new, less stringent dioxin standard."

YOUNG MAN RIVER

BY JESSICA SPEART

The 25-foot boat darted toward the Exxon tanker under cover of night, stealthily taking water samples of the liquid being discharged. For a half year, the tiny boat had trailed tankers along New York's Hudson River as they rinsed their tanks clean of sea water tainted with jet fuel—an illegal activity Exxon would live to regret. But back in 1983 few people knew that the Hudson River had recently acquired its very own watchdog: John Cronin, better known as the Riverkeeper.

As a boy, Cronin never paid much attention to the river. "To me, the good Lord put the Hudson there to separate New York from New Jersey," quips the 43-year old. Tall and lanky with blue eyes and a mop of curly blond hair, Cronin was working as a roofer in 1972 when he first heard of an environmental sloop named the Clearwater that would be sailing into Beacon, New York. There he met Pete Seeger, folk singer and activist, who was using the sloop in his fight to clean up the 315-mile river. The Clearwater crew still sails the Hudson today, giving people a firsthand look at the river's problems. Cronin soon joined Clearwater's "Pipewatch Project"; his subsequent investigative work, taking pipe discharge samples from an adhesive tape manufacturing company, resulted in the company being fined $50,000 for violating the 1972 Clean Water Act. Cronin was hooked. For the next 10 years he worked as a lobbyist, then a legislative aide on environmental issues in Albany. But Cronin missed the river. Quitting his job, he headed down to Nyack, New York to work as a commercial fisherman where he came face-to-face with the run-off, waste and sewage that fishermen on the Hudson were dealing with.

At about the same time, writer Robert Boyle coined an idea to protect the river, derived from the tradition of the old English riverkeeper who watched over private trout streams and protected them from poachers. Cronin seemed the perfect choice for the job. Within his first three months as Riverkeeper, Cronin nabbed several offending Exxon tankers. Settling out of court, Exxon contributed $250,000 to the Riverkeeper Fund, along with an additional $1.5 million to New York State to help clean up the river. The Hudson River Improvement Fund was established by Governor Cuomo with this money, and is still in existence today.

Cronin has been busy ever since, taking on landfills, nuclear facilities and sewage treatment plants. In doing so, he's made his share of enemies. "He's overcome by his own importance," claims Robert Kirkpatrick, former town supervisor of Newburgh, New York. Cronin had sued the town for illegally dumping alum (a toxic aluminum compound) into the river in the middle of the night. Cronin agrees he has little tolerance for those who pollute: "I'm uncompromising because somebody has to be. The area we've carved out for ourselves is to be unwavering in our enforcement of environmental law because the government is not doing it," responds Cronin.

Together with the Fund's full-time attorney, Robert F. Kennedy Jr., Cronin has won 60 cases in federal court since 1983. His focus is now on the power plants along the Hudson. "The Indian Point plant uses one million gallons of water a minute for cooling purposes and has been killing millions of fish a year," explains Cronin. Fish had been sucked in and crushed against the plant's intake screens. Cronin's suit forced Con Edison, an electric company, to spend $20 million on fish-saving equipment. Says Cronin, thinking aquatically as usual, "We may be a small fish in a big pond, but when it comes to the river, we mean business."

JESSICA SPEART *is an environmental writer living in New York City.*

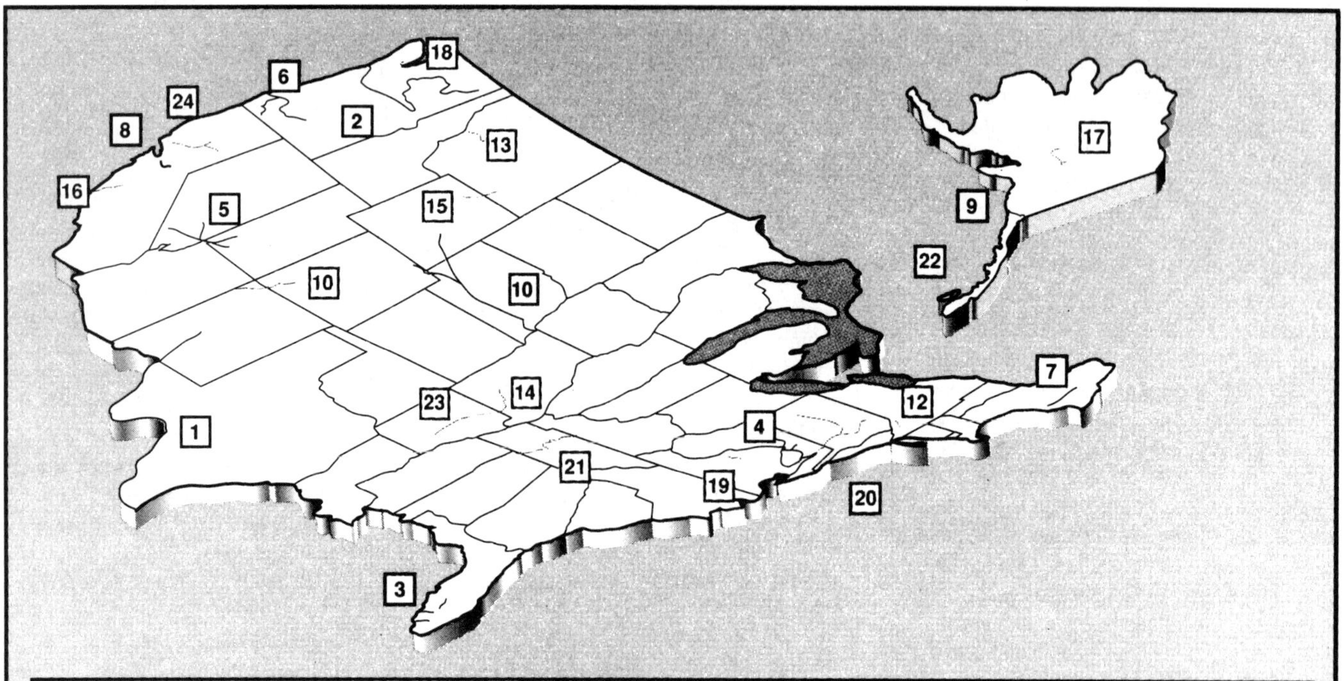

Endangered Rivers

1. Rio Grande and Rio Conchos River System, Colorado, New Mexico, Texas, Mexico
2. Columbia and Snake River System, Northwest U.S., Canada
3. Everglades, Florida
4. Anacostia River, Washington D.C., Maryland
5. Virgin River, Utah, Arizona, Nevada
6. Rogue and Illinois River System, Oregon
7. Penobscot River, Maine
8. Clavey River, California
9. Alsek and Tatshenshini River System, Alaska and British Columbia
10. Platte River, Nebraska

Threatened Rivers

11. Animas River, Colorado
12. Beaverkilt (lower) and Willowemec River System, New York
13. Blackfoot River, Montana
14. Eleven Point River, Missouri
15. Little Big Horn River, Wyoming
16. Los Angeles River, California
17. Moose Creek, Alaska
18. Skokomish River, Washington
19. St. Mary's River, Virginia
20. Susquehanna River, Pennsylvania
21. Tennessee River, Kentucky
22. Thorne River, Alaska
23. White River, Arkansas
24. Yuba South, California

Source: American Rivers

Bruce Kerr

"I'm in favor of more federal control when it comes to toxic discharges," says Nina Bell of NEA. "States are undercutting human and wildlife health in order to appeal to industry. There needs to be a provision in the Clean Water Act that recognizes some pollutants are so dangerous that there is no safe level for discharging them into our rivers. Why are we haggling over how much substances like dioxin should be diluted? Congress had to ban DDT, but it should have been eliminated through the Clean Water Act."

But focusing only on the worst pollution may create problems of its own. "Our national fixation on cleaning up the nation's most polluted water resources to minimally acceptable standards has blinded us to the imminent decline of existing pristine water bodies," says a 1992 report from the National Wildlife Federation. "If the current course remains unchanged, the consequence of continued neglect of outstanding water resources in the United States will be equally mediocre water quality everywhere."

Fulfilling the goal of the Clean Water Act, "to restore and maintain the chemical, physical and biological integrity of the nation's water," remains a daunting task, but many environmental leaders say it is still possible. It will require federal leadership and plenty of funding, and most important, a renewed commitment to the original idea of the Clean Water Act rather than to the bureaucratic quagmire that it now represents. It will also require compromise on the part of business, government and environmental groups, but the one thing that can't be compromised is the river itself. "I hate the word 'mitigate,'" says Neal Emerald, grassroots coordinator for Trout Unlimited. "You can't make up for pollution that's already gone into a river. It's much better not to mess it up in the first place. What it comes down to is having a commitment to protecting the environment instead of raping and pillaging our natural resources." And if we don't? Beautiful, healthy rivers will go the way of the Blackfoot, and become the stuff of fiction rather than real life treasures.

For information on what's being done to improve rivers and streams and how you can get involved, contact:

- *American Rivers*, 801 Pennsylvania Avenue SE, Washington, DC 20003/(202) 547-6900.
- *Clean Water Network*, 1350 New York Avenue NW, Washington, DC 20005/(202) 624-9357.
- *EPA Office of Wetlands, Oceans, and Watersheds*, 401 M Street SW WH-556F, Washington, DC 20460/(202)260-7166.
- *National Wildlife Federation*, "Keeping Clean Waters Clean" Program, 1400 16th Street NW, Washington, DC 20036/(202) 797-6800.
- *Northwest Environmental Advocates*, 133 SW Second Avenue, Portland, OR 97204/(503)295-0490.
- *U.S. Public Interest Research Group*, 215 Pennsylvania Avenue SE, Washington, DC 20003/(202)546-9707.

It Comes Down to the Coasts

ALONG THE SEAMS OF THE EARTH WHERE LAND MEETS SEA, BIOLOGICAL PRODUCTIVITY IS MUCH HIGHER THAN FOR THE REST OF THE PLANET'S SURFACE. IF THE COASTS ARE TO CONTINUE SERVING THEIR ESSENTIAL ECOLOGICAL AND ECONOMIC FUNCTIONS, WE WILL HAVE TO BEGIN ALTERING OUR PATTERNS OF HUMAN SETTLEMENT AND DEVELOPMENT.

Peter Weber

Peter Weber is a research associate at the Worldwatch Institute. He is author of Worldwatch Paper 116, Abandoned Seas: Reversing the Decline of the Oceans *(1993), and co-author of* State of the World 1994. *This article based on field research in the Netherlands, as well as on his previous work on the subject and on the sources listed below.*

What is a view of the ocean worth? The price of a night at an expensive hotel, or the purchase of a beachfront bungalow? Enduring a biting winter wind, or a beach-bound traffic jam on a sultry day in August? For many, the answer is: whatever it takes. Every year, half of the world's vacationers head for the sea.

But for many more people, being close to the shore is worth something more than an annual pilgrimage. It is worth the cost of leaving better-paying jobs, or ancestral ties, or friends—and moving their homes to the coast. Fully half the world's people live within 50 miles or so of saltwater. And their ranks are growing. In 30 years, the same number of people as are now on earth—some 5.5 billion—are expected to live in the coastal zone.

What is the attraction? The meeting of land and sea works a kind of magic that is more powerful than that of just scenic beauty. The soil on the coastal plain, laid down when the land was covered by the ocean, and subsequently replenished by sediments washed down from the mountains, tends to be particularly fertile. About 2 percent of the world's agricultural land, including some of its most intensively and productively cultivated land, was actually taken from the sea by people.

Offshore, the same nutrients promote the growth of aquatic plants, which in turn feed fish that now provide humankind's largest single source of animal protein—larger, even, than beef or chicken. The world's primary fishing grounds are in these fertile coastal waters, from which 90 percent of the marine catch is taken (see map). Farming and fishing are major coastal industries that employ hundreds of millions of people worldwide.
worldwide.

From *World Watch,* March/April 1994, pp. 20-29.

Coastal dwellers can also make a good living from international trade, 80 percent of which is carried by ship. That's one reason why nine of the world's 10 largest cities and 33 of the top 50 are near the coasts. And of course there are the vacationers bringing their portion of the *$1.9 trillion* annually spent on tourism worldwide. Although there are no estimates for coastal tourism alone, the Madrid-based World Tourism Organization estimates that tourism accounts for nearly one-tenth of the global economic output and is one of the fastest growing industries. The attraction of the coasts is as much economic as aesthetic.

It's not surprising, then, that the narrow ribbons of land and water that outline the world's continents and islands are widely used as development zones. The phenomenon is nowhere more vividly illustrated than in The Netherlands, whose crowded populace lives with the sea literally in its back yard. In fact, one-third of The Netherlands is land that used to be under the North Sea or its tributaries; because coastal land is so valuable to the Dutch, they have been diking and draining it continuously for over a thousand years. Their sea-hugging cities are now thriving centers of commerce and culture, and their farms are some of the most productive in the world.

All this activity may churn out money, but it is also churning up the coasts—as the Dutch have become acutely aware in recent decades. Draining wetlands has reduced the natural habitat for wildlife and has driven the Dutch national symbol, the stork, from the country (see cover story in the January/February *World Watch*).

But the problem is more than just a few endangered species. By choosing to concentrate its swelling population along the coasts, humanity is locating the ecological damage of its activities precisely where the world's most productive ecosystems are concentrated. The coastal zone, extending from the beginning of the coastal plain to the end of the continental shelf, accounts for only 8 percent of the world's surface area, but hosts 26 percent of the earth's primary (plant) productivity, **the world's major spawning and nursery grounds, and one of the earth's most diverse ecosystems, the coral reefs. As a result, coastal areas, which are approximately twice as productive on average as the inland areas, suffer roughly nine times more damage because of the number of people living there.**

HAZARDS AT THE CROSSROADS

Having chosen to live where land meets sea, humanity has greatly increased the difficulty of achieving a stable relationship with the Earth's environment. The intersection between human and biological activity has already scarred the coastal landscape by altering and destroying large portions of some of its most fertile habitat.

> The coastal zone accounts for only 8 percent of the world's surface area, but 26 percent of its primary (plant) production.

Not all coastal habitat is highly productive; about half of the world's 440,000 kilometers of coastline are lined by cliffs and ice, and another 20 percent are beaches, which have relatively low biological activity. However, wetlands and estuaries, where rivers turn brackish as they enter the sea, are among the most productive of all ecosystems. There, nutrients from land feed plant growth so abundant that mangrove forests, for instance, which cover only 0.4 percent of the world's surface area, account for 2.3 percent of plant productivity. That fecundity makes mangroves, other coastal wetlands, and estuaries particularly important as nurseries for marine species. Some two-thirds of all commercially caught fish spend their first and most vulnerable stages in estuaries and wetlands, and many more species go to these coastal ecosystems to feed.

These are also some of the most endangered ecosystems in the world. Estuaries are particularly vulnerable because they are naturally sheltered harbors, and therefore tend to be heavily used and polluted. Wetlands have traditionally been regarded as wasteland, and therefore are targets for city expansion. All over the world, there are coastal cities that have degraded nearby estuaries and wetlands through the combined effects of direct habitat destruction and pollution. Commercially burgeoning Singapore, for example, has removed almost all of its mangrove wetlands and reduced offshore water visibility from eight meters prior to 1960 to an average three meters in 1992. San Francisco Bay, the largest estuary in the western United States, has lost 60 percent of its water area to land reclamation over the past 140 years.

It is agriculture, however, not urbanization, that causes the most extensive destruction. The Dutch impound coastal wetlands with dikes, then pump them dry with windmills, primarily for the fertile farmland. The Chinese have been draining coastal wetlands for the rich soils they yield for 6,000 years. The densely populated delta country of Bangladesh has impounded at least 30,000 square kilometers of wetland for agriculture; it is no coincidence that Bangladesh has the world's highest population density for a mainland country, as well as the largest area of impounded farmland.

Other causes of extensive coastal habitat destruction include the rapidly expanding fish farming industry, timber extraction, and civil engineering projects that alter the flow of sediments and fresh water. The wetlands at the mouth of the Mississippi River are eroding away at a rate of 150 square kilometers per year, largely due to flood control and channeling projects in the delta and upstream. Worldwide, about half of all saltmarshes and mangrove swamps have been cleared, drained, diked, or filled, and few estuaries remain unpolluted or unaltered.

Offshore, coral reefs, kelp forests, seagrass beds, and other shallow water habitats are endangered by the combination of direct destruction and pollution from land. Coral reefs are of particular concern. They line more than 100,000 kilometers of coast and harbor a large portion of the coasts' biological wealth. Unfortunately, they are highly vulnerable to changes in their environment. If the normally clear tropical waters they form in are clouded by pollutants, for example, the corals can't photosynthesize to produce their food. They also recover slowly when damaged. Other offshore habitats, likewise, suffer from such habitat degradation. The pollution and harbor development off Singapore, for instance, has degraded the majority of the seagrass beds and all but 5 percent of the coral reefs.

The unique ecology of coral reefs makes them one of the world's most diverse ecosystems, second in density of unique species only to tropical rain forests; thus the widespread damage to these reefs constitutes a major blow to the Earth's overall biological diversity. Yet, 5 to 10 percent of the planet's coral reefs have essentially been ruined by pollution and direct destruction, and another 30 percent could be lost in the next 10 to 20 years. The most graphic examples are the extensive portions of reef that have been mined for construction materials in places like southern India and Sri Lanka, and the damage caused by fishers using explosives to kill and catch fish. But globally, pollution from burgeoning developments onshore is the more extensive and intractable threat to these and other coastal habitats.

The Demographic Squeeze

Without closer attention to the management and protection of these coastal ecosystems, the destruction is bound to accelerate. Because of steady coastward migration, coastal populations—and the environmental pressures they bring—may be growing even faster than the global population, which is climbing by some 90 million people a year.

One of the forces driving the trend is rural poverty. Like a pied piper, the promise of employment in cities draws people from depressed agricultural areas. The United Nations estimates that 20 to 30 million of the world's poorest people annually migrate from rural to urban areas, especially to Third World mega-cities, which are usually on the coasts. Rural coastal populations may also be increasing for similar reasons. In the Philippines, the coastal population is growing faster than that of the rest of the country in part because people who give up on farming often move to coastal areas to try fishing. While land is scarce, open access to fishing grounds gives poor people at least the hope of making a living.

In China, the coastal population may be increasing by 10 percent or more per year, though the country's overall growth rate is only 1.2 percent. Already the population density along the China coast is three times as high as the national average, and this region accounts for 70 percent of the country's gross national product. While the economic success along the coast will inevitably attract more Chinese, the government is encouraging this coastward migration by placing special economic development zones there.

In Southeast Asia, where marine biodiversity is particularly high, more than two-thirds of the population lives within the coastal zone. Coastal populations are also particularly high in southern Asia, Europe, southeastern Africa, and portions of North and South America. And as the global trend of rural flight and urbanization progresses, the challenge to protect the world's coasts will become more severe.

More Than Coastal Living

As if this pattern of human habitation weren't damaging enough, the thin ribbons of coast are also subject to devastating environmental assaults from both far inland and out at sea. Pollution from human activity outside of the coastal zone funnels into estuaries and coastal waters, while in an almost mirror image, the impacts of fishing and shipping become more concentrated closer to shore.

A surprising proportion of the pollutants entering coastal waters originates not from the adjacent coastal land but from more distant sources. Of the polluting nutrients, about half come from inland. In the eastern United States, for instance, the Chesapeake Bay has been overwhelmed by nutrients from inland sources. Farms contribute one-third and air pollution another one-quarter of the nitrogen pollution that has caused eutrophication, algal blooms, and oxygen depletion in this estuary—once one of the most productive in the world. The oyster

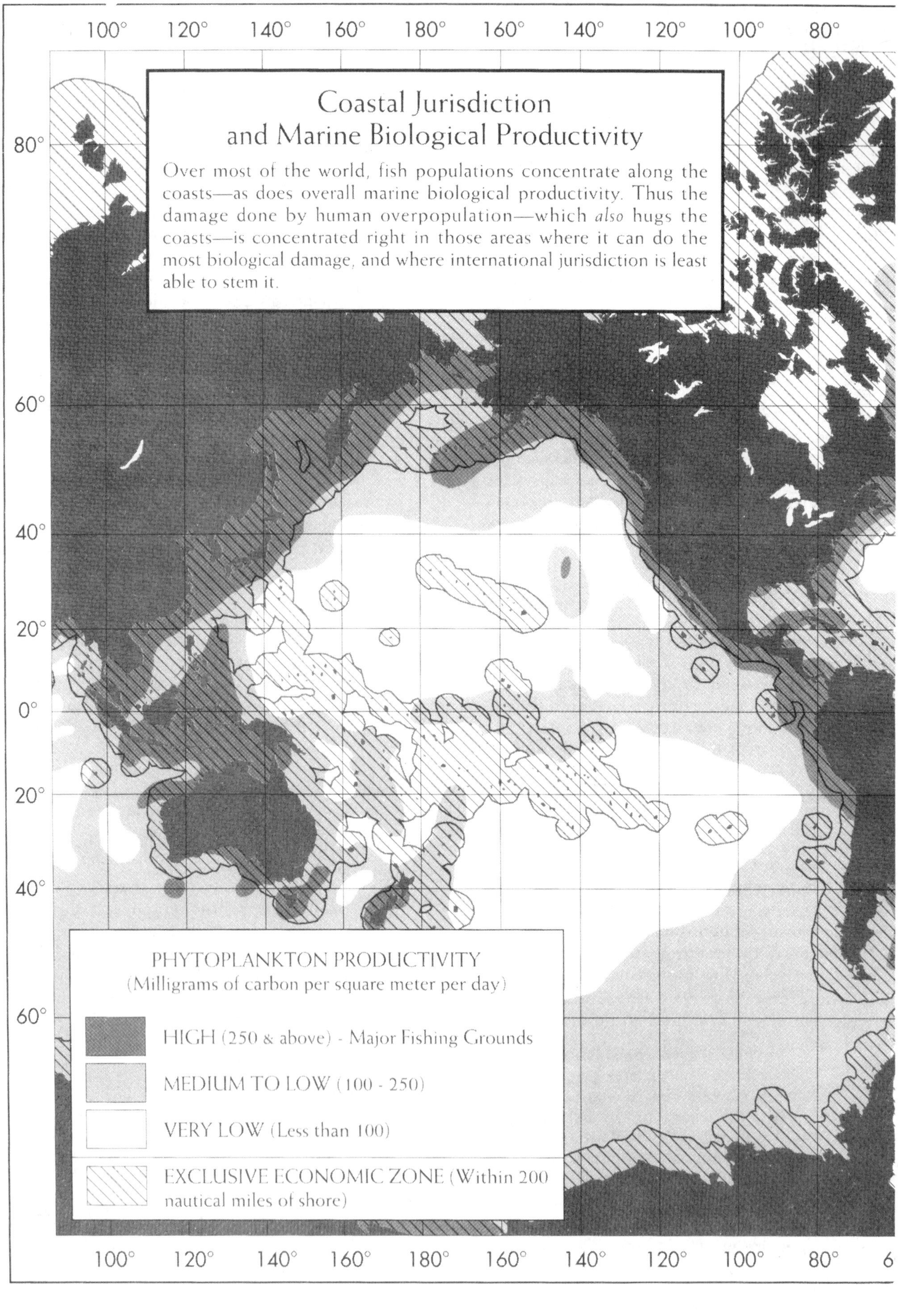
Coastal Jurisdiction
and Marine Biological Productivity
Over most of the world, fish populations concentrate along the coasts—as does overall marine biological productivity. Thus the damage done by human overpopulation—which *also* hugs the coasts—is concentrated right in those areas where it can do the most biological damage, and where international jurisdiction is least able to stem it.
100° 120° 140° 160° 180° 160° 140° 120° 100° 80°
80°
60°
40°
20°
0°
20°
40°
60°
PHYTOPLANKTON PRODUCTIVITY
(Milligrams of carbon per square meter per day)
HIGH (250 & above) - Major Fishing Grounds
MEDIUM TO LOW (100 - 250)
VERY LOW (Less than 100)
EXCLUSIVE ECONOMIC ZONE (Within 200 nautical miles of shore)
100° 120° 140° 160° 180° 160° 140° 120° 100° 80° 6

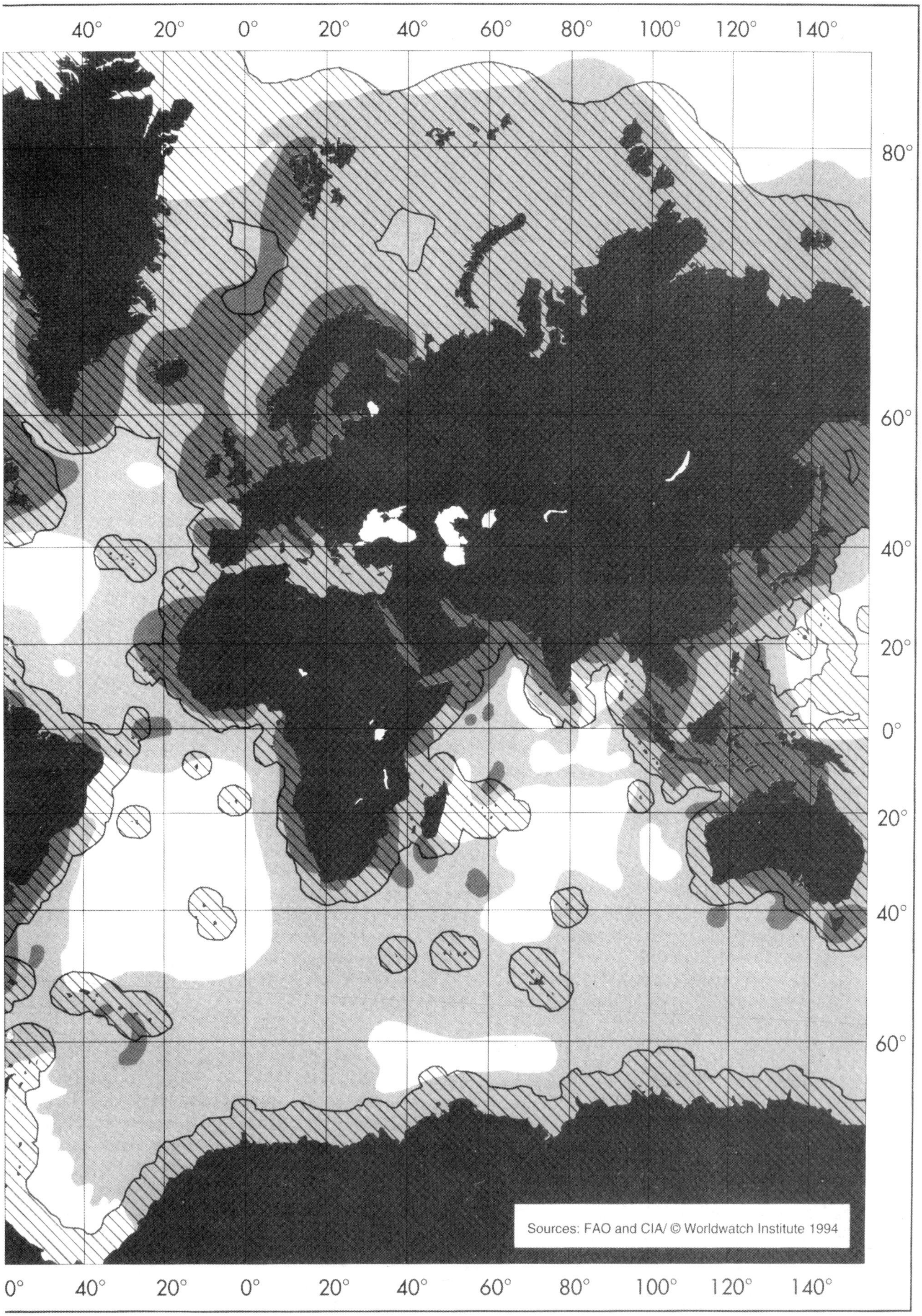
40°
20°
0°
20°
40°
60°
80°
100°
120°
140°
80°
60°
40°
20°
0°
20°
40°
60°
Sources: FAO and CIA/ © Worldwatch Institute 1994
0°
40°
20°
0°
20°
40°
60°
80°
100°
120°
140°

catch in the Chesapeake has fallen from 20,000 tons in the 1950s to under 3,000 tons in the late 1980s, at least partly as a result of this pollution.

In a study of samples from 42 of the world's major rivers, Jonathan J. Cole and his colleagues at the Institute of Ecosystem Studies at the New York Botanical Garden found that the level of pollution correlates uncannily with the level of human activity in the watershed. The Rhine, for example, has 10 times the population density of the Mississippi, and dumps 10 times more nutrients into the sea, even though the Mississippi drains an area 14 times as large (see graph on next page).

About one-third of the pollutants entering the marine environment come from air emissions, a large portion of which settle into coastal waters. For many heavy metals and volatile organic chemicals, air is the primary route to the sea. In the North Sea, about a quarter of the pollution, including the majority of PCBs and other chlorinated organic chemicals, comes from the air. In the Persian Gulf, the 4 to 12 million barrels of oil that the Iraqi army deliberately spilled during the 1991 Gulf War turned out to be only part of the total amount of oil estimated to have entered the Gulf as a result of the war. Another 4 to 5 million barrels are thought to have been carried into the Gulf by oil-laden smoke. Worldwide, about 10 percent of the oil that reaches the oceans is airborne.

Ironically, human industries and settlements are choking coastal waters with the very rivers that make these waters productive. The excess nutrients, sediments, pathogens, and persistent toxins come mostly from land-based sources. Even oil pollution, which is typically associated with accidents at sea such as that of the Exxon Valdez, is as likely to have flowed into the water directly from a car or factory on land as from a barge or boat.

On the ocean side of the coastal zone, overfishing has depleted some of the world's major fish stocks, along with the health of their ecosystems. There is a growing crisis in the world fisheries, as epitomized by the collapse of North Atlantic cod stocks off Canada. Although pollution and habitat destruction have played a role in this crisis, the main problem is simply that the capacity of the fishing industry—in numbers of people and in the efficiency of their high-tech equipment—has grown too large for the regenerative capacity of the oceans. Of the world's 17 major fishing grounds, all of which are primarily coastal, every one has been fished to its limits or beyond, according to the United Nations Food and Agriculture Organization (FAO), which tracks global fishing trends. Nine are now in serious decline because of overfishing.

As high-tech factory boats and traditional fishers alike have extracted larger and larger proportions of the biomass from coastal waters, whole ecosystems have begun to break down. In the Shetland Islands, Arctic terns, puffins, and other nesting birds failed to breed in the mid– and late 1980s, apparently due to overfishing of the sand eel, a small shoaling fish caught for fish meal and oil. The birds normally feed young sand eels to their chicks, but the fish's population declined with the commercial catch, which peaked at 56,000 tons in 1982 and then plunged to 4,800 tons in 1988. In a similar disaster, off the coast of Peru, guano birds abandoned their young when the Peruvian anchovy fishery collapsed. In Kenya, researchers found that heavy fishing of triggerfish on coral reefs allowed the proliferation of rock-boring sea urchins, which were endangering the entire ecosystem.

Global Implications

What happens to the coasts has effects that reach far beyond their local aquatic and human communities, however. Though they are among the most vulnerable of Earth's ecosystems, the coasts house biological processes and diversity that are essential to the health and stability of the biosphere as a whole.

The oceans, which are the *largest* ecosystems, rely disproportionately on the coasts for food. Although the coastal waters over continental shelves cover only 10 percent of the ocean surface, they account for 20 percent of the marine plant production. The energy captured in these waters' prolific plant growth feeds into the oceanic food chain, starting with small marine organisms such as copepods and other zooplankton, and moving out to sea with currents and migratory species. Unlike on land, animal life makes up the majority of biomass in the oceans, and its movement into the open ocean redistributes some of the disproportionate productivity of coastal waters.

This coastal productivity also helps to drive the oceans' "biological pump," the process by which the oceans help to regulate global climate. Scientists have found that the marine food chain moderates the atmospheric concentration of carbon dioxide, the primary heat-trapping gas. Carbon dioxide enters the churning upper layer of the oceans, where phytoplankton and other marine plants use it in photosynthesis to make simple sugars. While 90 percent of this carbon is recycled through the food chain, some falls into the deeper layers of the oceans as the detritus of decaying phytoplankton and other sea plants or animals. There, the carbon is stored in deep ocean currents that take about 1,000 years to bring it back to the surface as carbon dioxide.

HUMAN POPULATION AND COASTAL MARINE POLLUTION FROM MAJOR RIVERS

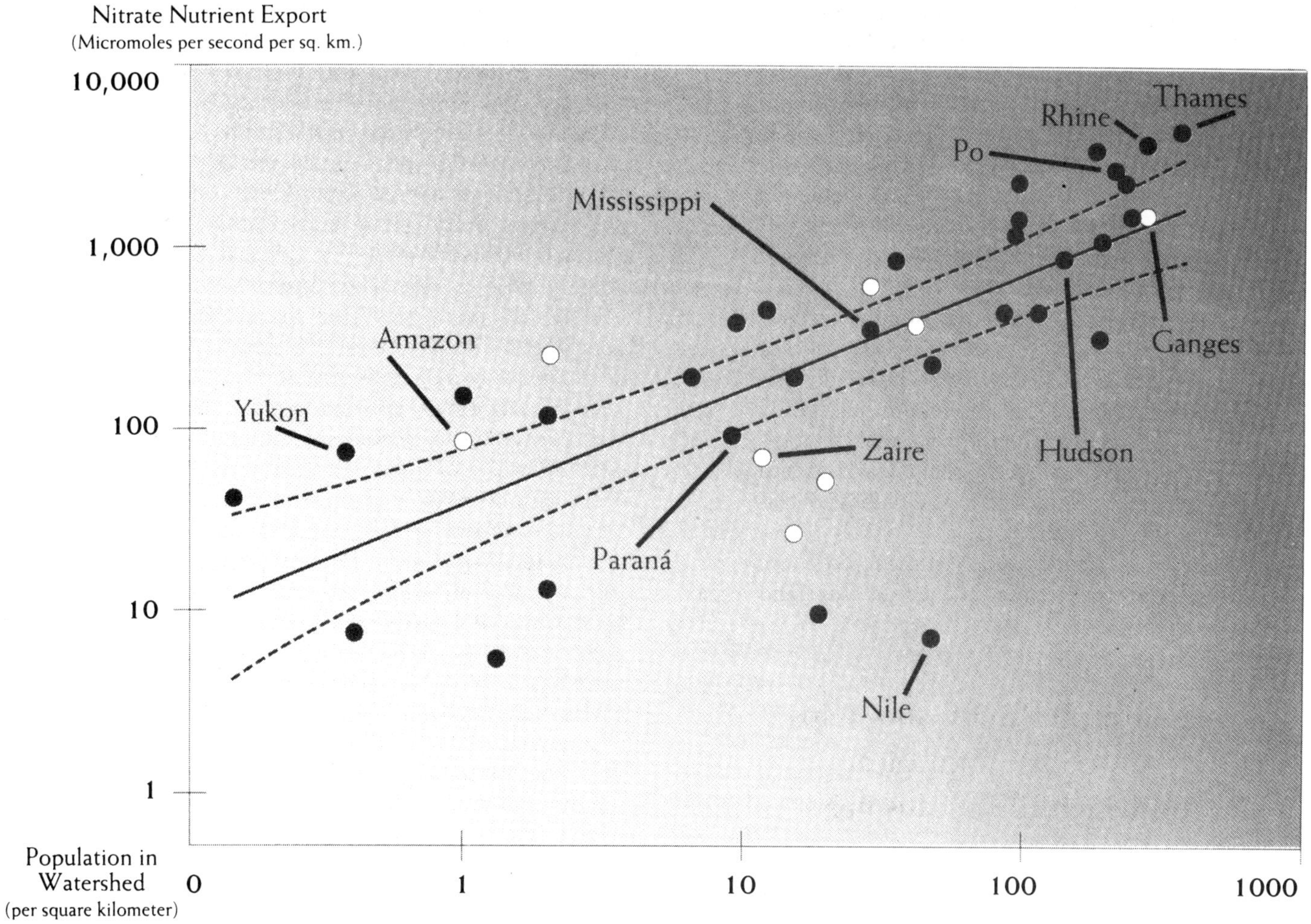

Each dot represents a different river. Open dots are tropical rivers (within 23.5 degrees latitude). Some are labeled for comparison; thus:

- The densely populated Thames watershed dumps 55 times as much nitrate pollution as the sparsely populated Amazon, even though the Amazon drains an area 700 times as large.
- The Rhine watershed has 10 times the population density of the Mississippi, and dumps 10 times as much pollution, even though the Mississippi drains an area 14 times as large.

Note: Both axes are logarithmic. The solid line is the trend using a least squares regression; the dashed lines mark the region of a 95 percent confidence for the trend.

Source: Jonathan J. Cole et al., "Nitrogen Loading of Rivers as a Human-Driven Process" in M.D. McDonnel and S.T.A. Pickett, eds., *Humans as Components of Ecosystems: The Ecology of Subtle Human Effects and Population Areas* (New York: Springer-Verlag, 1993)

The large amounts of biomass produced and consumed along the coasts, too, may play a major role in global warming. On one hand, some of the carbon dioxide captured by marine plants is stored in coastal sediments. On the other hand, some of the carbon trapped in organic matter flowing in from land is oxidized and rereleased to the atmosphere. Scientists are still uncertain whether the coasts are a net source or sink of carbon. But either way, altering coastal processes is likely to have a global impact because of the sheer quantity of carbon pumped through this zone.

The high biological diversity of the coasts helps to stabilize these global systems. Organisms ranging from bacteria to great blue whales play key roles. Copepods, for instance, are minute crustaceans that eat phytoplankton and are thought to be the most numerous animals in the oceans. They fill a critical link between the primary producers and the rest of the marine food chain. If ecological conditions change in a way that no longer permits copepods to perform this function, their disappearance could have devastating consequences.

But there's another dimension, as well, to the extraordinary diversity of coastal organisms. About 90 percent of the history of life on earth has taken place in salt water, making the oceanic gene pool an invaluable resource. Its species are the descendants of the 3 to 3.5 billion years of evolution that predated the appearance of plant life on dry land some 450 million years ago. Therefore, many coastal species have no evolutionary counterparts on dry land. These unique species make irreplaceable contributions to food production, medicine, and scientific research.

A large proportion of these species are housed in coral reefs. Only the deep ocean floor, which covers half the earth's surface, is thought to contain more. Within coastal waters, a general rule of diversity is that shallow waters harbor more diversity than deeper waters, rocky areas more than sandy or muddy ones, and the tropics more than temperate or polar zones. Coral reefs—shallow, rocky, and tropical—are believed to contain the highest density of unique species in the oceans.

Researchers are increasingly turning to these coastal waters in their search for medical cures and unique compounds. They have derived anti-leukemia drugs from sea sponges, bone graft material from corals, diagnostic chemicals from red algae, and anti-infection compounds from shark skin. Because marine life is relatively unstudied compared to terrestrial life, the oceans and coasts are a vast new frontier for research.

This coastal productivity also helps to drive the oceans' "biological pump," by which the oceans help to regulate the global climate.

Shoring up the Sea

Under the current international regime, protecting the coastal zone is up to coastal nations. Nearly two decades ago, international negotiations over the Law of the Sea, a United Nations-mediated treaty on the management of the oceans, gave rise to international acceptance of the concept of a 200-nautical-mile coastal area—called the Exclusive Economic Zone (EEZ)—within which the coastal country has exclusive rights to the natural resources (see map). By 1976, 60 countries had claimed EEZs of their own and the notion became an accepted part of customary oceans law.

The recent ratification of the Law of the Sea formalizes the EEZ construct and puts in force the treaty provisions that encourage coastal states to conserve and protect these waters. But the language is vague and probably unenforceable because of long-standing concerns over national sovereignty—the same issue that blocked international standards for coastal zone management at the 1992 Earth Summit in Rio de Janeiro. The delegates acknowledged the growing coastal crisis, but they shied away from infringing on national jurisdiction.

Of the three major threats to the coasts—coastal development, pollution from inland, and overfishing of coastal waters—it is development that warrants the highest priority for major changes in policy. The direct destruction and pollution of essential ecosystems is steadily undermining the coastal zone on every continent, and the surging of coastal populations means that these threats are worsening.

The single most effective change that could be made to slow the juggernaut of coastal development would be to eliminate subsidies such as government-sponsored insurance and funding for ocean-altering roads, dikes, and dams. The Netherlands, for instance, spends $400 million a year just to pump water and repair inland dikes, and new seawalls and dikes can cost hundreds of millions of dollars. These investments have come under domestic scrutiny, not only because they contribute to the loss of coastal habitat for the stork and other wetland-dependent species, but also because they may not be cost-effective. Some of the impounded agricultural land is often too wet to farm, and the Dutch don't need all of it because they are already producing more food than they can either use or sell abroad. As a result, expenditures on draining coastal land for farming can lead, absurdly, to still more expenditures on farm subsidies to cover excess production.

To save money and begin rehabilitating the coastal ecosystem, the Dutch government has made an extraordinary and courageous decision to return 150,000 hectares of farmland (15 percent of the total converted area) to rivers and estuaries over the next 25 years. Although the Dutch will continue diking and developing other parts of the coastal zone, this reversal reflects their growing concern over the degradation of their coasts.

In the early 1900s, the Dutch built a 30-kilometer-long earthen seawall across the mouth of the Zuider Sea in the northwest to protect the impounded farmland in the estuary from flooding. The barrier against the sea completely altered the original ecosystem, turning the giant brackish water estuary into a fresh water lake, now known as Lake IJssel. The country has continued to pursue this strategy of "coastal defense," but recent projects have been more ecologically sensitive. For instance, rather than building a similar earthen seawall across all of the estuaries in the rich coastal region of Zeeland in the southwest, the Dutch built mechanical seawalls that can be opened to allow relatively natural water flow, and closed in case of a strong coastal storm that threatens flooding.

As the Zeeland projects demonstrate, coastal development can be made less destructive. But the methods don't have to be high-tech engineering solutions. Natural buffer zones, for instance, can protect coastal habitat from nearby development. Wetlands trap toxins, pathogens, and excess nutrients and sediments as they move seaward, while also protecting coastal communities from coastal storms and sea surges. Coral reefs act as natural seawalls, reducing the erosive action of the ocean by absorbing the impact of waves.

Simple guidelines can make a significant difference. In Thailand's Ban Don Bay, for instance, the provincial government instituted building restrictions to protect the region's primary tourist attraction, the coral reefs. Developers now must build back from the beach and cannot use coral for construction material.

In Ecuador, which has lost 144,000 hectares of mangrove forests to shrimp ponds, the government is sponsoring a national program to manage coastal resources so that local communities can continue to profit from them without destroying them. Starting with a U.S. Agency for International Development pilot project, the Ecuadorean government has formed six special coastal management zones, with management committees composed of local and government people. In the case of the shrimp industry, which constitutes a sizable portion of Ecuador's exports and economy (nearly 80,000 metric tons of shrimp, worth almost $500 million in 1991), shrimp farmers were given special training on how to protect the coastal environment while maintaining their livelihoods.

Even if well-managed, however, coastal development could turn the world's coastlines into continuous strings of cities, farms, and resorts. Aside from the catastrophic ecological impacts, such an eventuality could take a heavy toll on those who live and invest there. As is becoming increasingly evident in places like the Eastern seaboard of the United States, coasts are dynamic. Portions are always eroding or shifting, and over the course of tens of thousands of years, changes in sea level can alternately expose and inundate the coastal zone. In the 10,000 years since the last ice age, the sea level has been rising as the result of melting ice and glaciers and thermal expansion of the oceans. Most of the world's low coasts continue to retreat due to the recent rate of sea level rise of 1 to 2 millimeters per year, or 10 to 20 centimeters per century.

With the increase in greenhouse gases and the threat of global warming, coastal living in the coming century will become more precarious. Sea level is projected to rise by 60 centimeters in the next 100 years, and storms are likely to grow stronger. Governments may need to consider restricting or even prohibiting further coastal development altogether.

For information on what you can do to influence coastal policy in the United States, contact the Coast Alliance, 235 Pennsylvania Avenue, SE, Washington, DC 20003. Tel. 202/546-9554.

KEY SOURCES

Fan Zhijie and R.P. Côté, "Population, development and marine pollution in China," *Marine Policy,* May 1991.

P.M. Holligan and H. de Boois, eds., *Land-Ocean Interactions in the Coastal Zone,* The International Geosphere-Biosphere Programme: A Study of Global Change of the International Council of Scientific Unions, Stockholm, February 1993.

Joint Group of Experts on the Scientific Aspects of the Marine Pollution (GESAMP): *The State of the Marine Environment,* UNEP Regional Seas Reports and Studies No. 115 (Nairobi: United Nations Environment Programme, 1990).

United Nations Food and Agriculture Organization, *Marine Fisheries and the Law of the Sea: A Decade of Change,* FAO Fisheries Circular No. 853, Rome, 1993.

H. Jesse Walker, "The Coastal Zone" in B.L. Turner II et al., *The Earth as Transformed by Human Action* (New York: Cambridge University Press, 1990).

The Deforestation D · E · B · A · T · E

Estimates vary widely over the extent of forest loss

RICHARD MONASTERSKY

As tales of burning forests captured headlines in the late 1980s, a string of rock stars, movie actors, and even ice cream makers joined the fight to save tropical woodlands, helping to transform the awkward term "deforestation" into a household word. But recent studies have produced markedly different estimates of the pace of clearing, raising questions about the accuracy of deforestation figures that have floated around policy circles in recent years.

While tropical forests are certainly vanishing at a disturbing rate, the widespread disagreement over deforestation estimates makes it difficult for government officials and scientists to assess the problem. That, in turn, hampers efforts to gauge the threat of related issues, such as habitat destruction and global warming.

Concerns about previous deforestation estimates emerged in the last few years as researchers from a number of countries looked into the problem, often using more reliable methods than before. Most recently, a study published in the June 25 SCIENCE confirmed suspicions that several earlier assessments had drastically overestimated the rate of forest destruction in the Brazilian Amazon basin, thereby inflating some global estimates.

The Brazilian case provides a dramatic example of how different researchers can arrive at markedly divergent conclusions concerning the extent of deforestation. In 1988, Alberto Setzer of Brazil's National Space Research Institute (INPE) used data collected by infrared sensors on a U.S. weather satellite to gauge the number and extent of fires within the legally defined Brazilian Amazon — an area that includes only part of Brazil's tropical forests. Assuming that 40 percent of the fires occurred on recently cleared forest, Setzer's team calculated that 8 million hectares of forest were cleared during 1987 within the legal Amazon — an almost unfathomable amount equal to 2.2 percent of the forest.

Although contested by other researchers, that alarming number found its way into several global deforestation estimates at the time. In particular, the Washington, D.C.-based World Resources Institute (WRI) included Setzer's Amazon figure in a 1990 worldwide assessment. The high number for Brazil drove up WRI's global estimate for tropical forest loss, which was calculated at 16.4 to 20.4 million hectares per year.

Despite the controversy over the Brazilian estimate, WRI's global total seemed to agree with a provisional number issued by the United Nations Food and Agriculture Organization (FAO), which put tropical deforestation at 17 million hectares per year for the period 1981 to 1990 (SN: 7/21/90, p.40).

Brazil emerged from the WRI study and others looking like the ultimate forest destroyer, responsible for roughly one-third to one-half of the global deforestation total. That triggered a round of international finger-pointing, focusing criticism on Brazil for allowing such rapid clearing of the Amazon. Brazil, however, complained that the estimates were inaccurate and that deforestation rates had never reached such heights, says Jayant A. Sathaye, an energy and forestry analyst at the Lawrence Berkeley (Calif.) Laboratory.

More recent studies have backed up Brazil's claims. In the last few years, researchers at INPE and the National Institute for Research on Amazonia, based in Manaus, Brazil, challenged Setzer's fire-counting technique and began gauging deforestation by mapping cleared areas on images taken by Landsat satellites. Studies that relied partly on this technique indicated that deforestation within the Brazilian Amazon averaged 2.1 million hectares per year between 1978 and 1989 and 1.4 million hectares from 1989 to 1990.

The newest estimate for Brazil goes even lower. David Skole of the University of New Hampshire in Durham and Compton Tucker of NASA's Goddard Space Flight Center in Greenbelt, Md., studied some 200 Landsat images covering the entire Brazilian Amazon for 1978 and 1988, allowing them to map the extent of forest and cleared land for those two years. The images showed that deforested areas covered 7.8 million hectares in 1978 and 23 million hectares in 1988, implying an average annual loss rate of 1.5 million hectares, Skole and Tucker report in their recent SCIENCE paper.

Conventional wisdom holds that Brazil's deforestation slackened dramatically after peaking in 1987, in part because the country's economy slowed, reducing the land speculation that had motivated people to clear forest for new farms or rangeland. If true, that standard theory could explain why Setzer and others found so much more deforestation going on at the peak period than others have seen in the last four years.

But Skole dismisses that explanation. "A lot of people are using it as a convenient excuse for being wrong," he contends. Although he, too, finds that deforestation rates have dropped in Brazil, he says the average for the late 1980s did not range much above 2 million hectares per year — not high enough to explain the earlier estimates.

If Brazil's actual rate of forest loss is so much lower than studies had previously suggested, how accurate are the various global estimates? Skole, for one, has little faith in the sea of numbers. "All of the published global studies do not use a systematic approach," he says. "They use secondary and tertiary sources, anecdotal reports, different time periods, different methodologies, different terminology. It's the state of affairs right now in deforestation monitoring. It's kind of a sad state of affairs, but people are using whatever resources they have, which are not adequate."

Before deforestation gained widespread attention in the late 1980s, most researchers relied on an estimate by FAO, which concluded in 1981 that tropical deforestation worldwide averaged 11.3 million hectares per year during the late 1970s. That number stood uncontested because it was the only figure available.

Since 1989, FAO has been working to update that global estimate. In 1990, it released a provisional figure of 17 million hectares of deforestation per year; but this March it lowered the global total to 15.5 million hectares per year for the period 1981 through 1990. K.D. Singh, leader of FAO's forestry assessment team in Rome, explains the change by saying that his organization's 1981 study overestimated the amount of forest remaining in the tropics at that time, a mistake that had inflated its 1990 estimate.

By all accounts, the latest FAO assessment represents the most comprehensive global study to date, having collected scattered data from individual countries or provinces and woven them together using a mathematical model based on information about forest conditions, population density, and ecological zones. Singh says his team has striven to find the best data available, although the quality and type of data vary from one region to another. Some local and national governments have conducted forest surveys using satellite images, while others have used ground-based approaches for estimating deforestation.

The success of the FAO effort remains uncertain, however. Forestry researchers cannot yet check the new global assessment against other studies because FAO released only regional deforestation estimates and has not yet issued tallies for individual countries.

For instance, the FAO numbers reported in March include 6.2 million hectares of forest lost annually in tropical South America from 1981 through 1990. That region includes Brazil and six other nations. To some researchers, the South American total appears unrealistically high. If FAO chose the best data available at the time (the Brazilian estimates of 2 million hectares lost annually in the legal Amazon during the 1980s), that would leave more than 4 million hectares cleared each year outside the Brazilian Amazon.

Where, then, is all that missing South American deforestation? That is precisely the issue raised by an international committee of researchers called the Intergovernmental Panel on Climate Change. In a 1992 report, the panel questioned FAO's South American estimate (which has since decreased slightly), saying, "This seems to ascribe a very high proportion (about 70 percent) of the total deforestation in South America in the late 1980s to the region outside the Brazilian Amazonia, even though this region accounts for very little of the total amount of forest on the continent."

But FAO's Singh says researchers have not appreciated the extent of South American deforestation in the open forest outside of the rainforest of the Brazilian Amazon. "This has been one of our main findings – that the deforestation outside the legal Amazon basin is quite high," he told SCIENCE NEWS. The open forest faces a greater threat because it is more accessible and because more people live there than in the rainforest, Singh says.

Beyond those hints, Singh says he cannot respond fully to criticisms of the new deforestation assessment until FAO publishes its more complete report, which will include a breakdown of figures for individual countries. The report should come out in late summer, he says. Singh also hopes to submit the study to a panel of scientists for peer review.

Some researchers, however, wonder whether the FAO will delay releasing the long-awaited numbers, perhaps indefinitely, in hopes of avoiding the intense scrutiny that will descend on this study.

Ken Andrasko, chief of a forestry section in the Environmental Protection Agency's climate change division, suggests that deforestation studies have acquired political significance in the wake of last year's Earth Summit in Rio de Janeiro, where countries signed treaties on biodiversity and climate change. The climate change convention requires all countries to provide an inventory of their greenhouse gas emissions, including those caused by deforestation. Since future treaties may call for all countries to limit their emissions, the deforestation estimates will partly determine how much a country needs to cut back.

"It's going to be increasingly difficult to publish those individual country [deforestation] estimates. If the number is higher or lower, it has very real political consequences now," Andrasko says.

DEFORESTATION HOT SPOTS

Region	Forest remaining as of 1990 (thousands of hectares)	Annual deforestation 1981-1990 (thousands of hectares)	Annual rate of deforestation (percentage)
Africa	527,586	4,100	0.7
East Sahel Africa	65,450	595	0.9
West Africa	55,607	591	1.0
Central Africa	204,112	1,139	0.5
Tropical Southern Africa	145,868	1,345	0.9
Asia	310,597	3,904	1.2
Continental S.E. Asia	75,240	1,314	1.6
Insular S.E. Asia	135,426	1,926	1.3
Latin America	918,115	7,407	0.8
Central America and Mexico	68,096	1,112	1.5
Tropical South America	802,904	6,173	0.7
World Total in Tropics	1,756,297	15,411	0.8

Source: Food & Agriculture Organization

That lesson was not lost on Brazil, which released its own deforestation data on the eve of the Rio summit. Such studies, as well as the one by Skole and Tucker, show that while Brazil may still be number one, it no longer sits in a category of its own, far and above every other nation on the list of forest destroyers.

Although the FAO did not provide estimates for individual countries, the data released earlier this year clearly indicate that tropical forests are shrinking worldwide. Indeed, parts of other continents are losing a greater percentage of their forests than is South America, which has much more intact forest than other parts of the globe. According to FAO, the highest percentages of deforestation during the 1980s occurred in southeast Asia, Central America and Mexico, and West Africa.

Looking beyond the problem of absolute deforestation, experts say fragmentation and degradation of remaining forests also present substantial threats, especially to the diversity of plant and animal life in some of the most biologically rich habitats on Earth. Indeed, Skole and Tucker found that the area of disturbed habitat surrounding cleared areas grew by more than 4 million hectares per year in Brazil's Amazon, much faster than the pace of deforestation there. "Even though the rate of deforestation was much lower than previous estimates, the effect on biological diversity was much greater," says Tucker.

To address such concerns, the second phase of the FAO study will examine the extent to which people have broken up forest or removed trees without stripping an area bare. As part of this work, Singh's team has purchased high-resolution satellite images for 117 randomly selected regions corresponding to about 10 percent of the forest-covered land in the tropics. For quality control, his group also used these satellite images in the first phase of the study to improve its deforestation estimates.

Ideally, FAO would purchase satellite images for the entire tropical belt. But Singh says the organization cannot afford the thousands of images needed to cover the tropics.

An ongoing NASA project may help complete the picture. In a program called Landsat Pathfinder, NASA is funding the purchase of satellite photos covering some three-quarters of the world's tropical rainforest. According to Skole, a participant in the project, it will provide the most accurate assessment of deforestation to date. As with the Brazilian case, the research done with satellite data could show that past estimates have been inflated. But Skole says the new study may also uncover much more deforestation than had been suspected.

The NASA effort does have some critical limitations. Because it focuses mostly on tropical rainforest, it will not include all open forests and dry forests, which cover just as much territory as do rainforests. Moreover, the project is a one-shot deal, not to be repeated. Experts say periodic updates are needed, not only to assess the changing deforestation threat but also to gauge the resulting increase in concentrations of carbon dioxide.

Despite its drawbacks, however, the NASA project should finally provide a means of checking the global estimates. "I feel confident," says Skole, "that in the next two to three years, as our work comes forward, we will have a much better idea because we are applying a consistent method."

Threat of Encroaching Deserts May Be More Myth Than Fact

William K. Stevens

Common wisdom has it that the deserts of the world are on the march, steadily expanding, permanently converting pastures and croplands to sand dunes, and that human mistreatment of the drylands that flank the deserts is responsible.

But scientists using the most up-to-date investigative techniques have found no evidence that this is true, at least in the case of the Sahara and its immediate environs, everyone's favorite and most serious example of what is called "desertification." In view of the lack of evidence, many experts suspect that the threatening image of encroaching deserts may be more myth than fact.

The findings, based largely on satellite measurements, are forcing a reassessment of just what is happening in the arid and semi-arid drylands along the desert's perimeter, which have turned out to be more resilient than once thought. And even as talks on a multinational treaty to deal with desertification enter an important phase at the United Nations this week, some leaders of the international effort to halt drylands degradation have backed away from the idea that deserts are expanding. In fact, they and others say, the very term desertification confuses the issue and obscures what is really going on in the drylands.

No one denies that what is taking place in the drylands is serious. As in much of the rest of the world, growing population and economic pressures are depleting the soil, damaging vegetation and natural ecosystems, depressing agricultural yields and threatening the future survival of those who live in the regions between deserts and more humid grasslands. Drylands' sparse rainfall and inevitable droughts make them more vulnerable than more humid regions.

The degradation is serious enough to the 900 million people who live in these regions, which cover a quarter of the earth's land mass. But are the drylands turning into permanent deserts? Not likely, according to the emerging scientific evidence.

Images obtained by the National Aeronautics and Space Administration from meteorological satellites show that from 1980 through 1990, the boundary between the Sahara and the Sahel drylands region on its southern border—actually a vegetative transition zone rather than a sharp line—did not move steadily south, as conventional wisdom would have it.

Rather, the vegetation line moved back and forth in conjunction with rainfall patterns, creeping northward in wetter years and southward in drier ones. The shifts from one year to the next ranged from 30 to 150 miles along the border, but no overall trend could be discerned one way or the other.

Swedish scientists at the University of Lund, combining a variety of data collected by satellites and aircraft with ground observations, examined the Sahara-Sahel border in the Sudan for the period 1962 to 1984, when the border was thought to be moving southward. The studies found that this was not happening. The Swedish scientists also found, contrary to what some had argued, no evidence that patches of desert were spreading outward from villages and water holes within the drylands area of the Sahel. And they found no changes in vegetation cover and crop productivity that could not be explained by variations in rainfall.

Major oscillations between extended dry and wet climate patterns are a normal and governing fact of life in the drylands, said Dr. James E. Ellis, an ecologist who heads the Center for Environment and Sustainable Agriculture, a research group in Morrillton, Ark., run by the Winrock Corporation, a private voluntary organization.

Long-term rainfall records show that the climate in Africa's drylands has shifted back and forth between periods of extended drought and

From the *New York Times*, January 18, 1994, pp. C1, C10.

higher rainfall for at least the last 10,000 years. On the basis of long-term studies in Kenya, Dr. Ellis believes that climate keeps the drylands in a continual state of disequilibrium, and is a bigger influence on the dynamics of drylands ecology than people are.

Role of Climate

While the evidence taken together suggests that climate is the major influence on crops and natural ecosystems in the Sahel, it does not yet prove the case. The scientific record is too sparse and short at this point, says Dr. Compton J. Tucker of the space agency's Goddard Space Flight Center, who conducted the 1980–1990 satellite studies. Forty to 50 years of observations may be necessary to determine for sure whether the desert is spreading and, if so, whether climate or human activity is most responsible.

The evidence does not mean that deserts are not spreading, but simply that "we can't find it," says Dr. Ulf Hellden, the leader of the Swedish team. Nevertheless, he said, "our hypothesis is that climate is responsible for whatever land degradation is taking place" in the Sahel. "We know we can explain 70, perhaps 80 percent of the food productivity variability with rainfall statistics, which leaves another 20 to 30 percent we cannot explain," he said.

The prime candidate for explaining that 20 to 30 percent is human activity, argues W. Franklin G. Cardy, a Canadian who directs the Nairobi-based desertification control program of the United Nations Environment Program, or UNEP, which has led the struggle to halt drylands degradation. Scientists have identified a number of factors contributing to land degradation in the Sahel and other arid regions. Cattle, camels and goats overgraze the land. Excessive grazing and cultivation by fast-growing populations reduce vegetation and encourage soil erosion by wind and water. In wet years in some localities, herders move farther north in search of new stretches of greener grass. Farmers move in behind them and plow up the land. When dry years return, the herders return to find the land plowed up, while the farmers cannot get a crop and the soil blows away, just as it did in the American dust bowl of the 1930's.

"There is no doubt in my mind" that excessive grazing and cultivation are causing serious land degradation in drylands, said Dr. David Hillel, an environmental scientist, hydrologist and soil expert at the University of Massachusetts at Amherst.

Not least of the problems is that when precipitation does return to degraded land, it takes only a little rainfall to cause much erosion. One problem, Mr. Cardy said, is that it is "extremely difficult" to measure land degradation scientifically.

"It's invisible, essentially," he said. "The farmer knows he or she has less and less crop, knows that it's not going to be sustainable. The farmer will tell you, but not quantifiably."

Lack of Rain

In the Sahel, the problem has been exacerbated in the last 25 years by below-average rainfall, according to the conclusions of international experts who met in Sweden to examine the situation in 1990. This has led some experts to wonder whether any concern over desertification would have emerged had the last quarter-century been a wet cycle rather than a dry one.

The group that met in Sweden also concluded that scientific evidence did not confirm any human-made trend toward desert-like conditions. Rather, it supported the view that dryland ecosystems are resilient and bounce back after a drought. The scientists noted that population growth could reduce this resilience, but they added that outward migrations when conditions got bad enough could allow the land to recover. The scientists did not rule out the possibility of a future trend toward desert conditions as a result of human activity.

The proposition that deserts are expanding dates to the early years of this century. The idea that regenerating drylands on the edge of the deserts would stop the spread emerged at about the same time. Over the years, anecdotal evidence convinced many scientists, development experts and much of the public that deserts were indeed advancing. By the 1970's, this view had long since moved into the mainstream; in 1972, the United States Agency for International Development asserted that the Sahara was moving southward at 30 miles a year. But many scientists in time came to see the anecdotal evidence as unconvincing. Go to the drylands in the dry season of a drought year, they pointed out, and the land will certainly look like a desert. But in many cases, they added, the same land would look different in a wet year.

As the new evidence has emerged in the last decade, UNEP, for one, has modified its view considerably. Mr. Cardy calls the concept of expanding deserts and advancing sand dunes "largely invalid." And he believes, along with Dr. Hillel and others, that the term "desertification" should be jettisoned.

It persists, Mr. Cardy and others say, mainly as a political artifact, a way to call attention to one regional expression of the global problem of land degradation, and thereby attract financial assistance. African countries, in fact, extracted the promise of a desertification treaty at the 1992 Earth Summit in Rio de Janeiro as the price of their support of other countries on other issues.

And so the term desertification hangs on, though its definition was enlarged in Rio to encompass more than human activity as a cause of deterioration of drylands. The definition adopted by the Rio delegates reads: "Desertification is land degradation in arid, semi-arid and dry subhumid areas resulting from various factors, including climatic variations and human activities." No mention of desert encroachment.

A Proposed Strategy

Definitions aside, Mr. Cardy said, the practical issue is what to do about human impact on the drylands, whatever the influence of climate and whether or not the desert is advancing. Some experts say that if the drylands are mostly hostage to climate, it might be best to concentrate resources and effort on improving wetter, more productive lands where the costs would be lower and the returns in terms of agricultural yields would be much greater.

"That's a good economic argument," Mr. Cardy said, "but where are the people who live in the drylands going to go? As populations grow, are we going to say that because it's tough we'll turn our backs on them? It doesn't make sense. People have been making a living in those areas for millennia."

Until now, Mr. Cardy acknowledged, efforts to stem drylands degradation have had mixed results at best. One reason, he says, is that solutions have too often been imposed from above and from outside, ignoring the experience and perceived needs of the people who live there.

Dr. Ellis provides an especially telling example. "In the past," he said, "we've attempted to intervene in these systems in ways consistent with our perspectives on North America." Specifically, herders have been encouraged to attach themselves to a single piece of land, on the model of North America, where greater rainfall keeps growing conditions relatively stable. But in the unstable ecology of the drylands, in times of drought herders must be able to move their animals freely across wide expanses, as they traditionally did, to take advantage of scarce grass wherever and whenever it appears.

An emerging new philosophy on management of the drylands seeks to tailor aid more closely not just to the climatic and ecological realities of the region but to local peoples' traditional strategies and tactics for coping with them. Mr. Cardy said these solutions could be as simple as the donkey cart provided to villagers in Burkina Faso so they could haul stones to create terraces to prevent erosion.

Climate seems to have more influence on drylands than people do.

Where there are successes, he said, they usually build on locally generated efforts to rehabilitate land. Aid might be partly directed simply toward helping inhabitants of drylands in these efforts and assisting them over rough spots by extending credit, for example, or by providing seed for the next growing season if drought forces families to eat everything they grow.

Rehabilitation of Lands

There is apparently no great secret about how to rehabilitate arid lands. Soil conservation, erosion control and protecting slopes are all "standard stuff," well illustrated by the rehabilitation of the American dust bowl, Mr. Cardy said. And some strategies to beat drylands drought have precedents at least as old as the Bible: Dr. Hillel cites Joseph's building of the granaries to tide Egypt over its seven lean years.

Before any solutions can be adopted, scientists say, it is essential to understand the drylands for what they are. But the full picture remains elusive, given the gaps in knowledge that still exist and the lack of definitive proof about desert expansion and the causes of drylands degradation.

Unless the characteristics of the drylands are documented according to scientific standards, said the scientists who met in Sweden in 1990, "there is a risk that the desertification issue will become a political and development fiction rather than a scientific fact."

Environmental Problems of the Danube Delta

Europe depends on the Danube River for shipping, power, agriculture and municipal water; downstream, the river's delta reflects the environmental problems of the entire region

Catherine Pringle, George Vellidis, Francis Heliotis, Dan Bandacu and Sergiu Cristofor

Catherine Pringle is an assistant professor at the Institute of Ecology, the University of Georgia. She received her B.S. in botany, her M.S. in resource ecology and her Ph.D. in aquatic biology from the University of Michigan. George Vellidis is assistant professor in the Biological and Agricultural Engineering Department at the University of Georgia. Francis Heliotis is associate professor of biology at George Mason University. Dan Bandacu is a Scientific Researcher with the Danube Delta Research Institute in Tulcea, Romania. Sergiu Cristofor is Senior Scientist II and biologist at the Braila Hydrobiological Station, the University of Bucharest. Address for Pringle: Institute of Ecology, University of Georgia, Athens, GA 30602. Internet: pringle@zookeeper.zoo.uga.edu.

Environmental problems routinely disregard national boundaries, but scientists seeking solutions to such problems cannot. Whether pollution takes the form of a plume billowing from a smokestack or nutrients entering a river from agricultural runoff, the effects may be experienced both locally and at great distance from the source. Thus efforts to restore and manage damaged ecosystems require an interdisciplinary approach to understanding the events and processes that have led to current environmental problems. Often these are intricately tied to national politics and economic strategies, requiring the collaborative efforts of ecologists, agriculturalists, resource managers, economists and other specialists to work toward solutions.

As Europe's largest wetland, the Danube Delta provides a case in point. Fed by the Danube River, which stretches 2,860 kilometers through nine nations and serves the watersheds of four more, the delta receives the drainage from 810,000 square kilometers—about 70 percent of the area of Central Europe. On average the Danube delivers 6,300 cubic meters of water per second through the delta and into the Black Sea.

Among European rivers the Volga is longer, but the Danube carries more navigation, making it one of the world's busiest rivers. The Danube River provides the only access to the sea for Austria, Slovakia and Hungary, and it links four national capitals: Vienna, Budapest, Belgrade and Bratislava. With the recent completion of the Main-Danube Canal, which has been under construction for 30 years, the Black Sea and the North Sea are now linked through the Main (a tributary of the Rhine) and the Danube.

The Danube's vital role in Central European economies, however, has been a major source of environmental problems in its delta. In addition to providing transportation and drinking water for inhabitants along its course, the Danube's waters are tapped for hydroelectric power, industrial processes, irrigation of agricultural land, and disposal of municipal and industrial waste. Production-oriented strategies in former socialist countries often failed to incorporate into management practices science-based environmental protection and conservation. The effects of these uses upstream have fallen heavily on the Danube Delta and its inhabitants.

Formed nearly 8,000 years ago, the Danube Delta exhibits the classic delta form—a broad, flattened cone with its apex at the point where the river's main channel divides into three main branches: the Bratul Chilia, the Bratul Sulina and the Bratul Sfintu Gheorghe. Between these branches lies a mosaic of shallow lakes and channels, rooted

From *American Scientist*, July/August 1993, pp. 350-361.

Figure 1. Danube Delta, Europe's largest wetland, is a nesting area for mute swans *(Cygnus olor)* and more than 160 other species of birds, many of which migrate on European Flyways. Threats to their habitat include water-quality deterioration from heavy nutrient loads, pesticides and engineering works; the drainage of wetlands for agricultural production and aquaculture; coastal erosion; and predation from feral animals. The plight of birds is one of the most visible of the delta's environmental problems, which are a result of influences both within its confines and far upstream. The problems actually reflect those of the area the Danube River drains—much of Central and Eastern Europe. (Photo courtesy of The Cousteau Society, copyright 1991.)

emergent vegetation, and natural and artificial levees. During times of very high flow, the branches lack sufficient capacity, and the entire delta floods.

Almost 80 percent of the delta's area (580,700 hectares) is located within Romania (459,000 hectares); the remaining portion (121,700 hectares) is in Ukrainian territory. Romanian geographers divide the delta into three zones: the lake complex (Lakes Razim, Colvita, Zmeica and Sinoe); the fluvial (river-deposited sediment) zone stretching from the lakes to the Letea-Caraorman-Crasnicol sand dunes, which originated as barrier islands around 3,500 B.C.E.; and the maritime zone, extending from the dunes to the Black Sea.

The delta contains a variety of habitats and species, many of which are seriously threatened throughout the rest of Europe, making it an area of unique ecological significance. Fisheries in the delta have long played a pivotal role in the Romanian economy. Many birds that migrate on European flyways stop at the delta. One of the delta's most distinctive habitats is its reed beds, the largest single area of reeds in Europe, covering 284,000 hectares in Romania alone.

Environmental stresses on delta wetlands have increased markedly in the past few decades. The volume of agricultural runoff and municipal waste flowing into the Danube River upstream from the delta has increased, and engineering works have reduced the river's ability to retain those effluents along its course. As the river has delivered greater loads of plant nutrients to the delta, the wetlands' ability to cycle these materials has been compromised by development. Efforts to exploit the delta for mechanized agriculture and aquaculture have reduced or eliminated natural water flow in many areas, severely disturbing aquatic ecosystems. The delta has become physically smaller as well, owing to severe coastal erosion.

Romanian scientists began documenting delta environmental problems more than a decade ago, but few data

Figure 2. Danube River runs through nine Central European nations and serves the watersheds of four more. The river offers access to the Black Sea for the land locked nations of Austria, Czechoslovakia and Hungary and is linked to the North Sea through the Rhine-Main Canal.

have been published outside Romania. As a first step toward making those data more generally available and developing new wetlands research and restoration efforts, a U.S.–Romanian collaboration was launched in 1991. Under the joint sponsorship of the U.S. and Romanian National Academies of Sciences, 10 U.S. and 11 Romanian ecologists, agricultural engineers, biogeochemists, biologists, entomologists, ichthyologists and restoration biologists lived and worked for three weeks on a river barge towed to various research locations in the delta. In the second phase of the exchange program in 1992, Romanian scientists visited the United States to continue research collaborations and proposal writing, and to examine analogous environmental problems in the Mississippi Delta. This article is one result of the collaboration.

The Roots of Environmental Decline

The complex and varied ecosystems of the Danube Delta have deteriorated dramatically over the past few decades. Studies have identified four primary causes of this decline: high nutrient loads in the Danube River as it enters the delta; hydrologic changes in the Danube River—primarily the elimination of the river's floodplain in the nine nations that abut it; hydrologic changes within the delta resulting from engineering works such as drainage programs, dikes, impoundments and channel dredging; and nutrient and pesticide

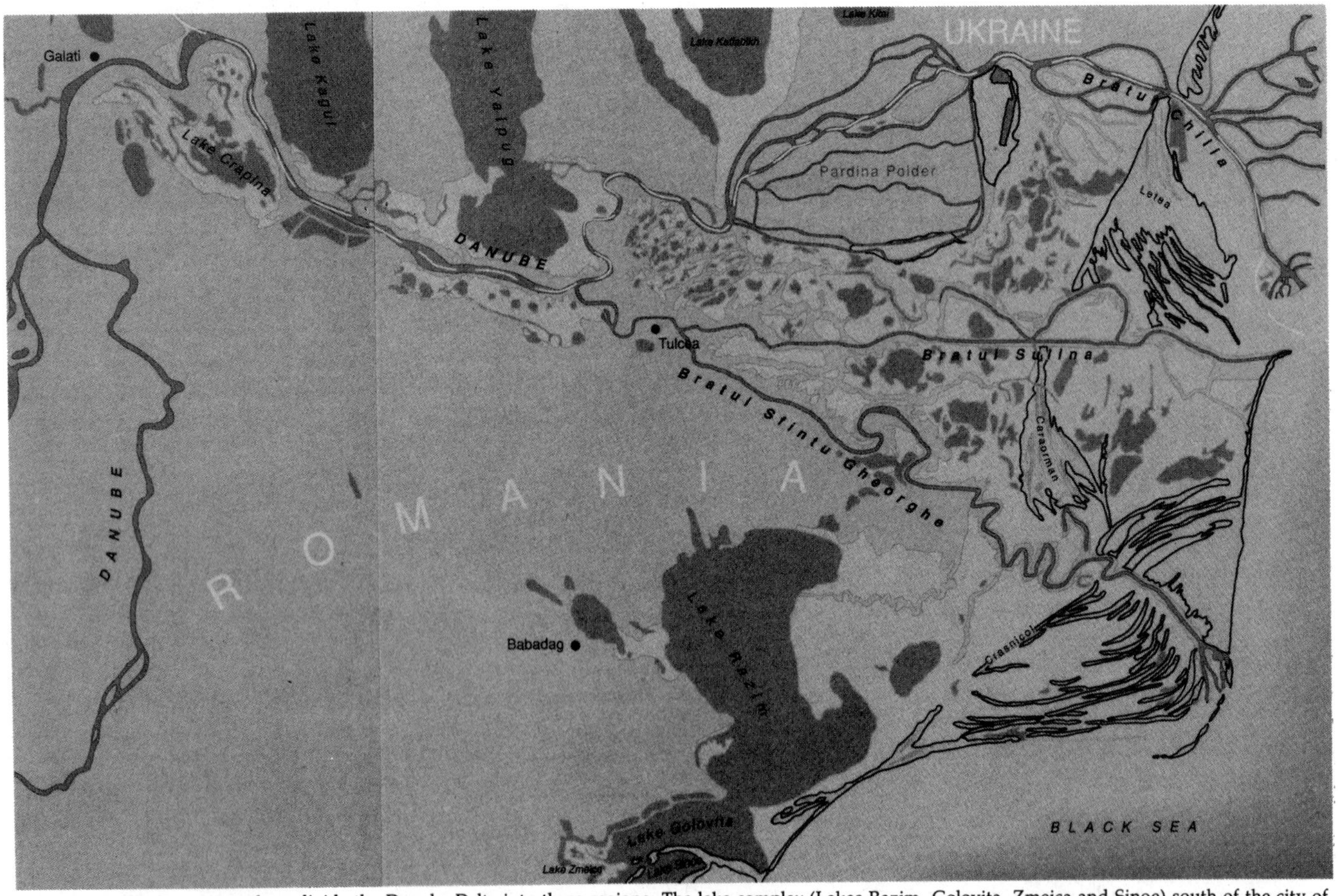

Figure 3. Romanian geographers divide the Danube Delta into three regions: The lake complex (Lakes Razim, Golovita, Zmeica and Sinoe) south of the city of Tulcea; the fluvial (river-deposited sediment) zone stretching from Tulcea and the lakes to the Letea-Caraorman-Crasnicol sand dunes (areas outlined in black), and the maritime zone, extending from the dunes to the Black Sea. North of the Danube River, in Ukraine, lie several lakes that have been hydrologically isolated from the Danube River by engineering works.

Figure 4. Broad beach-barrier complexes grow through the action of current and waves transporting sand southward along the Danube Delta's coastline. In addition to building subdeltas of the Danube branches, these beach-barrier islands are important breeding grounds for many species of birds, including terns and gulls. (Photo courtesy of the Cousteau Society, copyright 1991.)

Figure 5. Half of the Palearctic population of the white pelicans *(Pelecanus onocrotalus)* nests in the Danube Delta. The drainage of wetlands and the construction of dikes have destroyed much valuable habitat for these birds, which were common in the delta's Pardina region (Figure 7) until the area was drained. At the beginning of this century reported numbers were at least ten times higher than at present. (Photo courtesy of The Cousteau Society, copyright 1991.)

loading from agricultural activities inside the delta.

Pollutant loadings in the Danube River are very high. The human population within the river basin is roughly 86 million, about 12 percent of all Europeans, and many major cities and small towns along the river lack even primary sewage treatment facilities for domestic and industrial waste. Budapest, the capital of Hungary, for example, empties an estimated three-quarters of its sewage untreated into the Danube.

At the same time that contamination has increased in the Danube, hydrologic modifications along the river's course have compromised its capacity for self-purification. Numerous hydroelectric projects have sprung up along the river, bringing with them channel diversions and impoundments. Currently more than 30 dams span the Danube before it reaches the delta.

These and other engineering activities along the Danube's main channel have disconnected the river from its usual floodplain. Within the Romanian stretch of the river, embankments built between 1963 and 1967 reduced the floodplain by 290,000 hectares, which corresponds to a loss of 4.3 cubic kilometers of water-retention capacity. As a result, the Danube has lost a portion of its capacity to retain nutrients and heavy metals locally; they are now carried in the river to the delta.

Another negative effect of hydrologic modifications in the river system is coastal erosion. The natural accretion of sediment on the Black Sea coast near the mouths of the Danube branches has ended, and severe coastal erosion is taking place. The shoreline is receding at a rate of up to 17 meters per year, threatening tourism and the economic base of coastal cities such as Constanta. Coastal erosion is a natural and inevitable process as waves pound against the shoreline, but in the past it was offset by sediments dropped from the river at its outlets and pushed ashore by the Black Sea. Dam construction and other hydrologic changes have reduced the transport of sediments, disturbing the balance between erosion and accretion.

Exploitation of the Delta

Traditionally, the Danube Delta was the least-populated and least-developed region of Romania because of its harsh climate, its inaccessibility, and spring and winter floods. In 1983, however, the leadership of the former communist regime implemented a plan for the management and exploitation of the delta. This plan envisioned large-scale changes in the wetland that would make the region a center for agricultural production. In fact, however, the economic exploitation of the delta began much earlier and can be segmented into five distinct phases, of which former President Nicolae Ceausescu's program is only one.

The Romanian naturalist Grigore Antipa recognized the economic potential of the delta's natural reed beds (*Phragmites australis*) as far back as the turn of the century. Commercial exploitation of the reed beds for high-grade cellulose and for sugar for yeast production began in 1908 and continued at a sustainable pace until the mid-1950s. In 1958 a new cellulose factory doubled the demand for reeds from the delta, and an intensive program of reed cultivation was undertaken within specially constructed, diked polders (areas separated from normal water circulation by manmade embankments). Production reached a peak of 226,000 tons from 213,000 hectares in 1965, of which 136,000 hectares were in managed polders.

This high productivity was short-lived, however, as the reed harvest plummeted to 40,000 tons over the next decade, owing to a lack of seed regeneration in the polderized areas. Regeneration was hampered by the design of the polders, which limit water flow and exclude sediments and nutrients usually supplied to the reed beds by flood water. Reed marshes require a free flow of river water through them, especially during the crucial periods of plant development during spring and early summer. Standing water can produce soil conditions that are toxic to the reeds in their budding phase, when they depend on a slightly oxidized upper soil layer. Also, the poor nutritional status of the reeds provided the opportunity for other plants, such as reedmace (*Typha*), to replace them. As reed production failed in the polders, they were converted to aquaculture or drained for conventional agricultural production or for cellulose production from fast-growing trees.

Attempts to improve fisheries in the delta began as early as 1903, when two small river courses were excavated to bring Danube water to Lake Razim. Extensive further efforts to increase water circulation and oxygen content in smaller lakes were undertaken between 1930 and 1965. Fish-polder construction began in the 1950s, and the area dedicated to polders grew steadily until 1970, when aquaculture became the focus of the government's economic strategy in the delta. Between 1970 and 1990, the area in fish polders nearly doubled to 53,007 hectares.

Despite the commitment, aquaculture was not successful in the delta, and many polders were abandoned. Shortages of basic materials—such as feed for the fish and spare parts for the pumps—inadequately trained personnel and the introduction of fish species ill-suited to the delta contributed to low yields, which averaged 23,000 tons per year. During the same period, catches by local fishermen plunged from 7,000 to 9,000 tons per year to 4,000 to 5,000 tons

Figure 6. Intense competition from native reeds (*Phragmites australis*) is one of the main reasons that attempts to convert Danube Delta wetlands to conventional agricultural production have been unsuccessful. Here corn seedlings are being overwhelmed by reed shoots growing from residual rhizomes. Heavy applications of herbicides have failed to hold back the reeds. (Photo by George Vellidis.)

Figure 7. Dikes and drainage canals such as those in the Danube Delta's 28,000 hectare Pardina polder were used to convert wetlands to agricultural crop and forage production. The need for intensive fertilization and pesticide use has made such efforts at agriculture in the Danube Delta uneconomic, and the damage to sensitive delta ecosystems has been extensive. (Photo by George Vellidis.)

Figure 8. Traditional delta agriculture in the Danube region consists of small (up to one-quarter hectare) plots in silt deposits along river channels. This sustainable approach has supported small delta communities for centuries. (Photo by Catherine Pringle.)

per year. This decline has been attributed to the loss of fish habitat and the general deterioration of water quality in the delta. Although the Danube still accounts for 50 percent of freshwater fish production in Romania, the drop in catches has affected food supplies and the livelihood of the 500 to 600 fishermen who live in the delta.

Traditional small-scale agriculture has long been practiced in the delta. Subsistence farmers cultivate small (up to one-quarter hectare) plots carved from silt deposits along the smaller river channels around their villages. Large-scale agriculture came only recently. As fish and reed polders failed, they were drained and converted to forestry or conventional mechanized agriculture as part of the complex plan for the economic development of the delta. These plots range from 2,800 to 28,000 hectares, and the primary crops are barley, corn, wheat, flax and sunflowers (for oil) and various fruits. With the arrival of mechanized agriculture, the amount of land under cultivation grew tremendously. In 1970, 35,355 hectares (7.7 percent of the delta) were in production; by 1990 the area had grown to 61,604 hectares (13.4 percent of the area). Under former President Ceausescu's regime, an unsuccessful attempt was made to turn 100,000 hectares of the delta into farmland.

The Danube Delta is not ideally suited to large-scale, intensive agriculture. Production from polders is hindered by low rainfall, sandy soils, dropping water tables from lack of replenishment, soil salinization from evaporation, wind erosion, soil acidification, peat fires and intense competition from reeds that grow from residual rhizomes and seed banks in the soil. Overcoming these limitations has required energy-intensive practices that demand fuel for mechanical cultivation, planting, harvesting and irrigation and heavy use of fertilizers and pesticides. Because of severe shortages of these materials, as well as what appears to be a conscious decision by the post-communist government to reduce the intensity of agriculture in the delta, large-scale agriculture there faces an uncertain future.

From 1990 to 1991 the delta area devoted to intensive agricultural production dropped from 38,394 hectares to 36,800 hectares. Since the fall of the Ceausescu government in 1989, large tracts are being converted to silviculture, and others are being completely abandoned. Production seems to be shifting back toward traditional labor-intensive practices, but the economic and environmental effects of these changes have not been quantified.

The Ukrainian portions of the Danube Delta have also seen economic-

Figure 9. Large-scale aquaculture became the goal of the Romanian government's plans for the Danube Delta beginning in 1970. Despite a major commitment to construction of new polders, the effort was a failure, largely because of shortages of fish feed and fuels to run equipment. Shown here is an abandoned aquaculture operation in a polder. (Photo by Catherine Pringle.)

development efforts that have changed hydrology and had detrimental effects on water quality. The four largest Danubian lakes north of the Chilia Channel (Kagul, Yalpug, Katlabikh and Kitai) originated as lagoons of the Danube River. They were cut off from the river between 1940 and 1960 by a series of dams constructed primarily to eliminate seasonal water-level fluctuations that limited irrigation supplies to the nearby Odessky region.

As a consequence, annual water exchange between the lakes and the river is now one-third to one-half what it was, causing major increases in salinity and other forms of mineralization. Scientists have documented a dramatic deterioration of floral and faunal habitats over the past decade. Nutrient loads from agricultural activity in the lakes' watersheds have led to high levels of eutrophication, or lake enrichment. In a eutrophic lake a few plant and animal species become dominant, and the oxygen content of subsurface waters may drop to levels lethal to aquatic life. This, combined with influxes of agricultural chemicals and heavy metals from industrial waste, has made the water in three of the four lakes unsuitable for human consumption. It can be used for irrigation only after extensive and expensive treatment. Despite these problems, agricultural and industrial development has intensified in the surrounding watersheds over the past decade.

The Delta Today

Increasing nutrient, heavy-metal and pesticide inputs into the Danube and its delta, in combination with changes in surface water flow and sediment loading, have increased the eutrophication and turbidity of the water serving the delta's aquatic ecosystems. This degradation of water quality has led to reductions in biodiversity, major shifts in the structure of ecosystem primary productivity—from rooted aquatic plants to phytoplankton (floating algae)—and large economic losses from declining fish yields.

Anthropogenically produced loads of nitrogen and phosphorus in the Danube River have increased steadily since 1980. Chemical oxygen demand (a measure of the potential for oxidizing reactions to use up the dissolved oxygen in water) has increased sharply. A corresponding increase in hydrogen-sulfide concentration indicates the existence of anaerobic conditions in river sediments.

Over the past decade large influxes of nitrogen and phosphorus into the delta have overwhelmed its ability to cycle these plant nutrients, producing eutrophic or polluted conditions in

Figure 10. Fish harvests by the 500 to 600 Danube Delta fishermen who use traditional methods dropped by nearly half, severely affecting their livelihood, at the same time that aquaculture efforts failed in the delta. (Photo by Catherine Pringle.)

Figure 11. Intense algal blooms have become common in the Danube Delta as nutrient loads have increased over the past two decades. These and other threats to water quality in delta wetlands and lakes have accompanied significant declines in populations of rooted plants, shellfish and fish. (Photo courtesy of The Cousteau Society, copyright 1991.)

Figure 12. Feral livestock often disturb bird-nesting areas along the Black Sea. In the background, erosion-control engineering works have been installed to help slow the recession of the coastline, which is eroding as rapidly as 17 meters per year. (Photo by Catherine Pringle.)

many lakes and associated nuisance blooms of algae. These blooms deplete oxygen, typically consist of algal species unsuitable as food sources for fish, and shade out submerged rooted plants that are important habitat for species such as pike.

Within the delta, regular sampling along the Sulina Branch shows little reduction in nutrient, metal and pesticide concentrations compared to the Danube River above it. This reflects the fact that channels such as the Sulina, which have been straightened and dredged, are bypassing the filtering capacity of the wetlands. Instead, the branches have become conduits for the delivery of concentrated pollutants to the Black Sea. Levels of dissolved nitrogen and phosphorus in lakes and secondary channels of the delta are lower than those measured in the main channels but have been increasing at the same rate over the past 10 to 20 years. Already those levels are well above the threshold for algal growth and for the decline of larger aquatic plants.

Studies indicate that the delta's waters are in an advanced state of eutrophication. Most lakes and secondary channels show a marked decrease in rooted aquatic-plant density and an increase in algal blooms—primarily blue-green algae (Cyanophyta)—over the past decade. The diversity of bottom-dwelling macroinvertebrates such as shellfish has dropped dramatically over the same period, and in one lake, numbers of midge larvae (Chironomidae) have decreased by 90 percent. Although it is difficult to assess the effects of pesticides on the delta ecosystem, data suggest that the aquatic food web is affected by pesticide runoff from sources both inside the delta and upstream in the Danube River. Residues of the insecticides HCH (also known as lindane) and DDT are present at significant levels in polder soils in the delta, and in the sediment, plankton and fish of delta lakes.

The Danube Delta supports large populations of bird species that are generally widespread across Europe. More than 160 bird species breed in the delta, including pelicans, herons, ibises and terns. The drainage of wetlands, river channelization, impoundments, pollution and feral livestock have degraded the habitat quality to the point where bird populations are a fraction of their historical numbers.

Beyond the delta, the eutrophication of the Danube has been responsible, at least in part, for declining water quality in the Black Sea. The Sea is currently in a very eutrophic state and was described as being "within an inch of falling into a coma" by specialists who attended the Ecoforum Peace Conference in Moscow in 1990. Its waters are highly stratified, and the chemocline (the depth below which water is stagnant and very low in dissolved oxygen) has risen from 170 meters to 110 meters below the surface over the past few years. Because few fish can live below the chemocline, its rise has destroyed valuable fisheries.

The Outlook for Improvement

There is some hope that the rate of environmental degradation in the delta is easing. Political changes in Romania following the revolution of 1989 have given the Romanian portion of the delta a reprieve. In February 1990 President Ion Iliescu decreed a halt to all agricultural and hydrologic development in the delta, and the area was made a Biosphere Reserve by national decree in August 1990. More than 50 percent of the reserve was declared a World Heritage Site by the United Nations Educational, Scientific and Cultural Organization (UNESCO) in late 1991. As a result, the surface area of the delta within Romania devoted to agriculture is no longer increasing. Furthermore, pesticide use is restricted through the Danube Delta Biosphere Reserve Authority, a management and research unit established in 1990 by the Ministry of Environment.

Upstream from the delta, hydroelectric projects now under construction, such as the Bos-Nagymaros dam, have proved highly controversial and have been delayed because of public concern about deleterious environmental effects. Measures to reduce the introduction of untreated waste and agricultural runoff to the Danube River and to restore its floodplains, however, have been limited. In 1985 the nine nations through which the Danube River passes signed the Bucharest Declaration, an agreement to cooperate on water management and pollution control, but socioeconomic and political problems in the nations of the Danube basin have stifled progress.

Although it is clear that water-quality issues in the entire Danube River watershed must eventually be addressed if the environmental decline of the delta is to be reversed, current efforts focus on the more practical matter of restoring aquatic ecosystems within the delta itself.

The World Bank, through the Global Environment Facility (GEF), has recently approved an advance to provide technical assistance and equipment to the Romanian government to prepare for a project on biodiversity conservation in the delta. The $4.2 million (U.S.) project, Danube Delta Biodiversity, will support local authorities in their efforts to manage the delta as an ecological system, including the development of environmentally sustainable economic activities such as fisheries, small-scale agriculture and tourism. Divided into Romanian and Ukrainian subprojects, these efforts will be connected to two regional GEF projects, Environmental Problems of the Danube River Basin, and the Black Sea Environmental Program.

Figure 13. Abandoned aquaculture and sand-mining and processing complexes at Caraorman in the Danube Delta demonstrate the degree to which delta wetlands geography has been changed by human activities. More than 23,000 hectares of fish polders have been constructed in the delta since 1970. (Photo courtesy of The Cousteau Society, copyright 1991.)

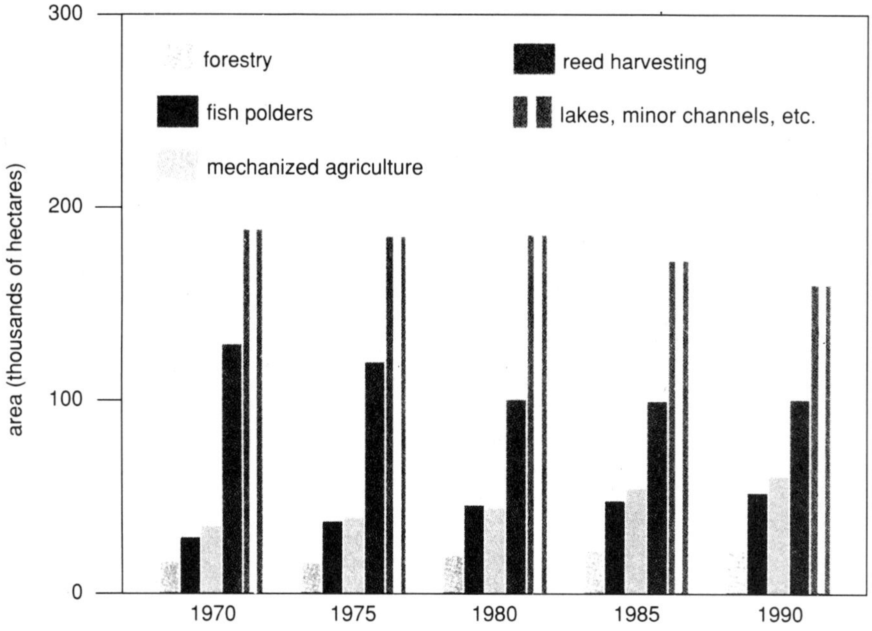

Figure 14. Changing patterns of land use over the last two decades show clearly the conversion of lakes and minor channels in the Danube Delta to agricultural and aquacultural uses. Increased forestry is largely in abandoned reed polders.

One goal of the preparation phase of the Romanian phase of the biodiversity project is to identify two medium-scale (100 to 500 hectares) restoration sites for converting deserted agricultural polders or fish ponds into wetlands. Plans will also include a program to monitor changes in the rehabilitated areas and the surrounding environment.

Another important goal of the project's preparation phase will be to increase the control of human activities in the delta. The Danube Delta Ecological Guards (Corps) was established in November 1990 to protect the Danube Delta Biosphere Reserve. The Corps is responsible for enforcing harvest regulations, eradicating domestic and feral animals from protected areas, excluding people from sensitive bird-nesting areas and educating the people who live in the delta about environmental concerns. Unfortunately, there is little money to support this fledgling program. Thus cadets are under-trained, under-equipped and underpaid. The World Wildlife Fund International has provided some basic equipment for the Corps, but the most crucial need is financial support to train and pay the wages of cadets, who currently earn the equivalent of only $20 per month.

Research into Wetlands Restoration

Local restoration is crucial for delta rehabilitation. Both the Romanian government and local inhabitants have begun to acknowledge that large-scale agricultural production in most of the polderized areas is not sustainable and that restoring such areas to wetlands will have substantial benefits. Research has shown that drained wetlands in the delta are probably the major cause of both its inability to handle nutrient loads and its declining fisheries. These findings prompted Marin Gomoiu, governor of the Danube Delta Biosphere Reserve, to give high priority to restoration of reed beds in selected areas.

The ideal way to return polderized land to a condition suitable for natural reed beds would be to raze completely the retaining dikes, restoring original water depths and flow patterns. In reality, however, fiscal constraints will drive restoration efforts, and polder dikes likely will be breached in strategic locations to establish the necessary hydrologic conditions. High flow rates will require more openings in the dikes and significantly larger budgets. Water-depth regulation may require supplementary excavation or water-level control structures to accommodate elevation changes from earth moving or soil subsidence.

Because the science of wetland creation and restoration is in an early stage of development, the knowledge necessary to make informed management decisions is not currently available. To avoid the mistakes of the past, therefore, it is important that we gain fundamental information about restoration before attempting the large-scale reconversion of polders to wetlands. The best way to acquire such information is through experiments that allow manipulation of key environmental variables.

The technical problems of restoring reed beds converted to agricultural land are not insurmountable. Such areas generally retain their seed banks, and the dispersal of plant species is facilitated by waterfowl that use these wetlands. As long as there are no other severe disturbances, reed beds recover naturally once crop planting stops and the natural water flows are restored. It is not known, however, which hydrologic regime will most effectively bring about rapid establishment of highly productive reed stands; natural reed stands in the delta have many natural hydrologic conditions.

Scientists of the Danube Delta Research Group, consisting of the 21 participants of the 1991 and 1992 workshops sponsored by the U.S. and Romanian National Academies of Sciences, have proposed a dual experimental approach for determining feasible restoration techniques for drained lands currently in unsustainable agricultural production.

The first approach, currently being implemented by scientists from the Danube Delta Research Institute, involves flooding selected small polders (4.9 hectares of agricultural polders and 10.2 hectares of fish polders) by breaching the retaining dikes in one or two locations without any other hydrologic modification. Over the next two to three years, periodic measurements will be made to determine the recovery of wetland functions.

The second approach, a rigorous experimental study by Romanian and U.S. scientists, is still in the formative stage. Experimental plots will be established in a series of large earthen basins, and various water depths and flow-through velocities will be tested. In addition, some elements of the natural hydrologic cycle will be replicated within the experimental basins. Nonfloating reed beds in the delta are typically inundated for several months each year when the river rises from mid-April through the first week of June and again from mid-November through the first week of December. During the spring flood—

which lasts longer and has greater volume, making it more important for reed growth and regeneration—the Danube River discharges a third of its annual flow.

The success of restoration efforts will be assessed with intensive water-quality, soil, vegetation and aquatic-biota sampling. To better understand how the quality of Danube River water influences restoration success, simplified nutrient budgets will be developed by estimating, based on collected data, annual nutrient inputs, outputs and sinks for each basin. Results from both studies will be used to establish guidelines for the successful implementation of the large-scale restoration projects anticipated in the Danube Delta Biosphere Reserve in the coming years.

Restoration will provide benefits at both the population and ecosystem levels. At the population level, flora and fauna that require a wetland habitat will be re-established. Many of these species—reeds, for example—have economic value. At the ecosystem level, restored wetlands will provide spawning and nursery habitat for fish and shellfish, which will support commercial, recreational and subsistence fisheries in the delta and in the Black Sea.

Restoring Danube Delta wetlands and associated ecosystems is a necessary first step toward achieving environmental security for the entire Danube Basin. By showing that environmental restoration can provide direct and indirect economic, environmental and social benefits—not only to the delta but also to the nine nations the Danube River runs through, as well as other nations dependent on the Black Sea for fisheries, tourism and other economic activities—it may provide the catalyst that leads regions to tackle environmental problems on an ecological, rather than a national, scale.

Acknowledgements

The authors gratefully acknowledge the support of the U.S. National Academy of Sciences and the Romanian Academy of Sciences and the participation of other members of the Danube Delta Research Group in the U.S.–Romanian workshop: A. Chiorascu, R. Dorel, I. Gheorghe, C. Griffin, L. Guta, B. Harvey, B. Howes, J. Hanganu, D. Kogalniceanu, K. Lajtha, B. McKee, V. Mitache, M. Palmer, L. Platica, G. Risnoveanu, G. Ruzsa, M. Staras, A. Zale and M. Zamfir. We would like to extend special thanks to Stephen Deets of the National Research Council's Office of Central and Eastern European Affairs, who played a key role in facilitating and organizing both phases of the U.S.–Romanian Young Investigators Program.

Bibliography

Bacalbaca-Dobrovici, N., C. Nicolau and M. Nitu. 1990. Conception, evolution on fisheries hydraulic management of the Danube Delta. Management of freshwater fisheries. In: *Proceedings of a Symposium Organized by the European Inland Fisheries Advisory Committee*, Goteborg, Sweden, 31 May–3 June 1988. PUDOC, Wageningen. pp. 447–461.

Botnariuc, N., Gh. Ignat, I. Diaconu and A Vadineanu. 1987. L'evolution de l'etat trophique des ecosystems aquatiques caracteristiques du Delta du Danube. 5. La structure et la dynamique de la faune benthonique. *Revue Roumaine del Biologie Animale* 32(2):121–127.

Calinescu, M., and V. Tismaneanu. 1991 The 1989 revolution and Romania's future. *Problems of Communism*. 40:42–59.

Cristofor, S. 1987. L'evolution de l'etat trophique des ecosystems aquatiques caracteristiques du Delta du Danube. 6. Responses de la vegetation submerse en fonction de la reserve de nutrients et du regime hydrolique. *Revue Roumaine de Biologie Animale. 32(2):129-138.*

Fekete, G. 1967. Wirtschaftliche Bedeutung der Donau: Schiffahrt. In: *Liepolt* vol. IV, pp. 49-59.

Fossi, C., S. Focardi, C. Leonzio and A. Renzoni. 1984. Trace metals and chlorinated hydrocarbons in bird eggs from the Danube Delta. *Environmental Conservation* 11:345–350.

Gastescu, P., and B. Driga. 1983. Les caracteristiques du regime hydrique du Danube a son embouchure dans la Mer Noire. *Revue Roumaine Geologie Geophys. Geographie** 25:55–60.

Griffin, C., et al. 1991. *Scientific Report of the U.S. Romania Summer Program for Young Investigators in Ecology and Environmental Sciences.* Internal report of the National Academy of Sciences.

Haas, P.M. 1990. *Saving the Mediterranean: The Politics of International Environmental Cooperation.* New York: Columbia University Press.

Ignat, Gh., A. Vaadineanu and N. Botnariuc. 1986. Role of Chironomus plumonus depending on environmental fluctuations in the Danube Delta. *Hidrobiologia* (Bucharest) 19:221–226.

International Union for the Conservation of Nature and Natural Resources. 1991. *Report on the Status of the Danube Delta.* IUCN Mission 17–27 September 1990.

Kusler, J. A., and M. E. Kentula. 1990. *Wetland Creation and Restoration: The Status of the Science.* Covelo, Calif.: Island Press.

Murray, J. W., H. W. Jannasch, S. Honjo, R. F. Anderson, W. S. Reegurgh, Z. Top, G. E. Friederich, L. A. Codispoti and E. Izdar. 1989. Unexpected changes in the oxic-anoxic interface in the Black Sea. *Nature* 338:411–413.

National Research Council. 1992. *Restoration of Aquatic Systems.* Washington: National Academy Press.

Perczel, K., and G. Libik. 1989. Environmental effects of the dam system on the Danube at Bos-Nagymaros. *Ambio* 18:247–249.

Pringle, C.M. 1991. U.S.–Romanian environmental reconnaissance of the Danube Delta. *Conservation Biology* 5:441–445.

Rich, V. 1989. Danube neighbour's travails. *Nature* 341:377.

Rudescu, L., C. Niculescu and I. P. Chivu. 1965. *Monografia Stufului din Delta Dunarii.* Editura Academiei Republicii Socialiste Romania.

Schweitzer, G. E. 1991. The future of scientific research in Eastern Europe. *Technology in Society* 13:39–51.

Vadineanu, A., and S. Cristofor. 1987. L'evolution de l'etat trophique des ecosystemes aquatiques caracteristiques du delta du Danube. 1. Le regime hydrologique, la transparence secchi et la reserve de phosphore et d'azote. *Revue Roumaine del Biologie Animale* 32(2):83–91.

Westing, A. H. 1989. Environmental security for the Danube basin. *Envirorimental Conservation* 16:323–329.

AN ACTION Plan TO Clean UP THE Baltic

Janusz Kindler and Stephen F. Lintner

Janusz Kindler served as vice chairman of the Helsinki Commission's ad hoc high-level task force and is a professor of water and environmental systems at the Warsaw Technical University in Poland. He is currently a water resources planning specialist at the World Bank in Washington, D.C. Stephen F. Lintner served as the World Bank's representative to the Helsinki Commission's ad hoc high-level task force and is currently its representative to the Programme Implementation Task Force. He is also a senior environmental specialist at the World Bank. The views presented in the article are solely those of the authors and should not be attributed to the World Bank or the Helsinki Commission.

The largest body of brackish water in the world, the Baltic Sea, has severe problems of water pollution and environmental degradation.[1] As late as 1950, the Baltic Sea was still regarded as environmentally "healthy." Since that time, however, the situation has changed dramatically. In spite of numerous protective efforts, the Baltic Sea's rich biodiversity is threatened by environmental pollution that could cause irreversible damage to a sea that is an important source of economic activity and recreation for more than 80 million people who live along its coast and within its catchment area.

The Baltic Sea catchment area, or drainage basin, is home to 14 nations (see Figure 1). Nine of them share the Baltic's coastline: Sweden and Finland to the north; Russia, Estonia, Latvia, and Lithuania to the east; Poland to the south; and Germany and Denmark to the west. The catchment area also includes parts of Belarus, Norway, Ukraine, the Slovak Republic, and the Czech Republic because some of the rivers flowing into the Baltic find their sources there. Many of these countries are undergoing dramatic political, economic, and social changes. As the division of Europe into Western and Eastern blocs vanishes and the countries in the eastern and southern Baltic region lose their peripheral position, the region has a chance of regaining its historical position as one of the major crossroads of economic exchange, as in the time of the Hanseatic League—a mercantile organization of towns along the Baltic Sea and the North Sea from the 13th through 18th centuries that allowed trade to flow across the Baltic Sea without political obstacles. Certainly, such present cooperation as the recent establishment of the Union of the Baltic Cities and the Baltic Council of Ministers of Foreign Affairs confirms this possibility (see box "Union of the Baltic Cities").

The Baltic Sea is important in several ways. Its coast is a popular vacation area; therefore, the demand for tourist and recreation services is very high. The coastal areas also serve as spawning, nursery, and feeding grounds for several species of marine and freshwater fish. Marine species such as herring, sprat, and cod dominate in open waters, and both marine and freshwater species inhabit coastal areas. The value of the catches, which amounts today to about 540 million European currency units (ECU) per year, is an indication of the considerable economic importance of the Baltic fishery. But above all, the Baltic Sea has an environmental significance

From *Environment*, Vol. 35, No. 8, October 1993, pp. 7-15, 28-31. Reprinted with permission of the Helen Dwight Reid Educational Foundation. Published by Heldref Publications, 1319 Eighteenth Street, NW, Washington, DC 20036-1802. © 1993.

of its own: It is a shared heritage to be preserved and managed as a common resource.

Causes of Degradation

The Baltic Sea has a total surface area of 415 square kilometers and is naturally vulnerable to pollution because of its semi-closed character and particular hydrography. The link with the North Sea is very narrow, with the shallowest sill being only 18 meters deep. Because of this narrow link, the Baltic Sea is dominated by freshwater inputs. Vertical variations in salinity cause permanent stratification, hampering the exchange of oxygen in the deeper parts of the sea. In some years, as much as 100,000 square kilometers, close to one-fourth of the whole sea, approaches "dead bottom" conditions.

The natural vulnerability of the Baltic Sea has been seriously aggravated by the destruction of its wetlands, particularly in the western parts of the catchment area. During the 19th century, coastal wetlands were ditched and drained to meet the demands of expanding agriculture. Wetlands have also been dredged or filled to make room for urban and industrial developments, including harbors. The consequences of these activities were not readily visible until the environmental situation in the Baltic Sea had further deteriorated.

Pollution reaches the Baltic Sea by a wide diversity of pathways. Diffuse "nonpoint" sources include airborne emissions and agricultural runoff, while point-source pollution from urban areas and industry—including untreated sewage from 30 million people, wastewater from pulp-and-paper and other industries, toxic substances, and heavy metals—is either directly discharged into the sea or carried into it by rivers. This devastating influx can be attributed to a host of different factors, including economic inefficiency, poor legislation, lack of enforcement, and institutional weaknesses. In general, however, Denmark, Finland, Norway, Sweden, and the western federal states of Germany present a different set of problems than do the once centrally planned economies. In the former, municipal and industrial pollution loads have been significantly reduced over the last few decades, and product control measures have reduced the use of hazardous compounds. There is, however, still scope for improved control in some industries, such as pulp-and-paper. The total farming area in these countries is much smaller than in other parts of the basin, but intensive agricultural practices involve high use of chemicals, and better policies are needed to control nutrient releases.

STEPHEN F. LINTNER

Forty percent of the arable land in the Baltic's catchment is in Poland, where small family farms like this one predominate.

In the countries that used to have centrally planned economies, pollution loads from various sources are still heavy although declining somewhat because of new control measures and the overall slowdown of economic activities in the past few years. In the past, the economic structure of these countries became skewed toward heavy industry dominated by large, state-owned monopolies. These industries used as much as two to three times more water and energy per unit of output than did similar industries in other countries of the basin. The input intensity and high concentration of industries (especially in such large industrial basins as Upper Silesia in Poland and Ostrava in the Czech Republic), coupled with inadequate wastewater treatment and limited emission control, resulted in very high levels of water and air pollution as well as large quantities of solid wastes.

The principal pollution sources for the Baltic Sea are municipalities, industries, and agriculture that are located not only on the coast but deep in the interior as well.

Municipalities

In the formerly centrally planned economies, most of the water bodies, such as rivers, natural and man-made lakes, and groundwater aquifers, receive excessive amounts of untreated or insufficiently treated municipal wastewater. Existing facilities, including sewer systems and treatment plants, are generally inadequate, overloaded, and poorly maintained and operated. Moreover, large quantities of highly toxic industrial wastewater and chemical liquid wastes are discharged into the municipal sewage systems. For example, in the late 1980s, the city of St. Petersburg was responsible for

FIGURE 1. The Baltic Sea catchment.

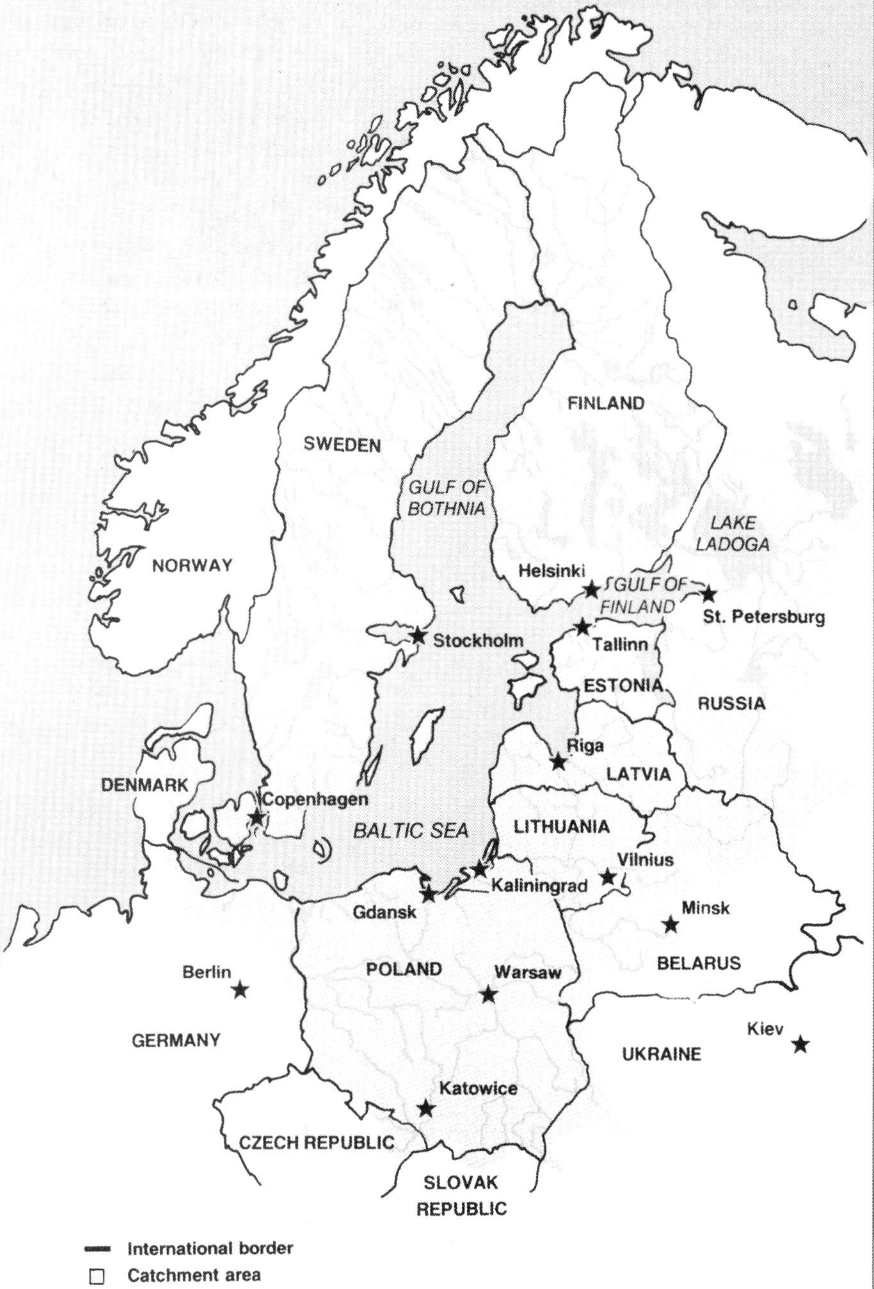

SOURCE: Helsinki Commission, The Baltic Sea Joint Comprehensive Environmental Action Programme, Helsinki, 1993.

about 90 percent of all copper and chromium discharged into the Gulf of Finland. Pretreatment of industrial effluent is generally insufficient for biological treatment processes to operate efficiently. Without either pretreatment or the separation of noxious industrial wastes from household sewage, serious problems with sludge disposal also arise. Another important source of water pollution, and one which is attracting increasing attention, is storm water runoff from urban areas.

In the Nordic countries and in the western states of Germany, there have been substantial reductions in the pollution load discharged by municipalities during the last 20 years. The load of organic substances has been reduced from 50 to 5 percent and that of phosphorous from 25 to 10 percent of the amount generated by municipalities. For example, in Sweden and Finland, the average reduction efficiency for biochemical oxygen demand (BOD) and phosphorus in municipal sewage treatment plants exceeds 90 percent.

Industries

Industrial restructuring is taking place in the formerly centrally planned economies, but it will take many years for the environmental effects of this process to become more visible. For the time being, industry continues to play a significant role in the discharge of polluting substances directly into the sea and inland waters. Metallurgical and chemical industries discharge a variety of inorganic wastes that affect water in diverse ways, including rendering it completely toxic. Synthetic chemical production creates new and more exotic types of waste. Many technologies are obsolete, the most dramatic examples being the paper mills in Kaliningrad, Russia, that were built at the end of the 19th century. Wastewater treatment installations typically suffer from the same problems as sewage treatment plants—insufficiency, overloading, and poor operation and maintenance.

The pulp-and-paper industry, in particular, plays a significant role in the discharge of oxygen-consuming, nutrient-rich, and slowly degradable substances into the sea and river waters in the Baltic region. Most of the old mills are located in the Karelian, St. Petersburg, and Kaliningrad regions of Russia, Estonia, Latvia, Lithuania, and Poland. In Sweden and Finland, pulp-and-paper mills are located primarily in the catchments of the Bothnian Sea, Bothnian Bay, and the Gulf of Finland. Some of the mills already have closed circulation of process water in chemical bleaching; intensive research and development seeks to find further substitutes for chlorine- and sulfur-containing chemicals.

In the Baltic's catchment area, about 400 million tons of solid waste

STEPHEN F. LINTNER

Catches of the Baltic's marine and freshwater fish are important to the economy of Estonia and its neighbors.

of industrial and municipal origin are generated annually. In Denmark, Finland, Sweden, and the western states of Germany, hazardous wastes are handled separately from both household and regular industrial waste and are properly treated. Unfortunately, this is not the case in the remaining countries of the region, where thousands of poorly maintained or uncontrolled dumping sites contribute significantly to contamination of local aquifers, lakes, rivers, and ultimately the Baltic Sea. The lack of separation of various kinds of wastes is a major problem. Furthermore, the effects of past practices are monumental. For example, landfill and dumping sites around St. Petersburg contain about 200 million tons of mineral waste. In Poland, accumulated solid waste is estimated at 1,500 million tons.

Agriculture

Important agricultural areas are located in Russia, Estonia, Latvia, Lithuania, and Poland, with the latter accounting for about 40 percent, or 19.5 million hectares, of the arable land in the catchment. Except in Poland, large, formerly state-owned farms dominate; their average size is more than 5,000 hectares. In Poland, the ownership structure is different; about 80 percent of agricultural land is in small family farms with an average size of about 5 hectares (although the number of large private farms is growing).

Agriculture in Denmark and southern Sweden relies quite heavily on fertilizers. Farming operations in the Danish part of the Belt Sea catchment, which has a total area of about 12,400 square kilometers, annually discharge about 30,000 tons of nitrogen into the sea, while operations in the much larger Vistula River basin, whose 166,000 square kilometers cover two-thirds of Poland and small portions of Belarus, the Slovak Republic, and Ukraine, discharge some 50,000 tons. As agriculture intensifies in Poland and other formerly communist countries, the overuse of chemical fertilizers and pesticides must be avoided and alternatives developed. Otherwise, nutrient loading of the Baltic Sea will increase dramatically.

At present, inputs of nitrogen and phosphorus from agriculture contribute significantly to the overall nutrient load of the Baltic Sea. They originate from ammonia volatilization, nitrogen leaching (nitrate and organic nitrogen), phosphorus leaching, soil erosion, and the discharge of farm wastes, such as effluents from animal houses, manure storage, and silage heaps. Animal manures produced not only in the Baltic catchment but also in the North Sea catchment in Germany, Belgium, the Netherlands, Luxembourg, and France release ammonia into the atmosphere that is eventually deposited in the Baltic Sea. Nitrate leaching is mainly the result of inadequate handling and inefficient use of commercial fertilizers. Although livestock density is generally low, large animal farms—for example, hog farms with 100,000 to 150,000 animals—cause the most serious and difficult problems in handling animal manure.

A Framework for Regional Action

The Baltic Sea's environmental problems have been the concern of the surrounding countries for several decades. In 1974, inspired by the 1972 UN Conference on the Human Environment, the governments of the region signed the Baltic Marine Environment Protection Convention, known as the Helsinki convention. Its implementation began immediately on a provisional basis, and the convention formally entered into force in May 1980. The Helsinki Commission (HELCOM) is the steering agency for the convention. Unfortunately, until the relatively recent political changes in the Baltic region, the activities of HELCOM concentrated on the open sea. As long as the coastline was shared by countries belonging to different military blocs, the coastal waters were largely inaccessible, and only extremely limited data on land-based pollution sources were available.

About 15 years after signing the initial Helsinki convention and as soon as the political situation in the region had changed, the prime ministers of Poland and Sweden invited their colleagues from the other countries in the Baltic catchment to a conference held in Ronneby, Sweden, in September 1990. The participants at the Ronneby conference adopted the first Baltic Sea Declaration, which sets out a number of principles and priority actions necessary to enhance the Baltic environment. Most importantly, the conference signaled the launching of a concrete effort to "assure the ecological restoration of the Baltic Sea, ensuring the possibility of self-restoration of the marine environment and preservation of its ecological balance."[2] That effort is the Baltic Sea Joint Comprehensive Environmental Action Programme. The program was developed from 1990 to 1992 by a HELCOM ad hoc high-level task force (HLTF), which was a joint endeavor of the Baltic Sea countries (Denmark, Estonia, Finland, Germany, Latvia, Lithuania, Poland, Russia, and Sweden), the countries of the catchment area (Belarus, the Czech

STEPHEN F. LINTNER

The obsolete technologies used in many industries in the formerly communist countries, such as this sulfur mine in Poland, have helped pollute the Baltic.

Republic, the Slovak Republic, Norway, and Ukraine), the Commission of the European Communities, and four international financial institutions (European Investment Bank, European Bank for Reconstruction and Development, Nordic Investment Bank, and World Bank). Also invited to attend HLTF meetings were several organizations that acted as observers, including the International Baltic Sea Fisheries Commission, the Coalition Clean Baltic, Greenpeace, and the World Wide Fund for Nature. The task force used a variety of studies and sources of information to develop the program, including national plans prepared by all Baltic countries and eight major prefeasibility studies covering the eastern, southern, and southwestern parts of the catchment.[3] The prefeasibility studies and special topical studies[4] were financed by grants totaling 5 million ECU from the Commission of the European Communities, the governments of Denmark, Finland, Germany, Norway, and Sweden, the Nordic Project Export Fund, and Sweden's World Wide Fund for Nature. In April 1992 in Helsinki, the Diplomatic Conference of Ministers of the Environment revised the 1974 Helsinki convention and approved the Baltic Sea Joint Comprehensive Environmental Action Programme.

The Joint Comprehensive Programme

Nearly 20 years of scientific work by HELCOM committees and studies conducted for the HELCOM task force have followed ecological developments in the Baltic Sea catchment. This preparatory work for the program concluded that preventive and curative actions are necessary in all of the countries in the catchment to reduce the pollution load reaching the sea. Some of these actions are already under way: Some state-owned enterprises with polluting production activities have shut down; wastewater treatment plants are planned or partly constructed; new protected areas have been created; and environmental controls have been strengthened. These ongoing activities require support; in particular, new environmental policies and pollution control programs should be formulated and adopted in the formerly Eastern-bloc economies.

The Strategy

The underlying strategy of the Baltic Sea Joint Comprehensive Environmental Action Programme consists of actions by each concerned government to carry out needed policy and regulatory reforms; to build capacity; and to invest in controlling pollution from point and nonpoint sources, safely disposing of or reducing the generation of waste, and conserving ecologically sensitive and economically valuable areas. To complement these activities, the program also includes elements to support applied research, environmental awareness, and environmental education. These actions will be phased in to keep pace with the gradually increasing capacity to raise funds and pay for the recurrent costs of environmental management in the transforming economies. For the first few years, emphasis will be placed on creating the enabling policymaking environment and institutional arrangements, on making limited investments in the highest priority projects, including pilot and demonstration projects, and on promoting private investment and initiative through concessions and incentives. Environmental investment programs in the northern and western parts of the region are also an integral part of the joint comprehensive program and are expected to be financed from local resources.

Program Components

The program consists of six components that comprise broad and distinct areas of action. The first component is a set of policy, legal, and regulatory reforms that establish a long-term environmental management framework in each country, including macroeconomic policies and incentives; financial facilities, policies, and controls; environmental standards and laws; and the appropriate systems for monitoring and enforcing these laws. To accomplish these goals, the program will encourage participating

UNION OF THE BALTIC CITIES

By Piotr Krzyzanowski

For hundreds of years, people living by the Baltic Sea were unified by their common work—fishing. Although the importance of this industry has diminished in the region, the spirit of the oldest traditions of the Baltic region—families and local associations working together to fish, rescue the drowning, and build houses, roads, and harbors—has survived. In September 1991, despite years of divisions and political barriers, representatives of 32 towns and cities on the Baltic Coast met in Gdansk, Poland, to form the Union of the Baltic Cities. The union was established to encourage and contribute to positive democratic and economic development in the region.

The goals of the Union of the Baltic Cities are far-reaching and include cultural awareness, improved transportation and telecommunication, and environmental protection. Member cities are encouraged to enter into twin-city relationships with each other so that cities with extensive needs can benefit from the knowledge, experience, and willing partnership of highly developed cities. The union also acts as a clearinghouse to match the needs of such member cities with the resources of others.

Environmental protection of the Baltic is a priority for the union. Much of the region's environment is undergoing increasing degradation because the speed of economic development has severely strained the ability of nature to accommodate it. The countries surrounding the sea have been abusing its resource for too long; in essence, the Baltic Sea has been treated as a waste collector of unlimited capacity.

Although much of the policymaking necessary to restore the Baltic is the responsibility of officials at the national and international levels, such matters as improved sewage treatment, district heating systems, and handling of refuse are usually dealt with by individual cities. Thus, the union could be instrumental in arranging the transfer of environmental protection technologies between member cities. For example, the Danish Environmental Association has developed the Baltic Sustainable Cities Programme on behalf of the member city of Aarhus, Denmark. The program has instituted partnerships between eastern cities, such as Elblag, Kaliningrad, Klaipeda, Riga, and Tallinn, and western cities to provide assistance and expertise in planning and implementing environmental projects.

The activities of the Union of the Baltic Cities are numerous and varied so that it can fulfill its goal of helping the Baltic region to enter the 21st century as a new civilization of democracy, respect for rights and duties, and balanced economic development.

Piotr Krzyzanowski is the Polish representative to HELCOM and the deputy chairman of the Union of the Baltic Cities.

governments to undertake studies of new legal regulatory arrangements and drafting of governmental and parliamentary decision documents; policy studies of options, costs, and benefits; investment in new monitoring equipment, upgrading of laboratory equipment and procedures, and upgrading of data processing and analytical capacity; and development of new organizational structures and arrangements to carry out management functions. The program will also promote the use of a range of economic measures for the management of environmental quality, such as adoption of the "polluter pays principle," adoption of realistic user charges, and introduction of cost-sharing principles in the case of transboundary pollution. In addition, the program will seek to promote the adoption of the best environmental practices and the use of the best available technologies to prevent pollution at the source, consistent with the 1992 Helsinki convention (an update of the 1974 convention that was signed at the Diplomatic Conference) and HELCOM recommendations. Actions that facilitate the transfer of technology between and within cooperating countries will also be encouraged.

The second component of the program is institutional strengthening and human resources development: building the organizational and human capacity to enforce regulations; planning, designing, and implementing environmental management systems, including infrastructure; and managing natural resources efficiently. The program focuses on training people to use new concepts of management and new technology and developing the organizational and administrative framework for people to work effectively and efficiently. Priority will be given to support for environmental planning, river basin management, coastal zone management, and protected areas management. Consistent with the objective of decentralizing environmental management, the program will support the development of effective local authorities that are responsible for water supply, wastewater, and disposal of solid wastes. The program will also support the development of local capacity to carry out environmental audits by training personnel from local industries, consulting firms, and regulatory organizations.

The third component is a program for infrastructure investment in specific measures to control point and nonpoint sources of pollution and to minimize and dispose of wastes. These measures include the rehabilitation and modernization of existing infrastructure; the development of new infrastructure; and the conservation of environmentally sensitive areas and resources. This program includes investments in three areas:

- Investments in municipal environmental management will emphasize the collection, treatment, and disposal of wastewater. Existing municipal water systems in the region commonly include all or most of the industrial wastewater within the service area of the sewer network, which means that they are functioning as combined municipal and industrial wastewater systems. The program

FIGURE 2. Environmental hot spots in the Baltic Sea catchment.

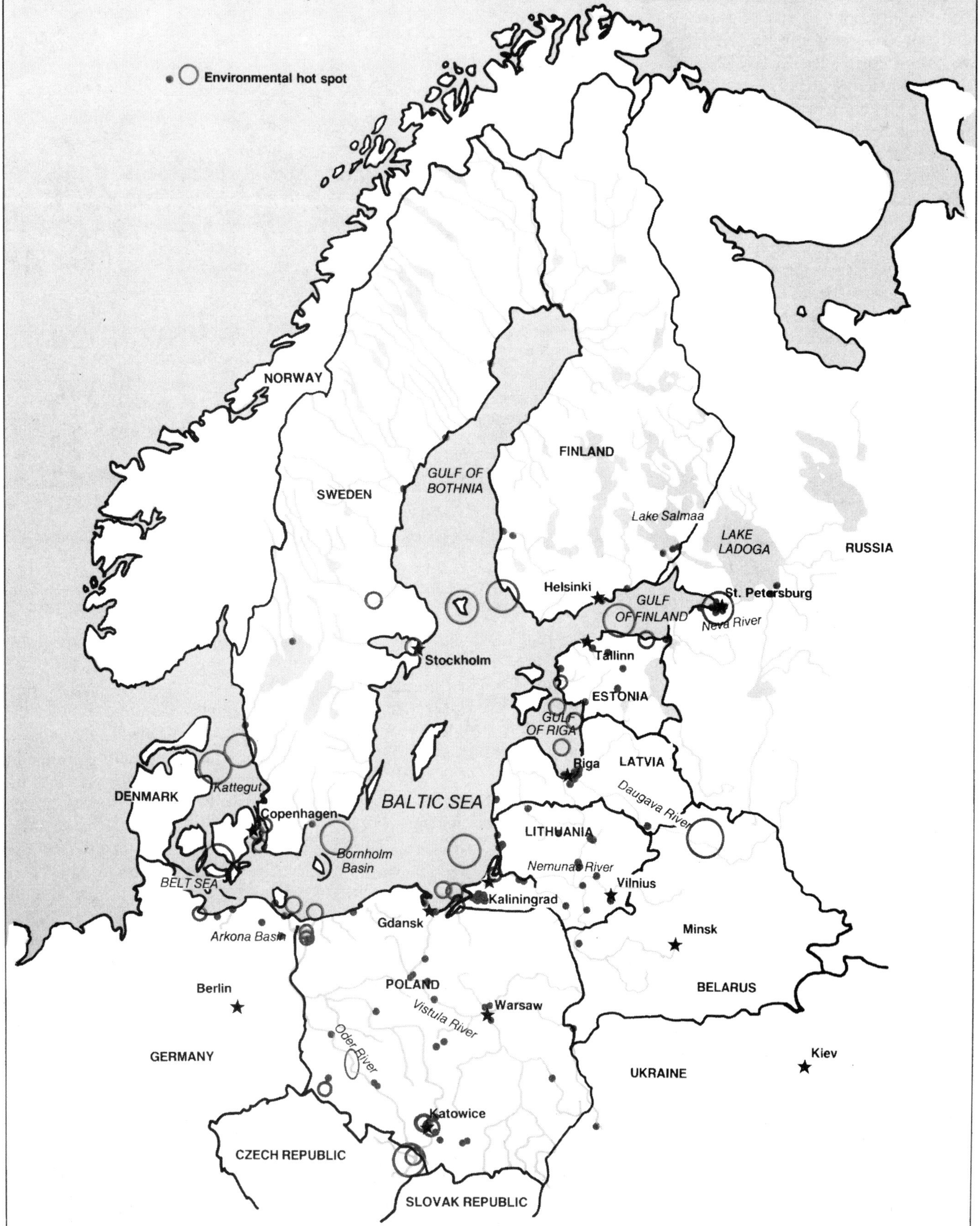

SOURCE: Helsinki Commission, The Baltic Sea Joint Environmental Action Programme, Helsinki, 1993.

will support national and local activities to rationalize municipal water consumption and to reduce leakages and unaccounted-for water. Support will also be provided for the completion of facilities already under construction, subject to design modification (taking a least-cost approach) and replacement of any substandard civil works. There are a number of such projects under way in the region's "hot spots," including Kaliningrad, Klaipeda, Liepaja, Tallinn, and Vilnius. Key operational problems, such as inadequate plant instrumentation and energy-inefficient equipment, will also be addressed.

• Industrial waste management at specific sites and complexes will also be financed. These projects are primarily for wastewater management, but they also address waste minimization, safe disposal of solid wastes, treatment and safe disposal of various forms of hazardous and toxic wastes, and environmental restoration from past degradation. Particular attention will be given to the pulp-and-paper industry, which has special significance in the region. Although this industry is perhaps most modern in the northern and western parts of the region, it is arguably one of the most outdated and inefficient in the eastern and southern portions. In both cases, the pulp-and-paper industry produces serious pollution problems, particularly persistent organic chlorinated substances. In addition, priority will be given to addressing wastewater treatment in the chemical and metal production and processing industries.

• Controlling polluted water runoff and discharges from agricultural lands, large livestock operations, and rural settlements is also an investment priority. Agriculture and livestock are major contributors of nutrient loads to the sea. Control measures will involve a wide range of changes in farming practices, including modifications in the timing of manure application and tillage; improvements in farm infrastructure, such as larger capacity and more secure storage for fertilizers, manure, and farm wastes; changes in water use; and new equipment, such as manure spreading and waste handling equipment. The program will also support investment activities to reduce pollution problems resulting from fish farming.

STEPHEN F. LINTNER

Although the Baltic Coast, including this spot in Lithuania, has long been a popular vacation area, pollution has closed several beaches and reduced the tourist trade.

The fourth component of the program is to aid in the management of coastal lagoons and wetlands. These environmentally sensitive and economically valuable areas serve as important buffers of pollution before it reaches the sea and provide critical habitat for diverse flora and fauna, including commercially important fisheries. The management systems will include land-use controls and limited infrastructure and, in some cases, will be integrated with compatible ecotourism and recreation developments, possibly through joint public and private ventures or private investment. The program will support the development of a series of demonstration activities concerning the use of natural and constructed wetlands for wastewater treatment and storm water retention and as traps for nutrients and other pollutants.

The program's fifth part is supporting applied research to build the knowledge base needed to develop solutions, transfer technology, and broaden understanding of critical problems. Specific priority topics include environmental trends; systems ecology; development and application of the "critical load" concept for different pollutants in the Baltic Sea and its subregions; assessments of risks to human health; agricultural development patterns in the Baltic Sea basin; future trends in transportation and its environmental management; and management of critical ecosystems, such as coastal lagoons and wetlands.

Finally, the program will encourage public awareness and environmental education to develop a broad and sustainable base of support for the implementation of the other components. The participation of nongovernmental organizations reaching the grassroots level and the development of effective environmental education programs are essential to promoting public awareness and political commitment. Efforts to promote and expand environmental education, particularly in the context of local environmental cleanup activities, will be given priority.

The 1992 Baltic Sea Declaration that was signed at the April 1992 Diplomatic Conference mandated that the key elements of the Joint Comprehensive Environmental Action Programme be initiated in 1993. Although the main responsibility for implementing the program will rest with the governments concerned, coordination of many program activities is needed. Such activities include monitoring pollution and the impact of the program, maintaining databases, reforming policies and regulations, providing technical assistance, planning research programs, and exchanging information, as well as periodically updating the program. To this end, the Programme Implementation Task Force has been set up within the framework of HELCOM.

The Costs and Financing of the Program

The total cost of the 20-year program for all countries in the Baltic Sea catchment is estimated to be about 18 billion ECU (about $25.6 billion),[5] and phase 1, from 1993 to 1997, is projected to cost about 5 billion ECU (about $6 billion). (See Table 1.)

The program will focus on remediating 132 "hot spots" (see the map on page 101), 98 of them located in Russia, Estonia, Latvia, Lithuania, Belarus, Ukraine, Poland, the Czech Republic, and the Slovak Republic. These 98 actions will cost about 8.5 billion ECU, out of which 6.5 billion ECU will go toward 47 "priority hot spots," including 26 municipal spots, 9 industrial spots, and 12 others. The remaining 34 hot spots, located in Denmark, Finland, Germany, and Sweden, have been selected by these countries themselves, and their remediation will cost approximately 1.5 billion ECU. In Poland, which has the largest land area and population in the Baltic Sea catchment, the estimated cost for remediating the 40 recommended hot spots and priority hot spots exceeds 4.0 billion ECU (see "Report from Poland: Politics in the Midst of Environmental Disaster" in the March 1991 *Environment*).

In phase 1 of the program's implementation, the needs of 29 priority hot spots will be addressed, 19 in the Vistula and Oder river basins and 10 in Russia, Estonia, Latvia, and Lithuania. In addition, major reductions in discharges of adsorbable organic halogens are planned for the pulp-and-paper industry in Finland and Sweden.

The immediate costs for the program total about 30 million ECU for the feasibility studies of the highest priority projects. Financial arrangements for the implementation of these projects cannot be completed without the results of these studies. In addition, the governments in the eastern and southern parts of the catchment will need to arrange for local and external support to carry out the required policy and regulatory reforms. Timely implementation of the program critically depends on those and other noninvestment activities. To complicate matters, nearly two-thirds of the hot spots are located in countries whose current economic situation makes ordinary loans and commercial financing difficult. Therefore, some combination of normal and concessional development lending, supplemented by outright grants, will be needed from bilateral and multilateral

TABLE 1
ESTIMATED COSTS OF THE BALTIC SEA JOINT COMPREHENSIVE ENVIRONMENTAL ACTION PROGRAMME

Program element	Phase 1 1993–1997 (millions ECU[a])	Phase 2 1998–2012 (millions ECU)	Total 1993–2012 (millions ECU)
Policies, laws, and regulations	5	5	10
Institutional strengthening and human-resource development	70	140	210
Investment activities			
Point-source pollution			
Immediate support and warning systems	50		50
Municipal wastewater treatment	1,000	2,000	3,000
Combined municipal and industrial wastewater treatment	1,600	4,000	5,600
Pulp-and-paper industry wastewater treatment	400	1,000	1,400
Environmental control at other industries	300	1,000	1,300
Solid and hazardous waste management	200	800	1,000
Air quality management	460	1,200	1,660
Nonpoint-source pollution[b]	800	2,700	3,500
Management programs for coastal lagoons and wetlands	100	120	220
Applied research	10	20	30
Public awareness and environmental education	5	15	20
Total	**5,000**	**13,000**	**18,000**

[a]European currency units

[b]Nonpoint-source pollution includes runoff from agricultural and livestock operations and rural settlements.

SOURCE: Helsinki Commission, The Baltic Sea Joint Comprehensive Environmental Action Programme, Helsinki, 1993.

financing agencies. Varied approaches to project financing are also needed, including enhanced local sources of revenue from taxes and user charges, user taxes on potentially polluting substances, and private investment that supplements traditional public-sector borrowing and budgetary resources.

In March 1993, at the High Level Conference on Resource Mobilization for the Baltic Sea Joint Comprehensive Environmental Action Programme in Gdansk, Poland, the participants stressed that availability of local or foreign funds is not the only constraint to program implementation; several mutually related factors also limit the mobilization and flow of, and the capacity to use effectively, the funds that are available. Several important observations were made at the Gdansk conference.[6] First, the greatest proportion of project financing must come from local resources; however, despite the efforts on the part of governments of the formerly communist countries, local resources will remain limited in the short term. Slow progress in this regard has been largely due to the precarious position of the economies in transition. Nevertheless, according to those at the conference, "early action should be taken to support the establishment of financing mechanisms and incentives, to develop the institutional capacity to implement them, and to create greater public awareness of their importance."[7] The principal local sources of funds available to support activities under the program include user charges, pollution fees, budgetary allocations and nonbudgetary incentives, domestic loans, and, potentially, private investments. Domestic loans may not be a major factor in the near term because local financial institutions, such as capital markets and banks, have not been sufficiently developed to support environmental improvements.

Under the current economic conditions, however, the concerned countries, municipalities, and enterprises have sought increased support for program financing from external sources. Although some of the potential donor countries are suffering from a protracted recession, "there will be a critical need, at least for the short term, for continued and better coordinated support from bilateral donor organizations to implement the Programme, especially to support policy, institutional development and investment project preparation activities."[8] Grant and concessional funding from the Commission of the European Communities and bilateral donors, from both within and outside the region, has been an important source of support for program activities in recent years.

In addition, the conference participants anticipated that "the international financing institutions will continue to provide loans and implement projects for selected priority actions under the Programme consistent with the requests of the borrowers and within lending limits established by their creditworthiness."[9] The level of investment by international financing institutions is determined by the priorities of the borrowing country, the levels of borrowing and indebtedness that present and anticipated economic conditions are able to support, the balance of investment activities between priority sectors, the quality of the proposed investment, and the related characteristics and conditions of the borrower.

During phase 1 of the program's implementation, special emphasis "must be put on comprehensive feasibility studies that yield economically and financially feasible and affordable investment projects, and that devote more attention to the assessment of the current institutional framework and the formulation of measures to strengthen that framework to support project implementation and operation."[10] Several actions will require special attention in phase 1, including local fundraising, support for institutional reforms, support for industries in transition, and the phasing in of investments requiring long development periods.

The conference also acknowledged that, in the formerly communist countries, pollution control "at the source" will have to be incorporated into the ongoing privatization, restructuring, and modernization of industries. In the municipal sector, innovative approaches—such as joint ventures with foreign capital and long-term concessions—will be needed to attract capital financing, especially from private and commercial sources. Investments in municipal wastewater treatment plants must be seen within the broader framework of developing autonomous self-financing municipal and regional water and wastewater utilities, whether public or private.[11]

The environment ministers and other representatives of the governments of the Baltic Sea countries and the representative of the Commission of the European Communities assembled at the Gdansk conference jointly decided to make all efforts to mobilize local, national, bilateral, and multilateral financial and other resources for the implementation of the program.[12]

Progress in Implementation

Phase 1 investment activities will concentrate on improving combined municipal and industrial wastewater treatment to reduce organic pollution loads. High-priority projects are the completion of unfinished or inoperable treatment facilities, the installation or improvement of pretreatment of industrial wastewater discharges into the municipal sewage systems, and the expansion of safe disposal of sludges. In the formerly centrally planned economies, nutrient-removal facilities (tertiary treatment) at municipal wastewater treatment plants will be deferred until more substantial progress is achieved in nutrient reductions in the agricultural sector.

As discussed at the Gdansk conference,[13] initial program activities have emphasized the establishment of priorities at the national level and detailed preparation of projects, including feasibility studies. Out of the 29 priority hot spots to be addressed in phase 1, detailed feasibility studies are under way or are planned at 17 of the 26 priority municipal hot spots; and environmental audits have been carried out at 6 of the 9 priority industrial hot spots. In addition, an economic and environmental assessment of the region's pulp-and-paper industry was completed, which reviewed market prospects and cost competitiveness at the region's 34 pulp-and-paper mills and focused on 12 mills that are candidates for feasibility studies and possible investment support.

The development of control programs for nonpoint source pollution in the agricultural and livestock sectors requires a different approach. The emphasis in phase 1 is on establishing an effective institutional framework and on developing and implementing well-designed pilot and demonstration activities. Seven pilot studies and programs have been established for the control of agricultural and livestock runoff in hot spot areas of Russia (at a major hog farm in the St. Petersburg region), Estonia (protection of groundwater from agricultural pollution), and Latvia, Lithuania, and Poland (testing ecotechnologies in small catchment areas). Thirteen surveys, studies, and pilot programs have been established or are planned in the most important wetland areas and in the key coastal lagoons, which are mostly in Estonia, Latvia, Lithuania, and Poland. In addition, the World Wide Fund for Nature, in cooperation with the countries of the region, is developing a regional program for managing coastal lagoons and wetlands, focusing on central Matsalu Bay in Estonia, the north coast of Latvia, and Putsk Bay, which is a subsection of Gdansk Bay in Poland.

Although several factors have combined to slow the rate at which resources are committed to and used for various program activities, the first year of implementation has demonstrated that, despite all difficulties, a great deal can be accomplished. The foundations established during this early phase will ensure the long-term success of the Baltic Sea Joint Comprehensive Environmental Action Programme.

Expected Environmental Benefits

The program is expected eventually to have a major impact on the rivers in the Baltic Sea catchment, which are the principal source of water supply for industry, agriculture, and about 80 million people. Reducing pollution loads and restoring aquatic ecosystems will increase the quality and reliability of water resources and benefit the health and well-being of the local population.

The coastal waters are expected to improve most rapidly, which would allow several contaminated beaches to open again and contribute to re-establishing favorable conditions for tourism and local recreation. The overall reduction in the load of nutrients should reduce algal blooms, assist in lowering eutrophication levels, and improve oxygen conditions. These improvements should have a major positive impact on fishery resources, including an increase in the number and diversity of commercially valuable fish species, such as whitefish, cod, and plaice. The quality of the open sea will be restored more slowly, however, because of the difficulty in controlling long-range atmospheric transportation of various pollutants.

Another benefit of the program to Baltic countries is the strengthening of local capacities to plan, finance, and manage environmental measures. The strategic gains from capacity building for environmental cleanup will be of particular importance in the formerly centrally planned economies, which are undergoing profound institutional as well as economic changes.

Given the current state of the Baltic Sea environment, however, the program cannot be expected to make any major impacts for about 20 years. But gradual and visible improvements, both environmental and economic, can be realized in the relatively near future.

NOTES

1. The information contained in this article is based principally on the findings and recommendations of the Helsinki Commission (HELCOM) ad hoc high-level task force and the HELCOM Programme Implementation Task Force.
2. Ronneby Diplomatic Conference, Baltic Sea Declaration, 1990.
3. The national plans were worked out in the first six months of the operation of the task force, on the basis of nationally available data and information. They included information on the 1985 pollution loads discharged into the Baltic Sea, environmental policies and regulations currently in force, and major pollution control programs and initiatives. The eight prefeasibility studies carried out in the Baltic Sea catchment covered St. Petersburg, the St. Petersburg region, Karelia, and Estonia; the western coast of Estonia; the Gulf of Riga and the Daugava River basin; the Lithuanian coast and the Nemunas River basin; the Kaliningrad region and the Pregel River basin; the Vistula River basin and the Baltic coast of Poland; the Oder River basin; and the north German Baltic coast.
4. Topical studies included Atmospheric Deposition of Pollutants; Agricultural Runoff; Wetlands and Coastal Lagoons; and several special studies concerning selected environmental problems in Estonia, Latvia, Lithuania, Poland, and the St. Petersburg region of Russia.
5. The exchange rate used is 1 European currency unit (ECU) equals U.S. $1.20.
6. The Baltic Sea Joint Environmental Action Programme, conference document no. 2 (Background paper for the High Level Conference on Resource Mobilization held in Gdansk, Poland, 24–25 March 1993).
7. Ibid.
8. Ibid.
9. Ibid.
10. Ibid.
11. W. Stottman, "World Bank Activities in the Municipal Water/Wastewater Sector" (Background paper presented at the Baltic Sea Joint Environmental Action Programme, High Level Conference on Resource Mobilization, Gdansk, Poland, 24–25 March 1993).
12. The Baltic Sea Joint Environmental Action Programme, "Declaration on Resource Mobilization for the Baltic Sea Joint Comprehensive Environmental Action Programme, 1993" (Gdansk Declaration).
13. The Baltic Sea Joint Environmental Action Programme, note 6 above.

The Region

The region is one of the most important concepts in geography. The term has special significance for the geographer, and it has been used as a kind of areal classification system in the discipline.

Two of the regional types most used in geography are "uniform" and "nodal." A uniform region is one in which a distinct set of features is present. The distinctiveness of the combination of features marks the region as being different from others. Examples of these features include climate type, soil type, prominent languages, resource deposits, and virtually any other identifiable phenomenon having a spatial dimension.

The nodal region reflects the zone of influence of a city or other nodal place. Imagine a rural town in which a farm implement service center is located. Now imagine lines drawn on a map linking this service center with every farm within the area that uses it. Finally, imagine a single line enclosing the entire area in which the individual farms are located. The enclosed area is defined as a nodal region. The nodal region implies interaction; regions of this type are defined on the basis of banking linkages, newspaper circulation, and telephone traffic, among other things.

The articles in this unit present examples of a number of regional themes. These selections can provide only a hint of the scope and diversity of the region in geography. There is no limit to the number of regions; there are as many as the researcher sets out to define.

"The Rise of the Region State" suggests that the nation-state is an unnatural and even dysfunctional unit for organizing human activity. "Africa's Geomosaic under Stress" reviews the independence movement of states in Africa and draws attention to core-periphery problems in South Africa, a nation torn by cultural strife for decades. Saul Cohen's article on the Middle East highlights the changing geopolitical position of this region in the post–cold war era.

"Prairie Potholes," by Bjorn Sletto, addresses attempts to reclaim a vast region of wetlands in the prairies of North America. The next article points out that a major environmental catastrophe is occurring with the literal demise of the Aral Sea, as water is diverted for irrigation agriculture. The article "Does It Matter Where You Are?" considers aspects of geographical location principles in the context of the new global economic systems. "Low Water in the American High Plains" focuses on mismanagement of a valuable water resource in the United States.

Finally, an article from *World Press Review* suggests a possible return of the Soviet Empire.

Looking Ahead: Challenge Questions

To what regions do you belong?

Why are maps and atlases so important in discussing and studying regions?

What major regions in the world are experiencing change? Which ones seem not to change at all? What are some reasons for the differences?

What regions in the world are experiencing tensions? What are the reasons behind these tensions? How can the tensions be eased?

Why are regions in Africa suffering so greatly?

Is the nation-state system an anachronism?

Unit 3

THE RISE OF THE REGION STATE

Kenichi Ohmae

Kenichi Ohmae is Chairman of the offices of McKinsey & Company in Japan.

The Nation State Is Dysfunctional

THE NATION STATE has become an unnatural, even dysfunctional, unit for organizing human activity and managing economic endeavor in a borderless world. It represents no genuine, shared community of economic interests; it defines no meaningful flows of economic activity. In fact, it overlooks the true linkages and synergies that exist among often disparate populations by combining important measures of human activity at the wrong level of analysis.

For example, to think of Italy as a single economic entity ignores the reality of an industrial north and a rural south, each vastly different in its ability to contribute and in its need to receive. Treating Italy as a single economic unit forces one—as a private sector manager or a public sector official—to operate on the basis of false, implausible and nonexistent averages. Italy is a country with great disparities in industry and income across regions.

On the global economic map the lines that now matter are those defining what may be called "region states." The boundaries of the region state are not imposed by political fiat. They are drawn by the deft but invisible hand of the global market for goods and services. They follow, rather than precede, real flows of human activity, creating nothing new but ratifying existing patterns manifest in countless individual decisions. They represent no threat to the political borders of any nation, and they have no call on any taxpayer's money to finance military forces to defend such borders.

Region states are natural economic zones. They may or may not fall within the geographic limits of a particular nation—whether they do is an accident of history. Sometimes these distinct economic units are formed by parts of states, such as those in northern Italy, Wales, Catalonia, Alsace-Lorraine or Baden-Württemberg. At other times they may be formed by economic patterns that overlap existing national boundaries, such as those between San Diego and Tijuana, Hong Kong and southern China, or the "growth triangle" of Singapore and its neighboring Indonesian islands. In today's borderless world these are natural economic zones and what matters is that each possesses, in one or another combination, the key ingredients for successful participation in the global economy.

Look, for example, at what is happening in Southeast Asia. The Hong Kong economy has gradually extended its influence throughout the Pearl River Delta. The radiating effect of these linkages has made Hong Kong, where GNP per capita is $12,000, the driving force of economic life in Shenzhen, boosting the per capita GNP of that city's residents to $5,695, as compared to $317 for China as a whole. These links extend to Zhuhai, Amoy and Guangzhou as well. By the year 2000 this cross-border region state will have raised the living standard of more than 11 million people over the $5,000 level. Meanwhile, Guangdong province, with a population of more than 65 million and its capital at Hong Kong, will emerge as a newly industrialized economy in its own right, even though China's per capita GNP may still hover at about $1,000. Unlike in Eastern Europe, where nations try to convert entire socialist economies over to the market, the Asian model is first to convert limited economic zones—the region states—into free enterprise havens. So far the results have been reassuring.

These developments and others like them are coming just in time for Asia. As Europe perfects its single market and as the United States, Canada and Mexico begin to explore the benefits of the North American Free Trade Agreement (NAFTA), the combined economies of Asia and Japan lag behind those of the other parts of the globe's economic triad by about $2 trillion—roughly the aggregate size of some 20 additional region states. In other words, for Asia to keep pace existing regions must continue to grow at current rates throughout the next decade, giving birth to 20 additional Singapores.

Many of these new region states are already beginning to emerge. China has expanded to 14 other areas—many of them inland—the special economic zones that have worked so well for Shenzhen and Shanghai. One such project at Yunnan will become a cross-border economic zone encompassing parts of Laos and Vietnam. In Vietnam itself Ho Chi Minh City (Saigon) has launched a similar "sepzone" to attract foreign capital. Inspired in part by Singapore's "growth triangle," the governments of Indonesia, Malaysia and Thailand in 1992 unveiled a larger triangle across the Strait of Malacca to link Medan, Penang and Phuket. These developments are not, of course, limited to the developing economies in Asia. In economic terms the United States has never been a single nation. It is a collection of region states: northern and southern California, the "power corridor" along the East Coast between Boston and Washington, the Northeast, the Midwest, the Sun Belt, and so on.

From *Foreign Affairs*, Vol. 72, No. 2, Spring 1993, pp. 78-87. © 1993 by Kenichi Ohmae. Reprinted by permission.

What Makes a Region State

THE PRIMARY linkages of region states tend to be with the global economy and not with their host nations. Region states make such effective points of entry into the global economy because the very characteristics that define them are shaped by the demands of that economy. Region states tend to have between five million and 20 million people. The range is broad, but the extremes are clear: not half a million, not 50 or 100 million. A region state must be small enough for its citizens to share certain economic and consumer interests but of adequate size to justify the infrastructure—communication and transportation links and quality professional services—necessary to participate economically on a global scale.

It must, for example, have at least one international airport and, more than likely, one good harbor with international-class freight-handling facilities. A region state must also be large enough to provide an attractive market for the brand development of leading consumer products. In other words, region states are not defined by their economies of scale in production (which, after all, can be leveraged from a base of any size through exports to the rest of the world) but rather by their having reached efficient economies of scale in their consumption, infrastructure and professional services.

For example, as the reach of television networks expands, advertising becomes more efficient. Although trying to introduce a consumer brand throughout all of Japan or Indonesia may still prove prohibitively expensive, establishing it firmly in the Osaka or Jakarta region is far more affordable—and far more likely to generate handsome returns. Much the same is true with sales and service networks, customer satisfaction programs, market surveys and management information systems: efficient scale is at the regional, not national, level. This fact matters because, on balance, modern marketing techniques and technologies shape the economies of region states.

Where true economies of service exist, religious, ethnic and racial distinctions are not important—or, at least, only as important as human nature requires. Singapore is 70 percent ethnic Chinese, but its 30 percent minority is not much of a problem because commercial prosperity creates sufficient affluence for all. Nor are ethnic differences a source of concern for potential investors looking for consumers.

Indonesia—an archipelago with 500 or so different tribal groups, 18,000 islands and 170 million people—would logically seem to defy effective organization within a single mode of political government. Yet Jakarta has traditionally attempted to impose just such a central control by applying fictional averages to the entire nation. They do not work. If, however, economies of service allowed two or three Singapore-sized region states to be created within Indonesia, they could be managed. And they would ameliorate, rather than exacerbate, the country's internal social divisions. This holds as well for India and Brazil.

The New Multinational Corporation

WHEN VIEWING the globe through the lens of the region state, senior corporate managers think differently about the geographical expansion of their businesses. In the past the primary aspiration of multinational corporations was to create, in effect, clones of the parent organization in each of the dozens of countries in which they operated. The goal of this system was to stick yet another pin in the global map to mark an increasing number of subsidiaries around the world.

More recently, however, when Nestlé and Procter & Gamble wanted to expand their business in Japan from an already strong position, they did not view the effort as just another pin-sticking exercise. Nor did they treat the country as a single coherent market to be gained at once, or try as most Western companies do to establish a foothold first in the Tokyo area, Japan's most tumultuous and overcrowded market. Instead, they wisely focused on the Kansai region around Osaka and Kobe, whose 22 million residents are nearly as affluent as those in Tokyo but where competition is far less intense. Once they had on-the-ground experience on how best to reach the Japanese consumer, they branched out into other regions of the country.

Much of the difficulty Western companies face in trying to enter Japan stems directly from trying to shoulder their way in through Tokyo. This instinct often proves difficult and costly. Even if it works, it may also prove a trap; it is hard to "see" Japan once one is bottled up in the particular dynamics of the Tokyo marketplace. Moreover, entering the country through a different regional doorway has great economic appeal. Measured by aggregate GNP the Kansai region is the seventh-largest economy in the world, just behind the United Kingdom.

Given the variations among local markets and the value of learning through real-world experimentation, an incremental region-based approach to market entry makes excellent sense. And not just in Japan. Building an effective presence across a landmass the size of China is of course a daunting prospect. Serving the people in and around Nagoya City, however, is not.

If one wants a presence in Thailand, why start by building a network over the entire extended landmass? Instead focus, at least initially, on the region around Bangkok, which represents the lion's share of the total potential market. The same strategy applies to the United States. To introduce a new top-of-the-line car into the U.S. market, why replicate up front an exhaustive coast-to-coast dealership network? Of the country's 3,000 statistical metropolitan areas, 80 percent of luxury car buyers can be reached by establishing a presence in only 125 of these.

The Challenges for Government

TRADITIONAL ISSUES of foreign policy, security and defense remain the province of nation states. So, too, are macroeconomic and monetary policies—the taxation and public investment needed to provide the necessary infrastructure and incentives for region-based activities. The government will also remain responsible for the broad requirements of educating and training citizens so that they can participate fully in the global economy.

Governments are likely to resist giving up the power to intervene in the economic realm or to relinquish their impulses for protectionism. The illusion of control is soothing. Yet hard evidence proves the contrary. No manipulation of exchange rates by central bankers or political appointees has ever "corrected" the trade imbalances between the United States and Japan. Nor has any trade talk between the two governments. Whatever cosmetic actions these negotiations may have prompted, they rescued no industry and revived no economic sector. Textiles, semiconductors, autos, consumer electronics—the competitive situation in these industries did not develop according to the whims of policymakers but only in response to the deeper logic of the competitive marketplace. If U.S. market share has dwindled, it is not because government policy failed but because individual consumers decided to buy elsewhere. If U.S. capacity has migrated to Mexico or Asia, it is only because individual managers made decisions about cost and efficiency.

The implications of region states are not welcome news to established seats of political power, be they politicians or lobbyists. Nation states by definition require a domestic political focus, while region states are ensconced in the global economy. Region states that sit within the frontiers of a particular nation share its political goals and aspirations. However, region states welcome foreign investment and ownership—whatever allows them to employ people productively or to improve the quality of life. They want their people to have access to the best and cheapest products. And they want whatever surplus accrues from these activities to ratchet up the local quality of life still further and not to support distant regions or to prop up distressed industries elsewhere in the name of national interest or sovereignty.

When a region prospers, that prosperity spills over into the adjacent regions within the same political confederation. Industry in the area immediately in and around Bangkok has prompted investors to explore options elsewhere in Thailand. Much the same is true of Kuala Lumpur in Malaysia, Jakarta in Indonesia, or Singapore, which is rapidly becoming the unofficial capital of the Association of Southeast Asian Nations. São Paulo, too, could well emerge as a genuine region state, someday entering the ranks of the Organization of Economic Cooperation and Development. Yet if Brazil's central government does not allow the São Paulo region state finally to enter the global economy, the country as a whole may soon fall off the roster of the newly industrialized economies.

Unlike those at the political center, the leaders of region states—interested chief executive officers, heads of local unions, politicians at city and state levels—often welcome and encourage foreign capital investment. They do not go abroad to attract new plants and factories only to appear back home on television vowing to protect local companies at any cost. These leaders tend to possess an international outlook that can help defuse many of the usual kinds of social tensions arising over issues of "foreign" versus "domestic" inputs to production.

In the United States, for example, the Japanese have already established about 120 "transplant" auto factories throughout the Mississippi Valley. More are on the way. As their share of the U.S. auto industry's production grows, people in that region who look to these plants for their livelihoods and for the tax revenues needed to support local communities will stop caring whether the plants belong to U.S.- or Japanese-based companies. All they will care about are the regional economic benefits of having them there. In effect, as members of the Mississippi Valley region state, they will have leveraged the contribution of these plants to help their region become an active participant in the global economy.

Region states need not be the enemies of central governments. Handled gently, region states can provide the opportunity for eventual prosperity for all areas within a nation's traditional political control. When political and industrial leaders accept and act on these realities, they help build prosperity. When they do not—falling back under the spell of the nationalist economic illusion—they may actually destroy it.

Consider the fate of Silicon Valley, that great early engine of much of America's microelectronics industry. In the beginning it was an extremely open and entrepreneurial environment. Of late, however, it has become notably protectionist—creating industry associations, establishing a polished lobbying presence in Washington and turning to "competitiveness" studies as a way to get more federal funding for research and development. It has also begun to discourage, and even to bar, foreign investment, let alone foreign takeovers. The result is that Boise and Denver now prosper in electronics; Japan is developing a Silicon Island on Kyushu; Taiwan is trying to create a Silicon Island of its own; and Korea is nurturing a Silicon Peninsula. This is the worst of all possible worlds: no new money in California and a host of newly energized and well-funded competitors.

Elsewhere in California, not far from Silicon Valley, the story is quite different. When Hollywood recognized that it faced a severe capital shortage, it did not throw up protectionist barriers against foreign money. Instead, it invited Rupert Murdoch into 20th Century Fox, C. Itoh and Toshiba into Time-Warner, Sony into Columbia, and Matsushita into MCA. The result: a $10 billion infusion of new capital and, equally important, $10 billion less for Japan or anyone else to set up a new Hollywood of their own.

"Political leaders, however reluctantly, must adjust to the reality of economic regional entities if they are to nurture real economic flows."

Political leaders, however reluctantly, must adjust to the reality of economic regional entities if they are to nurture real economic flows. Resistant governments will be left to reign over traditional political territories as all meaningful participation in the global economy migrates beyond their well-preserved frontiers.

Canada, as an example, is wrongly focusing on Quebec and national language tensions as its core economic and even political issue. It does so to the point of still wrestling with the teaching of French and English in British Columbia, when that province's economic future is tied to Asia. Furthermore, as NAFTA takes shape the "vertical" relationships between Canadian and U.S. regions—Vancouver and Seattle (the Pacific Northwest region state); Toronto, Detroit and Cleveland (the Great Lakes region state)—will become increasingly important. How Canadian leaders deal with these new entities will be critical to the continuance of Canada as a political nation.

In developing economies, history suggests that when GNP per capita reaches about $5,000, discretionary income crosses an invisible threshold. Above that level people begin wondering whether they have reasonable access to the best and cheapest available products and whether they have an adequate quality of life. More troubling for those in political control, citizens also begin to consider whether their government is doing as well by them as it might.

Such a performance review is likely to be unpleasant. When governments control information—and in large measure because they do—it is all too easy for them to believe that they "own" their people. Governments begin restricting access to certain kinds of goods or services or pricing them far higher than pure economic logic would dictate. If market-driven levels of consumption conflict with a government's pet policy or general desire for control, the obvious response is to restrict consumption. So what if the people would choose otherwise if given the opportunity? Not only does the government withhold that opportunity but it also does not even let the people know that it is being withheld.

Regimes that exercise strong central control either fall on hard times or begin to decompose. In a borderless world the deck is stacked against them. The irony, of course, is that in the name of safeguarding the integrity and identity of the center, they often prove unwilling or unable to give up the illusion of power in order to seek a better quality of life for their people. There is at the center an understandable fear of letting go and losing control. As a result, the center often ends up protecting weak and unproductive industries and then passing along the high costs to its people—precisely the opposite of what a government should do.

The Goal is to Raise Living Standards

THE CLINTON administration faces a stark choice as it organizes itself to address the country's economic issues. It can develop policy within the framework of the badly dated assumption that success in the global economy means pitting one nation's industries against another's. Or it can define policy with the awareness that the economic dynamics of a borderless world do not flow from such contrived head-to-head confrontations, but rather from the participation of specific regions in a global nexus of information, skill, trade and investment.

If the goal is to raise living standards by promoting regional participation in the borderless economy, then the less Washington constrains these regions, the better off they will be. By contrast, the more Washington intervenes, the more citizens will pay for automobiles, steel, semiconductors, white wine, textiles or consumer electronics—all in the name of "protecting" America. Aggregating economic policy at the national level—or worse, at the continent-wide level as in Europe—inevitably results in special interest groups and vote-conscious governments putting their own interests first.

The less Washington interacts with specific regions, however, the less it perceives itself as "representing" them. It does not feel right. When learning to ski, one of the toughest and most counterintuitive principles to accept is that one gains better control by leaning down toward the valley, not back against the hill. Letting go is difficult. For governments region-based participation in the borderless economy is fine, except where it threatens current jobs, industries or interests. In Japan, a nation with plenty of farmers, food is far more expensive than in Hong Kong or Singapore, where there are no farmers. That is because Hong Kong and Singapore are open to what Australia and China can produce far more cheaply than they could themselves. They have opened themselves to the global economy, thrown their weight forward, as it were, and their people have reaped the benefits.

For the Clinton administration, the irony is that Washington today finds itself in the same relation to those region states that lie entirely or partially within its borders as was London with its North American colonies centuries ago. Neither central power could genuinely understand the shape or magnitude of the new flows of information, people and economic activity in the regions nominally under its control. Nor could it understand how counterproductive it would be to try to arrest or distort these flows in the service of nation-defined interests. Now as then, only relaxed central control can allow the flexibility needed to maintain the links to regions gripped by an inexorable drive for prosperity.

Africa's Geomosaic Under Stress

H. J. de Blij

University of Miami, Department of Geography, Coral Gables, Florida, and Georgetown University, School of Foreign Service, Washington, DC.

In 35 years, the colonial map of Subsaharan Africa has been transformed into a patchwork of four dozen independent states, many subject to severe devolutionary stresses. Domino effects hastened the decolonization process; a short-lived but significant buffer zone slowed it in southern Africa. During the period of Africa's transition, polarization in South Africa (socially as well as spatially) intensified. Core-periphery contrasts in the republic deepened; whereas integration and modernization increasingly mark the South Africa's core areas, the prospect for the periphery is bleak and instability may develop. Insurgencies, refugee flows, and environmental stresses buffet a politico-geographical framework that may appear stable on maps, but which may collapse from within. **Key words: domino theory, buffer zone, insurgent state, devolution, boundaries, core-periphery, centripetal-centrifugal forces, front line states.**

In less than two generations, the political geography of Africa has been transformed. In the late 1940s, European powers, recovering from the effects of World War II, laid plans to reassert and consolidate their control over African colonial empires. In the early 1990s, Africa's last colony, South West Africa, became the independent state of Namibia, and South Africa faced the realities of the Africa of the future. Four decades of change saw what British Prime Minister Harold Macmillan called Africa's "Wind of Change" sweep southward from West Africa and the Sudan toward the Cape of Good Hope.

During the decade from the mid-1950s to the mid-1960s, developments in Africa rivaled cold-war competition for world attention. African leaders in the struggle for independence, such as Kwame Nkrumah, Patrice Lumumba, and Jomo Kenyatta, rose to international prominence in a manner not unlike Lech Walesa and Vaclav Havel today. President Kennedy appointed a secretary of state for African affairs, and his Peace Corps initiative, while a global venture, was directed principally toward Africa. Many academics were euphoric. I remember hearing a leading political scientist, addressing a convention of the APSA, describe political prospects for Ghana and Nigeria as "guaranteed" by the tested models on which their new constitutions were based. Ghana would become the embodiment of the Westminster model for Africa, and Nigeria would lead the continent with a federal system that was to be the vanguard for other states burdened with regional centrifugalism (Rothchild 1960). Shortly thereafter, I heard a future East African Union depicted as having "limitless opportunities for growth and development (once freed from the colonial yoke)...on a par with Western Europe." African leaders visited the United States and lectured at universities; African students in unprecedented numbers enrolled in American colleges. African studies centers, programs, and institutes arose at dozens of U.S. institutions. Funding for field research in Africa expanded, and scholarly journals in their contents reflected the new era.

In Africa, elation at the demise of colonialism and optimism about the future, fueled in substantial part by the sometimes careless predictions of non-African scholars, led to a revolution of rising expectations. The arts, especially literature, blossomed as perhaps never before. An outpouring of prose, poetry, and plays by African authors writing in English and French conveyed African feelings to European and American audiences. Leopold Senghor, a respected poet and author, became the first president of newly independent Senegal. The knowledge, judgment, and wisdom contained in works from this period seemed to confirm the favorable prospects and bright potentials for Africa's future (Nyerere 1961, 1963; Nkrumah 1957, Houphouet-Boigny 1957, Rooney 1988).

But even as the tide of African nationalism and independence swept eastward and southward from its West African sources, the salient problems that were to dash the dream of a peaceful, stable, prosperous Africa became manifest. Ghana achieved sovereignty in 1957 with a strong agricultural and industrial base, good educational and medical facilities, an adequate transport system, the highest per capita income of any tropical African country, substantial foreign currency reserves derived mainly from cocoa exports, a comparatively efficient civil service, and a dynamic political leadership. President Nkrumah spoke and wrote of pan-African unity and cooperation based on common interests and aspirations (Nkrumah 1963). Less than a decade later, the Ghanaian army had staged a coup, President Nkrumah was exiled, graft and corruption were rife, foreign reserves were depleted, the infrastructure was deteriorating, and living standards were in decline. Only part of this was due to the drop in cocoa prices

From *Journal of Geography,* Vol. 90, No. 1, January/February 1991, pp. 2-9. Reproduced with permission of the National Council for Geographic Education.

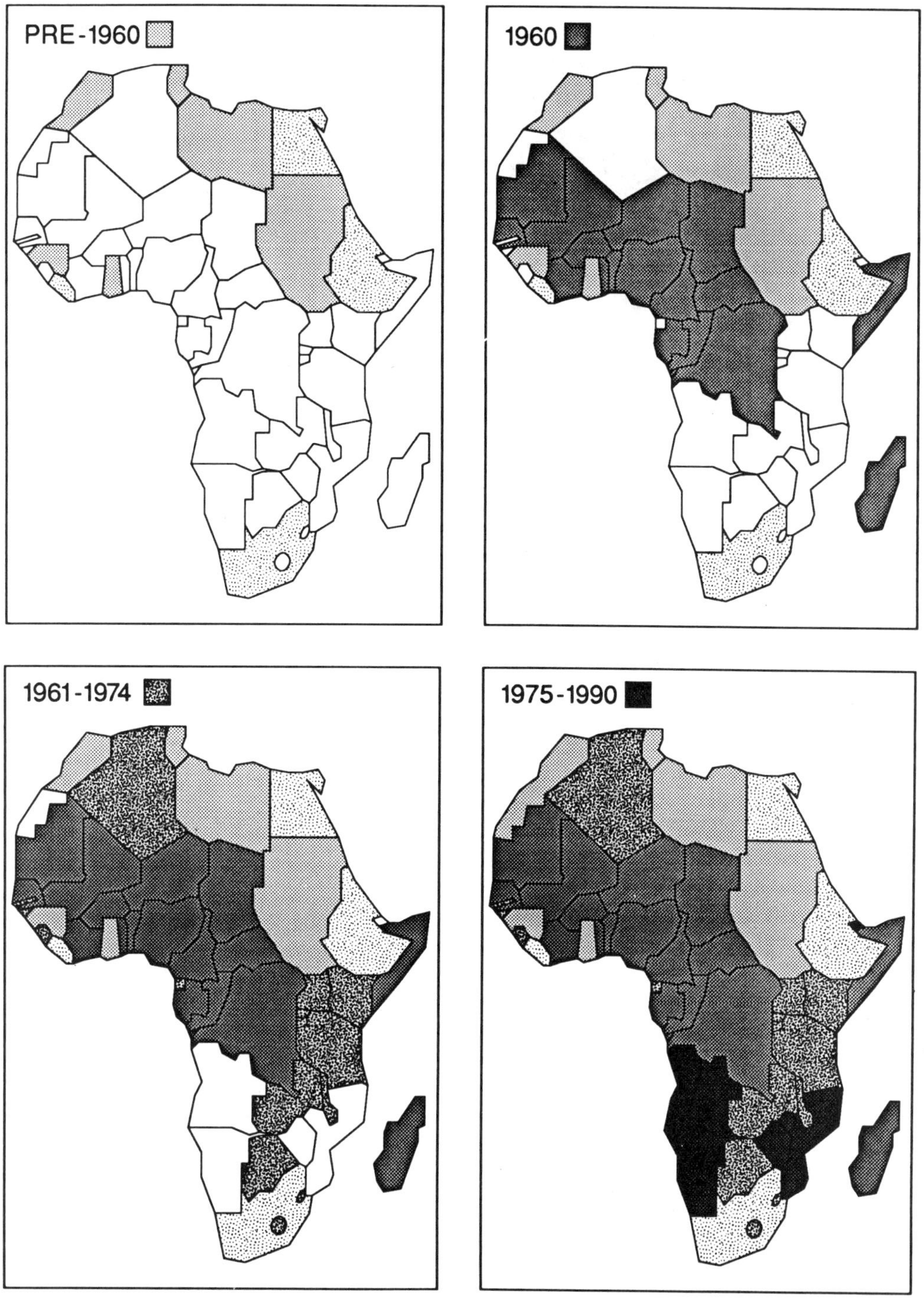

Figure 1. The progression of African independence in four stages. Before 1960, only Egypt, Ethiopia, Liberia, and South Africa were independent states not subject to decolonization.

on world markets. Economic mismanagement, political misjudgments, grandiose engineering and building projects, internal corruption worsened by dealings with corrupt multinational corporations, and inexperience all contributed to the collapse of black Africa's first great hope (Hadjor 1988).

Nigeria, Africa's most populous country and the regional cornerstone of West Africa, in 1960 became independent as a three-region federal state: North, West (really the southwest), and East (southeast). The federal parliament was regionally apportioned according to population, and the future depended on a delicate demographic balance (Azikiwe 1961). The first post-independence census, in 1962, showed the Northern Region to outnumber the other two regions combined, and a bitter controversy arose. As the 1965 elections approached, Nigeria plunged into anarchy that led to a military coup.

Following the military intervention, a wave of genocide occurred against Easterns living and working in the North. Eastern Nigeria responded by declaring itself independent as the state of Biafra. More than three years of devastating civil war ensued, setting Nigeria back severely despite the coinci-

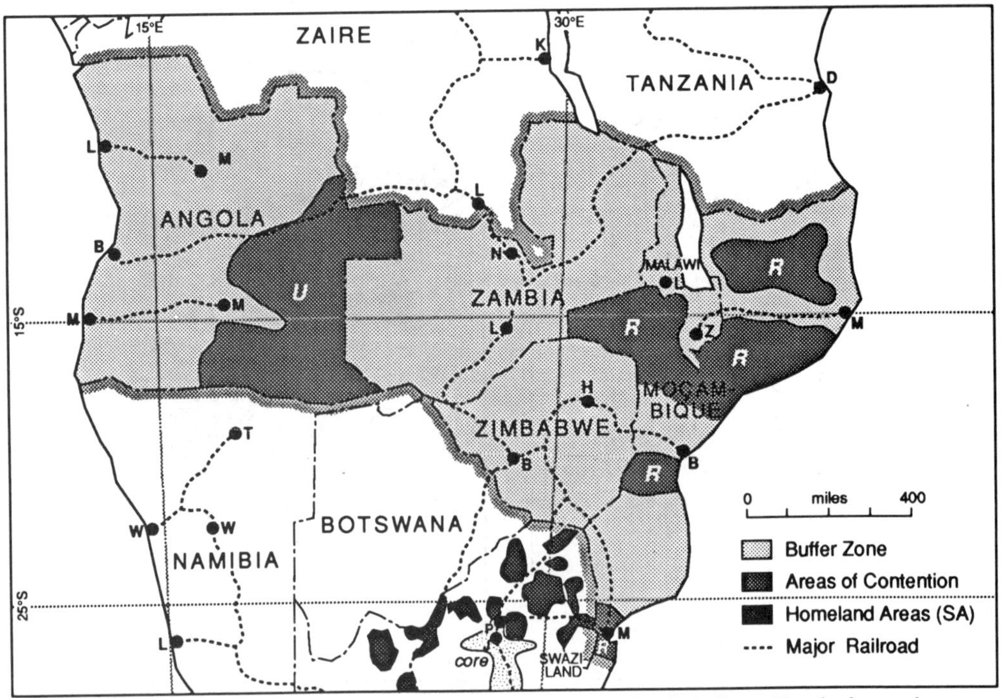

Figure 2. The buffer zone in its earliest stage. The stage of contention is indicated by the lettered areas: "U" for the UNITA movement in Angola, "R" for the RENAMO movement in Moçambique.

dental expansion of its oil industry. Thus, even before decolonization had reached southern Africa, disaster lay in its wake.

Domino Theory

The spatial sequence of decolonization in Subsaharan Africa suggests that the notion of a domino effect has merit despite fulminations to the contrary (O'Sullivan 1986). Simply defined, the domino theory holds that destabilization, or other significant transferable change, in one country or territory can affect the stability or normalcy of an adjacent state, and that this process can, in turn, affect other contiguous entities. The domino effect was much debated during the Indochina War, and it would be difficult to sustain the position that the conflict in Vietnam did not contribute to the disruption of neighboring Laos or Cambodia or, to a lesser degree, Thailand. More recently, observers have commented on the apparent domino effect in the Eastern Europe of the 1980s; Poland is often identified as the first "domino," and Albania as the last.

In Africa, Ghana was first in the 1950s, followed by East Africa in the 1960s and southern Africa in the 1970s and 1980s. British progress in West Africa made the French position untenable, and De Gaulle seized the initiative and moved not only Algeria, but also French West and French Equatorial Africa quickly toward independence in a "community" association with France (Houphouet-Boigny 1957). So rapidly was this process set in motion that Francophone Africa became independent in the same year long-prepared Nigeria did. Only Sekou Tourés Guinea chose to go it alone, asserting sovereignty in 1958 (Toure 1959). Zaire became independent following a violent upheaval in 1960; adjacent, landlocked, Belgian-administered Rwanda and Burundi were decolonized in 1962. In East Africa, where the British had faced the Mau Mau uprising in Kenya, it was Tanzania that led the way (1961), followed by Uganda (1962) and Kenya (1963). To the north, Somalia had become independent in 1960; to the south, Malawi and Zambia waited until 1964. Kenya's early independence, despite substantial opposition among its white minority, is especially relevant in the domino context. Nearly encircled by independent states and in control of Uganda's outlet to the sea, Kenya's sovereignty could not be deferred (Fig. 1).

The British awarded nominal independence to Botswana and Lesotho in 1966 and to Swaziland in 1968, but the key southern African territories—the Portuguese dependencies of Angola and Moçambique as well as still-British Southern Rhodesia—slowed the Wind of Change nearly to a halt. Indeed, change in Angola and Moçambique, in further affirmation of the domino effect, did not accelerate until insurgents could secure safe haven in adjacent Zaire and Tanzania, respectively. For several years, the Moçambique nationalist movement, FRELIMO, had headquarters in Dar es Salaam, Tanzania's largest city. One of Angola's three insurgent movements, FNLA, received protection as well as fiscal support from Zaire across the border. The presence of insurgents in newly independent Zaire and Tanzania had severe impact on these countries and their economies. In the case of Zaire, the conflict in Angola disrupted the outflow of minerals from the reserves in the southeastern interior, which during colonial times had moved across the Portuguese territory to the port of Lobito. Tanzania suffered not only from the effects of war in Moçambique, but also from the disastrous events that occurred in its neighbor to the northwest, Uganda.

Eventually Tanzanian armed forces entered Uganda in the aftermath of Amin's murderous regime, placing a heavy burden on an already impoverished economy.

Independence in Moçambique and Angola came in 1975, and again the domino effect came into play. Landlocked Rhodesia, where the white minority had declared unilateral independence (UDI), and which was under international economic sanctions, lost security along its eastern flank when the Portuguese withdrew from Moçambique. Immediately, its internal conflict widened into Moçambique, where insurgents now found safer haven and where Rhodesian forces engaged in hot pursuit. Britain's last domino fell in 1980; even South African support could not prolong UDI.

Angola's independence exposed Africa's last colonial domino, Namibia, to the full force of the Wind of Change. Despite continuing civil war in Angola, Namibia's rebel movement SWAPO (South West African People's Organization) used Angola's territory in its struggle against South Africa. Independence was achieved.

Buffer Zones and Front Line States

The slowdown of Africa's drive for independence could be prophesied in the early 1960s, based on the dimensions and influence of white minorities in southern Africa and upon the capacity of South Africa to affect regional power balances (De Blij 1962). From the beginning, it was clear that the ultimate objective of black Africans would be the termination of white minority rule in what was then still the Union of South Africa. In less than ten years following Ghana's independence, the Wind of Change had penetrated southern Africa. But Portugal did not match British or French flexibility; and Angola at the time of Zaire's independence had the second largest European minority in all of Subsaharan Africa. Moçambique, on the opposite coast, had a white minority more than three times as large as Kenya's. And landlocked Rhodesia, situated between Angola and Moçambique, was in position to slow the advance of African nationalism by thwarting British plans for decolonization. Together, these territories, astride the northern tier of southern Africa, created a buffer zone that for more than a decade separated South Africa from independent black Africa (De Blij 1973).

The southern African buffer zone had several consequences, some of which are outlasting its existence. First, by keeping the so-called Front Line States territorially removed from South Africa, the republic was able to implement its grand design of "Separate Development" with an impunity it would have been denied under other circumstances. Second, South Africa was given time to plan and organize support not only for the minority colonial regimes in the buffer zone, but also for movements that would later emerge as opponents of newly installed black African governments. Third, South Africa could prepare for the eventual breakdown of the buffer zone by exporting its Separate Development program to Namibia, by intimidating Botswana through cross-border raids (and by other means), and by strengthening its presence in the northern Transvaal. South Africa's geopolitical action(s) during this period leave no doubt that the republic was intent on substituting an internal buffer zone for the external one once the latter collapsed. Northern Namibia, Botswana, the northern Transvaal's Bantu Homelands, and the Kruger National Park all were part of this preparation for the time when the so-called Front Line States would abut South Africa itself rather than its neighbors to the north.

The appellation "Front Line States" originated in the southward march of African independence alluded to previously. While the external buffer zone remained intact, Tanzania and Zaire were Front Line States, both supporting insurgent movements in the Portuguese colonies; and Zambia was on the front line opposite white-minority-ruled Rhodesia. Malawi, although adjoining Moçambique and certainly affected by the strife in this Portuguese dependency, never played a comparable role ideologically, a posture dictated by its conservative ruler, Hastings Banda. But all of the Front Line States paid a price for their relative location. Revolutionaries, refugees, and retribution spilled across boundaries into these countries, themselves still searching for post-independence stability. A prominent Moçambique leader, Eduardo Mondelane, was killed in a bomb attack in Dar es Salaam, Tanzania's capital. Zaire's Kasai province was seriously destabilized by cross-border warfare. The then-outlawed (South African) African National Congress set up headquarters in Zambia, where South African paramilitary forces repeatedly attacked it.

When Portugal yielded, and Angola and Moçambique became independent states (1975), these flanks of the buffer zone now became Front Line States themselves—confronting not only South Africa, but, in the case of Moçambique, revolution-ravaged Rhodesia as well. Immediately, both countries were drawn into regional as well as superpower conflicts. Even as three factions vied for control over Angola, the government in Luanda proclaimed the country a Marxist state; a similar position was taken by the new government in Maputo (the renamed capital of Moçambique). In Angola, the movement called UNITA, ostensibly an anticommunist, "democratic" organization, received support not only from South Africa and from the United States but also from China—because the Chinese wished to counter Moscow's influence in the region. The Luanda government received proxy support from Cuba as tens of thousands of Cuban soldiers rallied to the Marxist side. By the mid-1980s, the UNITA movement had created an insurgent state in eastern and southern Angola (McColl 1969). In Moçambique, the RENAMO movement challenged the Maputo government, inflicting terror and dislocation on a rural population already ravaged by famine and disruption. RENAMO, supported by South Africa, never achieved the territorial success of UNITA; it controlled several sections of the country including parts of the hinterlands of both Maputo and Beira (Fig. 2). The conflict in Rhodesia also damaged Moçambique severely. The port of Beira, the landlocked neighbor's nearest outlet, was in disrepair. The Beira corridor to the interior lay devastated: bridges, roads, dams, railroads, and power lines were destroyed. The cost of front-line location was incalculably high.

When the struggle in Rhodesia ended and the independent state of Zimbabwe appeared on Africa's map (1980), the

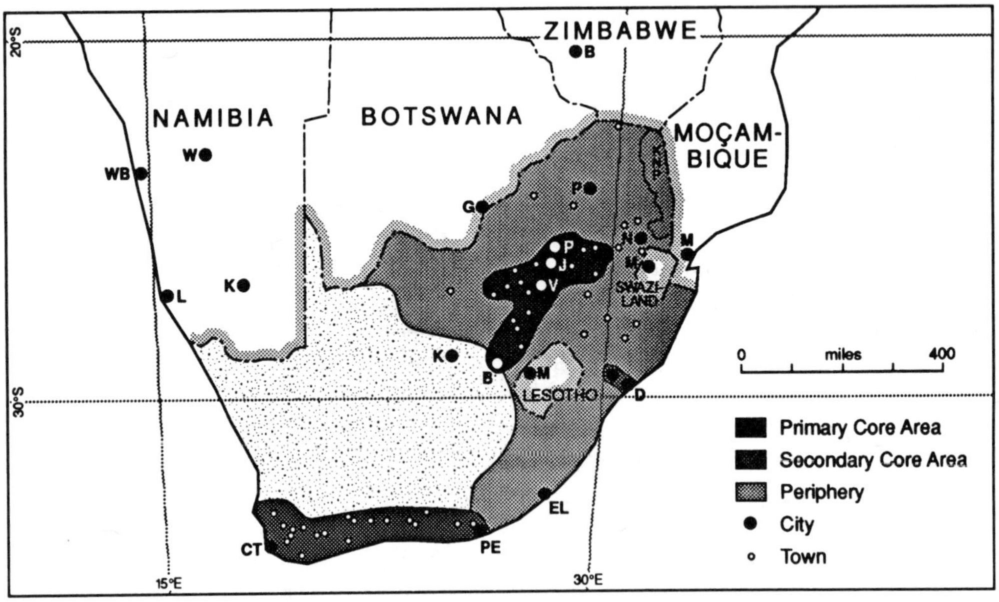

Figure 3. Core and periphery in South Africa. The lightly stippled area in the west is South Africa's emptiest quarter. Approximately 90 percent of the African population is located in the horseshoe-shaped zone enclosing the core area, and in the core area itself.

breakdown of the buffer zone was complete and South Africa confronted Front Line States across the entire length of its boundary except in the west, where Namibia still was under its control. At that time, the republic still pursued its campaign in Angola (in support of UNITA and in opposition to the Namibian independence movement, SWAPO) with enthusiasm. However, the cost of the war, both militarily in the field and politically at home, contributed to a search for settlement of the Angolan as well as the Namibian issue. The independence of Namibia in March 1990 with SWAPO members in the majority in the elected government, made Namibia a Front Line State and ended colonialism—not counting the domestic form within South Africa—on the continent.

South Africa's campaigns of support for UNITA and RENAMO in Angola and Moçambique, respectively, and of sabotage and disruption in Zimbabwe, were attempts to influence the geostrategic situation in the now-defunct buffer zone, intended to sustain conditions that had existed there previously. As long as the Front Line States were preoccupied with internal problems, they would be less able to cause or promote difficulties for South Africa. But in fact, the republic in the 1980s faced domestic challenges that could not have originated in the Front Line States. Urban insurrections, labor resistance, civil disobedience campaigns, and other forms of mass opposition to apartheid and Separate Development (and these systems' legal foundations) led to concessions that, in time, will be seen as the beginning of South Africa's political transformation.

Core, Periphery, and Front Line

The geopolitical situation in southern Africa in 1990 thus limited the roles of the final Front Line States in contributing to change within South Africa. Moçambique's primary objective was recovery. Zimbabwe, its economy the healthiest among regional states, was engaged in internal political reorganization. Botswana, many of its inhabitants dependent in one way or another on revenues earned in South Africa, was in no position to risk South African retribution. Namibia had become independent early in the year, its ties with (and dependence upon) the republic virtually unchanged as yet.

Should further change in South Africa take a revolutionary course, however, the relative location of the Front Line States would be likely to revive the role implied by their collective name. Cosmetic as well as consequential changes in the apartheid system have mainly affected the social geography of South Africa's heartland, its major cities, and their hinterlands. This has intensified core-periphery contrasts in a country where such regional disparities already are very strong (Fig. 3). The periphery was the scene of the establishment of the black homelands in the Separate Development scheme, and the horseshoe-shaped zone of ethnic "states" that partially envelops the republic's core area spatially defines much of the periphery. In much of this zone, South Africa resembles the poorer rural parts of the continent rather than the comparatively rich country that average-reporting statistics suggest it to be.

In Zimbabwe, the geographic situation was somewhat similar; there were no Bantustans in the South African sense, but core-periphery definitions and contrasts were sharp. It was in the periphery where the insurgencies of the 1970s arose and could not be suppressed. In South Africa, the periphery also will be vulnerable to insurgency—and the periphery marks the zone of contact between the republic and its front-line neighbors. Briefly during the 1980s, the vulnerability of this border area was underscored when land mines, planted by insurgents allegedly based in (or operating from) Zimbabwe, caused a number of casualties on Limpopo Valley farms. The South African government responded by compelling farmers to occupy their holdings for a substantial part of the year rather than leasing them to tenants. An increased military presence plus pressure on Zimbabwe suppressed the threat, but the potential for more serious problems along the republic's margins had been revealed.

The present Front Line States are strongly affected by their powerful neighbor—economically as well as politically. Their location relative to the geopolitical structure of South Africa will enmesh them in any revolutionary change the republic may undergo.

The Realm's Boundary Framework

Black Africa became independent partitioned by a boundary framework that was defined and delimited by colonial powers. Whatever the merits and demerits of this framework, it was decided by the member states of the Organization of African Unity that boundaries inherited at independence should be respected, and changed only by bilateral or multilateral consent (Brownlie 1979). Today, nearly four decades after the dawn of independence, the framework of African boundaries is substantially intact. Prescott (1987) attributes this to two causes: the colonial boundaries were defined with greater care and foresight than has generally been suggested, and African states have handled boundary conflicts with restraint.

In the early 1990s, the most serious boundary and territorial conflicts continue to afflict the Horn of Africa. The Ogaden question remains unresolved, and the Eritrean war appears on the verge of resurrecting the relic boundary between Eritrea and Ethiopia. Should the Eritreans' war for independence succeed, Ethiopia would become a landlocked country. This is undoubtedly the most consequential issue in black Africa's northeast today.

As a comparison between the maps of 1957 and 1990 shows, few boundary changes have been made during the period of decolonization. The boundary between former British and Italian Somaliland has been eliminated, and the Nigeria-Cameroon border was repositioned following a plebiscite in the borderland. Zanzibar was united with Tanganyika, eliminating a maritime boundary and resulting in the name Tanzania. In mid-1990, the issue of the South African exclave at Walvis Bay, on the coast of newly independent Namibia, remained unresolved. A United Nations resolution urged South Africa to yield the port and its immediate hinterland to Namibia, and there are indications that Pretoria will agree to a transfer. In that case, the exclave boundary will become a relic.

Given the intense fragmentation of Subsaharan Africa, the number of boundary disputes in the realm is small. Armed hostilities have occurred along the boundary between Mali and Burkina Faso, where a zone about ten miles wide and 100 miles long is contested. Nigeria and Chad have been in conflict over their boundary in Lake Chad, but this dispute has been overtaken by Chad's civil war involving Libya. In 1990, a boundary dispute erupted along the border between Senegal and Guinea-Bissau following the publication of reports that the area may contain fossil fuel reserves. And there is a disagreement between Zaire and Zambia over their joint boundary where it reaches Lake Tanganyika. Finally, the position of the border between Malawi and Tanzania at the northern end of Lake Nyasa has given rise to intermittent negotiations.

Considering the origin of Africa's boundaries, the purposes they initially served, and the number of landlocked states they created, this is a low incidence of border conflict indeed. A larger number of functional disputes have arisen, such as that between Kenya and Tanzania, which closed this East African boundary for more than six crucial years (1977 to 1983); but none of these has led to positional conflict. These functional problems, moreover, have generally been of short duration.

There are, however, signs that Africa's boundary framework may yet change significantly—not by boundary repositioning, but as a result of devolutionary stresses within African states. The Ethiopian-Eritrean case is only one of a substantial number of internal problems of this kind. The possibility of a north-south fragmentation in the Sudan grows as Khartoum's capacity to control secessionism in the south diminishes. The war in Chad has underscored the fundamental contrasts between north and south in this landlocked state as well. Strong and intensifying centrifugal forces are affecting Nigeria, where Muslim fundamentalism is fueling Islamic-Christian discord. In 1987, the worst religious riots in memory ravaged the northern regions (Brooke 1987). Devolutionary forces also are strong, as noted earlier, in Angola and in Moçambique. And the possibility of Natal's secession from South Africa, now mentioned by Zulu conservatives, is nothing new: it was proposed as an option in the early 1950s, when the Nationalist government's apartheid policies were first imposed on that multiracial, mainly non-Afrikaner province.

Given Africa's strongly fragmented cultural mosaic, its ideological divisions, and the growing awareness of ethnic and historic identity among peoples ranging from the Zulu nation in Natal to the Muslim Hausa of northern Nigeria, the potential for the balkanization of postcolonial Africa exists—and not only in the larger, more populous countries. Rwanda and Brundi, the small but populous countries wedged between Tanzania and Zaire, have been the scene of such deathly tribal conflict between Tutsi and Hutu that the compartmentalization of these territories has been seriously advanced as a means to reduce the carnage. The African reaction to ethnic complexity of national populations has been the imposition of the one-party state; in early 1990, there were 18 one-party governments (and 17 military regimes). But the centrifugal forces inherent in Africa's anthropogeography will not be permanently accommodated by such centralization of authority. Many leaders in postcolonial Africa were much impressed by Soviet-style political control and economic policies (Ghana's Nkrumah was among the first), and the Soviet model is much in evidence in the African one-party state. The Soviet struggle to adjust to the realities of devolution will be equally relevant to African states trying to cope with similar stresses.

While boundary changes have been few, population shifts, mainly in the form of refugee movements, have been numerous and devastating. Both in terms of absolute numbers as well as per capita, Africa has the world's largest body of dislocated people. Again the northeast has been most severely afflicted. Ethiopia's long-term conflict with its ethnic Somali peoples has driven nearly a million Somali across the border into Somalia, where they live in squalid, inadequate camps. Another million Eritreans and Ethiopians, victims of the war for Eritrean independence, live, and starve, in the Sudan. The turmoil in Uganda produced 200,000 refugees, most of whom fled to the Sudan; many have returned to their home areas as Uganda stabilizes. Nearly a half million refugees are encamped in Zaire, where they seek safety from strife in Rwanda, Burundi, and Angola. By 1988, nearly a million inhabitants of Moçambique had fled into neighboring countries ill-equipped to accommodate them. Africa's refugee camps are places of misery, disease, malnutrition, and starvation. Because their occupants, in some areas, are perceived to support a political cause, governments have attacked and destroyed relief operations, condemning hundreds of thousands to death. Not even the most ruthless colonial rule (Portugal's in Moçambique probably was the most atrocious) caused such horrors.

And the numbers above do not begin to reflect the dimensions of dislocation in Africa. In Moçambique, for example, an estimated 1.2 million people have left their rural homes to seek protection from the civil war in towns and cities. Liberia, Chad, Uganda, Angola, and other strife-torn countries have seen their villages and towns swell from a rural exodus. The combination of deserted farmlands and overgrown urban centers spells economic disaster and political trouble. Thus, governments are impelled to take draconian action to protect the interests of their citizens. In 1983, the Nigerian government summarily expelled 2 million Ghanaian workers who had come to Nigeria from their dictatorial homeland and its collapsing economy, to find jobs. The hardship faced by Africa's dislocated people mocks the stability of the realm's international boundary framework. Whatever the OAU decided, changes are bound to come.

Geography, Demography, and Environment

The transformation of Africa's political geography has taken place against a background of population explosion and environmental deterioration. In 1957, the year Ghana became independent, Subsaharan Africa's population totaled just 200 million. In 1990, the realm counted 500 million inhabitants; the projected figure for 2000 is just under 700 million. No other world geographic realm even approached such a growth rate; Kenya during the 1970s and 1980s became the world's fastest-growing country at about four percent annually, a doubling time of approximately 17 years. The TFR (total fertility rate) in the early 1980s was an estimated eight children per woman in Kenya. In Kenya as in other African countries, hopes for economic progress and improvement were dashed by growing costs and burdens of larger numbers.

And yet, viewing the numbers in global perspective, Africa is not, in general, densely populated. India alone has a much larger population than Africa's nearly four dozen countries combined; India's area is one-seventh that of Subsaharan Africa. According to FAO statistics, Indians and Africans, in the early 1960s, consumed, on average, about the same number of calories (slightly over 2000) daily. By the late 1980s, the average intake in India had risen to 2150; in Africa it had declined to 1870. Dietary balances had improved in India, but deteriorated in Africa. The population explosion, plus the social dislocation discussed earlier, contributed to this. But more important was the failure to transfer the Indian "green revolution" to Africa. Western agricultural advisers' obsession with high yields and cash crops led to the introduction of farming systems that worked in India's fertile Punjab, but not in most of Africa's low-yield countryside. Irrigation schemes and fertilizer-dependent crop varieties could not be afforded—either by governments or by subsistence farmers. African farmers need more roads and market systems to move farm produce from the remote, sparsely settled, land-abundant areas to the food-deficient population clusters. Without an improving infrastructure to help traditional farmers, no massive dam-and-canal schemes could solve Africa's food problems. So the African farmer lost ground in every direction: the newly independent governments mostly had their eyes on other, more prestigious sectors of the economy, and Western-devised green-revolution techniques, often involving irrigation projects and labor-intensive cultivation systems, were inappropriate for the realm's needs. In the meantime, millions of Africans remain utterly dependent upon overseas food supplies.

Even as the political transformation proceeded and the population explosion gained momentum, Africa's regional environments also changed dramatically. There can be no doubt that human intervention (through the opening of marginal land and the herding of livestock into fragile ecosystems) played a significant role in this. But nature also dealt Africa a series of blows during the second half of the century. The Sahara's southward expansion created the Sahel crisis of the 1970s and its enormous cost in human and animal lives, but it was not all people's doing. The desert also spread northward, even where no human activity contributed to its advance. The evidence suggests that the Sahara during this period was embarked on one of its natural expansion phases. The Inter-Tropical Convergence (ITC), a bellwether for West African moisture conditions, made its northward move later and started its coastward retreat earlier, facilitating the Saharan advance in the interior and reducing the wet season in the coastal countries. The human (and livestock) presence exacerbated the environmental situation in the Sahel, but it was not the disaster's sole cause.

While attention was focused on the Sahel crisis, other areas of Africa also experienced droughts, including East and South Africa. Regional droughts in Africa have several consequences that last long after the dry spell has ended: people and livestock are induced to destroy a widening area of natural vegetation, and the loss of this vegetation appears to hinder the return of normal, average conditions. We have studied maps of climatic regions, rainfall distributions, and vegetative associations, perhaps taking insufficient account of the degree to which the mapped phenomena are interrelated. The evidence from the Amazon Basin suggests that, in areas where the forest has been cut down, the exposed surface reflects more sunlight back into space, creating layers of dry air close to the ground. Since as much as half of all rainfall comes from moisture evaporated from the land and plant surfaces, such a dry layer would absorb evaporated moisture without yielding beneficial "return" rains. This, in turn, inhibits the revival of vegetation. Break the ecological balance, the evidence suggests, and the maps may have to be redrawn. In Africa, the destruction of natural vegetation may worsen permanently an already severe water shortage. Rainforest and savanna destruction are widespread. The Sahel problem (which extends all the way across the north from Senegal to Ethiopia) is only part of a larger environmental threat.

Environmental problems can have politico-geographical consequences. While the Sahel drought affected primarily the states and peoples of the Sahara margin, coastal West African countries were involved as well. Bassett (1988) describes the impact of a group of Fulani herders who drove their cattle from the desiccating Sahel zone into greener Ivory Coast. The government of Ivory Coast welcomed these pastoralists, who would make beef supplies more dependable and cheaper than they had been previously. But the local farmers saw it rather differently: the Fulani's cattle trampled their crops of cotton, corn, rice, millet, and yams. They resented the inadequate protection from the capital, and a violent conflict erupted. When finally the government decided to allocate parcels of pastureland to the Fulani, these were inadequate and the Fulani left the country. In the meantime, much of northern Ivory Coast was in disarray, a victim of the Sahel crisis hundreds of miles away.

Directly and indirectly, environmental change has had political repercussions in other areas: northern Nigeria, northeastern Kenya, and highland Lesotho are examples. The long-term impact of environmental change on the African political framework has just begun to be felt.

Conclusion

The final chapter in the transformation of Africa's political geography is now being written. South Africans could see the dominoes fall and the buffer zone collapse, but until the mid-1980s the minority government pursued a course that was destined to make future accommodations more difficult. That future is now here, and the question is whether Africa will witness still another violent struggle for power (and not necessarily an exclusively black-white conflict) or if a negotiated transition can be achieved. Then, perhaps, South Africa could become the regional force it should be, the provider of products and technologies, the example of a successful, multiracial African economy, the leader in finance and investment. Preoccupation with the South African situation has done much to screen the problems of the rest of Subsaharan Africa from world view and world opinion. Africa, the cradle of humankind, is now its sickbed, literally and figuratively. No geographic realm is so severely afflicted by disease (the total AIDS cases may number 3 million; some demographers are predicting an actual population decline in some areas as a result). No geographic realm has witnessed comparable economic and political failure; none is as hurt by falling commodity prices on world markets as is Africa.

The Wind of Change carried from Senegal to South Africa. Let us hope that a counterforce will soon emanate from the south, radiating the potential of a renewed republic, a prosperous Zimbabwe, and a stabilized Angola northward, eastward, and westward to redirect the destinies of a troubled realm.

References

Azikiwe, N. 1961. *Zik: a Selection from the Speeches of Nnamdi Azikiwe.* Cambridge: Cambridge University Press.

Bassett, T. J. 1988. The political ecology of peasant-herder conflicts in the Northern Ivory Coast. *Annals of the Association of American Geographers* 78:453-472.

Brooke, J. 1987. Moslem-Christian rioting tears Northern Nigeria. *New York Times*, 22 March, 25.

Brownlie, I. 1979. *African Boundaries: a Legal and Diplomatic Encyclopedia.* London: Hurst.

De Blij, H. J. 1962. *Africa South.* Evanston: Northwestern University Press.

__________. 1973. *Systematic Political Geography.* 2nd ed. New York: Wiley.

Hadjor, K. B. 1988. *Nkrumah and Ghana: the Dilemma of Postcolonial Power.* London: Kegan Paul International.

Houphouet-Boigny, F. 1957. Black Africa and the French Union. *Foreign Affairs* 35:579.

McColl, R. W. 1969. The insurgent state: territorial bases of revolution. *Annals of the Association of American Geographers* 59:613.

Nkrumah, K. 1957. *Ghana.* New York: Thomas Nelson.

__________. 1963. *Africa Must Unite.* London: Heinemann.

Nyerere, J. K. 1961. The African and democracy. In *Africa Speaks*, eds. J. Duffy and R. A. Manners. Princeton: Van Nostrand.

__________. 1963. A United States of Africa. *Journal of Modern African Studies* I:9

O'Sullivan, P. 1986. *Geopolitics.* New York: St. Martin's.

Prescott, J.R.V. *Political Frontiers and Boundaries.* London: Allen and Unwin.

Rooney, D. 1988. *Kwame Nkrumah: the Political Kingdom of the Third World.* London: Taurus.

Rothchild, D. S. 1960. On the application of the Westminster model to Ghana. *Centennial Review* 4:465.

Touré, S. 1959. *Toward Full Re-Africanization.* Paris: Présence Africaine.

Middle East Geopolitical Transformation: The Disappearance of a Shatterbelt

by Saul B. Cohen

DEPARTMENT OF GEOLOGY AND GEOGRAPHY, HUNTER COLLEGE, NEW YORK, NEW YORK.

The cold war's end has brought about major global geopolitical restructuring. It also is cause for regional geopolitical reordering. The gulf war and its aftermath are but one expression of Middle Eastern disequilibrium. This shatterbelt region has been caught up in both intraregional tensions and the post-World War II history of competition between the Maritime and Eurasian Continental realms. Now the Middle East is becoming strategically reoriented to the West. While powerful centrifugal forces still prevail, the reduction of external competitive pressures permits centripetal forces to become more salient. In addition to Arabism and Islam, these include migration and capital flows and water and oil transportation lines. A new balance among the Middle East's six regional powers can be fostered but not dictated by the outside world. Equilibrium can best be promoted, not by a Pax Americana, but by the United States and the European Community acting as two competitive but allied stabilizers. **Key words:** *capital flows, geopolitical equilibrium, Gulf War, migration, oil pipelines, shatterbelt.*

Introduction

The Persian/Arab Gulf War was heralded by many as a "defining" war, whose aftermath would be a new Middle Eastern order. The allied victory over Iraq was overwhelming and unprecedented. It was the first genuinely high-technology conflict that the world has known. Its devastating consequences will long be felt by Iraq, and the lessons learned will surely become a textbook for strategy and weaponry in future regional wars.

While the immediate allied objectives, freeing Kuwait and eliminating Iraq as a military threat to its neighbors, were speedily realized, the "new order" has yet to be achieved. We are learning, once again, that military victories do not translate into immediate and enduring political success. A decisive war is a one-time event. A decisive peace, however, can come only from a succession of reinforcing events.

Thus, the early aftermath of the 44-day war was the failed attempt by the Shia and Kurds of Iraq to overthrow Saddam Hussein. This was followed by the savage repression that triggered a massive wave of refugees fleeing the Iraqi troops—up to 1.75 million Kurds into the Turkish and Iranian borderlands and 100,000 Shia into Iran and the allied occupied South.

The allied effort to provide relief for the Kurds in a northern "safe-haven" zone, and the positioning of a United Nations' observer force to replace U.S. soldiers in the south, is part of the longer-term process of restoring stability to Iraq. It is not clear whether Saddam Hussein will retain his dictatorial powers or will be toppled, and whether a federated form of government that offers greater autonomy to the northern and southern provinces will emerge. As forceful as was United States leadership in "demonizing" Saddam during the war, it has been far more ambiguous in pursuing measures that would now drive him from office. What is clear, however, is that Iraq is in flux.

The same uncertainty holds true for an environmentally devastated Kuwait. Increasing pressures on the ruling Sabah family to open the country to political and economic reform could well lead to democratization of the kingdom. Moreover, the war may compel the Kuwaitis to forge a new kind of national identity in which they take responsibility for operating their own state, rather than depending on outside workers, as in the past.

Other questions about the post-war era have to do with whether the American initiative to bring the Arabs and Israel to the negotiating table will bear fruit and whether the Syrian-backed Lebanese government will be able to reunify the country. Finally, there is the danger that a new United States-sparked arms race in the Middle East will snatch defeat from the jaws of victory, making a mockery of the calls for a new Middle Eastern order.

If, then, the immediate aftermath of the Persian/Arab Gulf War is doubt and uncertainty, need one be pessimistic about long-term prospects for stability? A geopolitical assessment of the region offers an encouraging note. The Middle East is in disequilibrium because it has experienced not just the Gulf War, but more profound change—the impact of the end of the cold war. While the region remains a shatterbelt, it is now tilting geostrategically towards the Maritime Realm.

Still highly divided and immature, the regional system can gain in cohesiveness as forces promoting spatial interaction acquire greater salience. A coordinated effort between the United States and the European Community, as well as widespread fears throughout the Middle East, can create the conditions for long-term equilibrium. The reference is to equilibrium not order, for equilibrium is dynamic and order is

From *Journal of Geography,* Vol. 91, No. 1, January/February 1992, pp. 2-10. Reproduced with permission of the National Council for Geographic Education.

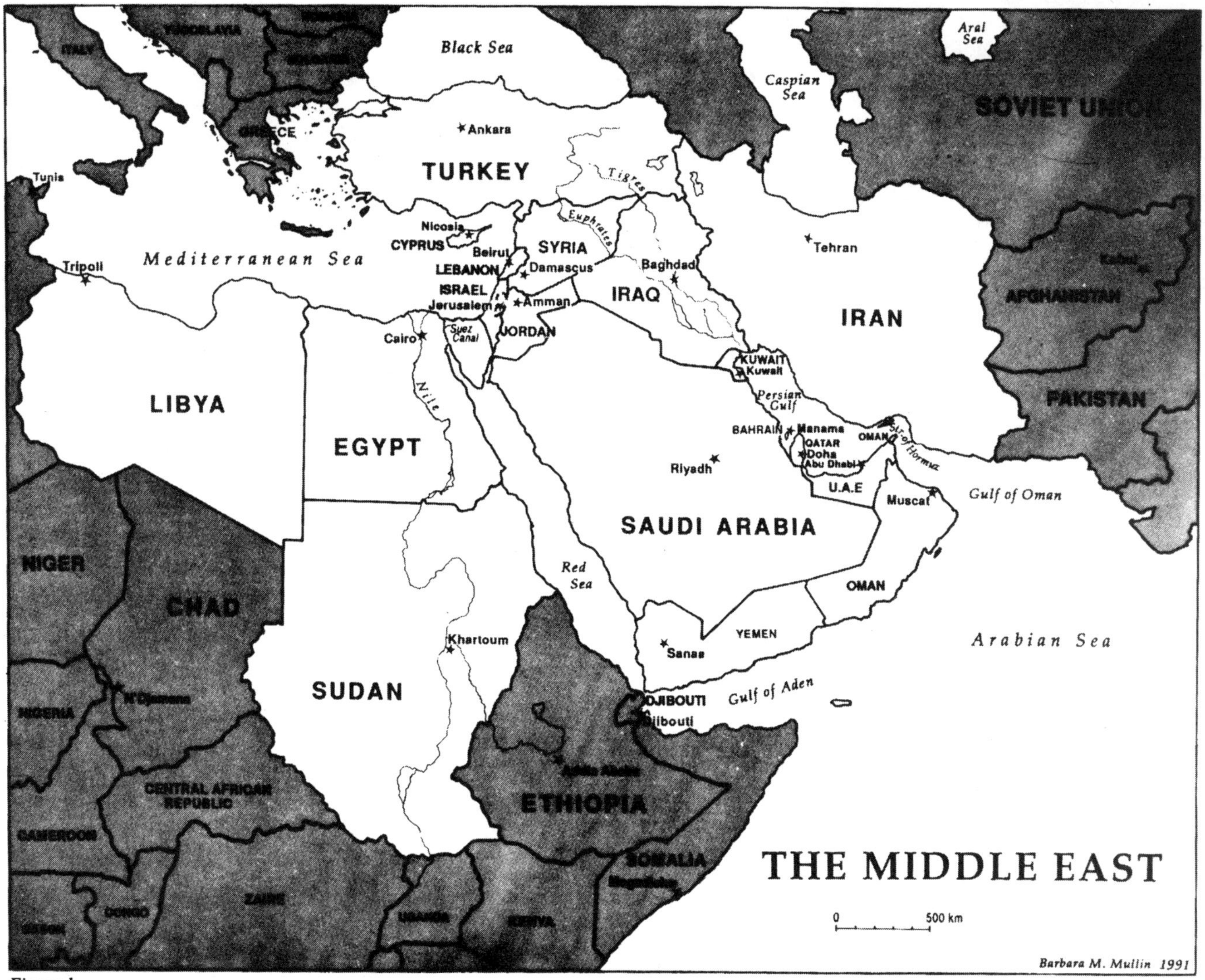

Figure 1.

static. The Gulf War has accelerated the process of geopolitical change within the region, but it is not the basic cause of such change. The war occurred because the Middle East had already begun to experience a fundamental geopolitical restructuring.

It is the end of the cold war that is responsible for the changing geopolitical status of the Middle East. Indeed, if it were not for the end of the cold war, we would not have had a "hot war." The diminished role of the USSR created a power vacuum. Disappearance of the restraining hand of the former Soviet Union gave the Iraqi dictator the opportunity to seize Kuwait and to seek domination over his neighbors to the south. Soviet disengagement also enabled the United States to move quickly on both the political and military fronts to respond to the Iraqi aggression. The Soviet Union continues to play a role in Middle East diplomacy, but lacks the military, economic, and ideological capacity to go beyond its efforts to mediate the Gulf War, which while they failed were not wholly without influence.

Geopolitical Evolution of the Middle East Region

When we speak of the Middle East, we refer to the area that extends from Turkey through Iran, and from Libya through the Sudan (Figure 1). This is a relatively new geographical region. There was no Middle East in its current outlines in either the folk or the scholarly regional consciousness of the 1920s and early 1930s. While the term was introduced by Alfred Mahan in 1902 and used by Sir Mark Sykes in British parliamentary speeches in 1916, it did not gain currency until the Second World War (Lewis 1966). Then, in 1941, the British created the Middle East Supply Centre, to embrace a single-purpose logistics and transportation region.

For most of its five millennia of recorded history, this juncture of three continents was not a distinct region. The Nile and Mesopotamia were worlds unto themselves, meeting each other in the Levant in times of war and peace. Overlapping and injecting themselves into these areas were powers from the adjoining highlands and deserts of Western and Central Asia, as well as from the interpenetrating Mediterranean and Arabian seas.

The Forging of a Region

Several modern-era forces led to the creation of the Middle East as we now know it. They include Great Britain's strategy for empire building, the discovery of oil, and the evolution of transportation and communications technology. They overlay the political-cultural frameworks of Arabism, Islam, and the Ottoman Empire.

By 1800, the British had become the dominant commercial force in the Persian/Arab Gulf, for the purpose of supporting and enhancing their interests in India. Then in 1839 Aden was acquired to reinforce the route to South Asia.

At the western end of the region, Britain began to build a power bastion in Egypt. British and Turkish troops forced Napoleon out of Egypt in 1801, thwarting French plans to use the country as a military base against India. British influence grew rapidly, culminating in the building of the Suez Canal (1869) and the military occupation of Egypt (1882).

In effect, Great Britain had brought together the Persian/Arab Gulf, the southern Arabian peninsula, and the Nile in a military, economic, and political framework. In addition, it extended its sphere of influence into southern Persia, countering the Russian pressures upon Persia, which Britain perceived as a threat to India.

The 1909 discovery of petroleum in southern Persia (Khuzistan), followed by oil finds in northern Iraq in 1927, triggered another region-creating force. This is expressed in today's system of oil-producing and transporting states that embraces every part of the Middle East. To transport Iraqi petroleum, the Iraq Petroleum Company built a pipeline in the mid-1930s from Kirkuk to the port of Haifa and a new refinery at Haifa Bay. This was the forerunner of a vast network of region-linking lines that has subsequently emerged.

A third early example of region formation was the railroad. The Germans acquired a concession for the Anatolian-Baghdad railway as early as 1902. The plan was stymied by British resistance. However, British engineers began to build an Iraqi system during the First World War. By the 1930s, Baghdad was connected to the Mediterranean via Mosul and the Taurus section of Turkey. At the western end, Egypt was connected by rail to Turkey via Palestine, Lebanon, and Syria when the Haifa-Beirut line was completed in 1943.

Britain's building of the port of Haifa (1929-33), and its deep dredging in 1930 of the Shatt al Arab, on which Basra is located, was further evidence of a colonial military and economic strategy to knit the region together. All of these efforts, when added to the power of the ideal, if not the reality of the pan-Arabism that was stirred by the Arab Revolt against the Ottomans (1916), were the underpinnings of the modern Middle East.

When the Middle East assumed definable regional form after the Second World War, what kind of region was it? It was clearly what we geographers describe as a shatterbelt. A shatterbelt is a region that is highly fragmented politically as a result of internal divisiveness and of the pressures of external great powers in pursuit of their own geostrategic interests (Cohen 1973).

Superpower competition made the Middle East a shatterbelt. The previous imperialistic domination by Britain and France, each of which had carved out its discrete sphere, provided a stabilizing influence. In contrast, the competition between the United States and the USSR for regional influence destabilized the scene. The external shatterbelt element was provided by the region's unique global location. The Middle East lies between the world's two geostrategic realms—the trade-dependent Maritime and the Eurasian Continental. This location and the new-found petroleum wealth made it a natural battleground between the two superpowers. Each lined up allies and satellites in the struggle for regional dominance. The fact that the superpowers dealt with highly unstable states whose governing regimes were frequently overthrown and switched alliances added to the general regional turmoil.

While superpower competition was fierçe, it was constrained by the fear of war and its nuclear consequences. The United States and Soviet Union acted in concert to bring an end to hostilities in two major instances: in the 1956 Sinai War and in the October 1973 war between Israel and Egypt. In both cases, the superpowers resisted being drawn into situations which might escalate into nuclear war.

The cold war fanned existing hatreds among the region's different national, religious, and ethnic groups through the supply of arms, equipment, and resources by the Soviet Union and the United States, and by other western and eastern bloc nations seeking political and economic gain. This supported the ambitions and rivalries of Middle Eastern states bent upon achieving regional or local hegemony. The instability stemming from conflict and shifts in alliances kept the region in constant geopolitical upheaval.

Now, four decades after its emergence as a shatterbelt, the Middle East is on the verge of a major change in geostrategic affiliation. It is tilting towards the Maritime Realm. The collapse of communism in Eastern Europe and the former USSR and the erosion of Soviet central authority have eliminated the new Commonwealth of Independent States as a major military and economic player within the region, at least for the foreseeable future, and relegated it to the important but not decisive role of mediator. Heartlandic Eurasia will remain sensitive to events along its 1,400-mile land and sea borders with Turkey and Iran, but its era of broad and enveloping regional penetration through naval and air bases in the Red and Arabian seas and the Eastern Mediterranean seems over.

In the geopolitical reordering now underway, it is Maritime Europe that is likely to become America's equal. While the United States still has a decisive military voice in the Western alliance, economic factors are changing the world power balance. Europe has an even greater strategic, economic, and historic stake in the Middle East than does the United States. It is dependent on the region for oil, is a major importer of Middle Eastern products and capital, and exports goods, capital, and other financial services to the countries of the region. The economic vitality and political structure of the European Community should lead to a more vigorous and independent pursuit of its Middle East interests in the post-Gulf War era. Evidence of this in the months following the war's end include Britain's initiative in formulating the Kurdish "safe haven" concept and Germany's lead in developing a Western presence in Iran to aid the refugees there.

If the United States and Maritime Europe can agree on certain vital issues like the Arab-Israeli conflict, the future of Iraq, and the acceptance of Iran as a full participant in shaping the region's future, the Middle East will probably shift to the Maritime orbit. If, however, there is serious disagreement between these two major power centers, then the region will remain a shatterbelt, particularly since this will provide Russia and/or Muslim Central Asian states with a new window of opportunity for intervention. Whatever the case, because the Maritime geostrategic realm is no longer dominated by a "Pax Americana," it is not possible for the United States to take unilateral action in reshaping the map of the Middle East.

With the end of the Gulf War, the military arsenals that were built up within the region, in part by exploiting the United States/Soviet rivalry, will seriously impede efforts to resolve the other conflicts that engulf the region. If the arms race is renewed, rather than dampened, destabilization will persist. However, if the outside powers draw up and fully comply with post-war agreements to restrict arms sales to all of the region's states, the capacities of hostile parties to use war rather than negotiations to address their differences will be considerably reduced.

Middle Eastern Regional Characteristics

Regional Immaturity

The internal divisions that contribute so greatly to Middle Eastern regional immaturity cannot be quickly or easily erased. While social and religious differences are the roots of much of the region's fragmentation, part of the problem is economic inequality. The uneven distribution of natural resources—land, fresh water, soils, and minerals; imbalances in population density, manpower pools, and educational/technological levels; and inequalities in health and living standards—are sources of continuing tensions within and among the nations of the Middle East.

Until now, the wealthy states of the Middle East have done little to allay poverty in other lands. Most of their gifts and loans have been devoted to supporting militaristic adventures (Iraq's invasion of Iran) and terrorism (the PLO's activities against Israel), or to humanistic relief efforts (maintenance of refugee camps). Very little has gone to genuine economic development projects. A positive result of the Gulf War is that the "have not" nations of the anti-Iraqi Arab coalition, Egypt and Syria, will be the immediate beneficiaries of some wealth-sharing, unless they squander it on arms purchases.

Parts-to-Whole Relationships

In spite of all the past divisions, and those likely to persist into the future, we can begin to anticipate the Middle East as a geopolitically unified, if not yet cohesive, unit. The parts that constitute the region cannot disentangle themselves, they cannot turn their backs upon one another. Thus, there cannot be a "Persian/Arab Gulf strategy," there can only be a "Middle Eastern strategy"—for the United States and the United Nations, for Iraq and Egypt, for Turkey and Iran, for Jordan and Israel.

Even if it suited some countries to try to opt out of the region, they could not. Turkey cannot arbitrarily declare itself European, nor can Israel and Egypt shift from being Middle Eastern countries to being Eastern Mediterranean by describing themselves as such in their tourist brochures. As long as Anatolia is home to half the Kurdish people, Turkey cannot detach itself from events in Iran and Iraq. As long as it has a northeast Mediterranean Sea coast and especially the Bay of Iskenderun, it cannot escape its geographical role as a land bridge for pipelines from Mesopotamia and ultimately Iran, or as a base for the U.S. warplanes that were used against Iraq. As long as it remains the source of the Tigris and Euphrates rivers, its water policies will be a major focus for interaction with Syria and Iraq.

Egypt was the lead Arab nation among those in the Middle East confronting Iraq. It will be in the forefront of the Arab states involved in enforcing a Gulf peace, because of its size, military power, traditions of regional leadership, and stake in regional stability.

Israel's present and future is inextricably entwined with, not simply the Palestinian Arabs, but also with the war and peace strategies of Egypt, Jordan, Lebanon, Syria, Iran, and Iraq. The Scuds that landed in Greater Tel Aviv, Haifa, and the south were launched from western Iraq, not from the sea to Israel's west.

Forces of Regional Interaction

There is no doubt that centrifugal forces have torn the region apart, especially with the advent of modern nationalism. The important question is: can centripetal forces develop enough momentum to override the divisive character of the region.

Of the various geopolitical forces that have the near-term capability for giving greater unity to what is becoming a holistic region are regional migrations, capital flows, and water and petroleum transitways. These are modern expressions of historical movement—unifying ties that are more tangible than the regional overlay of Arabism and Islam, which, because of internal tensions, cannot guarantee the region's integration.

Of course, pan-Arabism and Islam strongly influence the nature of Middle Eastern politics. However, they do not define the region geopolitically. During the Gulf War, rallies in the Arab states of northwest Africa may have expressed popular solidarity with Iraq, but the fate of the Maghreb is strategically and economically tied to Western Europe. In fact, France's greatest fears were that the anger of Algerian masses against French participation in the Gulf War would strengthen Muslim fundamentalism and increase political unrest to the point that there would be new large-scale Algerian migration to France. Immigration, not the rupture of Franco-Algerian relations, remains the concern, as is also the case for Spain. Similarly, Muslims in Pakistan may have vented their anger at the American military effort in the Persian/Arab Gulf, but Pakistan's geopolitical destiny is with South Asia.

Migration and Capital Flows

Two elements flow relatively freely throughout the region,

people and capital, even in times of war. Because of its locale as a global transitway, the Middle East has been a focus for migration throughout the ages. Today's important Middle Eastern migrations are essentially intra-regional, with the exception of Turks, who have sought temporary work in Western Europe, and Jews from Europe, Asian-North African lands, and the former Soviet Union, who have found haven in Israel.

While there is some daily transborder movement in the region, macro-intraregional migration is the more significant integrator. Egyptians have migrated to Iraq, Kuwait, Saudi Arabia, and Libya in the millions. It is estimated that Egyptian workers left 12 billion dollars behind as they fled Kuwait. Prior to the invasion of Kuwait, there were two million Egyptian workers in Iraq. More than half have left, and the exodus is likely to continue as the shattered Iraqi economy has less need for foreign labor. On the other hand, the number of Egyptians in Saudi Arabia has increased to over one million; over 700,000 Egyptians were issued visas from September 1990 to March 1991 to replace Yemenis and Palestinians. Hundreds of thousands of Palestinians had successfully integrated themselves into the Saudi Arabian and Gulf states' economies, parallel or subsequent to being absorbed into the mainstream of their first countries of refuge—Jordan, Lebanon, Syria, and Egypt. The number of Yemeni working in Saudi Arabia and the Gulf countries may have approximated four million in recent years, and one million Sudanese work outside their country's borders.

The Gulf crisis wreaked havoc with all migrants, forcing many to flee. When the crisis is over, many of the Middle Eastern foreign workers will doubtlessly return. However, Palestinians now hold far fewer jobs in Kuwait than before, as they have been permanently replaced by Asians or Egyptians, or social change within Kuwait brings more Kuwaitis into the job market. The same holds true for Palestinians in Saudi Arabia. The chronic labor shortages of the oil-rich states will require labor in the rebuilding of their economies, and widespread unemployment and underemployment in the sending countries will be a compelling "push" factor. But the welcome mat has been pulled from under the Yemenis and the Palestinians, at least until the outlines of a peace are clear.

Raw statistics of migrant numbers mask the significance of these individuals to the economies of their home countries. For Egypt, cash remittances either sent home to relatives or brought back as savings have amounted to four billion dollars per annum or up to eight percent of gross national product—Egypt's single largest source of revenue. Cash remittances have also been vital to the economies of Yemen and Jordan—in the case of Yemen, 40 percent, and Jordan, 34 percent of gross national product.

Water

A major element in both the economy and the politics of the region is water. There are several measures that could rationalize the supply of water for the whole region, but only if there is genuine peace.

For example, Turkey's freshwater withdrawals are under 10 percent of potentially available water. In order to increase its usable supply, Turkey has recently completed the Ataturk Dam on the Euphrates River. This is part of a 20-billion-dollar network of 22 dams along the Euphrates and Tigris rivers, which will provide irrigation and hydroelectric power to Turkey's dry southeast. These dams also represent a potential for exporting stored water by pipeline to the arid, dusty plains of northern Syria and Iraq, when political conditions warrant, and even to Jordan and Saudi Arabia.

Libya now withdraws far more water than is available to it from groundwater and rainwater—which means that it relies upon expensive distillation processes. Under peaceful political conditions, Egypt could pipe to Libya some of the several billion cubic meters of water that now escape into the Mediterranean, or, alternately export it to Gaza and Israel's Negev. The amount of the diversion would depend upon how much water is needed to maintain a strong flow in the Nile distributary to prevent siltation from occurring where the delta meets the Mediterranean.

Better use of irrigation waters in Egypt, such as through the drip technology that Israel has developed, could free Nile water for export to other countries. So would technologies for reducing evaporation loss from waters stored in Lake Nasser.

Israel is highly dependent on the headwaters of the Jordan River, but makes very limited use of the Yarmuk River, which forms the border between Syria and Jordan, and Israel and Jordan, before emptying into the Jordan River. At present, there are few reservoirs to capture and store most of the Yarmuk's winter floodwaters. A cost-effective measure would be to divert the Yarmuk to the Sea of Galilee in Israel, from which the waters could then be fed southward to Jordan's Ghor Canal, benefiting both countries. Jordan would remain the major user of the Yarmuk, and would have far greater quantities available to it than it now has (Ben-Shahar 1989). Another mutually beneficial water project could involve Lebanon and Israel in using the waters of the Lower Litani River that now flow out to the sea largely unused. Finally, as a result of a persistent drought in Israel, the shipment of fresh water in tankers from Turkey to Israel is being discussed by leaders of both countries.

These shared water projects are not possible in the present climate of tension and conflict. Only if the nations of the region place the mutual benefits of Middle Eastern economic integration above the potential gains of war can economic development receive the priority that it deserves.

Oil Pipelines

When we think of the Middle East, we think oil. The network of oil pipelines, existing and proposed, operational and non-operational, forges a critical set of regional links, as indicated on the map (Figure 2) (McCaslin 1989). These ties reflect such geographical variables as distance, terrain and optimal exit points, as well as international prices and political conditions. The direction taken by pipeline routes may also, in the future, reflect environmental hazard concerns, although to date these have not been significant factors.

The earliest transregional pipeline was, as previously

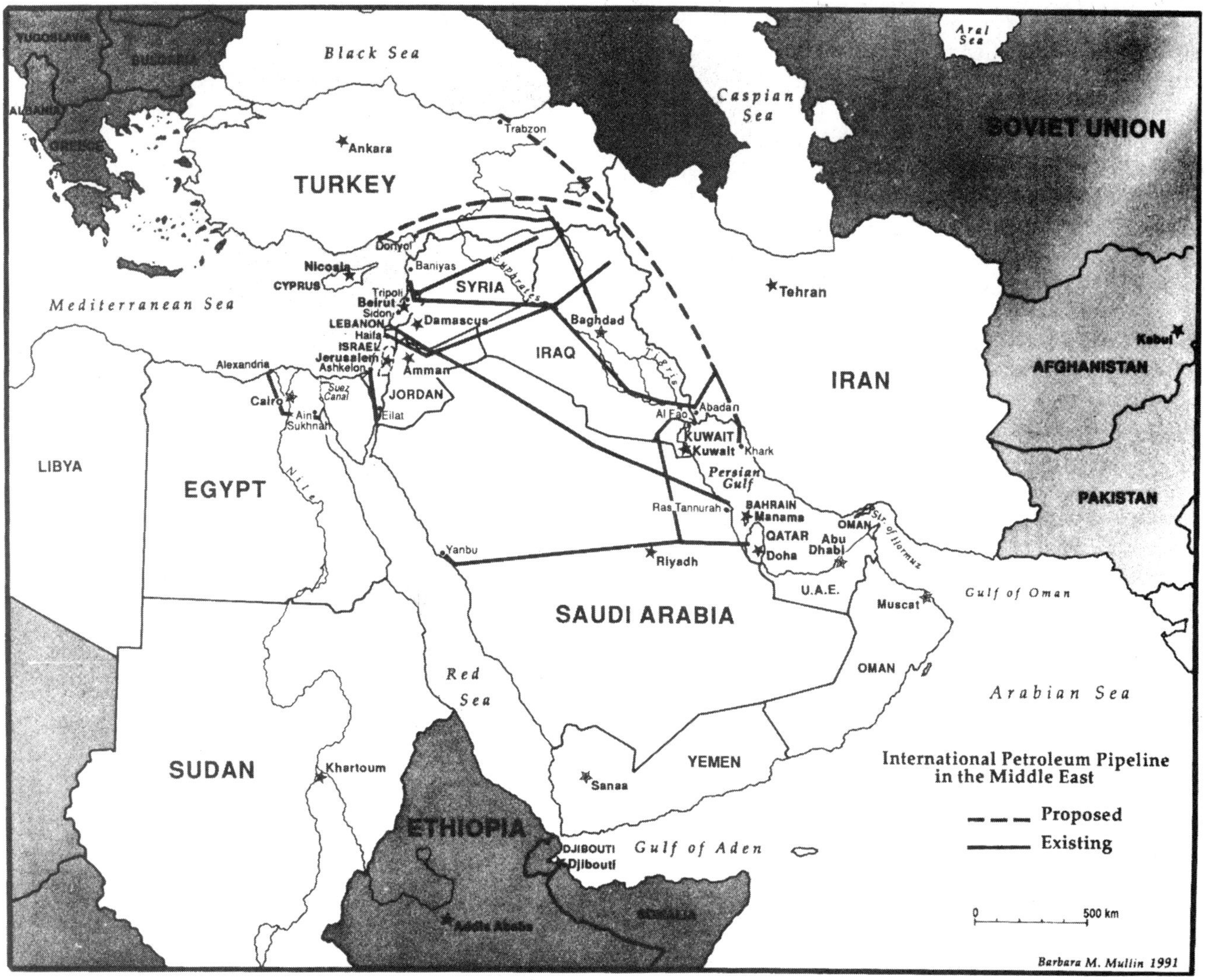

Figure 2.

noted, the Iraq Petroleum Company's (IPC) 12-inch line from Kirkuk to Haifa. It spawned a major refinery and petrochemical industry in Haifa Bay. The second major line, the 30/31" TAP-line, was completed in 1947. Originating in northeastern Saudi Arabia, at Ras Tannurah on the Gulf, the line was to have terminated in Haifa. However, the 1948-49 Arab-Israeli conflict caused TAP-line to be diverted to Sidon in Lebanon. Its capacity of 25 million tons has never exceeded 17 million, and it is now unused. In place of its prewar line to Haifa that was closed by that conflict, the IPC built two lines to Tripoli in Lebanon in 1952 (12 inch and 16 inch), to which was later added a 30-inch line to Banias in Syria.

Other key routes that have been developed in recent years are the Trans-Saudi 48-inch pipeline from Buqayq in northeastern Saudi Arabia to Yanbu on the Red Sea, built in 1981, and the line from Rumailah in southern Iraq, which was linked to the Yanbu carrier. The flow of oil from Iraq has been shut off by the Saudi government as a result of the current crisis.

When the Suez Canal was closed to Israel-bound shipping (from 1949 to 1975), a pipeline to carry Iranian oil was built from the Gulf of Aqaba port of Eilat to Israel's Mediterranean port of Ashdod. It is no longer operational. Also, when Iraq's Persian/Arab Gulf tanker traffic was interdicted by its war with Iran and tensions with Syria, Iraq developed a pipeline from Kirkuk in its northern fields to Cizre in Turkey and then west via the piedmont region of southern Turkey to the Bay of Iskenderun on the Mediterranean. It is now closed to Iraq. A second line was planned northward from Kirkuk to link up with a Turkish pipeline from Turkey's Batman oil fields to Iskenderun. Finally, when the Suez Canal was blocked during the 1967-75 period as a result of the Arab-Israeli conflict, Egypt built a bypass line that took oil from tankers off-loading at the Gulf of Suez and carried it to Alexandria on the Mediterranean via Helwan.

Suggested routes include a line from the oil fields of southwestern Iran to Urmiyeh in northern Iran and west across the border to join up with the Turkish network, or north for a distance of 300 miles across Anatolia to Trabzon on the Black Sea. Other proposed projects, dependent upon resolution of the Arab-Israeli conflict, would reopen TAP-line, building an extension from Mafraq in Jordan to Haifa, and reopen the Eilat-Ashkelon line, extending it northward to Haifa. The latter line would take oil shipped by tankers from Yanbu.

What is unique to the Middle East is that its historic

political centers have persisted into contemporary times, resulting in a greater number of evenly balanced power centers than in other parts of the world. There are six such power centers—Egypt, Iraq, Iran, Israel, Syria, and Turkey. Even if Saddam had succeeded in keeping Kuwait, his mastery over the Arab world, let alone the Middle East, was hardly assured. Egypt is a powerful competitor to any Arab state that seeks to dominate the Arab world. Its peace agreement with Israel enabled it to gain support from the U.S. and freed it to devote political and military energies to other regional affairs, particularly in Arabia and the Levant. Now, of course, the aftermath of the Gulf war has increased Saudi dependence on Egypt. Moreover, Iraq's defeat has benefited Syria. Having backed the wrong side among the Arabs in the Iraq-Iran war, Syria has regained its regional stature by lining up on the allied side. The defeat of Iraq has strengthened Syria's influence in Lebanon and will enable it to regain a prominent role in Jordanian and Palestinian affairs. Even a defeated Iraq will remain a regional power.

Whether the Baath party maintains control (with or without Hussein), or whether some kind of new, federated state emerges from the ashes of war, Iraq will remain an important regional presence. It has oil, water, agricultural resources, and a population large enough to provide all of the needed human resources without the burdens of overpopulation.

In the six-power competition in the region, there will continue to be shifting alliances among Egypt, Syria, and Iraq, and between these and subordinate states. For the present, however, an Egyptian-Syrian pact could have the desirable effect of facilitating an agreement between Syria and Israel over the Golan, and between Israel, the Palestinian Arabs, and Jordan over independence for the West Bank and Gaza. The prospects for a West Bank confederation with Jordan are strong as an aftermath of the emergence of a West Bank entity.

The process of striking a balance among these six regional powers is complex. There are profound difficulties in finding a security arrangement that will stabilize the regional balance of power. While the United States and other outside agents can help in the process, particularly by pressing for elimination of nuclear, chemical, and biological weapons and reduction of armaments, they cannot guarantee against continued turbulence. The challenge will be to manage regional turbulence, since it cannot be eliminated.

A litmus test of genuine commitment to post-war reduction of arms transfers to the Middle East is whether the United States itself will refrain from a new round of highly sophisticated conventional arms transfers to its Arab allies and Israel in the name of making up for war-time material loss and wear. The region has accounted for 60 percent of all world arms exports and a continuation of this trend can only be destabilizing. Given the U.S. administration's intentions to promote such sales, it is up to the U.S. Congress to exercise the necessary wisdom and courage to block such a move.

Important to the arms flow, and therefore the balancing process, is America's stand on OPEC oil-pricing. There is strong sentiment within the American administration to support an OPEC policy designed to raise prices on the grounds that this will protect United States domestic oil production and provide the Gulf Arab states with necessary funds for their rehabilitation efforts. Historically, the Arab OPEC states have used their oil profits for massive military arms purchases. There is no evidence that they will not continue to do so. American opposition to OPEC price-rigging would, on the other hand, contribute realistically to reducing the regional arms race. Lower oil prices would also give major relief to Third World oil-importing nations that are now the chief victims of high petroleum costs.

Planning for a post-war balance must take into account the ephemeral nature of alliances between and among the regional powers. Since the 1950s every one of the states concerned has abrogated formal or tacit alliances with one or more other regional power or powers. Former enemies have joined hands to balance off other regional states, e.g., Egypt and Israel, Egypt and Iraq, Syria and Egypt.

When the two opposing superpowers were the base supports of the regional seesaw, the shifts among the six regional powers were rapid and unpredictable, but some degree of equilibrium was maintained because there were two stabilizers, not one dominating superpower (Figure 3). For the moment, there is only one balancer, the United States, and the region is in high geopolitical flux.

In the post-Gulf War world, there are likely to be two major external stabilizers again—this time the United States and the European Community. Since they are allied, rather than opposing forces, the shifts of the seesaw should be less frequent and less violent. The former USSR will have only a secondary role in this balancing process. Moreover, the future influence of the outside powers is likely to be more indirect, with front-line, peace-keeping efforts being assigned to a combination of inter-Arab and United Nations forces. It would be a mistake, in the immediate post-war period, for the United States to retain some sort of military presence to help assure Gulf security, unless that presence is shared with its allied European powers. Just as there was need for a Western-Arab coalition for war, so will there be a need for the West to act in unison in the peace.

As Europe once again becomes a major player in the Middle East, it is likely to pursue its own agenda far more aggressively, filling the vacuum left by the partial withdrawal of the former Soviet Union. A greater European presence will probably be felt in both Iran and a rehabilitated Iraq, facilitating a "cold peace" between the two former enemies. Hostility towards the United States is likely to move both Iraqi and Iranian regimes in the direction of Europe; also, the oil industries of the two countries are strongly oriented to Europe. Egypt and Syria's pairing should become stronger; Turkey can be expected to seek a position that bridges American and European interests. Israel, while tied to the American camp, will have to be more responsive to European economic and, therefore, political pressures.

Relations among the six regional states are affected, not only by their ties to outside powers, but also by their relationships with smaller neighboring countries and peoples. Over-

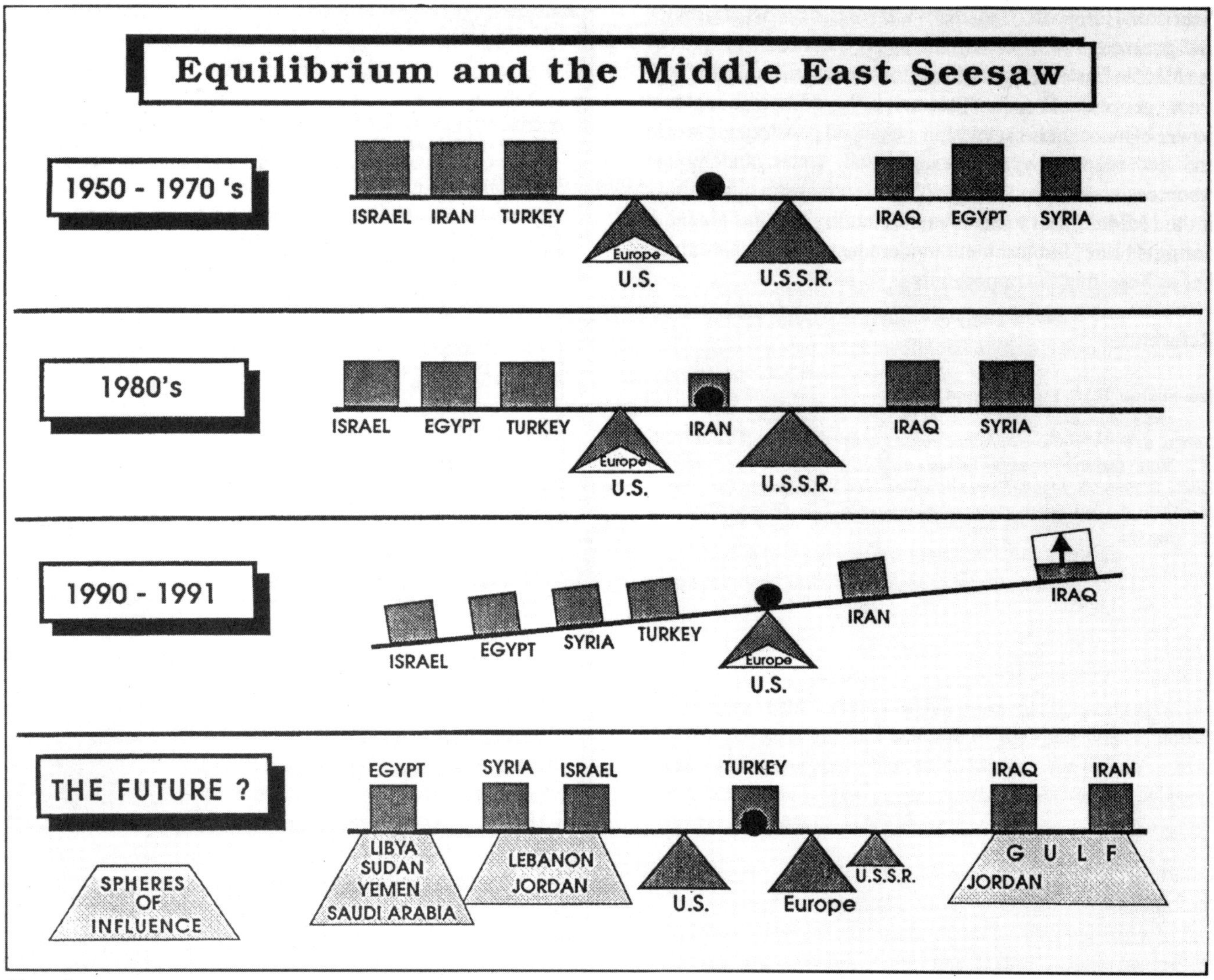

Figure 3.

lapping spheres of influence lead to tensions and potential conflict. The map of local spheres shows that all of the regional powers, save Turkey, have military and economic interests in their neighbors, which add to the complexity of balancing the system, but also contribute certain safety valves to the process. Mutual interests or vulnerabilities have led to tacit understandings between rivals, such as Israel and Syria in South Lebanon, and Israel and Iraq and Jordan at the northern end of the Gulf of Aqaba.

Jordan, Lebanon, and the Persian/Arab Gulf remain the most volatile areas of influence overlap, and the role of external powers, essentially those of the Maritime Realm, including Japan, can help to minimize the friction of overlap. Although geopolitical speculation is risky, I believe that the post-War Middle East will follow geopolitical developmental principles of specialization, integration, and hierarchy.

Conclusion

Historical events still play a key role in shaping the new Middle Eastern order. But the past is only a guide to the future. New resources, new technologies, and new modes of societal organization present challenges for which history cannot provide answers.

Would-be pharaohs and Nebuchadnezzars are unlikely to succeed in dominating the entire Middle East because it is geostrategically part of a larger realm which sets limits on the ambitions of regional overlords. The region also has a geopolitical structure whose patterns and features are shaped by a multiplicity of evenly balanced power cores that offer little comparative advantage to those who would seek gain through war. Around these nodes a network is being woven that can enhance the interests of individual states while furthering regional needs. The shock of this war has brought home the acute need to deal with water, food, and energy resources, to safeguard fragile environments, and to further the development of regional transitways in an atmosphere of peace, if not harmony.

The resources that were mobilized to wage the Gulf War were immense. If only a portion of the materials, money, diplomatic energy, and human costs would be dedicated to the war's aftermath, the peace can be won—in the Gulf, in the West Bank and Gaza, in Lebanon, in Kurdistan, and in the Sudan. A single outside power, the United States, cannot impose its designs on the region. However, the combination of

American, European, Japanese, and former Soviet assistance and guarantees, reinforcing the finely balanced strengths of the Middle East's indigenous regional powers, can help forge a new geopolitical order. This will be based upon a regional power balance that is set within a changed geostrategic world and tied together by a sharing of oil, water, and human resources across open borders. This is a historic opportunity for the Middle East to achieve the stability that has eluded it during its brief but turbulent modern history as a shatterbelt. Let us hope that the opportunity is seized.

References

Ben-Shahar, H., G. Fishelson, and S. Hirsch. 1989. *Economic cooperation and Middle East peace.* London: Weidenfeld and Nicholson.

Cohen, S. B. 1973. *Geography and politics in a world divided.* 2d ed. New York: Oxford University Press.

Lewis, B. 1966. *The Middle East and the West.* New York: Harper Torchbooks.

McCaslin, J. 1989. *International oil encyclopedia.* Tulsa: Pennwell Publishing Co.

PRAIRIE POTHOLES

On the North American prairie, the glaciers of the last ice age created 20 million acres of ponds and marshes. Today, these wetlands are an important but dwindling part of the prairie ecosystem.

Bjorn Sletto

Bjorn Sletto is a freelance writer and photographer based in Texas who frequently covers environmental topics.

The prairie pothole region of North America sweeps southeastward from the semiarid wheat country of south-central Canada to the verdant corn fields of northern Iowa. This 300,000-square-mile zone of shallow ponds and lakes functions as a natural water-treatment and drainage system, helping to replenish aquifers, filter impurities from agricultural runoff and prevent catastrophic flooding. These wetlands also provide critical nesting areas for North American waterfowl and way stations for migrating South American shorebirds.

But today, the region is under attack. Nearly half of the unique wetlands have been drained by surface ditching or underground conduits — principally to make way for cultivation. Only 40 percent of North Dakota's original 5.5 million-acre share of the prairie pothole wetlands remains. And in some heavily settled midwestern states, the toll of drainage is far more severe: Minnesota, for example, has lost 95 percent of its original prairie potholes.

Reflecting the steady loss of wetland habitat, waterfowl populations have thinned. Shorebirds that rest in the pothole region while migrating from South America to northern Canada have experienced declines as

As part of a study of prairie wetlands in North Dakota, U.S. Fish and Wildlife researcher Ned Euliss checks an amphibian trap in a shallow prairie pothole. Another researcher marks a salamander.

Bjorn Sletto

Bjorn Sletto

great as 80 percent. North America's ducks have also suffered: pintails have fallen by 55 percent, and even the ubiquitous mallard has declined by 25 percent.

Long before European settlers unpacked their plows, prairie potholes provided nesting and nourishment to countless waterfowl and other wildlife. This ecologically rich system of shallow depressions emerged during a period of repeated glacial expansion and retreat that ended 12,000 years ago, when the ice sheet of the Wisconsin glaciation retreated.

The lay of the land was quite different at the beginning of the Pleistocene Epoch, 1.6 million years ago, before glacial processes of erosion and deposition sculpted the prairie landscape of today. As the first glaciers grew southward from Canada's Hudson Bay, today's topographically undramatic northern plains were adorned with rolling hills, cascading rivers, low-lying swamps, and sharp-hewn cliffs.

The underlying foundation of the pothole region consists of limestone, sandstone, shale and siltstone — sedimentary rock laid down before the beginning of the Pleistocene. The expanding ice sheets easily eroded this bedrock. Much of what is now the pothole region sloped upward to the northeast, intensifying the grinding force of the glacial ice against the sloping terrain. This blunted high spots and filled in low-lying areas with glacial drift — a mantle of stone fragments and "rock flour" — that reached 400 feet (120 m) thick.

As the Pleistocene came to a close with the end of the Wisconsin glaciation, blocks of ice became trapped under these deposits. Entombed within this insulating layer, the ice remained frozen for as long as 3,000 years after the ice sheets melted. When the buried ice finally thawed, the overlying blanket of glacial drift collapsed, leaving behind a land pockmarked with tens of thousands of potholes of all shapes and sizes.

The size of these glacial remnants varies from a living-room-sized prairie oasis to a full-blown 40-acre lake or marsh. Fed by snow melt, rainwater or local aquifers, potholes become living wetlands, filling to a depth of two to five feet. Different mixes of plants establish a foothold, depending on the depth of the pothole, the length of the wet season and the chemical makeup of its water.

To impress some order on this complexity, scientists have developed systems for classifying potholes. To hydrologists, the most important distinguishing factor is the dynamic relationship between prairie wetlands and the local water table. Potholes exchange between 5 and 25 percent of their water with local aquifers — sometimes in either direction, sometimes in both — depending on the depth of the local water table, the pothole's elevation and the time of year.

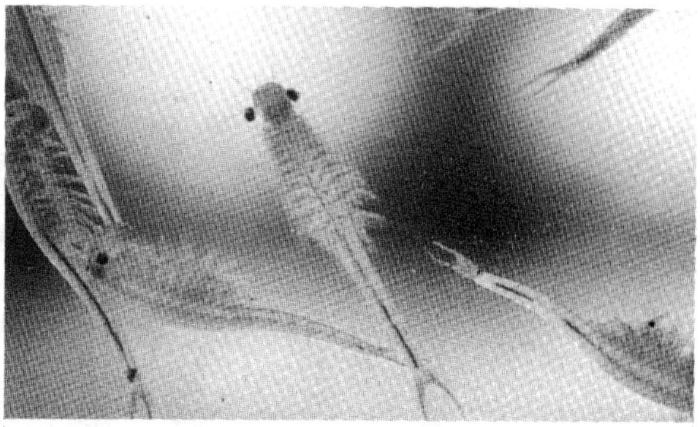

Photos courtesy U.S. Fish & Wildlife Service

Like oases in the desert, prairie potholes shelter a rich diversity of life in a region of low rainfall. Fairy shrimp (above) are an important food for waterfowl migrating through the pothole region in spring. Waterfowl also depend on amphipods (below), crustaceans that live in permanent and semipermanent prairie potholes.

Classified according to their interaction with groundwater, prairie potholes fall into three groups. The most common type, called flow-through potholes, simultaneously drain into and are fed by groundwater, which seeps in or drains through the walls and floor of the pothole. Recharge potholes, which often lie on high ground, funnel spring runoff and rainwater into the water table. In contrast, discharge potholes receive a large fraction of their

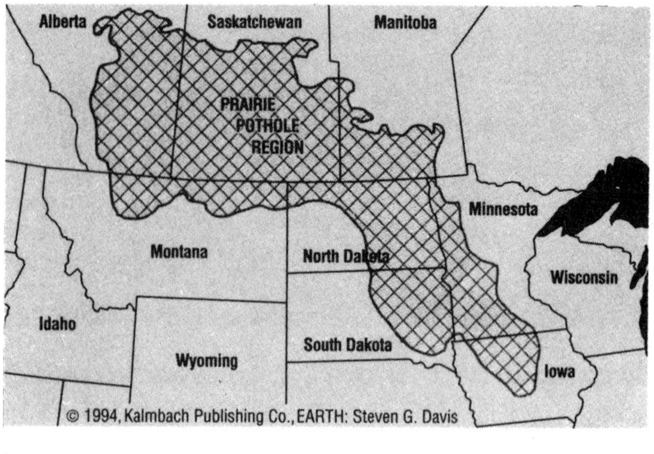

The prairie pothole region extends southeastward from Alberta to Iowa, covering parts of five U.S. states and three Canadian provinces.

Robert J. Long, Ducks Unlimited, Inc.

Among the many species of waterfowl that depend on prairie potholes for food, water and rearing young are the northern shoveler (above) and the canvasback (below).

Glenn D. Chambers, Ducks Unlimited, Inc.

water supply from the ground and are often found in low-lying areas.

The flow of groundwater creates important chemical differences among individual potholes. In a discharge pothole, for example, most of the water is lost through evaporation or plant transpiration. Over time, dissolved salts in the groundwater concentrate in the pothole's lining of muck. As a result, some discharge potholes become twice as briny as seawater.

Because some plants are more salt-tolerant than others, differences in water chemistry between potholes is matched by differences in vegetation. Recharge potholes, the least salty, are often colonized by sedges and smartweed. In brackish flow-through potholes, plants such as rushes, reedgrass, sago pondweed and sloughgrass thrive. And discharge potholes — the briniest of the three — support saltgrass, sago pondweed, muhly grass, and sea blite.

Ecologists classify prairie potholes by how long they stay wet each year. Like water chemistry, pothole permanence affects the types of plants that establish themselves: the smallest potholes, which dry up soon after the spring thaw, support different vegetation than flow-through potholes, which are large and retain their water throughout the year.

According to a system developed for the prairie pothole region by the U.S. Fish and Wildlife Service, wetlands are divided into four classes, arranged in order of increasing size and permanence. So-called ephemeral potholes, which cover an acre or two, are sucked dry in days or weeks by evaporation and thirsty plants. Temporary potholes, also an acre or so in size, are somewhat longer-lived, remaining wet for about two months after the spring thaw. Seasonal potholes, which are typically up to five acres in extent, may endure well into the dog days of summer. Finally, semipermanent potholes, which are generally bigger than five acres, maintain significant water levels throughout all but the driest years.

A pothole's character may shift with natural cycles of drought. This in turn can cause profound changes in the kinds of vegetation that thrive in a pothole wetland. In drought years, even large wetlands can nearly dry up, exposing mud flats rich in minerals and nutrients. The seeds of cattails and certain other plants, which in wet years lay inactive in the mud, take advantage of this rare germination window.

"A lot of species need to have a sloppy wet mud flat in order to germinate," says Chip Euliss, a research biologist with the U.S. Fish and Wildlife Service's Northern Prairie Wildlife Research Center in Jamestown, North Dakota. "The water has to be drawn down at some point for these plants to become established." Plant communities can also change when the water table beneath a pothole falls, transforming a brackish flow-through pothole into a freshwater recharge basin. In such a case, says Euliss, cattails might gain a foothold in waters where salt-tolerant bulrushes formerly thrived.

The diversity and great number of potholes are vital to the continued survival of North America's ducks. Nesting ducks are fiercely territorial, and the pothole wetlands offer innumerable face-saving opportunities for them to avoid turf battles. The entire region — about the area of the Great Lakes combined — contains only 10 percent of North America's total breeding habitat. Yet it contributes more than half of the continent's ducks in an average year.

In April, which is springtime for much of the northern prairie, the dabbling ducks (which feed on the surface of the water) begin to arrive, including mallards, pintails and northern shovellers. At this time, the largest wetlands are still frozen. This does not deter the dabbling ducks, however, because they nest away from the water and then return later with their hatchlings in tow. Fortunately, many of the temporary and seasonal potholes, which are smaller, are already charged with water and ready for ducks. The mud ringing these small wetlands is alive with wriggling bloodworms (the larval form of the midge fly) — a critical food for nesting ducks of all species.

Later in the spring, canvasbacks, redheads and other diving ducks (which feed underwater) sweep in from the south. Their arrival coincides with the thawing of the large, semipermanent potholes, the preferred nesting habitat of diving ducks, which nest directly over water. At this time of year, these wetlands are also thick with bloodworms and other tasty invertebrates.

During the hot months of summer, many potholes dry up. Ducks move as needed to find potholes that still contain water, food and enough plant cover to hide fledglings from predators. In the fall, the ducks prepare for migration by congregating in the few wet potholes remaining. Thus, to nest, raise young and then fatten up for the fall migration, each duck species requires a dozen or more different wetlands over the course of a single season.

Studies show that the number of ducks born and raised in an average year is directly related to the number of potholes available. Simply put, fewer potholes means fewer young ducks. Anything that disrupts the diverse mixture of ephemeral, temporary and seasonal potholes can cause a precipitous drop in the local waterfowl population.

"The great variability between potholes of different size, vegetation and salinity is very important for ducks," says Jim Almendinger, a hydrologist at the U.S. Geological Survey station in Mounds View, Minnesota. "It means that some wetlands will have water the same year that others are dry, and the reverse could happen the next year. So ducks flying north or south have a pretty good chance of finding wet potholes somewhere at all times."

Although ducks — and duck hunters — are the most obvious beneficiaries of prairie potholes, these wetlands make an equally valuable contribution to the health of the land by helping to recharge aquifers. Research on this issue is still sketchy, but wetland scientists have turned up considerable evidence that draining wetlands, particularly in dry regions like North Dakota, may ultimately lower the water table. And draining discharge potholes, which serve as a pressure-relief valve for mineral-laden groundwater, can cause that water to accumulate in the soil instead. As it evaporates, the overall salinity of the soil rises, thereby harming agriculture.

Perhaps more important, prairie potholes collect and clean surface runoff before it mixes with groundwater or drains into rivers. In a 1981 study, scientists compared the concentration of fertilizer by-products in the water entering and leaving a large, 900-acre wetland in an agricultural area of Iowa. The research showed that natural processes had broken down or filtered many of the fertilizer remnants carried by field runoff into the wetland. Indeed, the water leaving the wetland contained 86 percent less inorganic nitrates and 78 percent less ammonium. This clean-up is important because fertilizer chemicals cause algae blooms in lakes and rivers, destroying aquatic ecosystems, killing fish and often threatening human health.

Potholes also serve a vital function as a flood-control mechanism, drawing up excess surface water before it has a chance to build to dangerous levels. In parts of the region largely undisturbed by human development, the capacity of the land to absorb water during heavy rains is far greater than in areas where the potholes have been drained.

"Potholes are important to farms in the prairie pothole region, and it's unwise to drain too many of them," Euliss says. "The more potholes are drained, the greater the risk of flooding and crop damage." For instance, the frequency of flooding along Canada's Red River has more than doubled since 1958, when pothole draining began in earnest.

However, the events on the Red River pale in comparison to the flooding of South Dakota's Lake Thompson marsh. There, years of pothole draining had drastically reduced the water-holding capacity of the area. In 1985, after four years of heavy rain and snowfall, the 9,000-acre Lake Thompson marsh swelled to 325,000 acres and became a full-fledged lake, swallowing entire farms and roads in the process.

This calamity turned into a small victory for prairie wildlife enthusiasts. After studies determined that artificially lowering the water table beneath South Dakota's newest lake would be prohibitively expensive, Lake Thompson became a project under the Prairie Pothole Joint Venture, part of a U.S.-Canadian effort to conserve six million acres of prime waterfowl habitat and restore the number of ducks, geese and swans in North America to 1970 levels.

Thanks to this international project, the Lake Thompson wetland has begun its metamorphosis from maligned swamp to natural treasure. To attract waterfowl, project staff encourage local farmers to adopt cultivation methods designed to reduce the amount of sediment carried from fields to wetlands by surface runoff and erosion.

The soul of the plan, however, is pothole restoration. By plugging up pothole drainage ditches and pipelines, the Lake Thompson project aims to restore 10,000 acres of wetland. When the ancient potholes have been restored and Lake Thompson has regained its ecological balance, flooding will become a distant memory in this small corner of South Dakota, and the spring skies will fill once again with the sound of a thousand wings.

The aral sea basin

A critical environmental zone

V. M. Kotlyakov

V. M. KOTLYAKOV is director of the Institute of Geography at the Soviet Academy of Sciences in Moscow.

Among today's severely damaged ecological zones, the Aral Sea region is one of the most notorious.[1] The Aral, a large, desert-bound sea in south central Asia, was brought to life by the abundant Amu Darya and Syr Darya rivers, which drain into the Aral Sea basin from tributaries deep in Soviet central Asia and Kazakhstan (see Figure 1). But the sea, once comparable in size to one of the larger Great Lakes in North America, has been shrinking at an alarming rate over the last 30 years.

The process taking place in the Aral region may be called anthropogenic desertification because the sea is, in effect, drying up as a consequence of the development of irrigated agriculture in the basin. Its river deltas and other natural habitats, the local climate, and regional hydrology have all been similarly affected. Moreover, these negative ecological changes have been accompanied by grave socioeconomic costs: deteriorating human health, increasing unemployment as resource-based economic activity declines, and decreasing production of cotton, rice, and other agricultural crops. The fate of the Aral basin bears watching by other regions in the world prone to desertification.

In the 1950s, the Aral Sea covered an area of 66,000 square kilometers, containing 1,064 cubic kilometers of water with a mean salinity of 1.0 or 1.1 percent. At the time, the mean depth of the Aral was 16 meters, and 90 centimeters of water evaporated from its surface annually. The sea's water balance was maintained by an annual inflow of 56 cubic kilometers of water from the Amu Darya and Syr Darya rivers, supplemented by 5 cubic kilometers of atmospheric precipitation.

But early in the 1960s, rapid development of irrigated agriculture began, and water withdrawals from the Amu Darya, Syr Darya, and their tributaries greatly increased. By 1965, 4.5 million hectares in Soviet central Asia were irrigated, consuming 50 to 55 cubic kilometers of water annually. In the next quarter century, another 2.6 million hectares were irrigated, using an additional 50 cubic kilometers of water annually.

Since the early 1960s, the area of irrigated lands has increased by 50 percent in the Uzbek and Tadzhik republics, by 70 percent in the Kazakh Republic, and by 140 percent in Turkmenia. Today, a total of 7 million hectares in the Aral region are irrigated, with annual withdrawals of 60 cubic kilometers of water from the Amu Darya and 45 cubic kilometers from the Syr Darya.

With the rapid expansion of irrigated lands, the total inflow of water to the Aral decreased sharply, and the sea's level dropped (see Table 1). Between 1961 and 1970, the mean decline was 0.21 meters per year. The annual decline was 0.58 meters during the 1970s and as much as 1.09 meters during the 1980s. By 1990, the sea level had fallen more than 14 meters from the 1960 level, the area of the sea had shrunk by more than 40 percent, and its volume had decreased by more than 60 percent.

The mean inflow of river water to the

From *Environment,* Vol. 33, No. 1, January/February 1991, pp. 4-9, 36-38. Reprinted with permission of the Helen Dwight Reid Educational Foundation. Published by Heldref Publications, 1319 Eighteenth St., NW, Washington, DC 20036-1802.

Aral Sea between 1971 and 1980 was only 16.7 cubic kilometers per year, and early in the 1980s, it practically ceased altogether. In 1987 and 1988, there was a relative abundance of water: the Syr Darya delivered 1.2 and 6.2 cubic kilometers of water to the Aral, and the Amu Darya delivered 8 and 16 cubic kilometers. In 1989, the inflow from the Syr Darya dropped to 4.2 cubic kilometers, and that of the Amu Darya fell to only 1.1 cubic kilometers.

By the end of 1989, the Aral Sea had receded into two separate parts. The level of the southern "Greater Sea" dropped to 38.6 meters, and that of the northern "Lesser Sea" dropped to 39.5 meters. Now the area of the Greater Sea is about 33,500 square kilometers with a volume of 310 cubic kilometers and mean salinity of 3.0 percent. The Lesser Sea covers approximately 3,000 square kilometers with a volume of 20 cubic kilometers. The salinity of its waters varies in different parts from 1.8 to 3.5 percent because of the freshening effect of water from the Syr Darya.

The trend is clear. Without drastic measures, the Aral Sea is destined to become a small brine lake of between 4,000 and 5,000 square kilometers.

Ecological and Health Impacts

As a consequence of the physical changes, the Aral Sea now has almost completely lost its productive fisheries. The Aral once contained more than 20 species of fish, including 12 game species. Now all but a few have died out as shallow spawning grounds have dried up and food reserves have disappeared. If the present trend in salinization continues, by the year 2000, the salinity of the sea water will reach 3.8 to 4.2 percent. This high concentration will exclude the possibility of colonization by new species of fish and the organisms they feed on that might have acclimatized to the saline conditions.

The exposed sea bottom of the Aral is becoming a salty (solonchak) badlands, a source of constant wind-blown sand. Dust storms that are so powerful that they can be observed from space have become common in spring. In addition to fine particles of soil, the dust contains salts—primarily sulfates and chlorides, which are poisonous to plants. The dust clouds, which stretch for 150 to 300 kilometers, are particularly harmful to desert oases and pastures during spring flowering.

During the last 25 years, the duration of dust storms in the coastal areas of the sea has increased 2 to 3 times.[2] Based on preliminary estimates, the Aral region is the source of from 15,000 to 75,000 tonnes of atmospheric dust annually. Each year, each hectare in the lower Aral basin receives 340 kilograms of dry salt and an additional 180 kilograms of salt in precipitation for a total of 520 kilograms of salt deposited per hectare. The mineral content of precipitation in the basin was 3 times higher in the 1980s than it was in the 1960s and 1970s.

Before its level dropped, the Aral Sea influenced the climate of the land within 100 to 200 kilometers of the sea. But as the sea and its river deltas have dried up, that influence has diminished, and the continentality of the basin's climate has increased—that is, the climate has become more like that of a continental interior, with decreased precipitation and greater swings in temperature. Early in the 1980s, the difference between the mean monthly temperatures of January and July increased by 1.5° to 2° C. Frosts are now more likely to occur later in spring and earlier in fall. The frost-free period in the Amu Darya delta, a cotton-growing region, has shortened to as few as 170 days, far fewer than the minimum of 200 frost-free days required for growing cotton.

As spring floods on the Amu Darya and Syr Darya stopped and the deltas dried up, the natural landscapes of the region were destroyed. During the past 20 years, the 550,000 hectares of reeds on the floodplains of the Amu Darya shrunk to 20,000 hectares, and the productivity of pastures and haying grounds dropped by roughly 20 percent. More than 50 lakes in the Amu Darya delta—about 10 percent of the region's lakes—have dried up, as have the floodplain forests known as *tugai*. As a result, the region's biodiversity has been greatly impoverished. Only 168 of 319 species of bird continue to nest in the delta, and only 30 of 70 mammalian species remain.

A considerable part of the mineralized and polluted drain water from the surrounding expanse of irrigated fields returns to the Amu Darya and Syr Darya. This run-off has critically lowered the water quality in the river deltas. The problem has been exacerbated by the salinization of croplands because water is used to wash away the salts. The mean consumption of water between 1978 and 1982 in Uzbekistan was about 17,500 cubic meters per hectare. In Karakalpak and Khorezm, it reached 36,000 cubic meters per hectare.

In the lower reaches of the Amu Darya, the mineral content of the river water from run-off of drain water and fertilizers is already about 1.5 grams per liter. In some years, the mineral content of the water in the lower stretches

TABLE 1
HYDROLOGIC PARAMETERS OF THE ARAL SEA FROM 1960 TO 1989

Year	Sea level (meters)	Sea area (thousand square kilometers)	Sea volume (cubic kilometers)	Mineral content (grams per liter)	Total river run-off into sea (cubic kilometers)
1960	53.3	67.9	1,090	10.0	40
1965	52.5	63.9	1,030	10.5	31
1970	51.6	60.4	970	11.1	33
1975	49.4	57.2	840	13.7	11
1980	46.2	52.4	670	16.5	0
1985	42.0	44.4	470	23.5	0
1989	39.0	37.0	340	28.0	5

SOURCE: D. B. Oreshkin, "Aral'skaya Katastrofa," (The Aral Catastrophe), *Nauka o Zemle*, no. 2 (1990):41.

of the Syr Darya reaches 2.5 grams per liter. One liter of water from these rivers contains up to 6 grams of phosphates, 3 milligrams of ammonia, 2 milligrams of nitrites, and 6 milligrams of nitrates. The chlorinated hydrocarbon pesticides applied to agricultural fields in the basin can be detected in the water of both rivers.

Leaked and surplus irrigation water often ends up not back in the rivers but in local depressions and irrigation reservoirs at the periphery of irrigated zones, where the water evaporates. Such reservoirs have become particularly numerous along the lower reaches of the Amu Darya, where more than 40 large water basins annually lose from 6 to 7 cubic kilometers of water to evaporation. The largest reservoir of Sarykamysh receives 3 to 4 cubic kilometers of irrigation wastewater annually, increasing its total volume to 30 cubic kilometers.

Because of these reservoirs, bogs and boggy patches not typically found in desert habitats are forming. The bogs displace valuable pastures, which are adapted to scant precipitation. The bog water itself is wasted through evaporation, thereby increasing the salinization of the land.

The anthropogenic desertification of the Aral and its region, initially an ecological problem, in recent times has turned into a human health problem. Much illness has resulted from the use of highly toxic chemical pesticides, which accumulate in drainage waters that flow into the rivers and contaminate local drinking-water supplies. The deterioration of the drinking water, furthered by inadequate purification plants, piping, and sewage systems, has greatly impaired the health and sanitary conditions of the people in the Aral region. In the last 15 years, the incidence of typhoid fever has increased almost 30 times and that of hepatitis, 7 times.[3] There are also considerable increases in the incidences of kidney disease, gallstones, and chronic gastritis. Many babies are born weak and ailing, and child mortality is more than 50 per

FIGURE 1. The Aral Sea region.

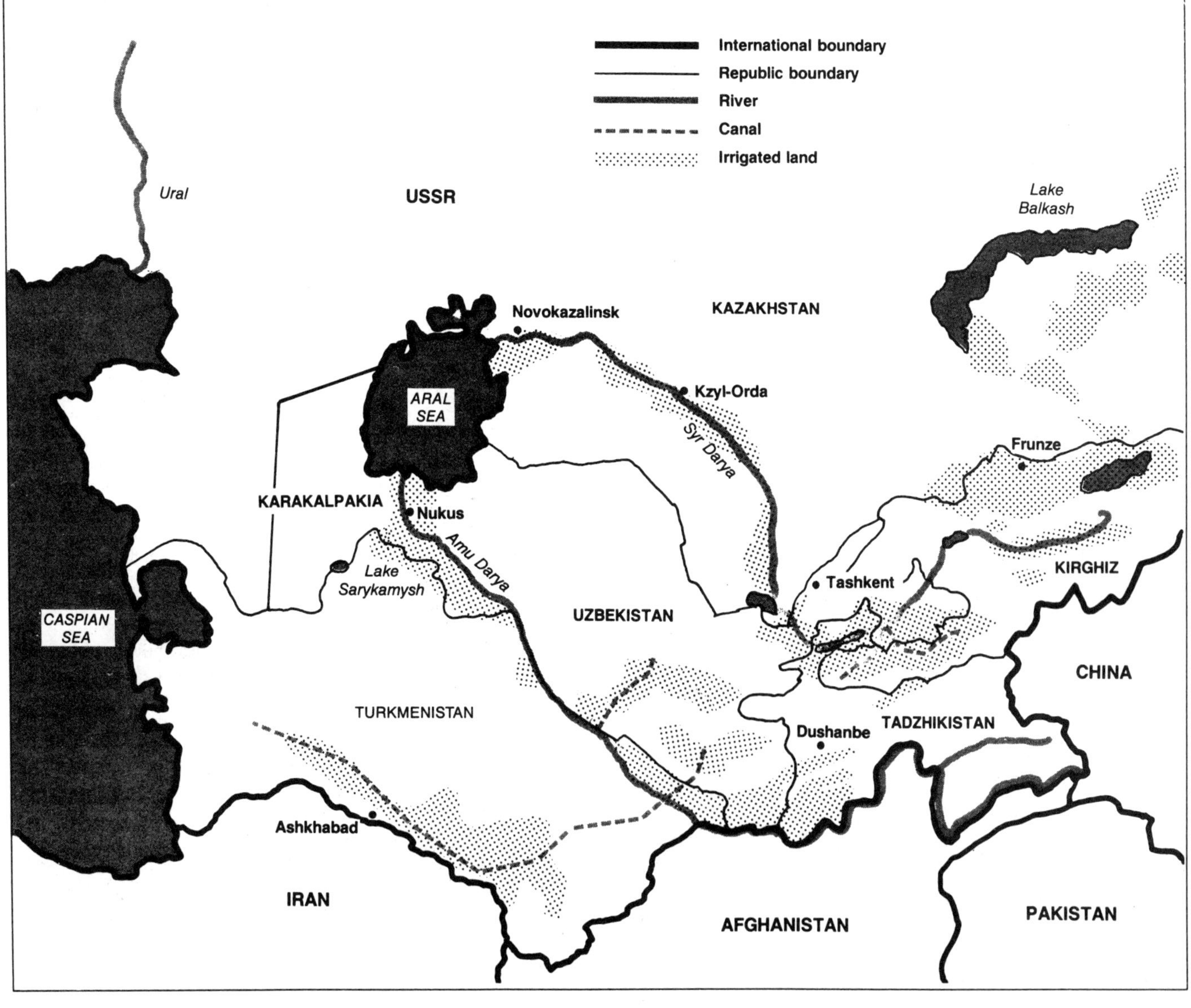

1,000 births. A recent appeal by scientists to improve the health of the region's children appears in the box on this page.

The Path of Development

The desertification of the Aral region is a direct result of the socioeconomic development of Soviet central Asia and a considerable part of Kazakhstan. For example, the current direction of agricultural development in the region is toward water-intensive production. The agriculture is characterized by a predominance of cotton monoculture, an absence of crop rotation, and overly large plantations of water-intensive rice. Marginal lands are being developed, producing low harvests but abundant salt-laden runoff. As a result, despite the increase in irrigated areas, the gross yield of cotton in the central Asian republics and in Kazakhstan (excluding the Tadzhik Republic) has not increased. For example, Uzbekistan produced 3.9 million tonnes of raw cotton in 1970 and 5.3 million tonnes in 1975, but only 5.1 million tonnes in 1985.[4]

Despite the rapid salinization of soils because of excessive water application with insufficient drainage, attempts to economize water are inefficient. The accepted quotas of water consumption per irrigated hectare are excessive because specific soil and plant types and the actual consumption and mineralization of irrigation water are not fully taken into account. Often, the actual volume of water supplied to fields is even greater than the quotas; in different central Asian republics, the excess varies from 20 to 100 percent. Yet as mineralization of the river water used for irrigation increases, irrigation quotas are raised even further, resulting in still greater water withdrawal. An increase in water mineralization by 0.1 grams per liter is offset by applying an additional 1,000 cubic meters of water per hectare.

If the anthropogenic desertification of the Aral region is not stopped, all environmental factors will be affected. The Aral Sea will be replaced by a 60,000-square-kilometer salt-and-sand

WOMEN SCIENTISTS' APPEAL FOR IMMEDIATE ACTION TO SAVE CHILDREN IN THE ARAL ECOLOGICAL CRISIS REGION[1]

We, the women participants in the first international symposium, "The Aral Crisis: Origins and Solution," held in Nukus, Karakalpak ASSR [Autonomous Soviet Socialist Republic], on 2–5 October 1990—specialists in the areas of ecology, medicine, geography, sociology, and demography—have concluded from analysis of data gathered from field observations that the Aral Sea region is one of ecological catastrophe that is especially hazardous to children.

The mortality rate of children in the Karakalpak ASSR is among the highest in the world and is growing each year: from 47.3 percent in 1978 to 59.8 percent in 1989. The maternal death rate in Karakalpakia has tripled in the last 5 years. More than 80 percent of women suffer from anemia, and every third [pregnant] woman gives birth prematurely. The dispensary system has revealed that in 1989–1990 almost 70 percent of the children in Karakalpakia fall into health categories II and III—i.e., [they are] practically sick. The number of children suffering from nervous and psychological disorders has tripled in the last 2 years.

The primary reasons for so sharp a decline in public health as to threaten the survival of the population are degradation of the environment, qualitative and quantitative depletion of the supply of potable water, microbial contamination of water, pesticide concentration, and protein and vitamin deficiency.

The situation is aggravated by the lack of necessary medical services and ecological education. We are extremely concerned by the slow pace, bordering on criminal, of [remedial] action. The knowledge already accumulated is sufficient to justify urgent action. We demand immediate action to save the population of the Aral region and other ecological disaster areas.

We call upon the government and the peoples of the USSR and the republics of central Asia and Kazakhstan, at all administrative levels of the country and the region; we call upon the United Nations, its specialized institutions—UNICEF [United Nations International Children's Emergency Fund], WHO [World Health Organization], and UNEP [United Nations Environment Programme] —and all organizations concerned with problems of public health and survival; and we call upon all of the world's women to render emergency assistance to save the lives of children in the Aral region and to declare this region an ecological disaster zone. During 1990–1991,

- provide the population with clean drinking water and food as well as necessary medical assistance;
- hasten the development and implementation of a plan of action for solving the Aral problem;
- immediately shut down all hazardous production;
- place under tight control and decrease use of all pollutants, toxic chemicals, radioactive materials, and ozone-depleting substances;
- provide *glasnost* [complete reporting] of ecology-related information;
- spread energy-, water-, and resource-conserving technology; and
- prohibit use of child labor in cotton fields.

We send our appeal from Nukus, the burning center of ecological disaster, but we know that similar problems are emerging in an ever increasing number of areas encompassing the whole world.

Working women in all fields and at all levels—teachers, physicians, engineers, writers, and artists—we must step up our efforts to maintain normal environmental conditions to ensure the health of our children.

Here in Nukus, we are creating a committee of women scientists and other specialists, "Mothers, Save Your Children." The primary purpose of the committee is to gather and disseminate knowledge needed for emergency action to restore the environment in the Aral region and the other most degraded areas in the world.

We will not allow the killing of our children!

Please direct inquiries about membership in the committee or suggestions for enhancing the effectiveness of our work to Nina Maksimovna Novikova, Coordinator, "Mothers, Save Your Children" Committee, USSR Academy of Sciences Commission on Ecological Problems, Sadovaya-Chernogradskaya 13/3, Moscow 103064, USSR.

1. Before being edited, this appeal was translated by Katya Partan.

RESOLUTIONS OF THE INTERNATIONAL SYMPOSIUM "THE ARAL CRISIS: ORIGINS AND SOLUTION"[1]

The international symposium "The Aral Crisis: Origins and Solution" was held on 2-5 October 1990 in Nukus, Karakalpak Autonomous Soviet Socialist Republic. More than 200 leading specialists and scientists participated. Among these were 27 foreign scientists from the United States, England, Canada, Australia, Germany, and Spain, representing international research institutions specializing in hydrologic, health/sanitation, and biomedical problems in arid zones. Also in attendance were about 100 scientists from institutes of the USSR Academy of Sciences and the academies of sciences of Uzbekistan, Turkmenia, Tadzhikistan, and Kirgizia and from Moscow University and other leading institutions of higher learning in the USSR, and more than 50 representatives from the conservation committees of the central Asian republics and Kazakhstan, the USSR State Hydrometeorological Center, social and economic organizations, and foreign companies.

The symposium included presentations of more than 40 papers and reports, as well as a Nukus–Muynak–Aral field trip. The presentations focused on the deteriorating ecology of the region, the resultant declining health of its population, decreasing efficiency in economic management, and growing social tension. The medical/hygienic and socioeconomic aspects of the Aral problem were discussed in connection with environmental pollution, improper use of pesticides and fertilizers, insufficient medical facilities, and the lack of a modern water-supply system. Attention was also focused on imprudent water use, insufficient water resources, and conservation and restoration of the Aral Sea.

The scientists of the central Asian republics and Kazakhstan reached a unanimous conclusion as to the reasons for and ways to resolve the Aral crisis:

1. The scientists consider it necessary to request that the supreme soviets of the central Asian republics and Kazakhstan, as well as the Supreme Soviet of the USSR, declare the lower reaches of the rivers in the Aral basin to be an ecological disaster area and confer a corresponding status on the region.
2. The fundamental causes of the Aral crisis are erroneous choices of strategies for developing the region's productive forces; extensive development of water resources and agriculture; low standards for planning, construction, and operation of irrigation systems; and indiscriminate use of chemicals in agriculture.
3. Ecological restoration is impossible without stabilizing the level of the Aral Sea. To accomplish this, it will be necessary to perfect a complete water-management system.
4. A combination of urgent measures is necessary to restore the ecological conditions in the Aral Sea basin. The most urgent of these must be completed during the period 1993 to 1995, as delaying their implementation may have unforeseen and irreversible consequences. These measures are economic/organizational in nature and are aimed at restructuring industry and agriculture. Immediate measures must be taken to improve the health of the population and the quality and quantity of potable water and to impose strict controls on the use of pesticides and fertilizers.
5. To solve the problem, the following measures must be implemented in stages:
   - Strictly limit intake of water by the republics, with consideration for the need to introduce water-conserving technology in all areas of the economy.
   - Strictly prohibit expansion of the land area under irrigation and new siting of water-retaining industry, thus freeing river flow for preserving the Aral Sea.
   - Immediately revise the structure of cultivated land and crop composition to limit rice culture, remove low-yielding irrigated land from cultivation, and end cotton monoculture, thus freeing the land for development of orchards, viticulture [vineyards], and seed alfalfa.
   - By the end of 1992, complete the removal of outflow from the region's [water] collection/drainage networks to the sea and reassess the continued use of lowland, valley, and container reservoirs, which lose 5 cubic kilometers of water annually.
6. Concomitantly, it is necessary to accelerate a comprehensive reconstruction of land-reclamation systems based on progressive water conservation and irrigation technology and coupled use of ground and surface water, which in many cases will provide waste-free use of irrigation waters.
7. Use of newly available water for unorganized flooding of high deltas and creation of polders are inadvisable. Feed crops should be grown only on land that has long been used for pasture or been under irrigation.
8. Construction of collectors to divert outflow to the Aral and Caspian seas from collection-drainage networks in the middle basins of the Syr Darya and Amu Darya is impermissible.
9. Current projects for redistributing flow between basins are scientifically unfounded. Fundamental research is needed to provide water to the Aral basin by alternate means.
10. Inasmuch as incomplete study of many important problems has made decisionmaking impossible, it is necessary to strengthen basic research and to create a specially funded comprehensive program to solve the Aral problem.
11. The leadership of the union's sovereign republics of central Asia and Kazakhstan is requested to create an interrepublic committee to coordinate joint activities, including scientific investigations, to solve the Aral Sea problem.
12. It is recommended that the republics of the union create scientific research subdivisions in their respective academies of sciences for ecological and water problems.
13. A program should be developed and implemented to increase ecological awareness in the population at large and to train personnel skilled in the area of ecology.
14. The conference considers it expedient to enlist the cooperation of international and foreign scientific organizations as well as individual foreign scientists in researching the Aral problem.
15. The participants in the international symposium support requesting the Union of Red Cross and Red Crescent Societies of the USSR to assist the population of the Aral region in improving [medical] service, the health of mothers and children, and supplies of good quality drinking water, and [they] appeal to governments, social organizations, and foundations to assist in these humanitarian activities.

1. Before being edited, these resolutions were translated by Katya Partan.

desert generating dust that will harm the desert oases. Salt that formerly went to the Aral, which was the main salt repository for the whole region, will be deposited in the oases, which will shrink under the burden of salt and dust and, eventually, disappear.

The Search for Remedies

The ecological problems of the Aral Sea and its basin have worried scientists since the end of the 19th century. The Institute of Geography of the Soviet Academy of Sciences has participated in research on the Aral since 1976. At that time, many specialists thought that the ecological and socioeconomic consequences of the development of large-scale irrigation in the Aral Sea basin—primarily, the drop in the sea's level—would be insignificant and ignorable. However, geographers at the institute thought that the socioeconomic consequences could be serious and must be taken into account. Recent events have shown that position was correct.

It is now realized that the problems of the Aral basin affect the health and life of a vast territory. Their solution requires new approaches and decision-making based on a profound and integrated analysis of the numerous direct and feedback relationships between the sea and the land; the fate of one cannot be divided from the other.

The Aral region is in a state of ecological crisis in which the natural processes and ecological links have been disturbed so profoundly and the degradation has become so serious that the human population can no longer live and work as it once did. An ecological catastrophe is fast approaching wherein the degradation would be irreversible and life and work in the region impossible. The urgency of the situation must be realized. Only a short time remains to provide the population with clean drinking water, to ban the application of highly toxic pesticides, and to clean up the mineralized and polluted drainage and river waters.

Also, the current practice of adjusting water use to meet the demands of agricultural production development must change. On the contrary, the problems of water use should be the deciding factor in agricultural production plans. The role of cotton in the country's economy also should be reconsidered to increase the production of foodstuffs and to introduce more salt-resistant and less water-intensive crops.

The water resources of Soviet central Asia and Kazakhstan must be inventoried. Special attention should be given to increasing the efficiency of water-economizing systems, decreasing irrigation quotas by 15 to 20 percent, optimizing drainage systems to reduce water consumption by several thousand cubic meters per hectare, and improving regulation of run-off. The water freed in this way should be used primarily for resolving ecological imbalances to reinstate the normal conditions of life and health for local populations. If necessary, the water supply for agriculture could be increased by introducing water-saving technologies such as drip irrigation, by planting protective forest belts, by decreasing evapotranspiration, and by desalinizing water resources, primarily drainage waters. A combination of measures for increasing the productivity of irrigated and nonirrigated lands is needed to increase agricultural production without expanding irrigated areas or water consumption.

Saving the Aral region and resolving its tangle of ecological, hydrological, and socioeconomic problems will require a new attitude and an entirely new approach to economic activity throughout Soviet central Asia. Agriculture and other branches of the economy should be allowed to return to their traditional forms, which have been destroyed over the past decades, and attitudes toward water use should be changed. A number of new economic laws already have been adopted to change economic and social relationships in the USSR in principle; changes in practice will naturally take time.

Global Connections

The problems of the Aral Sea region are not unique on Earth. They are part of the universal problem of desertification that is occurring in many regions of the world, especially in Africa.[5] Hence, the search for a solution to the complex problems of the Aral region is of general and global significance.

Indeed, international organizations already have begun to work cooperatively on the problems of the Aral Sea basin. In cooperation with Soviet specialists, the United Nations Environment Programme has set up a research project and formed a small working group on the problems of the Aral Sea. The group is expected to provide specific recommendations for action in two years. The executive committee of the International Geographical Union also has formed a research group that is working on the problem of critical ecological zones. The investigations of this group will embrace several critical zones, but one of the most important will be the Aral Sea region.

This past fall, an international symposium on the state of the Aral Sea basin was held in Nukus, the capital of Karakalpak. (The symposium resolutions may be found in the box on the previous page.) The symposium, organized by the Aral Research and Coordination Center with the participation and assistance of the International Geographical Union Study Group on Critical Environmental Zones and Global Change, was an important landmark in cooperation on the Aral. The symposium launched a serious effort to gather the data needed to conceptualize scientifically grounded socioeconomic development in Soviet central Asia. In the end, such thinking can be the only way to resolve the problems of the Aral Sea.

NOTES

1. P. P. Micklin, "Dessication of the Aral Sea: A Water Management Disaster in the Soviet Union," *Science* 241 (1988):1170-76.

2. T. I. Molosnova, O. I. Subbotina, and S. G. Chanysheva, *Klimaticheskiye Posledstviya Khozyaistvennoi Deyatel Nosti v Zone Aral'skogo Morya* (Climatic Consequences of Economic Activity in the Zone of the Aral Sea) (Leningrad: Gidrometeoizdat, 1987).

3. D. B. Oreshkin, "Aral'skaya Katastrofa," (The Aral Catastrophe), *Nauka o Zemle*, no. 2 (1990):41.

4. See also, F. I. Khakimov, *Pochvenno-Meliorativnye Usloviya Opustynivaniya Del't* (Soil-Meliorative Conditions of Desertification of Deltas) (Pushchino, 1989).

5. H. E. Dregne, "Aridity and Land Degradation," *Environment*, October 1985, 16.

Does it matter where you are?

The cliché of the information age is that instantaneous global telecommunications, television and computer networks will soon overthrow the ancient tyrannies of time and space. Companies will need no headquarters, workers will toil as effectively from home, car or beach as they could in the offices that need no longer exist, and events half a world away will be seen, heard and felt with the same immediacy as events across the street—if indeed streets still have any point.

There is something in this. Software for American companies is already written by Indians in Bangalore and transmitted to Silicon Valley by satellite. Foreign-exchange markets have long been running 24 hours a day. At least one Californian company literally has no headquarters: its officers live where they like, its salesmen are always on the road, and everybody keeps in touch via modems and e-mail.

Yet such developments have made hardly a dent in the way people think and feel about things. Look, for example, at newspapers or news broadcasts anywhere on earth, and you find them overwhelmingly dominated by stories about what is going on in the vicinity of their place of publication. Much has been made of the impact on western public opinion of televised scenes of suffering in such places as Ethiopia, Bosnia and Somalia. Impact, maybe, but a featherweight's worth.

World television graphically displayed first the slaughter of hundreds of thousands of people in Rwanda and then the flight of more than a million Rwandans to Zaire. Not until France belatedly, and for mixed motives, sent in a couple of thousand soldiers did anyone in the West lift so much as a finger to stop the killing; nor, once the refugees had suddenly poured out, did western governments do more than sluggishly bestir themselves to try to contain a catastrophe.

Rwanda, of course, is small (population maybe 8m before the killings began). More important, it is far away. Had it been Flemings killing Walloons in Belgium (population 10m) instead of Hutus slaying Tutsi in Rwanda, European news companies would have vastly increased their coverage, and European governments would have intervened in force. Likewise, the only reason the Clinton administration is even thinking about invading Haiti is that it lies a few hundred miles from American shores. What your neighbours (or your kith and kin) do affects you. The rest is voyeurism.

The conceit that advanced technology can erase the contingencies of place and time ranges widely. Many armchair strategists predicted during the Gulf war that ballistic missiles and smart weapons would make the task of capturing and holding territory irrelevant. They were as wrong as the earlier seers who predicted America could win the Vietnam war from the air.

In business, too, the efforts to break free of space and time have had qualified success at best. American multinationals going global have discovered that—for all their world products, world advertising, and world communications and control—an office in, say, New York cannot except in the most general sense manage the company's Asian operations. Global strengths must be matched by a local feel—and a jet-lagged visit of a few days every so often does not provide one.

Most telling of all, even the newest industries are obeying an old rule of geographical concentration. From the start of the industrial age, the companies in a fast-growing new field have tended to cluster in a small region. Thus, in examples given by Paul Krugman, an American economist, all but one of the top 20 American carpet-makers are located in or near the town of Dalton, Georgia; and, before 1930, the American tire industry consisted almost entirely of the 100 or so firms carrying on that business in Akron, Ohio. Modern technology has not changed the pattern. This is why the world got Silicon Valley in California in the 1960s. It is also why tradable services stay surprisingly concentrated—futures trading (in Chicago), insurance (Hartford, Connecticut), movies (Los Angeles) and currency trading (London).

HISTORY'S HEAVY HAND

This offends not just techno-enthusiasts but also neo-classical economics: for both, the world should tend towards a smooth dispersion of people, skills and economic competence, not towards their concentration. Save for transport costs, it should not matter where a tradable good or service is produced.

The reality is otherwise. Some economists have explained this by pointing to increasing returns to scale (in labour as well as capital markets), geographically uneven patterns of demand and transport costs. The main reason is that history counts: where you are depends very much on where you started from.

The new technologies will overturn some of this, but not much. The most advanced use so far of the Internet, the greatest of the world's computer networks, has not been to found a global village but to strengthen the local business and social ties among people and companies in the heart of Silicon Valley. As computer and communications power grows and its cost falls, people will create different sorts of space and communities from those that exist in nature. But these modern creations will supplement, not displace, the original creation; and they may even reinforce it. Companies that have gone furthest towards linking their global operations electronically report an increase, not a decline in the face-to-face contact needed to keep the firms running well: with old methods of command in ruins, the social glue of personal relations matters more than ever.

The reason lies in the same fact of life that makes it impossible really to understand from statistics alone how exciting, say, China's economic growth is unless you have physically been there to feel it. People are not thinking machines (they absorb at least as much information from sight, smell and emotion as they do from abstract symbols), and the world is not immaterial: "virtual" reality is no reality at all; cyberspace is a pretence at circumventing true space, not a genuine replacement for it. The weight on mankind of time and space, of physical surroundings and history—in short, of geography—is bigger than any earthbound technology is ever likely to lift.

Low Water in the American High Plains

David E. Kromm

David E. Kromm, professor of geography at Kansas State University, has authored and coauthored numerous articles and one book on water management issues.

Depletion of the Ogallala Aquifer once threatened to return the region to a Dust Bowl, but much is being done to conserve groundwater today.

Water defines many regions. It determines their character and sustains their well-being. Ironically, this is especially true of areas with an inherent water scarcity. What would Southern California and central Arizona be like without water imported from distant sources? The green fields and golf courses would give way to dry plains and hills, populated more by grazing animals than by people.

A huge dry area in the middle of the United States depends no less on water to transform a dusty outback into a productive garden. This is the High Plains overlying the Ogallala Aquifer.

There exists widespread concern that America's largest underground water reserve is drying up. The vast Ogallala Aquifer that underlies 174,000 square miles of the High Plains from west Texas northward into South Dakota has been partially depleted as more than 150,000 wells pump water for irrigation, municipal supply, and industry. In some areas the wells no longer yield enough water to make irrigation possible. In others there remains sufficient water, but it lies 300 or more feet below the surface. The cost of lifting water from such depths makes it uneconomical for many uses.

Touching base with some key words in the groundwater vocabulary helps tell the Ogallala story more precisely. One is *aquifer*. An aquifer is a zone of water-saturated sands and gravels beneath the earth's surface. It is not an underground lake or river. It is the porous rock structure that contains the water that we tap with wells. Some aquifers release water to wells readily, whereas others hold the water tightly. This affects the rate at which water can be withdrawn and is called the *specific yield* of a well. *Depth to water* describes the vertical distance from ground level to the aquifer. Together with the volume and quality of water, the depth and specific yield define the economic limit of water withdrawal. The fresh water in an aquifer is called *groundwater*, in contrast to surface waters such as rivers and lakes. Over half the nation's population depends on groundwater for its drinking water. Although there are several aquifers, the Ogallala ranks as the main formation in the High Plains aquifer system. Most people in the region refer to the entire system as the Ogallala.

The unconsolidated sand and gravel that form the Ogallala aquifer were laid down by fluvial deposition from the Rocky Mountains about 10 million years ago. More recent, near-surface deposits

This article appeared in *The World & I*, February 1992, pp. 312-319. Reprinted with permission from *The World & I*, a publication of The Washington Times Corporation.

of the late Tertiary and Quaternary ages compose the High Plains aquifer.

The volume of available water varies from place to place. Nebraska has about two-thirds (65 percent) of the High Plains groundwater, followed by Texas (12 percent), and Kansas (10 percent). The total water in storage is enough to fill Lake Huron or to cover the state of Colorado to a depth of 45 feet. Physical characteristics of the aquifer result in one farmer in a county having little or no access to water while another has substantial reserves. Ogallala water moves gradually from west to east, following the general slope of the land surface. This movement does not affect use or depletion, as it takes nearly a century and a half to flow a mere 10 miles.

The Ogallala Aquifer

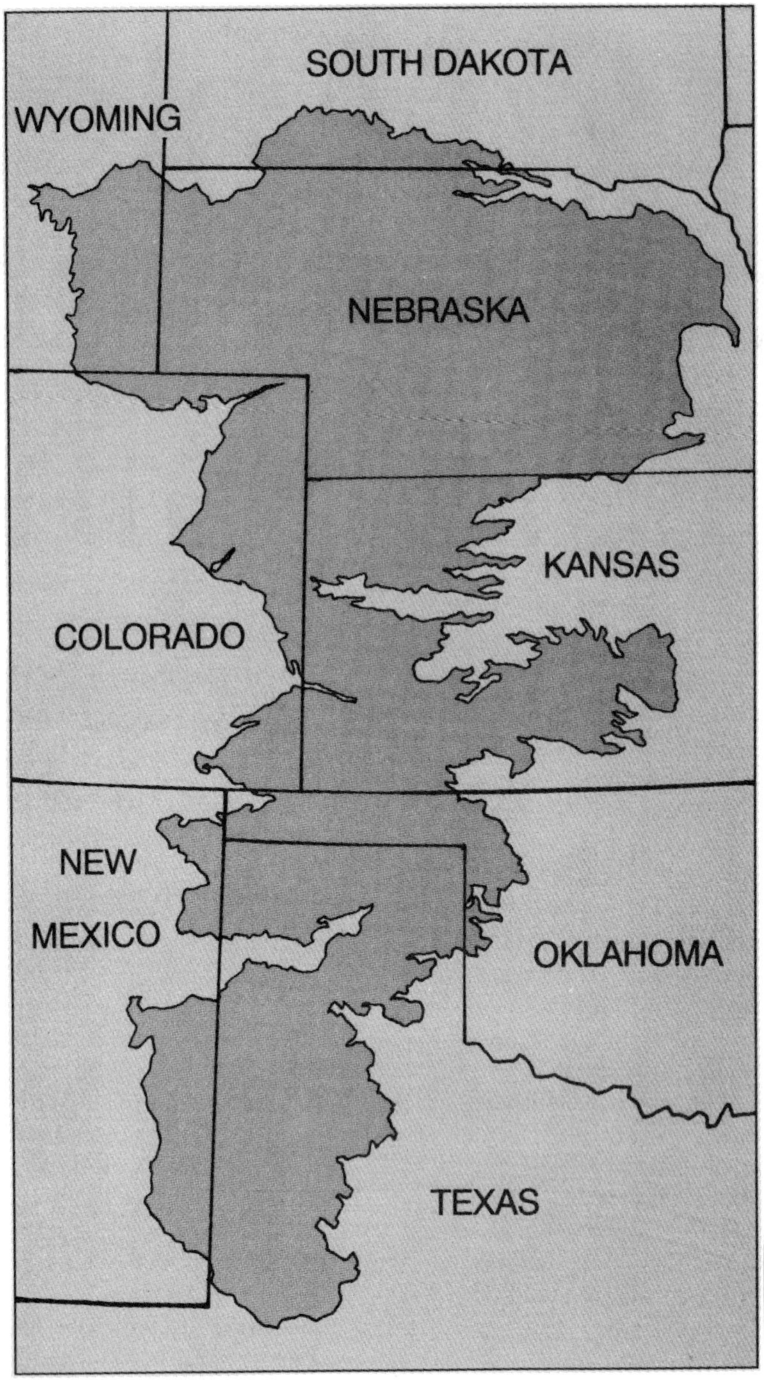

EMIKO OZAKI / THE WORLD & I

Changing views

When Stephen Long explored the region in the early nineteenth century, he discovered a sea of grass that contrasted with the trees that dominated landscapes to the east. Few lakes or rivers can be found. These signs of aridity led Long to name the area "The Great American Desert." Settlers on their way to rainy Oregon viewed the plains as worthless territory that had to be crossed in order to reach a land more promising. Even those few who attempted to break the prairie sod found it tough to plow. The native Americans and buffalo herds were initially displaced by cattle ranching, not by cultivation.

A whole new perception of the plains burst forth in the middle of the nineteenth century as railroads penetrated the region and touted its virtues. The promoters encouraged the development of farming communities that would depend on the rails for goods and the delivery of grain to eastern markets. New steel plows cracked the soil and many boosters came to believe that "the rain follows the plow." Once the ground was broken and crops planted, the aridity would end. Hopeful farmers took up homesteads from the government or bought lands directly from the railroad companies.

There ensued frequent dry years and just enough wet ones to allow many of the farmers to hang on. The rosy view of the High Plains as a garden was soon tarnished but never wholly abandoned. This changed with the 1930s. Everything went wrong. Depression weakened markets and reduced capital availability and drought destroyed the crops. A new name was coined for the

■ **The promotional railroad poster, 1887: the advantages of settling the High Plains.**

High Plains—the Dust Bowl. Outmigration swelled and the popular image was that of skies darkened by blowing dirt, desolate farmsteads surrounded by drifting soil, and impoverished families attempting to leave with whatever they could carry in their dilapidated vehicles. John Steinbeck chronicled the depth of misery in *The Grapes of Wrath.*

Emergence of a new Corn Belt

Even as the last settlers were taking up land in the 1890s, irrigation was beginning. It occupied small patches dependent on surface sources such as the Arkansas River or shallow wells. The Dust Bowl brought renewed interest in soil and water conservation and encouraged irrigation to create a stable moisture supply. Farmers suffered greatly from climatic variability in the High Plains. In a given year it might be a land of bountiful rain or a sun-drenched and parched desert.

Irrigation expanded in the 1930s and even more so in the dry years of the 1950s, as new technologies made possible large-scale tapping of the Ogallala aquifer. Pump engines came on the market that could lift large quantities of water from sources deep underground. New watering methods, such as center-pivot sprinklers, allowed irrigation of sandy and hilly areas. The green circles seen from aircraft flying more than 30,000 feet above the surface became the most prominent feature in the High Plains. The perception of the 1960s and 1970s was of a new Corn Belt flourishing in the land of the underground rain. Thanks to the Ogallala, stability had at last come to the High Plains.

Or had it? For the most part the Ogallala is a fossil water aquifer. It was formed millions of years ago and has been minimally recharged since. Only in a few areas such as the Nebraska Sandhills and the sand-sage prairie of southwestern Kansas was new water being added. Elsewhere, whatever was pumped out was forever gone. Wells sunk into zones with limited saturation thickness dried up early. Many were in west Texas, where large-scale irrigation began. By the late 1970s the whole High Plains region seemed threatened again, no less than it had been in the dirty thirties. Between 1978 and 1987, the irrigated area harvested in the High Plains sharply fell from nearly 13 million acres to 10.4 million acres.

Depletion ranks as such a serious problem that quality and streamflow issues are easily overlooked. In its natural state, the High Plains aquifer is generally of high quality. It is suitable for a wide array of uses without filtration. Where soils are sandy, however, precipitation can reach the water table, bringing with it nitrates from fertilizers and other surface contaminants. Abandoned water wells directly link pollutants and the aquifer. Where irrigation development is intense, decline in stream flows often follows. In Kansas, more than 700 miles of once permanently flowing rivers are now dry. The blue band on maps representing the Arkansas River in western Kansas hides the reality of a dry streambed.

An integrated agribusiness economy

Fears of impending disaster were real as the regional economy had expanded and grown relatively prosperous on the basis of irrigated agriculture. Except for the Platte River valley in Nebraska and Colorado, and minor surface sources in other places, groundwater sustained irrigation. In the southern reaches of the High Plains, irrigated cotton supports gins, oil mills, and a denim factory. Throughout most of the region farmers cultivate forage crops to

■ **Center-pivot irrigation has permitted the short-term cultivation of sandy, sloping land. Such areas are suitable only for grazing in the long term.**

feed cattle. Much of the cattle industry centers on huge feeder lots that collectively consume many tons of grain daily. The cattle in turn supply large meat processing plants, some of which are among the largest in the world.

Through the multiplier effect, irrigated agriculture affects all aspects of the regional economy. Where irrigation prevails, most rural towns seem vital, alive, and healthy. Where irrigation is absent, much less economic activity occurs, far fewer people are employed in commerce, and a decreasing volume and array of goods and services are available. Boarded-up storefronts provide visual evidence of the decline. One measure of civic progress in these communities is the tearing down of no longer needed buildings. Another is keeping the weeds under control in empty lots where structures once stood.

Observing this depopulation and decay, Deborah and Frank Popper of Rutgers University have recommended that the entire area be turned over to native grasses and animals. They call for a buffalo commons. The Poppers see a natural process of people moving away, with the population becoming so small and scattered that basic educational, medical, and commercial services could no longer be provided. To be fair, it should be noted that extensive cultivation and cattle ranching would continue to occupy the land, leaving little space for buffalo. Nonetheless, the reduction in the number of towns and farmsteads would approximate the appearance of the High Plains of more than a century ago. This general contraction of people and services occurs where dryland farming prevails. It could become the norm for irrigated areas, where scarcity results from high pumping costs as water is lifted from ever-greater depths, reduction in specific yield, or lack of water as wells are physically depleted.

The High Plains has exemplified what Wes Jackson, director of the Land Institute in Kansas, calls "the failure of success." The success of irrigation was sowing the seeds of its own destruction through depletion. Relying on a single water source also creates vulnerability. Take away the aquifer and the High Plains is without sufficient precipitation or surface water to sustain intensive agriculture or most other activities.

Responding to water scarcity

Few residents in the High Plains are standing idly by, merely watching a drama of decline being played out as irrigation becomes less and less a part of the regional economy. Water conservation has become more prevalent and is seen as the answer to sustaining irrigation and the integrated agribusiness economy it supports. Municipalities, factories, and other water users have lessened water use, but the major concern remains irrigation. More than 90 percent of the water consumed in the High Plains goes to irrigation. If irrigators are able to significantly reduce water consumption, for most there should be adequate and accessible water for many decades to come.

What are irrigators doing to conserve water? In 1988–90, with support from the Ford Foundation, the author and fellow geographer Stephen E. White looked into this question. A questionnaire was mailed to 1,750 irrigators in Texas, Oklahoma, Kansas, and Nebraska, asking them what water-saving practices they had adopted. Over 40 percent (709) returned a completed survey. Those who responded cited over 21 conservation practices now in wide use throughout the High Plains. Some of these techniques are: periodically checking pumping plant efficiency, planting drought-tolerant crops, replacing open ditches with underground pipes, and recovering runoff from fields. On the center-pivot sprinkler system, low-pressure heads are being installed on drop tubes to reduce overwatering and wind drift.

Several of the widely used practices are sophisticated, information-based techniques that can be highly effective. Scheduling irrigation based on moisture need serves as an example. The goal is to ensure that just enough water is in the root zone of a plant to accomplish the management objectives of the farmer. Soil water levels and plant stress are monitored so that the farmer can determine how much water to apply and when. The days of large amounts of water draining off the fields into ditches or leaching downward beyond the root zone are largely gone.

The days of large amounts of water draining off the fields into ditches or leaching downward beyond the root zone are largely gone.

Institutions play a major role in how the Ogallala and other aquifers are used and who controls the decisions affecting water use. Water law provides an example. Two general forms of water rights exist in the United States, and both function in the High Plains. In Texas, *riparian water rights* prevail, wherein the owner of land overlying an aquifer has the right to use the groundwater beneath. In the remaining states in the region differing forms of the *appropriation doctrine* exist. Under appropriation, the first party to establish the right to use a specified amount of groundwater (or surface water such as a river) has priority of use in times of scarcity. Junior rights may be reduced or even curtailed when they endanger senior rights. The doctrine may be summarized as "first in time, first in right." It has served the western states well, in that insufficient water is available to provide enough for all landowners, as is necessary to apply the riparian doctrine. Most states have developed a priority in water use, with domestic and livestock consumption usually ranking first.

These water rights are administered by various levels of organizations and agencies. Water largely falls under state control, but substate or local districts are often permitted by law. These authorities are formed usually to ensure that existing rights, often for irrigation, are protected. The authority of the local district varies from largely educational, establishing programs to advocate water conservation, to requiring a land-use plan or metering of water flow for all irrigators with water rights. Local districts frequently have enforcement authority. As a rule, a main goal of both state and local groups is to protect existing water rights, most of which are held by irrigators. Increasingly, water markets

COURTESY OF DAVID KROMM

COURTESY OF DAVID KROMM

■ **Different application strategies are helping conserve irrigation water.**

Top: **This standard center-pivot sprays water up into the wind.**

Right: **These low-energy precision application sprinklers have low-pressure heads attached to drop tubes, thereby minimizing wind drift.**

are being introduced that allow rights to be sold to other users. A farmer, for example, may sell a water right to a municipality or to a developer converting land from agricultural to residential use.

Much remains to be done, but the institutions and technologies of the High Plains show that the region is responding effectively. Most of the states now have water or resource management districts that are responsible for ensuring wise use of the Ogallala. A variety of policies have emerged. In various areas, wells are spaced so as not to interfere with each other, flow meters are required to measure water use, and drilling of new irrigation wells is prohibited. Although planned and orderly depletion constitutes the primary goal, one groundwater management district in western Kansas is considering a zero-depletion policy.

COURTESY OF DAVID KROMM

■ **This field of soybeans is irrigated using a "surge flow system" that wets the soil with intermittent impulses to reduce infiltration. Water-saving practices such as this are now being adopted by many irrigators tapping the waters of the Ogallala Aquifer.**

Innovation in irrigation technology has been striking. Many of the water-saving practices and devices used by farmers in the region and elsewhere were developed or first applied in the High Plains. Most are manufactured in the area. Land-grant universities throughout the region lead the way in developing techniques to conserve water. Nonprofit groups such as the Nebraska Groundwater Foundation support public education efforts. The High Plains ranks as a global center of technology and institutions for improving efficiency in irrigation.

What next?

Although numerous writers continue to cite the High Plains as a region where significant groundwater depletion occurs and where irrigation is doomed by its own excesses, current practices and conditions no longer support these views. Because of institutional and technical innovation, educational campaigns, and the land and water stewardship of most farmers, sustainable irrigation appears likely in the High Plains. The Great American Desert will not reappear as the Buffalo Commons.

A funny thing happened after the funeral

Return of the Soviet Empire

■ *In December, 1992, Russian Foreign Minister Andrei Kozyrev petrified a conference of European statesmen in Stockholm by threatening that Russia would use "all available means," including force, to defend its interests in its former empire. Then he explained that it was all a dead-serious joke to show what might happen if the wrong people took power in Moscow. These days, it's no joke—as the Russian intervention in Bosnia amply proves. What is more, the West shows no sign of stopping Russia from playing its great-power role. The cover package explores what's happening from the standpoints of observers in the west, in former Soviet republics and satellite states, and in Russia itself—where the once and future empire is a subject of much discussion.*

The **Guardian**

George Bush's poodle has died, and the most urgent foreign-policy question for President Bill Clinton and the other Western leaders is what kind of beast is replacing it. The bizarre anomaly of the past five years, in which one of the world's undisputed great powers has subordinated its foreign policies to the West's agenda, is over. Russia is again acting as an international player with its own interests and spheres of influence, and its new self-assertiveness has inspired a new school of American hawks who believe that we are watching the re-creation of the late and unlamented Soviet Union.

The arguments of the hawks can no longer be lightly dismissed. Russian troops are still in place in most of the ex-Soviet republics and, according to once-dovish Foreign Minister Andrei Kozyrev, will stay there so long as "dangerous vacuums" threaten to be filled by unfriendly forces.

Russian troops have already been deployed to stabilize four of the small states that Russians call their "near-abroad." They stopped the civil war in Tajikistan and installed an unpleasant Stalinoid regime. They intervened in the Georgian civil war to save the elected government of Eduard Shevardnadze, at the price of Georgia's humble re-entry into the Commonwealth of Independent States. They are now in Azerbaijan, poised to ensure that Armenia's success in the war over Nagorno-Karabakh does not topple the old Soviet Politburo member who now runs Azerbaijan. And Russia's 14th Army continues to squat over the tiny republic of Moldova, on the Romanian border.

Russia's new sphere of influence is economic as well as military. Belarus, on that edgy frontier between Poland and the old Soviet Union, has now beseeched and won economic re-integration with Russia. Kazakhstan, whose energy riches promised to make it the most viable of the former Soviet republics, has been told that Russia demands 20 percent of the takings from the Kazakh deal with the U.S. oil giant Chevron to develop the huge new Tengiz oilfield.

The U.S. security establishment is sounding the alarm. Senior officials point to the hard-line pressures on President Boris Yeltsin from the army, which saved him last October, and from the nationalist-conservative voting bloc in the new Russian Parliament. And after the defeat of the economic reformers in Yeltsin's government, the American hawks warn that the West will be dealing with a new Russia that looks and acts uncomfortably like the old Soviet Union.

This new American hawkishness is beginning to seep out from the Pentagon and State Department, but it is not yet American policy. The Clinton administration's policy toward Russia has been set by Strobe Talbott, Clinton's old Oxford roommate, who has more regular access to the president's ear than anyone except the president's wife. Talbott's policies are usually caricatured by his hawkish critics as "betting the farm on Boris," throwing all of America's weight behind Yeltsin as the embodiment of reform. Now that reform is being rethought, the hawks reckon their chance may be coming, and they can push for a different American strategy. The difficulty is that America's European allies are far from convinced that the hawks are right. A Western consensus has yet to emerge on Russia's ambitions in its near-abroad.

Even prostrate, Russia remains 150 million people in a traditional great power that still extends from the Baltic Sea

Reprinted from *World Press Review,* April 1994, pp. 8-13.

to the Pacific Ocean and commands a vast store of raw materials. The question the West has yet to answer is the degree to which Russia can now be allowed to have legitimate security interests beyond its borders and to act on them.

Britain and Germany are taking a realist line. If Russia is going to become a dangerous neighbor, it can be warned off. Until then, they reckon, Russia's legitimate interests will have to be defined and accepted so long as they follow the United Nations and other accepted rules of peace-keeping.

There are places, such as Caucasia and Central Asia, where the West might even welcome Russia's playing a stabilizing role that we all know—after Bosnia—the West cannot stomach. At the least, that means intervening only by invitation and with international approval, having a clear exit strategy, and operating under the eye of international observers.

The U.S. will not find it easy to swallow the Anglo-German realism. But the Americans have little choice. Now that we have buried Bush's poodle, everybody from the U.S. to NATO to Russia's worried neighbors will have to cooperate to ensure that its successor, nasty Rottweiler or friendly old golden retriever, is properly house trained.

—Martin Walker, "The Guardian" (liberal), London.

Polish Fears of a Russian-U.S. Axis

RZECZPOSPOLITA

In Poland, we have had our period of fascination with freedom and joy at liberation from Moscow's tutelage. Now we note painfully that America's version of the world order is again leading Poland into the sphere of Russian influence.

In Russian-American relations, one could always detect an atmosphere of cooperation between two great powers. During both world wars, there emerged something that could be called affection and understanding. Today, America is returning to these traditions. The U.S. wants a strong Russia, a partner in preserving a world order. Russia wants the same thing. "We want to be equal in everything, as it should be in relations between two great powers," said President Boris Yeltsin last December.

After the collapse of the Soviet Union, a sharp dispute went on in Moscow for months about how Russia was to fit into the new geopolitical system. In the winter of 1992, it became clear to Moscow that the new Russia could not start out by spewing superpower and imperialist slogans. So Yeltsin agreed to bury the U.S.S.R., retreating on all fronts without a struggle. But that was a tactical evasion.

Last year, Moscow began the process of rebuilding its sphere of influence. The most obvious spokesman of this change was Foreign Minister Andrei Kozyrev. Hounded quite recently by the nationalists and former communists for his tractability toward the West, he could now give lessons on how to treat Western politicians. After the success of [the neo-fascist] Vladimir Zhirinovsky in the recent elections, it was Kozyrev who said at a meeting with voters that certain postulates of the Russian fascists had to be taken into account and that Russian foreign policy had to be corrected.

All those who believed that, after the fall of the U.S.S.R., the era of hegemony of a great power also had ended were being unrealistic. I will say even more: These views were convenient for certain countries and political forces as arguments for limiting financial aid to the new states created by the Soviet collapse. Democratic Russia is different from the Soviet one, they said. We do not have to fear Yeltsin's Russia.

They did not want to see that during the seven-decade life of Soviet Russia, close economic ties and common interests were formed in this vast area. Russia had guaranteed stability of a sort over a huge part of Asia. These were not ties that could be broken in a day. Without help from abroad, the Baltic states will not find another supplier of raw materials for their energy needs; without such help, Ukraine has fallen into an industrial trap. The severing of economic ties is possible only when the new states are granted massive financial aid. But there is a shortage of those willing to grant such aid. In effect, Russia, as the largest state in the Commonwealth of Independent States, is building up its empire once again. Having patiently waited out the time for the storm to subside, Russia is returning to its role as a superpower. Perhaps there is nothing else it can do.

Western politicians, among others, seem to forget one important problem. Speaking of democracy in Russia, they see it in a Western light. But there is no democracy in Russia, and there will not be any for a long time. As it builds its economy—and it must begin with that—Russia will not take human rights into account. As in Indonesia and South Korea in the initial phase of their changes, so in Russia dictatorial and autocratic tendencies will increase. We will have more than one surprise like the parliamentary elections of last October, with successive incarnations of Vladimir Zhirinovsky.

—Ryszard Malik, "Rzeczpospolita" (business), Warsaw.

A Swaggering Bear In Central Asia

Moscow's Muscle Flexing

REVIEW

It was a cold and bleak winter in the capital of Kazakhstan, Alma-Ata, and Russians were holding the city for ransom. In the unheated terminal of the airport, the temperature had plunged to 4 degrees below zero. Hundreds of passengers huddled under blankets. They had waited three days for takeoff. All flights were canceled after Russia shut off the Siberian oil pipeline, which supplies Alma-Ata with fuel.

It was another week before the Russians opened the fuel tap. Meanwhile—and in a clear indication of just who remains boss around these parts—the Kazakhs continued to pump oil to Russia from their fields in the Caspian Sea about 1,500 miles away.

The Russian bear is once again throwing its weight around the vast Central Asian landscape. And as Moscow puts the pressure on the republics to toe its political line, it is once again being greeted with fear and loathing. Yet Russia remains the most crucial element in the economic, military, and even political survival of the region's five regimes. Moscow endorses all their present heads of state, and it has not attempted any serious destabilization in Central Asia. Many observers believe, however, that by pushing its own interests in the republics too forcefully, Russia is damaging its long-term credibility.

Moscow's leverage is built on its continuing military and economic influence in the region. In Tajikistan, 25,000 Russian troops call the shots as a Russian- and Uzbek-installed neo-communist government in Dushanbe fights Islamic rebels. In neighboring Turkmenistan, President Saparmurad Niyazov has succumbed to Moscow's pressure and rejoined the Russian-dominated economic union—the Commonwealth of Independent States (C.I.S.). And no republic, the Russians demand, should strike an economic or defense deal with its Muslim neighbors to the south without Moscow's concurrence.

But above all, Russia is tearing at the fragile ethnic fabric of all the republics by insisting that local Russians be granted dual nationality. The Uzbeks have rejected the demand outright. In Kazakhstan, despite unrelenting Russian pressure, a senior diplomat asks: "How can we agree to dual nationality for the Russians when they are 39 percent of the population and there are 100 other nationalities living here? It would destroy our country."

Local Russian chauvinism has been spurred by the election gains in Russia of the ultra-nationalist Vladimir Zhirinovsky's Liberal Democratic Party. Indeed, local Russians are in a strong position in the countries they controlled not too long ago. In Kazakhstan, they command key technical posts in the capital and dominate the wheat-farming belt in the north. Kazakh President Nursultan Nazarbayev has delayed a decision on dual nationality for a year. But Russian pressure on him has only increased following Turkmenistan's cave-in on the issue in December.

Only 12.6 percent of Turkmenistan's population is Russian, but ethnic Russians hold a disproportionate number of key positions in the infrastructure. Unless it agreed to dual nationality, the country faced a massive migration of trained Russians. "We are aiming next to persuade Kyrgyzstan to do the same," says a senior Russian diplomat. That won't be hard. Kyrgyzstan is the smallest Central Asian republic, and more than 20 percent of its population is ethnically Russian.

The Russians appear unconcerned that the dual-nationality issue is galvanizing local nationalism and increasing anti-Russian feeling across the region. Uzbekistan, which has refused dual nationality, is losing 700 Russians daily. But, says an Uzbek journalist: "If [President Islam] Karimov agreed to dual nationality, he would be finished. We hate the Russians." Yet Karimov is forced to play a dangerous double game. To flatter local sentiment, he regularly snubs Moscow's ambassador. This gets him good press locally. But the Uzbek president regularly makes up with the Russian envoy afterward.

Russia is also blamed for forcing Kazakhstan, Uzbekistan, and Turkmenistan to adopt their own currencies last fall and for insisting that oil- and gas-rich countries such as Turkmenistan and Kazakhstan consult Moscow before signing deals to build pipelines through Iran or Turkey to the sea. Russia remains the largest—and in many cases the only—market for unprocessed raw materials and the supplier of such essential goods as fuel and foodstuffs. Turkmenistan, for example, imports 60 percent of its food from Russia.

Zhirinovsky's statement that the former Soviet republics would soon "beg with tears in their eyes to be taken back into Russia" has struck a chord within the Russian military. Now Moscow's new military doctrine, adopted last October, asserts that its strategic domain includes Central Asia and that it must build a rapid-deployment force to quash regional conflicts.

At the December summit of the C.I.S. in Ashkhabad, Russia signed a military agreement with Turkmenistan stipulating that Russia will be allowed to intervene militarily in C.I.S. states when its interests are threatened. These interests include "protection of Russian minorities." Moscow wants to sign similar agreements with the other Central Asian republics. It will probably get its way.

—Ahmed Rashid, "Far Eastern Economic Review" (independent newsmagazine), Hong Kong.

A Tinder Box In the Crimea

Will Ukraine Take on Russia?

Wochenpost

The election of Yuri Meshkov to the presidency of the Crimea has plunged the political landscape of Ukraine into a surreal twilight. Meshkov was the candidate of the Russia Democratic Party, one of three organizations that have promised the Crimea's Russians to bring the Black Sea

In the Baltics, High Anxiety

THE INDEPENDENT

Like most Latvians, President Guntis Ulmanis is looking increasingly uneasy. "You tell me," he says, attempting a jocular tone. "Is there a deal being done over our heads? Is our sovereignty about to be sacrificed? Is the West going to let us down? We really would like to know."

Until recently, such comments might have been dismissed as typical of Latvia's almost obsessive fears of Russia and the possibility of a repeat of the 1939 Molotov-Ribbentrop pact, under which the Baltics were surrendered to Stalin.

The comments do not sound so fantastic now. Vladimir Zhirinovsky, the ultra-nationalist who made big gains in Russia's December elections, has made sure of that with his expansionist plans, which would include re-annexation of the Baltics. Ulmanis and his colleagues have been equally alarmed by some of Moscow's policy directives. On New Year's Day, President Boris Yeltsin said 1994 would mark a more "energetic" defense of the 25 million ethnic Russians in neighboring states.

Then a comment by Foreign Minister Andrei Kozyrev brought howls of protest all the way from Tallinn to Vilnius, the capitals of Estonia and Lithuania. Kozyrev told Russian ambassadors that, to prevent a "security vacuum" on Russia's borders, its troops should remain stationed throughout the "near-abroad," Moscow's term for the former republics of the Soviet Union. Although Foreign Ministry officials later said the comments had referred to the countries of the Commonwealth of Independent States—and not the Baltics—the damage had been done.

With 10,000 Russian troops still in Latvia and 3,000 in Estonia, the situation is tense. Early in January, Russian forces in Latvia were put on alert after an official in Riga seeking to reclaim army property arrested two Russian generals and ordered them to be deported. Ulmanis received a phone call from the commander of Russian forces in Latvia ordering him to hand back the generals within 30 minutes—or else. His security tracked down the arrested men and had them returned on time. The situation was calmed by the sacking of the official responsible for the arrests and an apology to Moscow.

Whatever lay behind it, the incident was an example of what one Western observer called the "time bomb" ticking in Latvia. Yeltsin warned of a tougher response should there be any more incidents. Pessimists see parallels with 1940, when, before the Red Army invaded, Soviet media castigated "provocative" actions by Latvian "extremists." That could easily happen again, they fear.

Optimists believe the situation will not come to that. Unlike nearly all the other former Soviet republics, they insist, the Baltics could resist being sucked back into Moscow's orbit. An encouraging sign is that Russian troops stationed in Lithuania have all gone and that those left in Latvia and Estonia are due to quit by the end of August.

The removal of what Latvians see as occupation forces will do much to ease tension. So, too, would the passage of a citizenship law clarifying the status and rights of the country's hundreds of thousands of non-Latvians. But according to Ulmanis, not even a full security guarantee from NATO would ensure Latvia's long-term independence. "In the end, our security will not depend on a physical border across the continent but, rather, on the symbolic border dividing the forces of reform and reaction in Russia itself. Europe will be safe only if democracy really wins through in Moscow."

—Adrian Bridge, "The Independent" (centrist), London.

peninsula back under the Russian roof. With this turn of events, almost all of the elements that triggered war between Serbia and Croatia are now in place in Ukraine. The only thing lacking is an expansionist government in Moscow. If the nationalist Vladimir Zhirinovsky were already in power there, conflict between Russia and Ukraine would be almost unavoidable.

The strategic consequences of a Russian-Ukrainian war could be much more serious than the nightmare in Croatia and Bosnia-Herzegovina. Admittedly, Russian President Boris Yeltsin controls the codes that activate the more than 1,000 atomic warheads stationed in Ukraine. But in Kiev, there are scientists eagerly prepared to crack those codes. And Dmitri Pavlychko, head of the foreign-relations committee of the Ukrainian Parliament, has warned: "If it comes to a conflict, we will fight—if necessary with atomic bombs."

Meshkov knows he doesn't enjoy great support in Moscow and that what support he can count on is equivocal. On the one hand, the new Crimean president maintains that he wants to function as "a bridge between Ukraine and Russia." On the other hand, he has proposed that a referendum on Crimean independence be held. The reaction to that idea was foreseeable. Vice Minister Aleksandr Piskun, Kiev's point man on "ethnic matters," warned that a referendum would unleash "a very serious conflict with Ukraine."

The sudden switch in public opinion in favor of independence for the Crimea signals a remarkable change of heart. In 1991, 54 percent of the Crimean population, a good 70 percent of whom are of Russian origin, were in favor of Ukrainian independence from the Soviet Union. Their commitment to the newly emergent state was based on the conviction that Ukraine's economic prospects were better than

Russia's. But since Ukraine was cut off from the huge Russian market and forced to pay for its energy imports from Russia in hard currency, its economy has been in steady decline. Inflation is running at a rate of 90 percent a month.

The economy of the Crimea is especially hard-hit. The wretched capital city of Simferopol corresponds exactly to the description Meshkov has offered of the whole peninsula: "an economic rubble heap." Although the Russian economy has certainly suffered enormous tensions, the reform program has begun to inject a vitality that is nowhere in evidence in Ukraine. Today, the Russian minority in eastern Ukraine looks longingly at the relative well-being of their countrymen on the other side of the border.

The tensions in the Crimea are aggravated by the fact that Ukraine's claim over the region is historically weak. Nikita Khrushchev got his political start in the Soviet Republic of Ukraine and, out of gratitude, transferred the Crimea to Ukraine in 1954. But by tradition, the peninsula stands closer to Russia.

If Russia mobilizes in the name of the Russian minority in Ukraine, the stability of the whole of Central and Eastern Europe could be destroyed. It's not for nothing that the CIA has recently sounded an alarm about the region. This shaky situation is also one of the reasons that the Poles and Hungarians were pushing so hard to be taken into NATO. Apart from the "hot war" in the former Yugoslavia, there is no conflict graver in Europe right now than the tensions in the economic rubble heap of the Crimea.

—*Misha Glenny, "Wochenpost" (weekly), Berlin.*

'Russia Can Only Be Reborn as an Empire'

No Need for Shame, a Historian Says

СОВЕТСКАЯ РОССИЯ

Our minds these days are ready to be manipulated, to accept false ideas and values without a murmur. Taking advantage of this, the haters of Russia are ridiculing the unique ideas and values that have always been part of Russian society.

Particular abuse has been heaped on the idea of empire and the Russian people's imperial instinct. Now even well-intentioned people often are ashamed to speak of the need to re-create the empire. It is time for us to stop being ashamed. We must declare unequivocally that Russia can only be reborn as an empire.

We are told that an empire is a type of state in which the dominant people oppress other peoples, in which the center (the metropolis) lives by plundering the out-lying regions (the colonies). There is no room for such a monster in the civilized world, the line goes. But any impartial person who is familiar with our history can see that the Russian (and then the Soviet) empire did not conform to this definition. Everything was the reverse in our case: It was not the center that prospered at the regions' expense; the regions developed thanks to (and sometimes even to the detriment of) the center.

The world knows two types of empires. One is a state based on the economic, political, or military dominance of one people over others. Examples were the British, Austrian, and German empires and both French empires. The Europeans who created these systems distorted the essence of the imperial principle because of specific psychic and religious factors. The other type of empire was developed in ancient Rome, was spiritualized by Christianity in Byzantium, and then, after the fall of Constantinople, was adopted and refined by Orthodox Russia.

A genuine empire is a great world power that incorporates various peoples who are tied into a single entity by a common higher culture, equality of all citizens before the law, and the supreme government. All the people in the empire enjoy the broadest rights of self-administration, as long, of course, as these rights do not harm the empire's general interests. The empire's meaning of existence comes from great-power status, which the state fulfills through two interconnected functions: keeping the peace and tranquillity between peoples inside the empire and keeping humankind from falling into an abyss of chaos and mutual annihilation.

The imperial principle does not at all require that the state be restored to its 1917 or 1991 borders. External restoration, of course, is desirable (geopolitically and economically) but by no means imperative.

The empire should be restored in the same way it was created. This means that peoples would be incorporated into the state voluntarily (with minor exceptions). Ethnic groups that adopt an aggressive stance toward the imperial nation cannot be allowed to join the state and must, accordingly, be deprived of any aid or support from the government. However, adherence to the principle of voluntarism in restoring the empire is a highly important guarantee of internal stability in the state. And so, restoring the empire means creating conditions (economic, social, and political) that encourage neighboring nations to join it on a voluntary basis.

—*A. Stepanov, "Sovetskaya Rossiya" (conservative), Moscow.*

Spatial Interaction and Mapping

Unit 4

Geography is the study not only of places in their own right, but of the ways in which places interact. Places are connected by highways, airline routes, telecommunication systems, and even thoughts. Geographers study these forms of spatial interaction because they are an important part of their work.

In "Transportation and Urban Growth: The Shaping of the American Metropolis," Peter Muller considers transportation systems, analyzing their impact on the growth of American cities. The next article deals with spatial interaction in the form of Hispanic migration in the United States. Then Roger Vickerman's article, "The Channel Tunnel," provides an insightful example of a significant change in spatial interaction and accessibility. The next two articles, from *American Demographics,* address aspects of migration in the United States.

How could geographers begin to describe in words the detailed spatial pattern of, for instance, the major agricultural regions in the world? Even photographs could not do the job adequately, because they literally capture too much of the detail of a place. There is no better way to present many of the topics analyzed in geography than with maps. Maps and geography go hand in hand. Although maps are used in other disciplines, their association with geography is the most highly developed.

A map is a graphic that presents a generalized and scaled-down view of particular occurrences or themes in an area. If a picture is worth a thousand words, then a map is worth a thousand (or more!) pictures. There is simply no better way to "view" a portion of Earth's surface or an associated pattern than with a map. How else could we see the entirety of South America, for example, in one glance?

J. Brian Harley and David Woodward provide interesting insights into early mapmaking and cartography and the impact of maps on society. Finally, the last two articles deal with current developments in the growth of geographic information systems (GIS) and their applications to land-use planning and management.

Looking Ahead: Challenge Questions

How would you describe the spatial form of the place in which you live? Do you live in a town or in a city, and why was that particular location chosen?

How does your hometown interact with its surrounding region? With other places in the state? With other states? With other places in the world?

How are places "brought closer together" when transportation systems are improved?

What problems occur when transportation systems are overloaded?

How do you think public transportation will be different in the future? Will there be more or fewer private autos in the next 25 years? Defend your answer.

Are you a good map reader? Why are maps useful in studying a place? How will the new technologies in satellite imagery improve mapping?

What changes in geography will be brought about by GIS innovations?

Transportation and Urban Growth

The shaping of the American metropolis

Peter O. Muller

In his monumental new work on the historical geography of transportation, James Vance states that geographic mobility is crucial to the successful functioning of any population cluster, and that "shifts in the availability of mobility provide, in all likelihood, the most powerful single process at work in transforming and evolving the human half of geography." Any adult urbanite who has watched the American metropolis turn inside-out over the past quarter-century can readily appreciate the significance of that maxim. In truth, the nation's largest single urban concentration today is not represented by the seven-plus million who agglomerate in New York City but rather by the 14 million who have settled in Gotham's vast, curvilinear outer city—a 50-mile-wide suburban band that stretches across Long Island, southwestern Connecticut, the Hudson Valley as far north as West Point, and most of New Jersey north of a line drawn from Trenton to Asbury Park. This latest episode of intrametropolitan deconcentration was fueled by the modern automobile and the interstate expressway. It is, however, merely the most recent of a series of evolutionary stages dating back to colonial times, wherein breakthroughs in transport technology unleashed forces that produced significant restructuring of the urban spatial form.

The emerging form and structure of the American metropolis has been traced within a framework of

From *Focus,* Summer 1986, pp. 8-17. Reprinted by permission of the American Geographical Society. © 1986.

Horse-drawn trolleys in downtown Boston, circa 1885. (Library of the Boston Athenaeum)

four transportation-related eras. Each successive growth stage is dominated by a particular movement technology and transport-network expansion process that shaped a distinctive pattern of intraurban spatial organization. The stages are the Walking/Horsecar Era (pre-1800–1890), the Electric Streetcar Era (1890–1920), the Recreational Automobile Era (1920–1945), and the Freeway Era (1945–present). As with all generalized models of this kind, there is a risk of oversimplification because the building processes of several simultaneously developing cities do not always fall into neat time-space compartments. Chicago's growth over the past 150 years, for example, reveals numerous irregularities, suggesting that the overall metropolitan growth pattern is more complex than a simple, continuous outward thrust. Yet even after developmental ebb and flow, leapfrogging, backfilling, and other departures from the idealized scheme are considered, there still remains an acceptable correspondence between the model and reality.

Before 1850 the American city was a highly compact settlement in which the dominant means of getting about was on foot, requiring people and activities to tightly agglomerate in close proximity to one another. This usually meant less than a 30-minute walk from the center of town to any given urban point—an accessibility radius later extended to 45 minutes when the pressures of industrial growth intensified after 1830. Within this pedestrian city, recognizable activity concentrations materialized as well as the beginnings of income-based residential congregations. The latter was particularly characteristic of the wealthy, who not only walled themselves off in their large homes near the city center but also took to the privacy of horse-drawn carriages for moving about town. Those of means also sought to escape the city's noise

Electric streetcar lines radiated outward from central cities, giving rise to star-shaped metropolises. Boston, circa 1915. (Library of the Boston Athenaeum)

and frequent epidemics resulting from the lack of sanitary conditions. Horse-and-carriage transportation enabled the wealthy to reside in the nearby countryside for the disease-prone summer months. The arrival of the railroad in the 1830s provided the opportunity for year-round daily commuting, and by 1840 hundreds of affluent businessmen in Boston, New York, and Philadelphia were making round trips from exclusive new trackside suburbs every weekday.

As industrialization and its teeming concentrations of working-class housing increasingly engulfed the mid-nineteenth century city, the deteriorating physical and social environment reinforced the desires of middle-income residents to suburbanize as well. They were unable, however, to afford the cost and time of commuting by steam train, and with the walking city now stretched to its morphological limit, their aspirations intensified the pressures to improve intraurban transport technology. Early attempts involving stagecoach-like omnibuses, cable-car systems, and steam railroads proved impractical, but by 1852 the first meaningful transit breakthrough was finally introduced in Manhattan in the form of the horse-drawn trolley. Light street rails were easy to install, overcame the problems of muddy, unpaved roadways, and enabled horsecars to be hauled along them at speeds slightly (about five mph) faster than those of pedestrians. This modest improvement in mobility permitted the opening of a narrow belt of land at the city's edge for new home construction. Middle-income urbanites flocked to these "horsecar suburbs," which multiplied rapidly after the Civil War. Radial routes were the first to spawn such peripheral development, but the relentless demand for housing necessitated the building of cross-town horsecar lines, thereby filling in the interstices and preserving the generally circular shape of the city.

Before 1850 the American city was a highly compact settlement in which the dominant means of getting about was on foot, requiring people and activities to tightly agglomerate in close proximity to one another.

The less affluent majority of the urban population, however, was confined to the old pedestrian city and its bleak, high-density industrial appendages. With the massive immigration of unskilled laborers, (mostly of European origin after 1870) huge blue-collar communities sprang up around the factories. Because these newcomers to the city settled in the order in which they arrived—thereby denying them the small luxury of living in the immediate company of their fellow ethnics—social stress and conflict were repeatedly generated. With the immigrant tide continuing to pour into the nearly bursting industrial city throughout the late nineteenth century, pressures redoubled to further improve intraurban transit and open up more of the adjacent countryside. By the late 1880s that urgently needed mobility revolution was at last in the making, and when it came it swiftly transformed the compact city and its suburban periphery into the modern metropolis.

The key to this urban transport revolution was the invention by Frank Sprague of the electric traction motor, an often overlooked innovation that surely ranks among the most important in American history. The first electrified trolley line opened in Richmond in 1888, was adopted by two dozen other big cities within a year, and by the early 1890s swept across the nation to become the dominant mode of intraurban transit. The rapidity of this innovation's diffusion was enhanced by the immediate recognition of its ability to resolve the urban transportation problem of the day: motors could be attached to existing horsecars, converting them into self-propelled vehicles powered by easily constructed overhead wires. The tripling of average speeds (to over 15 mph) that resulted from this invention brought a large band of open land beyond the city's perimeter into trolley-commuting range.

The most dramatic geographic change of the Electric Streetcar Era was the swift residential development of those urban fringes, which transformed the emerging metropolis into a decidedly star-shaped spatial entity. This pattern was produced by radial streetcar corridors extending several miles beyond the compact city's limits. With so much new space available for homebuilding within walking distance of the trolley lines, there was no need to extend trackage laterally, and so the interstices remained undeveloped. The typical streetcar suburb of the turn of this century was a continuous axial corridor whose backbone was the road carrying the trolley line (usually lined with stores and other local commercial facilities), from which gridded residential streets fanned out for several blocks on both sides of the tracks. In general, the quality of housing and prosperity of streetcar subdivisions increased with distance from the edge of the central city. These suburban corridors were populated by the emerging, highly mobile middle class, which was already stratifying itself according to a plethora of minor income and status differences. With frequent upward (and local geographic) mobility the norm, community formation became an elusive goal, a process further retarded by the grid-settlement morphology and the reliance on the distant downtown for employment and most shopping.

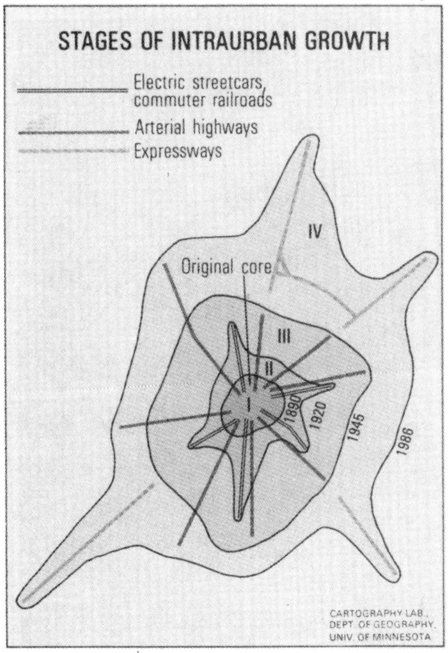

The ready availability and low fare of the electric trolley now provided every resident with access to the intracity circulatory system, thereby introducing truly "mass" transit to urban America.

Within the city, too, the streetcar sparked a spatial transformation. The ready availability and low fare of the electric trolley now provided every resident with access to the intracity circulatory system, thereby introducing truly "mass" transit to urban America in the final years of the nineteenth century. For nonresidential activities this new ease of movement among the city's various parts quickly triggered the emergence of specialized land-use districts for commerce, manufacturing, and transportation, as well as the continued growth of the multipurpose central business district (CBD) that had formed after mid-century. But the greatest impact of the streetcar was on the central city's social geography, because it made possible the congregation of ethnic groups in their own neighborhoods. No longer were these moderate-income masses forced to reside in the heterogeneous jumble of rowhouses and tenements that ringed the factories. The trolley brought them the opportunity to "live with their own kind," allowing the sorting of discrete groups into their own inner-city social territories within convenient and inexpensive traveling distance of the workplace.

By World War I, the electric trolleys had transformed the tracked city into a full-fledged metropolis whose streetcar suburbs, in the larger cases, spread out more than 20 miles from the metropolitan center. It was at this point in time that intrametropolitan transportation achieved its greatest level of efficiency—that the bustling industrial city really "worked." How much closer the American metropolis might have approached optimal workability for all its residents, however, will never be known because the next urban transport revolution was already beginning to assert itself through the increasingly popular automobile. Americans took to cars as wholeheartedly as anything in the nation's long cultural history. Although Lewis Mumford and other scholars vilified the car as the destroyer of the city, more balanced assessments of the role of the automobile recognize its overwhelming acceptance for what it was—the long-awaited attainment of private mass transportation that offered users the freedom to travel whenever and wherever they chose. As cars came to the metropolis in ever greater numbers throughout the interwar decades, their major influence was twofold: to accelerate the deconcentration of population through the development of interstices bypassed during the streetcar era, and to push the suburban frontier farther into the countryside, again producing a compact, regular-shaped urban entity.

Afternoon commuters converge at the tunnel leading out of central Boston, 1948. (Boston Public Library)

While it certainly produced a dramatic impact on the urban fabric by the eve of World War II, the introduction of the automobile into the American metropolis during the 1920s and 1930s came at a leisurely pace. The earliest flurry of auto adoptions had been in rural areas, where farmers badly needed better access to local service centers. In the cities, cars were initially used for weekend outings—hence the term "*Recreational* Auto Era"—and some of the earliest paved roadways were landscaped parkways along scenic water routes, such as New York's pioneering Bronx River Parkway and Chicago's Lake Shore Drive. But it was into the suburbs, where growth rates were now for the first time overtaking those of the central cities, that cars made a decisive penetration throughout the prosperous 1920s. In fact, the rapid expansion of automobile suburbia by 1930 so adversely affected the metropolitan public transportation system that, through significant diversions of streetcar and commuter-rail passengers, the large cities began to feel the negative effects of the car years before the auto's actual arrival in the urban center. By facilitating the opening of unbuilt areas lying between suburban rail axes, the automobile effectively lured residential developers away from densely populated traction-line corridors into the suddenly accessible interstices. Thus, the suburban homebuilding industry no longer found it necessary to subsidize privately-owned streetcar companies to provide low-fare access to trolley-line housing tracts. Without this financial underpinning, the modern urban transit crisis quickly began to surface.

Americans took to cars as wholeheartedly as anything in the nation's long cultural history.

The new recreational motorways also helped to intensify the decentralization of the population. Most were radial highways that penetrated deeply into the suburban ring and provided weekend motorists with easy access to this urban countryside. There they obviously were impressed by what they saw, and they soon responded in massive numbers to the sales pitches of suburban subdivision developers. The residential development of automobile suburbia followed a simple formula that was devised in the prewar years and greatly magnified in scale after 1945. The leading motivation was developer profit from the quick turnover of land, which was acquired in large parcels, subdivided, and auctioned off. Understandably,

Central City-Focused Rail Transit

The widely dispersed distribution of people and activities in today's metropolis makes rail transit that focuses in the central business district (CBD) an obsolete solution to the urban transportation problem. To be successful, any rail line must link places where travel origins and destinations are highly clustered. Even more important is the need to connect places where people really want to go, which in the metropolitan America of the late twentieth century means suburban shopping centers, freeway-oriented office complexes, and the airport. Yet a brief look at the rail systems that have been built in the last 20 years shows that transit planners cannot—or will not—recognize those travel demands, and insist on designing CBD-oriented systems as if we all still lived in the 1920s.

One of the newest urban transit systems is Metrorail in Miami and surrounding Dade County, Florida. It has been a resounding failure since its opening in 1984. The northern leg of this line connects downtown Miami to a number of low- and moderate-income black and Hispanic neighborhoods, yet it carries only about the same number of passengers that used to ride on parallel bus lines. The reason is that the high-skill, service economy of Miami's CBD is about as mismatched as it could possibly be to the modest employment skills and training levels possessed by residents of that Metrorail corridor. To the south, the prospects seemed far brighter because of the possibility of connecting the system to Coral Gables and Dadeland, two leading suburban activity centers. However, both central Coral Gables and the nearby International Airport complex were bypassed in favor of a cheaply available, abandoned railroad corridor alongside U.S. 1. Station locations were poorly planned, particularly at the University of Miami and at Dadeland—where terminal location necessitates a dangerous walk across a six-lane highway from the region's largest shopping mall. Not surprisingly, ridership levels have been shockingly below projections, averaging only about 21,000 trips per day in early 1986. While Dade County's worried officials will soon be called upon to decide the future of the system, the federal government is using the Miami experience as an excuse to withdraw from financially supporting all construction of new urban heavy-rail systems. Unfortunately, we will not be able to discover if a well-planned, high-speed rail system that is congruent with the travel demands of today's polycentric metropolis is capable of solving traffic congestion problems. Hopefully, transportation policymakers across the nation will heed the lessons of Miami's textbook example of how not to plan a hub-and-spoke public transportation network in an urban era dominated by the multicentered city.

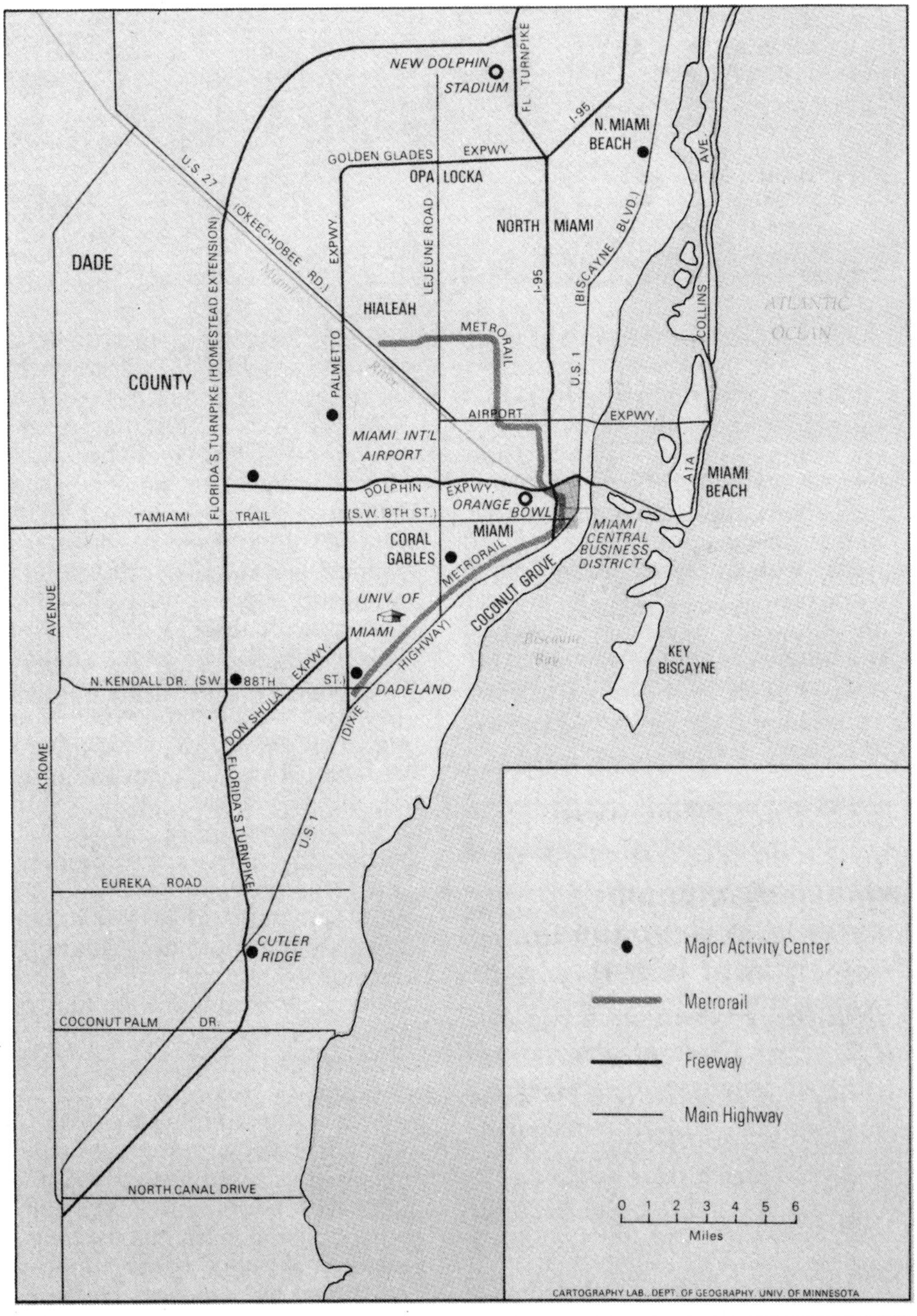

developers much preferred open areas at the metropolitan fringe, where large packages of cheap land could readily be assembled. Silently approving and underwriting this uncontrolled spread of residential suburbia were public policies at all levels of government: financing road construction, obligating lending institutions to invest in new homebuilding, insuring individual mortgages, and providing low-interest loans to FHA and VA clients.

Because automobility removed most of the pre-existing movement constraints, suburban social geography now became dominated by locally homogeneous income-group clusters that isolated themselves from dissimilar neighbors. Gone was the highly localized stratification of streetcar suburbia. In its place arose a far more dispersed, increasingly fragmented residential mosaic to which builders were only too eager to cater, helping shape a kaleidoscopic settlement pattern by shrewdly constructing the most expensive houses that could be sold in each locality. The continued partitioning of suburban society was further legitimized by the widespread adoption of zoning (legalized in 1916), which gave municipalities control over lot and building standards that, in turn, assured dwelling prices that would only attract newcomers whose incomes at least equaled those of the existing local population. Among the middle class, particularly, these exclusionary economic practices were enthusiastically supported, because such devices extended to them the ability of upper-income groups to maintain their social distance from people of lower socioeconomic status.

Nonresidential activities were also suburbanizing at an increasing rate during the Recreational Auto Era. Indeed, many large-scale manufacturers had decentralized during the streetcar era, choosing locations in suburban freight-rail corridors. These corridors rapidly spawned surrounding working-class towns that became important satellites of the central city in the emerging metropolitan constellation. During the interwar period, industrial employers accelerated their intraurban deconcentration, as more efficient horizontal fabrication methods replaced older techniques requiring multistoried plants—thereby generating greater space needs that were too expensive to satisfy in the high-density central city. Newly suburbanizing manufacturers, however, continued their affiliation with intercity freight-rail corridors, because motor trucks were not yet able to operate with their present-day efficiencies and because the highway network of the outer ring remained inadequate until the 1950s.

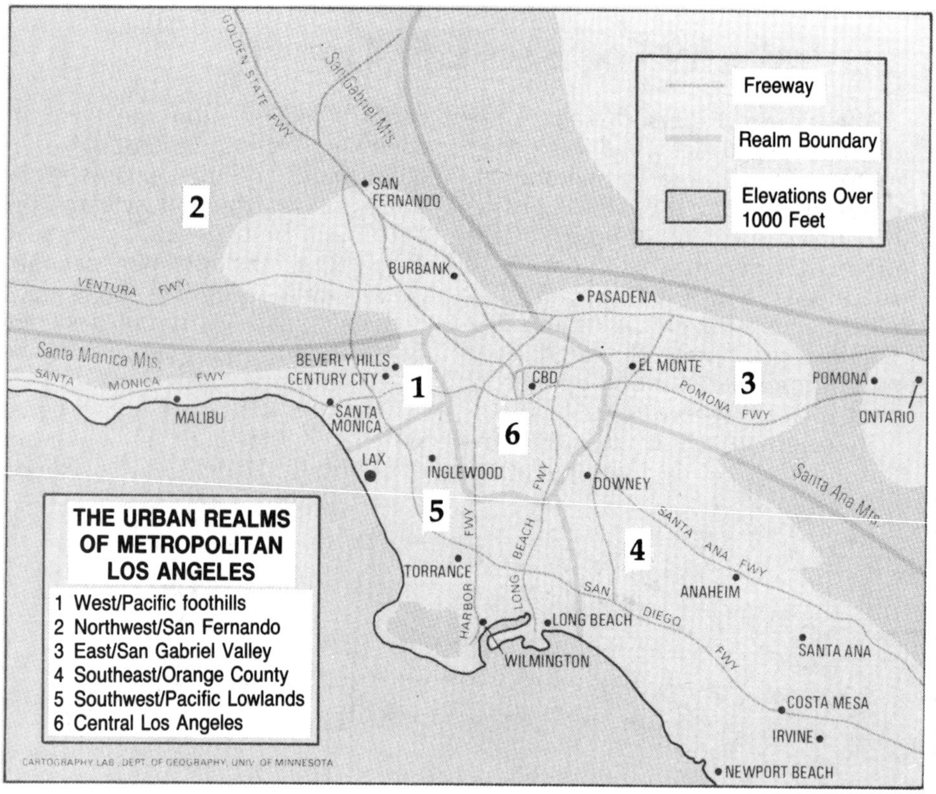

Retail activities were featured in dozens of planned automobile suburbs that sprang up after World War I—most notably in Kansas City's Country Club District, where the nation's first complete shopping center was opened in 1922.

The other major nonresidential activity of interwar suburbia was retailing. Clusters of automobile-oriented stores had first appeared in the urban fringes before World War I. By the early 1920s the roadside commercial strip had become a common sight in many southern California suburbs. Retail activities were also featured in dozens of planned automobile suburbs that sprang up after World War I—most notably in Kansas City's Country Club District, where the nation's first complete shopping center was opened in 1922. But these diversified retail centers spread slowly before the suburban highway improvements of the 1950s.

Unlike the two preceding eras, the postwar Freeway Era was not sparked by a revolution in urban transportation. Rather, it represented the coming of age of the now pervasive automobile culture, which coincided with the emergence of the U.S. from 15 years of economic depression and war. Suddenly the automobile was no longer a luxury or a recreational diversion: overnight it had become a necessity for commuting, shopping, and socializing, essential to the successful realization of personal opportunities for a rapidly expanding majority of the metropolitan population. People snapped up cars as fast as the reviving peacetime automobile industry could roll them off the assembly lines, and a prodigious highway-building effort was launched, spearheaded by high-speed, limited-access expressways. Given impetus by the 1956 Interstate Highway Act, these new freeways would soon reshape every corner of urban America, as the more distant suburbs they engendered represented nothing less than the turning inside-out of the historic metropolitan city.

The snowballing effect of these changes is expressed geographically in the sprawling metropolis of the postwar era. Most striking is the enormous band of growth that was added between 1945 and the 1980s, with freeway sectors pushing the metropolitan frontier deeply into the urban-rural fringe. By the late 1960s, the maturing expressway system began to underwrite a new suburban co-equality with the central city, because it was eliminating the metropolitanwide centrality advantage of the CBD. Now *any* location on the freeway network could easily be reached by motor vehicle, and intraurban accessibility had become a ubiquitous spatial good. Ironically, large cities had encouraged the construction of radial expressways in the 1950s and 1960s because they appeared to enable the downtown to remain accessible to the swiftly dispersing suburban population. However, as one economic activity after another discovered its new locational flexibility within the freeway metropolis, nonresidential deconcentration sharply accelerated in the 1970s and 1980s. Moreover, as expressways expanded the radius of commuting to encompass the entire dispersed metropolis, residential location constraints relaxed as well. No longer were most urbanites required to live within a short distance of their job: the workplace had now become a locus of opportunity offering access to the best possible residence that an individual could afford anywhere in the urbanized area. Thus, the overall pattern of locally uniform, income-based clusters that had emerged in prewar automobile suburbia was greatly magnified in the Freeway Era, and such new social variables as age and lifestyle produced an ever more balkanized population mosaic.

The revolutionary changes in movement and accessibility introduced during the four decades of the Freeway Era have resulted in nothing less than the complete geographic restructuring of the metropolis. The single-center urban structure of the past has been transformed into a polycentric metropolitan form in which several outlying activity concentrations rival the CBD. These new "suburban downtowns," consisting of vast orchestrations of retailing, office-based business, and light industry, have become common features near the highway interchanges that now encircle every large central city. As these emerging metropolitan-level cores achieve economic and geographic parity with each other, as well as with the CBD of the nearby central city, they provide the totality of urban goods and services to their surrounding populations. Thus each metropolitan sector becomes a self-sufficient functional entity, or *realm*. The application of this model to the Los Angeles region reveals six broad realms. Competition among several new suburban downtowns for dominance in the five outer realms is still occurring. In wealthy Orange County, for example, this rivalry is especially fierce, but Costa Mesa's burgeoning South Coast Metro is winning out as of early 1986.

The new freeways would soon reshape every corner of urban America, as the more distant suburbs they engendered represented nothing less than the turning inside-out of the historic metropolitan city.

The legacy of more than two centuries of intraurban transportation innovations, and the development patterns they helped stamp on the landscape of metropolitan America, is suburbanization—the growth of the edges of the urbanized area at a rate faster than in the already-developed interior. Since the geographic extent of the built-up urban areas has, throughout history, exhibited a remarkably constant radius of about 45 minutes of travel from the center, each breakthrough in higher-speed transport technology extended that radius into a new outer zone of suburban residential opportunity. In the nineteenth century, commuter railroads, horse-drawn trolleys, and electric streetcars each created their own suburbs—and thereby also created the large industrial city, which could not have been formed without incorporating these new suburbs into the pre-existing compact urban center. But the suburbs that materialized in the early twentieth century began to assert their independence from the central cities, which were ever more perceived as undesirable. As the automobile greatly reinforced the dispersal trend of the metropolitan population, the distinction between central city and suburban ring grew as well. And as freeways eventually eliminated the friction effects of intrametropolitan distance for most urban functions, nonresidential activities deconcentrated to such an extent that by 1980 the emerging outer suburban city had become co-equal with the central city that spawned it.

As the transition to an information-dominated, postindustrial economy is completed, today's intraurban movement problems may be mitigated by the increasing substitution of communication for the physical movement of people. Thus, the city of the future is likely to be the "wired metropolis." Such a development would portend further deconcentration because activity centers would potentially be able to locate at any site offering access to global computer and satellite networks.

Further Reading

Jackson, Kenneth T. 1985. *Crabgrass Frontier: The Suburbanization of the United States.* New York: Oxford University Press.

Muller, Peter O. 1981. *Contemporary Suburban America.* Englewood Cliffs, N.J.: Prentice-Hall.

Schaeffer, K. H. and Sclar, Elliot. 1975. *Access for All: Transportation and Urban Growth.* Baltimore: Penguin Books.

HISPANIC MIGRATION AND POPULATION REDISTRIBUTION IN THE UNITED STATES

The US Hispanic population has grown rapidly over the last two decades and remains geographically concentrated in nine states. Redistribution away from core states through internal migration has been largely offset by heavy immigration to traditional areas of Hispanic concentration. Geographical patterns of Hispanic migration show broad similarities to overall patterns of population redistribution in the United States. New York and California serve as key spatial redistributors or pivots in the Hispanic migration system. **Key Words: Hispanic concentration, Hispanic migration, population gateway, spatial redistributor.**

Kevin E. McHugh

KEVIN E. McHUGH (Ph.D., University of Illinois) is Assistant Professor of Geography at Arizona State University, Tempe, AZ 85287. His primary research interests are in migration and residential mobility.

The Hispanic population in the United States has grown rapidly over the last two decades, increasing from 9.1 million in 1970 to an estimated 18.8 million in 1987 (US Bureau of the Census 1988). Hispanics now represent the fastest growing minority in the nation. Between 1980 and 1987, the Hispanic population increased 30% while the non-Hispanic population grew less than 6%. Projections of the Hispanic population for the year 2000 range from 23 to 31 million (US Bureau of the Census 1986). According to the middle series projections, Hispanics will account for one-fourth of total US population growth between 1983 and 2000.

"Hispanic" is an umbrella term that refers to US residents whose cultural heritage traces back to a Spanish-speaking country (Valdivieso and Davis 1988). Other than having common ancestral ties to Latin America or Spain, peoples of Spanish origin in the US are highly diverse (Bean and Tienda 1988). Mexican-Americans, the largest group, account for 63% of US Hispanics in 1987; Puerto Ricans account for 12% and Cuban-Americans 5%. Hispanics with origins in Central America (excluding Mexico) and South America comprise 11%, and the residual category "other Hispanics" makeup the remaining 8% of US Hispanics (US Bureau of the Census 1988).

Hispanic immigration has received considerable scholarly attention, but Hispanic migration and population redistribution *within* the United States is seldom investigated (Garcia 1981). Some recent studies examine the geographical distribution of particular Hispanic groups, such as Boswell's (1984, 1985a, 1985b) work on Cuban-Americans and Puerto Ricans, Arreola's (1985) examination of Mexican-Americans, and Portes and Bach's (1985) longitudinal study of Cuban and Mexican immigrants in the United States. Bean et al. (1988) recently reviewed the geographical distribution and interregional migration of Hispanic groups. There has not been a comprehensive examination of place-to-place migration flows of Hispanics in the United States, partly due to the historical lack of information on Hispanic migration within the United States. Hispanic interstate migration for the period 1975–80 are the first place-to-place Hispanic migration data published by the Bureau of the Census (1985).

The purpose of this paper is to identify patterns of Hispanic migration and population redistribution within the United States. The paper focuses on whether Hispanics are becoming more or less geographically concentrated in the United States and on identifying recent migration patterns that are contributing to Hispanic population redistribution.

Hispanic population redistribution is examined in two ways. First, changes in the geographical distribution of Hispanics over recent decades are examined through state percentage shares of the total Hispanic population and state percentage shares of four major Hispanic groups: Mexican-Americans, Puerto Ricans, Cuban-Americans, and Central/South Americans. Shifts in the state shares over time indicate trends in the geographical concentration and deconcentration of Hispanic groups in the United States.

Second, I examine the role of immigration from abroad and internal migration within the United States in contributing to Hispanic population redistribution. These analyses provide insights into the relative importance of immigration versus internal migration in contributing to Hispanic population change at the state level. I also identify large net interstate migration streams within the US and compute the effectiveness of these streams in redistributing the Hispanic population. This shows the interstate connections most instrumental in redistributing Hispanics within the United States.

The paper draws upon the concept of spatial redistributors in contributing to a geographical understanding of the US Hispanic migration system. Spatial redistributors are places that exhibit asymmetry between patterns of in- and out-migration and thus serve as pivots in systems of population redistribution (Roseman 1977; Morrison 1977; Roseman and McHugh 1982). Key states should

* This research was supported by a Faculty Grant-in-Aid, Office of the Vice President for Research, Arizona State University. I thank Barbara Trapido for drafting the map.

From *The Professional Geographer,* Vol. 41, No. 4, November 1989, pp. 429-439. © 1989 by the Association of American Geographers. Reprinted by permission.

TABLE 1
TOP NINE STATES IN HISPANIC POPULATION

State	1970 Population	% Dist.	1980 Population	% Dist.	1987[a] Population	% Dist.
California	2,369,292	26.1	4,544,331	31.1	6,249,000	33.3
Texas	1,840,648	20.3	2,985,824	20.4	4,207,000	22.4
New York	1,351,982	14.9	1,659,300	11.4	2,182,000	11.6
Florida	405,036	4.5	858,158	5.9	1,256,000	6.7
New Jersey	288,488	3.2	491,883	3.4	737,000	3.9
Illinois	393,204	4.3	635,602	4.4	692,000	3.7
Arizona	264,770	2.9	440,701	3.0	664,000	3.5
New Mexico	308,340	3.4	477,222	3.3	535,000	2.9
Colorado	225,506	2.5	339,717	2.3	347,000	1.9
Total for nine states	7,447,266	82.1	12,432,738	85.1	16,869,000	89.9
United States	9,072,602	100.0	14,608,673	100.0	18,790,000	100.0

[a] 1987 figures are estimates of the civilian, noninstitutional Hispanic population from the March Current Population Survey. They are not directly comparable to the 1970 and 1980 census populations.
Sources: US Bureau of the Census, 1982; US Bureau of the Census, Current Population Survey, March 1987, Public Use File.

serve as Hispanic spatial redistributors at the international and national scales. International redistributors are states that attract large numbers of Hispanics from abroad and redistribute Hispanics within the United States, thus serving as population gateways. Key states should also serve as internal redistributors of Hispanics, as indicated by large net interstate migration streams. The redistributor concept is particularly relevant to the geographic concentration and deconcentration of Hispanics in the United States.

I first summarize shifts in the geographical distribution of Hispanic groups in the United States. The second section examines Hispanic immigration from abroad and internal migration within the United States, emphasizing the role of key states as Hispanic population gateways. Geographical patterns of migration that contribute to Hispanic population redistribution within the United States are identified in the third section. The final section is a discussion of three key issues: (1) whether Hispanic groups are becoming more or less geographically concentrated, (2) determinants of Hispanic migration within the United States, and (3) linkages between Hispanic immigration from abroad and internal migration within the United States.

Geographical Distribution of Hispanics

The US Hispanic population is concentrated geographically. Nine states accounted for 82% of the total Hispanic population in 1970 (Table 1). This percentage rose to 85% in 1980 and an estimated 90% in 1987. The following states had 1987 Hispanic populations greater than 300,000: New York and New Jersey in the Northeast, Illinois in the Midwest, Florida in the Southeast, and California, Texas, Arizona, New Mexico, and Colorado in the Southwest.

There has been some redistribution between these nine states as measured by their share of the total US Hispanic population, most notably a seven-point rise in California's share, so that California now accounts for one-third of all Hispanics in the country. Texas, Florida, and Arizona have also increased their share of the Hispanic population over the last two decades. New York's declining share between 1970 and 1980 is noteworthy. Illinois, New Mexico, and Colorado also posted small declines in their share of the Hispanic population.

The US Hispanic population is diverse in nationality and cultural heritage. Disaggregating Hispanics by national origin and showing state percentage shares in 1960 and 1980 indicate trends in the geographic concentration and deconcentration of individual Hispanic groups (Table 2).

Hispanics of Mexican origin dominate in the southwestern states of California, Texas, Arizona, New Mexico, and Colorado, and also in Illinois. California and Texas in 1980 accounted for three-fourths of the Mexican-origin population in the United States. The most important shifts in the distribution of Mexican-Americans are the increase in California's share coupled with a declining share for Texas. This long-term trend began early in the twentieth century. In 1910, 60% of persons of Mexican stock in the United States resided in Texas, and California accounted for only 13% (Grebler et al. 1970). At that time, Texas had greater employment opportunities for the Mexican population, particularly in agriculture. Throughout the twentieth century, California's share of the Mexican-origin population steadily increased as job opportunities shifted to California, initially in agriculture and later through urban expansion (Jaffee et al. 1980).

Illinois is the only state outside the southwest with a large Mexican-American population. The Mexican-origin population in Illinois grew from less than 2% of the national total in 1960 to nearly 5% in 1980. The development of the Mexican-origin population in Illinois resulted from their "settling out" from midwestern migratory labor streams as well as from direct migration to Chicago in response to employment opportunities in railroad maintenance, steelmaking, meatpacking, and other manufacturing sectors (Grebler et al. 1970). In 1980, Chicago ranked third among metropolitan areas in Mexican-origin population, behind Los Angeles and Houston (Bean et al. 1988).

Puerto Ricans are the largest Hispanic group in New York and New Jersey. The most important redistribution of Puerto Ricans has been away from New York to nearby states in the Northeast, in addition to Florida and California. New York's share of the Puerto Rican population dropped from 72% in 1960 to 49% in 1980. Conversely, New Jersey, Massachusetts, Connecticut, Pennsylvania, Illinois, Florida, and California increased their share of Puerto Ricans. The deconcentration of Puerto Ricans away from New York resulted from declining employment opportunities, poor housing, and crime problems in New York City (Boswell 1984).

Cuban-Americans represent the largest Hispanic group in Florida, where they have become increasingly concentrated in south Florida, partly in response to the Cuban Refugee Resettlement Program (Boswell and Curtis 1984). Cuban-Americans resettled outside south Florida under this government-sponsored program began returning to Miami in the late 1960s. By the mid-1970s this return flow increased to a major migration stream. A survey commissioned by *The Miami Herald* in 1978 found that 40% of the population of Cuban origin in Dade County were returnees to Miami from elsewhere in the United States (Boswell and Curtis 1984).

The increased concentration of the Cuban-origin population in south Florida continues in the 1980s. The 1980 census figures do not include the estimated 125,000 Cuban "Marielito" refugees who arrived in Miami shortly after the 1980 enumeration. In addition, Cuban return movement to south Florida has continued in the 1980s. Boswell and Curtis (1984) cite estimates prepared by the Cuban National Planning Council that between 65 and 70% of Cuban-Americans reside in Florida.

Outside Florida, sizable numbers of Cuban-Americans reside in New York, New Jersey, and California. Before the Castro revolution in 1959, New York City was the primary destination of Cuban immigrants. New York's share of Cuban-Americans declined from 45% in 1950 to 10% in 1980. Cuban-Americans in New Jersey are highly concentrated in the area of Union City–West New York, across the

Hudson River from New York City. This concentration of Cuban-Americans is the largest outside Miami. California accounts for 8% of the 1980 Cuban-origin population. Los Angeles ranks fourth among urban areas in Cuban-American population (Boswell and Curtis 1984).

Hispanics with origins in Central America (excluding Mexico) and South America are concentrated in New York and California, with smaller concentrations in Florida and New Jersey. New York has a greater number of Hispanics with origins in South America and the Dominican Republic, while California has larger numbers of Central Americans (Allen and Turner 1988). Although fewer in number than Hispanics of Mexican and Puerto Rican origin, persons with origins in Central and South America represent the fastest growing Hispanic group in the United States, increasing an estimated 40% between 1980 and 1987 (US Bureau of the Census 1988). Much of the recent influx of Central Americans is a response to political turmoil in El Salvador, Nicaragua, and Guatemala (Allen and Turner 1988).

Hispanics are a highly urban population. In 1980, 81% of Mexican-Americans resided in metropolitan areas. Other Hispanic groups show greater levels of metropolitan concentration: 96% for Puerto Ricans, 94% for Cuban-Americans, and 96% for Central/South Americans. In comparison, 73% of non-Hispanic whites resided in metropolitan areas in 1980 (Bean et al. 1988). Twenty-nine metropolitan areas in 1980 had more than 100,000 Hispanics. Los Angeles and New York alone accounted for nearly one-quarter of the US Hispanic population (Davis et al. 1983).

Hispanics also show a propensity to concentrate in central cities within metropolitan areas. In 1980, 65% of Mexican-Americans, 81% of Puerto Ricans, 45% of Cuban-Americans, and 67% of Central/South Americans living in metropolitan areas were in central cities. The comparable figure for non-Hispanic whites is only 35%. Cuban-Americans have shown the greatest suburbanization, indicating their higher socioeconomic status relative to other Hispanic groups (Bean et al. 1988).

TABLE 2

GEOGRAPHICAL DISTRIBUTION OF HISPANICS BY NATIONAL ORIGIN, 1960 AND 1980[a]

	Percent of US total							
	Mexican		Puerto Rican		Cuban		Central/South American	
State	1960	1980	1960	1980	1960	1980	1960	1980
Massachusetts	—	0.1	0.3	3.8	0.7	0.8	1.6	1.8
Connecticut	—	—	1.6	4.5	2.1	0.7	1.9	1.1
New York	0.1	0.4	72.2	49.2	31.9	10.1	29.5	34.9
New Jersey	0.1	0.1	6.5	12.2	6.9	10.7	5.1	8.4
Pennyslvania	0.1	0.2	2.1	4.4	1.5	0.6	1.9	0.8
Ohio	0.2	0.5	1.3	1.7	0.8	0.4	1.7	0.5
Illinois	1.7	4.7	3.9	6.7	1.9	2.3	3.7	3.2
Michigan	0.6	1.2	0.3	0.5	0.2	0.4	1.7	0.6
Florida	0.1	0.7	2.1	4.8	43.0	58.4	5.2	9.1
Texas	38.7	32.4	0.7	1.0	1.1	1.7	3.3	2.8
Colorado	4.2	2.4	0.1	0.2	0.1	0.2	0.7	0.4
New Mexico	7.1	2.7	—	0.1	0.1	0.1	0.1	0.2
Arizona	5.7	4.7	0.2	0.2	—	0.1	0.6	0.3
Washington	0.4	0.9	0.1	0.2	0.7	0.2	0.8	0.4
California	38.7	42.1	3.1	4.4	3.2	8.0	24.9	25.4
Total for 15 states	97.7	93.1	94.5	93.9	94.2	94.7	82.7	89.9

[a] States listed have 100,000 or more persons of Hispanic origin, 1980.
Source: Bean et al. 1988.

TABLE 3

INTERNAL HISPANIC MIGRATION AND HISPANIC MOVERS FROM ABROAD, 1975–80[a]

	Internal migration			
State	Inmigration	Outmigration	Net migration	Number from abroad
Massachusetts	13,848	12,619	1229	20,118
Connecticut	11,148	10,005	1179	15,937
New York	27,552	133,061	−105,509	139,961
New Jersey	41,478	43,917	−2439	51,198
Pennyslvania	14,118	13,739	379	16,279
Ohio	9928	14,571	−4643	6355
Illinois	25,882	48,105	−22,133	66,124
Michigan	10,595	15,582	−4987	5958
Florida[b]	106,042	40,406	65,636	96,273
Texas	120,749	97,702	23,047	155,851
Colorado	28,578	27,137	1441	8596
New Mexico	32,485	31,036	1449	7535
Arizona	30,567	29,440	1127	15,229
Washington	24,051	11,826	12,225	8890
California	132,948	139,357	−6409	412,958

[a] States listed are those with 100,000 or more persons of Hispanic origin, 1980.
[b] Number of Hispanic movers to Florida from abroad, 1975–80, does not include the estimated 125,000 Cuban "Marielito" refugees who arrived shortly after the 1980 census enumeration.
Source: U.S. Bureau of the Census, 1985.

Hispanic Population Gateways

Immigration from abroad has contributed greatly to Hispanic population growth in the United States. Data on Hispanic immigration from abroad coupled with internal migration within the United States show that key states serve as Hispanic population gateways (Table 3). These data include immigration from abroad and internal migration within the United States, 1975–80, for 15 states with Hispanic populations over 100,000 in 1980. These migration data are not available for Hispanic groups defined by national origin and are based on Hispanics enumerated in the 1980 Census of Population. The actual number of Hispanic migrants, particularly from abroad, is greater because a significant share of undocumented immigrants were not enumerated in the 1980 census (Warren and Passel 1987; Bean and Tienda 1988). Migrants from abroad refer to persons of Hispanic origin residing outside the United States in 1975 and in the designated state in 1980. This calculation includes foreign immigrants as well as US citizens returning from abroad. The vast majority of Hispanic movers from abroad are immigrants.

As expected, California, Texas, and New York attract very large numbers of Hispanics from abroad; Florida, Illinois, and New Jersey also receive sizable numbers of Hispanic immigrants. These six states are the primary Hispanic gateways to the United States. Immigration from abroad more than offsets internal net migration losses for four of these states: New York, New Jersey, Illinois, and California. Despite internal migration away from these core states, they maintain or strengthen their Hispanic population concentrations through immigration. Florida and Texas, on the other hand, experienced both substantial immigration as well as net gains from elsewhere in the United States for the period 1975–80.

Geographical Patterns of Hispanic Migration

Geographical patterns of Hispanic migration within the United States can be seen by mapping the 25 largest net inter-

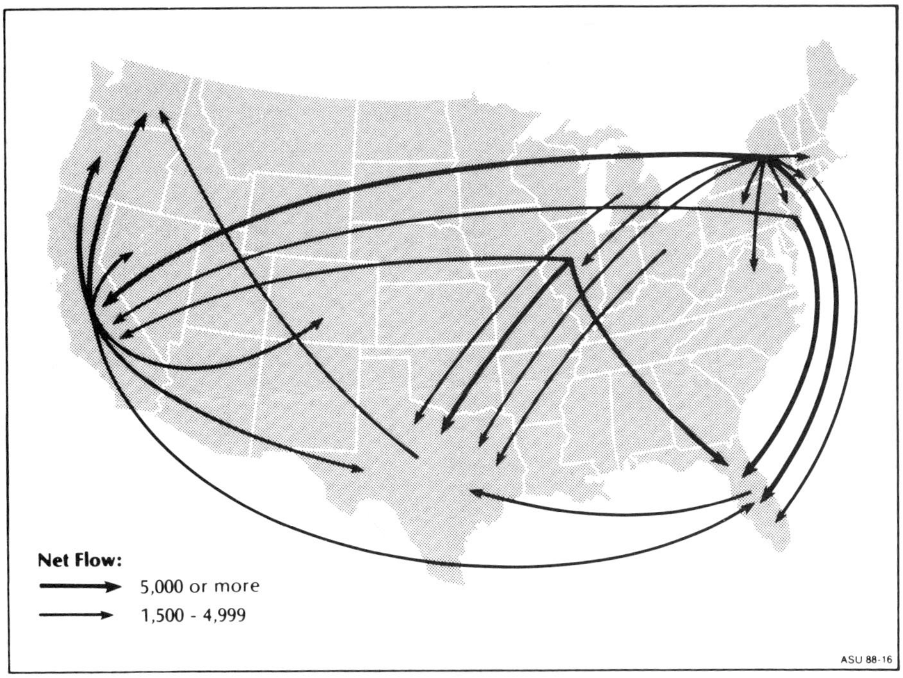

Figure 1. Large hispanic net interstate migration streams, 1975–80.

state migration streams for 1975–80, the most recent internal Hispanic migration data available (Fig. 1). In addition to the 25 net migration streams, the underlying gross migration flows and a percent effectiveness value for each interstate connection are reported (Table 4).

Percent effectiveness (Eij) indicates the level of net migration exchange between a pair of states relative to the size of the underlying gross migration flows. It is computed by dividing net migration by the sum of the gross migration flows in both directions, and multiplying the resulting ratio by 100:

$$Eij = [Nij/Mij + Mji] \times 100 \qquad (1)$$

where

Eij = percent effectiveness of migration from state i to state j
Nij = net migration exchange between state i and state j (Mij − Mji)
Mij = gross migration flow from state i to state j
Mji = gross migration flow from state j to state i.

In absolute terms, Eij varies from 0 to 100%. A 0% effectiveness indicates that equal numbers of migrants are moving in both directions resulting in no population redistribution between the pair of states. Conversely, an effectiveness value of 100% would mean that *all* movement is unidirectional (either Mij or Mji = 0). Thus, effectiveness values indicate strong currents in a migration system (Plane 1984).

Several patterns of Hispanic migration are evident (Fig. 1). Net movement from northeastern and midwestern states to the three large Sunbelt states—Florida, Texas, and California—is conspicuous. Northeastern states are linked most strongly with Florida. Net flows from New York and New Jersey to Florida are very large and highly effective in redistributing Hispanics (Eij = 83.6% and 75.6%).

New York stands out for registering highly effective Hispanic migration losses to Florida, Texas, and California (Table 4). This result parallels the overall trend of large migration losses for New York during the 1970s. In fact, currents of migration from New York to Florida and California, as measured by percent effectiveness values, were stronger among Hispanics than non-Hispanics.

Bean et al's. (1988) breakdown of Hispanic migration by national origin between New York and Florida, 1975–80, indicates why this stream is highly effective. Cuban-Americans constitute the greatest number of Hispanics in the New York-to-Florida stream. More than ten times as many Cuban-Americans migrated from New York to Florida as moved in the opposite direction. Many Cuban immigrants had been resettled from Miami to New York in the Cuban Refugee Resettlement Program (Boswell and Curtis 1984), so it is very likely that a substantial share of Florida-bound Cuban-Americans were returning to south Florida. Most Cuban-Americans returning to Dade County from outside Florida cite climate and a desire to be near family and friends as reasons for their return (Boswell and Curtis 1984). Net movement of people of Puerto Rican and Central/South American origin from New York to Florida is also significant, although these streams are not as effective as Cuban-origin movement to Florida (Bean et al. 1988).

The midwestern states of Illinois, Michigan, and Ohio are linked most strongly with Texas (Fig. 1). These Hispanic migration streams are overwhelmingly Mexican-American, and are moderately effective in redistributing Mexican-Americans from the Midwest to Texas, with effectiveness values of 38.8% for Illinois, 25.2% for Michigan, and 39.1% for Ohio (Table 4). Significant numbers of Hispanics from Illinois move to Texas, Florida, and California, although the connection to Florida is most effective.

New York and California serve as spatial redistributors of the Hispanic population within the United States (Fig. 1). In addition to sending large numbers of Hispanics to Florida and California, New York is a redistributor of Hispanics within the Northeast. Large numbers of Hispanics move from New York to nearby states, including New Jersey, Pennsylvania, Connecticut, and Massachusetts. These four net migration streams from New York have moderately high effectiveness values (Table 4). Puerto Ricans are the dominant group in these streams, although Cuban-Americans and Central/South Americans are also likely to be present, especially in the stream to New Jersey. Puerto Rican migration away from New York relates to declining manufacturing employment, particularly in the textile and garment industries (Bean and Tienda 1988). Boswell (1984) also cites poor housing and crime as additional push factors in Puerto Rican migration from New York.

California is also a spatial redistributor of the Hispanic population. California gains Hispanics from New York, New Jersey, and Illinois, but loses Hispanics to western states, including Washington, Oregon, Nevada, and Colorado (Fig. 1). Thus, California is emerging as an interregional Hispanic redistributor, just as it has served as an interregional redistributor among Anglos since the late 1960s (US Bureau of the Census 1973). Overall, California recorded modest net out-migration of Hispanics within the United States, 1975–80, as losses to western states more than offset gains from northeastern and midwestern states.

Examining place of birth for Hispanics in western states also provides evidence that California is a Hispanic redistributor. In 1980, 50% of Hispanics in California were native to the state and 40% were foreign born. Only 12% of California Hispanics were born elsewhere in the United States. On the other hand, 40 to 50% of Hispanics in Washington, Oregon, and Nevada were born elsewhere in the United States, most likely California (US Bureau of the Census 1985).

For 1975–80, Texas gained Hispanics from northern states as well as from Florida and California (Fig. 1). Net flows to Texas from California and Florida, however, are small relative to large gross migration exchanges. Effectiveness values for the net streams to Texas are only 7.9% for California, and 18.0% for Florida (Table 4). In fact, Texas may be losing Hispanics to Florida and California since the recent decline in the energy-based Texas economy.

TABLE 4
LARGE HISPANIC NET INTERSTATE MIGRATION STREAMS AND PERCENT EFFECTIVENESS OF STREAMS, 1975–80

State i	State j	Gross flow i to j	Gross flow j to i	Net gain state j	Percent effect.
New York	Florida	38,398	3431	34,967	83.6
New York	New Jersey	28,080	7098	20,982	59.7
New Jersey	Florida	18,071	2515	15,556	75.6
New York	California	16,960	3369	13,591	66.9
Illinois	Texas	12,949	5710	7239	38.8
Illinois	Florida	7806	1754	6052	63.3
California	Oregon	8344	2459	5885	54.5
California	Washington	10,005	4178	5827	41.1
California	Texas	32,234	27,494	4740	7.9
California	Nevada	6916	2234	4682	51.2
New York	Texas	5702	1187	4515	65.5
New York	Pennsylvania	5626	1141	4485	66.3
New York	Connecticut	5644	1617	4027	55.5
New York	Massachusetts	5701	1833	3868	51.3
Illinois	California	9387	5707	3680	24.4
Florida	Texas	8499	5910	2589	18.0
California	Colorado	7888	5476	2412	18.0
New Jersey	California	3906	1510	2396	44.2
Michigan	Texas	4925	2942	1983	25.2
Ohio	Texas	3411	1492	1919	39.1
Connecticut	Florida	2385	635	1750	57.9
New York	Virginia	2288	539	1749	61.9
New York	Illinois	2664	1009	1655	45.1
California	Florida	7160	5531	1629	12.8
Texas	Washington	3037	1512	1525	33.5

Source: U.S. Bureau of the Census, 1985.

Discussion

Are Hispanics becoming more or less geographically concentrated in the United States? There has been some redistribution of the Hispanic population through internal migration as a result of (1) movement from northeastern and midwestern states to Florida, Texas, and California; (2) net movement from New York to nearby states in the Northeast; and (3) net migration from California to other western states. Immigration from abroad, however, continues to traditional areas of Hispanic concentration. For several states, heavy immigration among Hispanics has more than offset migration losses to other places within the country. A complete understanding of Hispanic population redistribution will require examination of both immigration and internal migration, as well as consideration of differentials in natural population increase among Hispanic groups.

The Hispanic population remains geographically concentrated in nine states, but this overall view masks differences among individual Hispanic groups. Cuban-Americans and Hispanics of Central/South American origin are becoming more concentrated, the former in Florida and the latter in California and New York. The increasing concentration of Cuban-Americans in south Florida is partly attributable to return migration following the Cuban Refugee Resettlement Program and to the strength of the Cuban-American community in Dade County. It is not surprising that most Central/South Americans concentrate in California and New York, given their recent arrival in the United States.

Hispanics of Mexican origin show some deconcentration away from core states. Bean et al. (1988) reached similar conclusions through their analysis of dissimilarity indexes that compared the geographic distribution of Hispanic groups and the overall US population. They found that the concentration of the Mexican-origin population has become less pronounced from 1960 to 1980. Bean et al. (1988) also found that Puerto Ricans exhibit some deconcentration away from core states, especially New York, over the 20-year period. Recent interstate migration has played the dominant role in the deconcentration of Puerto Ricans away from their New York core.

Hispanic migration patterns are broadly similar to overall patterns of migration within the United States. Hispanic migration from northern states to Florida, California, and Texas is part of the larger population redistribution to the Sunbelt (Biggar 1979; Long 1988). Currents of migration to Florida, California, and Texas tend to be stronger among Hispanics than non-Hispanics, perhaps because of the greater concentration of the Hispanic population and opportunities in the three large Sunbelt states. Social networks defined on the basis of ethnicity probably serve to channelize Hispanic migration flows to Florida, California, and Texas.

New York and California have emerged as spatial redistributors of Hispanics, just as they have redistributed the Anglo population. California's emergence as an interregional redistributor in the late 1970s—attracting Hispanics from states in the Northeast/Midwest and losing Hispanics to states in the West—follows a similar trend among Anglos. New York and California are likely to continue as central pivots in the Hispanic migration system: both have large Hispanic populations and serve as gateways for large numbers of new immigrants to the United States.

Comparisons of immigration from abroad and internal migration of Hispanics within the United States should show that Hispanics born in the United States, or those residing in the United States for a number of years, are more likely to migrate than are recent immigrants. Recent immigrants are typically less familiar with the United States, know less English, and tend to be of lower socioeconomic status than longer-term residents. Recent immigrants tend to concentrate in ethnic enclaves for social and economic support. Grebler et al. (1970) found that Hispanics of Mexican origin showed greater rates of intercounty migration, 1955–60, the further they were removed from the immigrant generation.

Portes and Bach (1985) studied the link between immigration and internal migration through a six-year residential history of a sample of Mexican and Cuban immigrants who entered the United States in 1973. They found that Mexican immigrants were more likely to change residences after living in the United States for three years, and that less than 25% remained at the same residence over the six-year period, 1973–79. Slightly more than one-half of the Mexican immigrants remained in Texas (state of entry), one-fourth moved to other states in the Southwest, and 16% moved northward to Chicago. Return immigrants (those who had been to the United States previously) were more likely to move and showed a more dispersed pattern of settlement than first-time Mexican immigrants. This study demonstrates that experience in the United States as well as social and economic ties can be developed through circular migration between Mexico and the United States (Massey 1985). In contrast to the rather dispersed settlement pattern of Mexican immigrants, Portes and Bach (1985) found that the Cubans concentrated in Miami and remained there over the six-year period.

As the US Hispanic population grows, questions and issues relating to migration and population redistribution will be of increasing concern to social scientists and policy-makers at local, state, and federal levels. At the microlevel, there is a need for household level research that examines linkages between migration and socioeconomic and demographic status of Hispanics. Relationships between immigrant generation/length of residence in the United States, internal migration, and socioeconomic and demographic status will contribute to a broader theory of migration, adjustment, and assimilation.

At the aggregate level, Hispanic migration and population redistribution impacts labor markets and has important implications for the provision of educational and social services. The issue of geographic impacts is particularly important given the growth of the Hispanic population and uncertainties surrounding consequences of the Immigration Reform and Control Act of 1986.

Literature Cited

Allen, J. P., and E. J. Turner. 1988. *We the People: An Atlas of America's Ethnic Diversity.* New York: Macmillan Publishing.

Arreola, D. D. 1985. Mexican Americans. In *Ethnicity in Contemporary America: A Geographical Appraisal,* ed. J. O. McKee, 77–94. Dubuque, IA: Kendall/Hunt Publishing.

Bean, F. D., and M. Tienda. 1988. *The Hispanic Population of the United States.* New York: Russell Sage Foundation.

Bean, F. D., M. Tienda, and D. S. Massey. 1988. Geographical distribution, internal migration, and residential segregation. In *The Hispanic Population of the United States,* ed. F. D. Bean and M. Tienda, 137–77. New York: Russell Sage Foundation.

Biggar, J. C. 1979. The sunning of America: Migration to the Sunbelt. *Population Bulletin* 34:1–42.

Boswell, T. D. 1984. The migration and distribution of Cubans and Puerto Ricans living in the United States. *Journal of Geography* 83: 65–72.

Boswell, T. D. 1985a. The Cuban-Americans. In *Ethnicity in Contemporary America: A Geographical Appraisal,* ed. J. O. McKee, 95–116. Dubuque, IA: Kendall/Hunt Publishing.

Boswell, T. D. 1985b. Puerto Ricans living in the United States. In *Ethnicity in Contemporary America: A Geographical Appraisal,* ed. J. O. McKee, 117–144. Dubuque, IA: Kendall/Hunt Publishing.

Boswell, T. D., and J. R. Curtis. 1984. *The Cuban-American Experience.* Totowa, NJ: Rowman and Allanheld Publishers.

Davis, C., C. Haub, and J. Willette. 1983. U.S. Hispanics: Changing the face of America. *Population Bulletin* 38:1–44.

Garcia, J. A. 1981. Hispanic migration: Where they are moving and why. *Agenda: A Journal of Hispanic Issues* 2:14–17.

Grebler, L., J. W. Moore, and R. C. Guzman. 1970. *The Mexican-American People.* New York: The Free Press.

Jaffee, A. J., R. M. Cullen, and T. D. Boswell. 1980. *The Changing Demography of Spanish Americans.* New York: Academic Press.

Long, L. 1988. *Migration and Residential Mobility in the United States.* New York: Russell Sage Foundation.

Massey, D. S. 1985. The settlement process among Mexican migrants to the United States: New methods and findings. In *Immigration Statistics: A Story of Neglect,* ed. D. B. Levine, K. Hill, and R. Warren, 255–92. Washington, DC: National Academy Press.

Morrison, P. A. 1977. Urban growth and decline in the United States: A study of migration's effect in two cities. In *Internal Migration: A Comparative Perspective,* ed. A. A. Brown and E. Neuberger, 235–54. New York: Academic Press.

Plane, D. A. 1984. A systematic demographic efficiency analysis of US interstate population exchange, 1935–80. *Economic Geography* 60:294–312.

Portes, A., and R. L. Bach. 1985. *Latin Journey: Cuban and Mexican Immigrants in the United States.* Berkeley, CA: University of California Press.

Roseman, C. C. 1977. *Changing Migration Patterns within the United States,* Resource Paper No. 77-2. Washington, DC: Association of American Geographers.

Roseman, C. C., and K. E. McHugh. 1982. Metropolitan areas as redistributors of population. *Urban Geography* 3:22–33.

US Bureau of the Census. 1973. Census of population: 1970. *Mobility for States and the Nation,* Final Report PC(2)-2B. Washington, DC: Government Printing Office.

US Bureau of the Census. 1982. Census of population: 1980. *Persons of Spanish Origin by State: 1980,* Supplementary Report PC80-S1-7. Washington, DC: Government Printing Office.

US Bureau of the Census. 1985. Census of population: 1980. *Geographical Mobility for States and the Nation,* PC80-2-2A. Washington, DC: Government Printing Office.

US Bureau of the Census. 1986. Projections of the Hispanic population: 1983 to 2080. *Current Population Reports,* Series P-25, No. 995. Washington, DC: Government Printing Office.

US Bureau of the Census. 1988. The Hispanic population in the United States: March 1986 and 1987. *Current Population Reports,* Series P-20, No. 434. Washington, DC: Government Printing Office.

Valdivieso, R., and C. Davis. 1988. US Hispanics: Challenging issues for the 1990s. *Population Trends and Public Policy* 17:1–16.

Warren, R., and J. S. Passel. 1987. A count of the uncountable: Estimates of undocumented aliens counted in the 1980 United States census. *Demography* 24:375–93.

The Channel Tunnel

The opening of the Channel Tunnel adds another major link to the European transport network. This article analyses the effect of the tunnel on Europe's 'Capitals Region', the changing economic geography of European integration, and the project's regional and local impacts.

Roger Vickerman

Roger Vickerman is Professor of Regional and Transport Economics at the University of Canterbury.

The Channel Tunnel project was announced by the British and French governments in January 1986, after nearly 200 years of discussion and at least 25 previous attempts to restore the fixed link between Great Britain and the European continent which was severed in the last ice age. The tunnel project is interesting for legal, financial and economic reasons. The project involves a concession or franchise, in which the concessionaire, Eurotunnel, has been granted the right by the British and French governments to construct and operate a fixed link between the UK and France. Initially the concession ran for 55 years from 1987, when the primary legislation was passed in both countries. In late 1993 it was extended by a further 10 years as settlement of a claim by Eurotunnel against the governments for the cost of increased safety provisions. Eurotunnel's monopoly rights are protected until the year 2020. Eurotunnel has, however, to raise all the finance for the project with-

Figure 1 The Channel Tunnel in its wider regional context.

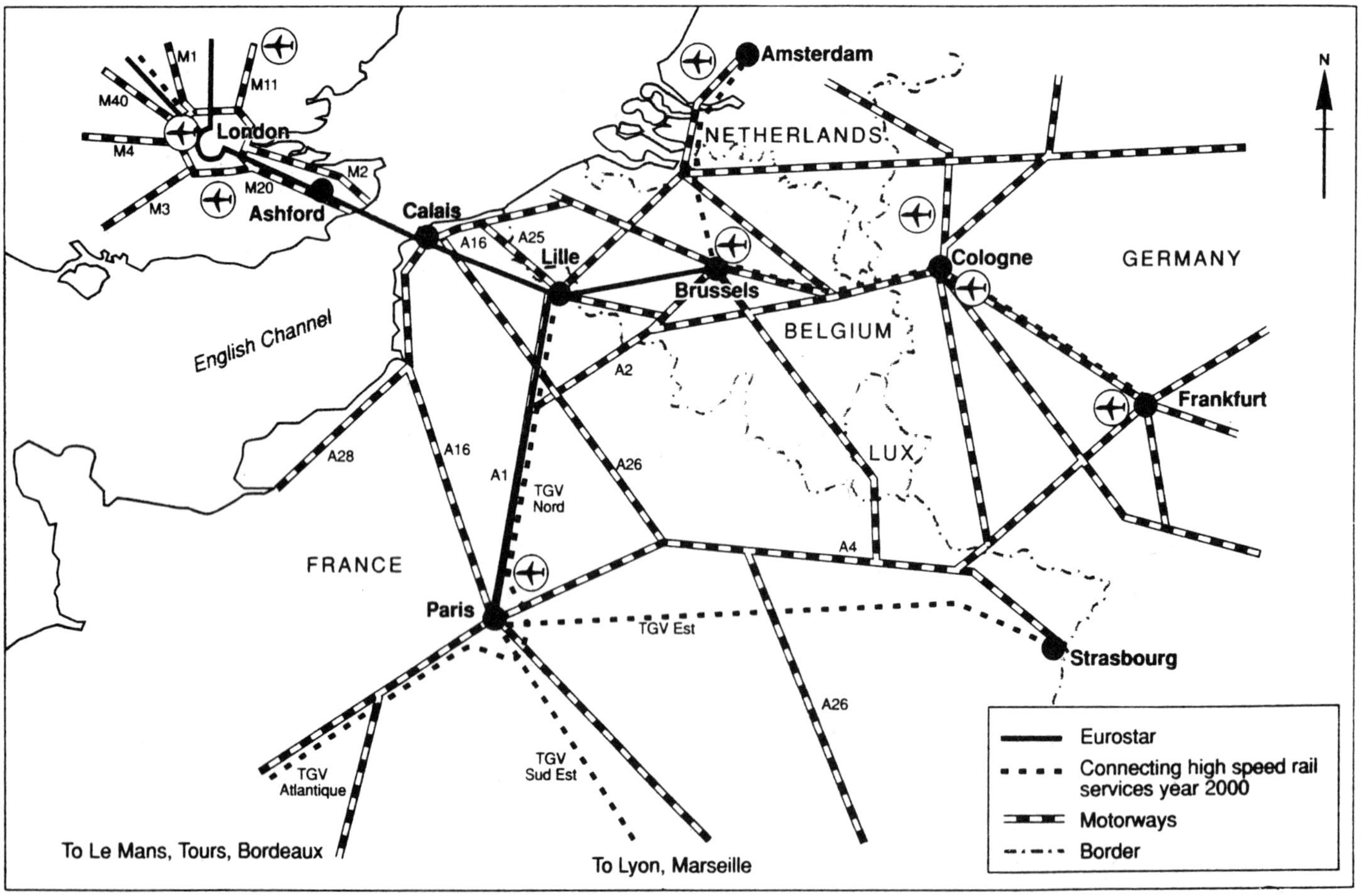

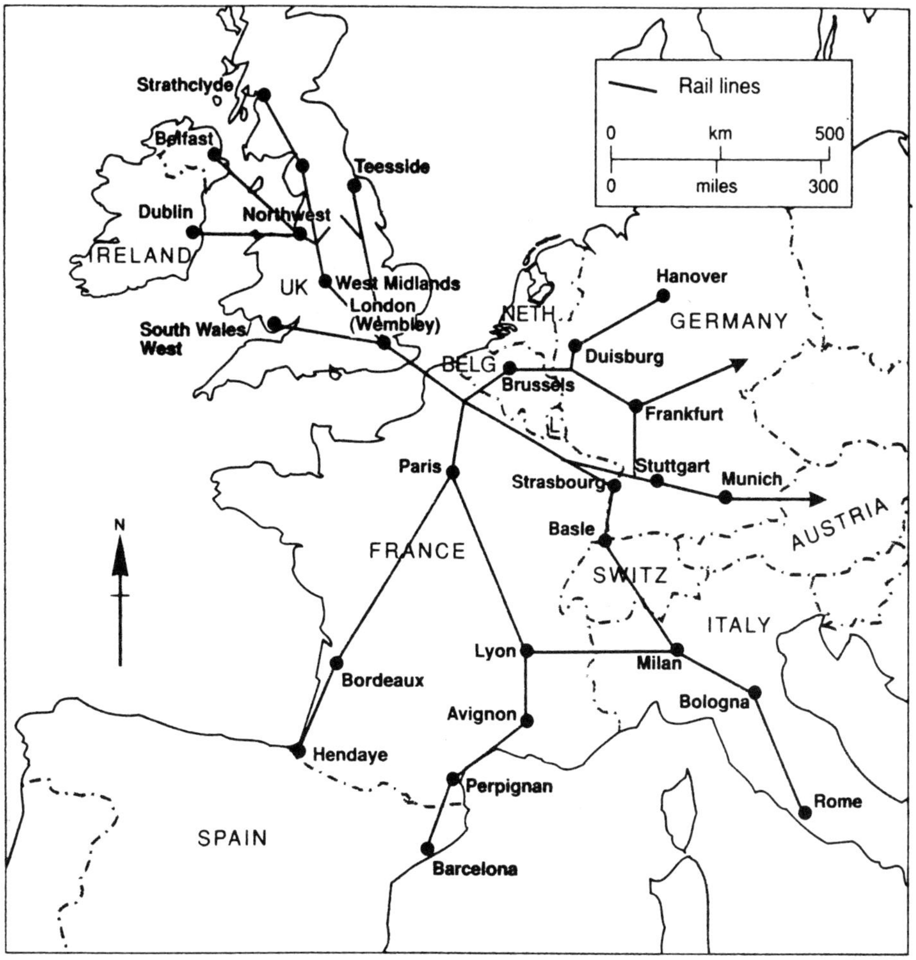

Figure 2 Proposed Channel Tunnel rail freight networks.

out the benefit of any government guarantees. This makes the Channel Tunnel the largest piece of public infrastructure ever to have been constructed entirely by the private sector. The final cost is still unknown, but the total construction and financing cost is likely to be in the order of £10 billion, more than double that originally envisaged in the 1985 proposal.

The tunnel consists of three 50 km tunnels, (two running tunnels and a service tunnel), 30 km of which are under the sea. These join two large terminals at Cheriton, near Folkestone, in Kent, and Coquelles, near Calais, in the French region of Nord-Pas de Calais. The terminals opened for service in stages during the first half of 1994. The tunnel provides four distinct types of service on its standard gauge, electrified railway track:

- *Le Shuttle* tourist shuttles for cars and coaches, linking the M20 motorway with the A16/A26 autoroutes. Terminal to terminal time is 35 minutes, motorway to motorway time 1 hour.
- *Le Shuttle* freight shuttles for accompanied lorries.
- BR/SNCF through freight trains for intermodal traffic (containers and swapbodies*) automotive traffic (new cars), and ultimately conventional wagon load (siding to siding) traffic, linking major centres in the UK with those in Germany, France, Switzerland and Italy.
- BR/SNCF/SNCB through Eurostar services for passenger traffic between London and Paris (3 hours) and Brussels (3 hours 10 minutes, until completion of Belgian high speed link in 1996 then 2 hours 40 minutes). Completion of a Channel Tunnel rail link in the UK could reduce these times by a further 30 minutes.

The economic geography of the tunnel can be assessed in four stages:

(1) the transport geography of communications in the European Union's European Capitals Region;
(2) the economic geography of European integration;
(3) the regional impacts on the UK;
(4) the local and regional planning impacts on Kent.

We can only hope to identify some of the main issues under each of these headings, but in all of them we have to assess how far the Channel Tunnel in itself is a marginal or non-marginal change to networks and accessibility, how far it depends on developments of other associated networks, and how far any wider regional or local impact depends on complementary planning decisions. The general message of this discussion is that, although on most criteria the impact of the tunnel is fairly small, when added together all of these marginal impacts could be quite significant.

THE GEOGRAPHY OF COMMUNICATIONS

The tunnel lies fairly centrally in the European Capitals Region. This region includes the cities of London, Amsterdam, Frankfurt, Brussels and Paris, with over 25% of the European Union (EU) population and over 30% of EU GDP. It also straddles six member states of the EU. Historically, nationally developed transport systems have many points where they are incomplete. Both road and rail systems tend to serve national needs, so that motorway-standard roads frequently finish close to a frontier rather than crossing it, and different electrification and signalling systems prevent easy through haulage of trains without a change of locomotive.

Within this system, land-based transport links to one of the EU's largest metropolitan regions, the southeast of England, have not only faced poor links to and from frontiers, but have required a change of mode at the frontier to cross the Channel. Good and improving communications are seen as vital to the continuing economic performance of all major conurbations. The importance of transport in this region is illustrated by the growth in cross-Channel passenger traffic, which grew from 9.6 million passengers in 1962 to 64.8 million in 1990, and is forecast to continue to grow to 113 million by 2003, and 150 million by 2013. Meanwhile, freight traffic is growing, if anything even faster, from 29 million tonnes in 1971 to 79 million

*Swapbodies are vehicles which can run on both road and rail.

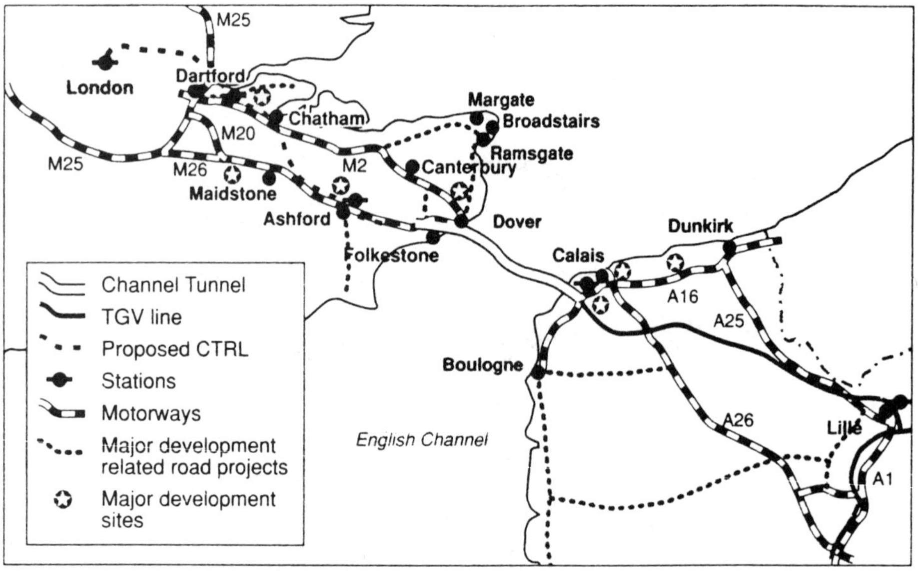

Figure 3 Major regional and local impacts of the Channel Tunnel.

tonnes in 1990, with forecast levels of 143 million tonnes in 2003 and over 210 million tonnes by 2013. Actual traffic levels have continued to outstrip forecast levels with great regularity over the past 30 years.

It is this incessant growth in traffic which makes the Channel Tunnel project economically viable. Even if the tunnel only takes some 40% of passenger traffic, and less than 20% of freight traffic, it is potentially viable, subject to the final out-turn of construction costs. The tunnel will, however, continue to face competition, both from ferries against *Le shuttle* and from airlines against the Eurostar through rail services. It remains to be seen whether an ordered market can develop, particularly for ferry and tunnel traffic, in the absence of the regulation which is so typically necessary in transport markets. The fear here would be of a price war, designed to exploit the tunnel's vulnerability during its early years of operation, while faced with the burden of its substantial debt. The problem for ferries, however, is that if they were to exploit this vulnerability to the extreme, the tunnel could become an even more formidable competitor if, by going bankrupt, it was relieved of its debt.

The best expectations are of a stable, if somewhat uneasy competitive outcome, with prices in the long run at a little, but not substantially, below those of current ferry fares in real terms. The prices announced by Eurotunnel for 1994 do not give a guide to this long-term situation since the limited capacity available in the first year of operation necessitates rather higher prices to avoid overcrowding on the turn up and go, no reservations service.

Such a situation has to be considered within the overall development of transport in the region, the key element of which is the PBKAL (Paris–Brussels–Kölun–Amsterdam–London) high-speed rail network. Growing congestion, both on roads and in air links, has placed a new emphasis on the development of high-speed rail links, which are optimal for distances up to 500–600 kilometres, roughly the distance between London and Paris. Linking London into the system is important for the rest of the network because it will ensure viable levels of flow on other links. Most of this traffic will divert from overcrowded airways and airports. The tunnel is a vital part of this network, but it highlights the key point that the significance of the tunnel depends on the rest of the network if it is to achieve this major improvement in transport flows.

The section from the tunnel via Lille to Paris came into service in 1993 and from 1994 will be linked to the existing two TGV lines to the southeast and southwest of Paris via the Paris Interconnexion. This also provides an interchange with Paris–Charles de Gaulle Airport. The link from Lille to Brussels is now under construction, for completion in 1996. The final authorisation for the mixture of upgrading and new line planned for the sections between Brussels, Amsterdam and Cologne is awaited, with completion expected for 1996–98. The new line between Cologne and Frankfurt am Main is due for completion around the same time. This leaves the final link from the tunnel to London, which awaits private finance and a lengthy period of authorisation following the final routes announcement in January 1994. Completion is not currently expected before 2002.

Given that Eurotunnel provides, in essence, both a road and a rail link, its position within the wider European road network is also of importance. From a position where access roads to the ports of Calais and Dover were relatively poor, the tunnel has acted as a catalyst to the completion of the M20 motorway in Britain. In France, both the A26 autoroute which leads south from Calais to Reims and on to Dijon and the Rhône Valley, and the A16 Rocade Littoral, which links the Belgian border via the Channel ports towards Amiens or Rouen, have been developed.

The essential impact of the tunnel is thus to act as a catalyst to the completion of important inter-metropolitan transport links, to remove a key bottleneck, but also to expose other weak links in the network. In this way it fits into the emergent trans-European networks for both rail and road, and also that for multi-modal transport.

THE GEOGRAPHY OF EUROPEAN INTEGRATION

A key issue in the economic integration of the European Union is the balance of centrality and peripherality in the union territory. One important measure of peripherality is that of accessibility. Reductions in travel time, and especially of excess times spent changing modes or trans-shipping goods (moving them from one mode of transport to another), tend to reduce peripherality. This has impacts on the directly affected regions, and they have an aggregate effect on the Union as a whole. Reducing the costs of transport within Europe enables the achievement of scale economies and increases the potential competitiveness of European industry.

The tunnel on its own does not of course achieve this, but, as one element in a series of attempts to remove communication barriers in Europe, is part of that process.

If we combine this point with the previous discussion of communications geography, there is a potential problem of introducing bias towards metropolitan development at the expense of intermediate regions. Transport is increasingly focused into corridors with limited access which concentrates their impacts on the end points. Thus high speed railways have impacts similar to that of air transport, concentrated around airports. We might expect therefore that bringing London, Paris and Brussels within 3 hours of each other, city centre to city centre by non-stop rail, may accentuate their positions relative to intermediate cities. It may also lead to fears of a European megalopolis, not as a continuous built-up area, but as a polycentric urban core to western Europe.

What of the periphery? In peripheral regions a similar process of centralisation into the major cities may also be taking place. This appears to be happening in city regions such as Dublin, Lisbon, Madrid and Athens which have good communications with the core region by air. These cities have accessibility which is as good or better than many intermediate cities, but it is achieved at the expense of their own hinterland. This has two relevant consequences: the high-speed rail network in the core becomes necessary to maintain its competitiveness; and the connections between the different parts of the European transport network become critical, because high-speed rail is not the answer for every link of a network. Distance and traffic volume will determine the best solution. But each city needs to have a competitive means of reaching every other city in the European network. In many cities having the triple linkage between air, high speed rail and regional (conventional) rail is a top priority. This is true of Paris, Brussels, Amsterdam and Frankfurt.

What of the secondary and non-urban areas? For them, links to the key network are critical. The Channel Tunnel confers a potentially improved link for the UK, but its significance depends on providing onward links to other regions.

REGIONAL IMPACTS ON THE UK

The centralisation debate for Europe as a whole applies particularly to the UK. A general fear has been that the Channel Tunnel naturally concentrates advantages on southeast England. However, with the possible exception of London this is not necessarily the case. Even for London, the absence of a Channel Tunnel rail link means that, although rail will now be competitive with air for journeys such as London to Paris or Brussels, the absolute level of accessibility of London will not be significantly improved. The major advantage will be an increase in capacity which should put competitive pressure on prices and improve reliability by reducing both airport and air traffic control congestion.

The completion of a Channel Tunnel rail link which enhances capacity, reduces time and increases reliability will have an important positive effect on London's accessibility relative to other European cities. This could have important consequences for the rest of the UK, depending to an extent on the well-being of the London economy for its own economic fortunes. A further impact is that a dedicated new rail link will enable faster through or connecting rail services from regions outside London through the Channel Tunnel, removing the inconvenient and time-consuming need to change stations and cross London. For passengers this will mean a major reduction in rail times to other centres. Although there may still be a disadvantage relative to air travel, again the increase in capacity and choice could lead to a significant improvement in accessibility.

For freight (around 80% of British exports by volume originate in regions outside the southeast) the major factor again is access to the network. Through rail-freight services to continental destinations will originate from specially developed freight villages in Scotland, the northwest, Teesside, south Wales and Bristol. A proposed site in West Yorkshire has run into serious planning problems. Since the depot for the southeast is at Wembley in northwest London, significant parts of the region to the east and south of London will have very poor access to this new rail network. Road freight will continue to dominate total trade, even though rail is expected to triple its volume to around 6 million tonnes. At about 8% of total trade, this is still only about half the share taken by rail in Europe as a whole. Road freight too needs to overcome the particular problem of congestion in and around London in getting to the Channel Tunnel or Channel ports for the short sea crossing. The development of east-west routes to the north of London, leading to better access to the east coast ports such as Harwich and Felixstowe or Hull, is thus an important priority. If nothing else, the Channel Tunnel has acted as a catalyst to the fundamental reappraisal of the transport needs of the British economy within Europe, although much of this has yet to find its way into a strategic transport policy.

REGIONAL AND LOCAL IMPACTS ON KENT

If the national regional picture is somewhat equivocal, with regions facing both positive and negative consequences, this is particularly true of the one part of Britain most directly affected, the county of Kent.

Contrary to popular belief, the economy of Kent, and particularly that of east Kent, is not typical of the image of the affluent southeast. The eastern part of the county has suffered from the long-term decline of traditional industries such as coal-mining, tourism and light manufacturing, whilst, despite the growth of port traffic, the need to seek enhancements in productivity has led to a decline in port and ferry employment. Construction of the Channel Tunnel did lead to a substantial boost in employment locally, but since the peak of construction in 1989–90 unemployment rates in the coastal belt of east Kent have risen continually. By December 1993 unemployment was 10.4% in Dover, 13.0% in Folkestone, and 16.4% in Thanet. It is therefore no surprise, if somewhat overdue, that these areas all received Assisted Area status during 1993. Thanet, one of the ten worst unemployment blackspots in the country, was also granted Objective 2 status for assistance under the EU Structural Funds.

In 1987 the Kent Impact Study estimated that, after a loss of 4,500 to 6,500 jobs in the port and ferry industries, new tunnel-related employment, and a range of secondary employment impacts in areas such as manufacturing, producer services, wholesale distribution, retail distribution and tourism, could lead to a net growth of between 9,500 and 13,000 jobs. These, however, were optimistic forecasts, made at a time of rapid growth in the British economy, and assuming that the existence of the tunnel would attract new businesses to locate nearby. By 1991, however, it had become increasingly clear that these forecasts were unlikely to be met. Economic downturn and reappraisal of the likely relocational impact of the tunnel, plus growing awareness of the mixed impact of the completion of the single European market, all suggested that the net gain in jobs would be lower, of the order of 2,600 jobs. As well as a lower forecast of new jobs, the prediction of job losses on the ferries in the light of their achieved productivity gains over the 1987–91 period rose to 7,500. To these figures need to be added the loss of almost 2,000 jobs in Customs and other frontier-related activities following completion of the single European market.

This led to an urgent need for policy intervention in the Kent economy, particularly in east Kent, to try and take some advantage of its new locational position. Following the announcement of the Channel Tunnel project the county had identified a number of key road schemes to link more peripheral parts of the county to the main road corridor of the M20 route. In addition, a number of sites had been identified for new business developments. These, however, only amounted to about the same total area as available at the French tunnel terminal. The major concentration of these sites is around Ashford, the site of the proposed international passenger station, which, although agreed by government from the start of the project, was only begun in the latter part of 1993. Thus far, the take up on the various business park developments has been relatively low.

The 1991 review gave renewed impetus to the plan for a more concerted development policy in east Kent, which materialised as the East Kent Initiative. This has helped to highlight the fact that the building of the Channel Tunnel really has little impact on the local economy, which continues to suffer from long-term structural problems. The flurry of construction activity between 1987 and 1990 did little to address these longer-term problems, and to some extent took attention away from them.

The Channel Tunnel rail link is an entirely separate project, but it needs to be discussed since the Tunnel itself is only as good as the networks of which it forms a part. The rail link is particularly important for Kent, since the environmental effects of its construction would be much more severe than those of the tunnel itself, which has had only a localised impact. The 1970s scheme for a Channel Tunnel foundered on the environmental opposition to the rail link, seen at that stage as an integral part of the tunnel project. On this occasion the UK government attempted to detach the tunnel project from any plans for a rail link. The capacity problems of the existing rail network in the southeast made such a link inevitable. The problem is to provide a link which is both environmentally acceptable and economically viable through a part of the UK which is both densely populated and abundant in areas where there are natural environmental constraints. After 6 years of debate, we are still awaiting a final government decision to introduce a Parliamentary Bill in 1994 to enable the construction of this link.

The Channel Tunnel and the rail link have both demonstrated the difficulty of devising a decision-making process which allows local input, is sensitive to national needs and is rapid enough to enable the introduction of private finance. This is not just a question of compensating the residents of Kent for the disturbance of new transport links designed to speed the residents of other regions through the county. A new rail link would enable the substantial improvement of rail services between east Kent and London, reducing times from Ashford by around 30 minutes and providing a fast, more comfortable, link for the towns in the east of the county, which is currently served by one of the poorest of the longer-distance commuter services in Network South East.

SUMMARY

The Channel Tunnel is a big project, but even so its likely impacts are so dispersed that it may be difficult to identify them. On most locations it may have both positive and negative consequences— this is true for places near to the tunnel, in Kent, and those further away. The exceptions to this are the big cities of the European core for which the tunnel and the associated high-speed rail developments provide a positive boost. The tunnel is also important as a multi-modal transport project—associated improvements in both road and rail are vital both to the tunnel's success and for it to have a positive impact on any location. The tunnel also has to be seen as just one of a number of major projects around Europe which, taken together, may be of much greater significance.

FURTHER READING

Holliday, I., Marcou, G. and Vickerman, R. (1991) *The Channel Tunnel: Public Policy, Regional Development and European Integration,* Belhaven Press, London.

'Spatial Perspectives on the Channel Tunnel', a theme issue of *Applied Geography,* Vol. 14, No. 1, January 1994.

Gibb, R. (ed.) (1994) *The Geography of the Channel Tunnel,* John Wiley, London.

In Focus—The Channel Tunnel, a set of structured bibliographies, The Channel Tunnel Group and University of Kent at Canterbury (available from Eurotunnel Exhibition Centre, St. Martin's Plain, Folkestone, Kent, CT19 4QD).

The New White Flight

SUMMARY **Migration flows are widening the demographic differences among states. In six states, minority immigration from other countries may be driving poor whites away, but not the college-educated. Florida and five other states that attract interstate migrants are magnets for the nation's most talented and skills workers. And states with heavy out-migration are especially likely to lose their best and brightest.**

William H. Frey

William H. Frey is research scientist and associate director for training at the Population Studies Center, the University of Michigan.

Immigrants exert a powerful influence on the U.S., but only in a handful of states. During the 1980s, newcomers from Mexico, China, and other countries flooded into Los Angeles, New York, and other major cities. As they moved in, large numbers of whites moved away from these areas. Minority-dominated in-migration combined with interstate "white flight" is leading to sharp differences in the racial and socio-demographic characteristics of different states.

The effect of migration on a state's population depends on three things: the size of the migration stream, its direction, and its source. A migration stream can be comprised of immigrants from abroad or of internal migrants from other states. In the U.S., the geographic patterns of international migrants and state-to-state migrants generally do not overlap. States with large immigrant streams, like California and New York, tend to have large existing settlements of earlier immigrants from Latin America and Asia. A somewhat different group of states, most of which are located in the South Atlantic, Pacific, and Mountain regions, are magnets for internal migrants.

Conventional wisdom says that people who move from state to state tend to be America's better-educated and affluent citizens. In the past, states with high out-migration have lost a disproportionately large share of their most educated and talented residents to states with high in-migration. But this rule does not apply to states with high rates of international immigration. In these states, low- and middle-income whites appear to be most likely to move away. Increased competition for low-skilled jobs, the indirect social cost of a growing population of immigrants (rising taxes, overcrowded schools, and language barriers), and simple fear of unfamiliar people may drive these migrants away. At the same time, the high-skilled jobs clustered in many high-immigration states also attract highly educated whites.

The race-migration dynamics associated with different migration streams can also be linked to trends in poverty status, educational attainment, and even the age distribution of different states. These trends are different in high-immigration states than in states that attract large numbers of interstate migrants, or in states that lose people to other states.

WIDENING DIFFERENCES

The internal migration flows of white Americans* are similar to the patterns of the nation as a whole. In the late 1980s, net white migrant gains were largely in the South Atlantic, Pacific, and Mountain regions of the country, and net losses were concentrated in states with high international immigration or declining economies. The broad pattern suggests an "emptying out" of whites from the upper Midwest region of the country. It also shows that whites left several Mountain

**The term "white" in this article refers to non-Hispanic whites. Minorities refer to all other population segments combined. The time period for net migration (the number of in-migrants minus the number of out-migrants) in this article is between 1985 and 1990. See "Behind the Numbers" at end of article.*

The New Golden Door

Several states that attract large numbers of international immigrants also have net out-migration to other states.

(states gaining more than 150,000 immigrants from abroad, 1985-90)

Migration From Abroad

150,000 or more | **Below 150,000**

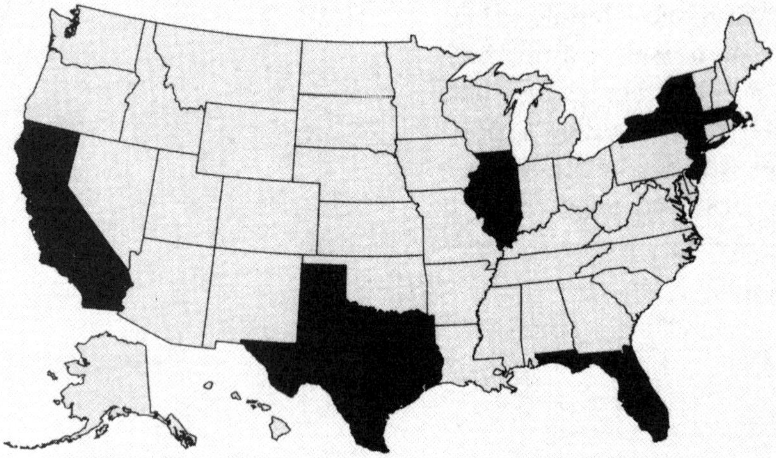

(states gaining 150,000 or more interstate migrants and states losing 100,000 or more interstate migrants, 1985-90)

Net Interstate Migration

Gains 150,000+ | **Losses 100,000+** | **Others**

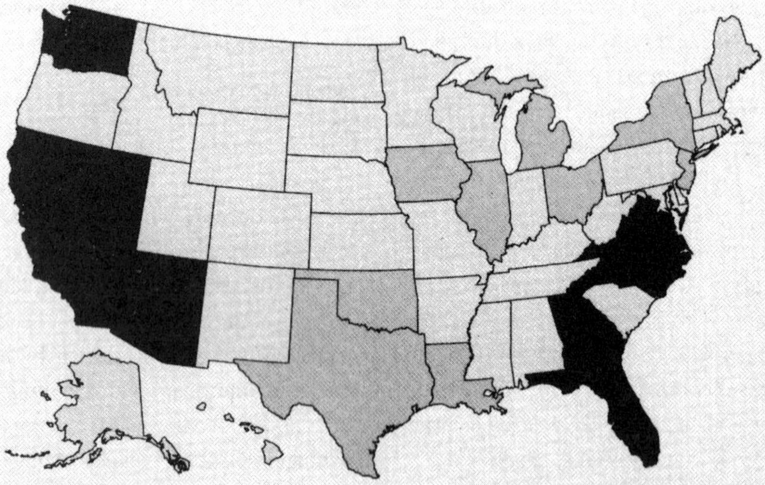

Source: 1990 census data compiled by the Population Studies Center of the University of Michigan

states that sustained economic downturns during the second half of the 1980s.

Florida continues to be a magnet for whites from many northern states, especially New York. A strong "spillover" of whites also occurred as New Yorkers moved into New Jersey. And whites in Massachusetts moved to New Hampshire. Between 1985 and 1990, a significant number of whites made the leap from Texas to California.

Minorities followed this pattern to some degree. Their gains in South Atlantic states are heavily concentrated in Florida and Georgia, and to a lesser extent in Virginia and Maryland. In the Pacific region, minority net gains are dominated by California, where Asians contributed substantially to interstate migration. Minorities and whites alike are moving away from New York, Illinois, Texas, and other states with declining or slow-growing economies. Unlike whites, minorities are moving away from Mississippi, Alabama, and Arkansas and filtering into Minnesota, Wisconsin, and Kansas. All six states in New England, including Massachusetts, experienced a net gain of minorities from other states.

Florida continues to be a magnet for whites from many northern states, especially New York.

Among minorities, five of the ten greatest migration streams flow outward from New York state. As with whites, the largest stream flows between New York and Florida. But New York also has a net loss of minorities to New Jersey, North Carolina, Virginia, and California.

Another important minority migration stream flows from Washington, D.C. to Maryland, as successful minorities seek new suburban homes. Minority migration streams are most likely to begin in states that are already home to large numbers of blacks, Hispanics, and Asians. They typically flow toward faster-growing, more economically vibrant areas of the South and West.

Minority patterns of migration differ subtly from those of whites. But the differences between low-income and higher-income whites are far more pronounced. Like internal migrants of all races, poor

The New Grapes of Wrath

Midwestern states are attracting interstate poverty migrants as they lose affluent whites.

(states ranked by net interstate migration of whites with poverty incomes, 1985-90)

Poverty Whites

Net In-Migration		Net Out-Migration	
Top 5 States	Other States	Top 5 States	Other States

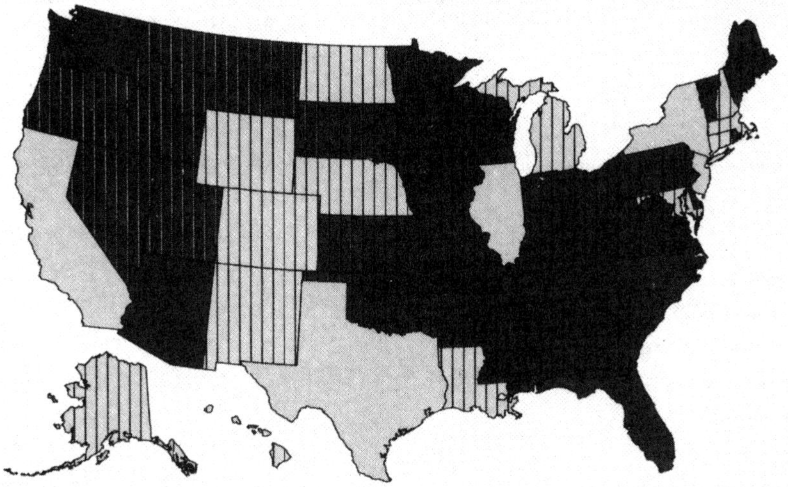

(states ranked by net interstate migration of whites with non-poverty incomes, 1985-90)

Non-Poverty Whites

Net In-Migration		Net Out-Migration	
Top 5 States	Other States	Top 5 States	Other States

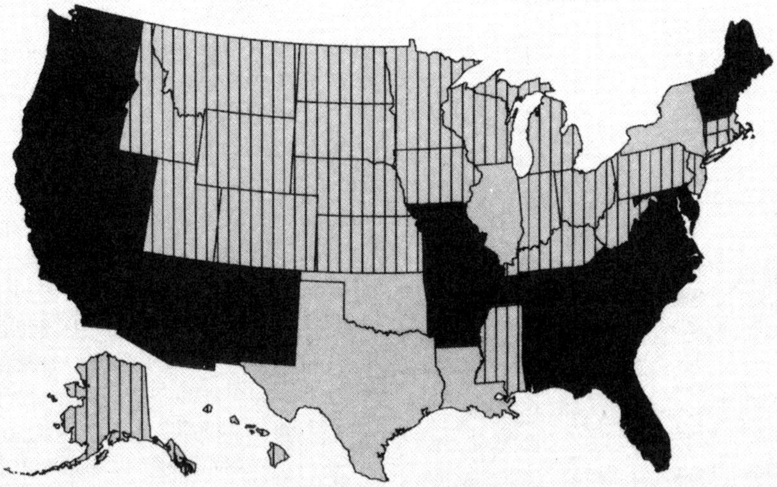

Source: 1990 census data compiled by the Population Studies Center of the University of Michigan

whites are leaving New York faster than they move in. But New York is not the leading exporter of poverty migrants, as it is for all other population segments. The outflows of poor whites are even greater from Texas, New Jersey, and California.

As poor whites migrate away from California and Texas, they move into the nearby states of Washington, Arizona, Oregon, Utah, and Arkansas. A large number of midwestern states are gaining poor whites even as they experience a net loss of all whites. In general, the white poverty population is spreading away from states with high levels of immigration. Still, Florida has had the greatest increase in poverty migrants, as it does for most other population groups.

Florida also leads the nation in the number of white college graduates it receives. California ranks ninth in attracting all whites and registers losses among poor white migrants, but it ranks number two in its ability to attract white college graduates. This pattern is more evidence of the "dual economy" found in many high-immigration states. Cities with large financial centers and other information-economy jobs often employ high-wage and low-wage service workers, with few posts available for mid-wage manufacturing workers.

The flow of white college graduates is particularly heavy from northern industrial and midwestern states such as Ohio, Pennsylvania, and Wisconsin. Strong one-sided exchanges appear to be directing college-educated whites away from these states toward Florida and California. More than other whites, college graduates are attracted to America's coasts.

Ohio, Pennsylvania, and Wisconsin are suffering heavy losses of college graduates.

The elderly population is another important contributor to white internal migration. While education and skills migrate from the interior states to the coast, elderly migration is more likely to flow from the Snowbelt to the Sunbelt. With the notable exceptions of California and Louisiana, a solid block of southern and western states receive a net gain of white elderly residents. Florida and Arizona top the list of gainers, while the losers are dominated by large northern states.

HIGH-IMMIGRATION STATES

Between 1985 and 1990, six states—California, New York, Texas, New Jersey, Illinois, and Massachusetts—experienced high immigration from abroad, but did not attract large numbers of internal migrants. In fact, California was the only one of this group that attracted more interstate migrants than it lost during the time period. Although California ranked seventh in attracting internal migrants, its population growth is clearly dominated by immigration from abroad.

Among the six high-immigration states, California best embodies the migration patterns of a dual economy. Its economy is attracting educated white workers but is losing unskilled whites perhaps because of increased competition for low-skilled jobs. Between 1985 and 1990, California gained over 100,000 white college graduates and a significant number of minority college graduates. It lost less-educated migrants.

Another truism in migration studies is that college graduates are more mobile than people with less education. After all, older Americans are less likely to migrate than younger adults, and they are also the group with the lowest educational attainment. But in five of the six high-immigration states, college graduates were less likely than high school graduates to move away between 1985 and 1990. The exception is New York, a state with high net losses for all whites and especially high losses for whites with college degrees. In all six states, immigration boosted population at both extremes of the education scale. But people with no college experience form the majority of immigrants from abroad and provide competition for less-skilled native-born whites. College graduates are more attuned to job markets and are more likely to respond to economic pushes and pulls.

California stands out because its net migration is positive for higher-income whites and negative for lower-income whites. New Jersey is noteworthy as well for its exceptionally high losses of lower-income whites. In California, New Jersey, and Illinois, minority out-migration is higher for minority poverty populations than for other minorities. In Massachusetts, poor minorities register significantly higher net migration gains than do minorities with higher incomes. Still, immigration rates in each state are higher among poverty than nonpoverty immigrants.

In all the high-immigration states except Texas, net out-migration rates of elderly whites are greater than those for younger whites. The strong pull of the Sunbelt for retirees accounts for the gains in Texas as well as the losses from northern states. But the loss of elderly migrants in sunny California comes as a surprise.

Once a strong magnet for the elderly, California is now the third biggest loser of elderly migrants. The state's higher cost of living makes it a less desirable destination for elderly whites, who are increasingly likely to choose Oregon and nearby states. Between 1985 and 1990, the net loss of elderly whites in California was 37,000.

For almost all groups studied—whites,

Moveable States

Seventeen U.S. states are intensely affected by migration: six because they attract immigrants from abroad, six because they are magnets for internal migrants, and five because they are losing population to other states.

(total migration from abroad and net interstate migration in thousands for states with high immigration, high internal migration, and high out-migration, 1985-90)

rank	state	migration from abroad	net interstate migration
HIGH FOREIGN IMMIGRATION STATES			
1	California	1,499	174
2	New York	614	-821
3	Texas	368	-331
4	New Jersey	211	-194
5	Illinois	203	-342
6	Massachusetts	156	-97
HIGH INTERNAL MIGRATION STATES			
1	Florida	390	1,072
2	Georgia	92	303
3	North Carolina	66	281
4	Virginia	149	228
5	Washington	102	216
6	Arizona	80	216
HIGH OUT-MIGRATION STATES			
1	Louisiana	30	-251
2	Ohio	69	-141
3	Michigan	74	-133
4	Oklahoma	32	-128
5	Iowa	17	-94

Note: Net interstate migration equals in-migration minus out-migration between 1985 and 1990. High immigration states are those where immigration from abroad exceeded net interstate migration. High internal migration states are those where net interstate migration exceeded immigration from abroad, and high out-migration states experienced negative interstate migration and were also not recipients of large numbers of immigrants from abroad.

Source: 1990 census data compiled by the Population Studies Center of the University of Michigan minorities, poor whites, higher-income whites, white college graduates, and elderly whites—California lost in its exchanges with Washington, Oregon, Nevada, and Arizona. This "spreading out" of American-born whites and minorities to nearby areas is a departure from traditional migration patterns. For decades, the nation's most talented and mobile citizens leaped across the interior states to reach California's economic promised land. The new pattern may be a response to demographic, economic, and social pressures exerted by the continuing large waves of immigrants into California.

A large influx of minority immigrants, coupled with substantial outflows of American-born whites, is the new pattern of white flight from high-immigration states. Minority immigrant flows dominate demographic change in all of these states. And in most cases, these immigrant in-flows are roughly equal to their interstate losses.

INTERSTATE MIGRANTS

The six states with the greatest net increases from interstate migration between 1985 and 1990 are Florida, Georgia, North Carolina, Virginia, Washington, and Arizona. With the exception of Miami and Seattle, cities in these states do not attract large waves of immigrants through traditional ports of entry. In every state, including Florida, the net in-migration of people from other states far exceeds immigration from abroad. A warm climate or other amenities help these states attract elderly retirees, new employers, and others.

The migration rates of higher-income whites into Florida, Georgia, and Virginia are greater than those of poor whites. In North Carolina and Arizona, the total numbers of migrants in these economic groups are roughly equal. But in Washington, poor white migrants outnumber the affluent. White immigration to Washington and Arizona is highly influenced by outflows from California. North Carolina's pattern is influenced by the return of migrants to the North whose efforts to find work were unsuccessful; it also attracts those in quest of economic opportunity in newly emerging southern job centers like Charlotte and Raleigh.

Once a strong magnet for the elderly, California is now the third biggest loser of elderly migrants.

Minority migration exhibits similar economic patterns. Both Washington and North Carolina have greater rates of gain for poor minorities than for those with higher incomes.

White in-migration by educational attainment follows the traditional rules in these states; all six are attracting the most educated interstate migrants. For five of the six states with high internal migration, rates of net migration for whites with college degrees are highest. Only in Arizona is it less apparent—and here the difference by education between the two groups is slight.

Clearly, the six high internal migration states are more than just magnets for snowbirds. In fact, significantly high net in-migration rates for elderly migrants are evident only in Florida, Arizona, and North Carolina. Florida's rates are high for both the elderly and younger movers. In North Carolina, younger migrants are increasing faster than those aged 65 and older. And in the other five states with high internal migration, substantially more younger than older whites are arriving. These trends are not surprising considering the strong economic gains in all of these states during the second half of the 1980s.

Florida draws more migrants than it exports in virtually every demographic category measured here, and it has a positive balance with most states. Yet Florida is losing elderly migrants to the western retirement magnets of Arizona and Nevada. And it is losing migrants in all categories to Georgia, North Carolina, and Oregon. As a result, Georgia and North Carolina are challenging Florida's dominance in the South Atlantic.

Like Florida, Georgia gains migrants from a majority of states in every demographic segment. Net in-migration to Georgia is particularly strong from the populous northern states of New York, Illinois, and Ohio. Georgia is also a regional draw for migrants from Florida and Texas. In fact, no state draws more migrants from Georgia than it supplies.

Georgia and North Carolina are challenging Florida's dominance in the South Atlantic.

The migration dynamics of the states with high internal migration contrast sharply with those of the high-immigration states. In the domestic-migration states, the influx of whites dominated population growth between 1985 and 1990. White interstate migration is particularly strong into Florida, Washington, and Arizona. American-born minorities—especially blacks—make up a sizeable proportion of the net in-migration flows to Georgia, Virginia, and North Carolina. Both Florida and Virginia attract significant numbers of immigrants from abroad, but white internal migration dominates their demographic outlook.

HEAVY OUTMIGRATION

A third class of states, including Louisiana, Ohio, Michigan, Oklahoma, and Iowa, have high out-migration. Among the states that did not receive large numbers of immigrants from abroad, these five experienced the greatest out-migration between 1985 and 1990. The out-migration from these states stems from the declining economies of the "oil patch," "rust belt," and "farm belt" regions in the late 1980s.

On most socio-demographic dimensions, Michigan is a loser in its migration exchanges. Elderly out-migration is more severe in Michigan than in the other states in this category. But Michigan's northerly location could be more responsible than its struggling economy for its losses. College graduates are more likely to leave Michigan than to move there, and the state's inflow of poor whites is slightly greater than its outflow.

Michigan's population gains in the late 1980s came from interior states, especially those in the "oil patch." Some of this gain was the return migration of former Michigan residents who moved out when jobs were plentiful in Texas and Oklahoma. People who leave Michigan frequently wind up in the fast-growing South Atlantic states.

In the other high out-migration states, the rate of elderly net out-migration is less than that of younger immigrants. This pattern will speed up aging in these states.

The race-migration dynamics in high out-migration states are the reverse of states with high internal migration. Out-migration of whites dominates demographic change in these states. In fact, with the exception of Louisiana, the heavy out-migration states are not losing minorities. Rather, they are losing large numbers of whites without replacing them with immigrants from abroad. And the whites who are leaving tend to be well-educated.

Michigan's population gains in the late 1980s came from interior states, especially those in the "oil patch."

Migration drives demographic change in all three types of states. In states with heavy overall losses, migration speeds up the aging of the population and robs employers of their most valuable labor resources. Educated whites and minorities are relocating to states with the most internal migration. These states are frequently magnets for elderly retirees, but younger people in search of greater employment opportunities are drawn to them even faster. States that attract many immigrants from abroad lose lower-income whites, even though they may still be attracting educated whites. Migration patterns are increasing the gaps between rich, poor, minority, and white.

Behind the Numbers The full report on this study (*Research Report No: 93-297, Interstate Migration and Immigration for Whites and Minorities, 1985-90: The Emergence of Multi-ethnic States*) is available from the University of Michigan Population Studies Center; telephone (313) 998-7141. The data were drawn from the 1990 census 5-percent Public Use Microsample (PUMS) files. The question about "residence five years ago" identified immigrants from abroad and net interstate migration (in-migration from other states minus out-migration to other states) between 1985 and 1990. White selectivity in migration and its potential implications for states is emphasized in this article. The term "whites" in this paper refers to non-Hispanic whites. Minorities include blacks, Asians, Hispanics, and all others.

Asians in the Suburbs

William P. O'Hare, William H. Frey, and Dan Fost

William P. O'Hare is a senior associate with the Annie E. Casey Foundation in Baltimore and a contributing editor of American Demographics. *William H. Frey is associate director for training at the Population Studies Center, University of Michigan, Ann Arbor. Dan Fost is a contributing editor of* American Demographics.

SUMMARY Forget Chinatown: most Asian Americans live in middle-class suburbs. The biggest markets for Asian suburbanites are in western states, but more than half of the top 25 Asian metros are elsewhere. Asian suburbs are diverse markets, ranging from Filipino Daly city to Chinese Monterey Park. And while suburban Asians are usually assimilated Americans, they also tend to preserve ancestral customs.

At first glance, Robert Lee, Rita Mah, and Jean B. Chan may look similar. These three Chinese Americans all live in suburban San Rafael, California, an affluent town just across the Golden Gate Bridge from San Francisco. But Lee is a fourth-generation American who grew up in suburban Burlingame, California, while Rita Mah grew up in New York City's Chinatown, and Chan grew up in China and Hong Kong. Their diverse backgrounds reveal the futility of trying to define even a segment of today's Asian-American population as a single market.

Asian Americans' diversity is also reflected in where they live. Cities are historically the gateway for new immigrants, but most Asian Americans now live outside the central city. If you're looking for affluent Asians, look in the suburbs.

In general, Asian Americans who live in the suburbs are more highly educated and have more disposable income than do those living in cities. The average household income of suburban Asian-American households was $56,300 in 1991, or 23 percent higher than that of Asian-American households in central cities, according to the Census Bureau's Current Population Survey. The gap is even wider in the nation's largest metropolitan areas, where most Asian Americans live. In metros with populations of 1 million or more, Asian-American average household income is 25 percent higher in suburbs ($59,000) than in central cities.

BIGGEST ON THE RIM

Twenty-five metropolitan areas in the U.S. had at least 25,000 Asian-American suburbanites in 1990. These metros accounted for 76 percent of all suburban Asian Americans. Los Angeles-Long Beach has the largest number of Asian-American suburbanites; its count (528,600) is almost twice as high as second-place Honolulu's (268,900). Oakland ranks third (196,800), followed closely by /Anaheim-Santa Ana (195,600).

Eight of the top-ten metros for suburban Asians are in the West, reflecting the destinations of recent as well as earlier immigrants. Yet more than half of the top-25 metros for Asian suburbanites are outside the West, and metros from all four census regions are on the list.

Some businesses prefer markets with a high concentration of their intended customers, rather than markets that offer sheer size. The most concentrated Asian suburbs are in Honolulu, where 57 percent of suburban residents say they are Asian-American (many are native Hawaiians). Honolulu is well ahead of second-place San Jose, where just 16 percent of the suburban population is Asian American. The next four areas are

Reprinted with permission from *American Demographics,* May 1994, pp. 32-38. © 1994 by American Demographics, Inc. For subscription information, please call (800) 828-1133.

also in California. The rest range from Washington, D.C. to Detroit, but all have far lower concentrations of Asian suburbanites than do the top six; none are over 5.8 percent.

High-growth areas for suburban Asians are spread across the country. Only four of the top ten are in the West.

A look at the fastest-growing Asian-American suburbs reveals even more geographic diversity. High-growth areas for suburban Asians are spread across the country, and only four of the top ten are in the West. In Atlanta, Riverside-San Bernardino, and Dallas, the number of Asian-American suburbanites more than quadrupled during the 1980s. In Middlesex-Somerset (New Jersey) and Houston, the number more than tripled.

DOZENS OF MARKETS

Asian Americans can be divided into dozens of markets. A suburban residence may indicate an Asian household's middle-class status, for example. But Asians also fall into at least a dozen distinct ethnic subgroups, and different groups dominate the suburban population in different metro areas. For example, Chinese Americans are almost one-third of Asian suburbanites in Los Angeles-Long Beach, but only 7 percent in Honolulu. Japanese Americans are one-third of the Asian suburban population in Honolulu, but only 4 percent in Washington, D.C. and 8 percent in Oakland. Koreans are 21 percent of the Asian suburban population in Washington, D.C., but only 3 percent in Honolulu.

Asian cultural ties may be less apparent in the suburbs than in dense urban neighborhoods. Yet they still exist, and they manifest themselves in different ways. Filipinos cluster in Daly City south of San Francisco, and Vietnamese shop in their own strip malls in Orange County's Westminster. In San Jose, the Lions Mall attracts suburban Chinese from Silicon Valley. And in Monterey Park, a once-sleepy farm town near Los Angeles, Asians are in the majority. Monterey Park had 38,000 residents in 1960, 3 percent of whom were Asian. Now it is a town of 60,000, 56 percent of whom are Asian.

"Monterey Park's Chinese residents reflect the changing pattern of Chinese immigration nationwide," writes sociologist Timothy P. Fong. "Chinese newcomers to Monterey Park and elsewhere are not analogous to the historically persecuted and oppressed male laborers who came to this country in the mid-19th century. They are men and women generally much better-educated and more affluent than either their Chinese predecessors or their white counterparts."

Wealthy Chinese were initially encouraged to move to Monterey Park during an economic slump in the early 1970s. The suburb developed the nickname "The Chinese Beverly Hills." Subsequently, Chinese immigrants of more modest means began to move in.

Monterey Park has enjoyed a boom in new business openings, says Fong. The businesses fall into three categories: small-scale restaurants and specialty shops run by new immigrants who speak little English and rely on free family labor; medical, legal, accounting, and real-estate offices run by well-educated, bilingual, Chinese-born entrepreneurs; and Chinese-owned and operated banks. Most of the new businesses cater to ethnic Chinese who live in the San Gabriel Valley and beyond, he says.

In the suburbs of San Francisco, a large middle-class group moved directly from the Philippines to the suburbs and stayed there. Daly City, in suburban San Mateo County, is a new homeland for Filipinos. It's "not like Chinatown, where people move out after making it," says Cherie Querol Moreno, managing editor of *Philippine News,* a newspaper with a national circulation of 120,000.

Filipino immigrants often move directly into suburban areas because they can assimilate quickly. Many of them learn to speak English in Filipino schools, and many travel to the U.S. on business—as Querol Moreno did before making a permanent move. "The United States is an extension of the Philippines for most people in Manila," she says.

While less-affluent Filipinos are likely to settle in San Francisco proper, Querol Moreno says that many others live in Hercules and Union City, east of San Francisco. In Daly City, Filipinos run small businesses and restaurants; others work as doctors, dentists, lawyers, realtors, and insurance brokers. "Daly City is not a bedroom community for Filipinos," says Querol Moreno. "Because of the high concentration of Filipinos, there's a captive market for restaurants and boutiques. If you want to eat Filipino food, the place to go is Daly City."

Filipino immigrants often move directly into suburban areas because they can assimilate quickly.

NATIVE CUSTOMS AND PRODUCTS

Suburban Asian Americans are more affluent than those in cities, but they are not more affluent than other suburbanites. On average, they had a per capita income of $15,600 in 1989, compared with $16,500 for suburbanites of all races. Among the top-25 metros for Asian suburbanites, only in Detroit is the per capita income of Asian suburbanites higher than the per capita income of the entire suburban population.

The highest Asian-American incomes are located in the larger suburbs of the eastern seaboard and the Midwest. Only two of the top ten—San Jose and San Francisco—are in the West. The most affluent suburban Asians tend to live in places where housing and land are much more expensive than in the central city. Older metros tend to have sharp city/suburb income disparities for all race and ethnic groups.

Living in the suburbs means success to

The Most Asian Suburbs

In six metros, more than 10 percent of the suburban population is Asian-American.

(metro areas ranked by percent of suburban population that is Asian-American, 1990)

rank	metro area	percent of suburban population that is Asian-American
1	Honolulu, HI	57.1%
2	San Jose, CA	15.6
3	San Francisco, CA	13.5
4	Oakland, CA	12.7
5	Los Angeles-Long Beach, CA	11.5
6	Anaheim-Santa Ana, CA	10.6
7	Washington, DC	5.8
8	Middlesex-Somerset, NJ	5.8
9	Bergen-Passaic, NJ	5.7
10	Seattle, WA	5.2
11	Sacramento, CA	5.1
12	San Diego, CA	5.0
13	Chicago, IL	3.8
14	Riverside-San Bernardino, CA	3.8
15	Houston, TX	3.7
16	New York, NY	3.6
17	Newark, NJ	3.2
18	Dallas, TX	2.7
19	Denver, CO	2.3
20	Boston-Lawrence-Salem, MA	2.2
21	Baltimore, MD	2.1
22	Atlanta, GA	2.0
23	Philadelphia, PA	1.9
24	Minneapolis-St. Paul, MN	1.6
25	Detroit, MI	1.5
	National average	3.0%

Note: Asians include Pacific Islanders.

Source: Compiled from the 1990 census at the Population Studies Center, University of Michigan

The Most Suburban Asians

Eight of the ten largest Asian suburbs are on the Pacific Rim.

(metros ranked by size of Asian-American suburban population in 1990)

rank	metro area	number of Asian-American suburbanites in 1990
1	Los Angeles-Long Beach, CA	528,608
2	Honolulu, HI	268,907
3	Oakland, CA	196,847
4	Anaheim-Santa Ana, CA	195,589
5	Washington, DC	178,890
6	Chicago, IL	121,011
7	San Francisco, CA	118,723
8	San Jose, CA	102,816
9	Riverside-San Bernardino, CA	81,066
10	Seattle, WA	70,697
11	Bergen-Passaic, NJ	64,719
12	San Diego, CA	63,326
13	Philadelphia, PA	58,413
14	Houston, TX	58,009
15	Boston-Lawrence-Salem, MA	55,694
16	Middlesex-Somerset, NJ	54,494
17	Sacramento, CA	50,306
18	Detroit, MI	47,269
19	Atlanta, GA	47,174
20	Newark, NJ	46,615
21	New York, NY	42,185
22	Dallas, TX	36,237
23	Baltimore, MD	34,247
24	Minneapolis-St Paul, MN	27,615
25	Denver, CO	26,129

Note: Asians include Pacific Islanders.

Source: Compiled from the 1990 census at the Population Studies Center, University of Michigan

Asian Americans, just as it does to everyone else. Paul Chow, a 65-year-old retired civil engineer, heads the Angel Island Immigration Station Foundation, a group trying to get San Francisco Bay's "Ellis Island of the West" declared a national monument. He was born in San Francisco in 1928, raised in Chinatown, and did not speak English until age 5. "The only white people I knew were the schoolteacher, the milkman, and the police officer," he says. "I never knew about the world outside." Then, as a young adult, Chow moved to San Francisco's Richmond District, a heavily Asian enclave of two- and three-story buildings with residential streets running off business-lined boulevards. "I had arrived," he remembers.

Fellow San Rafael resident Robert Lee attributes the upward mobility of Asian Americans to two factors: "the escalator of education and the elevator of real-estate investment." Until the mid-1960s, restrictive covenants often barred suburban homeowners from selling to Asians, he says. A taboo against intermarriage also waned in that era.

Social trends have certainly played a part in the movement of Asian Americans toward the suburbs, according to Eleanor Yu, president and chief executive officer of Adland and Adland Worldwide, a San Francisco-based agency specializing in the Asian market. "Historically, inner-city Chinatowns in Los Angeles, San Francisco, and New York were

Fastest-Growing Asian Suburbs

During the 1980s, suburban Asians increased more than fourfold in Atlanta.

(metro areas ranked by percent increase in suburban Asian Americans between 1980 and 1990)

rank	metro area	percent increase in suburban population 1980-90
1	Atlanta, GA	386.1%
2	Riverside-San Bernardino, CA	344.6
3	Dallas, TX	336.8
4	Middlesex-Somerset, NJ	268.3
5	Houston, TX	239.7
6	Anaheim-Santa Ana, CA	190.0
7	Boston-Lawrence-Salem, MA	189.3
8	Seattle, WA	174.1
9	Bergen-Passaic, NJ	173.4
10	Sacramento, CA	161.4
11	Washington, DC	157.2
12	Los Angeles-Long Beach, CA	153.9
13	Oakland, CA	150.4
14	Minneapolis-St. Paul, MN	135.1
15	Denver, CO	132.0
16	San Jose, CA	130.5
17	Newark, NJ	125.8
18	New York, NY	121.0
19	Philadelphia, PA	119.7
20	Baltimore, MD	108.3
21	Chicago, IL	103.7
22	San Diego, CA	101.1
23	San Francisco, CA	92.3
24	Detroit, MI	82.5
25	Honolulu, HI	24.4

Note: Asians include Pacific Islanders.

Source: Compiled from the 1990 census at the Population Studies Center, University of Michigan

Most Affluent Asian Suburbs

Asian suburbanites are most affluent in the Northeast.

(metro areas ranked by per capita income of suburban Asian Americans, 1989)

rank	metro area	Asian-American per capita income
1	New York, NY	$22,785
2	Bergen-Passaic, NJ	20,102
3	Newark, NJ	19,897
4	Detroit, MI	19,477
5	San Jose, CA	18,941
6	Middlesex-Somerset, NJ	17,820
7	Chicago, IL	17,538
8	Baltimore, MD	17,491
9	San Francisco, CA	17,172
10	Boston-Lawrence-Salem, MA	16,890
11	Philadelphia, PA	16,724
12	Oakland, CA	16,278
13	Washington, DC	16,123
14	Los Angeles-Long Beach, CA	15,694
15	Anaheim-Santa Ana, CA	15,587
16	Seattle, WA	14,295
17	Honolulu, HI	14,012
18	Houston, TX	13,819
19	Dallas, TX	13,631
20	Atlanta, GA	13,202
21	Riverside-San Bernardino, CA	13,029
22	Minneapolis-St. Paul, MN	12,164
23	San Diego, CA	12,028
24	Denver, CO	12,001
25	Sacramento, CA	11,468

Note: Asians include Pacific Islanders.

Source: Compiled from the 1990 census at the Population Studies Center, University of Michigan

created because of discrimination and because the Chinese were not ready to assimilate," she says. "Today, many Asians—even recent immigrants—*are* ready to assimilate. They speak English, they've been exposed to the culture, and they're buying estates in San Marino, Westchester, and Monterey Park." Wealthy Asian immigrants have global business interests, professional careers, and travel frequently, says Yu. They place their children in private schools or "the creme de la creme of public schools."

Although suburban Asians may be better educated and wealthier than their urban counterparts, Yu says that "they still prefer Asian food, music, and videos—Asian society. They're staying with their Asian identity, more by choice than out of necessity." The newest migrants to the suburbs may speak English, but they "prefer to speak, read, and receive information in their own language," says Yu. "They are not so assimilated that they predominantly rely on general media for information. They watch Chinese TV, even though other channels are available to them. You are sure to find stacks of Asian-language newspapers in the homes of suburban Asians."

"Asians in the suburbs assimilate like anyone else," Yu continues, "but they do maintain a certain level of Asianness. At Yaohan Plaza in Queens, 90 percent of the customers are Japanese. Although they live in a mixed neighborhood, Japanese are still attracted to Japanese stores.

This wasn't always the case. Paul Chow says that early Chinese Americans hid their culture to avoid the era's prevailing racism. "The first generation of Chinese Americans despised being Chinese,"

An Asian Mall in the Great Midwest

It may be the only supermarket in America where customers receive discount coupons for local motels. That's because Yaohan Plaza, in the prosperous Chicago suburb of Arlington Heights, draws Asian consumers from as far away as Michigan, Ohio, and Kentucky. "We cater to our customers' culture through retailing," says Yoshiyia Watanabe, a spokesman at Yaohan's U.S. corporate headquarters in Los Angeles. "We like to be as authentic as possible."

Yaohan Plaza caters not only to the Japanese Americans who account for half of its customers, but also to Chinese and Koreans (30 percent) and non-Asians (20 percent). Through a direct-mail list of 12,000 regular customers, the mini-mall announces sale and promotions that keep its parking lots full. Its appeal is the same as in bigger malls nationwide—variety. Shoppers come to the combination department store/supermarket for groceries, as well as books, liquor, newspapers, toys, videos, and airline tickets, all sold the way Asian consumers want them. "They don't have to go anywhere else—it's one-stop shopping, says manager Shuji Kono.

Service is key at Yaohan. The 61,000-square-foot pavilion exudes gracious cordiality. Customers who prefer not to speak English need not do so; employees speak Japanese, Korean, and Chinese fluently. "The customer is king," says Kono. He insists that all complaints be delivered directly to him for an immediate response. "If something is a problem, we have to do something right away. Right away."

What do people buy in an Asian mall in suburban Chicago? The answer is an intriguing mix of standard American products and imported items. Del Monte canned peas are stocked next to Azuki beans; Starkist tuna sits adjacent to broiled eel. Quantities sometimes seem larger than life with 25-pound bags of rice stacked on pallets and one-gallon cans of soy sauce. On the other hand, the Asian taste for junk food seems sated by unimpressively small bags of potato chips.

One obvious difference between an Asian supermarket and a typical American supermarket is in the seafood department. At Yaohan, fish and produce take up roughly equal amounts of space. Kono explains that his Japanese customers routinely prepare seafood in 10 or 12 different ways. They need different species and cuts—some for cooking and others to eat raw. Thanks to nearby O'Hare International Airport and four weekly shipments from California and Japan, Kono can offer such delicacies.

The supermarket is packed with items for non-Japanese Asians, too. Chinese come for jasmine rice, very sweet cookies, and special varieties of green tea. Koreans buy extra-thin-shaved beef and ribs for barbecuing, as well as dried cuttlefish. The store sells more than a dozen types of tofu and eight varieties of fresh mushrooms, even in the dead of a Midwest winter.

The physical features of the supermarket also strike the non-Asian shopper. The aisles are wider than in other grocery stores, and the shelves are as much as a foot lower to keep items within easy reach of small-framed customers. The store also offers unusual housewares seldom found in American supermarkets, such as the Panasonic Intimist, an electric appliance that attaches to a toilet. It has three settings: family, bidet, and dryer.

Founded in 1928 in Japan, Yaohan hopes to build as many as 1,000 stores in China. Although corporate plans to add to 10 existing U.S. stores are on hold because of economic conditions, the Yaohan Plaza in Arlington Heights is doing well. Kono says that revenues were up 12 percent last year in an extremely competitive retail environment. Even so, he laments that two local chains control 75 percent of the grocery market.

Kono hopes to expand his own customer base. "The Japanese people, they're happy," he says. "But that is not enough. We need American people." His strategy is simple and foolproof. "We're going to introduce Japanese culture with food."

—Mark D. Uehling

he says. "But now you have Asians growing up in white suburbs. By the time the kids get to college, they want to learn about their culture."

"When [our] children go to school, they're not exposed to Chinese culture," says Dr. Jean B. Chan of San Rafael, a mathematics professor. "They want to be like everyone else." That's why Chan is active in the Marin Chinese Cultural Group, which sponsors classes in Cantonese and Mandarin for young Sunday-schoolers, as well as a summer encampment at a state park. "We tell Chinese stories, have massage, and do arts and crafts. It's mainly for the children," she says.

Suburban Asians are "staying with their Asian identity, more by choice than out of necessity."

Robert Lee has taken things a step further. Although he sees some Asians trying to "be 105 percent more Yankee than the Yankees," he avoided that trap by taking his five children on a trip to China. "They had a sense of recovering their roots," he says. "They began to own them, not reject them."

Behind the Numbers In this study, suburban is defined as the portion of a metropolitan area outside the central city or cities. This analysis of census data used constant metropolitan-area boundaries for 1980 and 1990 to examine changes over time. Metropolitan Statistical Areas (MSAs) and Primary Metropolitan Statistical Areas (PMSAs) were used rather than Consolidated Metropolitan Statistical Areas (CMSAs) to provide more geographic detail. The Nassau-Suffolk MSA was excluded because it has no central city to compare with its wholly suburban population. The term Asian American here includes Pacific Islanders.

For more information about the Asian-American market, see *Asian Americans: America's Fastest Growing Minority Group*, by William O'Hare and Judy Felt, available from the Population Reference Bureau, Suite 520, 1875 Connecticut Avenue, NW, Washington, DC 20009; telephone (202) 483-1100. See also *The First Suburban Chinatown: The Remaking of Monterey Park*, by Timothy P. Fong, and *The Asian American Movement*, by William Wei, both available from Temple University Press, Broad and Oxford Streets, Philadelphia, PA 19122; telephone (800) 447-1656.

AN ALTERNATIVE ROUTE TO MAPPING HISTORY

J. BRIAN HARLEY AND
DAVID WOODWARD

J. Brian Harley is professor of geography at the University of Wisconsin-Milwaukee and director of the Office for Map History, American Geographical Society Collection. David Woodward is professor of geography at the University of Wisconsin-Madison.

THE SIXTEENTH-CENTURY GEOGRAPHER Hulsius once wrote, "Maps may be called the light or eye of history." It is in this role, as the primary documents for locating historical events, that early maps are still most used by the historians of the late-twentieth century. Nowhere are these uses more visible than in the study of the maps of what is sometimes still called the first great age of European exploration. J.A. Williamson, the distinguished historian of the Cabots, wrote discerningly in 1937 that "old maps are slippery witnesses." But for many researchers maps still hold out the prospect of locating the elusive landfalls of a Columbus or a Drake, of reconstructing the routes of navigators or tracks of the explorers, or perhaps of identifying a place described ambiguously in written texts. Maps are the coordinates of history.

During our researches in connection with the History of Cartography project and the Maps and the Columbian Encounter Exhibition program, we have come to understand the place of maps in early American history in some alternative ways. Maps can still be analyzed as credible and articulate witnesses to some aspects of the European voyages and explorations to America and in that sense we continue to interrogate them as a traditional record of events. But we are also discovering—as we reread them as a visual language to uncover new meanings—that they have yet more to contribute to a richer history of the Columbian encounter.

First, we are seeking a new perspective that focuses on the use of maps and on the social consequences of their making. The key question is "What happened when particular maps were made?" The research has shifted from a theoretical consideration of what maps were designed to do to what they actually did in society.

Inasmuch as Renaissance maps straddle a major transition in the history of European cartography—from the medieval to the modern—this question is especially fascinating. The dramatic shift in ways of thinking about the world, and in the way that vision was constructed, can be seen by comparing two of the dominant traditions of fifteenth-century cartography. The first tradition, the medieval *mappaemundi*, was allegorical, historical, and literary—a representation of the space of Christianity. Often centered on Jerusalem, these maps were introverted to the interior of the classical and medieval world by a circumscribing ocean sea. Beyond the pillars of Hercules there was nothing: *Ne plus ultra* (Nothing more beyond). The second tradition—represented by the rediscovered world maps of Ptolemy—by popularizing coordinates of latitude and longitude, led to a major conceptual shift in ways of fixing geographical positions and hence in visualizing and controlling the world. From the early fifteenth century onwards, after Ptolemy's *Geography* had been translated into Latin, the system of latitude and longitude—the symbol of modern cartography—began its ascendancy.

> From the *mappaemundi* to the Ptolemaic grid, maps have been both mirrors and catalysts of their times

From *Américas,* Vol. 3, Nos. 5/6, November 5, 1991, pp. 6-13. Reprinted with permission of Américas Press, Inc., 106 West 56th Street, New York, NY 10019.

The coordinate system derived from Ptolemy was quickly appropriated as an instrument of the first great age of European expansion into the overseas world. Whether or not such a seemingly humble innovation was a necessary condition for that expansion we cannot be sure. But by reversing the introspection of the *mappaemundi*, the Ptolemaic world map projected an image of extroversion. The numbered sequence of latitude and longitude values, known as the graticule, explicitly recognized the other half of the world. Even if it was not an accurate prediction of what was there, it was a rhetorical visualization of the unknown, an invitation to fill the blank space, and to explore that previously inauspicious West beyond the ocean sea.

The importance of the Ptolemaic grid in the visualization of the world is more difficult to assess at the level of individual historical actors. With Columbus—who, as nearly everyone now knows, began from the assumption that the world was round rather than proving that this was the case—we should be especially cautious. We know that he made careful comparisons of maps and first-hand observations to promote his voyage to America yet the Bible took its place as his authority along with the Classical geographers. In a moment of self-denial, he wrote that "reason, mathematics, and *mappaemundi* were of no use to me in the execution of the enterprise of the Indies," but this reflects his doubts about the meaning of his mission as well as the geography revealed by his voyages. Certain questions obsessed Columbus: the size of the earth; the longitudinal width of Asia and its relationship to Japan; the corresponding width of the Western Ocean.

The common denominator of the key maps available to Columbus is that they bore a graticule either drawn or implied. So it was with the "navigation chart" drawn by the Florentine physician and astronomer, Paolo Toscanelli in 1474, and a copy of which was later sent to Columbus. Toscanelli describes his map thus: "Although I know that the world can be shown in the form of a sphere, I have determined . . . to show the same route by a chart similar to those made for navigation . . . the straight lines shown lengthwise on the said chart show the distance from west to east; those across show the distance from north to south . . . " We are looking here at a map graduated with parallels and meridians, a grid that enabled the user to measure the distance across the Atlantic between Lisbon and Quinsay near the city of Cathay in China (26 spaces of 250 leagues each). It may not be an exaggeration to assert that Ptolemy's grid was a critical preconception for the events leading to the meeting of two worlds in 1492. The world maps by Henricus Martellus Germanus, of which the large manuscript map he made in 1489 is the most dramatic

COURTESY EDWARD E. AYER COLLECTION, THE NEWBERRY LIBRARY

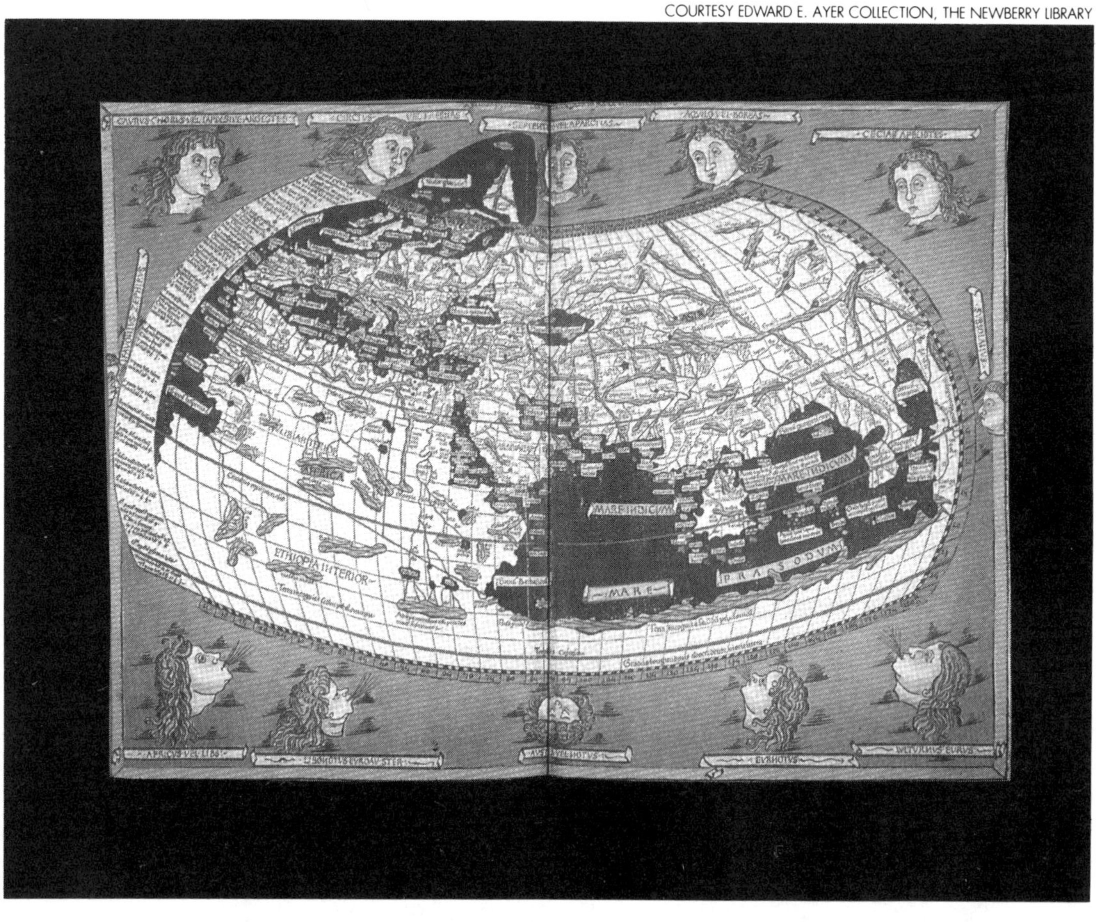

World Map, *from the Ulm 1482 edition of Ptolemy's* Geography, *reveals a world of the late Greco-Roman times with a closed Indian Ocean and a Mediterranean Sea twenty degrees too long*

example, are crucial for such an understanding. Its graduation in latitude and longitude implies that only 90 degrees of longitude—a quarter of the world—existed between the Canary Islands and Japan.

Second, we find that the often unintended results of making maps are as important as those that were intended. Once again Ptolemy's grid, rectilinear, abstract and uniform is a stimulus for other geographical actions. We do not know if Ptolemy in the second century AD could have foreseen what the eventual historical effects of his invention would be, but the potential of a system of spatial reference as a source of power and inventory was quickly grasped in the Renaissance. Roger Bacon had already stressed the proselytizing power of a global coordinate system to his patron Pope Clement IV in the thirteenth century. Likewise, Jacopo d'Angelo, in presenting to Pope Alexander V the first Latin translation of Ptolemy's *Geography* in the early fifteenth century, wrote in the dedication that he hoped the book would serve as "an announcement of his coming rule . . . so that he may know what vast power over the world he will soon achieve." And later in his book *The Cross*, John Donne recognized the religious symbolism of a mathematical coordinate system: "Looke downe, thou spiest out crosses in small things;/ Look up, thou seest byrds rais'd on crossed wings;/ All the Globes frame and spheres, is nothing else/ But the Meridians crossing Parallels." As Samuel Edgerton has put it, "the cartographic grid of the Renaissance was believed to exude moral power"; it expressed "nothing less than the will of the Almighty to bring all human beings to the worship of Christ under European cultural domination." The globe could now be grasped as a knowable totality and though finite, an expression of God's infinite wisdom.

The maps that carried the grid were also a super icon of this power to dominate. Initially, following Ptolemy, the "world map" had covered only the "inhabited" hemisphere of the Old World. The first map on which it extended to the whole world (globes excepted) was the *Cosmographia Universalis* made circa 1508 by Francesco Rosselli, a commercial printmaker in Florence. This small world map thus has an importance extending far beyond its modest appearance. Graduated with 360 degrees of longitude and 180 degrees of latitude, it is thus the earliest extant map of the world in the modern sense of "map" and "world." It takes on a special significance as drawn on an oval projection into which every point on earth could be theoretically plotted and upon which every potential route for exploration could be shown. The map had truly become a "totalizing device": it was a geographical idea of elegant simplicity.

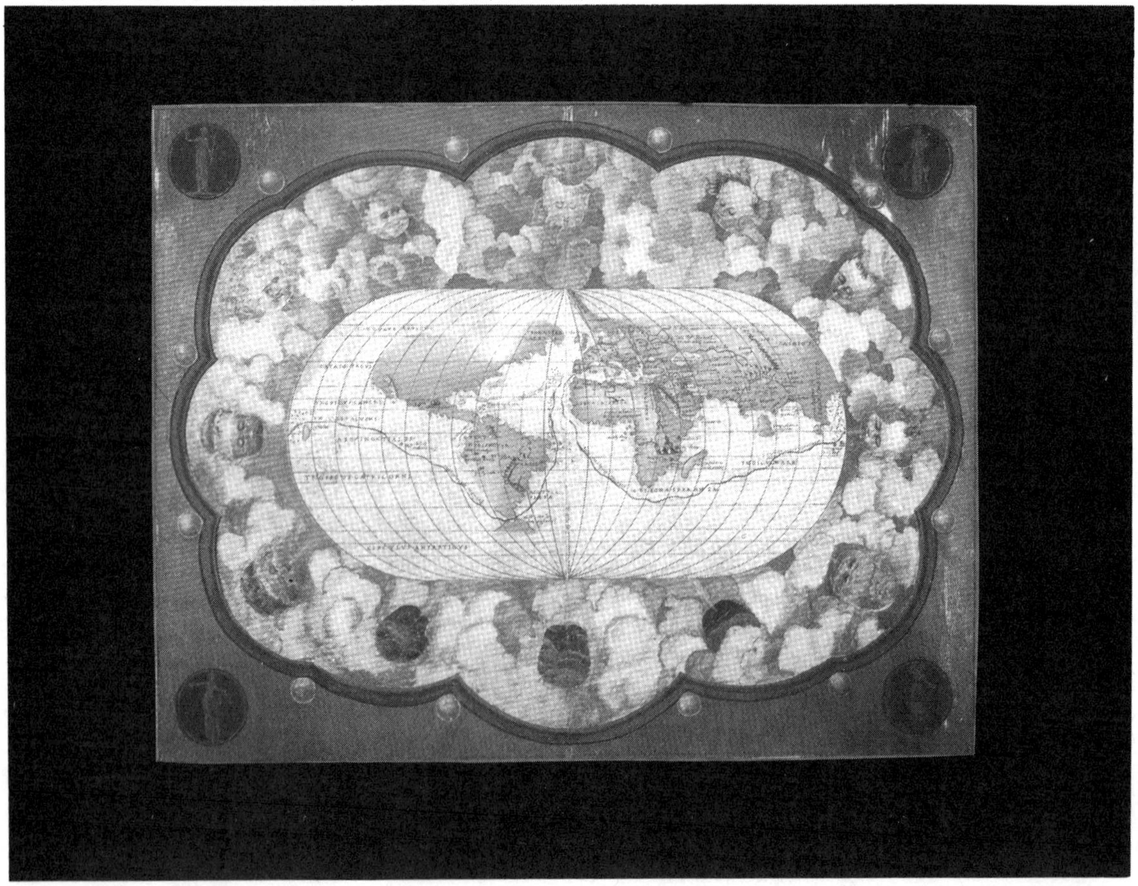

World Map, *1543–1545, from a portolan atlas by Battista Agnese, a Genoese cartographer active in Venice. Using the Ptolemaic grid, the map clearly shows Magellan's route around the world*

To the monarchs of early modern Europe bent on imperial and spiritual conquest, the map became a menu for colonization. As one chart maker put it in 1534, "With these charts, the reader may inform himself about all this new world, place by place, as though he himself had been there." The world could be carved-up on paper. By its abstracted simplicity and apparent objectivity, placing the viewer above the world even before the age of the astronaut, it also homogenized space and offered to the explorer and his patron a clean slate for exploitation. The Ptolemaic grid was the perfect cartographic instrument for collecting, collating and correcting geographical knowledge. Robert Thorne could boast in 1527, "there is no sea unnavigable, no land unhabitable." The circumnavigation of the world in 1522 had made everything possible. The world could now be viewed as a marked out stage, the *Theatrum Orbis Terrarum* of Ortelius' famous atlas of 1570 and the actors—the Europeans and the "Others"—could be assigned their place. Turn over its pages, and every map has a gridded backdrop on which the Europeanization of the world could be played out. The atlases of the sixteenth and seventeenth century increasingly became the symbols as much as the instruments of European power. Spatial imagery had acquired a new meaning and a new strength.

Our third point addresses the need to consider the maps of peoples on both sides of the Columbian encounter. It highlights the extent to which mapping, rather than being primarily a European preserve, has a significant native American dimension. In the early colonial period, the fullest evidence for the coexistence of Native American and European traditions of mapping relates to Mexico. What the Europeans found in Central America after 1520, though it was not recognized as such, was an independent cradle for the invention of cartography. The claim of pre-Columbian peoples—no less than those of Europe, the Middle East, or China—to have created their own tradition of cartography is confirmed not only by eye-witness reports, as when Cortés was given a "cloth [map] with all the coasts painted on it," but also by the survival of picture maps from both the pre- and post-conquest eras. Somewhat later, it is also confirmed by some of the local maps and plans *(pinturas)* in the *Relaciones Geográficas* of New Spain in the 1580s. Though often drawn and painted in a European style, some maps perpetuate purely native or hybrid traditions of representation.

Only relatively recently has the maplike character of Mixtec ritual and genealogical manuscripts been fully recognized. For instance, the pre-conquest Nuttall screenfold and comparable codices are now interpreted as spatial histories showing episodes of an ancestral migration and conquest of the Valley of Mexico. Among the place signs identified in the Nuttall Codex are many of those for hills (shaped like a bell and painted brown), those for buildings, fortified sites, and historical events, and the strings of footprints for routes taken by the conquering lords. Such pictorializations of the land are no less a map than the Peutinger map deriving from the classical Roman world or a fifteenth-century map of a European estate. When the place signs are deciphered and related to a modern map, using archaeological, oral and pictorial evidence, we can reconstruct some of the historical places within the pre-conquest landscape: rivers, lakes, and cities as seen through the lens of an indigenous culture. Mapping as geography and cosmography was by no means alien to the cultures of ancient America and for them, too, maps were the coordinates of history and an ideological perception of territory.

A striking contribution of Native Americans to the mapping of the Encounter—also revealed by recent research—lies in their often unacknowledged choreographing of European exploration. Beginning with Juan de la Cosa's world map of 1500, most European maps showing the New World conceal a hidden stratum of Indian geographical knowledge. It is difficult to imagine what some of the early European maps of America would have looked like had there been no Indian guides when the Europeans arrived in the New World. The extent to which Columbus and his contemporaries relied on Indian knowledge was considerable. As early as October 13, 1492, Columbus reported taking prisoners and on other occasions—alike by the Spanish, English, and French—Indians were kidnapped and taken back to Europe for interrogation. On their return they became the eyes of the mapmaker. A remarkable exchange of geographical information was in progress throughout the sixteenth century and much of it eventually given coordinates in European maps. Among those who had maps drawn for them by Indians are Cortés, Coronado, Escobar, Farfan, Captain John Smith, and Samuel de Champlain. Only a few European maps acknowledge these sources so that their existence has to be inferred from features such as large lakes, artificially straightened rivers running into the west, or the fabled "golden" cities such as Cibola, El Dorado, and Norumbega.

Nor should we picture Native American peoples as solely passive agents for European mapmakers. The mapping of America was not a one-way process in which colonized peoples offered no challenge to external surveys of their territory. It is true that in some regions native voices were quickly silenced and their maps were superseded by those of the politically dominant culture. But in other regions maps were used to help resist the imposition of colonial rule. A tradition of native mapping in Mexico—as part of native art in general—survived the Conquest. We glimpse the power articulated in European maps being partly resisted on native maps which offer an alternative cartography stressing the legitimacy of their own territory.

The pre-conquest Nuttall screenfold from the Mixtec culture depicts the story of an ancestral migration. Researchers have reconstructed the geographic elements identifying place signs and relating them to modern locations

Among the manifestations of resistance are the maps used by Indians in land claims, where they became documents for litigation in colonial courts. Elsewhere, the genealogy of ruling Indian families was inserted on maps as a way of seeking to restore land or to reduce onerous taxes. The Codex Xolotl—a narrative of the original conquest of the Valley of Mexico by the ruling family of Texcoco—is also a cartography. As the Indians sought to remake their own history through a map, it links time and space, seeking to prove ancient nobility rooted in territory. These "alternative cartographies" stood as a challenge to Spanish power.

In many of the European colonial maps we witness a process of silencing the indigenous culture. The imposition of a western way of seeing as the only valid form of representation excludes not only the Indians from the perception of their own land but also the Europeans from the perception of the Indians. If for the colonists cartography was psychologically enabling, for the colonized it let down a curtain on a familiar world. By insisting that the land will only appear in a certain way—and by affirming the "correctness" and "naturalness" of what it shows—European maps excluded the American way of seeing the land. The induction of this cartographic amnesia was a social projection of a future geography. Just as Indian maps were often destroyed, so too were the traces of an Indian geography frequently eradicated from the space of European maps. The maps increasingly convey, through the articulation of the blank spaces and *terra incognita*, the assumption of an uninscribed earth. Later, in North America, they would contribute to the myth of an empty frontier.

As we approach the 500th anniversary of the first voyage of Columbus in 1992, we are reaching toward an alternative cartographic history. Its tone is more reflective than celebratory. Although the maps of the Columbian era have been traditionally

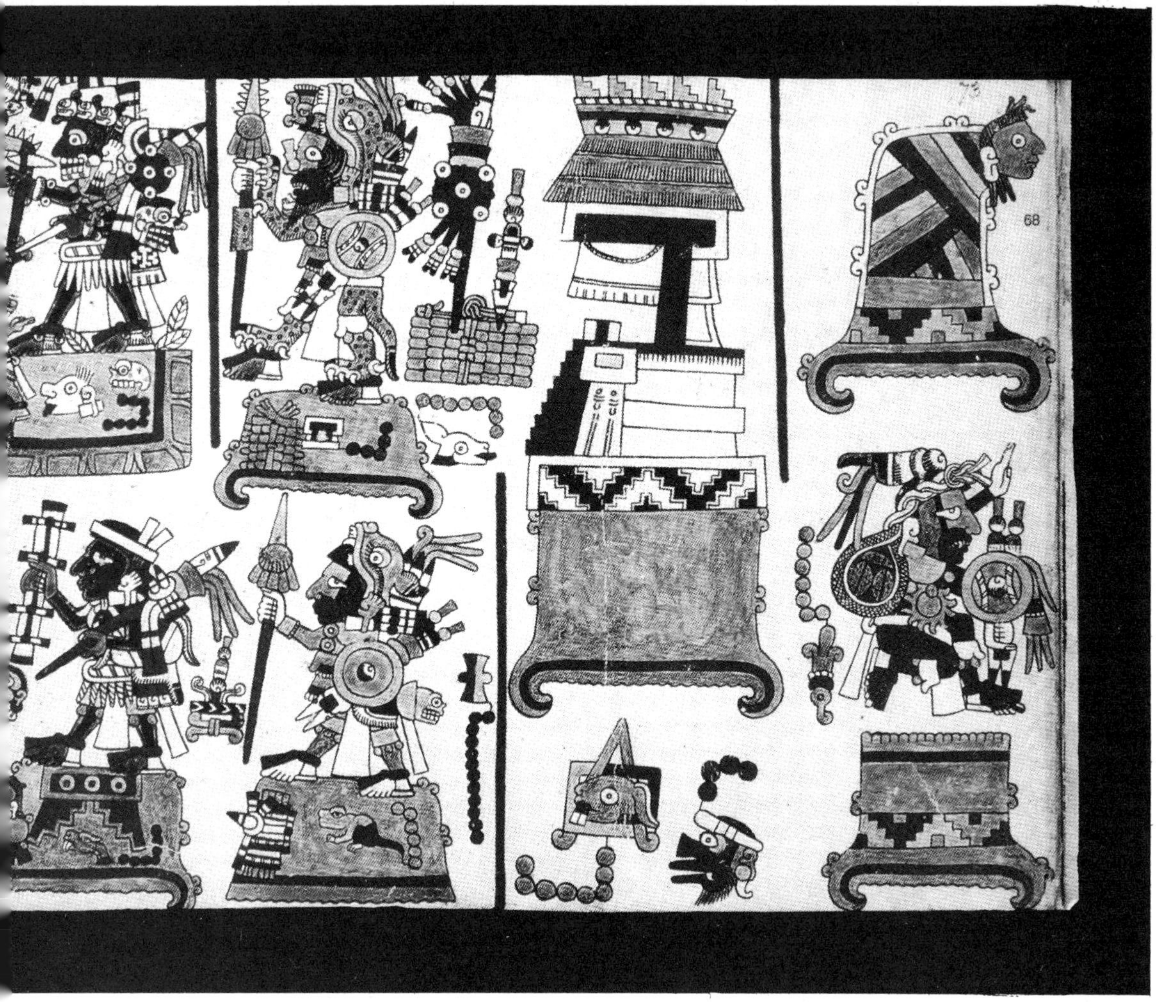

COLOR FACSIMILE FROM THE SPECIAL COLLECTIONS GOLDA MEIR LIBRARY, UNIVERSITY OF WISCONSIN—MILWAUKEE

viewed as eloquent witnesses of European geographical discoveries, they are much more than that. They also reveal a fundamental shift in thinking by the geographers of Renaissance Europe about the shape and size of their material world. The talisman of this enlarged world was the Ptolemaic grid. But as well as inventorying places discovered by Europeans and identifying a terrain for evangelization, the coordinated space of the new maps was instrumental in the symbolic appropriation of Native American territory. By recognizing Indian peoples as the victims of a European cartography we have also begun to reinstate their contribution into the cartographic record of American history. By reading between the lines of the map, a start has been made in writing a different account of the mapping of a New World that was already old when Columbus arrived.

Maps to the nth degree

J. Brian Harley and David Woodward have edited a multi-disciplinary world history of cartography being published by the University of Chicago Press in six volumes. The series, entitled *History of Cartography*, is supported by The National Endowment for the Humanities, The National Science Foundation, and private foundations and individuals. Volume 1, *Cartography in Prehistoric, Ancient, and Medieval Europe and the Mediterranean* was published in 1987; Volume 2, Book 1, *Cartography in the Traditional Islamic and South Asian Societies* is scheduled for publication in Spring, 1992.

The "Maps and the Columbian Encounter" supported by The National Endowment for the Humanities, has generated a traveling exhibition with a narrative about maps and their meaning from both sides of the encounter. It is described in an illustrated guide by J. Brian Harley, *Maps and the Columbian Encounter* (Milwaukee: Golda Meir Library, 1990), $12.95.

A sense of where you are

Powerful computerized maps are helping make order out of an increasingly complicated world

A map is more than lines and figures on a sheet of paper. It is a state of mind. From the days of the earliest explorers, map makers have drawn the terra incognita of the Earth into closer and closer focus, shaping world views as they sketched ever-more-accurate images of the planet. Artist Tom Van Sant of the GeoSphere Project in Santa Monica, Calif., recently took the process to its ultimate end with a bit of cartographic history: the first map of the world that is not drawn at all. Rather, it is pieced together entirely from satellite photos.

Van Sant's new view of the world is part of a cartographic revolution that is transforming flat and static maps into dynamic displays of information about the earth and its inhabitants. Using powerful computers, high-resolution video monitors and vast memory banks, a new generation of map makers is merging the crisp photo imagery from satellites and aircraft with volumes of data to create maps that are as vital a tool for navigating in the modern world as sea maps were for ship captains centuries ago.

Highlighted in a six-part television series called "The Shape of the World" airing on PBS this month, computerized maps are rapidly becoming an integral part of scientific research, business marketing and urban planning. The series is funded by IBM, one of many companies racing to become part of the rapidly growing business of supplying software and hardware for the new electronic map technology, known as "geographic information systems" or GIS.

Pioneered by such companies as the Environmental Systems Research Institute of Redlands, Calif., and Intergraph Corp. of Huntsville, Ala., GIS systems are already being used by city governments as the geographic equivalent of a "crystal ball." Municipal maps that combine data on water tables, residential housing and air-pollution levels help officials find an optimum site for a landfill, for instance, and computerized maps that show updated traffic information provide the fastest routing for ambulance and police service. The military is using highly detailed GIS maps of Kuwait City made prior to the gulf war to assess bomb damage and help restore power and phone lines, and the U.S. Fish and Wildlife Service used the new map technology to analyze the impact of an Alaskan oil pipeline on caribou migrations. In the future, scientists hope to use GIS to combine data from various earth monitoring satellites to keep track of global climate changes.

Boardroom mapping. By allowing map makers to easily merge almost any kind of data with a spatial map, GIS technology has become a key tool in corporate boardrooms as well. Petroleum companies use GIS technology to analyze geological formations and locate the best spots for drilling; the telephone company U.S. West is targeting its marketing of "call waiting" and other services with a GIS program that merges customer profiles with phone information; and a movie distributor uses GIS to analyze what kinds of films draw the best crowds in various neighborhoods. The new mapping technology is even being downsized to work on a typical personal computer: One system offered by MapInfo of New York is used by banks, for instance, to track the geographical distribution of their mortgages.

Merging maps with other data to create analytic tools has a proud tradition: During the Revolutionary War a French cartographer used hinged overlays to display troop movements during the Battle of Yorktown. In 1855, a British physician plotted the location of victims of cholera on a map of London to trace the source of the epidemic to a public water pump.

But it has only been with the advent of computers that map makers have had the power to merge vast reservoirs of data with highly accurate geographic displays. Typically, map makers start with a photograph from a satellite or an airplane. The geographical data are either scanned into the computer or entered by means of a handheld device that a map maker uses to "trace" a coastline, for instance, or follow the contours of a mountain range. Once in the computer, the geographic data can be merged with almost any existing database—basic census information, rainfall patterns, income distribution, the populations of various insect species, disease prevalence or a country's mineral resources.

For all their potential, the new map making techniques still come up short of a common map maker's dream: to be able to give a map gazer instant access to a wealth of information—past and future—about any spot on the globe. The sheer mass of data required for such a task would require highly sophisticated computer programs that do not yet exist, says Terry Smith of the University of California at Santa Barbara. Smith is an associate director of the National Center for Geographic Information and Analysis, a consortium of universities funded by the National Science Foundation that is developing computer programs and other technologies to handle the huge amounts of data needed for modern mapping. This task will become even more challenging in the near future, Smith says. Several Earth-monitoring satellites, planned for launch in the mid-'90s, will begin beaming down data on everything from weather to vegetation patterns to geological formations. Making sense of it all will be a herculean task, says Smith, requiring programmers to give computers what in essence amounts to a "map of the map" to help navigate through the data.

More honest maps? The sophistication of GIS notwithstanding, cartographers are quick to point out that the burgeoning mounds of data provide no guarantee that the new maps are any more accurate, or any less deceptive, than their predecessors. By their very nature, maps are selective presentations of information, with sprawling cities shown as round dots, hilly terrain smoothed to flat sheets of pastels and statistical mi-

"MENTAL MAPS"

The politics of cartography

All maps distort reality. Flattening a spherical world without misrepresenting some part of it is simply not possible. Map makers have long appreciated this fundamental paradox of cartography, but in recent years the distortions in maps have become increasingly political. Indeed, map making appears to be the most recent target of the political correctness movement that is currently sweeping through American education and publishing.

The political debate centers mostly on a 400-year-old map, the Mercator projection, the image of the world most familiar to American schoolchildren. Originally designed as a navigational tool, it still works fine for that purpose, but it gets the relative size of land masses dead wrong. The Soviet Union doesn't dwarf Africa, as the Mercator makes it appear. Nor is Europe larger than South America.

Maps of the mind. Such distortions are of more than passing significance, critics of the Mercator insist, because "mental maps" are crucial to cultural perceptions. "In our society," argues Salvatore Natoli of the National Council for Social Studies, "we unconsciously equate size with importance and even with power, and if the Third World countries are misrepresented, they are likely to be valued less."

The most provocative challenger to the Mercator is the Peters projection, named after its creator, German historian and cartographer Arno Peters. Although the map is nearly 20 years old, it is being heavily promoted today by the World Council of Churches and various United Nations organizations, which distribute the projection as "a map for our day" and as a politically sensitive replacement for the outdated Mercator. The Peters map is an "equal area" projection that claims to represent relative sizes of land masses more accurately. In publicizing his map, which noticeably elongates the Third World continents of Africa and South America, Peters has bitterly denounced the "European arrogance" of the Mercator map, saying that the cartographic profession has intentionally used it to foster European imperialist attitudes.

The Peters map has been roundly attacked by the cartographic establishment on technical and philosophical grounds, but publishers and educators appear to find the map's politics appealing. Despite an intense lobbying effort by leading cartographers that dissuaded Prentice-Hall from publishing the map, in October, HarperCollins Publishers in New York released the first American edition of a world atlas based on the Peters map.

The schools, too, are yielding to the tide of cartographic political correctness. More and more are using the Peters map not only to raise consciousness about the inevitability of map distortions but also to counter the strong European emphasis of the Mercator and other maps. The Texas Education Agency has required textbook publishers who sell books to Texan children to explain that the world does not really resemble the traditional Mercator image. Publishers of new texts must also include comparisons of different map projections. In Paramus, N.J., educators are using the Peters projection with other maps to get students to look at the world differently.

It is human nature for map makers to put their own interests at the center of the world and keep what is foreign peripheral. The enthusiastic reception that the Peters map is currently receiving suggests that the Third World's point of view is, if nothing else, politically fashionable.

BY SCOTT MINERBROOK

FRIENDSHIP PRESS

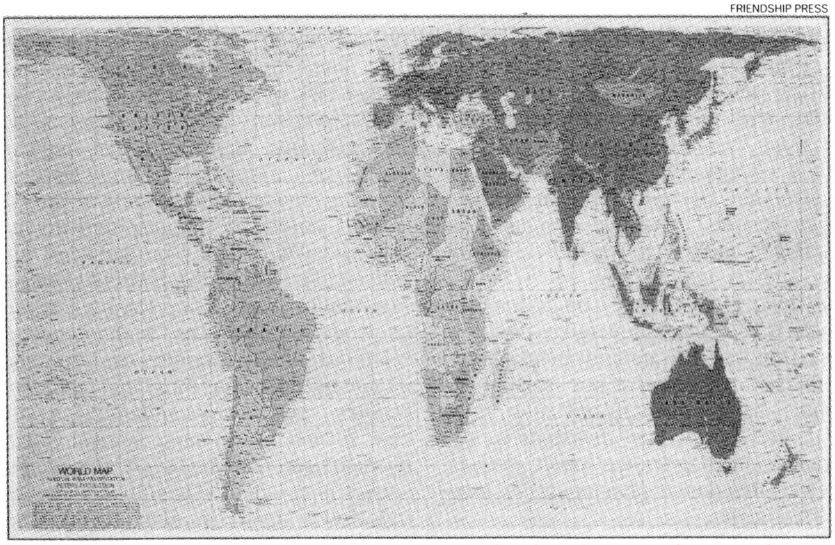

Stretching truths. *Arno Peters has campaigned for the adoption of a map that displays the world's continents at their true size, though not their true shape.*

nutiae lumped into coarse generalizations. "It's not only easy to lie with maps," notes geographer Mark Monmonier of Syracuse University, whose book *How to Lie With Maps* has just been published. "It's essential." With their fleet computers and access to vast stores of information, map makers have more rather than less power to skew their presentations, whether their goal is to show the "ideal" location to build a house or to demonstrate that a development project will have a negligible impact on the environment. The fact that these distortions can subtly shape public perception has not been lost on developers, advertisers and propagandists who promote maps with a view of the world that fits their particular agenda (see preceding page).

Nor is electronic cartography likely to supplant paper maps. Indeed, the result of the new technology will most likely be more paper maps, not fewer. Not only does GIS make it easier to update maps more frequently, it also makes it possible to produce customized, "one time" maps designed only for specific tasks. Paper maps will stay around for a more basic reason as well. They are a convenient method for bringing information to the most sophisticated computer on earth, the human brain. "The human visual system is extremely powerful," says Smith, and the brain's ability to organize the dots, lines and colors of a traditional map into meaning is unparalleled by any machine.

From the dazzling displays of electronic cartography to the intricately wrought scrolls of the ancient explorers, maps have long been a source of pleasure as well as information for a species whose most sophisticated sense is vision. By capturing the map maker's view of the world, maps touch the core of human curiosity that drives both art and science. Whether a cosmological theory of the universe or a simple block diagram in a shopping mall, maps provide a fundamental message that seems essential to the human condition: *You are here.* WILLIAM F. ALLMAN

THE NEW CARTOGRAPHERS

Gregory T. Pope

In a windowless chamber, scrubbed clean by hissing climate control, stand towers, racks, and cabinets of computing power. Here, in the U.S. Geological Survey's Reston, Virginia, headquarters, a nineteen-inch monitor winks on, revealing a three-dimensional relief map of the Loma Prieta area south of San Francisco. At the punch of a button the image wheels into motion, taking the viewer around the region's peaks and valleys on a ten second flying-carpet ride.

In a similar room at the SPOT Image Corporation, about a mile down Reston's tidy Sunrise Valley Highway, technicians are poring through data beamed down several days ago from *SPOT 2*, a commercial satellite that circles the globe every twenty-six days. These days, any mapmaker with as little as $500 to spare can freshen up an outdated map. By simply summoning a map on a computer screen, and superimposing a SPOT image over it, the computer whips through an automatic change-detection routine, shifting borders and other features to match the satellite picture.

It's fitting that both the Geological Survey and the SPOT Imaging Corporation—two driving forces behind today's cartographic revolution—call Reston home, a city of 32,000 that wouldn't have shown up on most maps twenty-five years ago. The landscape—and the art of cartography—change quickly now. Gone are the pens and sapphire-tipped gravers of yesteryear. More precise than ever before, thanks to computerization and satellite imagery, modern maps no longer stop at simply guiding the user from point to point. Like crystal balls, they must let the user gaze into the future to answer thorny questions: where to site a landfill, how to route a fleet of ambulances, how the terrain will look after an earthquake has rippled through.

New demands have compelled mapmakers to package geographical information in innovative ways. The new cartographers use software that translates spatial features—houses, street intersections, rivers, city blocks—into mathematical points, lines, and polygons. These geometric elements are identified and tagged as street names, zip codes, soil types, population figures, whatever, and are downloaded into a computer's memory. The result isn't a map in the traditional sense but rather an information pool where every feature is digitized and stored in a vast database. Such a database, called a geographic information system, or GIS, is the crux of the new cartography. Using a GIS, cartographers can analyze geographic information without ever looking at a map. Or they can unleash snazzy graphics routines to display the information in a more familiar maplike form.

The venerable mapmaking houses, whose profits hinge on the exactitude of their products, have wholeheartedly embraced GIS technology, largely because keying corrected digital data into a computer takes a lot less time than the traditional chore of scribing a whole new map onto a sheet of coated film. More than likely, a GIS database spawned the road map or world atlas you just bought.

The elite among the new cartographers sharpen their view of the world by employing a satellite capability known as remote sensing. *Landsat 1*, lofted by NASA in 1972, showcased the first glimpse of remote sensing's power, offering views of the earth unprecedented in their accuracy. Currently, *Landsats 4* and *5* can pick out objects the size of a baseball diamond from almost 700 miles above the planet.

But these days *SPOT 2*, launched and managed by the French space agency, boasts the keenest eyes in the sky available to civilian mappers, training high-resolution scanners on a continuous forty-mile ribbon around the earth's surface. Operating in multispectral mode (capturing red, green, and near-infrared wavelengths), SPOT's twin sensors can distinguish features sixty-five feet across; in black-and-white mode, they can resolve landmarks as small as thirty-two feet. The images are "rubber sheeted" by ground-based computers, a technique that stretches and doctors the data to compensate for the planet's curvature, the spacecraft's viewing angle, and other distortions. With aggressive marketing (Maps are lies, SPOT is truth, goes one unofficial corporate slogan), SPOT Image Corporation peddles its data in a variety of formats.

Among popular SPOT products are remotely sensed duplications of the U.S. Geological Survey's famous topographic maps. These break up the nation into standard rectangular map chunks known as quadrangles, or quads. SPOT quads provide an instant update of the Survey's quadrangles, some of which have fallen out-of-date. "You can't say they all reflect today's landscape," says University of South Carolina geographer David Cowen of the Survey maps. "It took the Survey a hundred years to map the country. SPOT quads help with fine-tuning." Aided by Cowen's department, South Carolina's government, for example, has mustered up-to-date SPOT coverage of the entire state, identifying new roads in rural regions to help plot economic development.

The one-two punch of high resolution and multispectral imaging has made SPOT the instrument of choice for mapping changes in land cover, especially encroachment on wilderness areas. Trees and tar, cornfields and concrete reflect the sun's radiation in distinctive spectral signatures that SPOT can measure. The U.S. Fish and Wildlife Service used a SPOT image to draw a vegetation base map of the Great Dismal Swamp National Wildlife Refuge, which straddles the Virginia-North Carolina border, in order to trace the shifting industrial and agricultural areas around the refuge. Meanwhile, planning new roads around Jacksonville, the Florida Department of Transportation employed SPOT data to distinguish sensitive wetlands from resilient uplands.

Yet even SPOT's acuity falls short of what some cartographers would like. Squint hard at a SPOT image and the geometry of streets and rivers stands out but you can't single out fence posts, electric pylons, manholes, and other small objects. In addition, objects viewed from space must be pinned to a matrix of longitude and latitude before they can be translated onto a map. Ground-based surveying teams, toting plane tables, theodolites, and trigonometric handbooks have traditionally fixed small features onto maps and continue to do so. Until remote-sensing satellites become more eagle eyed, their jobs are safe.

Just as mapmakers are turning to space-based tools, their counterparts in the surveying business also look skyward to refine their art. Many surveyors now rely on a fleet of military satellites called the Global Positioning System (GPS). These spacecraft broadcast meticulously timed digital pulses; a ground-based receiver, collecting signals from at least four satellites, can use these pulses to reckon its own longitude, latitude, and altitude.

The Pentagon designed GPS satellites to position soldiers and guide smart weapons to their targets. But GPS receivers were soon commercially available, alarming defense strategists: Anyone on the planet could tap GPS signals to steer a missile right into the men's room in the White House East Wing, for example. So last year the Department of Defense scrambled the signals so that only military receivers could use GPS to its full potential. (Ironically, the Pentagon had to lift GPS encryption during the Persian Gulf War because the military ran out of receivers, forcing them to equip soldiers with commercial GPS receivers.)

But surveyors have devised a neat trick to overcome the signal encryption. They place a GPS receiver on a landmark whose longitude and latitude is already known. They then walk around with another receiver to calibrate the degree of signal distortion. After adjusting for signal distortion, the receiver can establish its whereabouts to within three feet; stationary, to within inches.

The technique isn't cheap but for fast-growing areas in the Sunbelt it's worth the cost. Local communities have traditionally maintained a plethora of separate charts for tax assessment, property lines, police precincts, water and sewer lines, and so on. Many now want to scan the collection into a computer, coalescing the maps into a unified GIS to help plot growth. But there are problems. "The maps are supposed to fit together but sometimes old maps don't fit well because of the cartographic license they took back then, perhaps moving a stream's location or fudging a hill's placement so it would fit on the map," says Bill Daly, manager of mapping services for Huntsville, Alabama.

To resolve these inconsistencies, Daly's department turned to GPS. Surveyors laid out a GPS-derived network of control points using landmarks that stand out on different, but overlapping, aerial photographs. Guided by these landmarks, they could piece the different photos together. The result: a seamless, accurate base map of the area, detailed enough to show manholes, tiny streams, and other features. Cartographers then whisked the photographic map into a computer to generate custom renderings such as three-dimensional maps. Beyond giving the city the exact locations of its infrastructure, Daly's group has used the technique to identify slopes too steep or too aesthetically sensitive for proposed development projects.

Similar projects are underway at the U.S. Geological Survey's GIS Research Lab, where a staff of eight is developing maps that peer into the future. "There are a lot more uses for our data than just paper maps," says Nick Van Driel, chief of the GIS lab. For example, four years ago the Phelps-Dodge Mining Company offered to trade land with the Forest Service, hoping to sink an open-pit copper mine into terrain covered by Arizona's Prescott National Forest. The Forest Service called on the GIS Lab, where researchers loaded a computer with the Survey's own elevation data, a *Landsat* image, paper maps showing geology and water tables, land ownership boundaries, and the proposed mine plan. The computer responded with a three-dimensional view of the terrain, showing the mining operation's pits, ponds, and piles and spotlighting changes in drainage caused by the relandscaping. The image then swiveled to reveal how the proposed mine would stand out from different points along a nearby scenic road. Faced with this analysis, the land-swap deal collapsed.

The ability of GIS to model the future has given land-use planners powerful new capabilities. "There's a major transition going on right now," explains Douglas Gerull, executive vice president of the mapping sciences division of Intergraph Corporation, a leading vendor of computer-based mapping equipment. "First people used computers to make maps better, faster, and cheaper. Now they're using the data to manage the areas they mapped."

Managing data is a pet project of University of Wisconsin professor of landscape architecture Ben Niemann and his colleagues. Merging Landsat imagery with property-line maps and soil charts, they developed a GIS database that pinpointed sources of erosion in rural Wisconsin. Next they coupled the system with a water-quality assessment to model the impact of a proposed corporate headquarters on a nearby lake. Most recently they created a three-dimensional terrain map and trickled pesticides across the computerized landscape to illustrate how the chemicals would seep into bodies of water. "Before you implement a new policy," says Niemann, "you can predict its consequences on the landscape—you can ask, 'What if?' "

While local planners are benefiting from the new cartography, accurate geographic information is buoying the fortunes of modern commerce, just as improved navigational charts led Renaissance-era merchants to the riches of new worlds. Oil companies like Shell and Amoco siphon data from three-dimensional geological maps to keep track of exploration. For Federal Express and UPS, computerized maps deliver the fastest possible routes for package trucks. U.S. West, the phone company, calls on GIS to guide the marketing of premium services and the placement of new switching facilities.

The private sector's love affair with the technology has helped boost GIS into a big business. Sales of cartographic computers and software totalled $1.4 billion last year worldwide. But the explosive growth has lead to new concerns and disturbing trends.

True, the precision demanded by computer systems has prodded many cartographers to smarten up their data with remote sensing and other tools, but it's still possible, with some creative fudging, to shoehorn incompatible data into a single digital map. And when digital mapmakers have concocted a GIS from old maps without considering their original purpose, problems can multiply. "What happens when census maps are used for routing emergency vehicles? Who is liable when an ambulance runs into a dead end street?" asks Michael Goodchild, codirector of the National Center for Geographic Information and Analysis in Santa Barbara, California. "Maps are being held accountable relative to reality in ways they never should be." Other concerns are even more alarming. With we-know-where-you-live information so readily available, will the new cartographers turn from solving social problems to impinging on individual freedom? "The downside of the new cartography is that this is the technology of George Orwell," says Intergraph's Gerull. "If anything makes the Big Brother society possible, this will."

Easy access to geographic data has inspired a different perspective in the mind of Jack Dangermond, president of Environmental Systems Research Institute, or ESRI, a top seller of mapping software. Dangermond, considered a guru among the new cartographers, sees GIS as a means of opening windows for public scrutiny of governmental behavior. In short, as the technology becomes cheaper, the new cartographers will no longer just be bureaucrats—they'll be you and me. "We are the consumers of government," he argues. "Why not be a well-informed consumer?"

The current battle over congressional redistricting may furnish a proving ground for Dangermond's vision. With widespread use of GIS technology, state legislatures and governors' offices will no longer monopolize the tools to analyze the results of the 1990 census. As of April 1, 1991, the census data, which chart a block-by-block analysis of population, voting-age population, and racial makeup, has been publicly available on CD-ROM.

"Democrats, Republicans, caucuses, ethnic groups, anyone, can come up with their own proposal for reapportionment because the database is defined by public law," says Cowen of the University of South Carolina. "Equal access to the data elevates what was once a closed-door backroom deal to a level of democracy we've never seen before." In the case of redistricting, the new cartography stands to unlock a Pandora's box. But ESRI's Dangermond says that's just the point. He believes that digital mapping will allow people to grasp the connections between cultural, physical and geographic patterns. "We're reaching the ragged edge of sensitivity on this planet," he says. "Things are getting more complex, and there's not enough time to focus on them. GIS promises to interrelate things. Even if we can't solve our problems, we'll understand them."

Population, Resources, and Socioeconomic Development

Unit 5

The final section in this anthology includes articles on several important problems facing humankind. Geographers are keenly aware of regional and global difficulties. It is hoped that their work with researchers from other academic disciplines and representatives of business and government will bring about solutions to these serious problems.

Probably no single phenomenon has received as much attention in recent years as the so-called population explosion. World population continues to increase at unacceptably high rates. The problem is most severe in the less developed countries where, in some cases, populations are doubling in less than 20 years.

The first two articles in this unit deal with population policy in the developing world. The human population of the world passed the 5 billion mark in 1987, and it is anticipated that population increase will continue well into the twenty-first century, despite a slowing in the rate of population growth globally since the 1960s.

The following two articles discuss the related themes of population growth and food supply. As the human population increases, many more agriculturalists will be forced to depend on marginal land for growing food. Martha Farnsworth Riche's article follows, which discusses the radically changing ethnic composition of the U.S. population. David Aronson's article then deals with socioeconomic problems in sub-Saharan Africa. In the final unit article, Kathleen Newland addresses the tragic case of refugees in the world.

Looking Ahead: Challenge Questions

Are you personally affected by the population explosion? How?

Can you give examples of how economic development adversely affects the environment? Need this always happen?

What are natural resources? Give some examples.

How do you personally feel about the occurrence of starvation in developing world regions?

What might it be like to be a refugee?

Is colonialism a historic entity, or is it present today in certain forms?

How is Earth a system?

Are world systems sustainable? For how long?

What is your scenario of the world in the year 2000?

Population Policy Options in the Developing World

The population of the developing world is currently expanding at the unprecedented rate of more than 800 million per decade, and despite anticipated reductions in growth during the 21st century, its size is expected to increase from 4.3 billion today to 10.2 billion in 2100. Past efforts to curb this growth have almost exclusively focused on the implementation of family planning programs to provide contraceptive information, services, and supplies. These programs have been partially successful in reducing birth rates. Further investments in them will have an additional but limited impact on population growth; therefore, other policy options, in particular measures to reduce high demand for births and limit population momentum, are needed.

John Bongaarts

The author is director of the Research Division, The Population Council, One Dag Hammarskjold Plaza, New York, NY 10017, USA.

The arithmetic of global population growth has become numbingly familiar: 1 billion in 1800, 2.5 billion in 1950, and 5.5 billion today. In the past four decades more people have been added to the globe than in all of history before the middle of this century. And growth continues unabated. The world's population is now expanding at the unprecedented rate of nearly 1 billion per decade, and the United Nations and the World Bank project an additional 6 billion inhabitants by the end of the next century (*1, 2*). Virtually all of this growth is expected to occur in Africa, Asia, and Latin America; therefore, in this article I focus on the developing world.

Concern about the adverse effects of population growth on human welfare was expressed nearly 200 years ago by Thomas Malthus who concluded that "the power of population is indefinitely greater than the power in the earth to produce subsistence for man" (*3*). The result, he predicted, would be increasing deprivation and starvation as exponentially growing populations outstripped their food supply. Malthus was, of course, not without his critics who believed that increases in human knowledge and technological innovation would enable humankind to provide rising standards of living for growing populations. This debate has continued until today, with the optimists pointing to the notable successes in improving the welfare of much of humankind, whereas the neo-Malthusians emphasize the widespread poverty in the Third World and the many signs of stress in our environment: air, water, and soil pollution; global warming; and depletion of renewable and nonrenewable resources. Despite sharp disagreements about future prospects, there is broad agreement that a reduction in rapid population growth in the developing world will enhance the prospects for improved living standards of additional billions in the decades ahead. As a consequence, in recent decades concerted efforts to curb population growth have been undertaken in much of the developing world. An estimated $4 to $5 billion per year is now spent by the world on population programs in Africa, Asia, and Latin America (*4*).

In this article I review past approaches to population policy and assess alternatives available to governments of the developing countries. Such questions were discussed at the United Nations (U.N.) Conference on Environment and Development (the "Earth Summit") in Rio de Janeiro in 1992 and will be a focus at the U.N. International Conference on Population and Development in September 1994 in Cairo.

Population Policy Since 1950

The potential magnitude of the population problem became clear to demographers and a small group of development planners and activists in the early 1950s. Population had grown slowly over previous centuries, but a large expansion was expected after 1950. Although projections made in 1951 by the newly created Population Division of the U.N. considerably underestimated the actual course of growth (*5*), they led to strong concern about adverse effects of a large expansion of the human population on social and economic development in the developing world.

In response, organizations such as the International Planned Parenthood Federation (to link family planning programs appearing in many countries) and the Population Council (to serve as a scientific resource for the field) were created in 1952. India became the first country to adopt an official policy to reduce population growth by promoting family planning. However, on the whole, progress was slow initially, in part because birth control activists were not respected by the political establishment, and many governments were reluctant to intrude in the sensitive and private matters of human reproduction and sexuality. In addition, religious (mainly Catholic) and conservative groups strongly opposed birth control.

By the 1960s population growth had accelerated to more than 2.5% a year, and rates of growth were greater than 3% in many developing countries (*6*). The main cause was a decline in the death rate as a result of improved nutrition and public health measures such as immunization, antibiotics, and better sanitation. Birth rates remained high in much of the developing world. The threat of food shortages in the mid-1960s caused alarm about the race between food supply and population growth and provided an impetus for stronger government action, increased funding for population programs, and the establishment in 1967 of the U.N. Fund for Population Activities (UNFPA).

Governments concerned about the prospects of large increases in population typically responded by implementing family planning programs to provide information about and access to contraceptives. Newly available contraceptive methods, such as the birth control pill and the intrauterine device, greatly facilitated the delivery of family planning services. The rationale for this approach was largely provided by research on attitudes toward birth control and on knowledge and use of contraception. Surveys of women of reproductive age in the 1960s found that many women wanted to limit family size or space births but did not practice contraception (*7, 8*). This information reassured policy-makers of the acceptability of action programs.

By the early 1970s concern about the adverse consequences of population growth had increased to the point that family planning became a worldwide social movement. Several books as well as the extensive media coverage of the first U.N. Conference on the Human Environment held in Stockholm in 1972 raised global awareness of population and environment issues. This led to strong support for action and a large increase in funding from the developed countries, especially the United States (*9*). In addition, the health and human rights rationales for family planning became increasingly important. Numerous governments initiated family planning programs even though this approach remained politically sensitive and was a source of controversy. However, at the 1974 U.N.-sponsored World Population Conference, governments from the developing world resisted setting targets for lowering population growth and instead argued for a new international economic order to stimulate development. In the decade between the 1974 and 1984 World Population conferences, governments that were initially reluctant came to accept the importance of reducing population growth by implementing family planning programs (*10*). The Chinese government became so concerned about the consequences of population growth that it adopted a controversial one-child policy in 1978.

The implementation of family planning programs has in most countries been a key factor in assisting individuals in changing their reproductive behavior. In the developing world as a whole, the average number of children born per woman has declined from 6.1 in the mid-1960s to 3.8 in 1990, and the proportion of couples using contraception has risen sharply from less than 10% to 50% (*6, 11*). These averages conceal wide variations among regions (Table 1). The most rapid changes have occurred in East Asia where fertility has declined to 2.3 births per woman and contraceptive use is now at 75%—a level usually found in developed countries. In contrast, reproductive behavior has changed little in sub-Saharan Africa, although there are notable exceptions (for example, Botswana, Kenya, South Africa, and Zimbabwe) where fertility declines are now under way. These trends in reproductive behavior are also attributable to rapid social and economic development, which has reduced the motivation for large families. The relative contributions of family planning programs and socioeconomic development to fertility declines vary widely among countries. In a few (for example, China and Bangladesh), the effect of family planning programs predominates, whereas in many others socioeconomic development is more important.

Table 1. Estimates of total fertility rate and contraceptive prevalence rate for regions of the developing world, from 1960 to 1965 and in 1990 (*6, 11*).

Country	Total fertility rate (births per woman)		Contraceptive prevalence rate (% of married women)	
	1960 to 1965	1990	1960 to 1965	1990
Africa	6.8	6.1	5	17
East Asia*	5.9	2.3	13	75
South Asia†	6.0	4.3	7	41
Latin America	6.0	3.5	14	61
All developing countries	6.1	3.8	9	50

*Excluding Japan. †Including Southeast and West Asia.

By 1990 most governments of developing countries had adopted policies to reduce population growth, and 85% of the Third World's population now lives in countries in which the government considers the fertility rate too high (*12*). Most of these countries have implemented family planning programs, but the efforts and resources devoted to them vary widely (*13*), and the coverage and quality of services in many family planning programs need to be greatly improved.

Demographic Projections

Despite rapid changes in reproductive behavior during the past quarter century, population growth in the Third World continues at an unprecedented pace (Fig. 1). The population of the developing world is expected to grow from 4.1 in 1990 to 8.6 billion in 2050 and 10.2 billion in 2100, according to projections made by the World Bank (*2*). In 1990 Asia (excluding Japan, Australia, and New Zealand) had 3 billion inhabitants, nearly three quarters of the total of the developing world, and the population there is projected to more than double to 6.5 billion by 2100. Africa is projected to experience by far the largest relative growth: a nearly fivefold increase from 0.6 billion to 2.8 billion between 1990 and 2100. Latin America is the smallest of the three regions, and although its population size is expected to double to 0.9 billion over the same period, the absolute growth is substantially smaller than in Asia and Africa.

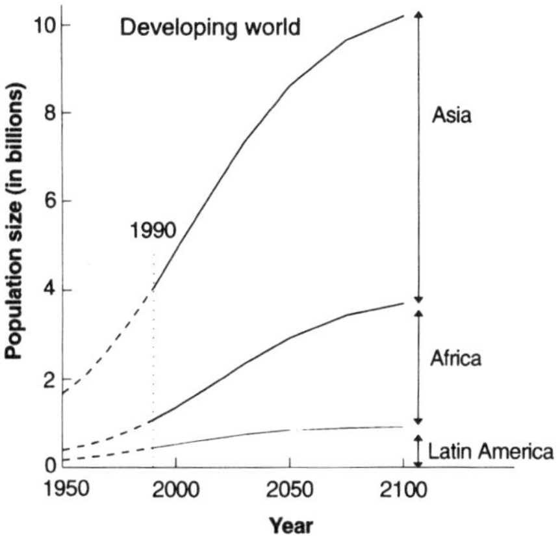

Fig. 1. Projections of population size for regions of the developing world, 1990 to 2100 (*2*).

The projected trend in population growth shown in Fig. 2 indicates that we are now at the climax of an unprecedented period of population expansion (*2*). Overall patterns of change in absolute annual additions to the population of the developing world (Fig. 2A) are similar to those in the rate of growth (Fig. 2B): At the beginning of this century, growth was low and it will again be low at the end of the next century, but there is rapid growth during the intervening years. Absolute annual population increments have been rising throughout this century, and during the 1980s, 774 million people were added to the Third World (*6*). More importantly, growth will likely exceed this level for the next three decades, adding 830 million in the 1990s and about the same again in the first two decades of the next century, before a decline is expected to occur as fertility reaches low levels.

Although the peak in absolute growth will occur in the next three decades, the rate of growth already reached its maximum in the late 1960s and has been declining since then. A declining growth rate is consistent with a growing absolute increment in population because the base population to which the growth rate applies keeps growing. When the fact that the growth rate had peaked became widely known in the late 1970s, some observers concluded that we had defused the population bomb (*14*). That conclusion is obviously incorrect because population will likely more than double before stabilizing, but the declining growth rate is good news and it is consistent with the claim that efforts to reduce population growth have had an impact.

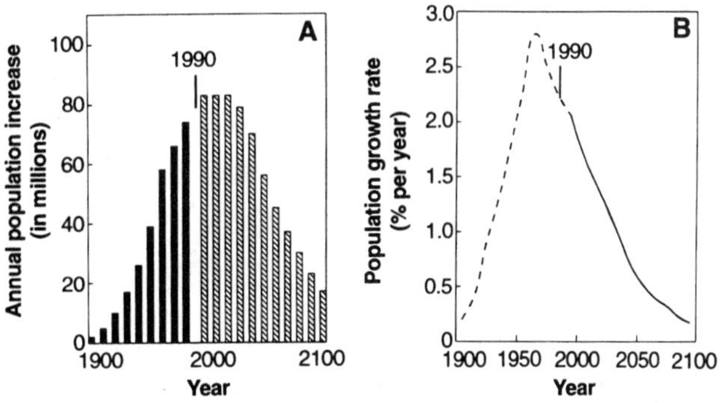

Fig. 2. Estimates and projections of (**A**) annual population increase and (**B**) population growth rate of the developing world (*2, 6*).

Future Policy Options

The already difficult task of reducing poverty and bringing about sustainable development in Africa, Asia, and Latin America will be made even more difficult by the expected addition of 6 billion people over the next century. Increased efforts to slow this population expansion are therefore desirable. Three broad policy options can be pursued.

1) *Reduce unwanted pregnancies by strengthening family planning programs.* The most direct way to bring about significant further fertility declines is by the implementation of comprehensive and high-quality family planning programs in all countries. Although past efforts have been substantial, services are still poor and limited in coverage in many countries. It is therefore not surprising that recent surveys in developing countries have found that many women who wish to delay or stop childbearing are not practicing contraception (*15*). Analysis of these findings suggests that one in six married women in the developing countries outside China has an unmet need for contraception—a total of about 100 million women (*16*). Estimates for unmarried women are not as readily available, but their needs are no doubt also substantial. The unmet need for contraception is highest in countries of sub-Saharan Africa (averaging near 25%), but even in Asia and Latin America, where services are much more accessible, unmet need levels of about 15% are typical in the countries for which data are available. These estimates are conservative because they are limited to women who are currently nonusers. There are, in addition, substantial numbers of contraceptive users who are not satisfied with their current method or who practice relatively ineffective methods that put them at risk of contraceptive failure.

The causes of this unmet need for contraception include (i) lack of knowledge of contraceptive methods or sources of supply; (ii) limited access to and low quality of family planning services; (iii) side effects and inconvenience of contraceptive methods; (iv) disapproval of husbands, family members, and others; and (v) cost of contraceptive commodities and travel.

Several of these problems can be addressed if family planning programs are strengthened by expanding coverage to unserved or underserved areas, improving service quality, providing more understandable contraceptive information through the media and in one-to-one communication with service providers, and giving ready access to a wider variety of birth control methods including abortion. In addition, existing programs need to reach out to groups such as adolescents and the sexually active unmarried who are now often excluded. With the implementation of these measures, programs can substantially increase the demand for contraception and reduce unmet need.

As a consequence of this unmet need for birth control, many women bear more children than they want. Approximately one in four births in the developing world (excluding China) is unwanted (*17*). In addition, there are approximately 25 million abortions annually, a large proportion of which take place under illegal or unsafe conditions, or both (*18*). Many of these undesirable pregnancies can be prevented if women are given greater control over their sexual and reproductive lives.

The central goal of family planning programs is to provide women and men with the information and means to control fully their fertility and thus eliminate mistimed and unwanted pregnancies. In addition to directly benefiting women and their families, the absence of unwanted childbearing would have a substantial effect on fertility and hence on population growth. I estimated the potential demographic effect of family planning programs by making a hypothetical projection of future population growth in which all unwanted fertility is eliminated after 1995. An estimated 20% of fertility in 1995–2000 will be unwanted (*19*), and I assumed that the trend in wanted fertility in the future is the same as the trend in total fertility projected by the World Bank, that is, a slow decline to replacement fertility in the middle of the next century (*2*). The results (Table 2) imply that the elimination of unwanted births after 1995 would reduce population growth and that the population size of the developing world would reach an estimated 7.5 billion in 2050 and 8.3 billion in 2100. This projection is considerably below the standard projection of the World Bank. The difference between the two projections provides an estimate of the demographic impact of unwanted fertility: 1.1 billion (8.6 minus 7.5) in 2050 and 1.9 billion (10.2 minus 8.3) in 2100. It should be emphasized that these projections are theoretical upper limits on what can be achieved. In practice, resource constraints, imperfect technology, human error, and reluctance of governments to take appropriate action pose limits on the impact of family planning programs. Even in countries with good programs, a significant proportion of women are reluctant to adopt methods because of concerns about their health and other side effects and pressures from spouses and other family members. However, there is no doubt that improvements in the quantity and quality of these programs can bring about substantial future reductions in fertility and population growth. In addition, strengthened support for family planning will bring substantial social and health benefits to women and children.

2) *Reduce the demand for large families through investments in human development.* Although family planning programs now claim the bulk of the attention and resources of population policy-makers, the potential effect of programs that provide supplies, services, and information is limited to reducing the unmet need for contraception. Because such programs are voluntary, they cannot reduce fertility below the level wanted by couples (*20*). As a consequence, this so-called "supply" approach cannot reduce population growth to zero in countries where, on average, desired fertility still exceeds two. This is apparently the case in most developing countries. An extensive survey program conducted in 27 countries in Africa, Asia, and Latin America in the late 1980s found no country with a desired family size at or close to two (*21*). These surveys documented a preference for large numbers of children in sub-Saharan Africa, and the average desired family size was close to six

Table 2. Projections of the population size of the developing world with and without unwanted births.

Projection	Projected population size (billions) in year 2050	2100
Standard* (with unwanted births)	8.6	10.2
Without unwanted births	7.5	8.3
Effect of unwanted fertility	1.1	1.9

*World Bank projection as quoted in Bos *et al.* (*2*).

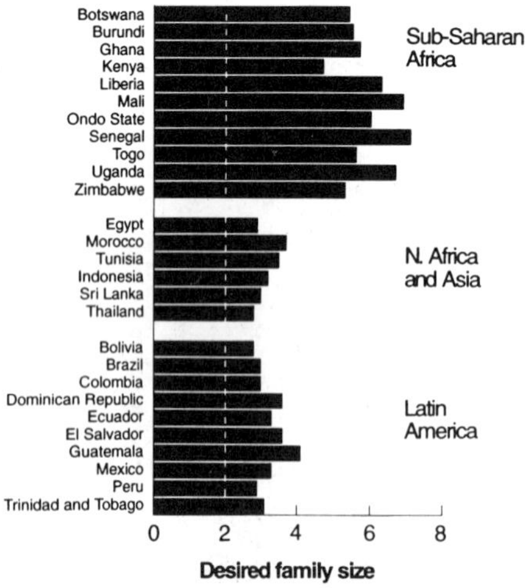

Fig. 3. Average desired family size among ever married women in selected developing countries, 1986 to 1989 (*15*).

(Fig. 3). Although the average desired number of surviving children in countries of Latin America, Asia, and North Africa was much lower, it still exceeded three in most cases. These preferences for high fertility remain one of the fundamental causes of high birth rates and rapid population growth.

A slow decline in fertility preferences is observable in most developing countries, and the expectation is that desired fertility will drop to around two children as these societies proceed through the transition from their traditional agricultural base to modern industrialized economies. Because this transition may take a long time, some policy analysts have advocated measures that reduce the demand for births through affirmative social and economic policies. The general objective is to change the costs and benefits of child rearing so that more parents will recognize the value of smaller families while simultaneously increasing the investment in children. Examples of factors potentially under government control include affecting (i) education levels, (ii) the status of women, and (iii) child mortality.

With regard to education, in traditional societies with largely agricultural economies, children are a valuable source of labor. The provision of educational opportunities, which require school attendance, lowers the labor value of children and raises their costs (for example, for books, uniforms, and school fees) (*22*). Of all the social and economic factors that have been studied for their potential effect on reproductive behavior, the level of education stands out as the most consistent (*23, 24*). This relation is attributable to shifts in the costs and benefits of children but also, and perhaps more importantly, to an acceleration in cultural change and the adoption of new, mostly western values that are facilitated by the introduction of mass schooling (*22*).

Improvements in the economic, social, and legal status of women can reduce desired fertility in several ways. Such improvements raise the cost of children by making nonmaternal roles more important. They also increase the willingness of women to make independent reproductive decisions and encourage them to engage in innovative contraceptive behavior. Empowering women is also likely to lead to reductions in the dominance of husbands (or other household members) over women, the societal preference for male offspring, and the value of (and thus need for) children as insurance against adversity (for example, in old age) and as securers of women's positions in families. Although the precise role of each of these effects varies among and within societies, there is little doubt that the overall effect of increasing gender equality significantly influences reproductive behavior (*25*).

A high death rate among children encourages high fertility for several reasons (*26*): (i) It makes the planning of families difficult because the number and timing of future deaths are unpredictable, thus contributing to fatalism. (ii) It discourages investments in children's health and education. (iii) It requires excess births to ensure that at least the desired number of children will survive to adulthood. All these effects can be counteracted by the implementation of public health measures to reduce infant and child mortality. The potentially important role of this variable is demonstrated empirically in that no population in the developing world has experienced a sustained fertility reduction without first having gone through a major decline in infant and child mortality.

Improving the education system, raising the status of women, and reducing child mortality are policy measures that are desirable in their own right. Indeed, most governments already pursue these socially desirable objectives independent of their potential role in lowering the rate of childbearing. The demographic benefits strengthen the rationale for intensifying these social policies.

Additional steps can be taken to encourage lower fertility. For example, monetary incentives for the adoption of specific birth control methods and disincentives for large families are features of population policies in a few countries (*27–29*). Although these measures can be successful, they raise serious ethical concerns and many governments are reluctant to adopt them (*29*). Another potential option for bringing about change in reproductive behavior is to increase a population's exposure to different life-styles through the media. Modern communication systems (radio, newspaper, and television) are powerful instruments for conveying ideas and messages about different nontraditional behaviors, family roles, and life-styles that are less compatible with large families (*30*). Although this exposure to mostly western ideas is considered a crucial element in ongoing fertility declines, it is rarely considered as a policy option because it would undermine increasingly popular efforts to strengthen national and ethnic identities of countries.

The potential demographic effect of additional efforts to implement policies to reduce fertility demand can be assessed by a comparison of population projections with and without such efforts. For this comparison I used the second projection in Table 2 because it assumes that high wanted fertility is the only reason for fertility to exceed the replacement level in the future. I also made a hypothetical new projection to simulate the potential effect of additional demand policies. In this new projection, the successful implementation of such policies is assumed to reduce fertility in all countries to the replacement level of two surviving children per woman after 1995. According to the results from these two projections, substantial further reductions in future population size, up to 0.6 billion in 2050 and 1 billion in 2100, are achievable by stronger measures to lower desired family size (Fig. 4). The relative role of demand for large families as a cause of population growth varies among countries and regions; it would, for example, be much larger in Africa than is the case in the decomposition for all developing countries shown in Fig. 4.

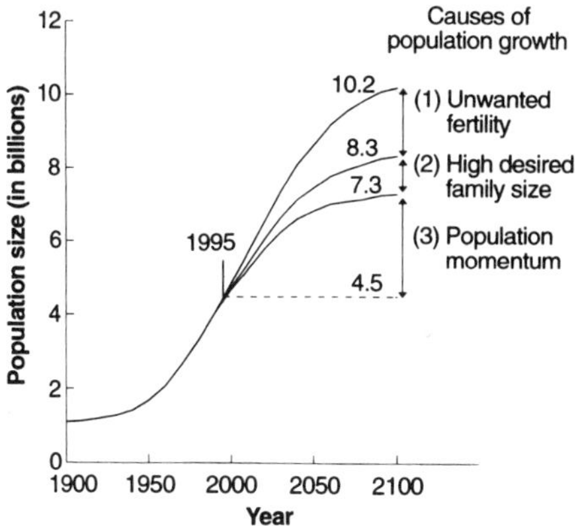

Fig. 4. Alternative projections of the population size for the developing world, 1995 to 2100, and three causes of population growth.

According to the standard projection of the World Bank (top graph in Fig. 4), the population size of the developing world will increase from 4.5 billion in 1995 to 10.2 billion in 2100. Aside from unwanted fertility and high desired family size, population momentum is responsible for the remaining growth over the next century (Fig. 4).

3) *Address population momentum*. Population momentum is the tendency of population size to increase for some time after fertility has reached a level consistent with long-range population stability (*31, 32*). As a result of the momentum, population growth would continue even if fertility could immediately be brought to the replacement level of two children per woman. Population momentum is primarily the consequence of a young population age structure (future mortality decline among adults is another, less important, cause of continued growth). Adjustments in the age structure after a decline in fertility take several decades to be completed, and it is only then that population size growth ceases. Unless efforts are made to reduce this momentum, the population of the developing world will grow to at least 7.3 billion. Attention to this neglected issue is essential because population momentum accounts for nearly half of the projected growth over the next century (Fig. 4).

There are two basic ways to bring about

Table 3. Simulated effect of delayed childbearing on population momentum if replacement fertility was reached in 1995.

Average age at childbearing	Population momentum* (billions)	Population in 2100, momentum only (billions)	Reduction resulting from delay (billions)
No change	2.8	7.3	0
Increase of			
2.5 years	2.2	6.7	0.6
5 years	1.6	6.1	1.2

*Momentum estimates include effect of future mortality decline.

Table 4. Average of median ages at marriage of ever married women ages 30 to 34 in 23 developing countries obtained from demographic and health surveys (*36*).

Level of education	Median age at marriage (years)	Median age at first birth (years)
None	17.6	19.3
Primary	19.1	20.2
Secondary	21.7	22.8

reductions in population momentum. The first involves additional declines in lifetime fertility to below the replacement level. In theory it is even possible to stop population growth completely by reducing fertility to the level needed to balance the number of births and deaths (assuming no migration). This is, of course, an undesirable option to implement because it would leave many women with only one birth, which is substantially fewer than most women want. It is unlikely that desired family size will drop substantially below two in most developing countries even with the demand measures discussed earlier.

A second option that has thus far received little attention is to raise the average age of women at childbearing. Research on the causes of fertility change in the United States has clearly demonstrated that the fertility in a given year is significantly affected by shifts in the timing of births. When successive age cohorts of women start their childbearing earlier and space their births closer together, fertility for that period temporarily rises. For example, Ryder concluded that much of the temporary rise in U.S. fertility in the 1950s (the "baby boom") was caused by changes in the timing of fertility rather than by variation in the desired fertility (*33*). Conversely, a delay in the onset of childbearing and wider spacing of births leads to a temporary decline in period fertility and hence in the population growth rate.

To determine the potential demographic effect of a rise in the age at childbearing, I used a simulation based on hypothetical population projections. I assumed that women over their life cycle bear children at the replacement level of two surviving births per woman, but that the mean age at childbearing is raised slowly over a 25-year period, from 1995 to 2020. Two postponements in timing were considered: 2.5 and 5 years (*34*). The results (Table 3) indicate that without changes in timing, the population momentum equals 2.8 billion in population growth between 1995 and 2100, that is, the difference between the 1995 population of 4.5 billion and the 7.3 billion projected for 2100 if fertility is kept at the replacement level (Fig. 4). This momentum would be reduced to 2.2 billion and 1.6 billion for delays of 2.5 and 5 years, respectively. Clearly, this approach to reducing population momentum has the potential for a substantial impact.

Governments that wish to encourage later childbearing have several options at their disposal. Legislation to raise the age at marriage has been moderately effective in a few countries (for example, Tunisia and China in the 1970s). However, legislation of this type has the drawback that it attempts to force rather than encourage changes in social customs. Indirect noncoercive approaches are preferable. An example of such an approach is greater investment in the education of girls, particularly at the secondary level. The longer girls stay in school, the later they marry and the greater the delay in childbearing. For example, in 23 developing countries, the median age of marriage of women with secondary education exceeded that of women with no education by 4 years (Table 4). This educational difference in age at marriage translates into a similar impact on the age at childbearing.

Another potentially effective approach is to address the neglected issues of adolescent sexuality and reproductive behavior. Many adolescents do not use contraception or use it sporadically when they become sexually active. As a result, childbearing often starts earlier than would be the case if young women had better information and services. Governments have been reluctant to address these problems of adolescents for social and political reasons.

Delays in childbearing can also be achieved by an increase in intervals between births. In general, however, the effect of a given increment in birth spacing on the mean age of childbearing (and hence on population momentum) is somewhat smaller than can be obtained by the same increment in the mean age at first birth, because spacing only affects subsequent births. Lengthening birth intervals also provides substantial health benefits for mothers and children; therefore, it should be encouraged for health as well as for demographic reasons.

Outlook

Past debates on alternative population policy approaches have frequently been contentious, with supporters of the supply and demand approaches each emphasizing their particular perspectives. In reality each of these approaches can be effective and neither of them should claim predominance. More importantly, the different approaches complement and reinforce one another. Reductions in demand for children or delays in childbearing that are achieved (for example, by increasing levels of education) do not by themselves reduce fertility. Instead, they raise the demand for contraception, and only if this demand is satisfied (for example, by services provided through family planning programs) will lower fertility be obtained. The fertility impact of the demand and delay strategies, therefore, depends to a significant extent on the availability of contraceptive information and services. Conversely, family planning programs are more successful in meeting couples' needs for contraception in societies with high levels of human development. For example, in a given supply environment, well-educated women satisfy their demand for contraception more effectively than their uneducated counterparts. The reasons for this are not entirely clear, but they presumably relate to the greater ability of educated women to control their lives as well as their superior knowledge of the fertility regulation methods and sources of supply. As a consequence, investments in family planning programs produce larger reductions in unwanted fertility when social conditions such as education and gender equality are favorable.

A comprehensive effort to implement all available policy options is required if humankind is to prevent the potentially severe, adverse consequences of continued rapid population growth. If the broad range of approaches proposed here is vigorously pursued, large reductions in future population growth can be achieved without resorting to the types of coercive measures that are objectionable to the majority of the world community.

REFERENCES AND NOTES

1. United Nations, Department of International Economic and Social Affairs (UNDIESA), *Long Range World Population Projections: Two Centuries of Population Growth 1950–2150* (United Nations, New York, 1992).
2. E. Bos, M. T. Vu, A. Levin, R. Bulatao, *World Population Projections 1992–93 Edition* (Johns Hopkins Univ. Press, Baltimore, MD, published for the World Bank, 1992).
3. T. R. Malthus, *Population: The First Essay* (1798; reprinted by Ann Arbor Paperbacks, Univ. of Michigan Press, Ann Arbor, MI, 1959).
4. *Effective Family Planning Programs* (World Bank, Washington, DC, 1993).
5. UNDIESA, *The Past and Future Growth of World Population: A Long-Range View* (United Nations, New York, 1951).
6. ———, *World Population Prospects 1990* (United Nations, New York, 1992).
7. R. Freedman, *Stud. Fam. Plann.* **18**, 57 (1987).
8. B. Berelson, in *Family Planning and Population Programs*, Proceedings of the International Conference on Family Planning Programs, Geneva, August 1965 (Univ. of Chicago Press, Chicago, 1966), pp. 655–668.
9. S. Conly and J. Speidel, *Global Population Assistance* (Population Action International, Washington, DC, 1993).
10. J. Finkle and B. Crane, *Popul. Dev. Rev.* **11**, 1 (1985).
11. UNDIESA, *Levels and Trends of Contraceptive Use as Assessed in 1988* (United Nations, New York, 1989).
12. ———, *World Population Monitoring Report 1991* (United Nations, New York, 1992).
13. W. P. Mauldin and J. A. Ross, *Stud. Fam. Plann.* **22**, 350 (1991).
14. For a comment on the related debate, see P. Demeny, *Popul. Dev. Rev.* **5**, 141 (1978).
15. C. Westoff, "Unmet need and the demand for family planning," *Demographic and Health Surveys, Comparative Studies No. 5* (Institute for Resource Development, Columbia, MD, 1991).
16. J. Bongaarts, *Popul. Dev. Rev.* **17**, 293 (1991).
17. ———, *ibid.* **16**, 487 (1990).
18. S. K. Henshaw and J. van Vort, *Abortion Factbook, 1992 Edition* (Alan Guttmacher Institute, New York, 1992).
19. For each country the proportion of fertility that is wanted (P) is estimated from the equation $P = 1.22 - 0.231\,TFR + 0.0252\,TFR^2$, where TFR is the projected level of the total fertility rate projected by Bos *et al.* for 1995–2000 (*2*). This equation was obtained by fitting a quadratic equation to estimates of TFR and P given in (*17*). Country-specific estimates of wanted fertility are calculated as $P \times TFR$, and their weighted average gives the level of the developing world as a whole. Because China is a special case, I assumed $P = 1.0$. The resulting estimate of 80% for the proportion of wanted births is, as expected, slightly below the 87% estimated for the United States in 1973 (*35*). The age-specific fertility rates in the baseline period (1995–2000) for age groups 15–19 to 45–49 were, respectively, 40, 147, 155, 111, 55, 17, and 2 births per 1000 women per year.
20. Some family planning programs also try to encourage couples to desire smaller families through information and education campaigns. Such efforts are considered to be relatively ineffective (*27*).
21. C. Westoff, "Reproductive preferences: A comparative view," *Demographic and Health Surveys, Comparative Studies No. 3* (Institute for Resource Development, Columbia, MD, 1991).
22. J. Caldwell, *Popul. Dev. Rev.* **6**, 225 (1980).
23. J. Cleland and G. Rodriguez, *Popul. Stud.* **42**, 419 (1988).
24. S. Cochrane, *Fertility and Education: What Do We Really Know?* (Johns Hopkins Univ. Press, Baltimore, MD, published for the World Bank, 1979).
25. K. Mason, *Sociol. Forum* **2**, 718 (1987).
26. C. Lloyd and S. Ivanov, *Stud. Fam. Plann.* **19**, 141 (1988).
27. B. Berelson, *Fam. Plann. Perspect.* **9**, 214 (1977).
28. P. Mauldin and S. Sinding, "Review of existing family planning policies and programmes: Lessons learned," *Working Paper No. 50*, presented at the United Nations Expert Group Meeting on Family Planning, Health, and Family Well-Being, Bangalore, India, 26 to 30 October 1992 (Population Council, Research Division, New York, 1993).
29. J. Cleland and W. Robinson, in *Family Planning Programmes and Fertility*, J. Phillips and J. Ross, Eds. (Clarendon, Oxford, 1992), pp. 159–177.
30. R. Freedman, in *International Encyclopedia of Population*, J. Ross, Ed. (Free Press, New York, 1982), vol. 1, pp. 450–451.
31. T. Frejka, in *ibid.*, pp. 950–451; T. Merrick, *Popul. Bull.* **41** (no. 2) (1989).
32. N. Keyfitz, *Demography* **8**, 71 (1971).
33. N. B. Ryder, in *Demographic Patterns in Developed Societies*, R. W. Hiorns, Ed. (Taylor and Francis, London, 1980), pp. 15–24. An analysis of the effects of changes in the timing of future childbearing on population growth in China is provided in J. Bongaarts and S. Greenhalgh, *Popul. Dev. Rev.* **11**, 585 (1985).
34. The estimates of the effect of delays in childbearing on future population growth are based on the assumption that current fertility levels in the developing world are not affected by changes in timing. Recent evidence of trends in age at first birth for Demographic and Health Survey countries suggests that this is a reasonable assumption (*36*).
35. L. B. Williams, *Fam. Plann. Perspect.* **23**, 212 (1991).
36. "An assessment of DHS-I data quality," *DHS Methodological Reports, No. 1* (Institute for Resource Development, Columbia, MD, 1990). Estimates of median ages at marriage and first birth are derived from computer data files for each country with a demographic and health survey.

Vicious Circles

African Demographic History as a Warning

TIMOTHY C. WEISKEL

Timothy C. Weiskel is Director of the Harvard Seminar on Environmental Values at Harvard Divinity School.

The terms of debate on global population issues have changed significantly in the last several decades. Theories which tried to isolate simple causes and define simple solutions have been discarded; we have come to recognize that the causes of population growth can only be found in the complexities of the international political economy and the ways it affects the cities and villages of the Third World. The "Developing World" is not developing along Western lines, nor does its demographic history mirror Europe's. Intelligent population policies must be informed by a thorough understanding of population dynamics and of the complex historical, cultural and economic circumstances within which they operate.

Human population growth was identified as a contemporary problem in the 1950s, with the advent of the post-World War II population surge. Initially, the use of birth control pills, condoms and other contraceptive techniques was thought to be the key to slowing population growth. Attention was thus focused on making these new technologies more widely available, especially in the Third World. Contraceptive technologies, however, proved less effective than originally promised. They were difficult to deliver and were resisted by local populations, who considered limits on their reproductive behavior to be limits on their potential livelihood. Rural populations in many parts of the Third World had come to depend upon large families to supply labor, create wealth and provide for the elderly. Thus, attempts to limit family size were regarded with mistrust and suspicion.

Attention eventually shifted to development and economic growth. The general correlation between higher levels of economic prosperity and lower birth rates seemed clear from analyses of global economic and demographic data—poverty appeared to cause excessive population growth. The strategic conclusion was that the population problem would solve itself if significant economic development occurred. With economists in the lead, population experts intoned in mantra-like fashion, "Development is the best contraceptive."

This thinking was guided by the model of "the demographic transition," a phenomenon observed in Europe as it underwent industrialization. One country after another moved from a pattern of high mortality and high birth rates to one of lower mortality and lower birth rates. This same demographic transition, it was thought, would occur throughout the world. The popularity of this model caused the goal of population stabilization to be subsumed by that of economic development. The problem with this approach, however, soon became clear: industrial development according to the European model was not inevitable or even probable in the Third World. Instead, many regions, particularly in Africa, experienced a decline in real GDP per capita. Unless unforseeable rates of economic growth were to spring forth miraculously in these regions, this demographic transition could not occur.

Furthermore, researchers have begun to notice that the presumed correlation between economic growth and declining birth rates is not as absolute as originally believed. Recent studies indicate that, despite a lack of economic growth, selected regions of India and Kenya have witnessed a marked decline in fertility. These studies challenge the idea that economic development is the primary cause of population stabilization. Women's status and education now appear to be far more significant than overall economic growth as a correlate of declining fertility. Many population experts have now embraced this insight, and it is likely to join economic development as a guiding

UN/Doranne Jacobson # 15321

Patterns of production based on cash crops impoverish developing nations.

principle in the formulation of population policy at the International Conference on Population and Development in Cairo this September.

Years of research and debate on population issues have failed to produce convincing mono-causal explanations or successful, unidimensional interventionist strategies; it is finally being accepted that there is no silver bullet. Neither birth control technologies nor development programs alone promise a solution to the population problem. Even programs aimed at improving women's education are not sufficient in themselves; they must be combined with sensitively designed family planning services and facilities.

The case of Bangladesh is instructive: in a poor, male-dominated society that deprives women of access to education, birth rates have been significantly slowed by family planning efforts. This led Jessica Tuckman Mathews of the Council on Foreign Relations to conclude in the *Washington Post* that, "the debate over which is more important, economic development or family planning, can finally be laid to rest. The slogan 'Development is the best contraceptive' stands exposed as the mindless rallying cry of people whose real agenda is opposition to family planning." It is now clear that more attention needs to be devoted to voluntary programs that address the reproductive needs of women.

Population growth is a bio-social problem embedded in the particular history and culture of a society. This realization leads to the awareness that simple mechanical models of causation ("A" causes "B") are inadequate tools for devising population policy. Such models posit that in order to effect a change in "B" one must attempt to change "A." This logic dominated both the contraceptive technology phase and the economic development phase of population policy discussion, but it is fundamentally unsuited to the problem.

We are coming to realize that population dynamics are not based on such simple relationships; their causality is cumulative, reciprocal and nested. It is *cumulative* in the sense that cultures are strongly bound to tradition. Accepted habits and norms of behavior change slowly and are influenced by the past at least as strongly as by prevailing contemporary circumstances. The causation of population growth is also *reciprocal*: while "A" may cause "B," it is equally true that, over time, "B" causes "A." For example, while having many children may reduce a family's welfare, declining family income may lead to a decision to have more children in an attempt to gain labor and eventually expand household income. Finally, this causation is *nested* because patterns of micro-behavior are conditioned by, and in turn, affect shifts in macro-behavior; local conditions are shaped by global circumstances and vice versa.

Population Growth in Africa: A Case Study

African demographic history provides an illustration of this three-fold framework for examining population dynamics. The magnitude of Africa's population expansion in recent decades is staggering. In 1950, the entire continent had an estimated population of 199 million.

By 1992, this figure had reached 682 million. The United Nations projects that by the year 2000 the continent will be home to 856 million people, and by the year 2025, 1.583 billion. How we account for this remarkable population surge will clarify some of the complexities of the population dilemma confronting us today.

At least five historical components have fueled African population growth. First, Africa's population grew during the slave-trade period. Very little is known about African demographics before the era of the European slave trade, but there is no doubt that the slave trade itself was a significant impulse for population expansion. The warfare and disorder involved in slave acquisition led to a state of generalized conflict in which maximum reproductive performance was highly valued and rewarded. All else being equal, larger families, villages and kingdoms survived more successfully in this state of insecurity than smaller ones.

We have blithely ignored the global patterns of economic integration, urbanization and migration that have conditioned and shaped local reproductive norms for the last five hundred years.

A further consequence of Europe's trade with the Americas was the introduction of foodstuff crops from the New World, like maize, groundnuts and cassava to West Africa. This new food supply made possible the growth of families and villages that, for reasons of self-defense, had become a necessity. Thus, the slave trade launched a fertility boom in Africa. But the fertility boom did not manifest itself as a population boom at the time for two reasons: mortality rates increased during the warfare engendered by the slave trade, and much of the added population was exported as slaves in what became known to demographers as "the largest non-voluntary migration in human history."

The slave trade and the warfare that it fueled lasted from roughly 1500 to 1850, establishing a pattern of large families; however, the impulse to have many children did not end with the close of the slave trade. Rather, European and American interactions with Africa in the latter half of the 19th century placed new demands on the continent's economy. These burdens motivated the second phase of African population growth. The "legitimate commerce" in palm oil, groundnuts, wild rubber and other tropical products put a premium on families that could mobilize large numbers of dependents in order to increase their household production. Thus, the cash-cropping boom of the 19th century—prior to formal colonial rule—maintained and extended the cultural logic that rewarded maximum reproductive performance.

The period of colonial conquest, from approximately 1885 to 1910, generated a third major component in Africa's population history. Much of this conquest was accomplished through destructive warfare. Moreover, in the wake of military intervention, African populations experienced a measurable decline from famine and epidemic disease. As is generally the case with catastrophes caused by famine, disease and warfare, Africa experienced a quick demographic rebound from these early colonial traumas. Thus, in many regions during the 1910s and 1920s a "baby boom" occurred which restored local populations to their pre-colonial numbers. International trade catalyzed this recovery. Based on the labor-intensive export of agricultural commodities, colonial cash-crop regimes—which continue to dominate African economies today, decades after the demise of colonial rule—gave even more support to the well-ingrained cultural preference for large families.

A fourth factor in Africa's population surge involved the gradual expansion of access to elementary hygiene and rudimentary medicine. Infant mortality rates were brought down by the investment in wells and sanitary water supplies for emerging African cities and the instruction in the use of that clean water. Large families (which, over the previous 400 years, had become culturally valued and economically rewarded) were now easier to maintain, since fewer infants died from childhood diseases.

The fifth historical factor contributing to Africa's contemporary population expansion was a remarkable period of urbanization. Whereas fewer than 12 percent of Africa's population lived in cities in 1950, nearly 25 percent did in 1980. This trend has continued; United Nations demographic indicators project that by the year 2010 more than 45 percent of Africa's population (440.9 million people) will be living in cities. In many parts of the world, urbanization is linked to declining fertility rates in the cities, but the impact upon the remaining rural populations is quite different. Many rural households view the loss of young adults to the cities as a "death," or at least as an export of labor. The net effect is to motivate rural households further to expand their dependent labor force by having more children.

Thus, a pattern of significant rural "out-migration" to the cities has actually served to motivate increased reproductive performance in rural areas. The growth of cities with their incessant demands for land, food, fuel and fodder has in turn accelerated the degradation of surrounding rural regions, driving more people off the land and into the cities, and further encouraging the rise of rural fertility rates. In Africa and elsewhere in the Third World, the growth of cities has had a very different impact on the demographics of society than it had in Europe. European urbanization, accompanied by industrialization, has led to marked *declines* in fertility on a society-wide basis. In the contemporary Third World, however, rapid urbanization may actually serve to stimulate society-wide *increases* in fertility, as rural areas seek to replace "lost" labor with more children.

Africa finds itself in what ecologists would call a massive "positive feedback loop." Having more children creates a vicious circle, the only perceived solution for which is to have even more children. Mobilizing greater amounts of dependent labor appears to be the only means households have to work their way out of poverty. The apparent solution is thus the source of the problem in the first place, and the vicious circle manifests itself as a cycle of decline.

African Demographics and the Global Economy

From an analytical perspective, Africa's contemporary population dynamics are best understood within the larger context of the continent's relation to the global economy. Mono-causal explanations do not account for Africa's population dynamics, and neither can these issues be adequately regarded as simply Africa's problem. Responsibility for Africa's population growth may be traced back hundreds of years; it is shared and should be acknowledged by those nations in Europe and the Western hemisphere whose economies have benefited from Africa's demographic history.

Once rural populations were drawn into this pattern of primary production, the local calculus of reproduction became intimately linked to the dynamics of the global economy.

Europe's expansion into Asia and the New World triggered massive demographic dislocations. The New World's population collapse, caused by the disease, famine and warfare engendered by early European encounters, created resource-rich but labor-scarce economies. Slaves from Africa supplied these economies with the means to build prosperity, and Africa became the specialized source for the production of human labor over a period of several hundred years. People were its most valued export commodity.

As European economies stopped demanding unskilled plantation labor and started demanding natural resource inputs for a growing industrial structure, Africa's expanding labor force was put to work in a succession of cash-crop booms. While the objects of this commerce may have changed from palm oil to wild rubber to coffee and cocoa, the underlying logic of expanding the household to expand prosperity was constantly reinforced.

In a broader sense, this pattern came to characterize the entire Third World, even those areas that were not formally absorbed into European colonial empires. While no other region became as involved in the export of labor as Africa did during the slave trade, cash-crop export economies linked to European industrial demand spread throughout Latin America, Asia and the Pacific. Once rural populations were drawn into this pattern of primary production, the local calculus of reproduction became intimately linked to the dynamics of the global economy.

Ironically, the very success of household production units has pressured them to expand their size. The Third World has produced surpluses of coffee, cocoa, tea, so high that the international glut of these commodities has led to a decline in their unit value. The result is what economists call "the primary producer's squeeze." The "squeeze" is simply this: in the face of the declining unit value of its commodity, the surest means available for a peasant household to maintain its income is to expand its production of that same commodity. This requires more labor, hence larger families. Yet, by expanding production in this manner, the primary producer contributes to an even greater glut of their particular commodity on world markets, which, in turn, leads to a further decline in its unit value. Receiving still less for the same volume of production, the peasant household is "squeezed" into expanding its production still further, and the vicious circle of population growth and subsequent emmiseration starts once again.

Urbanization and Population Growth

It is now becoming apparent that global patterns of urbanization are echoing those already manifest in Africa. Urban populations are increasing at rates that exceed average population growth. On a global scale, populations are continuing to grow, but, at an even faster pace, they are agglomerating in massive urban concentrations.

The evidence from Asia is the most dramatic in this regard. A recent report of the United Nations Economic and Social Council for Asia and the Pacific claimed that "by the year 2000, the population of Dhaka is expected to double to 12.2 million; Bombay, Calcutta, Delhi, Jakarta, Karachi, Manila and Shanghai [will] each gain four million people; and Bangkok, Bangalore and Beijing [will each gain] three million." There will be 21 cities with populations in excess of 10 million by the turn of the century, with 13 of these in the Asia-Pacific region. By the year 2020, the report estimates that 1.5 billion more people will be living in Asian cities: the equivalent of creating a new city of 140,000 people every day for the next thirty years.

In a similar vein, recent studies conducted by the Peace and Conflict Studies Program at the University of Toronto in cooperation with the American Academy of Arts and Sciences have drawn attention to rural out-migration in China. Citing Dr. Thomas Homer-Dixon, the author of one of these studies, the *New York Times* reported, "tens of millions of people are already trying to migrate to coastal cities from the country's rural north and interior which...cannot possibly support the next few decades' booming population." The result is the growth of these cities in a locally unsustainable manner; China's growing urban population will have to be supported by 25 percent less arable land per capita by the year 2010.

Chinese cities may therefore become dependent upon an international trade in surplus grains produced in Europe and the United States, as many African cities are today. Any sudden interruption of supply to these cities or continued environmental decline in rural areas could well rekindle age-old regional tensions or trigger ethnic conflict in Asia, as it already has in Africa. Dr. Homer-Dixon's

Population Council

Are growing cities one cause of rural population growth?

study suggests the emergence of a global pattern characterized by "falling grain prices and regional food surpluses in Western countries occurring simultaneously with scarcity-induced civil strife in parts of Africa and Asia." Recently reported rural strife in China is particularly troubling in this regard.

A newly published report of the International Food Policy Research Institute delivers another sobering message to population planners: "Over the next 20 to 30 years, farmers and policy-makers in developing countries will be challenged to provide food at affordable prices for almost 100 million [new] people every year—the largest annual population increase in history." Dr. Per Pinstrup-Anderson, the author of the Institute's study, *World Food Trends and Future Food Security*, quite bluntly claims, "Failure to significantly reduce population growth, particularly in sub-Saharan Africa, [within] the next 20 years will render all other development efforts insufficient to avoid greater human misery in the future." The report suggests that unless immediate commitments are made to undertake accelerated agricultural research, food production will not keep pace with population growth.

The problem we as population analysts face is our failure to develop a global understanding of population dynamics. Instead, we proceed with country-by-country demographic studies, expecting in each case that demographic change will mimic Europe's experience. We have blithely ignored the global patterns of economic integration, urbanization and migration that have conditioned and shaped local reproductive norms for the last five hundred years. In other words, we divide the world into the "West" and the rest—all those other people who are just waiting to pursue economic and social development on the West's terms.

However, Europe's "demographic transition" may prove to be the exception, not the rule. Similarly, while cities in the Western world have generally stabilized, this is surely not the trend in Third World areas. In the next twenty years 97 percent of world population growth will occur in what we now call the Third World—but perhaps should more accurately name the "Nine-Tenths" World.

Effective population policy can only emerge from a new understanding of the cumulative, reciprocal and nested character of population dynamics on a planetary scale. This expanded understanding of causation necessarily entails an enlarged sense of responsibility and a renewed sense of commitment to this issue on the part of all peoples and all nations. In effect, we face a global population problem without a global understanding of it. We persist in thinking that Africa or Asia have population problems—someone else, somewhere else, not us, not here. In reality, the world now has a human population problem that is most dramatically apparent in its weakest economies and most vulnerable ecosystems.

If we wish to survive as a global species, we must begin to think of ourselves as global citizens. In this context, who is "we"? Who is "they"? What is in our "national self-interest"? These are all concepts that will need to be re-cast as we struggle to forge a morally responsible world community.

Can the Growing Human Population Feed Itself?

As human numbers surge toward 10 billion, some experts are alarmed, others optimistic. Who is right?

John Bongaarts

JOHN BONGAARTS has been vice president and director of the Research Division of the Population Council in New York City since 1989. He is currently a member of the Johns Hopkins Society of Scholars and the Royal Dutch Academy of Sciences. He won the Mindel Sheps Award in 1986 from the Population Association of America and the Research Career Development Award in 1980–85 from the National Institutes of Health.

Demographers now project that the world's population will double during the next half century, from 5.3 billion people in 1990 to more than 10 billion by 2050. How will the environment and humanity respond to this unprecedented growth? Expert opinion divides into two camps. Environmentalists and ecologists, whose views have widely been disseminated by the electronic and print media, regard the situation as a catastrophe in the making. They argue that in order to feed the growing population farmers must intensify agricultural practices that already cause grave ecological damage. Our natural resources and the environment, now burdened by past population growth, will simply collapse under the weight of this future demand.

The optimists, on the other hand, comprising many economists as well as some agricultural scientists, assert that the earth can readily produce more than enough food for the expected population in 2050. They contend that technological innovation and the continued investment of human capital will deliver high standards of living to much of the globe, even if the population grows much larger than the projected 10 billion. Which point of view will hold sway? What shape might the future of our species and the environment actually take?

Many environmentalists fear that world food supply has reached a precarious state: "Human numbers are on a collision course with massive famines.... If humanity fails to act, nature will end the population explosion for us—in very unpleasant ways—well before 10 billion is reached," write Paul R. Ehrlich and Anne H. Ehrlich of Stanford University in their 1990 book *The Population Explosion.* In the long run, the Ehrlichs and like-minded experts consider substantial growth in food production to be absolutely impossible. "We are feeding ourselves at the expense of our children. By definition farmers can overplow and overpump only in the short run. For many farmers the short run is drawing to a close," states Lester R. Brown, president of the Worldwatch Institute, in a 1988 paper.

Over the past three decades, these authors point out, enormous efforts and resources have been pooled to amplify agricultural output. Indeed, the total quantity of harvested crops increased dramatically during this time. In the developing world, food production rose by an average of 117 percent in the quarter of a century between 1965 and 1990. Asia performed far better than other regions, which saw increases below average.

Because population has expanded rapidly as well, per capita food production has generally shown only modest change; in Africa it actually declined. As a consequence, the number of undernourished people is still rising in most parts of the developing world, although that number did fall from 844 million to 786 million during the 1980s. But this decline reflects improved nutritional conditions in Asia alone. During the same period, the number of people having energy-deficient diets in Latin America, the Near East and Africa climbed.

Many social factors can bring about conditions of hunger, but the pessimists emphasize that population pressure on fragile ecosystems plays a significant role. One specific concern is that we seem to be running short on land suitable for cultivation. If so, current efforts to bolster per capita food production by clearing more fertile land will find fewer options. Between 1850 and 1950 the amount of arable land grew quickly to accommodate both larger populations and greater demand for better diets. This expansion then slowed and by the late 1980s ceased altogether. In the developed world, as well as in some developing countries (especially China), the amount of land under cultivation started to decline during the 1980s. This drop is largely because spreading urban centers have engulfed fertile land or, once the land is depleted, farmers have abandoned it. Farmers have also fled from irrigated land that has become unproductive because of salt accumulation.

Moreover, environmentalists insist that soil erosion is destroying much of the land that is left. The extent of the damage is the subject of controversy. A recent global assessment, sponsored by the United Nations Environment Program and reported by the World Resources Institute and others, offers some perspective. The study concludes that 17 percent of the land supporting plant life worldwide has lost value over the past 45 years. The estimate includes erosion caused by water and wind, as well as chemical and physical deterioration, and ranks the degree of soil degradation from light to severe. This degradation is least prevalent in North

Chronically Undernourished Individuals

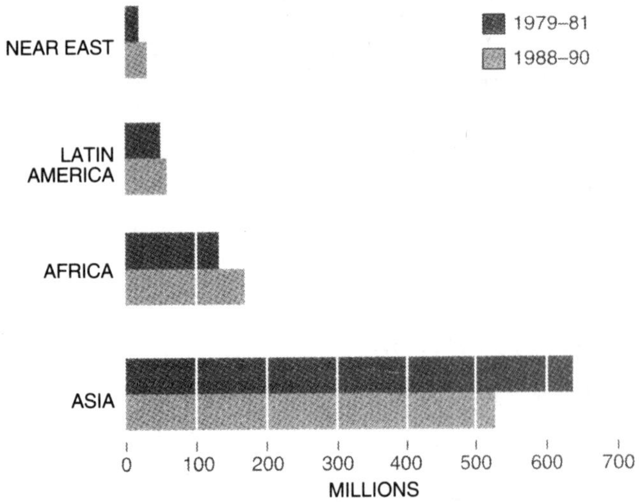

Crop Yields Needed in 2050

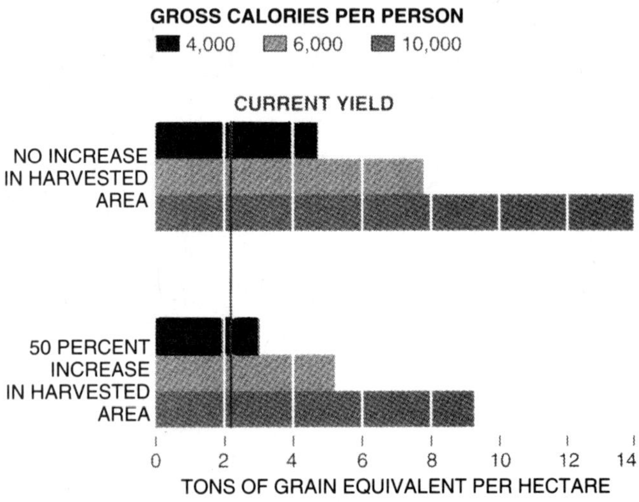

INCIDENCE OF CHRONIC UNDERNUTRITION fell in the developing world from an estimated 844 million sufferers in 1979 to 786 million in 1990, showing evidence of dramatic nutritional improvements in Asia (*left*). Agricultural productivity must improve to continue this trend (*right*). Even if more land is harvested in 2050, the average yield must rise sharply as well to offer the projected Third World population of 8.7 billion the current diet of 4,000 gross calories per day.

America (5.3 percent) and most widespread in Central America (25 percent), Europe (23 percent), Africa (22 percent) and Asia (20 percent). In most of these regions, the average farmer could not gather the resources necessary to restore moderate and severely affected soil regions to full productivity. Therefore, prospects for reversing the effects of soil erosion are not good, and it is likely that this problem will worsen.

Despite the loss and degradation of fertile land, the "green revolution" has promoted per capita food production by increasing the yield per hectare. The new, high-yielding strains of grains such as wheat and rice have proliferated since their introduction in the 1960s, especially in Asia. To reap full advantage from these new crop varieties, however, farmers must apply abundant quantities of fertilizer and water.

Environmentalists question whether further conversion to such crops can be achieved at reasonable cost, especially in the developing world, where the gain in production is most needed. At the moment, farmers in Asia, Latin America and Africa use fertilizer sparingly, if at all, because it is too expensive or unavailable. Fertilizer use in the developed world has recently waned. The reasons for the decline are complex and may be temporary, but clearly farmers in North America and Europe have decided that increasing their already heavy application of fertilizer will not further enhance crop yields.

Unfortunately, irrigation systems, which would enable many developing countries to join in the green revolution, are often too expensive to build. In most areas, irrigation is essential for generating higher yields. It also can make arid land cultivable and protect farmers from the vulnerability inherent in natural variations in the weather. Land brought into cultivation this way could be used for growing multiple crop varieties, thereby helping food production to increase.

Such advantages have been realized since the beginning of agriculture: the earliest irrigation systems are thousands of years old. Yet only a fraction of productive land in the developing world is now irrigated, and its expansion has been slower than population growth. Consequently, the amount of irrigated land per capita has been dwindling during recent decades. The trend, pessimists argue, will be hard to stop. Irrigation systems have been built in the most affordable sites, and the hope for extending them is curtailed by rising costs. Moreover, the accretion of silt in dams and reservoirs and of salt in already irrigated soil is increasingly costly to avoid or reverse.

Environmentalists Ehrlich and Ehrlich note that modern agriculture is by nature at risk wherever it is practiced. The genetic uniformity of single, high-yielding crop strains planted over large areas makes them highly productive but also renders them particularly vulnerable to insects and disease. Current preventive tactics, such as spraying pesticides and rotating crops, are only partial solutions. Rapidly evolving pathogens pose a continuous challenge. Plant breeders must maintain a broad genetic arsenal of crops by collecting and storing natural varieties and by breeding new ones in the laboratory.

The optimists do not deny that many problems exist within the food supply system. But many of these authorities, including D. Gale Johnson, the late Herman Kahn, Walter R. Brown, L. Martel, the late Roger Revelle, Vaclav Smil and Julian L. Simon, believe the world's food supply can dramatically be expanded. Ironically, they draw their enthusiasm from extrapolation of the very trends that so alarm those experts who expect doom. In fact, statistics show that the average daily caloric intake per capita climbed by 21 percent (from 2,063 calories to 2,495 calories) between 1965 and 1990 in the developing countries. These higher calories have generally delivered greater amounts of protein. On average, the per capita consumption of protein rose from 52 grams per day to 61 grams per day between 1965 and 1990.

According to the optimists, not only has the world food situation improved significantly in recent decades, but further growth can be brought about in various ways. A detailed assessment of climate and soil conditions in 93 developing countries (excluding China) shows that nearly three times as much land as is currently farmed, or an additional 2.1 billion hectares, could be cultivated. Regional soil estimates indicate that sub-Saharan Africa and Latin America can exploit many more stretches of unused land than can Asia, the Near East and North Africa.

Even in regions where the amount of potentially arable land is limited, crops could be grown more times every year than is currently the case. This scenario is particularly true in the tropics and subtropics where conditions are such—relatively even temperature throughout the year and a consistent distribution of daylight hours—that more than one crop would thrive. Nearly twice as many crops are harvested every year in Asia than in Africa at present, but further increases are possible in all regions.

In addition to multicropping, higher yields per crop are attainable, especially in Africa and the Near East. Many more crops are currently harvested per hectare in the First World than elsewhere: cereal yields in North America and Europe averaged 4.2 tons per hectare, compared with 2.9 in the Far East (4.2 in China), 2.1 in Latin America, 1.7 in the Near East and only 1.0 in Africa.

Such yield improvements, the enthusiasts note, can be achieved by expanding the still limited use of high-yield crop varieties, fertilizer and irrigation.

The Potential Impact of Global Warming on Agriculture

The scientific evidence on the greenhouse effect indicates that slow but significant global warming is likely to occur if the emission of greenhouse gases, such as carbon dioxide, methane, nitrogen oxide and chlorofluorocarbons, continues to grow. Agriculture is directly or, at least in some cases, indirectly responsible for releasing a substantial proportion of these gases. Policy responses to the potentially adverse consequences of global climatic change now focus primarily on hindering emissions rather than on halting them. But considering the present need to improve living standards and produce more food for vast numbers of people, experts doubt that even a reduction in global emissions could occur in the near future.

In a 1990 study the Intergovernmental Panel on Climate Change estimated that over the next century the average global temperature will rise by three degrees Celsius. The study assumes that agriculture will expand considerably. This forecast of temperature change is uncertain, but there is now broad agreement that some global warming will take place. All the same, the effect that temperature rise will have on human society remains an open question.

Global warming could either enhance or impede agriculture, suggest Cynthia Rosenzweig of Columbia University and Martin L. Parry of the University of Oxford. Given sufficient water and light, increased ambient carbon dioxide concentrations absorbed during photosynthesis could act as a fertilizer and facilitate growth in certain plants. In addition, by extending the time between the last frost in the spring and the first frost in the fall, global warming will benefit agriculture in cold regions where the growing season is short, such as in Canada and northern areas of Europe and the former Soviet Union. Moreover, warmer air holds more water vapor, and so global warming will bring about more evaporation and precipitation. Areas where crop production is limited by arid conditions would benefit from a wetter climate.

If increased evaporation from soil and plants does not coincide with more rainfall in a region, however, more frequent dry spells and droughts would occur. And a further rise in temperature will reduce crop yields in tropical and subtropical areas, where certain crops are already grown near their limit of heat tolerance. Furthermore, some cereal crops need low winter temperatures to initiate flowering. Warmer winters in temperate regions could therefore stall growing periods and lead to reduced harvests. Finally, global warming will precipitate a thermal swelling of the oceans and melt polar ice. Higher sea levels may claim low-lying farmland and cause higher salt concentrations in the coastal groundwater.

Techniques used to model the climate are not sufficiently advanced to predict the balance of these effects in specific areas. The most recent analysis on the impact of climatic change on the world food supply, by Rosenzweig and Parry in 1992, concludes that average global food production will decline 5 percent by 2060. And they anticipate a somewhat larger drop in the developing world, thus exacerbating the problems expected to arise in attempts to feed growing populations. In contrast, their report predicts a slight rise in agricultural output in developed countries situated at middle and high latitudes.

POSSIBLE BENEFITS OF GLOBAL WARMING ON AGRICULTURE

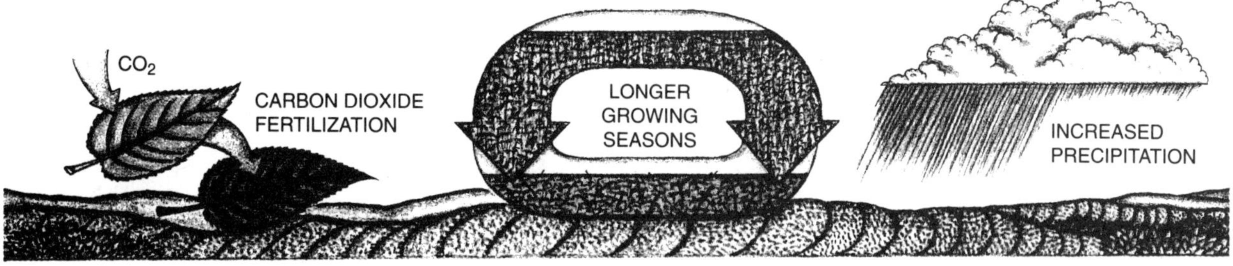

POSSIBLE DRAWBACKS OF GLOBAL WARMING ON AGRICULTURE

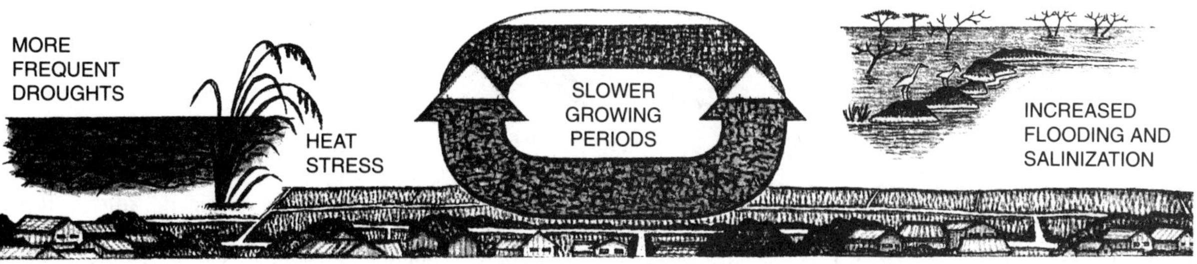

Change in Food Production between 1965 and 1990

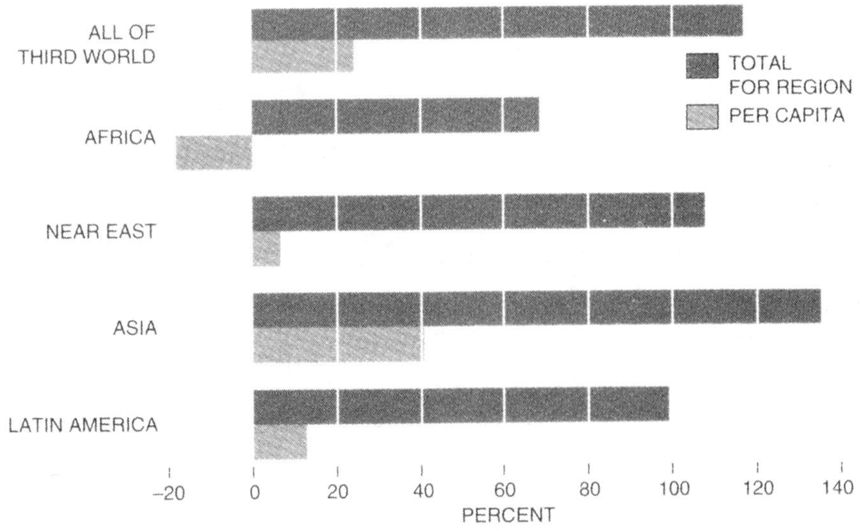

Soil Erosion of Vegetated Land

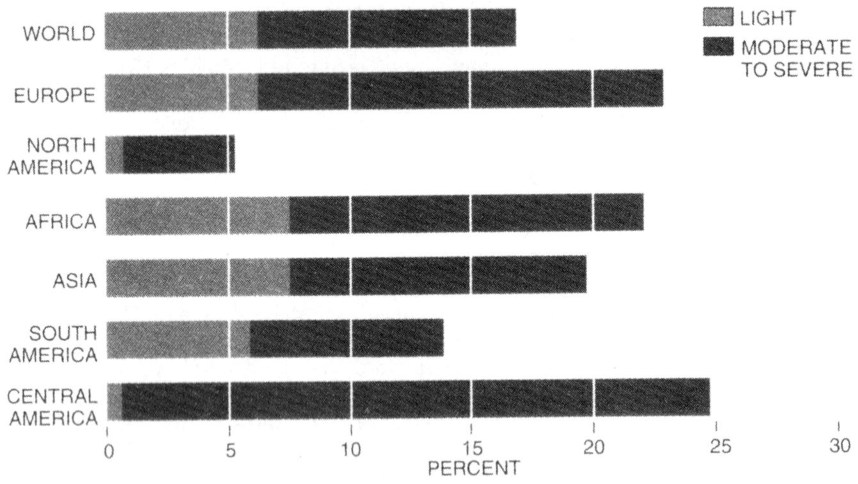

Arable Land

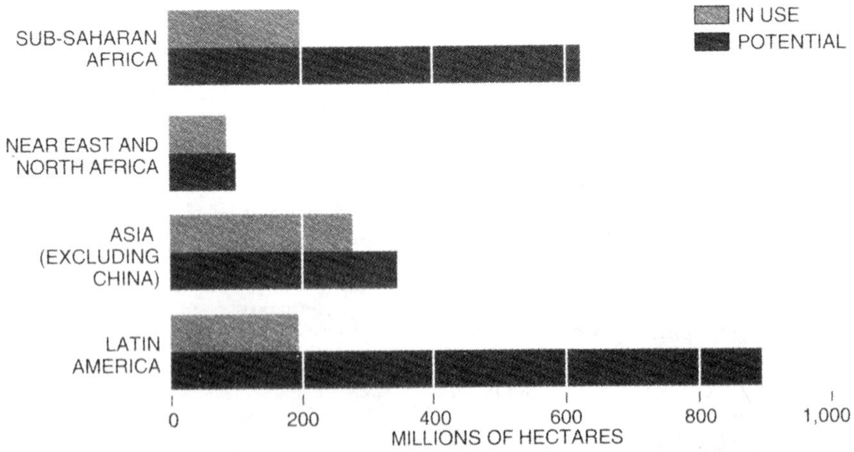

TOTAL FOOD PRODUCTION rose nearly 120 percent between 1965 and 1990 in the developing world. Per capita food production showed little change in regions outside Asia (*top*). Soil erosion has debased much of the land worldwide on which that food was produced (*middle*). But many Third World nations have vast holdings that could be farmed successfully if given more water and fertilizer (*bottom*).

In *World Agriculture: Toward 2000,* Nikos Alexandratos of the Food and Agriculture Organization (FAO) of the United Nations reports that only 34 percent of all seeds planted during the mid-1980s were high-yielding varieties. Statistics from the FAO show that at present only about one in five hectares of arable land is irrigated, and very little fertilizer is used. Pesticides are sparsely applied. Food output could drastically be increased simply by more widespread implementation of such technologies.

Aside from producing more food, many economists and agriculturalists point out, consumption levels in the developing world could be boosted by wasting fewer crops, as well as by cutting storage and distribution losses. How much of an increase would these measures yield? Robert W. Kates, director of the Alan Shawn Feinstein World Hunger Program at Brown University, writes in *The Hunger Report: 1988* that humans consume only 60 percent of all harvested crops, and some 25 to 30 percent is lost before reaching individual homes. The FAO, on the other hand, estimates lower distribution losses: 6 percent for cereals, 11 percent for roots and 5 percent for pulses. All the same, there is no doubt that improved storage and distribution systems would leave more food available for human nutrition, independent of future food production capabilities.

For optimists, the long-range trend in food prices constitutes the most convincing evidence for the correctness of their view. In 1992–93 the World Resources Institute reported that food prices dropped further than the price of most nonfuel commodities, all of which have declined in the past decade. Cereal prices in the international market fell by approximately one third between 1980 and 1989. Huge government subsidies for agriculture in North America and western Europe, and the resulting surpluses of agricultural products, have depressed prices. Obviously, the optimists assert, the supply already exceeds the demand of a global population that has doubled since 1950.

Taken together, this evidence leads many experts to see no significant obstacles to raising levels of nutrition for world populations exceeding 10 billion people. The potential for an enormous expansion of food production exists, but its realization depends of course on sensible governmental policies, increased domestic and international trade and large investments in infrastructure and agricultural extension. Such improvements can be achieved, the optimists believe, without incurring irreparable damage to global ecosystems.

Proponents of either of these conflicting perspectives have difficulty accepting the existence of other plausible points of view. Moreover, the polarity between the two sides of expert opinion shows that neither group can be completely correct. Finding some common ground between these seemingly irreconcilable positions is not as difficult as it at first appears if empirical issues are emphasized and important differences in value systems and political beliefs are ignored.

Both sides agree that the demand for food will swell rapidly over the next several decades. In 1990 a person living in the developing world ate on average 2,500 calories each day, taken from 4,000 gross calories of food crops made available within a household. The remaining 1,500 calories from this gross total not used to meet nutritional requirements were either lost, inedible or used as animal feed and plant seed. Most of this food was harvested from 0.7 billion hectares of land in the developing world. The remaining 5 percent of the total food supply came from imports. To sustain this 4,000-gross-calorie diet for more than twice as many residents, or 8.7 billion people, living in the developing world by 2050, agriculture must offer 112 percent more crops. To raise the average Third World diet to 6,000 gross calories per day, slightly above the 1990 world average, food production would need to increase by 218 percent. And to bring the average Third World diet to a level comparable with that currently found in the developed world, or 10,000 gross calories per day, food production would have to surge by 430 percent.

A more generous food supply will be achieved in the future through boosting crop yields, as it has been accomplished in the past. If the harvested area in the developing world remains at 0.7 billion hectares, then each hectare must more than double its yield to maintain an already inadequate diet for the future population of the developing world. Providing a diet equivalent to a First World diet in 1990 would require that each hectare increase its yield more than six times. Such an event in the developing world must be considered virtually impossible, barring a major breakthrough in the biotechnology of food production.

Instead farmers will no doubt plant more acres and grow more crops per year on the same land to help augment crop harvests. Extrapolation of past trends suggests that the total harvested area will increase by about 50 percent by the year 2050. Each hectare will then have to provide nearly 50 percent more tons of grain or its equivalent to keep up with current dietary levels. Improved diets could result only from much larger yields.

The technological optimists are correct in stating that overall world food production can substantially be increased over the next few decades. Current crop yields are well below their theoretical maxima, and only about 11 percent of the world's farmable land is now under cultivation. Moreover, the experience gained recently in a number of developing countries, such as China, holds important lessons on how to tap this potential elsewhere. Agricultural productivity responds to well-designed policies that assist farmers by supplying needed fertilizer and other inputs, building sound infrastructure and providing market access. Further investments in agricultural research will spawn new technologies that will fortify agriculture in the future. The vital question then is not how to grow more food but rather how to implement agricultural methods that may make possible a boost in food production.

A more troublesome problem is how to achieve this technological enhancement at acceptable environmental costs. It is here that the arguments of those experts who forecast a catastrophe carry considerable weight. There can be no doubt that the land now used for growing food crops is generally of better quality than unused, potentially cultivable land. Similarly, existing irrigation systems have been built on the most favorable sites. Consequently, each new measure applied to increase yields is becoming more expensive to implement, especially in the developed world and parts of the developing world such as China, where productivity is already high. In short, such constraints are raising the marginal cost of each additional ton of grain or its equivalent. This tax is even higher if one takes into account negative externalities—primarily environmental costs not reflected in the price of agricultural products.

The environmental price of what in the Ehrlichs' view amounts to "turning the earth into a giant human feedlot" could be severe. A large inflation of agriculture to provide growing populations with improved diets is likely to lead to widespread deforestation, loss of species, soil erosion and pollution from pesticides, and runoff of fertilizer as farming intensifies and new land is brought into production. Reducing or minimizing this environmental impact is possible but costly.

Given so many uncertainties, the course of future food prices is difficult to chart. At the very least, the rising marginal cost of food production will engender steeper prices on the international market than would be the case if there were no environmental constraints. Whether these higher costs can offset the historical decline in food prices remains to be seen. An upward trend in the price of food sometime in the near future is a distinct possibility. Such a hike will be mitigated by the continued development and application of new technology and by the likely recovery of agricultural production and exports in the former Soviet Union, eastern Europe and Latin America. Also, any future price increases could be lessened by taking advantage of the underutilized agricultural resources in North America, notes Per Pinstrup-Andersen of Cornell University in his 1992 paper "Global Perspectives for Food Production and Consumption." Rising prices will have little effect on high-income countries or on households possessing reasonable purchasing power, but the poor will suffer.

In reality, the future of global food production is neither as grim as the pessimists believe nor as rosy as the optimists claim. The most plausible outcome is that dietary intake will creep higher in most regions. Significant annual fluctuations in food availability and prices are, of course, likely; a variety of factors, including the weather, trade interruptions and the vulnerability of monocropping to pests, can alter food supply anywhere. The expansion of agriculture will be achieved by boosting crop yields and by using existing farmland more intensively, as well as by bringing arable land into cultivation where such action proves economical. Such events will transpire more slowly than in the past, however, because of environmental constraints. In addition, the demand for food in the developed world is approaching saturation levels. In the U.S., mounting concerns about health have caused the per capita consumption of calories from animal products to drop.

Still, progress will be far from uniform. Numerous countries will struggle to overcome unsatisfactory nutrition levels. These countries fall into three main categories. Some low-income countries have little or no reserves of fertile land or water. The absence of agricultural resources is in itself not an insurmountable problem, as is demonstrated by regions, such as Hong Kong and Kuwait, that can purchase their food on the international market. But many poor countries, such as Bangladesh, cannot afford to buy food from abroad and thereby compensate for insufficient natural resources. These countries will probably rely more on food aid in the future.

Low nutrition levels are also found in many countries, such as Zaire, that do possess large reserves of potentially cultivable land and water. Government neglect of agriculture and policy failures have typically caused poor diets in such countries. A recent World Bank report describes the damaging effects of direct and indirect taxation of agriculture, controls placed on prices and market access, and overvalued currencies, which discourage exports and encourage imports. Where agricultural production has suffered from misguided government intervention (as is particularly the case in Africa), the solution—policy reform—is clear.

Food aid will be needed as well in areas rife with political instability and civil strife. The most devastating famines of the past decade, known to television viewers around the world, have occurred in regions fighting prolonged civil wars, such as Ethiopia, Somalia and the Sudan. In many of these cases, drought was instrumental in stirring social and political disruption. The addition of violent conflict prevented the recuperation of agriculture and the distribution of food, thus turning bad but remediable situations into disasters. International military intervention, as in Somalia, provides only a short-term remedy. In the absence of sweeping political compromise, hunger and malnutrition will remain endemic in these war-torn regions.

Feeding a growing world population a diet that improves over time in quality and quantity is technologically feasible. But the economic and environmental costs incurred through bolstering food production may well prove too great for many poor countries. The course of events will depend crucially on their governments' ability to design and enforce effective policies that address the challenges posed by mounting human numbers, rising poverty and environmental degradation. Whatever the outcome, the task ahead will be made more difficult if population growth rates cannot be reduced.

FURTHER READING

POVERTY AND HUNGER: ISSUES AND OPTIONS FOR FOOD SECURITY IN DEVELOPING COUNTRIES. World Bank, 1986.

ENERGY, FOOD, ENVIRONMENT: REALITIES, MYTHS, OPTIONS. Vaclav Smil. Clarendon Press, 1987.

WORLD AGRICULTURE: TOWARD 2000. Nikos Alexandratos. New York University Press, 1988.

WORLD RESOURCES 1992–93. World Resources Institute. Oxford University Press, 1992.

THE LANDSCAPE OF HUNGER

We have seen the victims of mass starvation. We have shuddered at the images of millions of people arriving at remote camps for aid. Many of the world's famines result from wars or civil strife. But we rarely see that hunger also grows from environmental ruin.

BRUCE STUTZ

Bruce Stutz is features editor at Audubon. *He is the author of* Natural Lives, Modern Times.

The numbers alone are staggering: In 1990, 550 million people worldwide were hungry, 56 million more than in the early 1980s. During that time, the number of malnourished children in the developing world increased from 167 million to 188 million. And experts predict that the situation will only get worse as food production in the poorest countries continues to decline.

Deforestation, desertification, and soil erosion have devastating effects on food production. Where forests are cut down, the soils are washed or blown away. Where land is planted too often or grazed too long, it can no longer support crops or cattle.

Ironically, modern agriculture—the science of growing food—has had the greatest impact on the decline in the food supply. In the 1960s governments began encouraging nomads to settle in one place, to raise one cash crop instead of several, to herd only one kind of livestock, and the soils quickly became exhausted.

This "green revolution"—intensified farming of "improved crop varieties" with irrigation, chemicals, and pesticides—at first raised productivity, but the long-term results were just the opposite. According to Mostafa K. Tolba, former executive director of the United Nations' Environment Programme, the process "made agroecosystems increasingly artificial, unstable, and prone to rapid degradation."

Population growth and refugee migration add to the problems of environmental degradation. When the land becomes too crowded and the soil too exhausted to support life, farmers move into forests, slashing and burning new farms. As the land gives out, the people move on, again and again. Eventually, they find their way to the refugee camps.

At the 1972 United Nations Conference on the Human Environment in Stockholm, environmental issues were considered secondary to issues of economic development. But the 1968–74 drought in Ethiopia and the Sahel made it evident that the environmental costs of traditional economic development might be too high.

The Ethiopian government estimated that its highlands were then losing ap-

From *Audubon*, Vol. 95, No. 2, March/April 1993, pp. 54-63.

proximately 1 billion tons of soil a year through water and wind erosion. So when development experts convened at the United Nations Conference on Environment and Development (UNCED) last June, the agenda had changed. The environment had to be protected, it was decided. The diplomats finally recognized the simplest truth: The land that produces the food must be preserved.

The food web inextricably connects plants, animals, and people with the water, soil, and atmosphere of the planet; the hunger web begins as those connections are severed. Air and water pollution contaminate and ruin food sources. The predictions are that global warming will also have an effect, changing planting times, growing seasons, even the ability of crops to survive in their present ranges.

On the following pages *Audubon* examines the environmental causes of mass hunger and some possible solutions. Most do not involve high-tech, grand-scale megaprojects; the best of them are low-tech, local, modest in scale. The solutions may not be as dramatic as scenes of armies massing to feed millions. But they are sustainable—which means that in the future hunger may be defeated without the help of armies.

DEFORESTATION

Slash, Burn, Plow, Plant, Abandon

Forests now cover 27.7 percent of all ice-free land in the world. In 1990 wood was the main energy source for 9 out of 10 Africans, providing more than half of their fuel. By the end of this decade, according to Mostafa Tolba, 2.4 billion people will be unable to satisfy their minimum energy requirements without consuming wood faster than it is being grown.

As human beings encroach on the world's remaining woodlands, deforestation will exacerbate the problems of hunger. For when hillsides are denuded, soil erosion sets in.

In Haiti, where forests once covered most of the land, 40 to 50 million trees are cut each year to supply firewood, cropland, and charcoal. At the current rate of deforestation, Haiti's forests will cease to exist within two or three years.

Already, loss of forests has caused massive soil erosion, and when drought strikes, the quality of the remaining soil will decline. When rain finally *does* fall, runoff will be too rapid and farmers will be forced to abandon cultivation. Since the 1970s, food aid to Haiti has risen sevenfold.

In Bangladesh and India, deforestation has caused another kind of problem, increasing the frequency and force of floods. Bangladesh used to suffer a catastrophic flood every 50 years or so; by the 1980s the country was being hit with major floods—which wash away farms and rice paddies—every four years. Between the late 1960s and late 1980s, India's flood-prone areas grew from approximately 25 million hectares to 59 million. (One hectare equals 2.4 acres.)

PROTECT AND PRESERVE

Although some countries, notably Brazil and Costa Rica, have preserved tracts of their forested land, less than 5 percent of the world's remaining tropical forests are protected as sanctuaries, parks, or reserves.

Regenerating woodlands by replanting them would provide some measure of relief. Over the past 10 years, China has reforested some 70 million hectares of endangered landscape. The U.N. Food and Agriculture Organization estimates that 1.1 million hectares of trees are successfully planted each year worldwide.

Modifying wood stoves to make them more efficient and increasing use of solar cooking would slow the decline of forests by decreasing reliance on wood for fuel.

Using the forests sustainably—by tapping trees for rubber, for example, or developing environmentally sound tourism—would provide more revenue than slash-and-burn agriculture.

DESERTIFICATION
The Spreading Barrens

Every year nearly 6 million hectares of previously productive land becomes desert, losing its capacity to produce food. The United Nations defines desertification as "land degradation in arid, semiarid, and dry subhumid areas [drylands] resulting mainly from adverse human impact." Translated into human suffering, that phrase means that by 1977, 57 million people had seen their lands dry up. By 1984 the number had risen to 135 million worldwide. Today, one-sixth of the total world population is threatened with desertification.

When drylands—which make up about 43 percent of the total land area of the world—revert to desert, hunger follows almost axiomatically. Most crops can't survive in the parched landscape, and harvests fail. Further, withered root systems can't hold the soil, and winds finally erode whatever topsoil remains.

Arid landscapes are so fragile that they break down quickly. A drought can mean catastrophe. In Mozambique, for instance, civil war combined with a worsening drought last year to leave 3.1 million people in need of food aid, 1.2 million more than in 1991.

But Africa is not the only place where food supplies are threatened by desertification. In Russia, annual desertification and sand encroachment northwest of the Caspian Sea were estimated to be as high as 10 percent. Around the drying Aral Sea, the desert has been growing at some 100,000 hectares per year for the last 25 years, an annual desertification rate of 4 percent.

STAVING OFF DISASTER

Agroforestry—planting trees as windbreaks and shade to protect pastureland—contributes to the maintenance of hard-used fields. In Kenya, for example, the Green Belt Movement has embarked on a large-scale tree-planting program.

Massive irrigation projects, such as those tried in Nigeria (see "Death of an Oasis," [Audubon] May-June 1992), are less practical, benefiting only a few at great cost to the environment. Small-scale projects, as low-tech and low-cost as collecting and managing rainwater, are often slow and laborious, but according to the Bread for the World Institute on Hunger and Development, they have succeeded in reclaiming hundreds of hectares of degraded land.

SOIL EROSION
A Worldwide Dust Bowl

Worldwide, erosion removes about 25.4 billion tons of soil each year. Deforestation and desertification both leave land open to erosion. In deforested areas, water washes down steep, naked slopes, taking the soil with it. In desertified regions, exposed soils, cleared for farming, building, or mining, or overgrazed by livestock, simply blow away. Wind erosion is most extensive in Africa and Asia. Blowing soil not only leaves a degraded area behind but can bury and kill vegetation where it settles. It will also fill drainage and irrigation ditches.

When high-tech farm practices are applied to poor lands, the result is often a combination of soil washing away and chemical pesticides and fertilizers polluting the runoff.

In Africa, soil erosion has reached critical levels, with farmers pushing farther onto deforested hillsides. In Ethiopia, for example, soil loss occurs at a rate of between 1.5 billion and 2 billion cubic meters a year, with some 4 million hectares of highlands considered "irreversibly degraded."

In Asia, in the eastern hills of Nepal, 38 percent of the land area consists of fields that have been abandoned because the topsoil has washed away. In the Western Hemisphere, Ecuador is losing soil at a rate 20 times what would be considered acceptable by the U.S. Soil and Conservation Service. And even in the United States, 44 percent of cropland is affected by erosion.

DEFEATING THE ELEMENTS

According to the International Fund for Agricultural Development (IFAD), traditional labor-intensive, small-scale efforts at soil conservation—which combine maintenance of shrubs and trees with crop growing and cattle grazing—work best.

In the Barani area of Pakistan, a program begun by IFAD in 1980 to control rainfall runoff, erosion, and damage to rivers from siltation has resulted in a 20 to 30 percent increase in crop yields and livestock productivity.

POPULATION GROWTH
More Mouths to Feed

With a population growth rate of 1.7 percent, the world added almost 100 million people in 1992; an increase of some 3.7 billion is expected by 2030. Since 90 percent of the increase will occur in developing countries in Africa, Asia, and Latin America, the outlook is bleak: None of those countries can expect to produce enough food to feed a population increasing at such rates.

Population growth and environmental damage go hand in hand with poverty and hunger. In sub-Saharan Africa, for example, as colonial governments replaced pastoral lifestyles with sedentary farming, populations grew and farming and grazing intensified. Today, 80 percent of the region's pasture- and rangelands show signs of damage, and overall productivity is declining. Yet during the next 40 years the sub-Saharan population is expected to rise from 500 million to 1.5 billion.

Today only Bangladesh, South Korea, the Netherlands, and the island of Java have population densities greater than 400 people per square kilometer. (By comparison, the population density of the United States works out to 27 per square kilometer.)

By the middle of the next century, one-third of the world's population will probably live in overcrowded conditions. Bangladesh's population density could rise to 1,700 per square kilometer.

In Madagascar, population pressures have forced farmers to continuously clear new land. Virtually all the lowland forests in the country are gone. But cleared soil wears out quickly. Per capita calorie supply in Madagascar has fallen by 9 percent since the 1960s, probably the greatest decline anywhere in the world.

In Nepal, one of the world's poorest nations, increased population (700 people per square kilometer of cultivable land, the world's highest average) has forced villagers to expand their farm plots onto wooded hillsides. Marginal farmers rely on livestock, which they allow to graze in the remaining forests. Terraced soil once used for crop production has been abandoned for lack of nutrients, putting more pressure on ever-diminishing forest resources.

CHOOSING THE FUTURE

If a fertility rate of slightly more than two children per couple can be achieved by the year 2010, the world's population will stabilize at 7.7 billion by 2060. If that rate is not reached until 2065, world population will reach 14.2 billion by 2100.

According to a 1992 World Bank report, improving education for girls is an important long-term policy in the developing world. The more educated a woman is, the more likely she is to work outside the home and the smaller her family is likely to be. Choice also plays a role here: The United Nations' World Fertility Survey has found that women would have an average of 1.41 fewer children if they were able to choose the size of their family. Access to birth control methods could help lower the world's population by as many as 1.3 billion people over the next 35 years. During the Reagan-Bush years U.S. funding to programs offering such information was cut back; but President Bill Clinton has reversed that stand.

Somalia: An Ecopolitical Tragedy

Somalia's breakdown of law and order has created new waves of famine in recent months, but the groundwork for civil strife was laid by years of misuse of the nation's precious grazing lands and water resources.

Almost the entire country is categorized by the United Nations Environment Programme as susceptible to soil degradation, and most of the country is overgrazed.

Over the years the degradation was accelerated by the parceling out of communal grazing lands to private owners, which undermined traditional systems of land management. Private herds—which are generally larger than those owned communally—have stripped the hillsides bare, causing wind erosion during droughts and runoff during rains.

Building dams across valleys to halt water runoff in the north of the country has made matters worse by disrupting the natural drainage systems.

In the south the productivity of irrigated fields has been lessened by poor water management, which has created saline, waterlogged soils on the edge of the desert. There the salt will render the soil useless for food production in the decades to come.

—*Fred Pearce*

ENVIRONMENTAL REFUGEES
A Moveable Famine

The cycle of overpopulation, poverty, environmental ruin, and famine begins all over again when those trying to find a better life flee their ruined homelands. Land degradation is the largest cause of environmental-refugee movements.

According to Jodi L. Jacobson, a senior researcher at Worldwatch Institute, in Washington, D.C., 135 million people live in areas undergoing severe desertification.

But when those refugees move into areas that are already stressed by overpopulation or too intense agriculture, they place an added burden on the environment. Refugees need wood for fuel, water to drink, land on which to graze their livestock, and grain to eat—all of which are already scarce.

Jacobson estimates that some 10 million people worldwide are refugees from environmental ruin. "Competition for land and natural resources is driving more and more people to live in marginal, disaster-prone areas," she says, "leaving them more vulnerable to natural forces. Hence, millions of Bangladeshis live on *chars,* bars of silt and sand in the middle of the Bengal delta, some of which are washed away each year by ocean tides and monsoon floods."

CLIMATE CHANGE
Global Warning

Since 1800 atmospheric concentration of carbon dioxide (CO_2) has increased by about 25 percent and continues to rise each year. Over the same period atmospheric methane concentrations have doubled. Since the 1960s more than 100 separate studies have confirmed that a doubling of the CO_2 concentration would raise average surface temperatures by one to four degrees centigrade; three degrees is the figure used by the United Nations' Intergovernmental Panel on Climate Change.

Although a small number of scientists dispute these findings, weather and climate remain the biggest concern for farmers as warming begins to change growing seasons, irrigation needs, and land use. These changes will be especially serious in tropical regions, where farmland is already marginal and crops are growing near the limits of their temperature tolerance.

Those who live along shorelines will be hardest hit: The greenhouse effect could cause a global mean sea level rise of about six centimeters per decade. At that rate, many islands would become uninhabitable, and currently productive lowlands would be flooded. The developing countries that now experience the worst food shortages can expect to be hurt most by global warming. A study conducted by the University of Oxford and the Goddard Institute for Space Studies, funded by the U.S. Environmental Protection Agency, found that with an increase in average temperatures of three to four degrees centigrade, grain production in developing countries would decline by 9 to 11 percent by the year 2060, putting between 60 and 360 million people at risk from hunger—10 to 50 percent more than the currently predicted 640 million.

CLOSING THE GREENHOUSE

The use of renewable, or nonfossil, fuels—and more efficient use of all fuels—would go far to control the buildup of CO_2.

The World Bank recommends that governments remove energy subsidies and that they tax the use of carbon fuels. Maintenance of the world's large remaining forests would also help: Tropical deforestation accounts for 10 to 30 percent of the CO_2 released into the atmosphere.

The Oxford–Goddard Institute study found that slowing population increases could allow developing nations to cope more readily with the changing climate by changing land use and farming practices.

Hunger and the Ozone Hole

In early 1992 researchers from five U.S. marine-science institutes reported a drop of 6 to 12 percent in phytoplankton production under the Antarctic ozone hole. It appears that tiny marine organisms, which constitute more than half of all biomass on earth, may not be able to withstand harmful wavelengths of ultraviolet light—UV-B radiation—that penetrate the earth's thinning ozone layer.

When ozone holes form in the spring, most of the fish, shellfish, and crustaceans that humans harvest are in their larval, planktonic stages—floating in the topmost layer of the ocean. "Increasing intensities of UV-B radiation near the surface could negatively impact the reproductive potential of some of our most valuable marine resources, including tuna, pollock, cod, halibut, and flounder," wrote John Hardy, an associate professor at Huxley College, Western Washington University, in the November 1989 issue of *Oceanography.* Juvenile crabs, lobsters, shrimp, and anchovies are also vulnerable.

Just how such damage might move up the food chain is not known, but in Newport, Oregon, the Environmental Protection Agency's stratospheric ozone–depletion team found preliminary evidence of retarded growth in amphipods fed with phytoplankton that had been exposed to UV-B.

Although the leading industrial nations have agreed to halt production of the worst ozone-destroying compounds by 1996, ozone depletion is expected to continue for several decades as existing chemicals seep into the stratosphere. An ozone hole is likely to appear over the Northern Hemisphere, where ozone is dwindling at an estimated 1 percent per year. Each 1 percent decline in ozone is thought to increase exposure to biologically harmful ultraviolet light by at least 2 percent.

The United Nations Environment Programme warns that a 16 percent reduction in stratospheric ozone (which could occur in the next few years) would trigger a 6 to 9 percent drop in seafood production. Oceans now provide more than 30 percent of the animal protein eaten by humans.

—Brad Warren

We're All Minorities Now

SUMMARY Racial and ethnic diversity increases the differences between urban, rural, rich, and poor Americans. Children are most likely to be nonwhite or Hispanic, but the aging of diversity will have profound effects on consumer markets in the 1990s. Businesses can respond by using consumer information to unite diverse niches into profitable markets.

Martha Farnsworth Riche

Martha Farnsworth Riche is director of policy studies at the Population Reference Bureau in Washington, D.C.

The United States is undergoing a new demographic transition: it is becoming a multicultural society. During the 1990s, it will shift from a society dominated by whites and rooted in Western culture to a world society characterized by three large racial and ethnic minorities. All three minorities will grow both in size and share, while the still-significant white majority will continue its relative decline.

Whites represent eight in ten Americans, the 1990 census found, down from nine in ten as recently as 1960. Subtract white Hispanics, and you discover that only about three out of four Americans are non-Hispanic whites.

During the 1980s, the U.S. received 6 million legal immigrants, up from 4.2 million during the 1970s and 3.2 million during the 1960s. Few immigrants now are of European origin. Immigrants also tend to have more children than the non-Hispanic white population, as do Hispanics and blacks. Together, these two factors are boosting the share of minorities in the population.

All Americans are now members of at least one minority group.

These trends are also creating diversity within the minority population. According to the Census Bureau, the 1990 census missed 1 in 20 blacks and Hispanics. Nevertheless, it gives an accurate picture of the rapid growth in their numbers. In 1990, 12 percent of Americans identified themselves as black, 9 percent as Hispanic origin (some of whom are also black), 3 percent as Asian or Pacific Islander, 1 percent Native Americans, and 4 percent "other." The first three groups will continue to grow faster than the white population. As each group grows, diversity within them will grow too.

These trends signal a transition to a multicultural society. If you count men and women as separate groups, all Americans are now members of at least one minority group. Without fully realizing it, we have left the time when the nonwhite, non-Western part of our population could be expected to assimilate to the dominant majority. In the future, the white Western majority will have to do some assimilation of its own.

Government will find that as minority groups grow in size relative to one another, and as the minority population gains on the dwindling majority, no single group will command the power to dictate solutions. The debate over almost any public issue is likely to become more confrontational. Reaching a consensus will require more cooperation than it has in the past.

The new demographic transition may be particularly difficult for business because it parallels an equally momentous economic transition. As the economy moves away from manufacturing and phys-ical skills and toward services and knowledge skills, a real danger emerges. The economic transition is increasing inequality in both incomes and opportunities. This inequality happens within and across racial and ethnic groups, and it has the potential to polarize both consumers and employees.

YOUTH *equals* DIVERSITY

Most immigrants are young, and minorities generally have more children than whites. As a result, minorities are a progressively larger share of the population at younger ages.

(percent of population in each group by age)

	white	black	Hispanic	Asian/ Pacific Islander	American Indian	other races
0 to 9	74.8%	15.0%	12.6%	3.3%	1.1%	5.9%
10 to 19	75.1	15.1	11.6	3.3	1.1	5.4
20 to 29	77.3	13.1	11.5	3.3	0.8	5.5
30 to 39	79.9	12.0	8.9	3.3	0.8	4.0
40 to 49	82.9	10.4	7.1	3.1	0.7	2.9
50 to 59	84.4	10.1	6.4	2.6	0.6	2.3
60 to 69	87.4	8.8	4.8	1.9	0.5	1.5
70 to 79	89.3	7.9	3.5	1.4	0.4	0.9
80 or older	90.4	7.5	3.2	1.0	0.3	0.8
All ages	80.3	12.1	9.0	2.9	0.8	3.9

Note: Hispanics may be of any race; therefore, the percentages do not total to 100.

Source: 1990 census data

DIVERSITY DIFFERENCES

Immigration will add more Americans in the 1990s than it did in the 1980s, due to legislation enacted in 1990. The Immigration and Naturalization Service projects that legal immigration will exceed 700,000 per year starting in 1992. That compares with 600,000 immigrants per year as recently as the late 1980s. Illegal immigration will push the total even higher.

The 1990 law will also increase diversity among immigrants—notably at the upper end of the income scale. It allows people who have no family here to immigrate if they have highly prized work skills, or if they are ready to make a significant business investment. The law nearly tripled the number of visas (to 140,000 a year) for engineers and scientists, multinational executives and managers, and other people with skills in demand. This includes 10,000 visas a year for investor immigrants who will put at least $1 million into the economy and create ten jobs. (The entrance fee drops to $500,000 in rural areas and areas of high unemployment.)

Immigrants tend to join their peers, and their peers tend to live in large coastal cities. California, New York, Texas, Florida, Illinois, and New Jersey are expected to get three of every four new immigrants, who will be joining already-large minority populations in those states. In California, non-Hispanic whites will become a minority within the next two decades.

Central cities are still the front line for processing immigrants into society, and native-born minorities and older immigrants are also moving into suburban areas. Asians are most likely to integrate into white suburbs. Suburban blacks are still relatively segregated, according to research by Richard D. Alba and John R. Logan of the State University of New York at Albany. Hispanics fall somewhere in between.

These locational patterns ensure that multiculturalism will evolve unevenly across the country. As a result, many states and cities will become increasingly unlike the rest of the country.

Multiculturalism is not monolithic, either. The difference among Hispanic subgroups has been well documented; Cuban Americans are an economic and political dynasty in Miami, but no similar clout exists for Puerto Ricans in New York or Chicanos in Texas and California. One-quarter of the Hispanic population in 1990 was the product of immigration during the 1980s, if you include the children of immigrants. And 43 percent of Hispanics are immigrants from the 1970s and 1980s, according to Jeffrey Passel and Barry Edmonston of the Washington, D.C.-based Urban Institute.

Differences are even more pronounced in the fast-growing Asian American population. Passel and Edmonston report that 43 percent of the Asian American population in 1990 came from immigration during the 1980s, and 70 percent from immigration during the 1970s and 1980s. In 1970, the Asian American population was dominated by the Japanese. In 1980, the top group was the Chinese. Thanks to new immigration, the 1990 census found the Filipino American population had grown almost as large as the Chinese American population, and both grew far beyond Americans of Japanese origin. Both the Asian Indian and the Korean populations now rival the Japanese population in size.

Different patterns of childbearing also play a role in creating a more diverse society. Fertility rates are still higher for minority groups than they are for non-Hispanic whites. In 1988, Hispanic women had the highest rate, with 96 children per 1,000 women aged 15 to 44. Black women had a rate of 87 per 1,000, compared with 63 per 1,000 for white women. As a result, two-thirds of minority families had children in 1990, compared with fewer than half of non-Hispanic white families.

Hispanic and nonwhite women will still have higher fertility rates in the 1990s, primarily because they come from younger populations, according to Juanita Tamayo Lott, president of a Washington, D.C. consulting firm. But these rates should diminish as these populations age. Nonwhite and Hispanic fertility rates should resemble white rates by the mid-21st century, she says.

The trend is clear. If current conditions continue, the United States will become a nation with no racial or ethnic majority during the 21st century. This may happen as early as 2060, according to demographer Leon Bouvier of the Center for Immigration Studies.

THE AGING OF DIVERSITY

The engine driving the diversity trend is the relative youth of minority populations. In 1988, non-Hispanic whites were older than any minority group, with a median age of 31.4 years. Hispanics were the youngest, with a median age of 24 years. Blacks were second youngest, at 25.6, while "other" races (mainly Asians) had a median age of 27.

The median age is increasing for all racial and ethnic groups, but Hispanics and blacks will remain younger than non-Hispanic whites. According to Census Bureau projections, non-Hispanic whites will have a median age of 41.4 years in 2010. That's ten years older than the median age for blacks in 2010 (31.4 years) and 12 years older than for Hispanics (29.3). "Other" races will have a median age of 35.6.

As a result, different age groups are becoming multicultural at different rates. In 2000, 72 percent of Americans will be non-Hispanic white, according to Decision Demographics, a Washington, D.C. consulting firm. But fewer than two in three children will be non-Hispanic white. Non-Hispanic whites will account for 63 percent of children under age 8, 65 percent of children aged 8 to 13, and 66 percent of children aged 14 to 17. In contrast, nearly 80 percent of Americans aged 45 or older will be non-Hispanic white. Multicultural milestones show up first in the youngest ages.

Immigration will add more Americans in the 1990s than it did in the 1980s.

These differences in the composition of age groups combine with differences in life expectancy to make the elderly population disproportionately white. However, with the notable exception of black men, the gap in life expectancy between whites and nonwhites has been narrowing. All these trends will eventually increase the multicultural character of the older population.

Multiculturalism is seeping into every aspect of American society, including language. The battle to make English the official language of the United States seems to have fizzled out, as Spanish-speaking Americans make it clear that they intend to retain their native language. As a result, many English-speaking Americans are discovering with a shock that they cannot communicate when visiting certain sections of California, Florida, or Texas. Bilingual signs and forms are becoming commonplace in many parts of the country.

Next spring, the Census Bureau will release the first data on "linguistically isolated" households. These are households in which no member aged 5 or older reported speaking English "very well." The numbers of such households did not merit a separate tabulation in previous censuses. But the 1980 census found 23 million households that spoke a language other than English at home. It also found 10 million households that had a less-than-adequate command of English. These numbers will be considerably larger in the 1990 count, thanks to immigration, according to Census Bureau demographer Paul Siegel.

Other factors are influencing the evolution of racial and ethnic identities. More and more Americans are of mixed parentage, and they are demanding to be recognized as multiracial.

Communications technologies are also changing the way people identify with their ethnic roots. For example, African films are gaining a significant audience here, particularly among African Americans. VCRs, fax machines, and other new technologies create important opportunities for cultural exchange in both directions. At the same time, it reduces the impetus for immigrants to assimilate into the "mainstream."

More than ever, the way for minorities to gain broader opportunities in American society is to get a college education. But relative to whites, college enrollment rates actually declined for blacks and Hispanics during the 1980s.

In a multicultural society, businesses can thrive by finding common ground across racial and ethnic groups.

As educational attainment becomes increasingly important to individual success, differences in educational attainment will produce sharply different socioeconomic profiles for different racial and ethnic groups. This trend could create a population polarized by both race and economic opportunity. Whites and Asians could increasingly dominate high-income high-status occupations, leaving blacks and Hispanics with low-income low-status occupations.

Even if employment discrimination suddenly ceased to exist, the lower educational attainment of minorities would keep many of them from entering newly opened doors. Poorly educated young black men are already shut out of the broader society; nearly one in four of those aged 20 to 29 is behind bars or on probation or parole.

As America participates increasingly in the world economy, business leaders could use a multicultural work force as a powerful competitive edge. But the opportunities will not be distributed equally among different racial and ethnic groups. The challenge is to maximize our comparative advantage in the world economy while still offering upward mobility to all Americans.

HOW BUSINESS CAN RESPOND

"The typical consumer-citizen of California in the late 1990s may be a 38-year-old professional who does Zen meditation. At home, she listens to Celtic folk music because her grandparents were Scottish. But she spends her vacations in northern Mexico to study Tarahumara culture, after picking up a taste for ranchero music," says Paul Saffo, who follows technology for the Institute for the Future in Menlo Park, California.

In a multicultural society, businesses

thrive by finding common ground across racial and ethnic groups. Businesses that try to target each group separately will be stunted by prohibitive marketing costs. Others will meet this challenge by helping multicultural consumers mix and match their lifestyles. Multicultural consumers will take discrete cultural pieces and mix them into custom-tailored wholes.

Another common need is information and entertainment that explains the world to multicultural consumers from their point of view. Last year, a widely publicized journalism study faulted young Americans for their ignorance of important news figures and news events. But given their increasingly multicultural nature, it's no surprise that today's youth had little interest or knowledge in what was going on in Eastern Europe, but were up-to-the-minute on developments in South Africa.* Consumer information and entertainment businesses are going to have to reposition both their content and their advertising to appeal to today's multicultural youth as they become tomorrow's multicultural adults.

On every dollar bill is the phrase E pluribus unum, "from diversity comes unity."

Education is a major common need. The educational establishment has not adequately responded to the multicultural challenge, and that creates an opportunity for business.

Communications technology is building a new common ground for an increasingly multicultural population. We saw this during recent events in China and in Eastern Europe. We are going to see more of it as technological evolution lets our most recent arrivals keep close contact with their roots instead of cutting them off.

These developments create new opportunities for consumer businesses that can unlock culture from its origin and allow others to share in it. One example is the Japanese adoption of the Wild West, as Tokyo executives import log cabins from Montana and vacation on American dude ranches. As the world's first multicultural society, the United States is uniquely positioned to both understand and profit from the emerging global culture.

All this means that consumers are becoming simultaneously part of a global culture and a local community. It also means that these ties are based on common interests. Moreover, technology increasingly allows Americans to switch readily and frequently from one viewpoint to another. The marketer's new challenge is to find not only the right person with the right message but also to find them at the right moment.

Some of those moments will be global moments, as everyone in the world watches a soccer match, or a war. Some will be culturally specific moments, as Muslims or other groups share a moment that is invisible to everyone else. Some will be purely and simply local. But in every case, the common ground will be interests, concerns, and lifestyles.

Without necessarily realizing it, businesses have been preparing to meet this challenge by building detailed consumer information systems. Combined with attitude and behavior research, these systems can efficiently unite niches into markets. The systems' geographic specificity will extend marketing efficiency by allowing marketers to pay attention to the geographic variations in diversity.

For example, a Nissan television campaign featured a multicultural design team engineering cars "for the human race." The tag line made sense nationally, because it was broadly targeted image advertising. More directly targeted messages have to identify their audiences more closely. An ad that takes a multicultural society as a given is right for Los Angeles, but it might strike a strange note in rural Indiana.

Retailers can use locally based information systems to efficiently target specific demographic and market segments. Mark London is president and CEO of Equity Properties in Chicago, a firm that remodels and re-leases shopping centers whose trade areas have changed significantly. He recently analyzed an anchor store that was doing badly in a repositioned Miami mall. The store managers hadn't understood two crucial concepts. First, upscale Hispanic women don't have the same fashion preferences as other upscale women. Second, they don't have the same preferences as other Hispanic women. When the store learned to feature upscale Hispanic fashions, sales rebounded.

On every dollar bill is the phrase *E pluribus unum*, "from diversity comes unity." If this fundamental American belief can survive, our country will become a microcosm of an increasingly interdependent world. America can still offer hope to other countries, and to all of its citizens. But it can only work if we meet the multicultural challenge.

TAKING IT FURTHER

For more information about the changing makeup of minority populations, contact the Bureau of the Census's Data User Services Division at (301) 763-5820. A good general source of information on immigration is the *Statistical Yearbook* of the Immigration and Naturalization Service; telephone (202) 376-3066. For more on the impact of multiculturalism, contact the Institute for the Future at 2740 Sand Hill Road, Menlo Park, California, 94025; telephone (415) 854-6322. Reprints of this article may be purchased by calling (800) 828-1133.

*See "What's News with You," American Demographics, November 1990, page 2.

Why Africa Stays Poor
And Why It Doesn't Have To

David Aronson

David Aronson grew up in Nigeria and the Ivory Coast and spent a year in Zaire on a fellowship. He is a graduate of Wesleyan University and the University of Florida and is currently working on a book about Zaire.

The images are so familiar that we have become all but inured to them: starving African children outlined against a broad expanse of empty sky; ragged, impoverished families huddled together on a stony steppe. They could be Biafrans in 1968, Sahelians in 1973, or Ethiopians in 1985. The most recent pictures are from Somalia, a barren stretch of East African coastland that juts into the Indian Ocean. Once a consolation prize in the Cold War (the real trophy in the Horn was Ethiopia, a richer and more populous nation), Somalia has since disintegrated into fiefdoms of grizzled warlords armed with Kalashnikovs and AK-47s. Now 2,000 Somalis die every day from hunger and its attendant diseases, and reports from elsewhere in Africa suggest that Somalia is only the beginning; according to the United Nations, 20 million to 60 million people are at risk of starvation throughout the eastern and southern parts of the continent.

The news out of Africa has been so grim for so long that the continent seems hopeless, its problems ineradicable. Yet this perception—though it has been reinforced by endless images of famine, disease, and warfare—is both untrue and unnecessarily fatalistic. There are some good reasons, I will argue, for hoping that Africa's next 30 years will be better than the last three decades.

It must first be acknowledged, however, that Africa is in a dismal state. Though statistics cannot convey the miseries of living in a shantytown outside Lagos, or the hardships of wresting a subsistence from the leeched landscape of the Sahel, they can suggest the dimensions of Africa's problems. In the 1980s, per capita African gross national product declined by nearly 25 percent. African farmers produce 20 percent less food today than they did in 1970, and there are twice as many mouths to feed. (At its current rate, Africa's population will reach nearly three billion by the year 2050.) Direct private investment in Africa constitutes 2 percent of the world's total, and experts predict that much of that miniscule figure will be siphoned off as Eastern Europe and Asia rebuild. One French diplomat has written: "Economically speaking, if the entire black Africa, with the exception of South Africa, were to disappear in a flood, the global cataclysm would be approximately nonexistent."

By the late 1980s, most of Africa's states were facing outright financial ruin. The 1990 World Bank annual development report listed 27 African countries among the world's 40 poorest. It seemed to matter very little what path to economic growth these countries were ostensibly pursuing; political scientist Crawford Young argued as much in his book *Ideology and Development in Africa*. "Does ideology matter?" he asked. "My reading of the evidence does not lead to a single unambiguous conclusion." "Socialist" Zambia, Tanzania, and Ghana; or "capitalist" Zaire, Kenya, and Nigeria; the still verdant Congo or the desertified Mali—by 1990, all were mired in economic and political stagnation.

Africa's troubles are not just economic. Civil war and ethnic strife have erupted in over a dozen African countries. Liberia and Somalia have followed Chad and Mozambique into Hobbesian anarchy. Even Kenya and the Ivory Coast—long touted as the two "success" stories of black Africa—have been jolted by a series of anti-government demonstrations. Meanwhile, the AIDS pandemic looms over Africa like a modern-day bubonic plague; the World Health Organization estimates that the disease will kill 20 *percent* of Africa's working adults by 1996, including disproportionate numbers of the educated and successful. Perhaps the most sobering aspect of the AIDS crisis is the attitude of resignation that many Africans seem to have taken toward it. In a continent where 12,000 children die every day of hunger and hunger-related causes, that attitude is depressingly easy to understand: what to us is some horrific medieval plague to them is simply one more deadly infectious disease.

In the West, newspaper editors came up with the term *compassion fatigue* to describe their audiences' reactions to Africa's problems (and, one suspects, to justify their meager coverage of them). A famine in Mozambique, civil war in the Sudan, a slaughter of innocents in Burundi, chaos in Zaire and elsewhere—in the post–Band Aid era, the litany of Africa's woes was buried in the back pages of the press. The impression to be gleaned from this coverage was that Africa's problems were monolithic, insurmountable, and utterly alien—and therefore, presumably, not of pressing concern to us.

Though examples of African success are admittedly few, they provide much-needed evidence that the continent's current woes are not insurmountable. A few African countries made it through the 1980s with their economies and political systems reasonably intact: the Gambia and Botswana are islands of democracy; the Cameroon's economy grew by 8 percent per year through much of the decade; and Mauritius' economy grew by over 5 percent per head. And though Africa's problems seem nearly universal, they are far from monolithic.

Mobutu pillaged his country with scarcely a murmur of dissent from his Western sponsors—particularly the United States.

Zambia provides an instructive example of the continent's shifting fortunes. In 1964, when Zambia achieved independence under the leadership of Kenneth Kaunda, it was one of Africa's brightest prospects, with a highly developed infrastructure and abundant copper reserves that gave it some of the highest income levels on the continent. Kaunda himself was genial and charming, his political rhetoric an eloquent blend of socialism, pacifism, and pan-Africanism. Zambia became one of the world's largest per capita recipients of foreign aid. However, from 1965 to 1988, Zambia's average annual rate of growth was *minus* 2.1 percent, and today it is one of the poorest countries in the world—ranked eighteenth from the bottom in per capita GNP.

Belying his oft-proclaimed "humanistic philosophy," Kaunda officially declared Zambia a one-party state in 1972. Under the infamous Emergency Powers Act—a holdover from the colonial era—he regularly had dissenters jailed, beaten, or sent into exile. Kaunda also came to enjoy a life-style that few Zambians could have imagined, playing golf several times a week on a course adjoining his presidential estate and stocking his private zoo with peacocks and deer.

It was not, however, the gap between his professed idealism and his actual politics that brought Kaunda down—after all, any number of governments have survived telling more risible lies. Nor were Zambia's problems the result of outside pressures, though Zambia respected the African trade embargo against South Africa at considerable cost to its own economy. Rather, Kaunda's downfall was the result of economic policies that eventually boxed him in—policies that left him unable to fulfill the social contract he had established with his urban population.

Kaunda relied upon his nation's copper reserves to create a huge bureaucracy; at one point, nearly 40 percent of Zambia's wage earners received their checks from the government. At the same time, Kaunda poured money into the cities at the expense of the countryside. Schools, medical facilities, and subsidized housing were all available to the urban population; farmers had to make do with rigged, artificially low prices for their produce.

The economic consequences were as devastating as they were predictable. The rural poor moved to urban areas, where they came to rely upon subsidized food as part of the social contract; declining food production forced the government to spend an ever-greater percentage of its earnings on imported grain. Zambia borrowed heavily in the 1970s and early 1980s on the strength of its copper reserves and used the money to support urban consumption, to import food, and to keep afloat its bloated civil service. But as copper reserves dwindled and international commodity prices dipped, the government could no longer afford its part of the social contract. In 1990, rioting erupted in several cities, forcing Kaunda to allow elections. The results were overwhelming: in Kaunda's home seat of Nchanga, the vote went 20,680 for his opponent to only 637 votes for Kaunda himself.

In Zaire, Zambia's giant neighbor to the north, the pro-democracy opponents of President Mobutu Sese Seko have had a far rougher time of it. Mobutu has ruled Zaire since 1965, when he seized power in a CIA-sponsored coup after the conflicts of Zaire's early years. It is frequently claimed that, whatever Mobutu's sins, he at least brought unity to a war-torn country; in fact, the government in place at the time had already made peace with all but one minor rebel group when Mobutu staged his coup. If Mobutu brought unity to Zaire, it is a unity born of Zairians' near-universal hatred of his regime.

Under Mobutu, Zaire's economy fell through the floor. In 1990, per capita annual income was $170; real wages had plummeted to one-tenth their 1960 levels. In Mobutu's 27 years in power, not a single hospital has been built. The road network that linked Zaire together in 1960 has crumbled; the country is larger than the United States east of the Mississippi, yet there are now fewer miles of paved roads in all of Zaire than there are in Toledo, Ohio. Only 3 percent of the central government's budget goes to health and education; 23 percent goes to the military, and 50 percent to lining the pockets of Mobutu and his ruling elite. Mobutu Sese Seko—his adopted name means "the cock that leaves no hen untouched"—has accumulated a dozen French and Belgian chateaux, a Spanish castle, and a 32-bedroom Swiss villa. His net worth is variously estimated at $3 billion to $7 billion. Meanwhile, one out of every two children born in Zaire dies before the age of five.

Mobutu pillaged his country with scarcely a murmur of dissent from his Western sponsors—particularly the United States. There were two reasons for this: first, Zaire is an important supplier of minerals, including industrial diamonds, copper, and cobalt (needed for the alloys used in military aircraft); and second, Mobutu allowed his country to be used as a base for covert American military and diplomatic expeditions into Angola and Chad. His stature as one of America's most important assets in the region was underlined in 1988 when Mobutu became Africa's first head of state to meet with President George Bush.

In 1990 and continuing through most of 1991, pro-democracy agitators put Mobutu on the defensive. Led by the popular long-time dissident Etienne Tshisekedi, they forced him to convene a national conference on the future of the country's leadership. Mobutu did all he could to disrupt the proceedings of the conference; in the ensuing riots, scores of people in various cities were killed by the military. Mobutu himself fled to a luxury yacht cruising the Congo River but retained control of the elite army troops and his security forces. Meanwhile, Zaire's economy and its political institutions have collapsed.

During the Cold War, diplomats and politicians in the West frequently justified their support for Mobutu by arguing that the alternative was a return to the chaos of Zaire's early years. This argument is founded, as I've indicated, on a willful misreading of history; it ignores the fact that the situation in Zaire was well past its crisis point when Mobutu took power, and it also implies that Western support for Mobutu was motivated, at least in part, by a humanitarian concern for Zairians. "We care," the diplomats seemed to be saying, "that Zairians not be forced to suffer again the internecine warfare that accompanied the birth of their nation." But since the confrontation between the national conference and Mobutu reached a stalemate, the West has done almost nothing to help resolve the situation; in the absence of Cold War exigencies, we seem to have lost interest in the country. What remains, as political scientist Rene Lemarchand has written, "is a country teetering on the brink of chaos—a devastated economy, an empty treasury, a peasant sector reduced to subsistence agriculture, an urban population at the edge of starvation, and hundreds of thousands of unemployed youth for whom life has nothing to offer." For years, we heard from our politicians and diplomats that it was "Mobutu or chaos." Now it is both.

Finally, there is Uganda, once known as the "pearl" of East Africa. No longer. The rolling green hills and fertile soil that so pleased the colonialists are still there, but since the 1971 coup that brought Idi Amin to power the country has lurched from one disaster to the next, bloodier one. Consider: there are half a million internally displaced people and over a quarter-million foreign refugees living in Uganda; it is probably the one country most hard-hit by AIDS in the world; its economy is in a shambles, with tea and other agricultural exports down to one-fifth or one-tenth of 1970 levels; and it has suffered from more or less continuous political unrest and warfare. Even by African standards, Uganda is a basket case.

The reasons for this startling decline are complicated. Before 1963, Uganda boasted a flourishing economy, a well-trained populace, extraordinarily fertile land, and a highly developed infrastructure. Makerere University was one of the best in Africa, and Kampala was among Africa's most cosmopolitan cities. For several years after its independence, Uganda seemed poised to fulfill the immense potential that was perceived for it. The economy flourished under the moderate leadership of Prime Minister Milton Obote, and with the *kabaka*, or king, of Buganda assuming the largely ceremonial role of president, the political situation seemed remarkably stable.

In fact, however, Uganda was built on the most fractured of foundations. Buganda was only one (albeit the principal one) of several traditional kingdoms the British had lumped together into one protectorate; and with independence came not only heightened ethnic rivalries but also religious, regional, and ideological tensions. To be sure, the challenges to nation-building represented by these divisions were to be found throughout the continent: the jigsaw puzzle of national boundaries the colonial powers left behind bore little relationship to pre-existing ethnic or linguistic identities. But in Uganda, these divisions were never overcome. No central authority ever managed to impose a national identity on the disparate groups competing for power, and the result was that no one group or party was ever seen as legitimate. The tensions within the polity could be submerged, but they could never be resolved.

Uganda's political history probably reached its nadir during the eight-year reign of Idi Amin, the notoriously brutal army sergeant turned international buffoon. But Uganda's problems neither began nor ended with Amin. Obote, Uganda's first prime minister, had spent most of his time in office trying to contain the forces that were tearing the country apart. In 1966, for example, he ousted the *kabaka* under pressure from radical youth groups in the capital; to keep the army happy, he tripled its share of the nation's budget. That did not prevent factions from developing within it, and eventually one of them—led by Amin—secured the patronage of Great Britain and Israel, who were dissatisfied with Obote's growing radicalism.

Amin's 1971 coup brought an end to Uganda's economic growth. During his bloody rule, coffee, tea, and cotton production fell to one-third their earlier levels, and industrial performance dropped 85 percent. Amin was finally overthrown in 1979, after an attempted invasion of Tanzania turned into a rout of the Ugandan army by the better-trained, better-led Tanzanian troops. But a succession of leaders proved unable to stop the anarchy that had characterized Amin's final years, and the economy continued to sputter. Under Uganda's current leader, Yoweri Museveni, there has been a modest economic recovery, and aid from the major donor nations has also begun to trickle in. But though a semblance of order prevails, it seems only a matter of time before the next political tremors erupt.

The national boundaries left behind by the colonial powers bore little relation to actual ethnic or linguistic identities.

Are there any observations to be made, any lessons to be distilled, from the divergent experiences of these three countries? The first is that it pays not to live near one of Africa's hot spots. Zambia respected the boycott against South Africa at enormous cost to its own economy. Other countries, particularly Mozambique and

Angola, endured South African–sponsored terrorism and civil war that effectively blocked any possibility of their own development. And though guerrilla movements in these countries have now acquired a momentum of their own, support from the apartheid regime was critical in launching them. Much the same could be said of the Libyans in Chad and the Ethiopians in Djibouti.

The second observation to be made is that it was the misfortune of certain African nations to come of age during the intellectual heyday of a certain kind of nondemocratic socialism. It is true that, with few exceptions, Soviet and Chinese ties to Africa were always considerably weaker than the cold warriors would have had us believe. Thus, Herman Cohen, the outgoing American Assistant Secretary of State for African Affairs, has now blamed *European left-wingers* for implementing in Africa "the biggest socialist fantasies that they weren't able to implement in their own countries." But Cohen's is a simplistic rendering of history—a piece of Reaganite revisionism. African countries like Ghana, Tanzania, and Zambia "went" socialist not from any affection for the leaden Stalinists (Soviet advisers were despised wherever they went), nor from European left-wingers' denunciations of their own bourgeoisie (we should be so lucky, thought the Africans), but for complex reasons of their own. Socialism represented the opposite of capitalism, the system of Africa's colonizers. It offered a blueprint for social and political mobilization that seemed more coherent and plausible to some African leaders, and, with its hazy vision of a utopian future, it fed into a hallowed conception of Africa's past—a vision of a prelapsarian (read: precolonial) Eden whose traditions contained all the promises of Western political thought but none of its painful contradictions.

> ***It was disastrous for Africa to come of age during the Cold War. Both the U.S.A. and the U.S.S.R. helped to install tyrants whose records are a blot upon the human race.***

Nothing, alas, could have been more impractical for these fledgling nations. To work at all, socialism requires an educated bureaucracy and a vigorous, disciplined central government—precisely the conditions that did not exist in post-colonial Africa. After 30 years, the verdict is unequivocal: capitalism's record is mixed, but socialism—at least of the sort practiced by Kaunda in Zambia, Nyerere in Tanzania, or Nkrumah in Ghana—has been an utter failure.

The third observation to be made is that it was disastrous for Africa to come of age during the Cold War. Both the United States and the Soviet Union helped to install and maintain tyrants whose records are a blot upon the human race. America's support for Mobutu in Zaire and the Soviets' for Mengistu in Ethiopia may (or may not) have been justified by the superpowers' national-security needs, but the price that ordinary Zairians and Ethiopians paid for that security lies beneath the gravestones of countless children. It is important to be blunt about this: we have a moral duty to acknowledge how much of our own putative security has been purchased with the blood of others.

A fourth observation concerns the extent of corruption in Africa. From the governor who pockets half the state's budget for public works to the nurse at the local clinic who demands a bribe before changing a bandage, corruption is so deeply entrenched and so endemic that it requires an explanation. Peter Wanyande, a Kenyan political scientist at Kenyatta University in Nairobi, suggests that corruption flourishes in Africa in part because there are few institutions aside from the state through which the gifted and the capable can rise. But in contrast to the tribe or the extended family, the state remains an abstraction, commanding neither loyalty nor affection. The dispensation of favors and the profitable manipulation of alliances thus become the *modus vivendi* for Africans on the make. In Nigeria, in Zaire, and increasingly in Kenya, corruption is not so much the grease that keeps the wheel turning as it is the wheel itself. This is not to justify the flagrant abuses of a Mobutu but, rather, to put them into context. The powerful in Africa steal because they can; the poor steal to survive. Corruption in Africa, then, was born of the structural weaknesses of African political and civil society, and it is now a cause as well as a consequence of African poverty.

A fifth observation is that, like the former Yugoslavia, many African countries are still wrestling with the demon of tribalism (a polluted term, no doubt, but more accurate than its euphemisms). Tribal conflicts simmer in Uganda, Rwanda, Burundi, Kenya, and Zaire, and they have boiled over in Chad and the Sudan. Tribalism hurts countries not only when blood is spilt; the energy expended on keeping the peace between rival ethnic groups represents a considerable distraction from the business of economic, political, and cultural development.

The culminating lesson is that, in Africa as elsewhere, the prerogatives of history are impossible to deny. Lumped arbitrarily into geographic units at the Berlin Conference of 1885 and launched toward independence 80 years later in entities that corresponded in no way to African realities or experience, the continent has limped behind the rest of the world—not because Africans are stupid or lazy or incapable of collective action, but because they are caught in structures that negate their strengths and frustrate their efforts. Africans remain poor because the states in which they live are artificial constructs, unmoored to the societies or people they govern, largely free of any constraint from civil institutions, and subject all too often to fracture along the substantive divisions of class, religion, and ethnicity.

Are there any grounds for hope, any reasons to believe, that Africa will do better in its next 30 years than it has in the last three decades? Certainly, there has been a veritable sea-change in African attitudes toward development. Nigerian statesman Olusagen Obasanjo is among the most eloquent:

> I believe that for us in Africa, our salvation lies in our own hands and nowhere else. Only we can be the architects of our future; as we have been the architects of our misfortune by and large for the past quarter of a century.

Then, too, some countries—most notably Ghana—have embarked on ambitious economic restructuring programs to eliminate waste, corruption, and mismanagement and to encourage private industry. The World Bank has been the driving force behind much of this movement, and there is, naturally, considerable debate about how fair these programs are and whether or not they will work. To a certain extent, the programs represent a recolonization of Africa by Western technocrats. This is not necessarily bad, some argue: at the helms of central banks, it is better to have the gnomes of Zurich than the kleptocrats of Kinshasa. But these programs also represent the third or fourth generation of development initiatives sponsored by the World Bank, and they share with the Bank's earlier initiatives a refusal to acknowledge the political environments in which they operate. In fact, economic policies prescribed with little regard for such realities may exacerbate—as they have in the past—both the political and the economic problems confronting Africans. This is an age-old criticism of the Bank, but one that, despite an abundance of evidence, it seems constitutionally incapable of attending. The Bank's charter, argue its defenders, is properly economic and deliberately apolitical. Zairians—who have seen the results of such "aid" in the Mercedes-Benzes driven by the political elite through that country's corroded streets—might be excused for wondering whether the intention has not been improperly political and deliberately uneconomic. Their president could, after all, pay off the country's entire national debt.

The end of the Cold War ought to be a tremendous spur to African political and economic development; the West no longer needs to support dictators simply because they happen to be *our* dictators. Smith Hempstone, the American ambassador to Kenya and a conservative of long standing, has not hesitated to agitate on behalf of Kenya's fledgling democrats, even though he has irked Kenyan President Daniel arap Moi considerably in doing so. Significantly, in the past three years, a half-dozen African countries have followed Eastern Europe into democracy, and another dozen or so are struggling to achieve it. It is no exaggeration to say that the democracy movement represents the most important political shift in Africa since independence. It is clear, moreover, that the democracy movement has far deeper roots than many observers could have imagined. "Throughout the continent, independent political and social forces have emerged to challenge moribund, authoritarian-patrimonial regimes of many varieties," says Peter Lewis. "The result has been a succession of movements pressing for fundamental political change." At every level of government, indigenous institutions are evolving as a response to popular demands. The shape and future direction of these institutions are still difficult to determine; all that can now be said is that they belong to Africa in a way that the pre-fab parliaments and constitutions left behind by the colonialists never did. Kwame Nkrumah's famous injunction—"Seek ye first the political kingdom"—is at last being realized.

The news out of Africa has been grim for so long that one hesitates to conclude on a dispiriting note. However, the battle between democratic and despotic governments in Africa is by no means won: in Togo, for example, the former dictator is back on his throne, and in Kenya, President Daniel arap Moi seems to have survived the recent election. Moreover, the United States continues to send the bulk of its economic assistance to tyrannical regimes. Randall Robinson, executive director of Trans-Africa, points out that, in the last fiscal year, the United States gave $130 million to Kenya, Zaire, and Malawi—"states where there is massive corruption, broad repression, and little if any appreciation of democratic values." On the other hand, countries like Benin, Botswana, and Namibia, which are now fully democratic, received just $30 million. (Namibia, with the most liberal and democratic constitution on the continent, received $500,000.)

What is to be done? Let me conclude by listing several things the West can and should be doing to help Africa. I use the word *should* advisedly—not to insist on Western culpability but, rather, on Western responsibility, which should derive from a decent regard for humankind.

First, Western nations—particularly the United States—can send more aid more selectively. The U.S. budget for all of sub-Saharan Africa is about $800 million, roughly one-third of what we give to better-off (but more "strategic") countries such as Egypt or Pakistan. We ought, furthermore, to be giving our aid to those countries which are making genuine political and economic reforms; whatever else aid does, it bestows official approval on a Third World country's government. There's no longer any reason (if there ever was) for the United States to support tyrants.

It is no exaggeration to say that the democracy movement represents the most important political shift in Africa since independence.

The largest incentive the West can offer Africa's reformers is the prospect of debt relief. Compared to Latin America's debt burden, Africa's has been ignored. The numbers involved are much smaller and don't pose a threat to the world banking system; yet, according to the *Economist*, Africa's burden is

50 percent greater as a percentage of gross domestic product than Latin America's, and the continent remains "profoundly, unsustainably indebted." Swapping debt for political and economic reform is one of the best and least costly ways for the West to help out.

Second, there should be more contact between Africa and the West: more student exchanges, more artistic conferences, more sister-cities and business conventions, and more professional colloquia. Ties between newspapers, universities, and community or religious groups should be strengthened. The West can and must find a way to encourage the institutions of African civil society; their continuing development represents the best hope for the continent's future.

Third, the early-warning system that is supposed to signal the potential for famine in Africa needs to be strengthened. Cobbled together by the United Nations after the Sahelian famine of the mid-1970s, it has not been an effective agency; it predicted major famine-related deaths in 1991, and when these failed to materialize, it lost much of its credibility. It needs a better intelligence network on the ground and more effective links to the wider community of Africanist scholars, diplomats, and journalists.

Fourth, U.N. troops ought to be empowered as a peace-making force, not just as peace-keepers. As in the case of Somalia and Yugoslavia, difficult decisions about the conflicting claims of various groups and issues of international law and human rights will need to be addressed. At what point does a regime so violate the accepted standards of international law that it forfeits its claims to sovereignty? How feasible or desirable is direct intervention in another country's affairs? What price is the West willing to pay to save the innocent victims of a murderous regime? My bias here is plain.

Finally, the press could do a far better job than it has covering African issues. It is one of the sadder ironies of our time that famines in Africa only make headlines when thousands have already died. Unlike earthquakes or typhoons, famines can be spotted months and even years in advance—when the rains fail, crops wither, and prices for grain shoot up. All these things take time and can be monitored. Given their pervasive influence, the media have a moral responsibility to alert the world to the potential of famine and to agitate aggressively, if need be, to ensure that the matter is attended to before people die.

Beyond the issue of famine, however, is the more mundane issue of poverty. In its quiet way, poverty—of the day-to-day sort that millions of Africans are mired in—is more destructive than the occasional spectacular famine. Every day, some 12,000 children in Africa die because their parents are too poor to buy them the food or medicine they require. Though the press duly takes note of Africa's rebellions, civil wars, coups d'etats, and corruption, the biggest story in Africa—the quiet struggle of ordinary people to survive against grim odds—has hardly been told at all. The media should find a way to bring this story home. In its global ramifications, the gap between the rich and the poor countries of the world is certainly one of the most important stories of our time—and yet, it is being largely ignored.

REFUGEES
THE RISING FLOOD

SPREADING VIOLENCE IS DRIVING GROWING NUMBERS OF PEOPLE FROM THEIR HOMELANDS, AND THE COUNTRIES OF ASYLUM ARE FINDING IT HARDER TO ACCOMMODATE THEM.

Kathleen Newland

Kathleen Newland is a senior associate at the Carnegie Endowment for International Peace, and principal author of the United Nations High Commissioner for Refugees' State of the World's Refugees 1993 *(Penguin Books, New York and London), from which much of this article is adapted. Formerly a senior researcher at the Worldwatch Institute, she is author of Worldwatch Paper 43,* Refugees: The New International Politics of Displacement.

Virtually every political upheaval in today's increasingly crowded and dangerous world uproots people from their homes and sends them fleeing from violence and persecution. Those who manage to cross an international border to seek protection are called refugees. Their numbers now approach 19 million worldwide. In addition, 2.7 million Palestinian refugees and their descendants live in Jordan, Syria, Lebanon, and the occupied territories. There are at least another 25 million people who have fled from violence and persecution but have not crossed an international border: the internally displaced. All told, roughly one of every 123 people on earth is among the dispossessed.

The number of refugees has been climbing for the past 30 years or more (see graph). The reasons are complex: an amalgam of political violence, conflict over economic resources, environmental degradation, ethnic or religious persecution, and abuses of human rights. Increasingly often, such turmoil takes place against a background of disintegrating governments—the very institutions that should be expected to mediate conflict, or at least shelter people from its worst effects. In many cases, the government itself is the agent of persecution.

The inability to count on the protection of their own governments is what sets refugees apart from other migrants, however desperate, and other people in need of humanitarian assistance. Refugees know that they cannot expect, at home, the protection of the police, access to a fair trial, redress of grievances through the courts, prosecution of those who violate their rights, or public assistance in the face of disaster. In a world made up of sovereign states, people who do not have access to the legal and social protection that a properly functioning government normally extends to its citizens, as best it can, must look to the international community for protection.

Refugee laws, laid down in international treaties and adopted into national legal codes, acknowledge and spell out legal obligations toward people whose own governments are unwilling or unable to protect them. These laws define a refugee as any person who, "owing to a well-founded fear of being persecuted for reasons of race, religion, nationality, membership of a

From *World Watch,* May/June 1994, pp. 10-20. © 1994 by the Worldwatch Institute. Reprinted by permission.

particular social group, or political opinion, is outside the country of his nationality and is unable—or, owing to such fear, unwilling—to avail himself of the protection of that country. . . ." The most fundamental obligation to refugees is to ensure that they are not sent back to a place where they would face persecution.

The international system of refugee protection was consolidated in the aftermath of World War II and during the tense early stages of the Cold War. To negotiators looking back to the Nazi persecutions and Stalinist repression, the causes of the refugee problems did not seem excessively complicated. A political consensus among Western democracies that the people of Eastern Europe were persecuted by their governments meant that the limited numbers who managed to flee were automatically granted asylum. As conflicts over decolonization in the late 1950s and 1960s—such as those in Algeria, Angola, and Zaire—generated large numbers of refugees, the causes again seemed self-evident.

But refugees' numbers escalated sharply in the 1970s, and set off a vigorous debate about the root causes of their movement. Although individually targeted persecution was still rampant, more and more people were fleeing from general violence, severe disruptions of public order, and the inability to feed themselves in the midst of armed conflict. Moreover, many refugees were intermingled with people who moved not out of fear for their lives and freedom, but in search of better economic opportunities. As the numbers continued to rise throughout the 1980s and into the 1990s, policymakers began to focus more sharply on how they could prevent conditions from deteriorating to the point at which people feel compelled to flee.

Political roots

The main instrument of international refugee law, the 1951 Convention Relating to the Status of Refugees, identified what is still a major reason that people are forced out of their native countries: persecution based on who the refugee is (race, nationality, membership in a particular social group) or what he or she believes (religion or political opinion). Persecution usually takes place when there are fundamental political disputes over who controls the government, how society organizes itself, and who commands the power, privileges, patronage, and perks that go with political control. These disputes are at their most heated during periods of intense change—in the aftermath of a revolutionary struggle (successful or failed), at the moment of a far-reaching change of regime, or at the emergence of a new state.

Virtually all of the conflicts that caused people to flee their homes during 1993 and early 1994 were civil conflicts. Weak states, such as Liberia or Haiti, are especially prone to internal violence, since credible mechanisms for resolving conflicts peacefully or seeking redress for violations of rights in such states have usually eroded or ceased to function altogether. The lack of representative political institutions, an independent judiciary, impartial law enforcement, or free elections may lead people to conclude that armed resistance is the only way to bring about change. In many cases, no party or faction is able to establish control, and political conflict degenerates into anarchy, with no one able to provide security to the people. Somalia, with its tens of thousands of dead, hundreds of thousands of refugees, and millions of internally displaced, is today's example of this kind of nightmare—but elements of the pattern have also been visible in Afghanistan, Haiti, and Liberia.

As the superpower rivalry of the Cold War all too clearly demonstrated, external political support for one side or the other prolongs internal conflict and raises the level of violence. The largest refugee movements of the last three decades—from Afghanistan, Vietnam, Cambodia, the Horn of Africa, Angola, and Mozambique—were exacerbated by superpower involvement. External intervention in local disputes often disrupts local traditions of bargaining and compromise by giving one party, clan, or faction a definitive upper hand. An outside patron may prop up leaders who have little if any domestic legitimacy, and give them the firepower to enforce their will. An infusion of military aid increases the destructiveness of confrontation, while economic aid raises the stakes in the contest for control of domestic institutions.

Economic roots

Economic tensions are among the major underlying causes of refugee movements, but the relationship is not as straightforward as it may seem. It is too simple to say that poverty begets refugees. In relatively static situations, extreme deprivation is as likely to breed resignation as resistance.

More combustible situations are produced by a deterioration of economic standing. Bitter disputes among national groups (such as the Serbs and the Croats in former Yugoslavia) arise from efforts to preserve or advance the standing of one group at the relative expense of others. Disputes over the distribution of resources during general economic decline are the most politically explosive. Leaders, trying to avoid the blame for deteriorating economic conditions, frequently turn to scapegoating, and minority groups often provide the most convenient targets.

Impoverishment undoubtedly exacerbates ethnic and communal tensions. To know that the number of rural poor has doubled since 1950, that per capita incomes have fallen steadily in a number of regions, and that malnutrition has risen, is to know that the stage is set for continuing floods of refugees—but this is only one part of the dynamic of people being forced out of their homes. Worldwide, nearly one billion people live in absolute poverty. Only a small proportion of them will become refugees. In fact, the total number of refugees amounts to less than 3 percent of the destitute. Economic deprivation interacts with other circumstances to heighten instability and aggravate conflicts, but is itself rarely a direct cause of refugee flows.

In near-subsistence economies, violent conflict disrupts food production and distribution even as it displaces people. When the conditions of daily life, precarious to begin with, are disrupted by war, the ensuing famine and disease often become greater threats to the population than the fighting itself. In Sudan's civil war, for example, 600,000 people are thought to have died so far, the vast majority of whom have starved or succumbed to diseases that they would probably have been able to resist had the situation been more stable.

It seems obvious that stagnation and decline aggravate conflict—but it is also true that rapid growth can have the same effect. Every process of change has winners and losers. The dislocations of development result in imbalances, with some classes, regions, or ethnic groups benefiting disproportionately. The ethnic Chinese led the boom in trade and manufacturing in many Southeast Asian countries. South Asians dominated trade in a number of African countries—Uganda being one example, until the entire ethnic group was expelled by Idi Amin. Such groups may become the targets of resentment, or may themselves assert a claim for self-determination in order to be free of what they see as the drag of less dynamic elements of society. The secession of Slovenia from Yugoslavia, and of Eritrea from Ethiopia, are examples of the latter. Either reaction may provoke violent confrontation.

ENVIRONMENTAL ROOTS

Millions of people have been forced to leave home because their land has become uninhabitable or is no longer able to support them. In some cases the cause is a natural disaster; in others, the catastrophe is caused by people. It may be sudden, as at Chernobyl or Mount Pinatubo, or as gradual as the spread of a desert or the retreat of a forest.

The terminology for describing this kind of migration is controversial. For many observers, "migration" does not convey the fact that the people affected are *forcibly* uprooted. And to call them refugees makes it clear that they left their homes involuntarily, for reasons not of their own making. Accurate use of the term "refugee," however, implies a need for international protection. Most people whose homes have become uninhabitable turn first to their governments and communities for recourse. Although they undoubtedly need assistance, they don't necessarily require the kind of international protection implied by the term "refugee."

Nevertheless, there are clear links between environmental degradation and refugees. Deterioration of natural resources, coupled with demographic pressure and chronic poverty, can *lead* to conflicts that force people to flee. Africa, for example, accounts for 10 percent of the world's population and hosts more than 25 percent of its refugees. It is no coincidence that those parts of the continent that are most affected by soil erosion, drought, and other environmental disasters are also the main theaters of armed conflicts, recurrent famine, and consequent refugee movements.

In the Sahel and the Horn of Africa, the combination of rapidly expanding populations, drought, and competition between nomads and settled agriculturalists has erupted into violence along a number of fronts. Fighting arising from disputes over irrigable land in the Senegal River basin has pushed thousands of Senegalese and Mauritanian refugees across their common border in both directions. In southern Ethiopia, incursions by certain clans into the traditional grazing lands of other clans have led to fierce and bloody clashes, and to a large, though temporary, flow of refugees into northern Kenya. Further south, in Mozambique, civilians already under severe pressure from the effects of civil war were pushed to the very edge of survival—and in many cases beyond it—by the effects of drought in 1992. More than 100,000 of them took refuge in neighboring Malawi in that year alone.

Occasionally, habitat destruction takes on the character of persecution—for example, if it occurs as a result of deliberate governmental action or gross negligence and no effort is made to compensate or assist the people affected. Indigenous people are particularly vulnerable to this kind of assault, as their way of life is often closely connected to a particular terrain. In extreme cases, for example in the southern marshes of Iraq, destruction of habitat may be used as a deliberate weapon of war. People who are uprooted because of willfully negligent or intentional destruction of the environment may indeed need international protection.

Long-term prevention should address the poten-

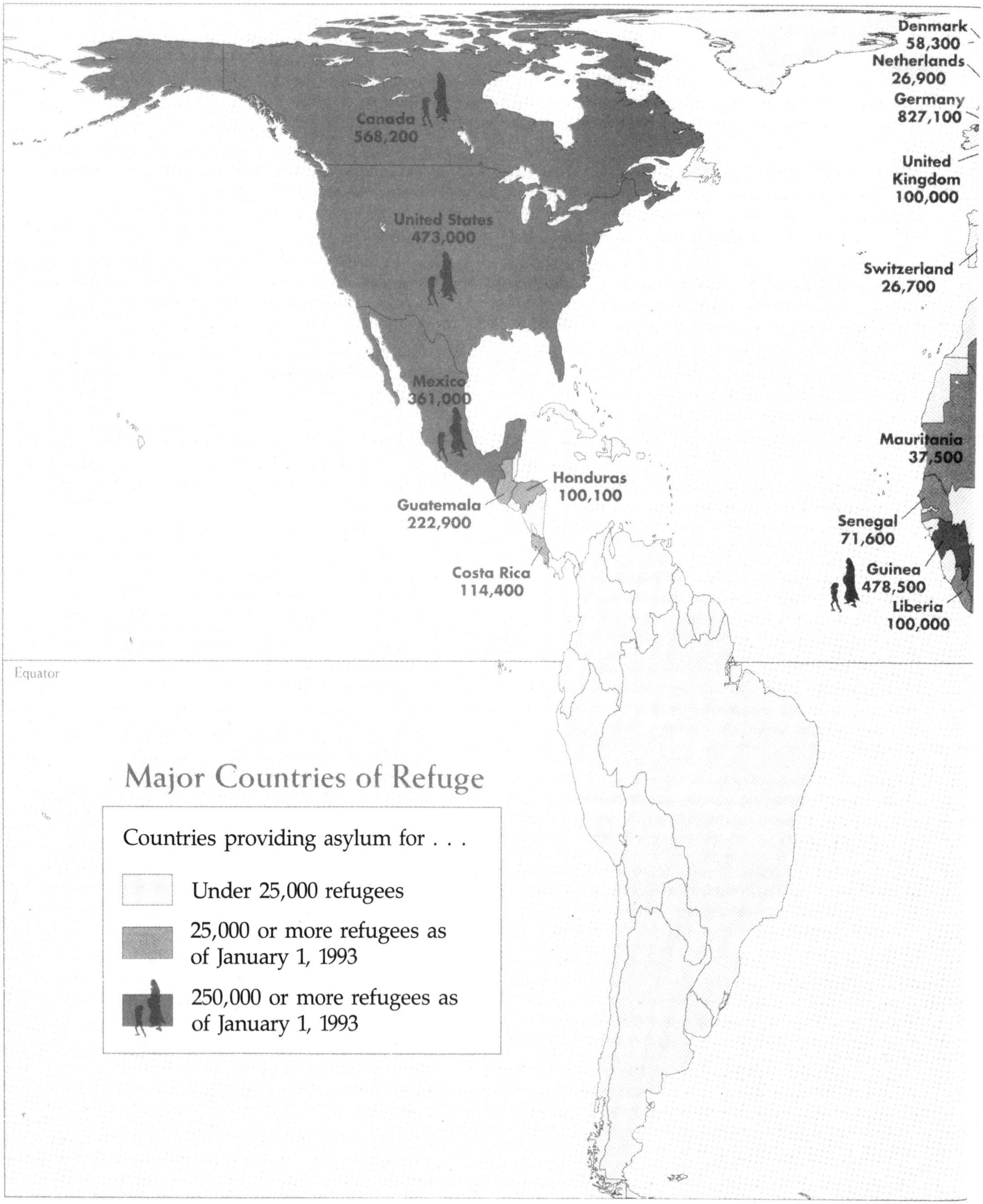
Denmark
58,300
Netherlands
26,900
Germany
827,100
United Kingdom
100,000
Switzerland
26,700
Canada
568,200
United States
473,000
Mexico
361,000
Honduras
100,100
Guatemala
222,900
Costa Rica
114,400
Mauritania
37,500
Senegal
71,600
Guinea
478,500
Liberia
100,000
Equator
Major Countries of Refuge
Countries providing asylum for . . .
Under 25,000 refugees
25,000 or more refugees as of January 1, 1993
250,000 or more refugees as of January 1, 1993

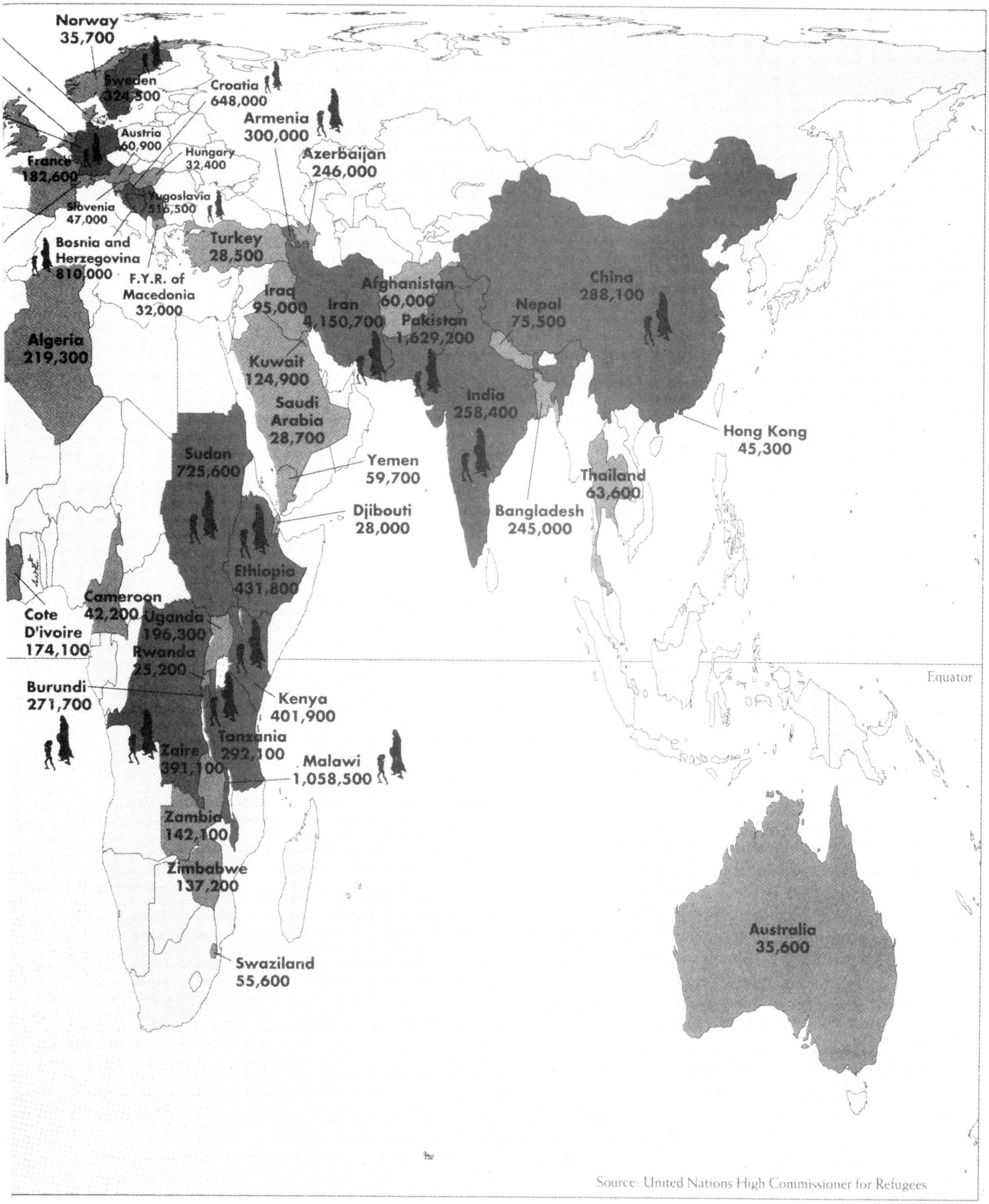

Source: United Nations High Commissioner for Refugees

tial role of environmental damage in refugee flight. There is no comfort in the realization that today only a minority of environmentally displaced people need international protection. The international community has every interest in responding to the need for assistance to preserve and rehabilitate the environment before degradation begets violence and persecution and produces a mass of homeless people who easily *do* meet the conventional definition of refugees.

Ethnic Tensions

Conflicts between ethnic groups have proliferated in recent years. Armenia and Azerbaijan, Burma, Burundi, Ethiopia, Georgia, Iraq, Sri Lanka, Sudan, and, of course, the former Yugoslavia are among a long list of countries where ethnic tensions have flared into civil war. Ethnic diversity is part of human geography almost everywhere: the 180 or so independent nations currently in existence are home to at least 5,000 ethnic groups. As a result, the notion of an ethnically pure nation-state is far-fetched—it could only be realized at an unacceptably high human cost.

Ethnic tensions can be seen as a root cause of refugee flows for two reasons. First, they are highly susceptible to political exploitation. Factions seeking to mobilize support commonly seek to fan ethnic antagonisms for their own ends. Ethnic conflict is a likely outcome when control of the state is captured by a single ethnic group that uses its power to further its own interests at the expense of others.

Second, despite the fact that most states contain a variety of ethnic groups, the ethnic identity of a single group is all too often made into a defining characteristic of nationality. Some minority groups may be seen as an obstacle to nation-building, incapable of fitting into a homogeneous national identity. Ethnic Albanians and Bosnian Muslims, for example, have no place in extreme nationalist visions of an Orthodox Christian "Greater Serbia." The ideology of *apartheid* in South Africa defined the non-white population out of citizenship. Members of groups other than the dominant one may be exposed first of all to discrimination, then to forced assimilation, persecution, expulsion, or even genocide. In many refugee crises, ethnicity is the criterion by which people are denied the protection of their national governments.

Recurrent conflict among ethnic or communal groups within a state calls for mediation by the central government. If the government is unwilling or too weak to perform this role effectively, "ethnic cleansing" or other forms of forcible segregation of populations may be the result, leading to a mass exodus—as in Palestine and the Punjab in 1948, and in Bosnia-Herzegovina today.

Ethnic tensions are also vulnerable to manipulation by external forces. Irredentism—the attempt to unite all territories occupied by a single ethnic group into one political entity—is the most obvious form of manipulation, and has played a large part in refugee-producing conflicts in the Horn of Africa and the former Yugoslavia, for example. Somalia's ambition to incorporate Somali-inhabited areas of the Ethiopian Ogaden led to a war in 1977, and the population of much of the region remains unsettled to this day, owing to a combination of political instability, ethnic tension, economic collapse, and recurring drought.

Throughout the Cold War period, superpower rivalry was a source of patronage for ethnic factions in many conflicts. Like European colonialism before it, the Cold War fostered or even created ethnic tensions. The recruitment of local factions into strategic alliances with East or West disrupted historical balances between groups, and artificially strengthened the position of client groups by arming them, arranging sanctuaries in neighboring countries, and providing diplomatic support for them. The Nicaraguan *contras* were given all three kinds of assistance from the United States.

Leaders trying to avoid the blame for failing economies frequently turn to scapegoating, and minority groups often provide convenient targets.

Members of certain ethnic groups were systematically co-opted to act as preferred proxies, intermediaries, or fighters—for example, the Hmong in Laos or the Miskitos in Nicaragua—thereby exposing the whole group to retribution. Local impulses toward accommodation or reconciliation were sometimes submerged by a powerful patron's interest in continuing the conflict. Refugees themselves became pawns in disputes that had little to do with their own immediate concerns.

If the Cold War era was dominated by ideological conflict, the fear is widespread that the 1990s mark the beginning of a new era of ethnic violence that will uproot additional millions of people from their homes. Already, refugees from dozens of ethnic conflicts look to the international community for material assistance and protection. Supposedly ancient hatreds, to which many people attribute the savagery of ethnic conflicts, can be invented, revived or kept from dying a natural death by opportunists who see in them a vehicle for personal or political profit. The Serbian strongman Slobodan Milosevic and other Serbian nationalists of the extreme right have made much of the entrenched enmity between Serbs and Croats, going back to (and indeed beyond) World War II, when the Croat allies of the Nazi regime in Germany inflicted great suffering on Serb communities. Yet in the post-war period, more than 20 percent of the adults of these two groups in the former Yugoslavia married someone from their "enemy" ethnic group—a testament to the mutability of supposedly immutable ethnic hatreds.

The challenge for modern nations is to alleviate ethnic tensions through mediation and prevent them from turning into violent conflict. This preventive role is set within a more positive responsibility: to manage ethnic diversity in a way that promotes tolerance within and beyond national borders.

Human rights violations

Forcing people to flee is a violation of the human right to remain peacefully in one's home. The direct denial of other basic rights, including the rights of civilians not to be targeted in military actions, often provides the immediate impetus for flight. Indirectly, protest about or resistance to human rights violations may provoke violent retaliation, or take a violent form itself. An accumulation of abuses accompanied by violence, which leads to further abuses and a general climate of fear, is a sequence that frequently sparks mass exodus. In Iraq, Bosnia-Herzegovina, Myanmar, Guatemala, and elsewhere, human rights violations have been at the core of major humanitarian emergencies.

The types of refugee floods that have occurred over the past decade cannot be handled solely by providing protection in countries of asylum.

A number of countries remain unwilling to acknowledge the growing international consensus on human rights standards, much less to subject themselves to international scrutiny. China, for example, rejects any attempt at international oversight of its policies in Tibet, or criticism of its treatment of Chinese dissidents. Premier Li Peng told the U.N. Security Council summit in 1992 that "the issue of human rights falls within the sovereignty of each country. . . . China is opposed to using human rights as an excuse for interference in the internal affairs of other countries."

But as refugee problems increase and come to be seen by many receiving states as a threat to international peace and security, the responsibility of governments toward their citizens is coming under closer scrutiny. Both humanitarian and security concerns have focused attention more sharply on the causes of mass exodus, bringing human rights out from behind the shield of national sovereignty. Responsibility toward one's own citizens is being extended to encompass a responsibility to the international community for the way those citizens are treated. Protection against the most threatening forms of abuse, such as arbitrary killings, detention, torture, and disappearance, can have a profound impact on the cycle of violence and fear that impels so many people to flee.

Human rights violations do not occur in a vacuum. Like other causes of refugee flows, they exist in a complex environment of economic strain, political instability, a tradition of violence, ecological deterioration, and ethnic tensions. One factor or another may dominate a particular situation while interacting with others. By the time serious and massive abuse of fundamental rights occurs, the chances of averting refugee flows are slim indeed.

Prevention

Prevention, where possible, is the most effective form of protection for people in danger of becoming refugees. As recent events have shown all too clearly, the international community needs to take earlier and more effective action if it is to prevent potential refugee-generating situations from degenerating to the point where people feel that flight is their only option. The crises in the Horn of Africa, the former Yugoslavia, the Caucasus, and elsewhere have followed a broadly similar pattern of evolution, albeit under very different circumstances: in each case, tensions arising from unresolved political, ethnic, religious, or nationality disputes led to human rights abuses that became increasingly violent. Left unchecked, this process has often developed into armed conflicts that force people to flee their homes, and often their countries, in search of safety. By then, it has proved too late to avert widespread suffering, and far more difficult to assist and protect people or to achieve lasting solutions.

The types of refugee floods that have occurred over the past decade or so cannot be handled solely by providing protection in countries of asylum. Of the three conventional solutions for refugees—local integration in the country of first asylum, resettlement in another country, or voluntary repatriation—the first two are under severe pressure because of the sheer magnitude of the exodus. The

GLOBAL NUMBERS OF REFUGEES: 1960-1992

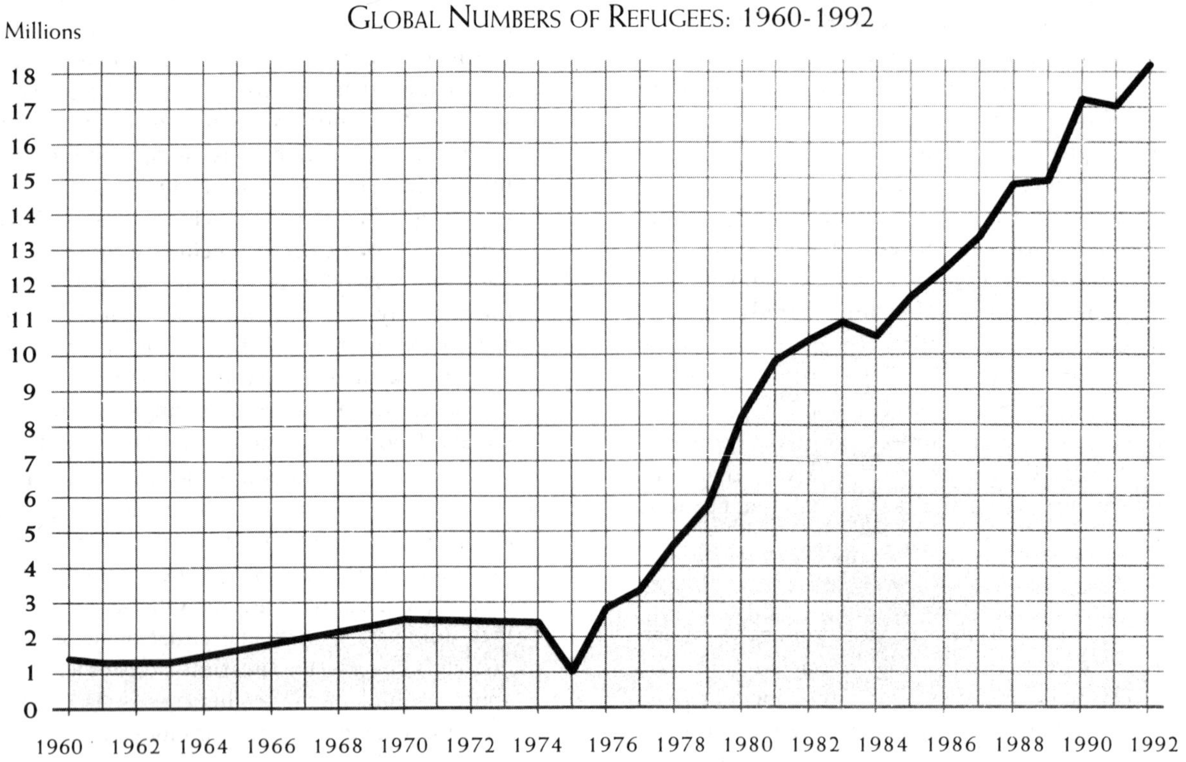

SOURCE: UNHCR, *State of the World's Refugees, 1993.*

developing countries that provide sanctuary for the vast majority of the world's refugees face economic, environmental, and political problems that make it increasingly difficult for them to shelter masses of people for long periods. Small and densely populated Malawi, for example, has hosted one million refugees from war-torn Mozambique—a number equivalent to 10 percent of its own population. Their presence has put a tremendous burden on the local economy and infrastructure—on eveything from schools to water supplies. The refugee settlements are located in some of the most ecologically vulnerable areas of the country, and their needs for fuel and building materials have exacerbated deforestation and land degradation; Malawi is losing about 3.5 percent of its forest cover each year. The peace plan that allowed the repatriation of Mozambican refugees to begin in 1993 came not a moment too soon for hard-pressed Malawi.

Wealthier countries also have faced pressures to adopt more restrictive policies toward asylum-seekers as their numbers have grown. In 1983, some 100,000 people requested asylum in Europe, North America, Australia, and Japan. By 1992, the number of applications passed 800,000. Germany was most seriously affected by the sharp increase, with asylum applications rising from 121,000 in 1989 to 438,000 in 1992. The surge, coinciding with the strains of German reunification, led to a drastic tightening of Germany's asylum law. Lawmakers in many other countries, including Austria, Switzerland, Canada, the United States, Britain, and Spain, have introduced similar legislation. Many of the countries that traditionally welcomed foreigners who wanted to settle there are showing greater reluctance. In some, there is an indiscriminate social backlash against all forms of immigration.

While very few people would argue with the truism that prevention is better than cure, in practice prevention is often controversial. The concept itself is open to misinterpretation, and even to misuse. Preventive action can take a positive or negative form. It can be aimed at protecting potential victims, promoting solutions to their problems before they are forced to flee. Alternatively, prevention can simply mean that a government throws up barriers to try to stop victims of persecution and violence from entering the country. Positive prevention aims to reduce or remove the conditions that cause people to flee, while the negative version—which should more properly be called obstruction—makes escape from persecution and danger more difficult, or impossible.

Unfortunately, obstruction is not uncommon. It ranges from forcibly turning back refugees at frontiers to intercepting them on the high seas and sending them back immediately, or to demanding that refugees show documentation in advance of entry. Pakistan has closed its border to further entries from Afghanistan, and the United States continues a policy of intercepting would-be refugees from Haiti on the high seas and returning them to Haiti without even a hearing on their claims to asylum. The United Kingdom requires Bosnians to hold a visa for direct entry to Britain, but does not have a consulate in Bosnia where they could obtain one—and will claim that those who go to a third country to apply should seek asylum in that country rather than Britain. Milder forms of obstructive prevention go under the name of "deterrence," a tactic that erects barriers to all immigrants and imposes harsh conditions upon reception, on the questionable assumption that economically motivated migrants will be discouraged while refugees will not. In reality, practices that raise barriers for one group raise them for all.

Prevention of refugee situations can be initiated long before, immediately before, or at various stages during the development of a crisis. At the most general level, prevention is—or should be—aimed at root causes, and goes far beyond the scope of humanitarian concerns alone. Displacement is the symptom of a host of the ailments of human society. Preventing the accumulation of social and economic strains that produce refugee-generating conflict and persecution is a many-faceted undertaking. It involves promotion of human rights, economic development, conflict resolution, the establishment of accountable political institutions, and environmental protection. It encompasses, in other words, virtually the whole agenda for constructing a sustainable society, with particular emphasis on the responsibilities of governments to care for all their people without discrimination.

In some countries there has been indiscriminate social backlash against all forms of immigration.

Truly massive, far-sighted prevention has rarely been attempted, and generally only on a remedial basis in order to prevent the recurrence of major disaster. Perhaps the most spectacular examples are the post-World-War-II reconstruction of West Germany and Japan, designed to avoid repeating the mistakes made in the aftermath of World War I, and the Marshall Plan for western European recovery. Of a lesser magnitude, but still important, are current programs to consolidate the peacemaking processes in Cambodia and Central America. These involve a very broad program of reconstruction and reconciliation, addressing issues as diverse as disarmament, land tenure, and human rights safeguards.

Rather than addressing root causes well before people are obliged to flee, most preventive efforts focus on immediate causes, when flight is imminent or has already started. Typically, they involve attempts to repair relations between people and their government before it is too late, and to provide supplementary or substitute protection until this can be accomplished. Efforts to stabilize internal population movements and provide protection and humanitarian relief to civilians within their home country involve, in many instances, the same measures that make possible the voluntary return of

Extreme deprivation is as likely to lead to resignation, as to flight. It is abrupt *deterioration* of status that causes refugee flows.

those who have already left. Finally, prevention involves helping states set up effective institutions, laws and procedures that enshrine the principles of national protection and guarantee the rights of minorities. The cost of failing to take preventive action can be very high, as illustrated by the situation of the Kurds and Shiites in Iraq, and of the Muslims in Bosnia and Herzegovina.

Responses

The once hospitable climate for refugees has cooled in many asylum countries. Economic difficulties, domestic political instability, the resurgence of ethnic tensions, and the rolling up of the West's ideological welcome mat for refugees from communist countries are among the explanations. There is also an increasing sense of weariness at the apparent intractability of refugee problems. In virtually all regions, the persistent growth in numbers of actual and potential refugees has prompted a more conservative approach. The authorities in many industrialized countries are increasingly inclined to interpret their obligations to refugees according to a narrow "persecution standard" and to apply a restrictive definition of what constitutes persecution. Fewer asylum countries remain willing to accept what they see as an unlimited obligation to people fleeing violence.

Maintaining a humane refugee policy in the current political and economic climate requires firm responses. To begin with, the refugee problem, large and growing though it is, must be kept in perspective. Worldwide, less than 20 percent of international migrants are refugees. In many countries, refugees make up a still smaller proportion of immigrants. For example, in the United States in the fiscal year that ended in September 1992, legal immigration amounted to 973,977 people. The much harder to measure number of illegal immigrants was assumed to be about 300,000. Of this total of perhaps 1.3 million, refugees and asylum-seekers whose claims have been accepted accounted for only 132,173. The often-invoked image of a country overrun with refugees hardly conforms to the facts.

The manageability of the refugee problem depends on four elements of policy, the first of which must be an insistence that treaty obligations be met. That means, first and foremost, that refugees should not be returned to the countries where they face persecution and should be allowed to seek asylum in safe countries.

Second must be the provision of tough, fair, and fast determination procedures for asylum seekers, so that the system meant to protect refugees is not clogged with people trying to use it as a back channel for voluntary migration.

Third is generous international support for refugee assistance programs, so that those states that live up to their obligations but are unlucky enough to be located next door to a refugee-producing country do not bear unfair burdens of a kind that might tempt them to slam the door on refugees.

Finally, a more activist foreign policy to prevent the causes of refugee flows from developing to the crisis stage, and to bring about conditions in which refugees may safely return to their homes, is the only framework in which the manageability of the global refugee problem can be maintained.

Achieving an international consensus on these points will not be easy, and no country can pursue them successfully in isolation. But there are few subjects on which the commonality of interests of people and countries across the entire economic and political spectrum is so apparent. Long-term solutions for refugees involve a basic rebuilding of societies' capacities to manage change—the same capacities that will be needed to solve the other major issues on the human agenda. The rapid growth in the global refugee population is symptomatic of the inadequacy of our efforts to date. Refugees are the human fallout of the explosive tensions that have been allowed to accumulate around economic maldistribution, environmental degradation, militarization, and a host of other ills. They are not the only people who have a stake in addressing the causes of their plight.

Index

Credits/ Acknowledgments

Cover Design by Charles Vitelli

1. Geography in a Changing World
Facing overview—Photo by Biblioteca Medicea-Laurenziana.

2. Land-Human Relationships
Facing overview—United Nations photo by King.

3. The Region
Facing overview—United Nations photo by Jeffrey Foxx. 143—Library of Congress illustration.

4. Spatial Interaction and Mapping
Facing overview—Photo by Digital Stock.

5. Population, Resources, and Socioeconomic Development
Facing overview—United Nations photo by T. Sennett.

PHOTOCOPY THIS PAGE!!!*

ANNUAL EDITIONS ARTICLE REVIEW FORM

■ NAME: ______________________________ DATE: ______________________________

■ TITLE AND NUMBER OF ARTICLE: ______________________________

■ BRIEFLY STATE THE MAIN IDEA OF THIS ARTICLE: ______________________________

■ LIST THREE IMPORTANT FACTS THAT THE AUTHOR USES TO SUPPORT THE MAIN IDEA:

■ WHAT INFORMATION OR IDEAS DISCUSSED IN THIS ARTICLE ARE ALSO DISCUSSED IN YOUR TEXTBOOK OR OTHER READING YOU HAVE DONE? LIST THE TEXTBOOK CHAPTERS AND PAGE NUMBERS:

■ LIST ANY EXAMPLES OF BIAS OR FAULTY REASONING THAT YOU FOUND IN THE ARTICLE:

■ LIST ANY NEW TERMS/CONCEPTS THAT WERE DISCUSSED IN THE ARTICLE AND WRITE A SHORT DEFINITION:

*Your instructor may require you to use this Annual Editions Article Review Form in any number of ways: for articles that are assigned, for extra credit, as a tool to assist in developing assigned papers, or simply for your own reference. Even if it is not required, we encourage you to photocopy and use this page; you'll find that reflecting on the articles will greatly enhance the information from your text.

We Want Your Advice

Annual Editions revisions depend on two major opinion sources: one is our Advisory Board, listed in the front of this volume, which works with us in scanning the thousands of articles published in the public press each year; the other is you—the person actually using the book. Please help us and the users of the next edition by completing the prepaid article rating form on this page and returning it to us. Thank you.

ANNUAL EDITIONS: GEOGRAPHY 95/96

Article Rating Form

Here is an opportunity for you to have direct input into the next revision of this volume. We would like you to rate each of the 37 articles listed below, using the following scale:

1. Excellent: should definitely be retained
2. Above average: should probably be retained
3. Below average: should probably be deleted
4. Poor: should definitely be deleted

Your ratings will play a vital part in the next revision. So please mail this prepaid form to us just as soon as you complete it.
Thanks for your help!

Rating	Article	Rating	Article
	1. The Four Traditions of Geography		20. Does It Matter Where You Are?
	2. The American Geographies: Losing Our Sense of Place		21. Low Water in the American High Plains
	3. The Coming Anarchy		22. Return of the Soviet Empire
	4. What's Wrong with the Weather?		23. Transportation and Urban Growth: The Shaping of the American Metropolis
	5. Beaches on the Brink		24. Hispanic Migration and Population Redistribution in the United States
	6. The New Downtowns		25. The Channel Tunnel
	7. Averting a Disaster		26. The New White Flight
	8. Is Our Climate Unstable?		27. Asians in the Suburbs
	9. Troubled Waters		28. An Alternative Route to Mapping History
	10. It Comes Down to the Coasts		29. A Sense of Where You Are
	11. The Deforestation Debate		30. The New Cartographers
	12. Threat of Encroaching Deserts May Be More Myth than Fact		31. Population Policy Options in the Developing World
	13. Environmental Problems of the Danube Delta		32. Vicious Circles: African Demographic History as a Warning
	14. An Action Plan to Clean Up the Baltic		33. Can the Growing Human Population Feed Itself?
	15. The Rise of the Region State		34. The Landscape of Hunger
	16. Africa's Geomosaic under Stress		35. We're All Minorities Now
	17. Middle East Geopolitical Transformation: The Disappearance of a Shatterbelt		36. Why Africa Stays Poor, and Why It Doesn't Have To
	18. Prairie Potholes		37. Refugees: The Rising Flood
	19. The Aral Sea Basin: A Critical Environmental Zone		

(Continued on next page)

ABOUT YOU

Name________________________________ Date__________

Are you a teacher? ☐ Or student? ☐

Your School Name ________________________________

Department ________________________________

Address ________________________________

City ______________________ State __________ Zip __________

School Telephone # ________________________________

YOUR COMMENTS ARE IMPORTANT TO US!

Please fill in the following information:

For which course did you use this book? ________________________________

Did you use a text with this Annual Edition? ☐ yes ☐ no

The title of the text? ________________________________

What are your general reactions to the Annual Editions concept?

Have you read any particular articles recently that you think should be included in the next edition?

Are there any articles you feel should be replaced in the next edition? Why?

Are there other areas that you feel would utilize an Annual Edition?

May we contact you for editorial input?

May we quote you from above?

No Postage Necessary if Mailed in the United States

ANNUAL EDITIONS: GEOGRAPHY 95/96

BUSINESS REPLY MAIL

First Class Permit No. 84 Guilford, CT

Postage will be paid by addressee

The Dushkin Publishing Group, Inc.
Sluice Dock
Guilford, Connecticut 06437